HISTORY
of the
TOWN *of* WOLCOTT
CONNECTICUT
from
1731 *to* 1874

WITH AN ACCOUNT OF THE
CENTENARY MEETING, SEPTEMBER 10TH AND 11TH, 1873;
AND WITH THE GENEALOGIES OF THE
FAMILIES OF THE TOWN

Rev. Samuel Orcutt

HERITAGE BOOKS
2011

HERITAGE BOOKS
AN IMPRINT OF HERITAGE BOOKS, INC.

Books, CDs, and more—Worldwide

For our listing of thousands of titles see our website
at
www.HeritageBooks.com

A Facsimile Reprint
Published 2011 by
HERITAGE BOOKS, INC.
Publishing Division
100 Railroad Ave. #104
Westminster, Maryland 21157

Index Copyright © 1991 Heritage Books, Inc.

Originally published:
Press of the American Printing Company
Waterbury, Connecticut
1874

To the families of the Ancient Parish of Farmingbury, now Wolcott, and their descendants at home and abroad, this work is inscribed, with sincere respect and esteem, by the author.

— Publisher's Notice —
In reprints such as this, it is often not possible to remove blemishes from the original. We feel the contents of this book warrant its reissue despite these blemishes and hope you will agree and read it with pleasure.

International Standard Book Numbers
Paperbound: 978-0-7884-5146-1
Clothbound: 978-0-7884-8646-3

PREFACE.

My acquaintance with the Town of Wolcott began in May, 1872. After preaching there a few Sabbaths, with no expectation of continuing in the place, I became interested in the history of the church by discovering that its Centenary would occur in 1873. I soon after accepted an invitation to supply the pulpit for one year. After a few months' labor in the parish, the idea of writing a brief history of the Congregational Church and Society was entertained, and the work was commenced with the expectation that it would not exceed two hundred pages. From that beginning the present volume has grown, and is, therefore, a little different in plan and style from what it would have been if the original design had included so large a field.

The work necessary to the making of this book has been performed with the greatest pleasure, though prosecuted, much of the time, under circumstances of disadvantage and discouragement. Now that it is done, I have no apologies to offer; nor have I any regrets to express, save that the people who form the subject of the volume have not received from my pen as high commendation as they deserve.

The labor has been performed within the space of two years, and has rather aided than hindered parish duties. In the commencement, it was as the Spring-time, full of buds and blossoms of hope; but in the closing it has seemed as Autumn. A shade of sadness has touched my mind as I have taken leave of one and another, individuals and families, when they passed from study and research; for, after so much thought expended upon them, it seemed as if they were friends and neighbors among whom I had spent my days, and I was at last attending their funeral services. The summing up of life, for each one of them, has seemed written in great characters before the mind, in the proverbial expression: " Born, lived, and died." And wherever the mind looks in review of the past, the epitome of history seems recorded in the repetition of this form. Yet in remembering the good of the past (and in fulfilling the responsive feelings of the heart), it is a comfort, if nothing more can be said, to repeat this form, and in it cherish the memory of those who have completed the routine of its unchangeable decrees: — " *Born, lived, and died.*"

The style of the work is without ornament, because the times and the character of the persons forming the subject-matter of the history are better represented thus than otherwise. Of the times and circumstances through which the early settlers passed, there can be but one opinion: they were rigorously hard. Although the number who lived to be over three score and ten is large, yet to most of them, life meant hard work with many privations, plain food with scanty allowance at times, little clothing, and that of the plainest kind, restricted to the fashion of two seasons. Of the character of these ancestors, a good summary, in a few words, is given by Dr. Henry Bronson, in his History of Waterbury: "Individually, our Puritan ancestors were very much such men as we are ; little better, no worse. They were bred in a rigorous age, and were exposed to peculiar hardships, dangers, and temptations. Yet, on the whole, they, like us, were average men."* In one thing, however, it seems to me they have the pre-eminence, namely, in faithfulness to moral and religious convictions. Modesty, honesty, and integrity in the profession of the Christian religion, might have been written over nearly every man's door, to be read by all the world.

It will be observed that the genealogy of a few families is wanting. The cause of this, in every case, is the want of sufficient information to make a respectable representation of the family. The Blakeslee family was among the first in the parish, but no records could be obtained until it was too late to introduce them in their proper order. I have hope of including them in the history of another town where their number is larger than in Wolcott. The Ponds and the Baileys were influential and leading families for some years. They are all now gone from the town, and no records have been obtained of them. A few families early in the parish, disappeared so soon that no connected account of them could be obtained. Also, a few came in about 1800, tarried a few years, then joined the grand army which for two or three generations has been steadily marching Westward.

The limited number of subscribers, and hence of copies printed, has compelled the laying aside of all illustrations, after considerable preparation had been made for their publication. This has been to myself and others a source of great regret.

In acknowledging my obligations to the very kind

---
* Page 323.

friends who have rendered special aid in this work, it is pleasant to say that all have cheerfully contributed information and encouragement as they were able, and have urged that the book be made as perfect as possible, even though the price of it should be increased. In fulfilling this last desire its publication has been delayed nearly six months.

I am specially indebted to Rev. Joseph Anderson, pastor of the First Congregational Church of Waterbury, who has taken much interest in the work from the first, and has rendered very valuable assistance. Also, to Frederick B. Dakin, Esq., of the Waterbury *American*, a practical book-maker, under whose supervision the volume was printed. The following persons have also rendered special service to the work: Messrs. A. Bronson Alcott, Frank B. Sanborn, and William Ellery Channing, of Concord, Mass.; Judge William E. Curtiss, of New York; Hon. Leman W. Cutler, of Watertown; Hon. Birdsey G. Northrop, of New Haven; E. Bronson Cook, Esq., Editor of the Waterbury *American;* Hon. Elihu Burritt, of New Britain; Rev. William H. Moore, of Berlin; Rev. Heman R. Timlow, and Messrs. Gad Andrews, Simeon H. Norton, and Isaac Burritt, of Southington; Rev. William R. Eastman, of Plantsville; the late Ralph L. Smith, Esq., of Guilford; Mr. Aaron G. Atkins, of Chenango County, N. Y.; Mr. Lucas C. Hotchkiss, of Meriden; Mrs. Lucina Holmes and Mrs. Lucina Lindsley, of Waterbury.

WATERBURY, November 10th, 1874.

CONTENTS.

CHAPTER I.
FIRST SOCIETY IN WOLCOTT.

First Settlers — Formation of the First Society — Assembly Act — Warnings — First Meeting — Adjourned Meetings.

CHAPTER II.
BUILDING A MEETING HOUSE.

Committee to Stick the Stake — Notification — Order of the Court — The Deed — The House Built — Officers Chosen in 1770, 1771, 1772, 1773, 1774.

CHAPTER III.
OBTAINING A PASTOR.

Grant of a Tax — First Call, Mr. Jackson — Second Call, Mr. Gillet — Organization of the Church — Declarations — First Members — The Ordination of Mr. Gillet.

CHAPTER IV.
MR. GILLET'S MINISTRY.

Graduate of Yale — His Father — A Library — Church Discipline — Revival — Results, Repairs on Meeting House, Singing. Additions — Mr. Gillet at Home — His Salary — He closes his Labors — Doings of the Council.

CHAPTER V.
MR. WOODWARD'S MINISTRY.

The Call — Letter of Acceptance — Subscription — His Labors — Completion of the Meeting House — Dedication — Mr. Woodward's Salary — Rate Bill — His Death.

CHAPTER VI.
REV. MR. HART'S AND REV. MR. KEYS' MINISTRY.

The Call — His Ordination — The Ball — His Labors — His Death — Mr.

CONTENTS.

Keys — Urgent Invitations — The Council — Dr. Beecher's Sermon — Sunday School — Efficiency of the Church — Mr. Keys' Resignation and Dismissal.

CHAPTER VII.
WITHOUT A PASTOR.

The Meeting House full — Payment of Debts — Improvement in Singing — Deacon Isaac Bronson — His Gratuitous Labors Five Years — Journal of Rev. Erastus Scranton — The Revival — Dr. Wm. A. Alcott — Sunday School — Procuring a Bell — Subscription — Improvement of the Meeting House — Rev. Nathan Shaw — Rev. Seth Sacket — Rev. W. F. Vail — Pew-holders according to Age.

CHAPTER VIII.
MINISTRY OF REVDS. J. D. CHAPMAN AND AARON C. BEACH.

Anti-slavery — Burning of the Meeting House — Second Society Organized — Efforts to Rebuild the Church — A Council Called, its Findings — Mr. Chapman Dismissed — Difficulties Settled — Rev. Zephaniah Swift — Rev. A. C. Beach — His Settlement — His Labors — His Dismissal.

CHAPTER IX.
REVDS. STEPHEN ROGERS, LENT S. HOUGH, W. C. FISKE.

Mr. Rogers' Settlement — His Illness — He Resigns — Rev. Lent S. Hough — Letter of Commendation — A Communion Service — Revised Articles of Faith — Mr. Hough Closes his Labors — Rev. Mr. Fiske — He Resigns after Three Years — Rev. S. Orcutt — The Home Missionary Society.

CHAPTER X.
OFFICERS AND MEMBERS OF THE CHURCH.

The List of Ministers — List of Deacons — Clerks of the Church — Moderators — Clerks of the Society — Treasurers — Prudential Committees — School Committes — Members of the Church.

PART II.— THE EPISCOPAL CHURCH.
CHAPTER I.
ORGANIZATION OF THE SOCIETY.

Episcopalians Early in Wolcott — Withdrawal from the First Society — Call for the First Meeting — Minutes of the First Meeting — Officers — Building a House of Worship — A Site Given by the Town — The House Built.

CONTENTS.   ix

CHAPTER II.

ORGANIZATION OF THE CHURCH.

Early Records — A List of Ministers — Clerks — Society Committees — Wardens — Vestry Men.

PART III.— CIVIL HISTORY.

CHAPTER I.

THE TOWN INCORPORATED.

Votes of the Society — A Memorial — Act of the Assembly —The Poor — First Town Meeting — Hills of Wolcott — Streams in Wolcott.

CHAPTER II.

THE FIRST SETTLERS.

Farmington Part — Waterbury Part — Wolcott Center in 1800 — The Public Green — The Will Place — Atkins' Will — Woodtick — Hotels — Highways.

CHAPTER III.

PUBLIC SCHOOLS.

The Districts — Expenses — Will of Addin Lewis — Whipping Post — Law — Small Pox — Burying Grounds — Yankee Peddlers — Taxes.

CHAPTER IV.

ROLL OF HONOR.

List of Freemen — Town Officers — State Officers — Revolutionary Soldiers — Soldiers in the Late War.

PART IV.— BIOGRAPHY.

	PAGE.		PAGE
John Alcock,	231	Timothy Bradley,	298
Capt. John Alcox,	233	Rev. James D. Chapman,	300
A. Bronson Alcott,	235	Rev. W. C. Fiske,	302
Dr. Wm. A. Alcott,	265	Judah Frisbie,	303
Rev. Wm. P. Alcott,	278	Rev. Alexander Gillet,	313
Joseph Atkins, Senr.,	279	Rev. Timothy Gillet,	322
Dea. Joseph Atkins,	280	Dea. Aaron Harrison,	326
Rev. A. C. Beach,	282	Rev. Lucas Hart,	330
Rev. J. W. Beach,	285	Lucas C. Hotchkiss,	332
Dea. Isaac Bronson,	287	Rev. Lent S. Hough,	336

B

CONTENTS.

	PAGE.		PAGE.
Capt. Heman Hall,	338	Rev. Nathan Shaw,	351
Ephraim Hall,	340	Seth Thomas,	352
Dr. Ambrose Ives,	342	Rev. Benoni Upson, D. D.,	354
Rev. John Keys,	344	Rev. Henry E. L. Upson,	356
Simeon H. Norton,	347	Rev. Israel B. Woodward,	358
Dr. John Potter,	350		

PART V.— THE CENTENARY MEETING.

Opening of the Meeting,	377
Remarks by Rev. A. C. Beach,	378
" " A. Bronson Alcott,	379
" " Editor E. B. Cook,	381
" " Hon. B. G. Northrop,	385
" " Rev. W. H. Moore .	386
" " Simeon H. Norton.	389
List of Aged Persons,	396
The Centenary Poem,	399
Wolcott People removed to Meriden,	403
Isaac Burritt's remarks,	404
Hon. Elihu Burritt's remarks,	410
Antiquities,	414
Judge W. E. Curtiss' remarks,	415
George W. Seward's "	416
Dea. Samuel Holmes' "	417
Rev. Mr. Hillard's "	418

PART VI.— GENEALOGIES OF FAMILIES.

	PAGE.		PAGE.
Alcott,	425	Churchill,	471
Atkins,	439	Curtiss,	472
Barnes,	446	Fairclough,	473
Bartholomew,	449	Finch,	475
Beecher,	450	Frisbie,	477
Bradley,	453	Frost,	480
Brockett,	456	Gillet,	482
Brooks,	457	Hall,	485
Bronson,	458	Harrison,	490
Brown,	464	Higgins,	497
Byington,	465	Hitchcock,	499
Carter,	467	Hopkins,	500

CONTENTS.

	PAGE.		PAGE.
Hotchkiss,	502	Rogers,	550
Hough,	506	Root,	552
Johnson,	508	Rose,	553
Kenea,	509	Scarritt,	555
Lane,	511	Seward,	556
Lewis,	513	Slater,	556
Lindsley,	519	Smith,	557
Merrill,	520	Somers,	558
Minor,	521	Sperry,	559
Moulthrop,	525	Stevens,	560
Munson,	528	Sutliff,	561
Nichols,	529	Thomas,	563
Norton,	531	Todd,	564
Pardee,	536	Tuttle,	570
Parker,	538	Twitchell,	575
Peck,	540	Upson,	578
Plumb,	541	Wakelee,	592
Potter,	544	Warner,	400
Pritchard,	545	Welton,	590
Richards,	548	Wiard	607

INTRODUCTION.

Amidst the rugged hills in the northernmost corner of New Haven County, just on the edge of the extensive granitic district which spreads through the western part of Connecticut, lies the town of Wolcott. It covers an area measuring six miles from north to south, by about three from east to west, and contains within its limits higher ground than any that lies south of it in the State. In its external features it is a good representative of those rural towns of New England which have failed, for whatever reason, to keep abreast of the age in its rapid onward movement. On the plateau at the center of the town stand two churches of that nondescript style of architecture so often seen amidst New England hills; one of them in good repair, through the kindness of outside friends, the other closed and going to decay. The Green which lies between these edifices is skirted by dwelling-houses, which have the look of having seen better times,—amongst these the remains of a flourishing country store, and of an equally flourishing tavern. There is the same look of incipient decay upon many of the houses of the town, some of which are still waiting for their first coat of paint. To one who wanders up and down these hills, on a sunless Autumn afternoon, the effect is monotonous and depressing, and even in the pleasantest Summer days there is but little that is interesting in these remnants of a farm life which must, at its best, have been unusually prosaic and dreary.

Not alone in its external appearance, but also in its

history, is Wolcott a fair specimen of the rural towns of Connecticut. There are the same noteworthy features in its earlier period; there is the same steady growth up to a certain point; and then, after the transition from agriculture to manufactures has fully set in in the State at large, there is the same gradual decline. The hills of Wolcott, although lying midway between Farmington and the *Manhan* or Meadows of the Naugatuck, received scarcely a passing thought from the pioneers who settled Waterbury, and whose chief attraction in this quarter consisted in the open meadow-land which they had here discovered stretching along both sides of the river. The first permanent settlement by the Farmington colonists was made in the valley, and it was only by slow degrees that the population spread backward from the central basin, and extended up the hills. In course of time, however, as more land for farming purposes was required, the hill country came to be occupied, and the territory lying between Farmington and Waterbury (and therefore called Farming-bury, according to the old Connecticut method of constructing place-names), naturally took the precedence in this respect. As early as 1731, there were residents within the limits of what is now called Wolcott, but it was not until eighty-two years after the First Church in Waterbury was organized that a separate church was established in Farmingbury; and not until 1796 was Farmingbury incorporated as a town, and named Wolcott (after the Lieutenant-Governor, who, as Speaker of the Assembly, gave it the benefit of his casting vote).

Attaining to the dignity of a separate existence so shortly before the great transition which has been referred to began, the period during which Wolcott could be considered a flourishing town was necessarily brief. As appears from several statements in the following pages, it attained its highest prosperity during the first decade of the present century. The parish was then one of the strongest in the county; the Society had over two hundred taxpayers on its list, and the attendance at public worship was so large that the meeting-house was habitually crowded. But the population of the town, which numbered nine hundred and fifty-two in 1810, diminished steadily from decade to decade, until, in 1870, it numbered only four hundred and ninety-one; so that at the last census Wolcott was in respect of population one of the three smallest towns in Connecticut. The population of Waterbury, on the other hand, which in 1800 numbered 3256, but which in 1810 had been reduced to 2784, or less than three times that of Wolcott, received within the next ten years a fresh impulse from the development of new industries within the limits of the town, and has continued to increase from year to year, until it now numbers over fifteen thousand, and is therefore thirty times as great as that of Wolcott. In comparison, then, with its sister town, not only, but in comparison with most of the towns in the State, Wolcott seems, even to its own inhabitants, insignificant,— so much so that the author of this volume was, in the course of his inquiries, frequently greeted with the remark, "What can you find here of which to make a history? What can you say of Wolcott — the last place on earth that will interest anybody?" It was difficult, indeed, to make people feel that such a place could have a history which any practical person would care to hear about. But this goodly volume, with its varied contents, proves not only that the old town upon the hills, now in its decadence, has a history, but that its history is of great interest and value,— partly because of the example its people have set of quiet, heroic living, and partly because of the impress it has made on the character and career of the nation by the men it has sent forth into other parts of the land.

In view of this last-mentioned fact, it is eminently proper that so large a part of this volume should be occupied with biographical sketches of men born and reared on the Wolcott hills. These sketches constitute one of the most interesting and valuable portions of the book. In the biographies of such men as the Rev. Messrs. Gillet and Woodward, Deacons Aaron Harrison and Isaac Bronson, Dr. Ambrose Ives, Seth Thomas, Judah Frisbie — a soldier of the Revolution — and, especially, Dr. William A. Alcott and Mr. A. Bronson Alcott, we find represented the utmost diversity of experiences and the most varied types of character. Some of these were remarkable for their intellectual ability, others for their enterprise, others for their philanthropic spirit or their piety; but, in the case of most of them, their broad and fruitful lives were in striking contrast with the sterile country and the contracted sphere in which they had their birth and training. In none of these men is the contrast more marked than in him whose biography fills the largest space in the following pages, but who still lingers amongst us, Mr. Bronson Alcott of Concord. It is a strange transformation, that by which the farmer boy of Spindle Hill, having served his time as a peddler of Yankee notions in eastern Virginia, becomes the father of educational reform in America, a leader of the Transcendental school of New England philosophers, the intimate friend of Thoreau and Emerson, and the silver-tongued conversationalist, whose monologues on lofty themes attract and charm the selectest spirits of the East and the West.

The biographical portion of the book, though large, is not the largest. Of its six hundred pages, a hundred and fifty-four are devoted to the history of the Congregational church and society; and this is the natural result not simply of the plan according to which the work was put together, but of the prominent position held by church and religion in the life of the people. In this, as in almost every old town in New England, the history of the community is to a large extent the history of the church, its meeting-houses and its ministers; and we are thus taught, more impressively than by any deliberate presentation of the subject, how the fathers of four score years ago devoted their thought to theology and their lives to religion.

Besides the history of the two churches, and the biographical sketches, we have in the volume an account of the civil history of the town, a full report of the varied exercises of the Centennial Meeting, and a hundred and eighty pages of genealogies. In each of these divisions of the work there is evidence of the industrious research and faithful labors of the author. He has brought to this work, not indeed a facile pen, but a great fondness for antiquarian investigation and a warm sympathy with old-time phases of life and thought; and the result is a book which is readable not because of its polished periods, but because of its pictures of the past, so full of local coloring, and for a certain simplicity and quaintness of style, imparting to the page that flavor so well known to all readers of town and county histories. Among such histories this volume is destined to hold a creditable place. The extent of the class of books to which it belongs, no one can apprehend until he examines the work of Ludewig on the "Literature of American Local History" (published in 1846), and considers how many local histories have appeared since that bibliography was compiled. To this extensive and steadily incerasing literature the present volume constitutes a substantial addition. It calls attention once more to the minutest details of the old Connecticut life; it increases the store of available materials from which the future histories of America must draw their most valuable facts and illustrations.

In scanning these pages, the reader is impressed not only with the prominence of the ecclesiastical element in the life of this old community, but also with the influence upon the people of the ecclesiastical system to which they adhered. The period most fully portrayed was one in which church councils, and the consociations which they represented, were recognized as possessing power. Their advisory function had all the force of authority, as may be seen in the declaration recorded on pages 120–122, and its reception by the Wolcott church and society. It was a time in which the fellowship of the churches was something more than a name and a formality. In all acts of fellowship between the Wolcott church and its neighbors, the church in Waterbury took part ; for this old parish held to the other the relation of mother and sister at once, and made its influence felt in a beneficent way. It is to the writer of this a gratifying fact that the pleasant relations so long existing have suffered no real interruption, and that he is permitted as the representative of the older organization, which still seems young and vigorous, to bespeak for the younger, as it seems to grow weak with age, the attention and sympathy of this new and busy generation. As pastor of the "First Church" of this whole region, I have a special interest in this history of the church and people of Wolcott; and I take pleasure in bidding this volume, in which a precious fragment of the past is treasured up, God speed on its useful errand. Its mission is not alone to the households scattered over the Wolcott hills ; it should find a place in homes and public libraries throughout our broad country. Whatever hands it may fall into, may it do a good work in reviving pleasant memories of other days, and rendering vivid to young eyes the sober pictures of the ancestral time. May it incline us to do honor to those New England fathers to whom honor is so largely due ; and may it deepen our reverence for the nation by showing us how its foundations were laid with toil and sweat and patience on New England hills.

JOSEPH ANDERSON.

Waterbury, Conn., Dec. 16th, 1874.

INDEX.

Atkins, Esther, . . 48
Joseph, Sen., 2, 3, 5, 6, 7, 8, 9
  11, 17, 18, 20, 21, 23, 27, 190
    194, 199
Dea. Joseph, 11, 23, 54, 61, 72
    175, 195
John S., ... 99
Levi, jr., . . . 2, 197
Samuel, . . . 47, 48
Alcock, John, Sen., 2, 3, 11, 38
  39, 188, 189, 190, 197
Alcox, Capt. John, 6, 185, 194, 199
Daniel, 6, 7, 8, 9, 17, 43, 45, 54
  61, 62, 158, 194, 196
David, . . 7, 47, 194
Jesse, jr., ... 158
Joseph, . . . 194
James, ... 194
David, jr., . . . 158
Joseph C., . . . 158
Jairus, ... 158
Alcott, A. Bronson, . . 210
Dr. Wm. A. . . 108
Johnson. 192
Thomas, . . . 210
Bailey, Dea. James, 70, 106, 176
Beach, Rev. A. C., . 122–125
David M., . . . 158
Joseph, ... 190
Barnes, Benjamin, . . 188
Nathan, . . . 70
Stephen, . 6, 7, 8, 17, 27, 47
Barrett, John, 7, 9, 25, 190, 192
James, ... 190
Bartholomew, Seth, . 7

Bartholomew, William, . 108
Beecher, Capt. Amos, . 7
Capt. Joseph, 7, 8, 17, 43, 60, 61
  70
Capt. Walter, . 60, 68, 177
Dr. Lyman, . 85, 88, 98, 102
John, jr., ... 99
Joseph, jr., . . . 177
Beckwith, Marvin, jr., . 158
Bement, Jonathan, . 185
Benham, Shadrick, . . 189
Isaac, ... 192
Samuel, ... 192
Birge, Elijah, . . . 191
Bishop, Bani, . . 190, 191
Bradley, Amos, . . 158
Brockett, Zuer, . . 12, 108
Brown, Levi, . . . 158
Bronson, Daniel, . . 8
Dea. Isaac, 40, 41, 48, 99
  100, 101, 102, 106, 179, 193
Dea. Irad, 90, 106, 108, 193
John, 6, 12, 23, 38, 188, 196, 199
John, jr., . . . 79
Levi, ... 7, 47
Byington, Daniel, Sen., 5, 6, 7, 11
  25, 199
Daniel, jr., 11, 23, 45, 60, 158,
  175, 176, 177, 181, 195
Samuel, 48, 50, 54, 177, 190
Carter, Isaac, . . 47
Jacob, 7, 12, 45, 47, 48, 53, 54
  61, 68, 181
Ensign Jonathan, 47, 48, 53, 54
  61, 70, 176, 177

INDEX OF NAMES.

Carter, Mary, . . . 48
   Major Preserve, . 71, 138
Chapman, Rev. James D., 117, 118
                                120, 122
Clark, Rev. Peter G., . . 166
Cowles, Asa, . . . 188
   Calvin, . 53, 54, 176, 181
   Josiah, . . . 158
   William, . . . 210
Covill, Rev. Mr., . . 166
Curtiss, Abel, . . 8, 190, 197
Deming, Phineas, . . 158
Dutton, Enos, . . . 70
Downs, Isaac, . . . 158
Fenn, Abijah, . . . 190
Finch, Daniel, . . 47, 199
Fiske, Rev W. C., . . 135, 136
French, Rev. Wm. G., . 166
Frisbie, Charles, . . . 177
   David, ... 101
   Elijah. 189
   Ira, ... 120
   Judah, . . 12, 38, 45
   Levi, ... 210
Frost, David, . . . 188
Gaylord, Levi, . . . 37
Gillet, Rev. Alexander, 32, 33, 38
     39, 40, 41, 45, 49, 50, 52, 53, 54
                             62
   Nathan, . . . 47, 62
   Capt. Zaccheus, . 39, 47
Grilley, Gehula, . 185, 189
Gregor, Rev. Mr., . . 166
Griswold, George, . . 99
Hall, Curtiss, . . 6, 8, 9, 23
   Ephraim, . . 108, 210
   Lieut. Heman, . . . 187
   Capt. Heman, . 12, 43, 188
   Levi, ... 158
   Orrin, . . 108, 196
   Richmond, . . . 158
Hart, Rev. Lucas, . . 79
Harrison, Dea. Aaron, . 5, 6, 7, 8
    11, 23, 24, 25, 27, 37, 54, 62
      190, 192, 193, 194, 199

Harrison, Aaron, jr., . . 192
   Benjamin, sen., . . 187
   Benjamin. jr., 39, 190, 192, 194
   David, ... 47
   Jabez, ... 192
   Jared, . . 7, 8, 47, 158
   Michael, . . . 194
   Mark, 45, 47, 48, 53, 54, 61, 64
     71, 72, 175, 176, 177, 181, 191
   Phebe, ... 48
   Samuel, . . . 47
   Stephen, . . . 94
Hitchcock, John, . . 70
Higgins, Lyman, . 158, 209
Holmes, Dea. Samuel, 132, 133
Holt, Daniel, . . 107, 112
Hopkins, Isaac, 9, 11, 25, 39, 60
                             70, 189
   Simeon, . 7, 43, 45, 62, 175
Hotchkiss, Abner, . . 107
   Asaph, . 191, 192, 194
   Chester, . . . 209
   Emerson M., . . . 196
   Harpin, . . . 158
   Holt, ... 210
   Jason, . . . 210
   Major Luther, . . 112
   Solomon, . . 190
   Timothy, . 158, 209
   Titus, . 158, 159, 160
   Wait, . . 7, 11, 190
Horton, Elijah, . . . 47
   Samuel, . . . 209
   Seth, ... 210
   Thomas, . . . 99
Hough, Ira, . 79, 101, 120
   Isaac, . . 185, 192
   Rev. Lent S., . 130–135
Ives, Ambrose, . . . 158
   Mrs. Wealthy, . . 134
Jackson, Mr. . . . 31
Johnson, Daniel, . 7, 25
   Salmon, . . . 158
Kenea, John J., . . 158
   Leverett, . . . 210

INDEX OF NAMES.

Keys, Rev. John, 82, 83, 88, 89, 92, 93, 94, 95, 97, 98, 99, 193, 196
Lane, Asahel, ... 70
Lewis, Capt. Nathaniel, 12, 43, 53, 68 175, 176, 181, 183, 188, 197, 199
    Nathaniel G., . . . 158
    Reuben, . . . 158
Lindsley, Lud, . . . 101
Loveland, Lewis, . . 158
Merrills, Caleb, . . . 158
Mills, Rev. Mr., . . . 41
Minor, Archibald, 109, 112. 158
    Jedediah, . . . 9, 199
    Joseph, . 47, 62, 70, 71, 158
    Marcus, . . . 158
    Marvin, ... 120
Mix, Eldad, . . . 189
Mott, Jonathan, . . . 188
Moulthrop, Levi, Sen., . 120
Norton, Abraham, 175, 190, 194, 196
    Cyrus, . . . 47, 48
    Daniel, . . . 45
    David, . 7, 11, 43, 61, 190
    Jerusha, . . . 48
    John, . . . 158, 194
    Noah, ... 47
    Ozias, ... 47
Orcutt, Samuel, . . . 136
Parker, Family, . . . 11
    Joseph, . . . 45, 189
    Joseph M., . . 47, 70, 71
    Levi, ... 158
    William, . . . 158
    Zephana, . . . 158
Peck, Daniel, . . . 45
    Dea. Justus, 7, 11, 53 175, 188
Pike, David, . . . 188
    James, . . . 188
    Samuel, . . . 188
Pond, Moses, Sen., . . 70
    Col. Moses, . . . 196
Powers, Barna, . . . 158

Potter, Ashbel, . . . 8
    Rev. Collis I, . . . 165
    Dr. John, 47, 54, 60, 61, 62, 70, 71, 176, 177, 192
Plumb, Family, . . . 12
    Ansel H., . . 132, 134
    Orrin, . . . 158
    Simeon, . 54, 60, 177, 199
Preston, Joseph, . . . 187
Pritchard, Dennis, . . 13, 194
    Roger, ... 189
Richards, Streat, 45, 48, 54, 71, 158, 175, 176, 177, 181, 195
Richmon, Jacob, . . . 8
Robins, William, . . 194
Roberts, Abiel, . . . 194
Rogers, Josiah, 6, 8, 11, 17, 25, 37, 43, 190
Sandford, Rev. David, . 166
Scarritt, James, . . . 158
    Jeremiah, . . 60, 70
Scott, Timothy, . . . 189
Scovill, Rev. Mr. . . . 157
Scranton, Rev. Erastus, 102, 103, 106
Seward, Amos, 6, 12, 25, 27, 43, 53, 54, 60, 175, 176, 189, 195, 199
Shaw, Rev. Nathan, . . 113
Smith, Eliakim, . . . 158
    Rev. John D., . . 166
Sperry, Jeremiah, . . 158
    Joseph, N. . . 99, 120
Steadman, Selah, . . 62
Stevens, William, . . 62
Stocking, Rev. Servilius, . 166
Sutliff, Joseph, Senr., . 11, 189
Talmage, Joseph, . . 9, 11
    Josiah, . . . 190
Terry, Eli, . . . 209
    Henry, . . . 209
    S. B. 43
Thomas, Seth, . . . 195
Thrasher, Elnathan, . . 195
Todd, Caleb, . . . 192
    Hezekiah, . . . 190

INDEX OF NAMES. xxi

Todd, Moses, 71, 190, 191, 192
    Jerry, ... 158
Twitchell, Isaac, . . 190
    Joseph, . . . 158, 196
Upson, Ashbel, . . 101, 107
    Capt. Charles, 43, 48, 53, 54, 60
        61, 63, 68, 70, 134, 175, 176
        177, 181, 191, 193, 195
    Gates, . . 79, 99, 102
    Dea. Harvey, . 107, 196
    Isaac, . . . 70, 195
    Jerry, ... 99
    Capt. Samuel, 7, 8, 9, 12, 17, 43
        45, 47, 53, 54, 61, 175, 177, 181
        196
    Samuel, Jr., . . 158, 196
    Samuel W., . . . 107
    Thomas, 1st, 38, 183, 187, 190
        197
    Thomas, 2d, 11, 99, 107, 112
        158, 195

Upson, Wealthy, . . 48
Warner, David, . . . 7
    Erastus W., . . . 192
    James, ... 8
Wakelee, David, . . 158
    Lewis H., . . . 79
Welton, Eliakim, 1st, 189, 197
    Eliakim, 2d, . . 157
    Oliver, . . 9, 157
    Thomas, . . . 189
    Richard F., . . . 62
    Rev. Ximenus A., . 166
Whiting, Adna, . . . 112
Wiard, Darius, . . 192, 193
    Matthew, . . . 192
    Thomas, . . . 196
Woodward, Rev. I. B., 60, 62, 65,
    66, 72, 76, 93, 158, 176, 191, 192
Woster, Abraham, 11, 19, 190, 193
    Rebecca, . . . 11

TOPICAL INDEX.

Academy, Southington, . 202
Articles of Faith, . . 134
Bell, Subscription for, . . 110
    Weight of, . . . 112
    New one, . . . 126
Beecher, Dr. Lyman's Sermon, 85
    Family, ... 88
Bronson, Isaac, Character and
    Gratuitous Labors, . 99
    Remarkable Eloquence, 100
    Reasons why he should have
    had some Salary, . 101
Beach, Rev. Aaron C., Or-
    dained, . . . 123
    Dismissed, . . 125
Burr, Rev. Z. B., A call, 128
Burying Grounds, The Center, 204
    Pike's Hill, . . . 206
    Northeast, . . . 208
    Southeast, . . . 208
    Southwest, . . . 208
Biographies, See Table of Con-
    tents.

Church, Congregational, Or-
    ganized, . . . 33
    First Members, . . 33
    Covenant Rules, . . 36
    Discipline, . . 41, 90
    Efficiency under Mr. Keys, 91
    List of Members, . . 148
    List of Officers, See Officers.
    Episcopal, Organization, 165
Clock-making, . . 209
Council, Ecclesiastical, Meet-
    ing of, . . 35, 42, 54
    To Ordain Mr. Hart, . 80
    Letter for, . . . 83
    Meeting of, . . 120, 123
Centenary Meeting, . 377
    See Table of Contents.
Chapman's Ministry begins, 117
    Dismissed, . . . 122
Communion Service, . . 133
Episcopalians, early in Wol-
    cott, ... 157

TOPICAL INDEX.

Episcopalians, Taxed by Law, 157
  Petition to General Assembly, ... 157
List who withdrew from First Society, . . . 158
Fiske, Rev. Warren C., hired, 135
Fever, the great, of 1810, . 76
Freemen, List of, . . 213
Genealogies, . . . 425
  See G, Table of Contents.
Green, the Public, . . 193
Rev Mr. Gillet, Settlement, 50
  His Marriage, . . 50
  Builds a House, . . 51
  His Salary, . . . 51, 52
  Closes his Labors, . . 53
  His last entries in Church Book, . . . 59
  His Biography, . . 313
Hart, Rev. Lucas, his Call, 79
  His Ordination, . . 80
  The Ball, . . . 81
  His Term of Service, . 81
  His death, . . . 82
Hough, Rev. Lent S., hired, 131
  Letter of Commendation, 131
  Closes his Labors,
Hills, of Wolcott, . . 181
Highways, . . . 196
Hotels, ... 196
Jack's Cave, . . . 197
Keys, Rev. John, his Call, . 82
  Installation, . . . 84
  A Communication, . . 92
  Resignation, . . 94
  Reasons for, . . 95, 97
Law in Wolcott, . . 203
Mill, Atkins', . . . 194
Mill Place, . . . 194
Meeting House, Voted to build, 14
  Stake fixed, . . 14, 16
  First Meetings in, . 24
  Description, . . . 24
  Its size, . . . 18, 19
  Deed for Land, . . 20

Meeting House, improvement, 44
  Seating by age, . . 45
  Pulpit, . . . 45, 46
  Its final completion, . 67
  Dedicatory Poem, . 69
  Pews first rented, . . 113
  Burning of, . . . 117
  Building a new one, . 119
  New one completed. . 124
  Repaired, . . 135, 136
  Episcopal, site given, . 163
  Built, ... 164
Mountain, Southington, . 49
Officers, of Cong. Church:
  Ministers, . . . 139
  Deacons, . . . 140
  Clerks, . . . 140
  Society, Moderators, . 140
  Clerks, ... 141
  Treasurers, . . . 141
  Committees, . . 142
  School Committees, . . 146
Officers of Episcopal Church:
  Ministers, . . . 167
  Clerks, ... 167
  Vestrymen, . . . 170
  Society, Committees, 160, 168
  Wardens, . . . 169
  Town Moderators, . 221
  Clerks, ... 221
  Selectmen, . . . 221
  Justices, . . . 223
  Representatives, . . 225
  Senators, . . . 226
Peddlers, Yankee, . . 209
Parsonage Built, . . . 124
  Bought by Society, . 127
Rogers, Rev. Stephen, installed, . . . 128
  Letter of resignation, . 129
  Dismissed, . . . 130
Revivals, under Messrs. Gillet and Mills, . . . 41
  Results, . . . 42
  Under Rev. Mr. Scranton, 103

TOPICAL INDEX. xxiii

Revivals under Rev. Jos. Smith, 129
    Under Rev. L. S. Hough, . 132
Roll of Honor, . . 213
Sabba' day Houses, . . 50
Sackett, Rev. Seth, . . 113
Scranton, Rev. Erastus, Journal, . . . 103
School, Public, Committee,
    First, ... 7
    Public, . . . 199
    Tax by poll, . . 7
    Expenses of, . . 200, 202
    Sunday, . . 88, 90
    Sunday Class, . . 109
Shaw, Rev. Nathan, . . 113
Settlers, First in New England, . . . 1
    Hartford and Farmington, 1
    Waterbury, . . 1
    Farmingbury, . . 38, 187
Singing, improvements in, 46, 48
         70, 94
Singers in the Gallery, . 48
Smith, Rev. David, hired, . 113
    Rev Joseph, hired, . 129
Small Pox, . . . 204
Society Congregational, preliminaries, . . . 3
    Assembly, Act for, . 3
    Warnings, . . 4, 5
    First Meeting, . . 6
    Measured, . . 8
    Vote for Meeting House, 8
    Offices, . . . 10
    First Officers, . . 25
    Annual Officers, . . 26, 27
    Incorporated as a Town, 71
    Rate List, . . . 73
    Cong., Second, Organized, 120
    Fund, . . . 137
    Episcopal, Organized, . 159
    Domestic Missionary, . 88
    Conn. Home Miss., 88, 91, 113
    Donations to Wolcott, . 137
Soldiers, Revolutionary, . 226
    Late Rebellion, . 226

Stoves, in the Church, . 118
Streams of Water, . . 185
Subscription for Gospel, according to age, . . 114
Swift, Rev. Z., hired, . . 122
Taverns, . . 50, 196
Taxes for Society, 7, 10, 28, 96, 98
         99
    To build a Meeting House, 23
    Twelve per cent., . 91, 92
    Assembly Act for, . . 29
    Order to collect, . . 44
    List of 1806, . . . 7
    List of 1789, . . . 211
    Grand Lists, . . . 210
    Episcopalians, . . 157
    A List, . . . 189
    For Singing, . . 70, 93, 94
Vail, Rev. Wm. F., hired, . 113
War of the Revolution, . 49, 50
    Late Rebellion, . . 49
Wheelock, Rev. Mr., hired, 109
Whipping Post, . . 202
Will of Addin Lewis, . 201
Wolcott like Land of Canaan, 51
    As a Business Centre, . 63
    In its Strength, . . 89
    Incorporated, . . 178
    Care of the Poor, . 181
    First Town Meeting, . 180
    The Center in 1800, . 190
Woodtick, . . . 195
Woodward, Rev. I. B. begins
    to preach, . . . 60
    Letter of Acceptance, . 61
    Ordained, . . . 62
    His Marriage. . 63
    Subscribers to his Settlement, . . . 64
    Salary, . . . 65
    His School. . . . 67
    Offers his Resignation, . 71
    His death, . . . 76
    His Gravestone, . . 77
    His Widow, . . . 77
    A Federalist, . 98

HISTORY OF WOLCOTT.

CHAPTER I.

FIRST SOCIETY IN WOLCOTT.

FIRST SETTLERS.

In the settlement of Connecticut, and other New England States, the settlers made their homes first in the valleys and along the rivers and streams of water. After fifty to seventy years' experience of decimation from fevers and sicknesses, caused by the fogs and malaria in these low lands, they began to climb the hills and mountains, and to make their homes where the sun rose *before* ten o'clock in the morning, and set *after* four o'clock in the afternoon; so that the first settlers came into Wolcott, upon the hills, fifty-seven years after the settlement of Waterbury, and ninety-one years after the settlement of Farmington.

The first settlers of Hartford reached that place in 1635, and "in 1640 the people of Hartford commenced a settlement at Farmington, it being the first made in Connecticut away from navigable waters. From this time to 1673, small beginnings were made at Norwich, Derby, Wallingford, Simsbury, Woodbury, and Plainfield." In the year 1674, "Articles of Association and Agreement" were signed by some of the people of Farmington for a settlement in Waterbury, but the first houses were not erected until the summer of 1678. The Indian "trail" or path by which the people of Farmington reached Mattatuck, now Waterbury, lay across the northwest corner of what is now Wolcott, and became, probably, the first "traveled" road in this town. It is the road that now passes Mr. Levi Atkins' dwelling house, and it is said that the millstones for the first Grist Mill in Woodbury were carried from Farmington on this road, on the back of a horse, the stones being in a sack balancing on each side of the horse, and the horse led by a footman. In 1731 Mr. John Alcock, of New Haven, settled in the west part of what is now Wolcott, he being the first settler there. In less than thirty years (in 1760) the people had become so numerous within this territory as to desire parish privileges, and so petitioned the General Assembly to make them a "Distinct Society." They stated that they "occupied a tract of land five miles square, were £2,000 in the list, and lived an inconvenient distance from places of public worship." Waterbury First Society remonstrated with arguments, and the petition was rejected, as was another with forty-three signers, in May, 1762. In October, 1762, the people, numbering thirty-eight, renewed their petition, and the old Society remonstrated, the chief reason given being the difficulty of supporting the First Society, if Farmingbury, West Farms, and South Farms, should be granted society privileges. Notwithstanding the cogency of this reasoning, the people of Farmingbury (so called at this time) were allowed to hire preaching five months in the year, and to set up a school, and in the meantime to be exempt from other society and school taxes. In the spring of 1767, thirty-one petitioners of the Winter parish requested society privileges, and asked that the limits of the society might be extended into New Cambridge (now Bristol). They said they numbered seventy-one families, and had a list of £3,872 8s. The petition was denied, as was also another in October, 1768.*

FORMATION OF THE ECCLESIASTICAL SOCIETY.

The organization of the First Ecclesiastical Society took place at the house of Mr. Joseph Atkins, on the 13th

---
* See History of Waterbury, pages 279–81.

day of November, 1770. This house stood south of the highway that now runs westward from the meeting-house, and stood about two hundred rods west from the present meeting-house, in what was then the town of Waterbury. The site may be recognized by a small part of the cellar-wall which still remains.

The preliminaries to this meeting were very carefully attended to according to the Colonial Law of that time, by a grant from the General Assembly, and by orders from the Courts, and legal warnings to the people. This grant formed the parish from the towns of Waterbury and Farmington, and gave it the name of Farmingbury.

Several efforts had been made between the years 1760-69 to form such Society, but without success. In the Spring of 1770 a petition, signed by forty-nine persons, was presented to the General Assembly, and was laid over until the next October, when the petition was granted.

The territory taken from Waterbury had been settled but a short time,—the first settler, Mr. John Alcock, of New Haven, having taken his residence on Spindle Hill, in March, 1731. So far as known all other settlers had come into this territory during the thirty-nine years intervening; and so far as known all the settlers in Farmington part of Farmingbury had come in after 1732.*

All the original papers issued for the purpose of forming the Society are preserved, though much changed by age and use, and are of such peculiar character that their insertion here will be particularly interesting. They are as follows:

ASSEMBLY ACT.

At a General Assembly of the Governor and Company of the Colony of Connecticut, holden at New Haven, on the Second Thursday of October, A. D., 1770:

Upon the Memorial of Joseph Atkins, of Waterbury, in the county of New Haven, and others living within the following limits and boundaries, viz.: Beginning half a mile west from the

---

* Mr. Thomas Upson, moved into the Southeast corner, in 1732-3.

northeast corner of the first "Long Lot" in said Farmington, next to said Waterbury; thence west about two miles and a half by the limits of Cambridge Parish to Northbury Society; thence southward to the middle of the dwelling-house of Caleb Barnes, of said Waterbury; thence to extend west to a line that is two miles west from the southwest corner of said Cambridge; thence south two degrees east, about three miles to a place two hundred rods north, two degrees from the four mile tree; thence southward to the middle of the dwelling house of Elijah Frisbie; thence a straight line to a line drawn west from the southwest corner of said Farmington three quarters of a mile; thence to said corner of Farmington; thence east on said Farmington south line to the east side of the original twenty rod highway; thence northward to the top of the mountain west of John Merriman's; thence a straight line to the first Station, — praying for society privileges, a committee was appointed [by] this assembly, who having reported in favor of the memorialists, which is approved of by this Assembly and accepted:

Resolved, by this Assembly, that the said Inhabitants living within said limits and boundaries as above described be and they are hereby made and constituted a distinct Ecclesiastical Society, and shall be called and known by the name of Farmingbury, with all the privileges and immunities to such societies usually belonging in the Colony, and the said Caleb Barnes hereby has liberty granted him of choosing whether he will be of said New Society or remain and belong to the First Society in Waterbury, and the same liberty is hereby given unto said Elijah Frisbie.

A true Copy of Record,

Examined by

SEALED.

GEORGE WYLLIS, *Secretary*.

Upon the reception of this grant, application was made to the officers in Farmington and Waterbury, and the execution of the several papers was attended to as follows:

To Jared Lee, Esq., one of his Majesty's Justices of the Peace in Farmington, in the County of Hartford:

The Honorable Assembly Having Constituted Part of Farmington and Part of Waterbury, to be a Distinct Ecclesiastical Society, In October, A. D., 1770, we the Subscribers, Principle In-

FIRST SOCIETY IN WOLCOTT. 5

habitants of said Society, Do as the Law Directs make application to the said Jared Lee, Esq., for a warning to the Inhabitants of said Society for a Society Meeting on Tuesday, the 13th day of November, inst., at 12 of the Clock, at the house of Mr. Joseph Atkins, in said Society.

JOSEPH ATKINS,
AARON HARRISON, } Principle Inhabitants.
DANIEL BYINGTON,

On the above said application of Mr. Joseph Atkins, Capt. Aaron Harrison, and Daniel Byington — these are therefore to command Capt. Aaron Harrison in His Majesty's name, to give lawful warning to all the Inhabitants in said Society In Farmington Part allowed by Law to vote, to meet at the Dwelling house of Mr. Joseph Atkins on the 13th Day of November, Instant, in said Society, at 12 o'clock of said day to Choose a Moderator and Society Clerk, and to do all other business Proper to be Done at said meeting.

Dated at Farmington, the 5th Day of November, A. D., 1770, and in the 11th year of his Majesty's Reign.

JARED LEE, Just. Peace.

Pursuant to this warrant, I have proceeded and given Legal warning to the Inhabitants of Farmingbury, in Farmington Part, for a Society Meeting at the house of Mr. Joseph Atkins, on Tuesday the 13th of November, inst., at 12 of the Clock on said Day.

AARON HARRISON, Inhabitant of said Society.

WARNING FOR WATERBURY PART.

To Mr. Daniel Byington of the Society of Farmingbury, in the Town of Waterbury, in New Haven County, Greeting :

Whereas, The Honorable General Assembly, in their Session in New Haven, on the 2d Thursday of October last made and constituted the said Farmingbury, consisting part of the Town of Farmington, in Hartford County, and part of the Town of Waterbury, in New Haven County, a Distinct Ecclesiastical Society, as appears of Record, and it is now necessary that the said Society be convened in Society Meeting for the Lawful Purposes thereof,—

These are therefore in His Majesty's name, to Require you to warn all the inhabitants of said Waterbury, within the Limits of said Society of Farmingbury, to meet at the Dwelling House of Mr. Joseph Atkins, in said Waterbury, on Tuesday, the 13th Day of Instant Nov., at twelve of the Clock on said Day, then and there to choose a Moderator, Society's Clerk, and other proper Officers, and to do and transact all other Business proper for said meeting according to law.

Dated at Waterbury the 6th day of Nov., 1770, and in the 11th year of His Majesty's Reign.

JOSEPH HOPKINS, Justice Peace.

JOSEPH ATKINS,
AARON HARRISON, } Inhabitants of said Society.
DANIEL BYINGTON,

Pursuant to this Warrant, I have Proceeded and given Legal warning to the Inhabitants of Farmingbury, in Waterbury Part, for Society Meeting at the house of Mr. Joseph Atkins, on Tuesday the 13th of Nov. inst., at 12 o'clock on said Day.

DANIEL BYINGTON, Inhabitant of said Society.

The foregoing Instruments are true copies of the warrants granted for the warning of the First Society Meeting in Farmingbury.

Certified by,

DANIEL BYINGTON, Society Clerk.

FIRST SOCIETY MEETING.

At a Society meeting holden in Farmingbury, the inhabitants being lawfully assembled on the 13th day of November, A. D., 1770, the following votes were taken. Capt. Aaron Harrison was chosen Moderator, Daniel Byington was chosen Society Clerk, Lieut. Josiah Rogers, Mr. John Alcox, Mr. Stephen Barnes, Mr. John Bronson, and Mr. Amos Seward, were chosen Society Committee for the year ensuing.

Voted, that we will procure preaching the year ensuing.

Voted, to lay a rate of two pence on the pound to be paid on the list of August, 1770, and that the said rate should be paid by the first day of September next. Curtiss Hall and Daniel Alcox were chosen to collect said rate.

At the same meeting Lieut. Josiah Rogers was chosen Society

Treasurer for the year ensuing. David Norton, Seth Bartholomew, Daniel Alcox, Amos Beecher, Joseph Beecher, Justus Peck, Capt. Aaron Harrison, and Stephen Barnes were chosen School Committee for the year ensuing.

David Warner, Wait Hotchkiss, Simeon Hopkins, Nathaniel Lewis, Capt Aaron Harrison, and Joseph Beecher, were chosen a committee to divide the Society into Districts. Voted to give Mr. Joseph Atkins £1 5s od for the use of his house to meet in on the Sabbath for the year ensuing, till the first of May next.

Jacob Carter, Levi Bronson, Jared Harrison, Stephen Barnes, and David Alcox were chosen Choristers for the year ensuing. Capt. Aaron Harrison and Mr. Amos Seward were chosen to read the Psalms for the year ensuing.

John Barrett was chosen Grave Digger. At the same meeting, voted to build a Meeting house. Joseph Atkins was chosen Agent to go to the County Court for a committee to stick the stake for said Meeting house. Capt. Enos Brooks, Capt. Enos Atwater, and Col. Hall were nominated a committee to stick the stake of said Meeting house. Voted to lay a rate Half Penny on the Pound to defray the Society Charges, and to pay the said half penny rate by the first day of February next, and Joseph Atkins and Jared Harrison were chosen to collect said half penny rate. Voted to adjourn said meeting to the last Thursday of Inst. November, at one o'clock in the afternoon.

ADJOURNED MEETING.

At the adjournment the Inhabitants did meet and voted as follows, viz. : To accept the doings of the committee in dividing the Society into Districts. Voted that the Schooling should be by the poll. Mr. Samuel Upson was chosen School Committee. Voted that each School committee shall collect their poll rate each one in his own District. Adjourned for one hour. At the adjournment the inhabitants did meet and voted to procure a Book for Records. Voted to adjourn the meeting to the Third Monday in December next at one o'clock in the afternoon.

Met according to adjournment. Daniel Johnson and Daniel Byington were chosen to take the marks of stray sheep the year ensuing.

Voted to have the Society measured by a County surveyor, and to reconsider the vote taken to lay a rate two pence on the pound in order to procure preaching. Voted to lay a half penny rate to pay for measuring the Society, and that said half penny rate be paid by the first day of February next. Joseph Atkins and Jared Harrison were chosen to collect said half penny rate. Sargent Samuel Smith and James Warner and Daniel Bronson were chosen chairmen, and Lieut. Ashbel Potter, County surveyor. Voted to lay a rate of one penny half penny on the pound to procure preaching, and to pay said rate by the first day of September next, and Abel Curtiss and Curtiss Hall were chosen to collect said rate. Voted to adjourn the meeting to the last Monday in Inst. December, at one o'clock in the afternoon.

Met according to adjournment and adjourned to the Second Wednesday of January next at one o'clock in the afternoon.

At the adjournment voted to adjourn half an hour, and then met and voted to confide in what the committee did in fixing a place for the Meeting house. Voted to have Society meetings on the first Monday of December annually. Voted to dissolve said meeting.

At a Society meeting holden in Farmingbury, on the 21st day of January, A. D., 1771, the inhabitants being lawfully assembled on said day, the following votes were taken. Capt. Aaron Harrison was chosen Moderator to lead the meeting. Voted to adjourn the meeting one hour, then met and voted to confide in what the late committee did in fixing a place for a Meeting house and dissolved said meeting.

At a Society meeting holden in Farmingbury, on the 22d day of April, A. D., 1771, the inhabitants being lawfully assembled on said day the following votes were taken. Capt. Aaron Harrison was chosen Moderator. Lieut. Josiah Rogers, Mr. Samuel Upson, Mr. Stephen Barnes, Mr. Joseph Beecher, and Mr. Daniel Alcox were chosen a Meeting house Committee. Voted to have all the land in the Society taxed. Voted to have the tax three pence per acre for four years. At the same meeting Capt. Aaron Harrison was chosen agent to apply to the Assembly to procure the said tax. Mr. Stephen Barnes was chosen for the same purpose. Voted to give Mr. Jacob Richmon his rate; also to give Mr. Jedediah Minor his two half penny rates, and also to give Mr. Joseph Talmage his two half penny rates. Voted to have preaching this summer, and to lay a half penny rate in addition to the penny half penny to be paid the first of September next. Adjourned to first Tuesday of June next at three o'clock in the afternoon.

At the time, met and adjourned to last Monday in September next, at one o'clock in the afternoon.

Met according to adjournment, and voted to have the said memorial for said land tax carried into the next Assembly, giving the agents leave to alter in respect to the Churchmen as they shall find best, and Mr. Samuel Upson and Mr. Daniel Alcox were chosen agents to apply to the Assembly to procure said tax. Mr. Joseph Atkins was chosen for the same purpose. Daniel Alcox and Stephen Barnes were chosen to collect said tax. Voted to have our meeting on the last Monday of November, annually, and to warn said meeting by setting up Notifications at these places, viz.: John Barrett's, Isaac Hopkins', Dan Tuttle's Shop, Curtiss Hall's, and Ensign Welton's. Voted to dissolve said meeting.

These several meetings, as recorded, show the effort and labor and patience expended in forming a new Society and bringing it into working order, and the manner of attending to such duties in those days. They also bring forward names that are prominent in these records for many years afterward, and names which will appear in various relations, and frequently, in the progress of this History.

Farmingbury did not become a Town till 1796. Hence many interests were attended to by the Parish Society which belonged properly to township authority, and not to the Church. In those days it was a principle of Christian duty to take special care of political matters and not to leave them in the hands of the neglecters of piety. This was supposed to be right and righteous, and human experience concurs with the supposition; for what would the unprincipled man like better than that he should take care of politics, while men of principle should sit at home to be governed like slaves, and then pay the expenses of government? What would the thief like better than that he should be left to make the laws and execute them at his own pleasure? This is not Church and State united, but church men in the state, *acting*. To demand that when a man embraces, personally, the benefits of the gospel, he shall forsake the political interests of his community and nation, leads only to the revival of the days of the Inquisition, that is, infliction of punishment for obedience to the Gospel.

From the first, Farmingbury Parish took supervision of the public schools; appointed the committees; voted how much "schooling" they should have each year; laid taxes for the support of schools, and directed how these should be collected, and appointed the collectors of these taxes. They appointed the "grave digger" and the keeper of the "key," and persons to take the "marks of stray sheep." In one instance only did they go to the Assembly for power to lay a tax, and that was for a church rate on all the lands "for maintaining the worship of God."*

---

*At a General Assembly of the Governor and Company of the Colony of Connecticut holden at New Haven, on the 2d Thursday of October, Anno Domini, 1771:

Upon the memorial of the Society of Farmingbury, prepared by Joseph Atkins, Samuel Upson, and Daniel Alcox, agents for said Society, representing to this Assembly that the list of said society is small and they unable to set up and maintain the worship of God among them without some further help, praying for a tax on all the lands within said Society, &c., as per memorial on file:

Resolved by the Assembly, that a tax of three pence on the acre for the term of four years, to be annually collected, be laid on all the lands within said Society which belong to the inhabitants living within said Society not being professors of the Church of England, and also on that part of the non-resident professors, which land is not put on the general list of such non-resident persons and subject to pay taxes in other societies and Towns; and Stephen Barnes of Farmington and Daniel Alcox of Waterbury, are hereby appointed and fully empowered to collect the said tax of the proprietors of such lands as aforesaid and the same to pay to the com-

FIRST SOCIETY IN WOLCOTT.

Thus was formed, organized, and put into effectual operation the First Ecclesiastical Society in Wolcott, which was as a tree in the wilderness and proved to be "a fruitful vine in the tops of the mountains." The families of the parish were very much scattered amidst the forests that then covered most of these hills and the small patches of low lands.

It is not certain that at the time of the formation of the parish, there was more than one house at Wolcott Center, that of Abraham Woster, all traces of whose family have disappeared from Wolcott long ago. He was a carpenter, and was "foreman" or "boss" carpenter at the building of the first Meeting house. His wife, Rebecca, united with the church on the 12th of January 1777, and on the 19th of the same month their son Lyman was baptized.

Mr. Joseph Atkins and his son Joseph lived in one house, a quarter of a mile west of Abraham Woster's house, or of the Center. Deacon Rogers lived half a mile west of the Center. Daniel Byington and his son Daniel lived at the "Mill Place." West of this were Mr. John Alcock and several of his children, settled on nearly one thousand acres of land. North of the Center on the "Bound Line" road there were no residents, except Mr. Talmage, nearer than Thomas Upson, the father of Charles, Esquire, and where Charles afterward resided. The Peck families lived further north-north-east. East of the Center less than half a mile lived Aaron Harrison (the first Deacon) with his father if then living. Southwest was David Norton ; then Wait Hotchkiss, Isaac Hopkins, the Sutliff family and Parker family. In Woodtick

---

mittee of said Society, to be improved to set up and maintain a Gospel ministry in said Society, and that the Secretary of the Colony shall issue and sign warrants for collecting of said tax in due form of law.

    A true copy of Record,
        Examined,
                By GEORGE WYLLIS, *Secretary.*

Judah Frisbie and others; and further east and south, on Bound Line, Amos Seward, and south of him Capt. Samuel Upson on the Turnpike. On the road from Wolcott to Cheshire were the Halls and Lewises, and east of this on Southington Mountain, the Carters; and further north the Beechers, Brockets, Plumbs, and others. John Bronson lived in the hollow half a mile directly east of the Center, and west of Southington mountain. It is said that at that time Southington Mountain was the best cultivated part of what is now Wolcott. And as the forests then consisted of "mighty trees" and the inhabitants were widely separated, it was in reality, "a church in the wilderness." The wild beasts made night hideous with their howlings, and it is told as a true story that the mother of the Halls used to relate, many years after, how careful she was at first, before putting her children to bed, to go to the bed and feel over the top of it, and under the blankets to see if, during the day, the "big snakes" had crept into the children's places.

Another difficulty at this time and for some years after was in the fact that there was not sufficient land cleared to produce food to supply the people, and hence many went to Southington, in summer time, and worked to earn provisions which they carried up the mountain on their backs, so as not to "starve in winter." Much is said at the present day about farming being hard work, but if we were to walk three miles down a mountain, and work from sunrise to sunset and then carry up the mountain three-fourths of a bushel of rye as the reward of such a day's labor we might think farming harder than it now is. Now, a man laboring by the day earns between two and three bushels of rye, but a hundred years ago he received only three-fourths of a bushel. The necessity for summer work was increased by the fact that very little could be done in the winter by which to get money or provisions. If they cut down the forests to clear the land, there was no demand for the wood; this must be burned in great heaps where it was cut. No mechanical work of any extent was required. The first wagon in Wolcott was brought in, in 1800, by Lucius Tuttle, and it marked a period of wonder and improvement. A little could be done by way of getting "logs to the mill" for lumber, but no great amount of work of this kind could be done, for there were but two "saw mills" in the town,— one where Mr. Pritchard's mill now is, and one at Woodtick,— and there was but little demand for lumber. In the house, the women were always at work. In the fall and beginning of winter they must make the clothes for the family for the year. As soon as "New Year's Day" was past they prepared to sit down at the "little wheel" to spin the "flax," and from New Year until April the "little wheel" occupied all the leisure time the mother and elder daughters could find. And in the latter part of spring and on into summer the "big wheel" usurped authority over the "little wheel" and the spinning of wool was the great extra work of the house.

Thus began the church in Wolcott.

CHAPTER II.

BUILDING A MEETING HOUSE.

At the first meeting of the Society, Nov. 13, 1770, action was taken in regard to a Meeting house. We find the following votes:

"Voted to Build a Meeting House. At the same meeting Joseph Atkins was chosen Agent to go to the County Court for a Committee to stick the stake for said Meeting House. At the same meeting, Capt. Enos Brooks, Capt. Enos Atwater, and Col. Hall were nominated a committee to stick the stake for said House. At the same meeting voted to lay a rate Half Penny on the Pound to defray the Society Charges [in this matter]. At the same meeting voted to pay the said Half Penny rate by the first Day of February next, and Joseph Atkins and Jared Harrison were chosen Collectors to collect said rate."

The energy with which Mr. Joseph Atkins moved in this matter is seen in the fact that the next day after this meeting and after his appointment as agent, he presented his memorial to the Court in Hartford, as appears from the following paper :

APPOINTMENT OF THE COMMITTEE.

"*At a County Court held at Hartford, in and for the County of Hartford, on the first Tuesday of November, A. D., 1770:*

Upon the Memorial of Joseph Atkins of Farmingbury and the Rest of the Inhabitants of the Parish of Farmingbury in said County showing to this Court that at a Society Meeting held in said Society on the 13th day of November, instant, it was voted (wherein more than two thirds of the Inhabitants were in the affirmative), to Build a Meeting House in said Parish, and thereupon appointed the said Joseph Atkins their Agent to apply to this Court, for the appointment of a Committee to repair to said Society to affix a stake in said Society, for said Inhabitants to Build a Meeting House upon, for Divine Worship, as per Memorial on file, dated the 4th day of November, 1770:

Whereupon this Court appoint Col. Benjamin Hall, Capt. Enos Brooks, and Capt. Enos Atwater, all of Wallingford, in New Haven County, a Committee with full power to repair to the Said Parish of Farmingbury, Notify the Inhabitants of said Parish, View all circumstances, and hear all Parties, and affix a stake upon some convenient spot of ground in said Society, for the Inhabitants thereof to Build a meeting House upon for the Purpose of Divine Worship, and make report of their doings herein to us at the next Court.

A true copy of Record,
Examined
By GEORGE WYLLYS, *Clerk*.

NOTIFICATION OF THE COMMITTEE.

To the Inhabitants of the Society of Farmingbury, Greeting:

Whereas, The Honorable County Court at Hartford in Their Sessions In November, Instant, appointed us subscribers a Comttee with instructions to repair to Said Society, Give warning to the Inhabitants, view their circumstances, Hear the Parties, &c., and affix a Place for said Inhabitants to build a meeting house upon:

These are Therefore to Notify said Inhabitants to Attend on said Comttee on The Last Tuesday of Instant November by Their Agents, Committees, or otherwise as They Shall Think fit in order to Enable said Comttee to Do The business assigned Them by Said Court, and Mr. Joseph Atkins of Sd Society is hereby Desired to Notify said Inhabitants accordingly. Dated at Wallingford the 23d of November, Anno 1770.

BENJAMIN HALL,
ENOS BROOKS,   *Comttee.*
ENOS ATWATER,

HISTORY OF WOLCOTT.

ORDER OF THE COURT.

At an adjourned County Court holden at Hartford, in and for the County of Hartford, on the fourth Tuesday of January, Anno Domini, 1771.

Whereas, upon the Memorial of the Inhabitants of the Parish of Farmingbury by their agent Joseph Atkins praying for a Committee to affix a place in said Society for the Inhabitants thereof to Build a Meeting House upon, for Divine Worship, the County Court at their sessions at Hartford within and for Hartford County on the first Tuesday of November, A. D., 1770, appointed Benjamin Hall, Esq., Capt. Enos Brooks, Capt. Enos Atwater a Committee to repair to said Society of Farmingbury—hear all parties and view all circumstances, and affix a place for the Inhabitants thereof to Build a Meeting House upon, for Divine Worship as by the records of said County Court fully appears.

The said Committee having Returned their report in the Premises therein setting forth that on the 27th, 28th, and 29th Days of November, 1770, the Said Parish before being Notified to attend them, did repair to Said Parish of Farmingbury and there heard all parties and viewed all circumstances, and there affixed a Place in said Society, and erected a stake thereon, with stones about it, viz.: on a Beautiful Eminence and on the line Dividing between the Towns of Waterbury and Farmington, a little Northerly of Mr. Abraham Worster's Dwelling House in said Society, near where the North and South Highways cross each other in said Society as per Report on file, Dated the 30th Day of November, 1770, which said report this Court accept and approve of, and thereupon this Court Order and Direct that the Place mentioned in the said report of the said Committee be and the same is hereby Established as the Place whereon the said Society Shall Erect and build a Meeting House, for the Purpose of Divine Worship accordingly.

A True Copy of Record,
Examined
By GEORGE WYLLYS, *Clerk.*

The Papers containing the above action of the Court are still preserved, and are signed in the hand writing of George Wyllys, Clerk of Records. After being folded, on one is written: "Copy of record for Mr. Joseph Atkins.

Court Fees 9 3
and Copying fee 6/ £0 15^s 3^d."

Mr. Atkins' name in these papers, and frequently in the church Records, is spelled Adkins. It is herein uniformly written Atkins; because when he signed the Deed to the Society, *he* wrote his name "Joseph Atkins."

This order of the court was given during the court term which began on the fourth Tuesday of January, 1771; but before the order was received by the Society, and probably before the court made the order, the Society took the following action on the report of the committee, in a Society meeting held on the Second Wednesday of January, 1771: "Voted to confide in what the late Committee did in fixing a place for the Meeting house." On the 21st day of the same month, in another Society meeting, they again "Voted to confide in what the late Committee did in fixing a place for a Meeting house."

In the next April, 22d day, at a Society meeting, the following persons were chosen a "*Meeting House* Committee:" Lieut. Josiah Rogers, Mr. Samuel Upson, Mr. Stephen Barnes, Mr. Joseph Beecher, Mr. Daniel Alcox.

This was a choice committee. These men were reliable, good men; equal, under ordinary circumstances, to the work committed to them; but the difficulties around and before them were peculiarly numerous. The Parish was new, not yet six months old, and had assumed nearly all the responsibilities of a Town, without the benefits. They had the work of dividing the parish into school districts, laying taxes for the support of these schools, providing school houses in some parts, and the ordering of the number of months school should be kept. They appointed a committee to survey the parish and fix the boundaries, and laid a tax to pay the expenses of surveying.

The Society meetings had voted, besides school tax and surveying tax, a tax for the committee to fix the stake for the Meeting house ; a tax of "one penny half-penny" to procure preaching, and the tax of three pence per acre granted by the Assembly, for "Maintaining of Divine Worship." Besides this, the country was new. Some of these men were born in Wolcott, but were the *first generation*. Their fathers all, as near as we can learn, immigrated to Wolcott. How were they to build a meeting house? If the house could be built at the cost of five hundred dollars, from whence was the money to come? This committee doubtless consulted together, and with the people of the Parish, and much desired to see that Meeting house, but we hear nothing of it for six months.

There was but one thing unfortunate about that committee ; the name of Joseph Atkins was not at its head. He never slept six months at a time ; when he moved others moved also. Whatever he touched seemed to rise to life, like the bones of the old prophet. As far as the record shows, he never failed but once, and that when sent by this parish as agent to the General Assembly in 1787 to secure town privileges. The united opposition of the adjoining towns of Waterbury and Southington was too strong for the energetic Joseph. Had he been on the committee there would have been some work done somewhere, and a report made at the next meeting; but as it was, they came to the meeting on the 22d day of next November, made Mr. Joseph Atkins moderator, and the first business done is recorded thus : "Voted to go about building a Meeting house forthwith." Voted to build said house 58 feet in length and 42 feet wide. Voted to have said house 24 feet between joints. Voted to face said house to the south. Voted to board the body of said house. Voted to shingle said house with chestnut shingles. Voted to clapboard said house with 'drent' oak."

On the first Tuesday of the next December, about two

weeks after the above meeting, they met and "Voted to take 12 feet from the length of the house, and 8 feet from the width, and two feet from the height." Also, "Voted that Abraham Woster should be master builder on said house."

Another meeting was held on the first Tuesday of January, 1772, when it was "Voted to add to the length of said meeting house six feet, and four feet to the breadth." After these last votes there appears to have arisen some further discussion about the Meeting house, when they voted to "Reconsider all the votes taken in said meeting, respecting building a Meeting house, and dissolved said meeting."

This last vote seems to have referred to all the votes taken in all the previous meetings in regard to the building of a Meeting house, for on the 20th day of the same month (January, 1772), they held another meeting, in which the only business recorded was concerning the Meeting house, as follows: "Voted to build a Meeting house 48 feet long and 36 feet wide. Voted to have the height of said house left with the carpenter. Voted to cover said house as the first proposed house was voted to be covered. Voted to give Mr. Abraham Woster 24 shillings for his services." From these records it appears that some work in making preparations, or estimates for building had been done by the master carpenter, and also by others, towards the building of the house. We are not informed as to the method pursued in building, except it appears that the work was not let by the job, but done by the day, as to the master builder. Whether work or lumber and materials were given by the parishioners, we are not directly informed, but the probability, from the facts mentioned, is that much was given in this way.*

---

* The frame of the Meeting house was, probably, raised about the first of April, 1772, but no record is found concerning it, except the following, which was written on the inside of the back cover of the Society Book, without date: "Capt. Hopkins, Ensign Beecher, Daniel Byington, Isaac

On the first Monday in March next a meeting was held and further action taken. "Voted to lay the underpinning of the Meeting house in lyme mortar. Voted to have the window frames made of chestnut, and to have 24 panes of 7 by 9 glass in each window."

The next meeting was held on the first Monday of April, one month later, when they "Voted to lay a rate of two pence on the pound, to defray the Meeting house charges, and that said rate should be paid by the first of October next."

It is very probable that from the first Mr. Joseph Atkins agreed to give the land on which to build a Meeting house, but now that that house was in process of construction, and probably the frame was standing in its place, and a tax was to be collected to pay for the building of the house, it was very proper that it should rest on a good title of land, so that no trouble should arise from this direction. Therefore Mr. Atkins proceeded to execute the deed. And here again is seen the character of Joseph Atkins. Instead of giving a plot of ground one hundred feet by fifty, he gave two acres. This land was given, as is seen by the deed, from the noblest impulses and for the noblest ends. And when thus devoted to the publishing of "good tidings" to lost men, it is saddening to know that on one corner of this square was erected a "whipping post," and that at this post were whipped several persons, and among them one woman, for stealing.

THE DEED.*

"To all people to whom these presents shall come greeting. Know ye that I, Joseph Atkins, of Waterbury, in the County of New Haven, in the Colony of Connecticut, in New England, for the Consideration of the love and good will which I have and do

---

Twitchell, Joseph Atkins, Jr., Abraham Woster, Isaac Cleveland, Elijah Gaylord, to sell liker and vitels During the time of Raising the meting House, and any Body Else that is a mind to."

* The original deed is preserved.

BUILDING A MEETING HOUSE.

bear to the Society of Farmingbury, part of which is in Waterbury aforesd, and part in Farmington, in the County of Hartford, do give, grant, convey, & Confirm unto David Norton, Amos Seward, Daniel Alcox, Stephen Barnes, and Joseph Beecher, as they are Society's Committee for sd Society and their Successors in Quality of Society's Committee, and to the rest of the Inhabitants of the Society of Farmingbury aforesd, to be Used & improved for the only purpose of Building and continuing a Meeting House for the Public Worship of God thereon, and for needful and convenient accommodations around the same, Two acres of Land. That is to say, one acre at the Southwest corner of the forty-first Long lot in the West Division in the Township of Farmington aforesd, Eleven Rods & an half wide at the West end, and nine Rods & an half wide at the East End, Extending East from the Line between the Towns so far as to make one acre buting West on the Line of Waterbury aforesd, South on Highway, East and North on the Remainder of the said 41st Lot.

And also one acre of land in the Township of Waterbury aforesd, lying West from the above described land adjoining to the Highway between sd Waterbury & Farmington Twelve Rods wide, North and South, to extend West so far as to make one acre, Buting Northward on Highway, West and South on my own land, & East on Highway; which Land Described as aforesd, I, the sd Atkins, make over to the Society of Farmingbury aforesd, for their use and benefit as above sd, & for the Church to be gathered, & which shall or may Worship in the sd House to be Erected according to the Method, Doctrines, & Discipline now owned and practiced by the churches in the Colony, whether Called Presbyterian, Congregational, or Consociated by way of Distinction from Episcopalians, Baptists, Separatists, or other Sectaries,— To have and to hold the above granted and given premises, with all the Privileges and appurtenances thereunto belonging, unto them the sd grantees and to their successors forever, to & for the use aforesd. And also I, the said Joseph Atkins, do for myself and my Heirs, Executors, and administrators, Covenant with the said Grantees and their successors, that at & until the Ensealing of these presents I am well seized of the premises as a good indefeasible Estate in Fee simple, and have good Right to give and Convey the same in manner and form as is above written, and that the Same is free of all Encumbrances whatever. And furthermore, I, the s^d Atkins, do by these presents Bind myself and my Heirs forever to warrant and Defend the above granted and given premises to them the s^d Grantees and their successors against all Claims and Demands whatever. In Witness, whereof, I have hereunto set my hand and seal, the 8th Day of June, in the 12th year of the Reign of our Sovereign Lord, George the Third of Great Britain, &c., King, A. D., 1772.

JOSEPH ATKINS. | L. S.

Signed, sealed, and delivered in presence of
JOSEPH HOPKINS.
LAURA HOPKINS.

N. B. The words Eleven Rods & an half Interlined in the 16th line, and the words nine Rods and an half Interlined in the 17th line, and the word eleven, Interlined in the 23d line, were wrote before the Deed was signed.

Waterbury, in New Haven County, the Day and Date above written, Personally appeared Mr. Joseph Atkins, Signer & Sealer of the foregoing Instrument, and acknowledged the same to be his Free act and Deed.

Before me JOSEPH HOPKINS, *Justs. Peace.*"

On the Deed, after being folded, is written :

" David Norton & others, Inhabitants of Farmingbury. Deed of Gift of Joseph Atkins.

Rec^d. June 12th, A. D., 1772, & is Recorded in Farmington, 17th Book of Records, page 427. Pr Sal. Whitman, Reg^r.

Rec^d also to Record in Waterbury, July the 6th, A. D., 1772.

And Recorded in Waterbury Land Records, Book 15th, Page 312. Pr Ezra Bronson, Recorder."

While Mr. Atkins was thus doing his part, the Meeting house was rising to perfectness in its place, and the people seemed ready to do their part as the cause might need. They were not only ready to pay the tax already assessed in behalf of the Meeting house, but they met

BUILDING A MEETING HOUSE.

again on the "Third Monday of August, following, and voted to lay a rate of four pence on the pound, to be paid the first of December next, said rate being to defray the Meeting house charges."

In order to know what an effort it was for the people to build this church, we must take a little survey of the parish. The territory was newly settled. The older, active men in the Society, such as Joseph Atkins, Sen., Curtiss Hall, and John Bronson, were born elsewhere, and had come into the community and settled as farmers. The younger men, like Aaron Harrison, Daniel Byington, Jr., Joseph Atkins, Jr., and many others who were active members in the Society, were born here, or a little time before their parents came here, and were just beginning in the world, having no fortune of money, or old homesteads left them. The sixteen thousand acres of land in the parish, with all other taxable property, amounted in the assessment on the tax list to about two dollars and fifty cents per acre, or forty thousand dollars, or £8,000. Some of this amount belonged to Episcopalians, and hence was not available to the parish. The parish proper contained about seventy-five families, and the $40,000 divided equally among them, gives them about five hundred dollars of farming capital each, in the assessment list.

If we were building a church to-day, and should find a family with only such a capital in farming, we would be moved to pass by without asking a dollar, even for the church. Yet they taxed themselves toward building the church equal to six dollars a family. Several of these families were building houses for their own shelter from the cold and the storm.*

How could they, with all other expenses growing out of the forming of a new parish, build and pay for a meeting house? Yet they did it, for the house was built at

---

* Quite a number of them were living in log houses.

that time, and we hear nothing of debts for a meeting house afterward.*

On the 26th day of October, 1772, at a parish meeting, they voted to have "our meetings for the future in the Meeting house." Here was the Meeting house so far completed that they could hold meetings in it. What a day of gladness to all who loved the "Hill of Zion" must that have been when they first assembled in that house!

This Meeting house stood on the north side of the "Green," or "Square," facing the Green, and also facing the south. The principal door was in the front, and there was a door also in each end, east and west. It is said that the house stood on the line that divided the towns from which the parish was formed,— half in Waterbury and half in Farmington. The house at first was not finished inside. The floor was laid, the frame-work of the gallery was put in its place, and the stairs were built. The gallery may have been used some on special occasions, and for the singers, in which case a temporary flooring must have been laid, but ordinarily the singers sat below. The house was furnished in the simplest manner for some ten years, there being neither pews, stationary seats, nor permanent pulpit.

There were probably but little if any dedicatory services, as they had no pastor, though they were trying to arrange with a Mr. Jackson to become their pastor; but in this they did not succeed.

Rev. Mr. Keys said, in an obituary notice, that Deacon Aaron Harrison made the first public prayer that was made in this house. This is all we can learn of dedicatory services.

At this time there were neither church organization nor church officers. The Society was organized, and had a Meeting house, and the parish had charge of many duties

---

* Since writing the above I have found that there was a small amount of indebtedness for the lumber, not paid till some ten to twelve years after.

which were attended to by town officers in other parts. In Westbury and Waterbury the town managed ecclesiastical matters for years, but in Farmingbury the Ecclesiastical Society conducted many interests belonging to the towns.

As illustrative of the many interests they attended to, we give a list of the officers chosen at some of the Society meetings for a few years after the organization :

OFFICERS CHOSEN NOV. 13, 1770.

Moderator, Capt. Aaron Harrison ; Clerk for the year, Daniel Byington, Sen.; Society Committee for the Year, Lieut. Josiah Rogers, Mr. John Alcox, Mr. Stephen Barnes, Mr. John Bronson, Mr. Amos Seward ; Collectors to collect the Society Rate, Curtiss Hall and Daniel Alcox; Treasurer, Lieut. Josiah Rogers ; School Committee for the year, David Norton, Seth Bartholomew, Daniel Alcox, Amos Beecher, Joseph Beecher, Justus Peck, Capt. Aaron Harrison, Stephen Barnes, and Samuel Upson ; Special Committee to Divide the Society into Districts, David Warner, Wait Hotchkiss, Simeon Hopkins, Nathaniel Lewis, Capt. Aaron Harrison, Joseph Beecher; To read the Psalms for the year, Capt. Aaron Harrison and Mr. Amos Seward ; Grave-Digger, John Barrett.

Voted that the schooling should be by the poll, and that each School Committee shall collect their poll rate in his district.

In December of the same year, 1770, at the adjourned meeting, they again elected officers :

To take the marks of Stray Sheep, Daniel Johnson and Daniel Byington ; Chainmen, to measure the Society, Sergt. Samuel Smith, James Warner, and David Bronson ; County Surveyor, Lieut. Ashbel Potter ; To collect the Rate to pay for Surveying the Parish, Abel Curtiss and Curtiss Hall.

1771.

At the annual meeting held in November, 1771, they elected the following officers :

Moderator, Isaac Hopkins ; Clerk for the year, Daniel Byington; Treasurer, Lieut. Josiah Rogers; Society Committee for the year, Mr. David Norton, Mr. Amos Seward, Sergt. Stephen Barnes, Mr. Daniel Alcox, and Mr. Joseph Beecher. Collectors, Heman Hall and Joseph Atkins, Jr.; To Collect the Churchmen's Rate, Ensign Oliver Welton; School Committee, Joseph Sutliff, Jr., Joseph Atkins, Jr., Ensign John Alcox, Amos Seward, Capt. Aaron Harrison, Jedediah Minor, Nathaniel Lewis, Samuel Plumb, and Daniel Finch.

Voted that each School Committee shall collect the poll rate.

1772.

At a meeting in March, 1772, a committee was appointed to "Fix a place or places for burying grounds, consisting of Ensign Welton, Capt. Harrison, Sergt. Barnes, Mr. Joseph Beecher, Mr. Israel Clark."

In November, 1772: Moderator, Capt. Isaac Hopkins; Clerk for the year, Daniel Byington; Society Committee, Mr. David Norton, Mr. Amos Seward, Lieut. John Alcox, Mr. Joseph Beecher, Mr. John Bronson, Mr. Stephen Barnes, and Daniel Alcox; Treasurer, Lieut. Josiah Rogers; School Committee, Mr. Simeon Hopkins, Jacob Carter, Capt. Aaron Harrison, Eliakim Welton, Jr., Joseph Beecher, Justus Peck, Daniel Byington, John Bronson, Samuel Upson.

Voted that the school shall be by poll, and that each School Committee shall collect the poll rate.

Special Collectors, Ensign Oliver Welton and Eliakim Welton, Jr.; Collectors for the year, Levi Gaylord and Justus Peck; Special Committee to try to secure Mr. Jackson as Pastor, Capt. Harrison, Mr. Hotchkiss, Lieut. Rogers, Sergt. Barnes, and Mr. Amos Seward.

1773.

Officers chosen in Society meeting, November, 1773:

Moderator, Capt. Hopkins; Clerk, Daniel Byington; Treasurer, Simeon Hopkins; Society Committee, Mr. Amos Seward, Mr. Joseph Beecher, and Sergt. Stephen Barnes; Collector, Justus Peck; School Committee, Stephen Barnes, Capt. Harrison, Joseph Beecher, John Bronson, Daniel Byington, Nathaniel Sutliff, Amos Seward, and Daniel Alcox; Grave Digger, John Barrett; To take the marks of Stray Sheep, Daniel Johnson and Daniel Byington; Extra School Committee, Lieut. Rogers, Capt. Harrison, Nathaniel Lewis, Samuel Upson, and Capt. Hopkins were chosen a Committee to "view the School Districts and alter them as they see fit."

The list of offices filled for the next year includes some in addition to those already given, and nearly completes the list of those appointed by the Society.

NOVEMBER 28, 1774.

Moderator, Deacon Aaron Harrison; Clerk, Daniel Byington; Treasurer, Simeon Hopkins; Society Committee, Mr. Amos Seward, Sergt. Stephen Barnes, Mr. Samuel Upson; Collectors, Mark Harrison and James Thomas; Grave Digger, John Barrett; Key Keeper, Daniel Alcox; School Committee, Justus Peck, Jessie Alcox, Deacon Harrison, Sergt. Stephen Barnes, Daniel Johnson, Amos Seward, Simeon Hopkins, Daniel Alcox, Eliakim Welton, Jr.

At the same meeting, "Voted, that we would try the affair respecting the land belonging in Southington." Here was a resolution to enter into a suit at law with Southington.

At an adjourned meeting held the week afte the above action, it was "Voted to reconsider the vote by which Samuel Upson was nominated Constable, and also that by which Eliakim Welton was nominated Surveyor."

By these votes it seems that the Parish sometimes nominated such officers; or that having done so once, it seemed wise to withdraw the nomination.

The energy and correctness with which these men entered upon this work indicates more than an ordinary business talent and spirit in the community, for I venture that few ecclesiastical societies and towns in this or any other State have kept as full records and attended to all items of public interest with greater care than has been the case here.

CHAPTER III.

OBTAINING A PASTOR.

At the first Society meeting, Nov. 13, 1770, the following record was made: "Capt. Aaron Harrison was chosen to read the psalms for the year ensuing. At the same meeting Amos Seward was chosen for the same purpose." At the same meeting five choiristers were appointed, and it was voted to "give Mr. Joseph Atkins £1 5s 0d for the use of his house to meet in on the Sabbath, for the year ensuing until the first of May next."

In the adjourned meeting held in December, about a month later, it was "Voted to lay a rate of one penny half penny on the pound to procure preaching."

At the meeting, the next April 22d, 1771, they "Voted to have preaching this summer," and, to sustain this, they voted to lay a "half penny rate in addition to the penny half penny" voted in December previous. As the tax list of the Parish amounted to about three thousand five hundred pounds, this tax brought them only one hundred and fifty dollars, and at five dollars a Sabbath, this would give them preaching thirty Sabbaths, or a little over two Sabbaths in the month during the year. Hence, because of this small sum with which to maintain public worship, they at this same meeting, April, 1771, "Voted to have all the land in this Society taxed," and appointed Captain Aaron Harrison and Mr. Stephen Barnes agents to procure a grant from the Assembly to this effect; but it was so late in the session that the application was not made till the next meeting of the Assembly in the Autumn. Hence at an adjourned meeting held on the last Monday of the following September they "voted to have the said memorial for said land tax to be carried into the next Assembly ; giving the agents leave to alter in respect to the Churchmen as they think best." Mr. Samuel Upson, Daniel Alcox, and Joseph Atkins were appointed agents to carry the Memorial to the Assembly. It was carried and the result appears in the following

GRANT OF THE ASSEMBLY.

At a General Assembly of the Governor and company of the Colony of Connecticut, holden at New Haven, on the 2d Thursday of October, Anno Domini, 1771 :

Upon a memorial of the Society of Farmingbury presented by Joseph Atkins, Samuel Upson, and Daniel Alcox, agents for said Society, representing to this Assembly that the list of said Society is small, and they unable to set up and maintain the Worship of God among them without some further help, praying for a tax on all the lands within said Society, &c., as per memorial on file :

Resolved by this Assembly, that a tax of three pence on the acre for the term of four years, to be annually collected, be laid on all the lands within said Society which belong to the Inhabitants living within the limits of said Society, not being professors of the Church of England, and also on that part of the lands of the non-resident Proprietors, which land is not put into the General list of such non-resident proprietors, and not holden to pay taxes in other Societies or towns : and Stephen Barnes, of Farmington, and Daniel Alcox, of Waterbury, are hereby appointed and fully empowered to collect the said tax of the Proprietors of such lands as aforesaid, and the same to pay to the Committee of said Society to be improved to set up and maintain a Gospel ministry in said Society ; and that the Secretary of the Colony shall issue and sign warrants for the collecting of said tax in form of law.

A true copy of record,
Examined
By GEORGE WYLLYS, *Sec.*

By this tax the Society raised, probably, four hundred and fifty dollars. If it had received a tax on all the lands within its bounds, at three pence per acre, it would have received about six hundred dollars, but the Episcopalians and some others were exempt.

Several persons were paying taxes for church support in Bristol and Waterbury and perhaps Southington. The Society, also, released every year quite a number of persons from paying their rate.

It was very soon after this grant of tax from the Assembly that this Society voted to "go about building a Meeting house forthwith," and it is possible that some of this tax money was used in building the Meeting house, which would be "setting up and maintaining the worship of God."

At the annual meeting, November, 1771, they "Voted to give John Atkins, Jr., ten shillings for the use of his house the summer past," and also to "Give Mr. Atkins and his son five shillings per month" for the future. And at the same meeting they "Voted to lay a rate of two pence on the pound, to be laid out for preaching the ensuing year."

Thus had they passed through the first year of ecclesiastical society work. That they had had preaching much of the time is quite evident from the fact of the use of the money raised for that special purpose; and, also, from the fact of laying another tax for the same purpose, besides that which was to come by the Assembly tax. To read the psalms the ensuing year, they had appointed Mr. Isaac Hopkins, Capt. Aaron Harrison, and Mr. Amos Seward. They meant "progress," and began to look more cheerfully for a minister who should become their pastor. In January, 1772, they met and made further arrangements for a Meeting house. In March they met again, and decided as to the laying of the foundation of the Meeting house. In April they held another meeting, and arranged further concerning the foundation.

THE FIRST CALL.

On the first day of June, 1772, in a Society meeting they "Voted to give Mr. Jackson a call on probation." He

OBTAINING A PASTOR.

had probably been preaching to them a few Sabbaths before this meeting was held, and he accepted this call on probation. On the second Monday of the next August they voted "to meet on the Sabbath at Mr. Upson's new house." Hitherto they had met at Mr. Atkins' house, but now they go to the new house, probably because it was larger and more commodious. Where this house was we cannot learn definitely, but the Upson families resided near the center on the north road, and it was doubtless on that road.*

The Society met again on the last Monday in the following September and voted to have Mr. Jackson on probation one month longer, and also that the Society's Committee should "go and treat with Mr. Jackson whether he will stay one month longer on probation, and likewise to ask him whether he will settle with us if we can agree on terms." At the end of the month, 26th of October, they came together and voted to settle Mr. Jackson if they could agree, and adjourned the meeting one hour. When they met, at the end of the hour, they agreed to give Mr. Jackson as a settlement 175 pounds and to be "four years paying said settlement," and to "give 50 pounds salary, to be paid yearly, four years," and then to raise it to 75 pounds; "to be continued during his continuing with us."

And it was at this meeting that it was voted to hold their meetings for the future in the Meeting house. Mr. Jackson did not accept this call, but appears to have continued to preach to the Society several weeks, for on the last day of November, 1772, a month later, they appointed a special committee to prevail with him to settle with them; and this committee did not succeed. In the next meeting, in January, 1773, they voted to "apply to some man to preach with us on probation a few Sabbaths."

---

* Since writing the above, we have learned that this house was that of Mr. Thomas Upson, and was the house where Charles Upson, Esquire, afterwards resided, and where Mr. Joseph H. Somers now resides.

Thus were they all "at sea" again concerning a Minister and Pastor.

A PASTOR OBTAINED.

On the second day of August, 1773, the record says: "Voted to continue Mr. Gillet with us as a preacher longer." "Voted to improve Mr. Gillet ten Sabbaths more, and on probation." On the second Monday of October next, before the ten weeks were ended, they gave Mr. Gillet a call, agreeing to give him as a settlement 175 pounds, and to be four years paying the settlement, and to pay him 50 pounds salary yearly for four years, and then raise it to 75 pounds yearly, which was $250 a year for four years, and after that $375 a year.

Mr. Gillet accepted this invitation, as appears from the fact that the Society held another meeting about six weeks after the invitation was given (Nov. 29th), and voted to have the "ordination on the 29th day of December next," and voted also that "All that is due to Mr. Gillet shall be paid the first of March next; and all that shall become due between this time and the first of said March, together with one-quarter of the settlement proposed by the Society."

The minister thus found by the Society could not be installed over a church until a church should be organized, and to this work Mr. Gillet gave his attention. Here were scattered sheep in the wilderness, and duty was laid on him to look till he should find them, and gather them into one fold. Some were members in Waterbury, some in Southington, and other places. Of this there is no specific record, only that they were "members of several churches."

The only ceremony at the organization was the signing of "The Covenant of Confederation," in a meeting held for that purpose on the 18th of November, 1773. The original paper which they signed is not preserved; that which we have is the record which Mr. Gillet wrote in

OBTAINING A PASTOR.

the Church Book five years after he was installed. This book, the first used for church records, is a paper-covered, foolscap-size, unruled book of twenty-four sheets. It is literally "crammed" with writing, except parts of a few pages. The last record made was in 1830, by Deacon Isaac Bronson. On the first page of this book Mr. Gillet wrote the following statement, in an elegant handwriting: "A Book of Church Records from the year 1774, or December 29th, 1773, for Farmingbury Church. Alexander Gillet, Pastor."

The third page of this book contains the record of the formation of the church, and we give it just as Mr. Gillet wrote it, excepting the ornamental part :

"THE FOUNDATION OF THE CHURCH AT FARMINGBURY.

Their Covenant of confederation, assented to at Farmingbury, November 18th, 1773.

We, who are members of several churches, desiring to be built up a spiritual house on the foundation of the Apostles and Prophets, Jesus Christ being the chief corner-stone, in order to offer spiritual gifts and sacrifices acceptable to God through Christ, and being united in the bonds of Christian love, and in the faith of the gospel of Christ, do this day renewedly dedicate ourselves to God, acknowledging our great obligation to walk in all the commandments and ordinances of the Lord blameless,— and in the presence of God, angels, and men, do enter into covenant obligation with each other, as members in particular of one distinct and entire church, for all the purposes of Christian edification; promising, by the grace of God, to treat each other with all the tenderness, faithfulness, and watchfulness, which become members of the same body of Christ, humbly depending on, and begging grace from God, that we may find so much favor in His sight as to be found faithful to these our solemn obligations, through Jesus Christ our Lord. In confirmation of which we here subscribe our names. November, &c.

Aaron Harrison, Deacon, and Jerusha his wife.
Josiah Rogers, Deacon, and Sarah his wife.
Isaac Hopkins, and Mary his wife.

Joseph Atkins, and Abigail his wife.
Thomas Upson.
Joseph Sutliff.
Amos Seward, and Ruth his wife.
David Norton.
John Alcox, and Mary his wife.
Samuel Upson.
Wait Hotchkiss, and Lydia his wife.
Nathaniel Butler, and Rebecca his wife.
Elizabeth Porter.
Daniel Alcox, and Elizabeth his wife.
Joseph Hotchkiss and Hannah his wife.
Judah Frisbie.
Israel Clark, and Mahetable his wife.
Daniel Lane, and Jemima his wife.
Stephen Miles.
Stephen Barnes, and Sarah his wife.
Zadoc Bronson, and Eunice his wife.
Lucy Peck, the wife of Justus Peck.
Rebecca, wife of Nathaniel Hitchcock.
Esther Barrett.
Joseph Benham, and Elizabeth his wife.
Josiah Barnes.
Admitted by letter, &c., December 22d, 1773,—William Smith, Anne, wife of James Bailey; John Bronson, David Frost.
January 2d, 1774, Samuel Bradley.
By letter, Ephraim Pratt and his wife.
Elizabeth, wife of Ebenezer Wakelee.
Admitted January 16th, 1774, Sarah, wife of Isaac Clark, Martha, wife of Aaron Howe.
January 30th, Daniel Byington.

These names, with the above "covenant," fill the third page of the book. They are given entire, as an illustration of Mr. Gillet's method of church work.

Of these persons, there were forty-one who united in organizing the church; four united with the church one month later, in December, and seven united during January following.

The church being organized, their next step was the ordination of a pastor. There is no record of any action of the Church separate from that of the Society, yet it is evident that the Church united cordially with the Society in calling an ordaining Council.

OBTAINING A PASTOR.   35

The record of the ordination is as follows:

At an Ecclesiastical Council at Farmingbury, on Wednesday, the 29th of December, 1773, invited by the church in said Farmingbury for the purpose of the solemn separation of Mr. Alexander Gillet to the pastoral charge of said Church, and to the work of the gospel ministry in said Society,—convened according to letters missive: Present, Elders,— John Trumbull, Mark Leavenworth, Samuel Newell, Timothy Pitkin, Joseph Strong, Andrew Stores, Rufus Hawley. Messengers,— Thomas Matthews, Esq., Deacon Andrew Bronson, Deacon Stephen Hotchkiss, Deacon Seth Lee, Judah Holcomb, Esq., Deacon John Warner, Joseph Hart, Esq.

Rev. John Trumbull was chosen Moderator, and Timothy Pitkin chosen Scribe. This Council, having been certified by attested copies from records, both of this Church and Society, of their respective united invitations of Mr. Alexander Gillet to be their pastor, and his acceptance of their invitation, proceeded to examine Mr. Gillet as to his regular church membership, and his views and ends in entering into the sacred work of the gospel ministry, and qualifications therefor, are of opinion that the way is clear for this Council to proceed to the solemn separation of Mr. Alexander Gillet to the work of the gospel ministry and pastoral office in this place.

The Rev. Mr. Stores to make the prayer before the sermon, Rev. Mr. Strong to preach the sermon, Rev. Mr. Leavenworth to make the prayer before the charge, and Rev. Mr. Trumbull to give the charge; the Rev. Mr. Newell to make the prayer after the charge, and Rev. Mr. Hawley to give the right hand of fellowship.

Passed in Council,
Test. TIMOTHY PITKIN, *Scribe*.

On the same day that the Council was convened the Church held a meeting, and adopted some statements

CONCERNING CHURCH DISCIPLINE.*

At a church meeting held in Farmingbury December 29th, 1773, after mature consideration, the church agreed and voted in y^e

---

*Two or three samples only of the spelling and literal methods of writing in olden times are given in this book; all else is put into modern style as nearly as possible.

following plan of ch^h discipline : That this ch^h takes ye word of God to be the only sure and unerring rule of ch^h Discipline; neither do we think that any platform of human composure, without just exceptions. However, we agree that ye platform drawn up by ye Elders & Messengers of ye ch^hs of Connecticut, convened at Saybrook, A. D., 1808, in ye main is agreeable to ye Word of God & a good Directory. But,

1st. We are not well satisfied that ye 7th article in ye heads of agreement, drawn up by ye Elders & Messengers aforesaid, and ye first article in ye administration of ch^h discipline are without just exceptions; but we are of opinion y^t ye administration of ch^h discipline is communicated jointly to Pastor & church. However, as Pastors or Elders are worthy of double honor, so we believe they ought to have and be allowed a double vote in all acts and votes of ye ch^h.

2^ly. We are not satisfied with ye 7th article, that a ch^h in ye calling of a council, ought to be confined to ye consociated ch^hs of ye circuit to which they belong; but we believe that ye ch^hs when they so agree, have a right to call in a promiscuous Council.

3rd. With respect to ye 8th article we are not satisfied. But we think an offending brother has no liberty of appealing to a Council, either before or after excommunication from ye ch^h, unless ye Pastor & church judge that ye nature of ye case require it, and will join in calling a Council.

4^thly. With respect likewise to ye 4th article, we are not very well satisfied, for we believe that whenever a Council is called, nothing ought to be deemed an act of it which hath not ye major part of ye Elders separate, and likewise of ye Messengers present.

5^thly. Lastly, we are not satisfied with ye 14th article ; for tho' we allow it to be expedient, yet destitute and bereaved ch^hs, in ordinary cases, consult ye association, and take their advice concerning those persons who are fit to be called and settled in the gospel ministry among them; yet notwithstanding, as we believe y^t ch^hs have a right of choosing their own officers, so we do not look upon it they are absolutely bound to adhere to such advice at all times; but there may be cases in which they have a right to judge for themselves, and act without it.

Concerning ye rest of ye articles in Saybrook Platform, we are so far satisfied with them as to agree in taking them as a good help to understand ye mind of God in ye administration of ch^h discipline, and we agree to act in conformity to them till God please to give us further light.

At a ch^h meeting, Farmingbury, April 15th, 1779, the ch^h voted to adopt ye above plan of ch^h discipline.

Test. ALEXANDER GILLET, *Pastor*.

Thus was the first gospel minister settled in Farmingbury, afterwards Wolcott, to feed the flock of God and publish glad tidings to lost sinners. The scattered sheep had waited long for a fold, for they began to petition the General Assembly for such privileges, in 1760, and had continued their toils and oft-repeated petitions until the desired object was obtained and they had a Zion in the midst of them. One thing remained yet to be done to make complete the outward working of a church,— the election of deacons, and the consequent orderly administration of the sacraments.

The sacrament of baptism was administered the first time, in January, 1774, to a child: Eunice, the daughter of Stephen and Zilpha Pratt.

On the 29th of January, 1774, the church met for the purpose of electing deacons, and elected Captain Aaron Harrison for their first deacon, and Lieutenant Josiah Rogers for their second. They also "voted that the Sacrament of the Lord's Supper be observed once in two months ; the first to be on the first Saturday of February ensuing." It was probably observed on the 6th of that month, when Levi Gaylord and Lois his wife united with the church.

CHAPTER IV.

DURING MR. GILLET'S MINISTRY: FROM 1773 TO 1791.

The ministry of Mr. Gillet, as a settled pastor, began on the first Sabbath of January, 1774, with a church membership of forty-five persons, and a parish numbering scarcely seventy-five families, the greater part of whom had come into the territory within the twenty years preceding the organization of the church; so that the whole parish was only a new settlement.

The settlement was began, in Waterbury part, in 1731, by Mr. John Alcock. Mr. Thomas Upson removed into the south-east corner of the parish territory in 1732 or 1733, but most of the other families living in the eastern part of the parish in 1773 had removed thither after 1755, as nearly as can be ascertained. The comforts of these families, when Mr. Gillet's work began, were of the most restricted kind. Many of them resided in log houses, with no outhouses of any kind; a haystack with a fence around it was the only barn some of them possessed. Many years after, Mr. John Bronson, father of the Bronson families in this parish, quoted the text: "Is it time for you, O ye, to dwell in your ceiled houses, and this house lie waste?" and said he was not guilty of living in a ceiled house while the Meeting house was unceiled. In 1795, the Meeting house was ceiled; but Mr. Bronson's dwelling was not, until some time afterward. The western, or Waterbury part of the parish, was more advanced in settlement, but was mostly a wilderness of heavy timber. Mr. Judah Frisbie, one of the first settlers in Woodtick, if not the very first, purchased land there in the fall of 1773; the deed of the same being still preserved.

Mr. John Alcock had been in the parish territory thirty-two years when the church was organized; and some of his sons and daughters were settled on their farms before 1773. Mr. Isaac Hopkins and Benjamin Harrison (father of Deacon Aaron Harrison), and a few other families, had been in the parish about thirty years.

This was Mr. Gillet's parish. The remark is attributed to the oldest inhabitants, that when the Meeting house was raised, all the inhabitants in the parish could sit on its "sills." If those sills were of the length fixed upon by the Society in its first vote on the subject, they were 42 by 58 feet, and would not have seated over 140 persons,— men, women, and children.

Mr. Gillet graduated at Yale College, September, 1770. In 1771 he united with the church in Granby. After graduating, he taught school in Farmington a year or more, and may have studied theology during that time, under the direction of Rev. Timothy Pitkin, then pastor of the Farmington church. He was licensed to preach by the Hartford Association, on the 2d day of June, 1773, and on the 2d day of next August, the Society in Farmingbury "voted to continue Mr. Gillet ten Sabbaths more, and on probation." He had probably preached two Sabbaths, and these with the ten made three months, at the end of which he was installed. When he settled here he was unmarried, was twenty-four years of age, naturally of a quiet spirit, but devotedly, and what is often called deeply religious. The good order with which all church matters were arranged, indicates a qualification, both in maturity of thought and in devotedness to the work, equal to the position he had accepted. Many churches, directed by older men, have not been as well directed; and it is seldom that church records are as fully kept and as carefully preserved as these; and to this preservation of these first records is due, in a large degree, this book of history.

Mr. Gillet's father, Capt. Zaccheus Gillet, removed into

the parish soon after the installation of his son, and therefore it became home, indeed, to the young pastor.

Under Mr. Gillet's labors, the church, from the first, experienced a gradual growth, receiving members on profession of their faith from month to month, and some of the time from Sabbath to Sabbath. In June following the organization, there were sixty-two members. Ten years later, one hundred and three persons had united with the church. During his whole ministry, which lasted eighteen years, one hundred and forty persons were recorded as members of the church,—ninety-nine besides those who organized the church, and most of them by profession.

Through Mr. Gillet's efforts a library was formed for the parish. The only account of it which I have been able to procure is contained in an inscription in one of the books which has come into my hands : "This book belongs to the library in Farmingbury. Founded November 5, 1779. No. 50." This library was, after some years, scattered among the original contributors, and between 1820 and 1830, another was formed, which suffered a like fate.

In 1784, a larger number united with the church than in any other year during his stay in the parish. This was the result of some special efforts made in the previous year. From some writings left by Deacon Isaac Bronson, we learn that in 1783, "Mr. Gillet was unable to preach, and Rev. Edmond Mills preached here, and there was quite an awakening among the people, so that they had preaching three times on the Sabbath, and conferences three or four times a week ; " and " Mr. Gillet visited from house to house, and brought many good preachers here," so that the "awakening soon became general," and this continued, somewhat, during the summer, and on "August the 9th, on Saturday, while alone at work," Isaac Bronson became greatly awakened in his own behalf. This interest in the church "greatly animated Mr. Gillet," and his health began to improve, and after a few months he resumed his preaching.

By a vote of the Society, in June, 1783, Mr. Mills was hired to preach. No length of time is specified, but the probability is that he preached three or four months. At the next annual meeting of the Society Mr. Gillet's salary was made "the same as other years;" and while they paid two ministers, the Society received more than double benefit, for more members were added than during the five years preceding, and the church was greatly quickened, and the minister much encouraged in his work.

Previous to this revival there had been some things to discourage the minister and the church, and the community felt these influences more, even, than the church and minister. Deacon Isaac Bronson, speaking of the effort which Mr. Gillet made, in connection with the preaching of Mr. Mills, says : "A serious attention began to take place, which Mr. Gillet perceiving, was greatly animated himself, and brought many good preachers here, and went round to every house to visit his people, and alarm them from that stupidity which for a long time had grossly overspread the Society."

During the ten years since the organization of the church, there had been several cases of church discipline which caused much trouble, and as is usual, much deadness in church interests. The first case arose in June, 1774, peculiar in itself, because it related somewhat to the civil courts. It caused considerable difference of opinion, and some personal feeling, and in regard to it the church voted twice to call a council ; but they finally settled it among themselves by making "null and void all the votes that had been passed in regard to it," and likewise voted "to banish all differences which had been entertained, one towards another, and conduct themselves as forgiving Christian brethren."

In 1779, another difficulty arose, and continued till the autumn of 1781, when a council rendered its decision, and the church "voted to consent to the doings and advice of the Ecclesiastical Council," and "that all matters of past altercation, complaint, and uneasiness shall be laid aside ; and that the pastor and the church shall not receive any manner of complaint whatsoever from any person for anything that has been matter of complaint before the Council." But a further difficulty grew out of this same case, about one year after the above settlement, and caused some further feeling and dissatisfaction towards the minister and among the members of the church.

These troubles, doubtless, affected the sensitive mind of the pastor, and may have had much weight in discouraging him, and bringing him to that state of health in which he was not able to preach. Hence, when the signs of revival appeared among the people in 1783, it was the morning of a new life to pastor and people, and was, in effect, like the passing away of a very cold winter, and the coming of April showers ; all things began to spring into life and activity. The church had been overcome and trodden down by the spirit of the world. The revival was like the return of the captives from Babylon after seventy years. Jerusalem was all astir, and the walls of the city and of the temple began to rise from the dust and ruins with marvelous rapidity, and promise of final completion.

RESULTS.

Several things resulted from this revival worthy of notice. They proceeded to "improve the Meeting house." Hitherto the Meeting house had no stationary seats or pews. Their place was supplied with seats from various sources,—among others, some provided chairs for themselves. There is now in the possession of Mrs. Henry Carter a chair that was used by some of her ancestors for this purpose.

The gallery had no floor or seats in it, and there had been no plastering or ceiling done in the house. In December, 1783, the Society appointed "Lieut. Joseph Beecher, Deacon Josiah Rogers, Capt. Daniel Alcox, Capt. Samuel Upson, Esquire Stephen Barnes, Mr. Amos Seward, and Daniel Byington, a committee to settle the Meeting house accounts." These accounts had never been fully settled since the building of the Meeting house. There does not appear to have been debts of any great amount, but there was some trouble in adjusting these accounts among the different parties interested. This committee did not succeed in this matter, and in the spring (May 4, 1784), they appointed another committee, "with power to settle them according to their best judgment." This committee was the same as the former, except Mr. Simeon Hopkins in place of Deacon Rogers. At this meeting in May they "voted that we should do something to the Meeting house." "Voted that the joiner work to the lower part of the house should be done, and the front seats in the gallery, if there should be stuff enough." At the same meeting, Mr. David Norton, Capt. Nathaniel Lewis, and Lieut. Charles Upson were chosen a Meeting house committee. "Voted that the lower part of said Meeting house be ceiled up to the windows, and be made into pews, and the work to be done decent and plain. Voted to lay a rate of four pence (which was afterwards made to five pence) on the pound, to be laid on the list of 1783, to be paid by the first of October next, in wheat, rye, or Indian corn." At the same meeting Heman Hall and Nathan Stevens were chosen to collect said rate. This tax, with a one-penny addition laid on the list of 1784, to be paid the first of October, 1785, was, doubtless, for these expenses on the Meeting house.

Since writing the above a paper has been presented me by Mr. Silas B. Terry, of Waterbury, which was the order of the court for the collection of the tax for repairing the Meeting house. The list of assessments is not to be found, but reference to a town tax list in the history of the town, elsewhere in this volume, will give some idea of the tax to repair the Meeting house, only the Meeting house tax is double that of the town tax referred to.

THE ORDER OF THE COURT.

To Isaac Barnes, Collector of Society rate for the purpose of doing something to the Meeting house of the Parish of Farmingbury, in Waterbury, in New Haven County, greeting :

By virtue of the authority of the State of Connecticut, you are hereby commanded forthwith to levy and collect of the persons named in the annexed list herewith committed unto you, each one his several proportion as therein set down of the sum total of such list, being a tax or assessment granted by the inhabitants of the said Society of Farmingbury, regularly assembled on the 24th day of September, 1784, to defray the charge that shall arise in prosecuting the above said purpose, and pay or deliver such sum or sums which you shall so levy and collect unto the Society's treasurer for the time being of the said Society of Farmingbury, at or before the first day of October next ensuing the date hereof.

And if any person or persons shall neglect or refuse to make payment of the sum or sums whereof he or they are assessed and set in said list, to distrain the goods or chattels of such person or persons, and the same dispose of as the law directs, returning the surplus, if any be, unto the owner or owners ; and for want of such goods and chattels whereon to make distress, you are to take the body or bodies of such person or persons refusing, and him or them commit unto the keeper of the gaol of said county, within the said prison, who is hereby commanded to receive and safely keep him or them until he or they pay and satisfy the said sum assessed upon him or them as aforesaid, together with your fees ; unless the said assessment, or any part thereof, upon application made to the county court shall be abated, or otherwise as the law directs.

Dated at Waterbury, this 24th day of September, A. D., 1784.

JONATHAN BALDWIN, *Justice of the Peace.*

When the Meeting house was thus improved by pews, it became quite a serious matter how and where the people should sit. On September 24th, 1784, "voted to have the front seats done in the gallery." "Voted that Capt.

Samuel Upson, Capt. Nathaniel Lewis, Judah Frisbie, Simeon Hopkins, and Daniel Peck, be a committee to Dignify the Meeting house." "Voted to seat the Meeting house by age." "Voted to have men and women sit together." At the same meeting Daniel Norton, Mark Harrison, Daniel Byington, Jacob Carter, Capt. Daniel Alcox were chosen a committee to seat the Meeting house. One month after this meeting they met again and made further efforts to seat the Meeting house. "Voted to give the pew by the pulpit stairs to Mr. Gillet during the pleasure of the Society." "Voted to reconsider the vote that was taken to seat the Meeting house by age; and voted to seat the Meeting house by age and by list, allowing eight pounds to a year." "Voted that each man have one head, and only one, to be seated on." "Voted to have the aged widows seated in the first pew east of the pulpit." "Voted that Capt. Daniel Alcox, Daniel Byington, Jacob Carter, David Norton, and Ensign Streat Richards, and Simeon Hopkins, and Mr. Joseph Parker be a committee to seat the Meeting house as above." Two weeks after they met again, and voted that the seating of the Meeting house in regard to the money list, should be on the list of 1772. That is, if on that list a man paid taxes on forty pounds, he should have double honor in the church, compared with a man forty years old without any list. Also, at this adjourned meeting, they "voted to have a pew built over the stairs for the niggers." The seats made at this time in the gallery, were a row of "front seats," and some years after this, there were box pews made in the rear of these seats. The pews below were old-fashioned box or square pews. The pulpit stood on the north side of the church, opposite the front door, with a double window in the rear above it; and there was a door in each end of the church, east and west. The pulpit was very high, as was the custom in those days, and beneath it, and perhaps extending a little in front, were the seats for the deacons, and those important officers who noted the absentees from church, and especially those absent from the preparatory lecture and the Lord's Supper. The house thus arranged and well filled, as it probably was at this time, was well calculated to animate the speaker and secure the sympathy and attention of the audience. The pulpit was high, but so were the galleries on the three sides. The pulpit stood on the side of the house,—a great advantage over its being at the end, according to a more recent style.

This was as far as the Society could go at this time, and though the house was far from being furnished, it was a great improvement on the first ten years of its existence and use. The Society had some difficulty in paying for these improvements and settling the old accounts, for in November, 1785, they appointed another committee "to settle the old accounts in building the Meeting house."

Another interest arose from the improvements in the Meeting house. It was respecting the singing, and the singers. Soon after the house improvements were made,—that is, in November, 1784, at the annual meeting, they appointed three choristers, as they had been accustomed for several years, and voted that "the singers should have the front seats, if they chose to sit there." That is, probably, the front seats in the gallery.

The next April, at a Society meeting, they voted, that "it is our mind to have more help respecting setting the psalm," for by vote the church had decided to use Watts' Psalms in public worship. They also voted that the "singers should have liberty to choose their own leaders;" and then, frightened at this innovation, immediately reconsidered the vote and adjourned the meeting two weeks.

When they came together at the appointed time, they were over their fright, and more venturesome than before, and voted that "we will leave it with the singers to carry on singing as they think best, during the pleasure of the

DURING MR. GILLET'S MINISTRY.

Society." The Society had from the first taken special interest in singing, from the fact that they had, for a new farming community, a marvelous number of singers. Almost everybody could sing; and this heavenly talent is well continued unto the present day. The following list of choristers, chosen previous to 1785, will show somewhat the musical talent of the community; and several of them were not only singers, but musicians and poets:

1770.

Jacob Carter, Levi Bronson, Jared Harrison, Stephen Barnes, and David Alcox.

1771.

Samuel Upson, Levi Bronson, Jared Harrison, Jacob Carter, Samuel Harrison, Cyrus Norton.

1772.

Samuel Harrison, Jacob Carter, Cyrus Norton. And for bass singers, Mark Harrison, Samuel Atkins, Daniel Finch, and Jared Harrison.

1776.

Stephen Barnes, Samuel Harrison, Cyrus Norton, Mark Harrison, David Harrison, Ziba Norton.

1778.

Zaccheus Gillet.

1781.

Samuel Harrison, Cyrus Norton, Nathan Gillet.

1784.

Cyrus Norton, Isaac Carter, Nathan Gillet.

1785.

Samuel Harrison, Cyrus Norton, Isaac Carter, Mark Harrison, Dr. Potter, Jacob Carter, David Harrison, Ozias Norton, Joseph M. Parker, Joseph Miner, Jonathan Carter, Noah Norton, Elijah Horton. Thirteen.

This last array of choristers would frighten modern choirs, though many churches would be very glad to see the fright. Some persons now living in Wolcott remember having seen the front seats in the gallery of the old church on three sides nearly filled with singers, and with them the congregation joined in the singing. This was during Mr. Keys' ministry.

In 1787, the Society appointed "a committee to draw up a subscription for the encouraging of singing," consisting of Streat Richards, Mark Harrison, Cyrus Norton, Charles Upson, and Isaac Carter; and some years after they "laid a tax" for the same purpose. Such were some of the substantial and joyous results of one revival.

There came into the church at this time men who for many years were its leading members: among the more prominent of whom were Justus Peck, afterwards deacon, whose wife was one of the first members of the church; Charles Upson, afterwards justice of the peace in the town, and for quite a number of years an active man in the church and Society, Jacob Carter, Samuel Byington, Samuel Atkins, and Mark Harrison, afterwards justice of the peace, all active and reliable men for years, and some of them, many years. Isaac Bronson, though converted at the same time, did not unite with the church till 1788, and was afterwards made deacon and served the church and Society many years, in many offices. He also served the town in various offices, being elected Town Clerk and Treasurer, when the town was organized, and afterwards was Representative in the Assembly for many years.

There were also gathered into the church at this time a number of noble women who strengthened the church and did their part in the Redeemer's kingdom. Judah Frisbie was one of the formers and first members of the church; his wife was now also led into the fold, and the household was one in the church. Wealthy, wife of Charles Upson; Phebe, wife of Samuel Harrison; Mary Carter, wife of Jacob; Jerusha Norton, wife of Cyrus; Esther Atkins, wife of Samuel; and a number of others equally noted for their honorable lives, as Christian women.

It should be borne in mind that this revival occurred in

the year, and soon after the Declaration of Peace, and the acknowledgment of the Independence of the United Colonies in America. Mr. Gillet had not been settled three years when the war " broke out." He and his little band had held on their way courageously, considering the " trouble" of those years of sore conflict, privations, and fears. A number of his fellow citizens and parishioners " went to the war ;" some had returned, some never would return to the homes they had left. When the war began, Southington Mountain, lying just within the eastern boundary of Farmingbury, was the most flourishing district in the parish. The line of the mountain runs north and south ; and a road was constructed on the ridge or highest part of it, nearly the whole length, some two miles or more. Along this road were settled some of the most thrifty farmers in the parish, on some of the most beautifully located land, and most easy of cultivation, in the township.

It is said that the war made such desolation in these families, that those who were left began to move into other parts ; and the emigration continued untill a few years since, when the last inhabitant had fled. This whole district is now grown up into woods and bushes, except a few fields near the only remaining skeleton of a house, where stands, as a lonely sentinel, the "sweep" over the well ; the "old oaken bucket" having gone to the depths of the well many years ago.

The Revolution began this work of desolation with a strong hand, and now the end is fully come. Legends of the Revolution are still told, but they are thrown far into the shade by the sorrows of war in our own day. There is a family now in the parish whose grandfather was captain under Washington in Boston and on Long Island, and was in the battle which secured the surrender of General Burgoyne and his army, in 1777 ; but the remembrance of their only son and brother, who died in

Sherman's army, near Atlanta, Georgia, obscures all the victories of the Revolution.

Though the times of the Revolution tried every man's courage, and every woman's heart, yet through these years this little Society and its ministerial captan, passed securely and prosperously, and came out into a "large place, beside still waters."

When a people are in the way of improvements, it is easy to continue the same. The added comforts of the Meeting house may have suggested the idea of building "Sabba Day" houses, for we find a vote passed in 1788 appointing a committee to direct where such houses should be built on the land near the church, owned by the Society. Some few were built, but soon went out of use,—for I have some suspicion that the hotel or tavern was the "Sabba Day" house many preferred to any other, between sermons. And I find, also, that many of the business meetings of the Society were held at Mr. Samuel Byington's house, which was the "tavern;" and Samuel Byington was a member of the church, as were also many who came in to warm at his "fire."

MR. GILLET AT HOME.

Mr. Gillet recorded his own marriage in the Church book as occurring "Dec. 3, 1778." This fact is mentioned specially because in Sprague's Annals it is given as having taken place "December, 1779," which latter date would not look well along with the fact that his son, Timothy Phelps, was baptized in this church July 23, 1780. He married Adah Rogers, daughter of one of the deacons of his church, and a man very prominent in all the doings of the church and Society for many years. The marriage services were conducted by Rev. Samuel Newell, probably in the church. Mr. Newell preached a sermon from the following text, John ii : 1, 2. "And the third day there was a marriage in Cana of Galilee ; and the mother of Jesus was there. And both Jesus was called and his disciples to the marriage." Mr. Gillet's marriage was on the third day of the month and this made the text more literal to the occasion, and it is said that a minister once likened Wolcott to the land of Canaan ; possibly the audience at this time thought they were in that land, and if the audience did not, perhaps the bride and bridegroom did. Mr. Gillet and wife resided first about half a mile east of the church, in a house now entirely gone, part of the walls of the cellar only are remaining. He afterwards built a house on a farm, a quarter of a mile north of the church on the east side of the road. This house is still standing and is quite inhabitable, though no one resides in it ; and must have been a good home in those days when that street was inhabited by a number of the first families of the parish. It is not known at present what peculiar incident, if any, gave to this part of the community the eloquent name of "Puddin' street," but it certainly has had this honor from beyond the memory of any persons living. In this house Mr. Gillet probably resided but a few years, for the recollections of some of his children are connected much more with the old house now gone than this one north of the Meeting house. Mr. Gillet had four children baptized while pastor here. Timothy Phelps, July 23, 1780, afterwards pastor in Branford, Conn., over fifty years ; Asaph, Nov. 24, 1782 ; Esther, July 17, 1785 ; Adah, Jan. 27, 1788.

MR. GILLET'S SALARY.

When Mr. Gillet settled here his salary was to be fifty pounds a year, for four years, and seventy-five pounds yearly after that. The Society was faithful to this agreement. The nominal amount varied during a very few years, but varied because of the diminished or increased price of wheat, for wheat seems to have been the standard of value. His salary for the first four years (£50 per year) was paid regularly, with one-quarter of the £175 settlement, on the 1st of March. In 1778 they promptly voted

HISTORY OF WOLCOTT.

him £75 for the ensuing year, according to agreement. In 1779 they voted him £75, "to be paid in wheat, at six shillings a bushel." In 1780 it was £50, "to be paid in wheat at four shillings a bushel." In 1781 it was the same, £50, "to be paid in wheat, at four shillings a bushel." After 1781 it was £75, with one exception, till he closed his labors here. In 1787 they paid him £75 and twenty-five cords of wood, and in 1788 it was £70 and twenty-five cords of wood.

This salary, though apparently small, was larger than Rev. Mr. Leavenworth, Congregational minister in Waterbury, was receiving at the same time*. "In 1755, Mr. Leavenworth's salary was £65 "proclamation money," or its equivalent in old tenor; in 1759, £54; in 1761, £65; in 1762, £82; in 1781, £55; but on account of the burdens of the Society and the public taxes, Mr. L. agreed to accept £45. In 1782, the salary was £65, and £10 in wood; in 1791, £70; but Mr. L. gave the Society £5 of it."

These figures show that Mr. Gillet's salary, on an average, was about ten pounds a year more than Mr. Leavenworth's, and therefore was very honorable for a new society, compared with one more than ninety years old. From the fact that the Society voted twenty-five cords of wood in 1787, we infer that Mr. Gillet was then residing in his new house, on his own farm, and that that farm included no woodland; and hence, also, that the farm was a small one, which we learn to have been about ten acres. It was in this house, probably, that the New Haven West Association held its first meeting. May 31st, 1787.† "There were present, Messrs. Leavenworth, Williston, Foot, Edwards, Wales, Gillet, David Fuller, Fowler, Perry, and Martin Fuller. Mr. Leavenworth was moderator, and Dr. Jonathan Edwards was scribe."

---

* Bronson's History of Waterbury, p. 285.
† Kingsley's Eccl. Hist. Conn., p. 327.

The fact that this meeting was held at Mr. Gillet's house, indicates his interest in the neighboring ministers and churches; for this being the first meeting, there must have been some preliminaries, and in these he must have taken considerable part, and hence the propriety of going to his house for this meeting. This was in accordance with his character, for though naturally reserved in his manner, he heartily gave all attention and effort to build up the churches and spread gospel light, and his home was a home of welcome to all who toiled as ministers in the Master's kingdom.

MR. GILLET CLOSES HIS LABORS IN WOLCOTT.

At the annual Society meeting, the 29th day of November, 1790, it was "voted to send a committee to the Rev. Mr. Gillet, to discourse with him concerning the uneasiness there is in the Society with him as a teacher." The committee consisted of Mr. Jacob Carter, Captain Nathaniel Lewis, Deacon Peck, Capt. Samuel Upson, Mr. Amos Seward, Mr. Mark Harrison, Capt. Charles Upson, Mr. Calvin Cowles, and Mr. Jonathan Carter. No reasons are given as to the cause of this "uneasiness," except in the words "with him as a teacher," and afterwards it is said "with him as a pastor and teacher." This committee, doubtless, performed the work assigned it, and reported to the Society the information obtained, for from this time they held several adjourned meetings from week to week. On the 23d day of December, 1790, in a Society meeting, they "voted to have Mr. Gillet invited into the house." He probably came, and they had a conference together like brethren. About two weeks after this conference, the Society "voted that Mr. Leavenworth, Mr. Trumbull, Mr. Smalley, and Mr. Waterman, with their delegates, be an advisory Council respecting the uneasiness there is with Mr. Gillet as a public teacher," and that the Council meet on the "first Tuesday of February next, at nine o'clock in the morning, at the house of Samuel Byington," and that Capt. Samuel Upson, Jacob Carter, Lieut. Richards, Deacon Atkins, Capt. Charles Upson, Jonathan Carter, Mark Harrison, Capt. Daniel Alcox, Calvin Cowles, Simeon Plumb, and Dr. Potter, be a committee to attend on the Council."

This Council met, but of its doings I find no record, yet from several items afterwards recorded, conclude that it advised against a dismissal. On the first day of next September, the Society "voted that all those that are easy with the Rev. Mr. Gillet as a pastor and teacher signify the same. Yeas, 40 ; nays, 19." "Voted that all those that are willing the Rev. Mr. Gillet be dismissed, agreeable to his request, signify the same by lifting the hand. Yeas, 20; nays, 29." One week from this meeting they "voted to call the same Council that were here in February last, to meet at the house of Samuel Byington in said Farmingbury, on the fourth Tuesday of October next, at nine o'clock in the morning, then and there to hear, advise, and determine, on matters of difficulty between the Rev. Mr. Gillet and his people." Deacon Aaron Harrison, Deacon Peck, Deacon Atkins, Messrs. Amos Seward, Streat Richards, Jacob Carter, Jonathan Carter, Capt. Samuel Upson, Capt. Daniel Alcox, were chosen a committee to make provisions for the Council, and to represent the Society before them."

DOINGS OF THE COUNCIL NOVEMBER 9, 1791.

The original copy of the proceedings of the Council is preserved, in Mr. Trumbull's hand-writing, and a splendid hand-writing it is :

At an Ecclesiastical Council convened by letters missive, in Farmingbury, at the house of the Rev. Alexander Gillet, October 25, 1791, the Rev. John Smalley was chosen Moderator, and Mr. Trumbull, Scribe. The Council, considering the importance and difficulty of the matters to be laid before them and their own thinness, not half the members being present, judge it altogether inexpedient to proceed to business; and therefore voted that this Council be adjourned till Wednesday, the 9th of November, to meet at Mr. Samuel Byington's at 9 o'clock in the morning.

Farmingbury, November 9th, the Council met according to adjournment, and adjourned to the Meeting house. In the recess of this Council the Society of Farmingbury, at the desire of Mr. Gillet and a number of the disaffected members, voted their willingness, that the Rev. Noah Benedict and Dr. Jonathan Edwards, with delegates from their respective churches, should be called to sit with the former Council, to advise with them relative to the matters of difficulty subsisting among them; in consequence of which vote, and letters missive to said gentlemen, predicated upon it, the Rev. Mr. Benedict and Dr. Edwards, Deacon Daniel Sherman from the First Church in Woodbury, and Mr. Jeremiah Atwater from the Church in White Haven, joined the Council.

The Council thus formed consisted of the gentlemen above mentioned (Benedict, Edwards, Sherman and Atwater), the Rev. Messrs. Mark Leavenworth, John Smalley, Simon Waterman, and Benjamin Trumbull, and of delegates Joseph Hopkins, Esq., from the church in Waterbury, Colonel Isaac Lee from the church in New Britain, Mr. Elijah Warner from the church in Northbury, and Joseph Darling, Esq., from the church in North Haven.

The Council was opened with prayer by the Rev. Mr. Leavenworth.

The Rev. Mr. Gillet, a committee of the Society in Farmingbury, and a committee of the members of said Society who were dissatisfied with Mr. Gillet, appeared before the Council, and after considerable conversation a question arose between the parties, whether the Society had properly submitted the matters of difficulty to the decision of the Council. Some time was taken up in the discussion of that point, and the parties disagreeing on the subject, the Council adjourned till two o'clock, P. M.

Met according to adjournment, and found the Society in regular meeting, and that the question stated above had been largely debated in said meeting, but without any determination. However, towards evening, said Society "voted that the Council of ministers and delegates from the several neighboring churches, present, be a mutual Council, to hear and determine respecting any matters of difficulty between the Rev. Mr. Gillet, the said Society, or any disaffected persons."

The Council adjourned to Dr. Potter's. Met according to adjournment, and the parties appeared before the Council and began to make a statement of their difficulties. Adjourned to the Meeting house, to meet at 8 o'clock to-morrow morning.

Farmingbury, November 10th, the Council met according to adjournment.

The Rev. Mr. Gillet delivered to the council a paper, in which he submitted all matters of difficulty, and declared, that if this Council shall judge that there is not a prospect for his future usefulness and comfort in this Church and Society as their pastor, it is his honest wish to be liberated from their pastoral charge; and they continued the hearing.

Voted that this Council be adjourned to Deacon Harrison's. Met according to adjournment; continued and finished the hearing; in which it appeared to this Council, that though the Rev. Mr. Gillet has done nothing inconsistent with the Christian or ministerial character, and has through a long scene of controversy acted with great prudence, patience, and gentleness, yet there is about a third of the church and Society dissatisfied with his ministrations; that this dissatisfaction appears to be of long continuance and deeply rooted; that, therefore, on the most thorough consideration of the whole matter, in all its circumstances, there is not a prospect of his continuing in his present pastoral relation, with either usefulness to the cause of religion or comfort to himself; that he and some individuals have settled his temporal affairs to his satisfaction; and that if he should be advised to continue in his present situation, his continuance would, probably, be but temporary, and for which he would be removed with greater loss of property, with greater disadvantage as to his settlement in the ministry, and equal if not greater disadvantage to this Society. For these reasons this Council think it necessary for the interests of religion in general, and especially in this church and Society, and for the usefulness and comfort of Mr. Gillet and his family, that he be dismissed from his pastoral relation to this church and Society, and accordingly he is hereby dismissed, though we feel very tenderly for Mr. Gillet, for his family, and for those of this

Society who wish him to be continued as their minister; yet we are satisfied that they are called, in Providence, to the patient exercise of self denial in this instance; and we wish them to rest assured, that we advise to this dismission of Mr. Gillet in a full persuasion that it is necessary for their respective interests and spiritual prosperity as well as for the interests of true religion in general.

We take the liberty here to refer it to the consideration of this whole Society, whether this whole calamity has not, in a great measure, come upon them in consequence of the want of due care to supply Mr. Gillet and his family with the conveniences of life; and whether if he had been duly supplied in this respect, he would not have been free from those cares, embarrassments and labors which have been inconsistent with that habitual study and improvement which would have rendered him more respected both to his own and neighboring Societies.

With respect to Mr. Gillet, from all that has appeared concerning him in the course of the hearing, and from our acquaintance with him, we believe him to be a man of strict morality and sincere piety; and of such ministerial accomplishments, natural and acquired, as may, if Divine Providence open the way, render him useful in the ministry; and as such we recommend him to all churches and to all Christians wherever God may cast his future lot. Passed unanimously in Council.

Test. BENJAMIN TRUMBULL, *Scribe*.

Thus closed on the 10th day of November, 1791, the ministerial labors of the Rev. Alexander Gillet as an ambassador of the court of heaven over this his first parish,— a pastorate which continued nearly eighteen years.

The "finding" of this council is very plain and very suggestive. They say that "the Rev. Mr. Gillet has through a long scene of controversy acted with great prudence, patience, and gentleness;" and as a reason for this they say, "that this dissatisfaction appears to be of long continuance and deeply rooted," and the explanation to this is, a difficulty in the church in the first year of Mr. Gillet's labors here, and another in 1781, in regard to which the church called a Council. The first was a case in which the parties, a husband and wife of influential family connections, had been prosecuted in Court for "scandal" and were acquitted, and soon after applied to be received as members of the church. This difficulty continued over six months, and then the whole matter was dropped and the persons admitted. The other case was concerning parties also of influence who had been before "Esquire Baldwin" and then came into the church, which was settled once by a council and came up again a year after, in another form, and caused considerable trouble in the church and community, and as a result the minister was thought to be prejudiced against these parties. Because the minister valued the honor of the church he was censured and a prejudice was entertained against him to strengthen in the years to come in proportion to his faithfulness to God and the church.

From several things mentioned in the records I am persuaded that these were the beginning of difficulties that finally secured the dismissal of Mr. Gillet. But there were other things which would not be worthy of mention but for the lessons we are to learn from them ; the principal of which is stated thus by the Council: "We take the liberty here to refer it to the consideration of this whole Society, whether this whole calamity has not, in a great measure, come upon them, in consequence of the want of due care to supply Mr. Gillet and his family with the conveniences of life ;" and the supplying of which would have saved him from embarrassment and made him "more respected, both to his own and neighboring Societies." The secret is this : Mr. Gillet received his salary at the end of the year, only, according to agreement, and that on the first of March, and seldom received it promptly at that time. In 1787 he sent word to the parish meeting that if he could have his money at the first of May, he would give five pounds for twenty-five cords of wood, and accept sixty pounds in place of the seventy due him. In one case, at the annual meeting, he had not received his money, due nearly a year.

These are the things that made trouble in the home of the minister, and because of which we are told Mr. Gillet was not respected as he would have been, although he was not in fault. These things are suggestive and we leave them.

The last entries made by Mr. Gillet, in the church book were, "A marriage, Thanksgiving day, November 24, 1791 ; a baptism of a child, November 27, 1791, and the death of James Bailey, December 8, 1791.

His house and farm he sold to some individuals, who transferred it afterwards to the Society, it being valued at £250, and the Society gave two hundred pounds of it to Mr. Woodward, as we shall see, as his "settlement" in the parish.

Mr. Gillet was settled in Torrington, Conn., May, 1792, where he labored as pastor thirty-four years, till his death.

CHAPTER V.

REV. MR. WOODWARD'S MINISTRY: FROM 1792 TO 1810.

Mr. Woodward began to preach for this Society as a candidate about the first of February, 1792,— that is, two months and a half after Mr. Gillet left. On the 13th of February the Society voted: "That we would wish to continue Mr. Woodward with us as a preacher till the first of May next," which would, probably, make three months' service. This was the only business done at this meeting, and it then adjourned until the first Monday in April. Hence it is probable that the meeting was called for this one purpose, and that it was held soon after his first service among them.

When they met, according to adjournment, they voted, "That we are agreed in Mr. Woodward as a preacher; that we are desirous to continue Mr. Woodward with us as our minister;" also, "That we will give Mr. Woodward £80 salary and twenty-five cords of wood, yearly. Yeas 48, nays 7." Having passed these votes, the meeting adjourned for three or four days, then met and voted "That Capt. Walter Beecher, Dr. John Potter, Lieut. Joseph Beecher, Daniel Byington, Capt. Charles Upson, Capt. Isaac Hopkins, Mr. Simeon Plumb, and Jeremiah Scarritt be a committee to circulate the subscription paper in each school district for the purpose of raising a sum for Mr. Woodward's settlement." This meeting was adjourned from Friday to the next Tuesday, when they voted "to give Mr. Israel B. Woodward two hundred pounds as a settlement, as subscribed, to be paid according to the subscription," and appointed as a committee

Deacon Atkins, Capt. Samuel Upson, Capt. Charles Upson, Mr. Jacob Carter, and Capt. Daniel Alcox, to wait on Mr. Woodward and inform him what the meeting had done. The meeting adjourned to the "last Monday of inst. April," and then appointed a committee to receive Mr. Woodward's answer, after which it adjourned to the "second Monday of May next, at three o'clock in the afternoon."

When they met, according to adjournment, they voted "to give Mr. I. B. Woodward two hundred pounds, we heretofore voted as a settlement, out of the late farm of the Rev. Mr. Gillet, estimated at two hundred and fifty pounds." They then appointed a committee "to wait on Mr. Woodward to the meeting." At this meeting the whole matter of settlement was arranged, and they appointed a committee to complete the work, as follows: "Voted that Capt. Samuel Upson, Capt. Charles Upson, Mr. Amos Seward, Mr. David Norton, Lieut. Joseph Beecher, Mr. Jonathan Carter, Mark Harrison, Esquire, Dr. John Potter, Deacon Joseph Atkins, be a committee to agree with Mr. Woodward on the time of the ordination, and on the ordaining council, and to attend said business till the ordination is over."

Mr. Woodward's letter of acceptance is still preserved in his own hand-writing, and is as follows:

MAY 14, 1792.

To the Church of Christ, and to the inhabitants of the Society of Farmingbury:

Having some time since received from you a unanimous invitation to be your minister in the gospel of Christ, I have, as I hope, most seriously considered the subject, and asked of my God, in a matter of so great importance, that wisdom which is profitable to direct; and after soberly viewing the circumstances which the subject involves, I have though it my duty, should the unanimity heretofore expressed in the Society be continued, to accept of your proposals, and submit myself to the doings of an ordaining council, hoping that it may issue in the salvation of those that are lost; in building up the Redeemer's kingdom on earth, and in displaying the nature and glorious perfections of God; and wishing that grace, mercy, and peace may be multiplied among you through our Lord and Saviour, Jesus Christ, I subscribe myself your brother in the Christian faith.

ISRAEL BARD WOODWARD.

Near the end of May, 1792, the Society met and voted that "Mr. Woodward's salary should become due on the 1st day of March annually," also that Mr. Richard F. Welton, Wm. Stevens, Dr. John Potter, Aaron Harrison, Capt. Daniel Alcox, Selah Steadman, Nathan Gillet, Simeon Hopkins, and Joseph Miner be desired to make preparation to entertain the people on ordination day. No records of the installation have been preserved; but we infer from these votes that some time in June, 1792, Mr. Woodward was ordained as pastor of this church and Society. On the fourth Tuesday of June the Society made further provision for Mr. Woodward. Certain persons had purchased Mr. Gillet's farm, apparently as a favor to Mr. Gillet. The Society at this meeting assumed the obligations of these persons, relieving them from further responsibility to Mr. Gillet, and ordered the treasurer to pay to Mr. Gillet the several sums collected on Mr. Woodward's settlement. The amount of the settlement was two hundred pounds; the farm was estimated at two hundred and fifty pounds. Hence they "voted that the above said committee be empowered to put the Rev. Mr. Woodward into possession of said farm, taking surety of him for the fifty pounds overplus of said two hundred pounds settlement agreeably to an agreement now in the hands of Judge Hopkins." It is reported that the Society lost the whole value of this farm, which must be a mistake. They may never have received the fifty pounds "overplus" but anything more they could not have lost. Mr. Woodward resided on this farm until 1799, when he sold it to Charles Upson, Esq., and purchased the house east of the Meeting house where he resided until his death. This house is now owned by Mr. Ephraim Hall and his grandson, Charles Hall, and is the finest looking residence at Wolcott Center.

Mr. Woodward was not married when he settled here. He afterward married the daughter of Rev. Dr. Smalley, of New Britain, now Berlin, but died childless. After his death his widow received from her father a house in East Haven, where she resided many years. She is spoken of as "a very fine woman," of a cheerful temperament, and fond of society. It is said that she was often present with her husband at public balls, given at the Hotel, and that she sometimes took part in the dance. Her husband never danced, but engaged in the social chat with much animation.

When Mr. Woodward settled here, Farmingbury was a flourishing parish, a "wide awake" community with considerable enterprise and business energy. In those days the present park in the city of Waterbury was a swamp, and Wolcott was a business centre with several stores and other enterprises which attracted visitors and drew trade from the vicinity for many miles around. The Church was really a strong one ; it had in its membership men of talent and men of means. Several of these subscribed toward Mr. Woodward's settlement twenty-five dollars or more, and paid their yearly tax towards his salary, besides. This "settlement" was raised by subscription ; the salary was paid by tax. There seems to have been considerable opposition to this method of raising the salary ; so that, when Mr. Gillet closed his labors, the Society voted "that we are willing that those who find themselves willing, may have preaching by subscription for three months." But they were compelled to return to the tax rate in order to fulfil their engagement with Mr. Woodward.

The two hundred pound settlement was paid in three

installments, or in three yearly parts. This subscription was copied into the Treasurer's Book by Mark Harrison, Esq., who was Treasurer in 1794:

The several subscriptions for Mr. Woodward's settlement are as follows:
Nov. 5, 1794.

	£ s. d		£ s. d
Joseph M. Parker,	1 0 0	Moses Todd,	1 0 0
Zephana Parker,	1 10 0	Jesse Alcox,	1 0 0
Isaac Upson,	4 9 0	Aaron Harrison,	2 0 0
Joseph Minor,	4 2 0	Elijah Lane,	0 15 0
Nathaniel Lewis,	6 0 0	Ezekiel Upson,	1 10 0
Samuel Upson,	6 18 0	Richard Welton,	1 0 0
Obed Upson,	1 0 0	Nathaniel Lane,	1 0 0
Jacob Carter,	4 6 0	Calvin Cowles,	3 0 0
Wait Hotchkiss,	1 0 7	Amos Seward,	3 12 0
Solomon Alcox,	1 10 0	David Norton,	1 11 0
Heman Hall,	2 12 0	Thomas Upson,	8 12 0
Asahel Lane,	1 4 0	John Kenea,	0 10 0
David Alcox,	2 0 0	Isaac Hopkins,	3 1 0
Mark Barnes,	1 12 11	Joseph Smith,	1 0 0
Nathan Barnes,	1 5 0	Abel Curtiss,	2 15 0
David Norton, Jr.,	1 0 0	David Harrison,	1 0 0
Jesse Selkrigg,	1 0 0	Benoni Gillet,	1 10 0
Charles Frisbie,	2 12 0	Samuel Byington,	5 0 0
Daniel Byington,	4 9 0	James Bailey,	3 6 0
Joseph Beecher,	4 0 0	Joseph Beecher, Jr.,	1 10 0
Judah Frisbie,	2 12 0	Brainard Lindsley,	1 0 0
Elnathan Thrasher,	1 10 0	Ezra Stevens,	1 0 0
Farrington Barnes,	0 15 0	John Alcox,	2 0 0
Stephen Carter,	3 10 0	Amos Beecher,	0 10 0
Daniel Alcox,	1 10 0	James Thomas,	4 10 0
Ephraim Smith, Jr.,	4 0 0	Aaron Harrison, Jr.,	0 18 0
Streat Richards,	7 0 0	Benjamin Alcox,	1 0 0
Moses Pond,	1 10 0	Jonah Barnes,	0 15 0
John Bronson,	4 0 0	Joseph Freeman,	0 18 0
Mark Harrison,	6 12 0	Jeremiah Scarritt,	2 10 0
Charles Upson,	13 10 0	Ezra Mallery,	1 0 0
Simeon Plumb,	2 10 0	Timothy Bradley,	1 5 0
Samuel Plumb,	1 0 0	Asahel Bradley,	1 0 0
Solomon Plumb,	1 5 0	Amasa Bradley,	1 0 0
Justus Peck,	2 0 0	William Stevens,	1 6 0
Ashbel Upson,	2 5 0	Caleb Miner,	1 0 0
John Beecher,	2 0 0	Heman Byington,	1 0 0

REV. MR. WOODWARD'S MINISTRY. 65

	£	s.	d		£	s.	d
Joseph Sutliff, jr.,	2	0	0	Eli Roberts,	1	0	0
Noah Neal,	1	18	0	Abram Norton,	2	6	0
John B. Alcox,	1	0	0	Joseph Atkins,	1	10	0
Joseph Twitchel,	3	0	0	Ozias Norton,	1	8	0
James Alcox,	3	12	0	Jesse Alcox, jr.,	0	18	0
Selah Steadman,	1	0	0	Hezekiah Beecher,	0	18	0
Jonathan Carter,	4	18	0	Noah W. Norton,	0	18	0
Daniel Johnson, jr.,	0	18	0	Nathan Scarritt,	1	0	0
Nathan Gillet,	1	0	0	Elisha Horton,	0	18	0
John Norton,	1	15	0	John Wiard,	0	6	0
Walter Beecher,	4	0	0	Ebenezer Bailey,	0	6	0
Barnabas Powers,	1	0	0	Jerry Moulthrop,	0	12	0
Levi Johnson,	0	18	0	Enos Dutton,	0	18	0
John Talmage,	1	0	0	James Scarritt,	1	0	0
John Frisbie,	1	19	0	Luther Atkins,	0	18	0
Daniel Dean,	0	15	0	Nathan Stevens,	2	0	0
John Potter,	6	10	0	Ebenezer Johnson,	1	0	0

By this list it may be seen that most of these men, if not all, subscribed liberally. They paid Mr. Woodward 400 dollars salary and twenty-five cords of wood, and gave him in addition this 1000 dollars settlement. To make up this settlement several persons gave twenty dollars, others thirty, and one — Mr. Charles Upson — sixty-five; while some of those who gave smaller sums, doubtless gave more in proportion to their ability than the more wealthy. This subscription list is highly creditable to the community in which it originated; it shows the effort they made to sustain the institutions of the Gospel. But those were the days of strength in Wolcott; for from 1790 to 1820 the town was at the height of its prosperity, as regards wealth and population. At the time of Mr. Woodward's settlement the number of inhabitants was about 900. In 1800 it was 948; in 1810, 952; in 1820, 943; in 1830, 844; in 1840, 633; in 1850, 603. The church membership, when Mr. Woodward began his ministry, numbered about 100, and the congregation from 300 to 500, which must have filled the Meeting house. That the congregation was large may be inferred from the apparent difficulty the committee had in "seating the Meeting house." Besides, Mr. Woodward's preaching was calculated to attract the attention of the multitude more than Mr. Gillet's because of the apt and animating illustrations which he habitually introduced. The increasing esteem in which he was held is indicated by the three annual subscriptions which were raised for paying the settlement. The first amounted to sixty-three pounds, the second to sixty-seven, the third to nearly one hundred pounds, or almost thirty pounds more than the two hundred pounds first agreed upon.

Under Mr. Woodward's labors the membership of the church increased somewhat ; how much, we are unable to say, because there is no record to be found of those who united with the church from 1798 to 1811. In a list of members prepared by Mr. Keys in 1815, there are over forty names of persons of whose uniting with the church we have no record, but who must have become members during these twelve years.*

Mr. Woodward was more than ordinarily successful as a preacher, and was highly esteemed as a neighbor and citizen. He was easy and friendly in his manners, ever ready with some pleasant remark, and was therefore liked by all classes. Probably no minister in the parish was ever loved and confided in as a minister more than he, for to this day the remark of the people, as to all they ever heard of him, is in the highest tone of Christian love.

---

*A like difficulty is experienced in regard to baptisms. Deacon Isaac Bronson was appointed in 1811, to keep the church records, and he says : " Here seems to be a long chasm (from 1792 to 1811) as to the record of baptisms, but no further papers have as yet come to hand. I therefore begin at the time I received the papers." If Isaac Bronson could find " no further papers " sixty years ago, I may properly cease the search now. Yet it seems a little singular that Mr. Woodward should keep the record of additions to the church, and of marriages, from 1792 to 1798, and then continue the record of deaths as he did, to 1809 (a short time before his death) and omit the two former.

He had a school for several years that was very popular with young men. He usually had from four to six scholars boarding with him, and others came to recite. Benoni Upson, son of Thomas and brother of Charles Upson, fitted for college at this school. He resided about half a mile from Mr. Woodward's. Mr. Woodward had students from New Haven, from Waterbury and other neighboring places, and also from the Southern States.

The efforts of the parish to promote education were quite commendable for those times. In November after Mr. Woodward's settlement the Society voted that "we will keep eleven months school," and this length of term does not appear to have been an unusual thing. It is probable that Mr. Woodward was induced to commence his school, because of the large number of young men in the community needing opportunities of more advanced culture than the common schools afforded.

Immediately after the success of the subscription to pay Mr. Woodward's settlement, the people proceeded to complete the inside of the Meetinghouse.

At a meeting held on the first day of December, 1794, they voted first, "that we will do something to the Meeting house." Then they "voted that the Meeting house be finished in the following order, viz.: First, that the roof be shingled with pine, and the siding with whitewood. 2ndly, that the body of the house be painted white and the roof red. 3rdly, that the inside of the said house above and below be decently and properly finished, lathed, and plastered, and timbers capped; a row of pews built in the back part of each of the galleries, raised to a proper pitch to overlook the seats in front of said pews. Voted that the above described work be done and completed by the first day of November next, and that a committee be appointed to cause the house to be repaired as is above written or described, at their own discretion; and further, the said committee are to sell or dispose of any boards, shingles, or nails that may be taken off or out of the said house, for the benefit of the Society, or appropriate them for any use for which they may be proper in repairing said house as above; and further that the said committee exhibit a true and just account of all the expenses that shall arise in so doing, before the annual Society meeting in November next. Voted that Capt. Nathaniel Lewis, Jacob Carter and Capt. Charles Upson be a committee for the above purpose. Voted to lay a rate three pence on the pound on the list of 1794 to be paid the first of June next. Voted a tax on said list of three pence on the pound to be paid in cattle and sheep* the first of November next. Voted that John Beecher and Judah Frisbie be collectors to collect the above rates." In a meeting held in the last part of January next they added one penny to each of these taxes making them each four pence on the pound. At a meeting held on the 5th of next February they voted "that we are willing that there should be a steeple erected adjoining this house, at the expense of individuals; and that the overplus, if there be any, of the rates laid to do the Meeting house be laid out on the steeple." The steeple was not built at this time, but the rest of the work proposed was completed before July of 1795 and then for the first time Farmingbury had a finished Meeting house. There is one item we mention and leave the reader to interpret, for he will probably know as much about it as any one. In the Treasurer's book for 1797 we find the following record: "Capt. Walter Beecher debtor to an order on the Treasurer for one dollar. Contra, credit by making three pair of butterflies for the Meeting house." It is thought these were ornaments about the sounding board over the pulpit.

There were, probably, some services dedicatory of this house in the summer of 1795, but I have seen no record

---

*There was a ready market for these cattle and sheep at the Center. The hides were made into leather in Wolcott, and the beef was packed in barrels for foreign markets.

of them in the books. There is a hymn printed and preserved, said to have been composed by Mr. David Harrison especially for this dedication.*

"DEDICATORY POEM.

With joyful heart and tuneful song,
   Let us approach the mighty Lord,
Proclaim his honors with our tongue,
   And sound his wondrous truth abroad.

His glorious name on golden lyres,
   Strike all the tuneful choirs above,
And boundless nature's realms conspire
   To celebrate his matchless love.

The heaven of heavens is his bright throne,
   And cherubs wait his high behest,
Yet for the merits of his Son,
   He visits men in humble dust.

In temples sacred to his name
   His saints assemble round his board,
Raise their hosannas to the Lamb,
   And taste the supper of the Lord.

O God our King, this joyful day,
   We dedicate this house to thee;
Here would we meet to sing and pray,
   And learn how sweet thy dwellings be.

O King of saints, O triune God,
   Bow the high heavens and lend thine ear;
O make this house thy fixed abode,
   And let the heavenly dove rest here.

Within these walls may Jesus' charms
   Allure ten thousand souls to love,
And all supported by his arms,
   Shine forth in realms of bliss above.

There saints of every tribe and tongue
   Shall join the armies of the Lamb;
Hymn hallelujahs to the Son,
   The Spirit, and the great I AM.

---

*A copy of this poem is now in the possession of Mrs. Mark Tuttle.

Their songs seraphic shall they raise,
  And Gabriel's lyre the notes resound ;
Heaven's full toned organ join the praise,
  And world to world repeat the sound.

To Father, Son, and Holy Ghost,
  Be ceaseless praise and glory given,
By all the high angelic host,
  By all on earth and all in heaven.
            Hallelujah! Amen."

This hymn, sung by the large number of trained singers then in the community, must have given a sense of gratitude and joy worthy of the occasion. That they were trained singers is abundantly evident from the singing talent here, and the money they had spent in years past, and were spending for the "improvement of singing." In the last of November, 1793, the Society appointed "Joseph Minor, Lieut. James Bailey, Moses Pond, Isaac Upson, Enos Dutton, Joseph Beecher, Jr., Asahel Lane, Joseph M. Parker, a committee to circulate a subscription for singing, and procure a teacher according to the subscriptions they shall get."

In November, 1794, they appointed another committee: "Voted that we will do something to encourage singing. Voted that Dr. John Potter, Ensign Joseph Beecher, Capt. Charles Upson, Isaac Upson, Ensign Jonathan Carter, James Scarritt, Isaac Hopkins, Jr., Lieut. James Bailey, Nathan Barnes, Asahel Lane, and John Hitchcock, be a committee to get subscriptions to hire a singing master."

These committees were composed of substantial men, and the singing school was not to be a young people's pleasure meeting, but a school of thorough training in singing. And this old practice of "doing something to encourage singing" was continued for many years after the dedication of the church. In 1797, they "voted that we lay a rate of three mills on the dollar on the last August list, payable the first of March next, to be laid out to hire and pay some man to teach and instruct in singing ; that Dr. John Potter, Moses Todd, Mark Harrison, Esq., Capt. Streat Richards, Joseph Minor, Joseph M. Parker, and Preserve Carter, be a committee to procure a teacher in singing, and to see to the laying out the above rate."

With this spirit of industry and improvement in the minds of the people, success and prosperity came to their hands and homes from every direction. They had petitioned for some years for "Town privileges," and in the spring of 1796, the parish was incorporated as a town, and the effect was to relieve the Society of various cares and responsibilities, and encourage them in all good things.*

In November, 1800, Mr. Woodward sent a communication to the annual meeting which caused the following vote, and which is explained only in a vote taken a year after : "Voted that a committee be appointed to treat with Mr. Woodward on the subject of the communication

---

*At this place in the Society's history I must take leave of an acquaintance who at first sight and introduction, gave me considerable trouble and misunderstanding, but to whom, after six months' acquaintance, I am quite reluctant to say "good-by," for he has been of great service to me. Besides, when we are well acquainted with tried friends, we may well hesitate to change them for strangers, though the strangers may be clothed in exquisite style and beauty. For twenty-nine years the records of the Society were written by Daniel Byington — the first year by Daniel Byington, Sen., the other twenty-eight by Daniel, jr. In 1799 Isaac Bronson was elected Society Clerk, and to his most elegant writing I now come, and in so doing must leave the less elegant "hand" of Daniel. Apart from a little formality in the introduction of transactions, Mr. Byington was very nearly a model in the use of concise and appropriate terms, and of fidelity and honor in the office he held. It is, therefore, with great pleasure that I record my high appreciation of Daniel Byington, jr., as clerk of the Society of Farmingbury, whose writings I have consulted daily for much of the time for three months past, until I had become familiar with every turn of his pen, and every form of expression; and until it seemed to me as a communion of spirits, in which friend Daniel was helping me on in giving to the world a picture of twenty-nine years of Society life in Farmingbury. Good-by, Daniel, till I am introduced to you "on the other side of the veil."

by him made to this meeting, and that said committee report to this meeting at their adjournment." No report of the committee is recorded, and the matter went over till December 7th, 1801, when it was voted "that Charles Upson, Esq., Deacon Joseph Atkins, Mark Harrison, Esq., Major Streat Richards, and Isaac Bronson, be a committee to wait upon the Rev. Mr. Woodward and inform him that the Society, for various reasons, wish not to act upon the proposition by him made as to a dismission, particularly, as they are well pleased with his performance as their minister, and are by no means willing for a dissolution of the pastoral connection between him and them." This action is all that is recorded concerning this matter, unless it be a resolution passed soon after by the Society in regard to the payment of Mr. Woodward's salary when it should become due. The unusual rigor of this action may give us a suggestion of the reason why he desired a dismission,— namely, because the Society was so slow in paying his salary, even after waiting a year for it to become due. The first action reads thus: "Voted that if the Rev. Mr. Woodward's salary be not paid by the first day of March, annually, or any part of the same, such salary, or such part of it as is not paid, shall be upon interest until paid." But this, after three years' trial, did not remedy the difficulty as desired, and hence the second vote: "That execution be taken out against the Society collector at the end of ninety days next coming after the first day of March, yearly, and put into the officer's hands by the Society's Committee, unless said collector shall have paid the Rev. Mr. Woodward's salary in full by that time." After this it may be supposed that either the collectors or parishioners recognized the fact that a minister had a right to his salary after having earned it. It is proper to state here that the Treasurer's book shows that Mr. Woodward received part of his salary from time to time during the year. He received money (a very little), orders, notes, wheat, and other items, as individuals felt disposed to let him have, or to sell to him, but much of it went over from month to month after the end of the year, until being weary with delay he proposed to find another parish, or other work.

It may be thought that it must have been difficult to obtain a collector after a vote to "take out execution" against him but it was not. The first man elected after the above rule was passed was Selah Upson, and it is a singular incident that the assessment which he was to collect, with the order from the justice of the peace to collect it, have come into my hands just in time for insertion here:

To Selah Upson, Collector of the Society Rate in the Society of Farmingbury, in Wolcott, in New Haven County, Greeting:

By authority of the State of Connecticut, you are hereby commanded forthwith to levy and collect of the persons named in the annexed list herewith committed to you, each one in several proportion as therein set down of the sum total of such list, being a tax or assessment granted or agreed upon by the inhabitants of said Society of Farmingbury, regularly assembled on the 27th day of October, 1805, for defraying the ministerial and other charges arising within the same, and to deliver and pay the sum and sums which you shall so lay and collect, unto the Treasurer of the said Society, at or before the first day of March, 1806, and if any person or persons shall neglect or refuse to make payment of the sum or sums whereat he or they are respectively assessed and set in the above list, to distrain the goods or chattels of such person or persons, and the same dispose of as the law directs, returning the overplus (if any be) unto the owner or owners; and for want of goods and chattels whereon to make distraint, you are to take the body or bodies of the person or persons so refusing, and him or them commit unto the keeper of the gaol of the said county within the said prison, who is hereby commanded to receive and safely keep him or them until he or they pay and satisfy the said sum or sums assessed upon him or them as aforesaid, together

HISTORY OF WOLCOTT.

with your fees; unless the said assessment, or any part thereof, upon application made to the County Court, shall be abated.

Dated at WOLCOTT, this 28th day of February, 1806.

ISAAC BRONSON, *Just. Peace.*

John Alcox,	$1.00	Benham & Tuttle,	$3.07
Jesse Alcox,	2.31	Samuel Benham,	25
James Alcox, jr.,	1.94	Estate of Joseph Beach,	1.97
Mark Alcox,	77	Hannah Beach,	33
David Alcox,	2.08	Asa Barnes,	15
Solomon Alcox,	3.49	Bezaleel Bowen	02
Obed Alcox,	34	Solomon Barnes,	07
Jesse Alcox, jr.,	2.52	Stephen Barnes,	08
John B. Alcox,	2.95	Levi Brown,	37
Joel Alcox,	2.30	Estate Lois Blakeslee,	17
David Alcox, jr.,	1.00	Jared Burr,	94
Eldad Alcox,	1.00	Abel Curtiss,	3.41
Elisha Adams,	2.01	John Cooper,	07
Joseph Alcox,	32	Jacob Carter,	5.93
Edmund Bradley,	2.22	Stephen Carter,	4.44
Zebulon Byington,	20	Preserve Carter,	3.23
Daniel Byington,	3.23	Elihu Carter,	52
Joseph Beecher,	2.25	Stephen Carter, jr.,	1.28
John Beecher,	4.04	John & Dan Carter,	1.26
Hezekiah Beecher,	3.38	Ashbel Cowles,	45
Hezekiah Beecher, Woodbridge,	84	James Cowles,	1.75
Sylvester Beecher,	54	Hope Cobb,	07
James Bailey,	3.86	Allen Clark,	33
David Bailey,	39	Phineas Castle,	21
Glover Ball,	3.41	Phineas Deming,	1.95
Timothy Bradley,	1.20	Isaac Downs,	3.55
Amasa Bradley,	2.32	Prince Duplax,	1.30
Moses Byington,	1.69	Jesse Dutton,	77
Daniel Byington, jr.,	1.34	Ezra Doolittle,	17
Farrington Barnes,	2.32	Judah Frisbie,	3.43
Mark Barnes,	3.29	John Frisbie,	4.27
John Bronson,	3.00	Lydia Frisbie,	1.14
John Bronson, jr.,	45	Ransom Frisbie,	71
Hannah Bronson,	28	David Frisbie,	52
Isaac Bronson,	87	Reuben Frisbie,	08
Osee Bartholomew,	4.51	Daniel Frisbie,	44
James Bartholomew,	2.16	Sarah Granniss,	1.75
Heirs of Sam'l Bartholomew,	2.73	Heirs of Irujah Granniss,	23
Marvin Beckwith,	66	Stephen Granniss,	19

Joseph Holt,	$2.34	Lewis Loveland,	$1.88
Hotchkiss & Upson,	2.15	Elijah Lane,	09
Asaph Hotchkiss,	2.07	Laura Lane,	14
Timothy Hotchkiss,	2.27	Joseph Miner,	5.05
Titus Hotchkiss,	4.89	Archibald Miner,	20
Abner Hotchkiss,	2.23	Ichabod Merrills,	1.73
Mary Hotchkiss,	1.42	Caleb Merrills,	27
Luther Hotchkiss,	29	Amasa Mix,	28
Miles Hotchkiss,	1.79	Samuel Munson,	04
Mark Harrison,	5.74	Elihu Moulthrop,	20
David Harrison,	3.94	Susanna Norton,	37
Rollin Harrison,	32	Ozias Norton,	1.34
Leonard Harrison,	65	John Norton,	5.03
Isaac Hopkins,	3.18	Ziba Norton,	1.40
Estate of Isaac Hopkins,	1.54	Rhoda Norton,	14
Harvey Hopkins,	39	David Pardee,	2.32
Milly Hopkins,	95	Samuel Porter,	1.34
Elisha Horton,	2.62	John Potter,	4.07
Samuel Horton,	85	Joseph M. Parker,	2.75
Heman Hall,	1.19	Zephana Parker,	1.67
Levi Hall,	1.84	Amos Parsons,	1.99
Lyman Hotchkiss and Nathan Andrews,	28	Justus Peck,	3.62
		Simeon Plumb,	2.42
Uriel Holmes, jr., and Ephraim Root,	70	Gamaliel Plumb,	61
		Samuel Plumb,	55
William Robinson and Isaac Upson,	2.00	Joseph Plumb,	1.68
		Amariah Plumb,	14
Estate of Enos Hotchkiss,	25	Marcus Potter,	1.40
Abigail Hull,	73	Asahel Peck,	02
John Hitchcock,	2.54	Streat Richards,	4.04
David Hitchcock,	41	Elijah Royce,	1.36
Abel Ives,	1.47	Elijah Rowe,	1.12
Ebenezer Johnson,	39	Lydia Rogers,	28
Levi Johnson,	1.40	William Robinson,	1.74
John J. Kenea,	1.20	Jeremiah Scarritt,	94
Nathan Lewis,	4.41	James Scarritt,	2.48
Job Lewis,	09	David Scarritt,	25
Timothy Lewis,	22	Joseph Smith's Estate,	29
Lemuel Lewis,	66	Joseph Sutliff,	63
Jesse Lewis,	08	Titus Sutliff,	1.29
Nathaniel Lewis,	7.96	John Sutliff,	1.25
Reuben Lewis,	1.65	Jesse Selkriggs,	42
Royce Lewis,	1.38	Ephraim Smith,	1.30
Nathaniel Lane,	30	Timothy Scott,	19
Josiah Lane,	51	Truman Sandford,	15
Lud Lindsley,	3.01	Jared Smith,	1.20

James Smith,	$0.12	Manley Upson,	$2.48
James Stone,	10	Charles Upson,	8.06
Lucius Tuttle,	1.97	Washington Upson	1.14
Ichabod Talmage,	1.28	Lee Upson,	81
Jacob Talmage,	2.29	Gates Upson,	32
Josiah Thomas,	2.60	Benoni Upson,	52
John Thomas,	1.50	Ashbel Upson,	2.67
Seth Thomas,	1.43	Selah Upson,	1.55
Joseph Twitchel,	1.46	Jesse Upson,	3.50
Samuel Upson,	2.25	Freeman Upson,	37
Isaac Upson,	5.64	Amos Upson,	07
Harvey Upson,	3.73	Ephraim Winstone,	1.82
I. Upson and H. Townsend,	26	David Wakelee,	4.07
Obed Upson,	1.80	Silas Weed,	1.72
Samuel Upson, jr.,	2.26		

Aside from this one item, there seems to have been no "uneasiness" but great satisfaction with Mr. Woodward in the parish and in his own mind as to the parish; and with his school in a good degree of prosperity, he might well feel assured of filling an important position in his Lord's vineyard. For the last ten years of his ministry the Meeting house was so filled with hearers that there were extra committees appointed from year to year to seat the people and to provide seats for those who should become regular attendants.

It is painful to record the sudden close of such a ministerial service. In the Autumn of 1810, there prevailed somewhat, a peculiar and very fatal fever called typhoid. It was also called "the great fever." With this Mr. Woodward died after a sickness of but a few days.* In

---

*In the summer of 1810, the typhoid fever appeared in the family of Mark Harrison, Esq. Rev. Mr. Woodward attended this family and others in their sickness, as pastor and neighbor, and rendered great comfort in this time of fear and dread, for it is said to have been very difficult to get help to take care of the sick. Mr. Harrison's son Rollin died July 22d; his wife, Rebecca Miles Harrison, died August 20th; his son Michael died in New Haven, two days after his mother, he having been home and taken the fever. Reuben Beebe, son-in-law of Mr. Harrison, died in Waterbury, Sept. 26th, of the same fever, having taken it in rendering help to the sick in Wolcott. Several others died in Wolcott besides Mr. Woodward and members of Mr. Harrison's family.

the grave yard at Wolcott Center, stands a stone, on which is written not without ornament,

IN

Memory of

Rev. ISRAEL B. WOODWARD,

WHO DIED

Nov. 17, 1810, Æ. 43.

It is a singular fact that this grave is made directly and wholly across the walk or space between the two rows of graves adjoining; as though, when dead, this remarkably good man's body must lie in the path where men walk, to arrest their attention and preach to them still.

He had served this people for eighteen years, preaching more than a thousand sermons; he had welcomed to church membership about one hundred persons, many of whom were noble men in the church long after their leader left the toils of earth, and most of whom we doubt not have joined him again beyond the flood, where snows of winter, heat of summer, and the sorrows of earth will never come. It seems sad that one just reaching manhood's strength of intellect, and of whom we might properly expect thirty years more of efficient labor, should fall so soon; but so doeth He, who "doeth all things well."

His wife remained in the place during the winter and supplied the pulpit by inviting neighboring ministers to preach from Sabbath to Sabbath. This illustrates the ability and faithfulness of this noble woman. On the 15th of April, 1811, the Society voted, "that the Society's committee pay over to Mrs. Woodward, the widow of our late pastor, the same sum for each Sabbath which she had supplied the pulpit by the neighboring ministers that the Rev. Mr. Woodward's salary would have amounted to for the same term of time including next Sabbath." Mr. Woodward's salary was 80 pounds a year and 25 cords of wood until 1796, when the Society voted him 90 pounds without wood, and this continued, probably, until his death.

CHAPTER VI.

REV. MR. HART'S AND REV. MR. KEYS' MINISTRY: FROM 1811 TO 1822.

REV. MR. HART'S SHORT MINISTRY.

At the meeting on the 15th of April, 1811, when the Society voted the settlement with Mrs. Woodward, they also voted, "that the Society's committee be directed to procure a candidate to preach to or in said Society after the next Sabbath," and on the 27th of May next they voted "to request the Society's committee to employ Rev. Mr. Parmele to supply the pulpit for a time that they shall judge proper."

In August next they had another candidate; for on the 26th they voted, "that the Society's committee be requested and directed to agree with Mr. Lucas Hart to preach with us six Sabbaths after the next, on probation as it is termed, that is to say, if his performances and the prospect of his health are such as to be satisfactory to the Society and the Society to him, that he continue with us as our minister." At the annual meeting, Oct. 7, 1811, they voted "to give the Rev. Mr. Hart a call for a settlement with us as our minister. Voted, to give Mr. Hart four hundred and fifty dollars annually as a compensation for his services, if he see cause to accept the invitation to be our minister. That the Society's committee be directed to wait upon Mr Hart and inform him what the meeting had done." This meeting adjourned and met on the 4th of Nov., 1811, and voted, "that Lewis H. Wakelee, Gates Upson, Ira Hough, Lucius Tuttle, and John Bronson, Jr., be a committee, in conjunction with the church committee, to provide for the Council at the time of ordination, and to take all necessary measures for the well ordering and conducting the same in all respects on the part of the Society." An account of the ordination is preserved.

ORDINATION OF MR. HART.

"At an Ecclesiastical Council convened at Wolcott, by letters missive from the church and Society in said town, at the house of Mr. Lucius Tuttle, on the 3d day of December, 1811, for the purpose of ordaining Mr. Lucas Hart to the pastoral care and charge of said church and Society,— present : The Rev. Simon Waterman, from Plymouth; the Rev. Benoni Upson and Deacon Asaph Smith, Kensington; the Rev. Jonathan Miller and Deacon Seth Peck, from the church at Burlington; the Rev. Luke Wood and Mr. Stephen Hotchkiss, from the church at Waterbury; the Rev. Luther Hart and Deacon Jacob Heminway, from the church at Plymouth; the Rev. Jonathan Cone and Deacon Bryan Hooker, from the church at Bristol; and Deacon Benjamin Dutton, from the church at Southington.

The Council proceeded to appoint the Rev. Simon Waterman Moderator, Rev. Jonathan Cone, Scribe. Business was then opened by prayer by the Moderator. The Council then attended to the communications from the church and Society, and from Mr. Hart, relative to his call and its acceptance. Being satisfied with these communications, the Council voted that the way was prepared to proceed to the examination of the candidate. After a thorough examination into his doctrinal and experimental acquaintance with the Christian religion, and his views with regard to entering the ministry, the Council unanimously voted to proceed to the ordination of the candidate at eleven o'clock to-morrow, A. M. The exercises of the ordination were then appropriated as follows: Voted that the Rev. Luther Hart make the introductory prayer; Rev. Jonathan Miller preach the sermon; Rev. Simon Waterman make the consecrating prayer; during which the Rev. Messrs. Waterman, Upson, Miller, and Wood, are to impose hands; Rev. Benoni Upson give the charge; Rev. Luke Wood give the right hand of fellowship; Rev. Jonathan

Cone to make the concluding prayer. Voted to adjourn till half-past 8 o'clock to-morrow morning.

Wednesday, December 4th, the Council met according to adjournment. Voted that they approve the minutes of the Council.

Test SIMON WATERMAN, *Moderator*.
JONATHAN CONE, *Scribe*.

The exercises of the ordination were performed at the time and in the manner specified as above.

Test. JONATHAN CONE, *Scribe*."

On the evening of the day of the ordination of Mr. Hart, an ordination "Ball" was held at the house of Mr. Pitman Stowe, which was then a hotel, and was the house Mr. Keys afterward occupied as his residence. This ball is certified by most reliable witnesses and confirming circumstances. It is also stated that the young pastor gave a sermon soon after, that was a high reprimand for this ball festivity. It is not asserted that the same committee of the church and Society that provided for the ordination services was the committee of the ball, but that nearly the whole congregation attended the ball.

Mr. Hart's term of ministerial service was short. He was ordained Dec. 4, 1811, and died in East Haven, Oct. 16, 1813. When he was preaching here on trial his health was such that there was doubt whether he would be able to do the work of the parish. From all we can learn he was a very good and acceptable minister, with more ambition than health to perform the work of a pastor.

He received to the fellowship of the church fourteen persons; attended to a sad case of church discipline; kept the records of the church very carefully in all respects, and apparently was fully ready for the summons that called him to rest in the mansions of peace.

I find the following receipt preserved with other papers by the clerk of the Society:

WOLCOTT, December 9th, 1813.
Received of Mr. William Bartholomew three hundred and thirty dollars, in full of all demands, which I have against the Eccle-

siastical Society in the town of Wolcott, in favor of Rev. Lucas Hart, late of said Wolcott, deceased.

SIMEON HART, *Administrator.*

Since writing the above I have seen the record of deaths in East Haven, wherein I find the following : " From Wolcott, Oct. 11, 1813, Edward, son of Rev L. Hart ; disease, dysentery ; one year old ; buried in East Haven. Oct. 16, 1813, Rev. Lucas Hart, of dysentery, buried in East Haven, aged 29 years." Hence I infer that Mr. Hart was married, probably shortly after his settlement in Wolcott ; that he was visiting his kindred in East Haven ; his little son departed this life, and five days later, the father followed.*

REV. MR. KEYS' MINISTRY.

In February, 1814. a Mr. Stebbins was preaching here as a candidate, and the Society voted that "The meeting give Mr. Stebbins notice that it is their wish to have him continue with the Society if it is consistent with him and them," but no arrangement was made with him for a settlement.

On the 18th day of April next (1814) they had another candidate and voted: " That we are satisfied with the Rev. Mr. Keys as a preacher, and wish to settle or continue him as our minister. Voted that we will give Mr. Keys the sum of five hundred dollars each year that he shall serve us as our minister, as a compensation for his services."

On the 23d of May next they voted : " To renew the former call made to the Rev. Mr. Keys to settle with us as our minister, and to give him in addition to the sum already offered, the quantity of 15 cords of wood yearly, so long as he continues to serve as our minister." These fifteen cords of wood had weight in this matter, evidently, for Mr. Keys came again, and on consulta-

---

*See Biography.

tion the Society took the following action: "Voted that Lucius Tuttle, James Bailey, Pitman Stowe, William Bartholomew, Gates Upson, Clark Bronson, Mark Upson, and Harvey Upson be a committee to consult with the Rev. Mr. Keys respecting the time of installation, the council, etc., and make the necessary provisions and arrangements for their entertainment and convenience, and the ceremonies of the day."

It was nearly three months after this when the invitations for the Council were sent out, and a month intervened before the Council met.

THE LETTER OF INVITATION.

"*To the Church of Christ in Plymouth, etc., The Church of Christ in Wolcott sendeth Greeting:*

Whereas, the Congregational Church of Christ and Society of the town of Wolcott, have unanimously and in due form, given a call to the Rev. John Keys of the Presbytery of Albany, State of New York, to become their pastor and minister — and whereas, the said Mr. Keys has accepted their call, and with them is desirous of having the pastoral relation constituted — and whereas, they have agreed upon and appointed Wednesday, the twenty-first of September ensuing, for the installation to take place: This is therefore to invite and request you to attend, by your Rev. Pastor and delegate, at the house of Mr. Lucius Tuttle in Wolcott, on the day preceding, at eleven o'clock, A. M., then and there to assist in Council, and if the way shall be prepared for the installation of Mr. Keys, to take such parts as the Council convened shall assign.

Signed, JOHN KEYS, *Pastor Elect*,

ISAAC BRONSON and others of the committee, in behalf of the church and Society.

August 37 [27], 1814.

THE COUNCIL.

"The Council convened according to appointment. Several, however, who were invited did not attend, their reasons, afterward assigned, were deemed satisfactory. At an Ecclesiastical Council convened by letters missive from the church of Wolcott, on the 20th of Sept., 1814, at the house of Mr. Keys, pastor elect, in said place, for the purpose of installing the Rev. John Keys in the work of the Gospel ministry in said Wolcott—there were present, Rev. Messrs. Lyman Beecher, Litchfield; Luke Wood, Waterbury; Luther Hart, Plymouth; Jonathan Cone, Bristol; with Deacons Pomeroy Newell, Southington; Thomas Trowbridge, from the church in Litchfield; Jacob Heminway, from the church in Plymouth; Lemuel Porter, from the church in Waterbury; Charles G. Ives, from the church in Bristol.

The Council proceeded to choose the Rev. Luke Wood, Moderator, and Rev. Jonathan Cone, Scribe. Prayer was offered by the Moderator. The Council having attended to the call of the church and Society to the Rev. Mr. Keys, to settle with them in the work of the ministry, and likewise to his answer accepting the call, and also to his credentials relative to his ministerial standing, concluded to proceed to his examination. Having obtained full satisfaction as to his doctrinal and experimental knowledge of the gospel,—voted unanimously, that we approve of Mr. Keys, as a minister of the gospel, and that we proceed to install him in the ministry over this people.

The exercises of the installation were then appointed as follows, viz:

The Rev. Jonathan Cone to read the doings of the Council and make the introductory prayer; Rev. Lyman Beecher to preach the sermon and make the installing prayer; Rev. Luther Hart to give the charge to the pastor elect, and an exhortation to the church and people; and the Rev. Luke Wood to give the right hand of fellowship, and make the concluding prayer.

Voted to proceed to the exercises to-morrow at eleven o'clock, A. M. Prayer being offered, voted to adjourn till to-morrow at nine o'clock, A. M.

Wednesday, September 21, 1814, the Council met and the meeting was opened with prayer. Voted to accept the minutes of the Council.

LUKE WOOD, *Moderator.*
JONATHAN CONE, *Scribe.*

At eleven o'clock, according to the foregoing resolution, the exercises of the installation were performed as above appointed.

Test. JONATHAN CONE, *Scribe.*

This installation is memorable because of Dr. Beecher's sermon on the occasion; for the effects of that sermon have not ceased in Wolcott nor in Connecticut to this day. The subject of the sermon was,*

"THE BUILDING OF WASTE PLACES."

Text: Isaiah, lxi, 4. And they shall build the old wastes; they shall raise up the former desolations, and they shall repair the waste cities, the desolations of many generations.

In the introduction it is stated that: " The waste places of Connecticut, and the duty of building them, will be the subject of consideration in this discourse. The building of these wastes will include the propagation of the truth, the communication of strength to the feeble, and the restoration of fallen Societies to the order of the gospel. In the illustration of the subject it is proposed to consider,

" I. The cause of these desolations.

" II. The means of restoring them.

" III. The motives to immediate exertion for that purpose.

" I. The immediate causes are, evidently, the difference of religious sentiment and worship which prevail, connected with a criminal indifference to the institutions of the Gospel. There is not, in this State, a town or parish unable to support the Gospel constantly, and with ease, provided all the families in the limits of each were of one heart and of one way to serve the Lord. But the property, in many Societies, is divided between three or four different denominations, besides a part, which the love of money and indifference to the Gospel wholly withdraw from the support of divine institutions. . . . .
A remote cause of our present wastes is to be found in a very great declension of vital piety in the churches, which took place many years ago. . . . . . . One

---

*Only the outline of this sermon is given, from a volume of Dr. Beecher's sermons.

effect of this decline was the introduction into the ministry of men, who probably had never experienced the power of divine grace on their own hearts, and who, of course, would be prepared by native feeling to oppose the doctrines of the gospel." These innovations, the Dr. says, became at length almost universal throughout New England.

"As another cause of debility and desolation, may be noted the defection occasioned by the restoration of evangelical doctrine and discipline. The revivals of 1740 were the commencement of a reformation in this state, which has brought the churches back to the doctrines and discipline of our fathers.

"Another cause of desolation, more limited in its operation, but not less disastrous in its effects where it has operated, has been, the timid policy of forbearing to preach plainly those doctrines which offend, and of shrinking from a vigilant, efficient discipline in the church, lest these things interrupt the peace, and endanger the stability of the congregation.

"A later cause of decline and desolation has been the insidious influence of infidel philosophy."

Another cause, Dr. Beecher mentions, is "political violence and alienation." Another: "The direct enterprise of religious denominations to augment their numbers." Another: "The change made in the law for the support of the gospel, in order to accommodate it to the changes in religious opinions which had gradually taken place in the State." The last cause he mentions is: "The common policy, to settle a minister upon an incompetent salary, with the expectation that he will support himself in part by his own exertions."

"II. The means by which the wastes, in this State, may be built.

"1. The great utility of the occasional itineration of the stated pastors within the limits of each association."

"2. Another means may be found in the appointment of

evangelists; and to these must be added, in some cases, a permanent stated supply, until the work of restoration be consummated." To these he adds : " Special enterprise of ministers in the performance of pastoral duties," and especially " pastoral visits."

" 3. To parochial visits, it will be proper to add an efficient system for the instruction of children and young people in the doctrines and duties of religion,"

And last : " Earnest prayer among the churches, for the outporing of the Holy Spirit upon these desolations, and the revival of religion."

" III. The motives to immediate exertion.

" 1. Duty of the churches to help sister churches to rise.

" 2. Unless these desolations are built, they will become more desolate.

" 3. If these waste places are not built, they will exert a powerful influence to create other wastes, and extend the scene of desolation.

" 4. If these wastes are not built, they will undermine, ultimately, the civil and religious order of the state.

" 5. The time past is more than sufficient to have neglected our duty and slept over our dangers."

It was on that part of this sermon concerning the support of evangelists, who might be sent out, that Dr. Beecher made remarks which were suggestive to the ministers of the State, and which resulted in the change of the Missionary Society of the State to the Connecticut Home Missionary Society.

The "Missionary Society of Connecticut" was organized in 1798, the objects of which were : " To Christianize the heathen in North America, and to support and promote Christian knowledge in the new settlements of the United States." This did not include home evangelization. Doctor Beecher in this sermon recommended the formation of a "general society for this special purpose."

In 1815, about six months after the delivery of this sermon, the General Association of Connecticut took up the subject and appointed a committee who reported at the next annual meeting. "On their report it was resolved unanimously to form a Domestic Missionary Society, for Connecticut and its vicinity." This Society is now the "Connecticut Home Missionary Society" and is auxiliary to the American Home Missionary Society. So much for the State of Connecticut.

In this sermon, also, Dr. Beecher refers to the education of children, in the following words: "To parochial visits, it will be proper to add an efficient system for the instruction of children and young people in the doctrines and duties of religion." "It is almost unspeakably important, that a system of religious instruction adapted to the age and altered feelings of young people be provided, to succeed the shorter catechism." Here we perceive the largeness of the Doctor's plan. "A system of religious instruction, for children and young people." The present Sabbath-school system of instruction is intended to meet this "unspeakably important" demand.

This part of the sermon resulted in the commencement of Sunday-schools in the parish under Mr. Keys' administration.

So much for this sermon. It is frequently remarked that Dr. Beecher's thoughts were "Fifty years ahead of his day." It is now fifty-nine years since he delivered this sermon and we are only beginning to realize the systems of church work he planned out for us. Truly some men's works do follow them; and works of which they, and the world, need not be ashamed. What if there had been a thousand Dr. Beechers, and each with a family as numerous and noted for good as Dr. Lyman Beecher's! This may be thought no part of Wolcott history, but I assure such that without the Beecher family a large and very important part of Wolcott history would be wanting.*

---

* It is said that Capt. Joseph Beecher and his sister who married Capt. Herman Hall, and Capt. Amos Beecher (all of Wolcott) were cousins to Dr. Lyman Beecher.

It should be remembered that this sermon was preached in Wolcott when Wolcott was not a "waste place" but in its glory and strength. From 1790 to 1820, it was one of the strong Societies of the county. In 1806 it had over two hundred tax payers on the list of the Society, and this continued about the same for twenty years afterward; and the town had a reputation for agricultural products equal to any in the county. Then wheat grew on these hills more abundantly than in the valleys adjoining, and it would have been a disgrace to have imported corn into "Puddin' street."

Dr. Beecher did not preach this sermon, alone for Wolcott, but for *all Connecticut*, and that, too, for a century of time after he should cease preaching on earth.

Mr. Keys had moved into the parish before he was installed and was ready to move forward in his work when the exercises of installation closed, and he did it right well. The first thing that meets us in his work, is the fulness of the records he made of the doings of the church, a matter which had been almost wholly omitted by the pastors before Mr. Hart. Hence we have the names of all who made application to join the church; the reports of the examining committees, and the decision of the church on each report during Mr. Keys' pastorate. We discover, also, from these records that Mr. Keys was a man of church discipline, not afraid to try to preserve the honor of the church by attending to those delinquent cases that sometimes occur in regard to individuals of the highest standing in the community.

Mr. Keys was a good preacher, above medium, but not equal to Mr. Woodward; a good and faithful pastor and public school visitor, and was esteemed, and kindly cared for, by the parish during his stay among them. During his pastorate, forty-one united with the church,— thirty-five of them by profession; and every interest of the church seems to have been cared for faithfully to the close of his labors, and even after he was dismissed.

The following entry in the church book illustrates these statements:

"At a church meeting, July 2d, 1819, opened with prayer. . . . After some conversation on the duty of calling the brethren to account, for neglecting gospel institutions, and on the subject of setting up a Sabbath School, adjourned till our next preparatory lecture — conclude with prayer.

Attest. JOHN KEYS, *Pastor*.

In the church meeting of March 2d, 1821, we find the following entry: "After some free conversation and earnest exhortation by several of the members, on the present low state of our church, and on the importance of awaking to activity to some extraordinary exertions to revive our drooping graces and promote the cause of the Redeemer among us — adjourned."

Mr. Keys had more than an ordinary amount of church discipline to attend to, all of which was prosecuted by church vote in regular form, and it was the fact of these difficulties that led the brethren on this occasion to "earnest exhortations to the importance of awaking to extraordinary exertions to revive drooping graces and promote the cause of the Redeemer."

Also, from the first, Mr. Keys had been a faithful pastor in catechising the children at home and in the public schools; but now he was on the move towards the Sabbath-school, which he succeeded in holding two summers. Here he calls this enterprise a "Sabbath-school," and as far as I can learn, it was a "Sabbath-school full grown for those days, and to this Deacon Irad Bronson, now living, adds his testimony. The catechism was recited, verses of the Bible were committed to memory, for which the children received credit of so many mills for every ten verses, and at the end of the school a book, in value according to the credit standing to their several names. Addresses were made by pastor, deacons, and others, which, doubtless, were quite as appropriate and valuable as many are in these later days. Mrs. Mark Tuttle has now in her possession a little book given her by Rev. Mr. Keys on account of attendance at Sabbath-school. It is a paper covered book, 16 mo., printed in New York in 1810. The subject matter is: "The principles of the *Christian Religion*, in verse, for the use of children, by P. Doddridge, D. D., arranged for this object by Dr. Doddridge at Northampton, England, Oct. 31, 1743. One of the teachers in this school, Mrs. Hannah Plumb, is now living, and four women, who were then girls in her class,—Mrs. Mark Tuttle, Mrs. Johnson Alcott, Mrs. James Alcott, and Mrs. Isaac Hough,—are still living.

EFFICIENCY OF THE CHURCH.

During Mr. Keys' pastorate the church and Society were diligent and energetic. There was appointed, every year, a committee like the following, and for the same purposes: 1816, "Voted that Lucius Tuttle, John Potter, and John Frisbie, be a committee to provide seats for persons moving in [into the parish] and others as shall be necessary the coming year." Year after year this was attended to regularly, because then people removed *into* the community but now they remove *out*. The tax to provide for the support of the gospel, including "ministerial and other necessary charges," was four to six cents on a dollar, on the tax list; now the Connecticut Home Missionary Society requires "one per cent" to be paid before they render help to a church; but the assessment was much lower, on property then than now. In 1815 the tax was 5 cents; in 1816, 4 cents; in 1817, 6 cents; in 1818, 6 cents; in 1819, they "voted that a tax of 12 cents on the dollar be laid on the assessment list of said Society for 1819, payable to the Treasurer of said Society, immediately, to pay Mr. Keys' salary for 1820, and other necessary expenses."

This twelve per cent. tax, "raised a dust" in Wolcott, that ended in the dismissal of Mr. Keys, and in a vacant pastorate for many years. At the next annual meeting in October they voted to try to raise, by subscription, a sum sufficient to defray the necessary expenses of the Society for the year ensuing." During these years Mr. Keys' salary was five hundred dollars a year ; and other Society expenses very little. The Society went through this year on the subscription plan, and at the end of the year voted : "That a tax, payable on demand, be laid on the list of said Society for 1819, sufficient to raise the sum of three hundred dollars, to be applied wholly to the payment of the debts of the Society at that time due, or that were incurred that year." Yet they proceeded to try the subscription plan another year, and appointed " Ira Hough, Jesse Upson, David Frisbie, James Bailey, Ziba Norton, Samuel Plumb, and Josiah Thomas, a committee to solicit subscriptions." These were mostly new men in the business of the Society and doubtless were opposed to taxation and in favor of a free gospel.

What was the result? At the next annual meeting, Oct. 14, 1822, they "voted that David Frisbie, James Bailey, and Thomas Upson be a committee to consult with Mr. Keys and obtain from him the lowest terms upon which he is willing to preach for us the year ensuing, and whether, if the Society cannot find it possible to raise the stipulated sum, it would be agreeable to his feelings to be amicably dismissed." The committee waited upon Mr. Keys and returned with a written answer, whereupon the meeting adjourned.

This twelve per cent. tax was called for probably, from the fact that the Society had fallen in debt from year to year till something must be done to pay up.

MR. KEYS' COMMUNICATION.

" *To the Ecclesiastical Society in Wolcott :*

GENTLEMEN : Your committee have waited on me to know what proposition I have to make to the Society, to which I reply : 1st. I will accept for the current year of what sum you shall be able to raise, together with the usual quantity of wood, for which

I will supply the desk so many Sabbaths as that compensates for, at the rate of $500 the year. Or, 2d. If a dissolution of our relation shall be judged necessary — deeply as I deplore it, yet considering the situation of the Society, I shall consent on condition that they pay me two hundred dollars in money or in things necessary for the support of my family at cash prices, old arrearages being paid up. I propose this not as a compensation but as willing to bear a part of the burden which in Providence is fallen upon us ; or, 3d. I am willing to abide the decision of any disinterested Council. That you may be directed in the path of duty and come to such a result as may be for the glory of God and the best interests of Christ's kingdom, is the prayer of your sincere friend and servant in Christ.

JOHN KEYS."

Wolcott, Oct. 14, 1822.

It is often the case that when troubles come in a Society, the minister is thought worthy of a full share of the responsibility. In 1806 there were over two hundred tax payers in the Society and the largest sum paid by any one man was less than nine dollars a year, and only seven that paid over five dollars a year. The Society was not reduced by emigration as in after years, for the diminishing of numbers in the town began after Mr. Keys left. Quite a number withdrew from the Congregational and joined the Episcopal Society, but apparently nearly an equal number graduated, by age, into membership or removed into the parish. Besides, there was energy and ability in the church for other interests.

In 1815, they voted, "that a stove or stoves may be erected in the meeting house ; if one only, at the west door ; if two, then one at the east door, in the aisles, with pipes to convey the smoke out of the house in a convenient and proper manner." This resolution was executed, and one of those stoves is now used in Mr. Dennis Pritchard's saw mill.

The singing was improved at considerable expense. During Mr. Woodward's ministry a tax was laid several times for the "encouraging of singing." In 1815 they laid a tax of "six mills on the dollar to procure a teacher of singing;" and at a special meeting six months later they added 4 mills, making one per cent. "to pay the singing master." In 1816 they voted to accept the offer of Mr. Stephen Harrison, and directed the committee to pay him the sum of ten dollars upon his spending one half day in each week so long as it shall be necessary to initiate young beginners who shall attend, in the first rudiments of singing, and two evenings in each week for three months in teaching and perfecting the singing." In 1817, "voted that the Society's committee be authorized and requested to take such measures and expend such sums from the Society treasury as they shall judge proper for the encouragement of singing, the year ensuing." In 1817, voted " That the committee be requested to take such measures as they shall judge proper to encourage and keep up singing."

Notwithstanding this apparent prosperity, the Society had lost so much strength that it could not meet the engagements made with Mr. Keys.

In Oct. 28th, they voted that "under existing circumstances we are willing to dismiss the Rev. Mr. Keys from his service as our pastor and minister."

On November 5th, they appointed a committee to confer with the church and Mr. Keys, and if desirable to make arrangements for the Council.

Upon this Mr. Keys wrote the following letter to the church:

Beloved Brethren:

The painful hour seems now arrived, in the sovereign dispensations of Providence, when we must part. The course of your deliberations this day, unpleasant and trying as they are, is plainly marked out. I have judged it best not to be present; the task would be painful; but I think also, that prudence dictates, you should be by yourselves.

If you shall concur with the propositions of the Society, relative to a dissolution of the pastoral relation between me and this church and congregation, which propositions have already been communicated to me, by their committee, I hereby give consent, and am ready to unite with you in calling a Council to carry them into effect. You will not need my assistance in selecting a Council. Any of the neighboring churches may be sent to—I should suppose five would be sufficient; but I cheerfully submit the matter to your discretion.

The condition of each of us — of the church and Society, and myself,—must necessarily be very unpleasant and trying. A church without the stated ordinances, and the minister without the means of support. We can, therefore, and I trust do, mutually sympathize with each other. Let us remember, brethren, and let us receive the consolation of it: The Lord reigns.

While I have been with you, though one of the least of all saints, if a saint, and unworthy to be called to the pastoral office, yet I have endeavored to be faithful. I have many and strong ties of affection towards this church. I never can forget you, or cease, in my feeble, unworthy manner, to pray for you; and brethren, I hope and trust you never will forget to pray for me.

Our journey in this life is a thorny maze; every bush we pass inflicts a wound. Truly we may not look for our portion here below. But, blessed be God, our hopes reach beyond the grave. There may we meet, when the storms of life are o'er — free from sin, free from sorrow and pain and perplexity and disquietude, to dwell in the smiles of our God and Sovereign, forever.

That you, brethren, may be kept from falling; enabled to maintain the good fight of faith, walking in obedience to all God's commands, and be preserved through grace to the final coming of Jesus Christ in his kingdom, is the sincere prayer of your yet affectionate pastor and unworthy brother in Christ.

JOHN KEYS.

Wolcott, Nov. 11th, 1822.

No vote of the church in regard to this is preserved.

On the 18th of the same month, the Society voted, "That the only cause or reason which we have for our committee to lay before the Council as a ground of dismissing the Rev. Mr. Keys from his pastoral relation to us, is our being, from the smallness of our numbers, and already embarrassing circumstances, utterly unable to afford him a sufficient support."

There are no records of the session or decision of a Council, yet it is very probable that the Council was called and rendered its decision, and that Mr. Keys was regularly dismissed in the first part of Dec., 1822, having served the parish eight years and three months.

He had several children and a family that he could scarcely keep comfortable on five hundred dollars a year, and to be dismissed in December, the beginning of winter, was a sore trial, besides the fact that Mr. Keys was greatly attached to his church and people.

He made an entry in the church book in December, 1822, and signed it as "Late Pastor."

On Dec. 31, 1822, the Society voted "That we lay a tax on the list of 1821, to the amount of three hundred and twenty-five dollars for the purpose of discharging the claims of Mr. Keys against the Society."

CHAPTER VII.

WITHOUT A PASTOR.

It runs in the memory of some persons now living, as well as in the records of the Society, that before and after the dismissal of Mr. Keys, the Meeting house was crowded with hearers to such an extent that it was one of the great difficulties of the Society, to provide seats to accommodate and satisfy the people. One dollar per person, per year, from the regular attendants, would probably have paid the salary of Mr. Keys [$500], and yet they dismissed him, as they say, "for no other reason" than that the salary could not be raised, and had not been for a number of years, on which account the Society was in debt. At this time there was money enough in Wolcott, and if not, there were wheat, corn, and butter in abundance; for those were the days of prosperity in it. We are compelled to conclude that there must have been some radical cause for the unwillingness to support Mr. Keys. I am at a loss to know what it was, and have heard but one suggestion,— namely, that while Mr. Keys was an eminent scholar, and a man of diligence and energy, faithful in all his work, visiting families and public schools, catechising the children, attending social meetings, and preaching, yet the theology he preached was so imbued with the darker doctrines of Calvinism, that the people did not feel like paying heavily, nor even moderately, for it. Another fact deserving of consideration is that his dismissal occurred during the conflict of public sentiment in this town, between the two systems of supporting the gospel,— the one by levying a tax, and the other by subscription. There was much opposition to the taxing system; there had been for thirty years. But if this had been the cause of the failure to raise the money, I do not understand how it occurred that when the Society voted to raise Mr. Keys' salary by subscription one year, as they did two or three years before his dismissal, they should have incurred a debt of nearly three hundred dollars. I have not learned that Mr. Keys was an objectionable minister on account of discussing "politics in the pulpit." Mr. Woodward was a high toned Federalist, and Thomas Jefferson was criticised with spirit and energy, more especially because Mr. Jefferson was supposed to be an infidel, which was the highest wickedness to the good minds of the Puritans. But Mr. Woodward's commanding dignity and learning, and his genial good nature, disarmed opposition even on the part of political opponents. Yet a considerable number left the Society during his ministry; some for this cause and some for other reasons. But these questions do not appear to have effected the minds of the people during Mr. Keys' ministry, and hence some other cause must have brought the support of the gospel into disrepute.

Another singular fact is, that although when Dr. Beecher made it emphatic at the installation of Mr. Keys, that a Society could much better afford to pay for the preaching of the gospel than to go without it, this Society should dismiss Mr. Keys with the expectation of remaining without a minister for a length of time, though probably not as long as proved to be the case. For three years after the dismissal of Mr. Keys there is no mention of any vote of the Society referring to the matter of hiring a minister, or obtaining one in any way.* They attended regularly

---

* During the history of the Society for seventy years, or more, the committee never hired a minister or procured a candidate without a vote of the Society to that effect. It was left for committees of later days to hire ministers, continue them *ad libitum*, and dismiss them, without allowing the Society any voice in the matter; a clear violation of Congregational rules.

to all other interests of the Society. Soon after his dismissal (Dec. 31, 1822) they voted to lay " a tax on the list of 1821, to the amount of three hundred and twenty-five dollars, for the purpose of discharging the claims of Mr. Keys." In May next they voted that a tax be laid sufficient to raise the sum of two hundred and seventy dollars. They appointed Thomas Upson as agent to collect the several "notes and debts due the Society on old arrearages, and if possible to settle the debts of the Society due S. J. Hitchcock." They appointed yearly the seating committee to seat the people in the Meeting house, and appointed in 1823 a special committee to "dignify or number the pews anew."

In annual meeting, 1824, they voted, "That John S. Atkins, Joseph N. Sperry, Jerry Upson, John Beecher, Jr. and Thomas Upson be a committee, to solicit subscriptions for the encouragement of singing; lay out and appropriate the moneys obtained as they shall judge proper and best, and superintend the whole business." In 1825 they appointed another committee for the same purpose, consisting of Gates Upson, Thomas Horton, George Griswold, Jerry Upson, John S. Atkins, and Ira Frisbie. Here is evidence of energy and of ability to do almost anything they chose to do as a Society.

These facts bring to view the character and standing of Deacon Isaac Bronson. After Mr. Keys was dismissed Mr. Bronson became the minister, in fact, although not in form ; first, to fill the vacancy during the embarrassed condition of the Society, and after that, by the informal choice of the people. He had been a member of the church over thirty years ; had been a deacon seventeen years, being sixty-one years of age. He had not the advantages of high school or collegiate education,— Mr. Woodward's school having begun several years after Mr. Bronson was married. Yet Isaac Bronson attained to a very creditable education for those times.

We have now in the Ministers' Library of this parish

a book of "Mathematicks" containing "Arithmetick, Algebra, Geometry, Conick Sections, and Arithmetick of Infinites," which was owned by Rev. Alexander Gillet, (dated as "his book," 1767) and which Mr. Bronson bought of Mr. Gillet for six shillings.* Mr. Bronson was a Latin scholar, as may be seen in his writings as clerk of the church and the town. Some sketches of sermons of his have fallen into my hands which show unusual historical knowledge and very great familiarity with Bible history.

He is said to have been a man of remarkable eloquence in prayer, and in addressing a religious assembly, and with this all his writings now left correspond. Could he have had the opportunities of an early education, it is doubtful if the county or State could have boasted of a greater man than he. To this opinion all persons with whom I have conversed, in and out of Wolcott, agree. He was a man of great diffidence, but when called out by circumstances or peculiar occasions, he surpassed the expectations of all.

When, therefore, the Society in Wolcott was brought to extremities, Isaac Bronson became its leader and minister *without* ordination. Thus he continued for nearly three years, but for what "consideration" from the Society we have no means of knowing except by a vote passed at the end of three years, as follows: "That the Society's committee" (and others named,) "be a committee to circulate subscriptions to raise money to hire preaching." This indicates that no money was raised for this purpose during the three years, for in those times money was not raised except by vote of Society. It is further evident from the fact, that upon the passage of this vote Mr. Bronson refused to serve the Society, as before; as is

---

*The possession of books relating to advanced studies, and the fact frequently mentioned among the people, that often, when tired at night, he lay on the floor of his shop, with his head toward the fire, studying by firelight, indicate the methods by which he obtained knowledge.

evident from a vote of the Society two months later, as follows: "That Gates Upson, Lud Lindsley, Ashbel Upson, Ira Hough, and David Frisbie, be a committee to confer with Deacon Isaac Bronson in regard to the difficulties subsisting between him and the Society, and the cause of his unwillingness to serve the Society as heretofore." After conferring with him the Society in a meeting held one week later, voted to rescind the former vote to hire preaching, and that money be raised to hire preaching "for one third part of the year, beginning the first of April next." That is, they should *hire* preaching four months, and the remainder of the year Isaac Bronson should preach for nothing. How the men of the Society could be at ease in their consciences, and let one man, and he a poor man, carry the largest part of the burden of the church for three years without compensation is beyond explanation, except on the supposition that they had been educated to think that if a man were ordained, he should be paid for preaching, otherwise not, no matter how eloquent or successful the preaching, or how great the service rendered. Probably but few ministers were ever more highly appreciated, in their parish generally, than was Isaac Bronson during these years, and but for the prejudices of a few leading men, he would have been ordained and settled as pastor; and in that case would have served their Society with as great success as any man they had had.

There were peculiar reasons why they should have paid him something appropriate for his work in filling the place of a pastor. He had several children and a noble, patient wife, for whom he could scarcely provide the comforts of life which his neighbors possessed. He had been clerk of the Society for twenty-six years, and had served the church as clerk and treasurer for fifteen years; and as deacon for twenty years. His health had been so poor, from hemorrhage of the lungs, that his family often expected his speedy departure to the better land. He had taught school many years with small pay; and was constant in every good work, for religion, education, and the town and State in which he lived. The Society had prospered and the public feeling had improved, so that they began to feel like raising a minister's salary, and did proceed with a tax in Sept., 1826, of ninety dollars, to repair the Meeting house. In all righteousness among brethren why should they not have payed Deacon Isaac Bronson for his labors in preaching and attending to the other duties of a pastor?

Thus did the Society continue enjoying a gratuitous ministry for the space of five years. What was the result? They had all grown "lean" except Isaac Bronson. Dr. Beecher had told them they could better afford to pay a minister than go without one. They had now tried the latter, and to what effect? All were asleep, in religion, except when the voice of Isaac Bronson aroused them in church or "broke" their hearts at the funerals. The year before Mr. Keys left, twelve united with the church, and during his ministry of eight years, forty-one united, but during these five years of a vacant pulpit, not one united, as far as the books show. But in mercy God sent them a minister to awake them, for in the midst of their sleep, a voice was heard as of one "in the wilderness" calling them to repentance. How he came we know not, but certainly not by the call of the Society or church.* At a meeting held Oct. 28th, 1827, they voted that the "committee be directed to employ Mr. Scranton to preach for us until the end of May next."

On the 10th of next March they voted, "That seven persons, one in each school district, be forthwith appointed to solicit subscriptions for the support of the Rev. Mr. Scranton as a preacher of the gospel for the year next ensuing, after the first of June next." He

---

* We learn from his journal, left in the hands of Mr. Jarvis R. Bronson, that he came here on Saturday, June 16, 1827, to preach for a number of Sabbaths.

preached here two years and then departed; the only reason we find is that the Society failed to raise three hundred dollars for his support for the year, as he desired. The first winter he was here he taught school three months, and in the spring and summer following there was a general awakening, and many were added to the church. This carried them through the second year, but when an effort was made for the third year it did not succeed well, and the Society voted on July 7, 1829, "That the committee appointed on the 30th of May to solicit subscriptions to hire preaching, offer their papers on the terms that in case there is not enough obtained to raise the sum of three hundred dollars, then whatsoever is subscribed to be null and void." Soon after this, Mr. Scranton left. Mr. Scranton's labors were many and resulted in great good to the church and community. As proof of this and as evidence of the Lord's faithfulness to those who labor faithfully, we give some extracts from Mr. Scranton's journal, which was sent after his death to Mr. Jarvis R. Bronson. These labors were put forth amidst great difficulties and hindrances. The church was much divided, and great indifference to religion prevailed throughout the community. Indeed, when there began to be a stir about religion, some of the people spoke against it and ridiculed it.

JOURNAL OF REV. ERASTUS SCRANTON IN WOLCOTT, 1827 AND 1828.

June 16, Saturday; came here to preach several Sabbaths.

17. Preached, being unwell. I have not recovered from my dangerous illness in May. I found the Society feeble and disunited, but desirous to have steady preaching.

July 1st. Administered the Lord's Supper. It had not been celebrated here before, for a long time. It was a precious season to Christian people.

Great coldness among professors of religion—much immorality among the people.

Sept. Miss Orpha Thomas, who is about 16, has been

awakened and hopefully converted to Christ in the course of the summer. The preaching of the word is better attended than it was during the two months past. Administered the sacrament of the Lord's Supper.

Oct. 26. Maria, wife of S. Wheeler Upson, and Laura, wife of Linus Munson, admitted to the church. For several years there has not been an addition to the church. Mr. Upson, on seeing his wife come out and join the church, was led to reflect. It was the means of his conversion, 'tis to be hoped.

Oct. 30, Thursday. Returned from attending the conference of the churches at Waterbury; called on Wheeler Upson, and found him an awakened sinner. Attended meeting at Woodtick School House; preached from Jer. 17, 9.

In the course of the season past, Colonel Moses Pond has been awakened and hopefully converted. He did not let it be known, till his sickness. He has been in great distress at times, and found relief, I suppose, on Sabbath, Nov. 4, on his way home from meeting.

November, 1827. I have had repeated conversation with Mr. Upson, &c. He obtained hope about three weeks after his first awakening.

Nov. 4, Sabbath. Spoke to several young ladies that came in to Mr. Whiting's.

Nov. 14. Conferences begin to be full and solemn. We seem on the eve of an awakening here. There has not been anything like a general revival here at any time.* B. L. revive thy work.

December, 1827. Meetings still full and solemn. Some Christians awake and pleading for a revival.

January 15, 1828, Thursday. Miss Rebecca Hall came here with Miss Vesta Frisbie, to see me, being awakened three weeks ago at her Uncle Frost's. She talked as one under conviction; proposed to come to school.†

Jan. 18. Took tea at Mr. Mark Tuttle's — found his wife

---

* There was a general awakening in 1783 under the preaching of Rev. Messrs. Mills and Miller and the labors of Mr. Gillet, and this was therefore forty-four years before Mr. Scranton came here. But a forty-four years' sleep was probably long enough !

† Mr. Scranton taught school — I suppose a select school like Mr. Woodward's and Mr. Keys'.

awakened. She told me that my conversation at their house, when I and Capt. Gates Upson came there, two or three weeks before, first awakened her. She had never disclosed her anxious feelings to any one before. Preached in the East School House this evening — full and solemn meeting. It is now manifest that an awakening is begun in this place.

19, Saturday evening. I went to make a religious visit to Mr. Albert Boardman. He was absent, but I found her [his wife] awakened as I suppose. I then called to see Mr. J. N. Sperry, and found him more anxious than he ever was before, as he told me — his wife listened.

20, Sabbath. This evening called to see Mr. Clark Bronson and wife. I found her indulging a hope. I called at Eldad Parker's and found his wife thoughtful. She told me that 13 years ago, at Shenango, she was awakened, but grieved away the Holy Spirit. Has feeling, but no reason to hope.

Jan. 21. Monday evening. Mr. Boardman came to see me, in deep concern of soul. He tells me that he was first awakened last June.

Jan. 22, Tuesday. Conversed with Miss Rebecca Hall, at noon, who says her mind is relieved. In the evening I went to preach at Mr. Levi Atkin's. Heard that Mr. Newton Norton talks seriously.

25th. The center school house was full (though it rained hard), and the meeting solemn.

27th, Sabbath. Exchanged with Mr. Hart and preached at Plymouth.

29. In conversation I find Mr. Doolittle anxious. He has felt that religion is important since his sickness two years ago. He lacks decision.

Feb. 1, 1828, Friday. Martha Tuttle is still anxious. No hope.

3, Sab. To-day Col. Pond and Mr. Upson told me they had a wish to join the church.

7. Conference of the churches at Prospect.

8th, Friday. Held first inquiry meeting; present 10 persons — Col. Pond, Mr. Upson, Clark Bronson and wife, Mrs. Parker, Mrs. Moulthrop, Mary Upson, Charlotte Harrison, Gen. G. Doolittle, and Rebecca Hall.

11. Monday. Preached at Woodtick; meeting full and solemn.

13. Preached at South School House.

15. Preached in Center School House, and meeting solemn, and 70 present.

18, Monday. Anxious meeting here to-night and a very rainy evening — 6 only present, one of whom is Miss Clarissa Upson, rejoicing in hope.

March 2, Sab. Col. Pond and S. W. Upson joined church.

3. Monthly Concert. Full meeting and interesting.

12th. Preached at Woodtick, having closed my school to-day.

13th. Visited at Mr. Bement's, &c. Cyrus Fenn somewhat anxious.

17th, Monday. Anxious meeting.

15th. Esther Hotchkiss anxious some, and came to the anxious meeting.

23. Began a Bible class.

24. Went to N. Milford and found there had been 4 to 6 conversions.

30, Sab. Preached at Cheshire and came to Wolcott and preached in the evening at Center School House, where I heard that Lowman Upson has a hope. Church voted to invite the Conference.

April 1st, Tuesday. Went to N. Milford.

2d. Conference of churches at N. M. 78 delegates.

4th. Annual Fast. Snowed all day. Rode from Prospect (where I preached last night) to Wolcott.

6th. Report from the Conference was listened to by all the congregation. Many were affected to tears.

7th. Monthly concert. Asaph Hotchkiss came to see me, P. M., in distress — and sent for me to come to his house, &c. His wife and Esther and Wealthy interested.

8th. Preached at Spindle Hill.

9th. Preached at South District.

11th. Preached at Woodtick.

May 1st. Preached at South District.

Up to this time Mr. Scranton had urged forward this work without any formal action on the part of the church. On April 25th the church met, and voted, "That Deacons James Bailey, Isaac Bronson, and Irad Bronson, with Brethren Thomas Upson, Harvey Upson, Ashbel Upson, Lucius Tuttle, Daniel Holt, Abner Hotchkiss, and Samuel W. Upson be a committee to visit the several members of the church, male and female, and inquire the situation of their minds in a religious point of view, and whether any, and if any, what matter of offense lies upon their minds and against any brother or sister, and if any such exist, to use their influence that the same may be mutually and satisfactorily healed and settled in a Christian manner."

On May 1st, Mr. Scranton wrote: "The church committee began their visits to prepare for the Conference to be held among them, and it was ascertained there was a happy state of feeling among the brethren; a readiness to confess their sins and to renew covenant. Several meetings of the church were pleasant and humbling seasons. Some few are opposed to the Conference — call it a Methodist meeting; speak against a revival as a pernicious thing. W. A.; J. H.; J. A."

May 4th, Wednesday. The Conference met late in the day, owing to the great rain yesterday. The church and people were prepared to receive them with open hearts.

5th. The meetings last evening and this morning, in the several districts were full, solemn, and interesting. 30 churches represented and 40 delegates.

May 6, Friday. Went down to Mr. John Frisbie's and found him an awakened, distressed church member. Mrs. Frisbie was all in tears. Soon after, Sarah, their son's wife, came in and on my speaking to her she was much affected. I prayed, and it was a scene of deep interest.

Met Mr. Fitch Higgins 12 or 15 rods from his door, and he clasped my hand, and on being asked how he did, he exclaimed, "I am a poor sinner." His wife was under deep conviction. He said he had tried to work but could not.

At Mr. David Frisbie's was another deeply interesting scene, and a meeting was appointed at the school house in the evening, which was 'a full and solemn concourse.'

On arriving home I learned that Mr. Smith Atkins had been to see me, and was deeply distressed in mind and could not work.

May 7th, Saturday. Went to see James Alcott and Smith Atkins and wife. Met the two first on their way to see me. At Mr. Alcott's house several came in and I exhorted and prayed.

Two days later he was sent for to go to the north-east part of the parish, where several were in great distress of mind. The whole parish was moved on this subject,— and why not? Too long had the people been indifferent or greatly negligent as to these things.

Among the names he mentions, of those greatly interested at this time, are the Brockets, Lindsleys, Nortons, Ephraim Hall and wife, Orin Hall and wife, Anna Lewis, Lucius Tuttle, Jr., Maria Thomas, Mr. Bartholomew, and a number of others.

On May 11th, they held their "first public prayer meeting in the Meeting house, and a considerable number present, and a most solemn and impressive meeting— many in tears—the prayers appropriate, and Deacon Isaac Bronson's address was most weighty, powerful, and awakening."

Thus the church, after six years wandering in the wilderness, returned to her allegiance to the mission for which she was sent,— to save men. Had the church been faithful, there had been no occasion for such excitement, as it was there was no other way to salvation.

Mr. Scranton says, in his journal, March 23, 1828, "Began a Bible class." This, I think, was on a week day evening, and was additional to the Sunday-school which was held on the Sabbath, between services, Dr. William A. Alcott being superintendent. The school was organized for the first time under a superintendent and other officers and teachers, during the summer of 1827.

Deacon Irad Bronson, now living in Bristol, thinks, this was not an organized school; only two or three classes were organized with teachers, Dr. Wm. A. Alcott assisting, particularly in collecting books for the pupils of the classes to read. Others think Dr. Alcott was regularly appointed superintendent; for one of the class papers written by him is still preserved. These are the names: Ira H. Hough, Isaac Upson, Samuel Upson, Daniel H. Holt, Asaph Upson, Mahlon Hotchkiss, Leverette Alcott, Ambrose B. Alcott, John E. Alcott. These were then boys from eight to twelve years old; so says Mr. Ira H. Hough. This was class No. 3, taught by Lucius Tuttle, Jr., and afterward by L. C. Hotchkiss, who still holds the original class paper.

By vote of the Society, Rev. Mr. Wheelock was engaged to preach "for the term of one year" from Sept. 11, 1829; but in March next, 1830, they voted to "obtain from him the terms on which he is willing to settle with the Society for his past services and relinquish the contract for the future." To this he made a written reply, but the records do not show whether he continued longer or not. The reason for this movement on the part of the Society, I apprehend to have been the difficulty of raising the salary of Mr. Wheelock, and that an arrangement was made by which he relinquished so much of that as to continue the time for which he engaged. The Society and church were probably without a stated minister from Sept., 1830, till August, 1831. On January 31, 1831, a subscription was started to raise money for a cupola and bell, to be attached to the Meeting house. This subscription, in the elegant "hand-writing" of Mr. Archibald Minor is preserved, and the spirit of it, in one respect, is worthy of perpetuation, and in another respect so peculiar that I copy it:

"Whereas, the inhabitants of the town of Wolcott, feeling desirous to have a bell in said town, do propose to build a cupola on the Congregational Meeting house in said Wolcott for the purpose of hanging said bell, provided a sufficient sum can be raised to defray the expenses of the same; and wishing that if there be one provided it may be used for all denominations whatever, and that the same shall be freely used whenever it may be necessary for the convenience of any and every individual of said town; and hoping and trusting that a thing of this kind would be the means of uniting the people of this town rather than of dividing them; it is therefore to be hoped and trusted that the inhabitants of this town generally will take so deep an interest in an object of this kind that they will cheerfully and liberally contribute to effect said object. The bell to be always considered the property of the Town of Wolcott, and the ringing of the same to be directed by the inhabitants of said town in their annual town meetings. The weight of the bell to be determined by the subscribers or by a committee by them appointed.

WOLCOTT, January 31, 1831.

Therefore, we whose names are underwritten do agree to pay the several sums annexed to our names, respectively for the attainment of the object as above specified, to be paid to him or them, whom the subscribers shall appoint for that purpose.

NAMES OF SUBSCRIBERS AND AMOUNT SUBSCRIBED.

Moses Pond,	$25.00	George Griswold,	5.00
Daniel Holt,	25.00	Lydia Alcott,	1.00
Adna Whiting,	25.00	Josiah Thomas,	10.00
Lucius Tuttle,	25.00	Luther Andrews,	5.00
A. & H. Boardman,	15.00	John S. Atkins,	5.00
Archibald Minor,	20.00	Samuel Plumb,	1.00
Thomas Upson,	20.00	Mercy Beecher,	1.00
Marvin Minor,	5.00	Lud Lindsley,	10.00
Charles M. Upson,	1.00	Esther R. Hotchkiss,	2.00
Freelove Upson,	2.00	Rev. E. Scranton,	5.00
Caroline R. Byington,	2.00	Almon Plumb,	1.00
David Frisbie,	20.00	Joseph N. Sperry,	5.00
John Bronson,	8.00	George G. Alcott,	1.00
Hannah Bronson,	50	Wm. Blakeslee,	1.00
John Bronson, jr.,	5.00	Wm. F. Curtiss,	1.00
Lua S. Carter,	2.00	Alben Alcott,	2.00
Luther Hotchkiss,	20.00	Lewis Churchill,	1.00
Irad Bronson,	5.00	Mark Tuttle,	8.00
James Alcott,	16.00	Simeon N. Norton,	2.00
James Alcott, jr.,	4.00	Wm. Parker,	1.00
Anson G. Lane,	5.00	Ansel H. Plumb,	3.00
Leveritt Kenea,	10.00	Reuben Carter,	5.00
John Thomas,	5.00	Mark Alcox,	5.00

Nathaniel Lane,	2.00	Ira Frisbie,	10.00
Levi Atkins,	3.00	John Frisbie,	10.00
Samuel Horton,	5.00	Almus Wakelee,	10.00
Moses Bradley,	5.00	Jonathan Bement,	15.00
Wm. R. Bradley,	2.00	Erastus Nichols,	1.00
Eri Welton,	5.00	David Pardee,	1.00
Ira Hough,	20.00	Levi Frisbie,	4.00
Seth Norton,	5.00	Ashbel Upson,	10.00
Derius Hull,	1.00	Lowman Upson,	2.00
Joel Alcox,	4.00	Clark Bronson,	6.00
Elijah Royce,	2.50	Harley Downs,	1.00
Timothy Royce,	.50	Isaac Alcott,	1.00
Luther Bailey,	2.00	Ransley Minor,	2.00
Henry Beecher,	5.00	Henry Harrison,	1.00
Leonard Beecher,	7.00	Seth Thomas,	25.00
Titus Brockett,	5.00	Solomon Parker,	1.00
Salmon Upson,	3.00	Allen Wells,	1.00
Cyrus C. Upson,	5.00	Ambrose Ives,	5.00
Abner Hotchkiss,	1.00	Ransom Blakeslee,	1.00
Orrin Hall,	4.00	Martin Upson,	2.00
Erastus Atkins,	3.00	Alfred Churchill,	2.00
Rollin Tuttle,	2.00	Ives Bronson,	2.00
Ziba Norton,	4.00	Chester Andrews,	3.00
Elihu Moulthrop,	10.00	Joshua Minor,	1.50
Mark Upson,	5.00	Newel Minor,	1.00
Prosper Hull,	1.00	Miles Loveland,	3.00
Abram Norton,	3.00	Fitch A. Higgins,	8.00
John A Brady,	1.00	Hezekiah Mix,	1.00
Ephraim Hall,	5.00	Royce Lewis,	1.00
Wm. A. Finch,	2.00	Samuel B. Tuttle,	5.00
Selim Doolittle,	2.00	Pliny Bartholomew,	1.00
Selah Upson,	8.00	Thomas Barnes,	10.00
Reuben Lewis,	4.00	Susan Byington,	1.00
Harvey Upson,	10.00	Jerry Upson,	5.00
Marshal Upson,	2.50	John Beecher,	6.00
Marcus Upson,	1.50	James Bailey,	10.00
Wm. Bartholomew,	10.00	Eldad Parker,	2.00
Isaac Bronson,	2.00	Gates Upson,	5.00
Seth Peck,	1.00	Almon Alcox,	3.00
Timothy H. Hotchkiss,	2.00	Truman Price,	1.00

Subscription for painting and covering Meeting house, - - 51.00
L. Tuttle, jr., added - - - - - - - - 7.00

Amount, - - - - - - - - - $650.50

In fifteen days this subscription was raised and the subscribers in assembly voted " to apply the balance of the subscriptions already obtained over and above the expense of erecting cupola and procuring bell, towards covering and painting the house. Upon this the Society voted, " That we accept and approve of the proposals of the subscribers for the cupola to the Congregational Meeting house and placing a bell in the same, agreeable to the terms and upon the same principles as stated in the caption to the subscription paper now before the meeting. That the Society approve of the proposal of individuals and grant permission to have the outside of the house covered and painted, if the subscriptions shall furnish means sufficient. That the committee appointed by the subscribers to superintend the erection of the cupola, be authorized to superintend the covering, painting, etc." This committee consisted of Archibald Minor, Thomas Upson, Daniel Holt, Luther Hotchkiss, Adna Whiting. It is worthy of note that this project was carried on by the citizens as such, and not as members of the Society or church, and yet a very large part of the money came from members of the church. Why it was they would not do as well through the Society as through the Town I am unable to say; but the fact is very evident, and to complete the whole, the Society gave its own work into the hands of the special committee.*

On the 28th of June, 1831, the contractor gave a receipt in full for the pay for the work done on the house and cupola, $440. The bell, weighing 931 pounds, and the hangings cost at the foundry, Medway, Mass., $313.61. At the following Town meeting the cupola and bell were offered by the subscribers to the Town as Town property, but the Town refused to accept the same; after which the subscribers organized into a stock company,

---

* In 1826 the Society voted a tax to the amount of ninety dollars, for repairing and painting the house, but in 1827 they rescinded the vote and gave up the work, having failed to raise the money.

appointed officers and held the property several years. It was finally given to the Society. The first bell became fractured soon after it was put up. It was returned to the foundry, and another sent in its place, according to the stipulations made by Mr. Holbrook, the maker. It is believed, to this day, that the first bell was not properly used.

In August, Rev. Nathan Shaw was hired for four months, beginning 4th of July, previous; and a vote was passed by the Society to apply to the Home Missionary Society for aid in paying the minister. Eighty dollars were obtained and Mr. Shaw preached until July 4, 1832. He is said to have been a "very smart" preacher.

In October, 1832, the pews were offered for the first time, for rent for one year; "to be sold to the highest bidder, provided the sum bid amount to three hundred and twenty-five dollars, reserving the pew east of the pulpit." One year from this time they were rented again.

On the 12th of November, 1832, the committee were directed to "engage the Rev. David Smith for three Sabbaths." During the year 1833 there is no account of a minister being hired by the Society. Mr. Shaw may have preached part of the year and others the remainder; the Home Missionary Society appropriated 80 dollars for 1833. On April 10th, 1834, they voted, that "this Society will settle a minister provided the means can be obtained." On the 21st of the same month they voted "That the prudential committee be directed to wait on Rev. Seth Sackett and invite him to become our minister and that we on our part will pay him four hundred dollars yearly, and that at any time, either party giving six months' notice, the connection between them may be dissolved, without damage on either side." This proposition was not accepted, and Mr. Sackett preached two months and probably no longer.

In 1835 Rev. Wm. F. Vail was hired for one year, his term of service extending into the summer of 1836.

HISTORY OF WOLCOTT.

Several persons, not members of the committee, personally bound themselves for the payment of his salary. They circulated a subscription and obtained what they could, and at the end of the year made up the whole amount that was wanting, by paying, each, an equal proportion of the deficiency. These are the names of the persons so uniting : Fitch Higgins, Jonathan Bement, Ephraim Hall, Orrin Hall, Reuben Carter, Luther Bailey, Joel Alcott, Lud Lindsley, Selah Upson, Noah H. Byington, Lucius Tuttle.

The committee were directed on the 4th of August, 1837, to "hire Mr. Chapman six weeks after next Sabbath, as a candidate for settlement," and in September they voted to invite Rev. James D. Chapman to settle with them "as a gospel minister," and this invitation being accepted, Mr. Chapman was "ordained Pastor of the church and Society of Wolcott, on the 25th day of October, 1837," with a salary of "three hundred dollars and all that is realized from the Home Missionary Society, annually, so long as he shall continue our minister."

The following is a list of those who subscribed for the support of the gospel in 1837, who were seated in the Meeting house according to their age :

John Bronson, aged 102, July 16th.
John Frisbie, 75, April 8th.
Nathaniel Lane 73, May 4th.
Sarah Parker, 72, January 12th.
Theda Bailey, 72, May 7th.
Samuel Plumb, 71, July 13th.
Amy Tuttle, 70, March 14th.
Mehitable Upson, 69, January 24th.
Samuel Gaylord, 69, June 12th.
Lois Alcott, 68, April 6th.
Harvey Upson, 68, Nov. 11th.
Lud Lindsley, 67, Sept. 24th.
Abner Hotchkiss, 66, May 24th.
Hannah Bronson, 66, Aug. 24th.
Mark Alcott, 64, May 11th.
John Thomas, 64, Dec. 9th.
Rhoda Norton, 63, Nov. 6th.
James Alcott, 63, Dec. 5th.
Levi Atkins, 62, Jan. 14th.
Royce Lewis, 62, Feb. 1st.
Ruth Johnson, 62, Feb. 1st.
Luther Andrews, 62, April 16th.
Josiah Thomas, 62, Sept. 10th.
John Bronson, Jr., 61, Jan. 31st.
Joshua Minor, 61, May 9th.
Selah Upson, 61, May 26th.
Lydia Hall, 61, Aug. 14th.
Moses Bradley, 60, Sept. 25th.
Luther Hotchkiss, 59, Dec. 17th.
Elizabeth Alcott, 58, July 14th.
Titus Bracket, 58, Nov. 25th.
Elihu Moulthrop, 57, March 12th.

WITHOUT A PASTOR.

Gates Upson, 57, July 18th.
David Scarritt, 56, Dec. 22d.
Ziba Norton, 55, October 2d.
Ira Hough, 54, March 7th.
Wm. Bartholomew, 54, Nov. 13th
Archibald Miner, 53, May 23d.
Jonathan Bement, 52, August 28th.
Thomas Upson, 52, Sept. 23d.
Nathaniel G. Lewis, 51, April 2d.
Clark Bronson, 51, Dec. 6th.
Moses Pond, 50, January.
Eldad Parker, 50, July 24th.
Isaac Hotchkiss, 50, October.
Olive Wiard, 48, January 10th.
Almon Alcott, 47, February 29th.
Lucy S. Carter, 47, Dec. 2d.
Freelove Upson, 46, Feb. 2d.
Daniel Holt, 46, August.
Stephen Harrison, 45, Sept. 20th.
Amanda Perkins, 44, March 13th.
Reuben Carter, 44, March 18th.
Jedediah G. Alcott, 44, June 26th.
Hannah Plumb, 43, February 12th.
Lamburton Tolls, 43, August.
John Beecher, 42, May 5th.
Milo G. Hotchkiss, 42, June 13th.
Marvin Miner, 42, August 19th.
Stephen Meriman, 42, Sept. 20th.
Flavius Norton, 42, Nov. 27th.
Anson G. Lane, 41, March 19th.
William Plumb, 41, July 29th.
Orrin Hall, 40, October 11th.
L. L. Kenea, 39, June 21st.
Leonard Beecher, 39, Nov. 27th.
Ephraim Hall, 38, Sept. 15th.
Nelson Tuttle, 38, Nov. 21st
Florilla Hickox, 37, March 7th.
Chester Andrews, 37, Sept. 1st.
Joseph N. Sperry, 37, Sept. 5th.
Prosper Hull, 36, April 10th.
Timothy Bradley, 36, May 22d.
Alben Alcott, 36, October 5th.
David S. Bailey, 35, July 21st.
Mary Hotchkiss, 35, August 11th.
Abram Norton, 35, Sept. 15th.

Ansel H. Plumb, 34, Jan. 6th.
Wm. B. Bradley, 34, August 13th.
Salmon Upson, 34, Sept. 8th.
Mark Tuttle, 34, October 21st.
George Griswold, 34.
Sylvia Thomas, 33, Feb. 15th.
Ira Frisbie, 33, March 28th.
Alfred Churchill, 33, May 28th.
Johnson Alcott, 33, Dec. 10th.
Lydia Hotchkiss, 32, March 15th.
Carlos R. Byington, 32, April 24th.
Lucius Tuttle, Jr., 32, Sept. 17th.
Luther Bailey, 31, July 10th.
Encas Blakeslee, Jr., 31, Aug. 10th.
Wm. Blakeslee, 31, Oct. 22d.
Charles Welton, 30, April 30th.
L. M. Sutliff, 30, Sept. 15th.
David Scarritt, 30, Dec. 28th.
Anson H. Smith, 29, March 20th.
Jarvis R. Bronson, 29, April 5th.
Henry Beecher, 28, Jan. 24th.
Lenas Tolls, 28, May.
Charles Upson, 28, June 4th.
Benjamin Z. Lindsley, 28, July 31st.
Noah H. Byington, 28, Sept. 18th.
John Humiston, 28, Sept. 23d.
Henry D. Upson, 28, Oct. 5th.
Henry Harrison, 27, March.
James W. Norton, 27, March 24th.
Joel Alcott, 27, August 16th.
Henry Minor, 27, December 17th.
Levi Moulthrop, 26, Jan. 5th.
Roxannah Perkins, 25, Feb. 13th.
Augustus Rose, 25, May 25th.
Isaac Hough, 25, Nov. 23d.
Cyrus Wiard, 24, Jan. 13th.
Wm. Johnson, 24, April 25th.
George H. Plumb, 24, Oct. 15th.
Levi Atkins, Jr., 24, Nov. 5th.
Henry A. Pond, 23, January 13th.
David B. Frisbie, 23, June 17th.
J. B. W., 23, June 23d.
Ezra S. Hough, 23, August 9th.
Joel A. Hotchkiss, 23, October 26th.
Lucius Upson, 22, Feb. 13th.

Lucian Upson, 22, Feb. 13th. John C. Alcott, 17, March 24.
Elihu Moulthrop, Jr., 21, March 16th. Wm. Wiard, 16, Dec. 10th.
Hendrick Norton, 21, Dec. 11th. Rachel Lindsley.
Stiles L. Hotchkiss, 20, March 6th. Isaac Bronson.
Mary Ann Wiard, 19, Nov. 10th. Mr. Higgins.
Rufus Norton, 18, Feb. 18th.

CHAPTER VIII.

THE MINISTRY OF REV. JAMES D. CHAPMAN AND REV. AARON C. BEACH: FROM 1837 TO 1857.

REV. JAMES D. CHAPMAN.

Mr. Chapman's ministry was passed during troublesome times. The anti-slavery spirit was rising in the country and making itself felt in political issues. Wolcott was a strongly democratic town and Mr. Chapman was a strong anti-slavery man, and it was not long after his settlement that the conflicting elements gave forth their legitimate prophecies. In April, 1839, when Mr. Chapman had preached here but eighteen months, the Society "voted that a committee be appointed to confer with Rev. J. D. Chapman, with regard to the expediency of dissolving the pastoral relations existing between him and the Society." So strong was the sympathy of some with the "peculiar institution" of the South that they adopted the barbarous expedient of despoiling their neighbors' property in order to intimidate them to silence. As a consequence, Mr. Chapman's horse was sheared, mane and tail, and also the horses of several other members of the church, and one member who had no horse had his cow sheared.

The church was satisfied with Mr. Chapman, but several members of the Society, not members of the church, were very greatly opposed to him. The contest went on till the 11th day of December, 1839, when the Meeting house was burned to the ground. It is said in charity that the burning of the house was in part accidental. A notice had been given for an anti-slavery meeting to be held in the Meeting house. The evening before this meeting was to take place, a quantity of powder was placed in the stove with a slow match attached, and a little after nine o'clock in the evening a heavy explosion was felt and heard by the people residing near the Meeting house ; but the cause they could not discover. About 12 o'clock in the night they were aroused by the cry of fire, and found the house all in flames, and it was soon a heap of ashes. The next day the anti-slavery meeting was held, and the people gathered around the smouldering ashes to keep warm while they were addressed on the great subject of freedom. It is possible that the intention was not to burn the Meeting house, but to destroy the stove, and thus prevent the meeting ; for it is said that there was great opposition to having any stove in the house, and for this reason some wanted it destroyed. The first stove was put into the Meeting house about 1815 and was used till near 1829, when it was set aside. The stove destroyed by the fire was a new one, and had been in the house about one month. This event made great excitement in the town and through the county. Some persons were arrested and held to trial, but when the trial came the principal witness was wanting. This witness was well known, and declared that certain parties had told him that if he testified in the court against them they would certainly kill him. Believing this, he left the town just before the trial, and has never been seen in Wolcott since. These things are still asserted by several of the most trustworthy persons of the town. This was the tribute that Wolcott paid in those early stages of the great conflict between slavery and freedom, a tribute which, though it seemed great at the time, was but a tithe of what it paid years after, in the conflict that closed, in 1865, in the realization of freedom to all the subjects of this nation without distinction of race or color. And it is to the highest honor of many in this town that, although they held strictly to the Democratic party, when the flag of the nation was dishonored by her own sons, they then buckled on the soldier's pack, marched to the war, and acquitted themselves like men. At the annual meeting, held on the 26th of April, 1840, seventeen men withdrew from the First Society. They were the anti-slavery men, who had been true and faithful to the church and to church principles as maintained in the Congregational churches in New England. They were nearly, if not all, communicants, and among them was Deacon Isaac Bronson, the great and good man of this church.

When these persons had withdrawn, being strong friends of Rev. Mr. Chapman, and on the same side of the great question at issue, the Society at once "voted that the Society hereby notify the Rev. James D. Chapman that they wish that the pastoral relation may be dissolved between him and this Society agreeably to the contract entered into between him and this church and Society at the time of his settlement."*

An effort was made at this meeting, 26th of April, to raise a subscription to build a Meeting house, but did not succeed. On the 16th of May next they met again, and put forth the following statement as the heading of a subscription paper:

Whereas, the Congregational Society in the town of Wolcott have suffered a severe loss in the destruction of their house of public worship, inasmuch as they have been deprived of a suitable and convenient place to assemble for the public worship of God; and whereas certain individuals who have formerly belonged to said Society have withdrawn from the same, thereby rendering said Society, whose strength has always been small, still more enfeebled; and whereas it is believed that the erection of a house of public worship by said Society will greatly tend to unite the feelings and promote that peace and harmony throughout the parish which ought ever to exist amongst all ecclesiastical bodies; and whereas said Society are contemplating the erection of such

---

* The contract was that the relation between the parties should be dissolved on condition that either party give six months notice.

a house, and feeling in their present circumstances the necessity of soliciting the aid of all those who feel desirous of promoting so laudable an object; therefore we, the undersigned, for the purpose of assisting said Society to build said house, hereby promise to pay, on demand, to the treasurer of said Society, or his successors in said office, the several sums set opposite our respective names, to be used by said Society for the purpose aforesaid.

Fifteen men were appointed to circulate this subscription paper, and on the 20th of June they had succeeded so far that the Society held a meeting and appointed the following persons a building committee: Joseph N. Sperry, Marvin Miner, Ira Hough, Ira Frisbie, and Levi Moulthrop. "The house, including portico, to be 52 feet long; main body of the house 46 feet long by 36 feet wide; length of posts, 20 feet."

This effort to build a Meeting house did not bring back those persons who had withdrawn, and on the 10th of July, 1840, a Second Congregational Society of Wolcott was organized. Under these circumstances a Council was called, consisting of the "whole Consociation." The church united in calling the Council because the Society demanded the dismission of the pastor. On the 9th of November, 1840,— probably the day on which Mr. Chapman was dismissed,— the church, at a church meeting, took the following action: "Voted unanimously that we are well satisfied with the Rev. James D. Chapman as a gospel minister, both as to his preaching and personal deportment, and are desirous that the pastoral relation might be continued, but as the persons who now constitute the Society over which he was installed are anxious for his dismission, we reluctantly consent to it; provided the Rev. Consociation shall judge it meet and proper."

The Council met apparently on the 9th of November, 1840, and passed the following remarkable but just and high-toned declaration:

"Whereas, there have existed various difficulties in the church and Ecclesiastical Society in Wolcott, which have led to the formation of distinct congregations for public worship ; and whereas, the Consociation has been requested to act on the case, in which request both parties have acquiesced ; and whereas, the interests of religion must be seriously injured in the place by their continued separate existence ; and whereas, the Consociation anticipate no good result from investigation into difficulties complicated and of so long standing, which it would be impossible now wholly to settle ; therefore

Resolved, That as in the opinion of Consociation, a union of these two bodies may take place without any sacrifice of principle by either of them, a union ought therefore to take place on the basis of the following great principles and stipulations, to be solemnly assented to and forever faithfully observed by the parties herein before mentioned : —

The church, in Congregational usage, is a body distinct and independent of the Ecclesiastical Society, and as such, should in the settlement of a pastor, give a separate vote to be concurred in by the Society, if the Society see fit ; and moreover, may for sufficient reasons separate from the Society; but the separation never should take place except in peculiar emergencies and after seeking counsel of Consociation or the neighboring churches.

It is a cardinal principle that every pastor has a right to discuss in his pulpit those subjects, moral and religious, the discussion of which will in his judgment promote the cause of the Redeemer, and that it is an unreasonable and dangerous infringement on his right, for his church or Society to dictate to him, while their pastor, what moral and religious subjects he shall or shall not discuss ; while we fully admit not only that the exercise of this right should be governed by discretion and wise regard to the interests of religion in the community, but also that a church or Society if they deem themselves aggrieved by indiscreet and improper discussion in the pulpit may seek redress, but only by the regular ecclesiastical and civil processes.

The above principles of Congregationalism are fully established and admitted, which no Congregational church or Society can violate without injustice to others and unfaithfulness to their denominational obligations.

We, therefore, the Congregational church and Society in Wolcott, do hereby solemnly admit these principles and express our fixed intention to abide by them. We also acknowledge it to be the sacred right of all individuals to enjoy, undisturbed, their own views in respect to Moral Reform, Anti-slavery, Temperance, and kindred subjects, and that we will not disturb, and will use our influence to prevent others from disturbing, any public meeting held for the discussion of these subjects.

Resolved, That on the above principles and stipulations we will unite in good faith as one Society in finishing the House of Worship which has been commenced on the site of the former house, and endeavor hereafter to support the gospel therein in peace and harmony, it being mutually understood that said house shall be opened for the discussion of the above mentioned subjects whenever it shall be requested by a majority of the Church."

Upon this arrangement between the Society and the church, the pastor was dismissed with the full confidence of the church and Council, and the church and Society entered upon their engagement to complete the Meeting house.

During Mr. Chapman's first year of labor twenty-one persons united with the church, most of them by profession, so that the condition of the church and the congregation was prosperous and hopeful; and had the Society, or rather certain members of it, conducted themselves according to the Congregational principles which they finally bound themselves to obey, there would have been little if any of this difficulty.

This conflict of opinion was not peculiar to Wolcott, but occurred in many communities in the nation. It resulted from the persistent effort of a political party striving to please slaveholders, by intimidation and by formal attacks upon the faith and freedom of the gospel, as maintained by a very large portion of the Christian people of the nation.

REV. AARON C. BEACH'S MINISTRY.

During the interval between Mr. Chapman's dismission and the employment of Mr. Beach, the Rev. Zephaniah

MINISTRY OF REV. AARON C. BEACH.

Swift supplied the pulpit from nine months to one year, and seems to have given good satisfaction as a minister. Mr. Aaron C. Beach preached his first sermon in Wolcott on December 19, 1841, in the Center School House. On the 6th of September, previous, the Society voted to hold their meetings in the Meeting house, but it is probable, that as the Meeting house was not finished inside, and as there was no way to warm it sufficiently in December, they held their meetings in the school house. Mr. Beach was engaged to preach six months, at the end of which time he received a unanimous call to become the pastor.

He was ordained by New Haven West Consociation, on the 22d day of June, 1842. The members of Consociation present were: Rev. Zephaniah Swift, Rev. John E. Bray, Rev. Jason Atwater, Rev. Anson Smith. The delegates were: Brothers Eben Hotchkiss, of Prospect; Eli Dickerman, of East Plains; Nathaniel Richardson, of Middlebury; Amos R. Hough, of Mt. Carmel; George W. Shelton, of Derby; Andrew W. De Forest, of Humphreysville; Deacon Lucian F. Lewis, of Naugatuck.

Rev. Z. Swift was chosen moderator and Rev. A. Smith, scribe. Revs. S. W. S. Dutton, of New Haven, and E. Lyman, of Plymouth, being present, were invited to sit as corresponding members, and after the examination the ordination services were arranged as follows: Mr. Lyman to offer the introductory prayer, Mr. Dutton to preach the sermon, Mr. Bray to offer the ordaining prayer, Mr. Swift to offer the right hand of fellowship, and Mr. Atwater to address the people and offer the concluding prayer. The services were held in the Meeting house, under the "naked rafters," at 11 o'clock on Wednesday, June 22d, 1842. Mr. Beach graduated at Yale College, in 1835, was licensed to preach in 1838, and remained connected with Yale Theological Seminary till near the time when he began to preach in Wolcott. He had a wife and one child when he came here, and resided three or four years in the house which Mr. Keys had formerly occupied. After his settlement, the first great work was to finish the Meeting house, which had already been in process of building nearly two years. It was completed January 18th, 1843, and dedicated the next day, and has been a very comfortable and commodious house to the present time. During the year 1843 fifteen persons united with the church, and affairs presented a more promising and hopeful appearance than for some years before. Mr. Beach says of his labors here: "No extensive revival of religion occurred while I was in Wolcott, but more than once we enjoyed a pleasant season of quickened religious interest, which resulted in additions to the church at different times." Forty-four names were added to the list of members while he labored here; the church and Society worked together in great harmony, and the way was prepared for better days.

A very important work was accomplished by Mr. Beach in building the house now owned as a parsonage. He built it for himself, but when he closed his labors here the Society purchased it of him. The ground around it, about four acres, was given to him for the purpose of a home, and a hard piece of land it was. There were more than four acres of stones to be disposed of before much soil could be found. Money and work were contributed by the parish,—some say, over a thousand dollars in money, besides the work; but often such matters are over-estimated. Mr. Beach put in money of his own, to the amount of twelve hundred dollars, and when he left there was a debt of five hundred dollars, which the Society accepted, and on this condition Mr. Beach sold them the house. It is a good house, commodious, and pleasantly located, and there would be pleasure in the thought of the accomplishment of so good an object, but for the little item that somebody "paid too dear for his whistle." When they began to build this house, the house that Mr. Woodward had owned, with ten acres of land, and very commodious out buildings, was for sale at the low price of seven hundred dollars. The choice to-day between that and the parsonage would be in favor of the former. If that had been purchased, Mr. Beach might have saved his $1,200, and the Society its $500, and then put that in repair with the extra money over $700 and the labor expended on the parsonage grounds.

MR. BEACH DISMISSED.

At a church meeting held May 10th, 1857, the "church having appointed Deacon A. H. Plumb chairman, received a communication from their pastor, requesting the church to unite with him in calling the Consociation for the purpose of dissolving his relation to them as their pastor." This communication was as follows:—

"May 10, 1857.

To the Congregational Church of Wolcott:

Beloved: It is not without pain and sadness that I separate myself from such tried and faithful friends as you have been to me and mine, in health and sickness, in joy and sorrow, these fifteen years. But the serious and growing inadequacy of my salary constrains me to ask, and I do hereby ask, you to unite with me in calling the Consociation to dissolve my relations to you as your pastor. Affectionately, your fellow disciple,

AARON C. BEACH."

Upon the reception of this letter the church voted to "grant said request, and accordingly appointed Deacon Orrin Hall a delegate to the said Consociation whenever it shall be convenient for that purpose."

DOINGS OF CONSOCIATION.

At a special meeting of the Consociation of New Haven West, held at Wolcott, May 27th, 1857, there were present the following pastors and delegates:

Wolcott, A. C. Beach, pastor, Deacon Orrin Hall, delegate; Waterbury, P. W. Carter, delegate; Naugatuck, C. Sherman, pastor, Bro. David Hopkins, delegate; Oxford, S. Topliff, pastor; Woodbridge, J. Guernsey, pastor, Bro. Nelson Newton, delegate;

Hamden E. Plains, Deacon Eli Dickerman, delegate; Hamden, Mt. Carmel, Bro. Lucius Ives, delegate; Seymour, Bro. W. H. Tuttle, delegate.

Mr. Topliff was appointed moderator, and C. S. Sherman, scribe.

After full inquiry and discussion, Consociation voted unanimously that the pastoral relation between Rev. A. C. Beach and the Congregational Church and Society in Wolcott be dissolved, the dissolution to take place on the 22d proximo. In coming to this result, Consociation express their conviction of the self-denying work of Bro. Beach, in laboring fifteen years, under the embarrassments of an inadequate temporal support, to preach the gospel to this people, raising up men and women for usefulness in other places to which they have been constantly emigrating, and preparing saints here for heaven. We sympathize with him in the necessity of leaving a still warmly attached church and people. We sincerely commend him to the ministry and churches as an able and faithful minister. With this church and Society, in their destitute circumstances, we also heartily sympathize, bearing witness to their self-denying efforts to sustain the gospel among themselves. We pray the Great Head of the Church that the way may be opened, the means of support supplied, and a faithful servant of Christ be sent to them, and this place not be left waste, or the people be scattered as sheep having no shepherd.

Attest: C. S. SHERMAN, *Scribe.*

The above statements were very true as to the sacrifice and efforts on the part both of pastor and people to sustain the preaching of the gospel in this place. Those were the years of emigration from Wolcott. The building of the church was a heavy work for the people, and after the best that could be done in raising money to pay for it, there was a debt of $350, which they tried to liquidate in the autumn of 1843, but whether they succeeded or not we are not told. In 1846 they took up the subject of procuring a bell, in which they seem to have been successful, partly by the sale of the bell metal of the old bell which melted when the church was burned, and by a special subscription.

In 1847 they took up the work of procuring a parsonage, and voted that subscription papers be circulated for this purpose, but they did not succeed. In 1848 they voted to "issue subscription papers to raise $750, for the purpose of buying," for a parsonage, "the place now owned by Mrs. Finch, provided the amount be raised." But they did not succeed in getting the parsonage. Then, in 1849, we find another special subscription for the purpose of paying $100, "arrearages."

The efforts to secure a parsonage having failed, Mr. Beach engaged in building a house for himself, which he finished in good style; but alas, when he proposed to sell it, the Society could not refund the money he had put into it; for, to assume the five hundred dollars debt was all they could do, and that cost them many years of hard labor and sacrifice to pay.

Thus closed the labors of Rev. Aaron C. Beach, as pastor in Wolcott.

CHAPTER IX.

REV. STEPHEN ROGERS', REV. LENT S. HOUGH'S, AND REV. W. C. FISK'S MINISTRY : FROM 1858 TO 1872.

REV. STEPHEN ROGERS.

In the Spring of 1858, Rev. Z. B. Burr, of Weston, Conn., received a "call" from this church and Society, but a settlement was not secured with him. In January, 1859, a call was extended to Rev. Stephen Rogers, and in February next the Society concurred in the call, and he was installed, the Society Records say, on the 7th of March, 1859, but the Church Records, a copy of the scribe's paper of the proceedings of Consociation, says the 25th day of March, 1859. Probably the latter is correct.

Members of the Consociation and other churches invited, who took part in the exercises of installation, were as follows : (The list of ministers and delegates present is not preserved.)

Rev. Austin Putnam, moderator; Rev. E. W. Robinson, scribe.

Invocation, by Rev. Geo. Bushnell; Sermon by Rev. Jas. Averil; Installation Prayer, by Austin Putnam ; Charge to the Pastor, by Rev. Charles S. Sherman ; Right Hand of Fellowship, by Rev. Alexander D. Stowel; Address to the People, by Rev. E. W. Robinson ; Concluding Prayer, by Rev. E. C. Jones ; Benediction, by the pastor.

Mr. Rogers came from Northfield, and was a man advanced in life, of precarious health, but of noble spirit and of devoted mind. He found a quiet, peaceful parish, a good parsonage to live in, and a warm-hearted, working church. It must be noticed here that during the year 1858 the church was greatly revived under the preaching of Rev. Joseph Smith, who was engaged some months as a supply. I find no mention of him in the records of either church or Society, but he was a Methodist local preacher, not engaged regularly in the Conference of that denomination, and resided in or near Birmingham.*

During the year 1858, thirty-nine persons united with the church by profession, quite a number of whom remain to this day devoted and trustworthy members. Most of these persons united in May, 1858, but it is probable that Mr. Smith began to preach in the summer or autumn of 1857, and continued during the following winter, it being a time of general religious interest in the parish. Mr. Rogers came here less than a year after these thirty-nine persons (at one time) united with the church, and had the comforting advantage of a church wide awake in religious things. He did well, considering his state of health, and is remembered with great kindness by the people of the parish. The following communication received by the church explains the difficulty of parish work to him, and the cause of the dissolution of the pastoral relation.

MR. ROGERS' LETTER.

To the Congregational Church and Society of Wolcott:

Beloved Brethren and Friends:—God in his allwise providence has for a long time visited me with sickness, rendering me incapable of performing all the duties that are expected of one having the pastoral relation; and, as there is no reasonable prospect of seasonable returning health, I feel constrained for your good and my own, to ask that the relation existing between myself and the church and Society be dissolved, to take effect the 18th of

---

* Rev. Mr. Smith is now (1874) a member of the Methodist Episcopal Conference, and is a successful minister in his denomination. He is preaching in Derby, Conn.

April next. Grateful for the friendly relations that have existed between us from the first to this day, and for the sympathy and kindness manifested to me through all the months of trial through which I have been called to pass ; greatly desiring the prosperity of the church and Society, and the re-establishment of the pastoral relation, and that you may enjoy and abound in all the blessings of the Spirit, is the prayer of your unworthy servant.

STEPHEN ROGERS.

Wolcott, Conn., Sept 6, 1862.

ACTION OF THE CHURCH.

Wolcott, Sept. 6, 1862.

Church voted unanimously to accept the above request.

Voted, that we as a church deeply sympathize with our pastor, Rev. Stephen Rogers, in his protracted illness and inability to preach the gospel. And further that we have full confidence in his Christian character and integrity as a minister of the gospel and that we cheerfully recommend him to any church wherever in the providence of God he may be called.

The Society concurred in a vote to accede to Mr. Rogers' request for a dismissal by Consociation, and it is probable that he was regularly dismissed, though I find no record to that effect.*

Mr. Rogers removed to Woodbury, Conn., where he departed this life a few weeks after reaching that place.

REV. LENT S. HOUGH.

Rev. Lent S. Hough came to Wolcott in the Spring of

---

* Mr. Rogers donated to the church a library of about a hundred and thirty volumes, consisting chiefly of standard theological works. The idea of writing a history of Wolcott was first suggested to the author while examining a book in this library, entitled *Hayward's New England Gazetteer.* This book contains an account of Wolcott, but makes no allusion to the church,— as though it were a heathen community, or one in which the preaching of the gospel had been discontinued. The author was thus led to make special inquiry respecting the religious history of the town, and the present volume is largely occupied with the results of his investigations. If it were not for the strange omission in the *Gazetteer*, the history of Wolcott might never have been written.

1863. Mr. Rogers closed his labors on the 18th of April, and on the 27th of the same month the Society voted to raise three hundred and twenty-five dollars for the purpose of hiring " Rev. L. S. Hough to preach for one year, and that the salary should be paid semi-annually." On the 4th of May, following, the Society voted "to invite Rev. L. S. Hough to serve as acting pastor of this Society, and that we invite the church to unite with us in the request." There is no record of any action by the church. In the Society vote there is no mention of the time for which he was engaged, nor of the terms upon which he was to continue with them. Mr. Hough came from Westfield Society, in the town of Middletown, where he had been a settled pastor for seventeen years. The letter he brought with him from that Society shows the appreciation of him by that people. It is as follows :

The Fourth Congregational Church of Middletown, to the Congregational Church at Wolcott, Conn :

Beloved Brethren :—This is to certify that the Rev. Lent S. Hough and Hannah S. his wife, are esteemed members of the Fourth Congregational Church in Middletown, in good and regular standing ; and having signified their wish to remove their particular relations from us to yourselves, they are hereby recommended to your special care and fellowship, and when they shall be received into membership with you their particular connection with us will be considered as dissolved. Hoping that our beloved late pastor will find among you warm hearts and kind friends, and a liberal support, both in temporal and spiritual things, we recommend him, dear brethren, to your special love. And may his labors be as faithful and as successful with you as they have been with us, and may your prayers ever follow him, as ours certainly will, through all the troubles and trials he may still be called to pass before he shall finally reach his heavenly rest.

In behalf of the church,

HENRY CORNWELL, *Clerk.*

MIDDLETOWN, May 4, 1863.

Thus introduced, Mr. Hough went forward with the success of former pastors in this church, for three years, during which time nineteen persons united with the church, and other interests were proportionately prosperous. I am informed, however, that during the summer of 1866 he manifested great discouragement in regard to the religious condition of the church, and seemed ready to seek some other field of labor. It was during this summer that Deacon Samuel Holmes, of New York, with his family, made his home in this parish for a few months; a fact that will be remembered with gladness for many years to come. The larger part of the time had passed before Mr. Hough became really acquainted with Mr. Holmes, for as he said afterward, he supposed Mr. Holmes was one of the city people, and would scarcely take notice of a country pastor or his flock. Early in the autumn, while the church was still in a torpid state, and after Mr. Hough had passed through several attacks of illness, accompanied with most acute pain, he gave expression publicly to his feeling of despondency, and added that if any one present had any word of encouragement or exhortation he would be glad to have him speak. Upon this, Deacon Holmes arose, took his position by the table in front of the pulpit, and, referring to the pastor's feeling of discouragement, expressed the conviction that if efforts were put forth in cheerful hope, better days would dawn in Wolcott. To test the matter, he proposed that as the evenings were becoming longer, and the people had passed through the hurry of farm work, they should come together in a prayer meeting at a private house during the week. This proposal was eagerly adopted by Deacon Ansel H. Plumb, who invited them to his house. Between that day and the evening of the meeting, Deacon Holmes conversed with three young men on the subject of personal religion. He found one of them cherishing a hope, and the other two anxious in regard to their spiritual state. He persuaded them to come to the Thursday evening prayer meeting and state there what they had told him. When the evening came and the meeting was opened, Mr. Holmes made a few remarks, and called upon the young men to take up their cross. After they had spoken, there was no lack of interest in the meeting, nor in subsequent meetings of the church, for several months. For some few weeks, while Deacon Holmes remained in the place, regular prayer meetings were held, and sometimes special meetings, which resulted in the conversion of a number of persons. When Mr. Holmes left, he had engaged J. D. Potter, the "evangelist," to hold meetings here for one week, which engagement was fulfilled at the time with good success. The result was that at the first communion in 1867, on January 6th, twenty-seven persons united with the church, and at the next communion four more. This success in the church revived the courage of Mr. Hough for a time, but he still felt inclined to find another parish, and offered his resignation to that effect, but it was not accepted. Again, in the beginning of 1869, he offered his resignation, and it was at once accepted by the officers of the church, without calling a meeting either of the church or of the Society. This method of doing business by the officers, gave dissatisfaction to many; but it is said by the officers that the agreement with Mr. Hough was that "upon his giving a certain timely notice, he was to be allowed to go." It will be readily seen that if any persons were to vote, those who called him, or the Society, should have done it; so that the method adopted was clearly contrary to Congregational rules and usages.

A COMMUNION SERVICE.

In the year 1864, the church was the recipient of a valuable present, which will be cherished by it, probably for the next century at least, and the following entry in the Records explains itself:

At a meeting of the Congregational Church in Wolcott, duly held on this 18th day of April, 1864, it being the 70th birthday anniversary of our much esteemed friend, widow Wealthy H. Ives, of Waterbury, formerly of this town; there was presented from her to this church as a birthday free-will offering, an exceedingly rich and valuable communion service. Whereupon, it was voted: That we gratefully receive the highly prized offering, and tender to the kind donor our heartfelt thanks for it, hoping that in ministering to others she may be ministered to from on high, abundantly, and that finally she may meet *all* the recipients of her bounty in the general assembly of the church in heaven.

Mrs. Ives was born in Wolcott, and was the daughter of Charles Upson, Esquire, for many years one of the most influential men of the town.*

In 1867, Feb. 28th, the church voted unanimously " to donate our old communion service, not now used, to the Congregational church in Allegan County, Michigan."

REVISED ARTICLES OF FAITH.

On the 1st of February, 1865, a committee was appointed to revise the Articles of Faith and Covenant, consisting of Rev. L. S. Hough, Deacon A. H. Plumb, B. A. Lindsley, S. L. Hotchkiss, and Deacon L. B. Bronson. They made their report at the next communion, and the revised Articles and Covenant were adopted, and were afterward printed, together with a list of the ministers and deacons, and the surviving members of the church. The old articles were twelve in number, and were Calvinistic in their doctrinal statements; the new or revised articles are eight in number, and have not the slightest tincture of Calvinism in them. The wording of these articles, however, is so obscure that it is difficult to discern what doctrines are intended to be taught. The rules of the church, as published in this " Manual," are peculiar in this respect, that members are received without vote, on the negative condition that no one publicly objects.

---

* See Biography of Dr. Ives. Mrs. Ives died November 21st, 1868, in the seventy-fifth year of her age.

MINISTRY OF REV. WARREN C. FISKE.

Mr. Hough closed his labors in the Spring of 1869, and went to Salem, Conn., where he preached sixteen months. He then settled in Lyme, where after three years he is still successfully at work, notwithstanding the severe and peculiar afflictions experienced by himself and family.

During Mr. Hough's labors in Wolcott, important repairs were made on the Meeting house, inside and outside, and a cabinet organ was purchased to aid in the singing. The money for these improvements was secured, mostly, by the Ladies' Sewing Society of the congregation, and, as is often the case, the number of ladies engaged in the work of the Sewing Society was not large.

REV. WARREN C. FISKE.

The officers of the Society, having dismissed Mr. Hough without a vote of the Society or the church, proceeded in like manner to hire another minister. They secured Rev. Warren C. Fiske, of Barkhamstead, a good pastor and preacher. It is possible that the committee proceeded in this manner without intending any violation of Congregational order, but it is difficult to see how they could proceed in this manner, when it was well known that there was much dissatisfaction in the parish in consequence of their dismissal of Mr. Hough. Mr. Fiske came to Wolcott in May, 1869, and continued to serve the church very acceptably for three years, and then, at his own pleasure, closed his labors, with the intention not to take charge of a parish again,—for a time, at least.

The year 1870 was the one hundredth year of the organization of the parish Society, and in that year should have been held the centenary meeting ; but as far as I have learned, no one thought of it or proposed such a meeting.*

---

*If some persons were so capable of conducting such a meeting as they represented themselves to be in 1873, why did they not show a specimen of their skill in 1870?

No special revival occurred during Mr. Fiske's labors, yet the church kept up its meetings regularly, and attended to all the usual interests with earnestness and fidelity. The people speak in high terms of Mr. Fiske, his excellent wife, and agreeable family. He preached as he was able, in the school houses, but being subject to sudden attacks of a bronchial ailment, could not do as he otherwise would, in the work of preaching. He removed from Wolcott to Charlton, Mass., where he now resides, preaching only occasionally, being without regular pastoral work.

REV. SAMUEL ORCUTT

commenced his services in this parish as stated supply, July 1st, 1872, and as to his labors, this book, including the account of the Centenary meeting, must bear its testimony. He preached three Sabbaths as supply, without any purpose of continuing here. But on learning from the records that 1873 was the one hundredth year of the existence of the church organization, the idea of holding a Centenary meeting arose in his mind and became a special attraction, because of the great pleasure he takes in historic study. In regard to that meeting, he has but one regret, namely, that in consequence of the restricted notions of a few brethren in the church, he was obliged to omit several items which would have given greater interest to that very successful and long to be remembered gathering.

During his second year, the Meeting house was repaired, outside and inside, at a cost of over two hundred dollars, and chairs, tables, and a sofa were placed in the Meeting house and in the parsonage, to the value of one hundred and twenty-five dollars, besides a beautiful and durable clock, donated by Deacon Charles Benedict, of Waterbury, through the agency of George Bridgeman, Esq., of Wolcott, lately deceased. A large proportion of the funds to purchase this furniture was solicited by the kind favor of Miss Mary E. Cook, of the

MINISTRY OF REV. SAMUEL ORCUTT.   137

First Church in Waterbury, and was presented to the church through Mrs. Henry Minor and Mrs. Elihu Moulthrop, of Wolcott. Mr. Ephraim Hall contributed twenty-five dollars toward this fund ; the remainder was raised by subscription in sums of five dollars and under.

Preaching services have been held in each of the six School Districts in the parish ; and the whole number of sermons preached in the eighteen months, preceding January 1st, 1874, was two hundred and sixty, being an average of three and one-third a week for that time ; and while thus preaching, the duties of Acting School Visitor have been faithfully attended to. Much time and labor were bestowed, meanwhile, upon preparations for the Centenary meeting, and also upon the pleasing task of collecting materials for this history, and preparing it for the press.

The church has received aid from the Connecticut Home Missionary Society during the last forty-six years as follows :

1828,	$50.	1843,	$100.	1852,	$100.	1860,	$125.
1829,	80.	1844,	100.	1853,	100.	1861,	125.
1831,	70.	1845,	100.	1854,	100.	1862,	125.
1832,	40.	1846,	100.	1855,	100.	1863,	100.
1833,	80.	1847,	150.	1856,	125.	1864,	175.
1836,	75.	1848,	100.	1857,	125.	1872,	100.
1838,	75.	1849,	100.	1858,	100.	1873,	200.
1842,	150.	1850,	100.	1859,	100.	1874,	200.

The whole amount thus received being three thousand four hundred and eighty dollars, a sum for which all the people feel grateful, and which reflects great honor on the Missionary Society.

The Society has a small fund left to it by legacy, the interest of which is used for the support of the gospel in the parish. The following resolution was passed by the Society in regard to a part of this fund, in April, 1860, but whether that was the date of the reception of the same does not appear :

Resolved, That the legacy of one hundred dollars left by Major Preserve W. Carter for the Congregational Society of Wolcott, constitute a permanent fund to be kept for the benefit of said Society, in the Waterbury Savings Bank, until further action of said Society; the income to be appropriated for the support of the gospel.

The sum of two hundred and fifty dollars was given by Judge Bennet Bronson, of Waterbury, the income of which is used for the support of the gospel.

In addition to these items of aid, it is a fact that in order to maintain the gospel in the parish, the members of the church are paying yearly a sum equal to one and one-eighth per cent. on their assessment in the grand list, a sum much larger in proportion than is generally paid by the more wealthy churches.

CHAPTER X.

OFFICERS OF THE CHURCH AND SOCIETY, AND MEMBERS OF THE CHURCH.

MINISTERS.

Rev. Alexander Gillet, ordained Dec. 29, 1773, dismissed Nov. 10, 1791. Died in Torrington, Conn., Jan. 19, 1826.

Rev. Israel B. Woodward, ordained June, 1792. Died Nov. 17, 1810.

Rev. Lucas Hart, ordained Dec. 4, 1811. Died October 16, 1813.

Rev. John Keys, installed Sept. 21, 1814, dismissed December, 1822. Died in Dover, Ohio, 1868. Aged 86.

Dea. Isaac Bronson, read sermons most of the time five consecutive years, from 1822 to 1827.

Rev. Erastus Scranton, stated supply from June 1, 1827, to August, 1829.

Rev. Mr. Wheelock, stated supply from Sept. 7, 1829, to Sept. 7, 1830.

Rev. Nathan Shaw, stated supply from July 4, 1831, nine months.

Rev. Seth Sackett, stated supply, a short time.

Rev. Wm. F. Vail, stated supply one year.

Rev. James D. Chapman, ordained Oct. 25, 1837, dismissed Nov., 1840.

Rev. Zephaniah Swift, stated supply, probably one year.

Rev. Aaron C. Beach, ordained June 22, 1842, dismissed June 22, 1857.

Rev. Z. B. Burr, stated supply a short time.

Rev. Joseph Smith, stated supply, one year.

Rev. Stephen Rogers, installed March 25, 1859, dismissed April 18, 1863, and died the same year in Woodbury, Conn.

140   HISTORY OF WOLCOTT.

Rev. Lent S. Hough, stated supply from May, 1863, to May, 1869.
Rev. Warren C. Fiske, stated supply, from May, 1869, to June, 1872.
Rev. Samuel Orcutt, stated supply, from July 1, 1872, to May 17, 1874.

DEACONS.

Aaron Harrison, elected Jan. 26, 1774. Died Sept. 5, 1819.
Josiah Rogers, elected Jan. 26, 1774. Died Oct. 1, 1803.
Justus Peck, elected 1784, resigned Feb. 27, 1812. Died Nov. 23, 1813.
Joseph Atkins, jr., elected April 19, 1786, resigned and moved to Chenango Co., N. Y., in 1805.
Isaac Bronson, elected May 16, 1805. Died April 28, 1845.
James Bailey, elected Feb. 27, 1812. Died March 29, 1834.
Irad Bronson, elected June 3, 1825, resigned March 20, 1834.
    Removed to Cheshire, thence to Bristol, where he now resides.
Harvey Upson, elected May 12, 1832. Died Sept. 11, 1857.
Orrin Hall, elected May 18, 1835.
Ansel H. Plumb, elected Nov. 9, 1838. Died Aug. 20, 1870.
Lyman B. Bronson, elected June 3, 1864. Died May 27, 1866.
Miles S. Upson, elected March 1, 1867.
George W. Carter, elected Sept. 2, 1870.

CLERKS OF THE CHURCH.

Rev. Alexander Gillet, from 1773 to 1791.
Rev. Israel B. Woodward, from 1792 to 1810.
Rev. Lucas Hart, from 1811 to 1813.
Rev. John Keys, from 1814 to 1822.
Dea. Isaac Bronson, from 1823 to 1836.
Rev. James D. Chapman, from 1837 to 1840.
William Bartholomew, from Nov., 1840, to May, 1842.
Rev. Aaron C. Beach, from June, 1842, to May, 1857.
Stiles L. Hotchkiss, from March, 1858, to 1874.

MODERATORS OF THE ANNUAL SOCIETY MEETINGS.

Dea. Aaron Harrison, 1770, 1774, 1775, 1776, 1777, 1778, 1779, 1782, 1783, 1788, 1789, 1794, 1795.
Capt. Isaac Hopkins, 1771, 1772, 1773, 1785, 1786.
Capt. Samuel Upson, 1780, 1787, 1790.
Capt. Zaccheus Gillet, 1781.

OFFICERS OF THE SOCIETY.

Capt. Nathaniel Lewis, 1784, 1793.
Dea. Joseph Atkins, 1791, 1792, 1797.
Esq. Charles Upson, 1796, 1798, 1799, 1800, 1803, 1804, 1807, 1809.
Esq. Mark Harrison, 1801, 1802, 1805, 1806, 1809, 1811, 1814, 1815, 1816, 1820.
Jacob Carter, 1810.
Asaph Hotchkiss, 1812.
Lud Lindsley, 1813.
Doct. John Potter, 1817, 1818, 1819, 1822, 1823, 1827.
Capt Harvey Upson, 1821, 1828, 1829, 1834, 1837.
Thomas Upson, 1824, 1825.
Lucius Tuttle, 1826, 1830, 1831, 1842, 1852, 1854.
Luther Hotchkiss, 1832, 1833, 1835, 1838, 1841, 1844, 1846.
Clark Bronson, 1836, 1849, 1855.
Dea. Orrin Hall, 1839.
Ira Hough, 1840, 1843, 1845, 1847.
Dea. George W. Carter, 1848.
Dea. Ansel H. Plumb, 1850, 1856, 1863.
Jarvis R. Bronson, 1851, 1858, 1860, 1872.
Benjamin A. Lindsley, 1853, 1862, 1864.
Eldad Parker, 1861.
Mark Tuttle, 1865.
Stiles L. Hotchkiss, 1857, 1859, 1866, 1870, 1871, 1873.

CLERKS OF THE SOCIETY.

Daniel Byington, sen., was clerk one year, or, from 1770 to 1771.
Daniel Byington, jr., from 1771 to 1798, 26 years.
Dea. Isaac Bronson, from 1799 to 1831, 32 years.
Thomas Upson, from 1832, one year.
William Bartholomew, from 1833 to 1835, two years.
Mark Tuttle, from 1836 to 1838, two years.
Ezra S. Hough, from 1839 to 1842, 3 years.
Joseph N. Sperry, from 1843 to April, 1847, $3\frac{1}{2}$ years.
Stiles L. Hotchkiss, from April, 1847, to April, 1850, 3 years.
Dea. George W. Carter, from April, 1850, to May, 1874, 24 years.

TREASURERS OF THE SOCIETY.

Dea. Josiah Rogers, from 1770 to 1773, 3 years.

Capt. Simeon Hopkins. from 1773 to 1789, 16 years.
Capt. Charles Upson, from 1789 to 1790, one year.
Jacob Carter, from 1790 to 1793, 3 years.
Esq. Mark Harrison, from 1793 to 1797, 4 years.
Dea. Isaac Bronson, from 1797 to 1830, 33 years.
Ira Hough, from 1831 to 1832, one year.
Lucius Tuttle, from 1833, one year.
Clark Bronson, from 1834, one year.
Mark Tuttle, from 1835 to 1838, 3 years.
Ezra S. Hough, from 1838 to 1843, 5 years.
Stiles L. Hotchkiss, from 1843 to 1850, 7 years,
Dea. George W. Carter, from 1850 to 1874, 24 years.

PRUDENTIAL COMMITTEES.

1770 — Josiah Rogers, John Alcox, Stephen Barnes, John Bronson, Amos Seward.

1771 — David Norton, Amos Seward, Stephen Barnes, Daniel Alcox, Joseph Beecher.

1772 — David Norton, Amos Seward, John Alcox, Joseph Beecher, John Bronson.

1773 — Amos Seward, Joseph Beecher, Stephen Barnes.

1774 — Amos Seward, Stephen Barnes, Samuel Upson.

1775 — Samuel Upson, Stephen Barnes, Joseph Beecher.

1776 — Joseph Beecher, Samuel Upson, Amos Seward.

1777 — Amos Seward, Jared Harrison, Thomas Upson.

1778 — Daniel Byington, jr., Thomas Upson, Daniel Alcox. Jared Harrison.

1779 — Daniel Byington, Jared Harrison, Lieut. Alcox.

1780 — Daniel Byington, Deacon Rogers, Jared Harrison.

1781 — Daniel Byington, Charles Upson, Joseph Beecher.

1782 — Lieut. Beecher, Daniel Byington, Lieut. Peck, Simeon Hopkins, Charles Upson.

1783 — Lieut. Beach, Mark Harrison, David Norton.

1784 — David Norton, Justus Peck, Mark Harrison, Simeon Hopkins, Lieut. Beecher.

1785 — Justus Peck, David Norton, Mark Harrison, Joseph Beecher, Simeon Hopkins.

1786 — Abraham Norton, Jonathan Carter, Justus Peck, Simeon Hopkins.

OFFICERS OF THE SOCIETY. 143

1787 — Simeon Hopkins, Nathaniel Lewis, Amos Beecher, Joseph Atkins, Jonathan Carter.

1788 — Jonathan Carter, Amos Beecher, Simeon Hopkins.

1789 — Amos Beecher, Jonathan Carter, Samuel Byington, Charles Upson.

1790 — Mark Harrison, Streat Richards, Jonathan Carter.

1791 — Jonathan Carter, Abraham Norton, Jacob Carter, Samuel Byington, Walter Beecher.

1792 — Walter Beecher, Streat Richards, Mark Harrison, Esq., Simeon Hopkins.

1793 — Streat Richards, Mark Harrison, Walter Beecher, Charles Frisbie.

1794 — Mark Harrison, Streat Richards, Isaac Bronson, Charles Upson, Samuel Byington, Joseph Minor.

1795 — Judah Frisbie, Joseph Minor, David Norton, Isaac Upson, Isaac Bronson.

1796 — James Bailey, Samuel Clinton, Joseph Atkins, Isaac Bronson, Daniel Johnson.

1797 — Deacon Atkins, James Bailey, Stephen Carter, Daniel Johnson, Samuel Clinton.

1798 — Moses Todd, David Harrison, Stephen Carter, Samuel Clinton, James Bailey.

1799 — Stephen Carter, Charles Upson, Joseph M. Parker, Samuel Clinton, Preserve Carter.

1800 — Charles Upson, Preserve Carter, Joseph M. Parker, James Bailey, Isaac Upson.

1801 — Joseph M. Parker, Preserve Carter, James Bailey, Charles Upson, John Frisbie, Nathan Johnson.

1802 — Nathaniel Lewis, Joseph M. Parker, David Harrison, Elijah Rowe, John Frisbie.

1803 — Joseph M. Parker, John Potter, Jesse Upson, Samuel Horton, David Harrison, John Frisbie, Royce Lewis.

1804 — David Harrison, John Potter, Jesse Upson, Washington Upson, Royce Lewis, Farrington Barnes, Samuel Horton.

1805 — John Potter, John Frisbie, Israel Upson, Washington Upson, James Bailey, Mark Barnes, Farrington Barnes.

1806 — John Potter, Asaph Hotchkiss, Washington Upson, Elijah Rowe, Hezekiah Beecher, John Frisbie, Stephen Carter, jr., John Hitchcock, Farrington Barnes.

1807 — John Potter, Asaph Hotchkiss, Joseph M. Parker, Farrington Barnes, Harvey Upson, Stephen Carter, jr., John Frisbie, John Hitchcock, Hezekiah Beecher, Washington Upson.

1808 — Asaph Hotchkiss, Heman Hall, John B. Alcox.

1809 — Asaph Hotchkiss, Harvey Upson, Lud Lindsley, Abner Hotchkiss, Heman Hall.

1810 — Harvey Upson, Gates Upson, Lud Lindsley, David Frisbie, Lucius Tuttle.

1811 — Asaph Hotchkiss, Harvey Upson, David Frisbie.

1812 — Harvey Upson, Lucius Tuttle, Thomas Upson.

1813 — Lucius Tuttle, William Bartholomew, Pitman Stowe.

1814 — Lucius Tuttle, William Bartholomew, Pitman Stowe.

1815 — William Bartholomew, Luther Hotchkiss, Clark Bronson.

1816 — Gates Upson, Ira Hough, Daniel Holt.

1817 — Ira Hough, Daniel Holt, John B. Alcox.

1818 — Irad Bronson, Orrin Plumb, David Frisbie.

1819 — Thomas Upson, David R. Upson, Moses Pond, Lucius Tuttle.

1820 — Lucius Tuttle, Thomas Upson, William Bartholomew, Daniel Holt.

1821 — Lucius Tuttle, Irad Bronson, Daniel Holt, William Bartholomew.

1822 — Lucius Tuttle, William Bartholomew, Irad Bronson, Harvey Upson, Daniel Holt.

1823 — Ira Hough, Lucius Tuttle, Irad Bronson, William Bartholomew.

1824 — William Bartholomew, Gates Upson, Clark Bronson, Thomas Upson, Luther Hotchkiss.

1825 — Luther Hotchkiss, David Frisbie, Jonathan Bement.

1826 — Harvey Upson, Jonathan Bement, Ira Hough.

1827 — Ira Hough, William Bartholomew, Daniel Holt.

1828 — Thomas Upson, Luther Hotchkiss, David Frisbie, Clark Bronson.

1829 — Thomas Upson, Lud Lindsley, Clark Bronson.

1830 — Reuben Carter, Mark Tuttle, Ira Frisbie.

1831 — Asa Boardman, George Griswold, Mark Tuttle.

1832 — Gates Upson, Ira Hough, Lucius Tuttle, jr.

OFFICERS OF THE SOCIETY.   145

1833 — Ira Hough, Luther Hotchkiss, Mark Tuttle.
1834 — Fitch Higgins, Clark Bronson, Orrin Hall.
1835 — Leonard Beecher, Ephraim Hall, Albert Boardman, Ira Frisbie, Mark Tuttle, Orrin Hall.
1836 — Ephraim Hall, Ira Frisbie, Joel Alcox, Luther Hotchkiss.
1837 — Moses Pond, Gates Upson, Joseph N. Sperry.
1838 — Milow G. Hotchkiss, Charles H. Upson, Reuben Carter.
1839 — Gates Upson, Daniel Holt, Ira Frisbie.
1840 — Gates Upson, Ira Frisbie, Ira Hough.
1841 — Ira Hough, Joseph N. Sperry, Ira Frisbie.
1842 — Ira Frisbie, Ansel H. Plumb, Luther Hotchkiss.
1843 — Ansel H. Plumb, Orrin Hall, Stiles L. Hotchkiss.
1844 — Orrin Hall, Stiles L. Hotchkiss, George W. Carter.
1845 — Stiles L. Hotchkiss, George W. Carter, Isaac Hough.
1846 — Isaac Hough, Mark Tuttle, Carolus R. Byington.
1847 — Ansel H. Plumb, Mark Tuttle, George W. Carter.
1848 — Ansel H. Plumb, George W. Carter, Benjamin A. Lindsley.
1849 — Jarvis R. Bronson, Ansel H. Plumb, Miles S. Upson, Mark Tuttle.
1850 — Ansel H. Plumb, Jarvis R. Bronson, Stiles L. Hotchkiss, Miles S. Upson.
1851 — Miles S. Upson, Ansel H. Plumb, Benjamin A. Lindsley.
1852 — Ansel H. Plumb, Stiles L. Hotchkiss, Henry Beecher.
1853 — Ansel H. Plumb, Stiles L. Hotchkiss, Jarvis R. Bronson.
1854 — Ansel H. Plumb, Benjamin A. Lindsley, Ira H. Hough.
1855 — Ansel H. Plumb, Stiles L. Hotchkiss, Benjamin A. Lindsley.
1856 — Ansel H. Plumb, Benjamin A. Lindsley, Miles S. Upson.
1857 — Miles S. Upson, Ira H. Hough, Stiles L. Hotchkiss.
1858 — Miles S. Upson, Ira H. Hough, Benjamin A. Lindsley.
1859 — Miles S. Upson, Benjamin A. Lindsley, Ira H. Hough.
1860 — Miles S. Upson, Stiles L. Hotchkiss, Ira H. Hough.
1861 — Miles S. Upson, Stiles L. Hotchkiss, Ira H. Hough.
1862 — Miles S. Upson, Ira H. Hough, Joel W. Upson.

1863 — Miles S. Upson, Stiles L. Hotchkiss, Benjamin A. Lindsley.
1864 — Miles S. Upson, Benjamin A. Lindsley, Stiles L. Hotchkiss.
1865 — Miles S. Upson, Stiles L. Hotchkiss, Ira H. Hough.
1866 — Miles S. Upson, Stiles L. Hotchkiss, Albert N. Lane.
1867 — Miles S. Upson, Stiles L. Hotchkiss, Albert N. Lane.
1868 — Miles S. Upson, Stiles L. Hotchkiss, Albert N. Lane.
1869 — Miles S. Upson, Albert N. Lane, Stiles L. Hotchkiss.
1870 — Miles S. Upson, Stiles L. Hotchkiss, Albert N. Lane.
1871 — Miles S. Upson, Albert N. Lane, Benjamin L. Bronson.
1872 — Miles S. Upson, Albert N. Lane, Stiles L. Hotchkiss.
1873 — Miles S. Upson, Stiles L. Hotchkiss, Albert N. Lane.

SCHOOL COMMITTEES, AS APPOINTED BY THE PARISH SOCIETY.

1770 — David Norton, Seth Bartholomew, Daniel Alcox, Amos Beecher, Joseph Beecher, Justus Peck, Capt. Aaron Harrison, Stephen Barnes, Samuel Upson.

1771 — Joseph Sutliff, jr., Joseph Atkins, jr., Ens. John Alcox, Amos Seward, Capt. Aaron Harrison, Jedediah Minor, Nathaniel Lewis, Simeon Plumb, Daniel Finch.

1772 — Simeon Hopkins, Jacob Carter, Aaron Harrison, Eliakim Welton, jr., Joseph Beecher, Justus Peck, Daniel Byington, John Bronson, Samuel Upson.

1773 — Stephen Barnes, Aaron Harrison, Joseph Beecher, John Bronson, Daniel Byington, Nathaniel Sutliff, Amos Seward, Daniel Alcox.

1774 — Justus Peck, Jesse Alcox, Aaron Harrison, Stephen Barnes, Daniel Johnson, Amos Seward, Simeon Hopkins, Daniel Alcox, Eliakim Welton.

1775 — Daniel Johnson, Justus Peck, Jesse Alcox, Joseph Smith, Jacob Carter, Amos Seward, Eliakim Welton, jr., Joseph Hotchkiss, Daniel Alcox.

1776 — Lieutenant Cleveland, John Barrett, Wait Hotchkiss, Eliakim Welton, jr., Justus Peck, Jesse Alcox, Samuel Upson, Stephen Barnes, Stephen Pratt.

1777 — Reuben Frisbie, Deacon Rogers, Captain Alcox, Amos

SCHOOL COMMITTEES OF THE SOCIETY. 147

Seward, Nathaniel Hitchcock, Nathaniel Lewis, Joseph Beecher, Abel Beecher, Jared Harrison.

1778 — Josiah Rogers, Jared Harrison, Stephen Pratt, John Alcox, Nathaniel Lewis, Isaac Hopkins, Noah Neal, Samuel Upson, Zadoc Bronson.

1779 — Captain Gillet, Eliakim Welton, jr., Samuel Upson, Mark Harrison, Simeon Plumb, Simeon Hopkins, Timothy Bradley.

1780 — John Bronson, Heman Hall, James Alcox, Samuel Upson, Abel Beecher, Simeon Hopkins, Amasa Gaylord, Reuben Frisbie.

1781 — Reuben Frisbie, Levi Gaylord, Heman Hall, Stephen Carter, Elisha Horton, Jonathan Robins, Amos Seward.

1782 — David Warner, Eliakim Welton, jr., Ozius Norton, Nathaniel Lewis, Captain Upson, Jacob Carter, Elisha Horton, Joseph Atkins, Abel Beecher, Samuel Byington, Lieutenant Beach.

1783 — Jacob Carter, John Silkregg, Mark Harrison, Eliakim Welton, jr., Samuel Byington, Charles Upson, Simeon Plumb, Justus Peck.

1784 — Jacob Carter, Jonathan Carter, Charles Upson, Wait Hotchkiss, Nathaniel Lewis, John Alcox, Amos Seward, Simeon Plumb.

1785 — Simeon Plumb, Nathaniel Lewis, Joseph Atkins, Zadoc Bronson, Jonathan Carter, Charles Upson, Simeon Hopkins, David Warner, Amos Seward.

1786 — David Harrison, Simeon Plumb, Charles Frisbie, Calvin Cowles, Joseph Atkins, James Bailey, James Thomas, Josiah Warner.

1787 — Charles Upson, Stephen Carter, Jonathan Carter, David Warner, Eliakim Welton, jr., Daniel Dean, Deacon Peck, Zadoc Bronson, Samuel Upson.

1788 — Charles Upson, Jonathan Carter, Mark Harrison, Jesse Alcox, Charles Frisbie, Amos Beecher, Eliakim Welton, jr., Samuel Upson, Ephraim Smith, jr.

1789 — Dr. John Potter, Samuel Byington, Charles Upson, Heman Hall, Ozius Norton, Joseph Minor, Simeon Plumb, Nathaniel Lewis, Nathan Scarritt, Eliakim Welton, jr., Samuel Upson.

1790 — Abraham Norton, John Potter, Charles Frisbie, Luther Atkins, Deacon Peck, Mark Harrison, Captain Lewis, Nathan Scarritt, James Bailey, Zaccheus Gillet, Eliakim Welton, jr., Amos Seward, Joseph Minor, Samuel Byington.

1791 — Simeon Plumb, John Potter, Nathan Scarritt, Moses Pond, David Alcox, Judah Frisbie, Deacon Atkins, Daniel Johnson, jr., Samuel Upson, Nathaniel Lewis, Joseph Minor, Ezekiel Upson.

1792 — David Harrison, Nathaniel Lewis, Streat Richards, William Stevens, Nathaniel Sutliff, Jesse Alcox, Samuel Byington, Zenas Bracket, Joseph Minor, Nathan Seward, John Alcox, Samuel Upson, Ephraim Smith, jr.

1793 — Joseph Twitchel, Daniel Tuttle, Mark Barnes, Joseph Minor, John Frisbie, Jonathan Carter, Stephen Carter, James Scarritt, Zuer Bracket, Moses Pond, John B. Alcox, Samuel Upson.

1794 — Simeon Plumb, Heman Hall, Joseph Beecher, Joseph M. Parker, David Wakelee, Selah Steadman, James Alcox, Joseph Minor, John Talmage, Samuel Clinton, Samuel Upson, Giddeon Finch, Nathan Scarritt, Walter Beecher.

1795 — Heman Hall, Joseph Beecher, Simeon Plumb, Joseph M. Parker, Selah Steadman, David Wakelee, James Alcox, Joseph Minor, John Talmage, Samuel Upson, Samuel Clinton, Giddeon Finch, Nathan Scarritt, Walter Beecher.

1796 — Town organized.

MEMBERS OF THE CHURCH.

1773 — Aaron Harrison and Jerusha his wife, Josiah Rogers and Sarah his wife, Isaac Hopkins and Mercy his wife, Joseph Atkins and Abigail his wife, Thomas Upson, Joseph Sutliff, Amos Seward and Ruth his wife, David Norton, John Alcox and Mary his wife, Samuel Upson, Wait Hotchkiss and Lydia his wife, Nathaniel Butler and Rebecca his wife, Elizabeth Porter, Daniel Alcox and Elizabeth his wife, Joseph Hotchkiss and Hannah his wife, Judah Frisbie, Israel Clark and Mahetabel his wife, Daniel Lane and Jemima his wife, Stephen Miles, Stephen Barnes and Sarah his wife, Zadoc Bronson and Eunice his wife; Lucy, wife of Justus Peck; Rebecca, wife of Nathaniel Hitchcock; Esther Bar-

MEMBERS OF THE CHURCH.

rett, Joseph Benham and Elizabeth his wife; Josiah Barnes, William Smith; Anne, wife of James Bailey; John Bronson, David Frost.

1774 — Samuel Bradley, Ephraim Pratt and his wife, Elizabeth, wife of Ebenezer Wakelee; Sarah, wife of Isaac Cleveland; Martha, wife of Aaron Howe; Daniel Byington, jr., Cyrus Norton, Levi Gaylord and Lois his wife, Nathaniel Sutliff, Joseph Beecher and Esther his wife, Jesse Alcox and Patience his wife, Daniel Byington and Sarah his wife, Sarah Seward, Simeon Plumb; Zeruiah, wife of Joseph Sutliff, jr.

1775 — Stephen Pratt and Zilpha his wife, Abel Curtiss and Anne his wife, Joseph Atkins, jr., and Phebe his wife; Sarah R., wife of Thaddeus Barnes; Eunice, wife of Samuel Bradley; Sarah, wife of Ingham Clark.

1776 — Elizabeth, wife of Daniel Byington, jr.; Mary, wife of Ezekiel Upson; Eunice, wife of Luther Atkins; Rebecca, wife of Heman Hall.

1777 — Rebecca, wife of Abraham Wooster; James Alcox and Hannah his wife; Mary, wife of Jeremiah Scarritt; Wait Hotchkiss; Elizabeth, wife of Zaccheus Gillet, jr., Jared Harrison and Hannah his wife, Zenas Brackett, Calvin Cole and Miriam his wife; Hannah, wife of Reuben Frisbie.

1778 — Susanna, wife of Noah Neal; Sarah Jones, widow; Mrs. Josiah Hart.

1779 — Josiah Hart.

1781 — Isaac Barnes and Lucy his wife; Rebecca, wife of Amos Beecher; Sarah, wife of Capt. Zaccheus Gillet; Joseph Mallery and Eunice his wife.

1783 — Justus Peck, Charles Upson and Wealthy his wife; Elizabeth, wife of Joel Lane.

1784 — Ruth, wife of Reuben Frisbie; Joseph Smith, Jacob Carter and Mary his wife, Samuel Byington and Olive his wife, Jonathan Carter and Abigail his wife; Phebe, wife of Samuel Harrison; Sabra, wife of Asa Alcox; Sibyll, wife of Archibald Pritchard; Jerusha, wife of Cyrus Norton; Samuel Waters and Sarah his wife, Samuel Atkins and Esther his wife; Esther, wife of Joseph Smith; Hannah, wife of Judah Frisbie; Hannah, wife of Ebenezer Johnson.

1785 — Mrs. Nathan Stevens; Mary, wife of Charles Upson; Mark Harrison and Rebecca his wife.

1786 — Triphene Carter, Abraham Norton; Betty, wife of Jeremiah Smith.

1787 — Sarah, wife of Nathaniel Lewis; Catharine, wife of John Sutliff.

1788 — Miriam, wife of Ozias Norton; Esther, wife of Joseph Beecher, jr.; Isaac Bronson, Ephraim Smith and his wife; Rachel, wife of Curtiss Hall.

1789 — Mrs. Selah Steadman.

1791 — Adah, wife of Rev. Alexander Gillet; Sarah, wife of Josiah Barnes.

1792 — Eunice, wife of Streat Richards; Hannah Talmage, widow.

1793 — Sally, wife of Rev. J. B. Woodward; Lois Hopkins, widow; Heman Hall, David Harrison.

1794 — James Bailey; Pamela, wife of Solomon Alcox; Lydia, wife of David Harrison.

1794 — Isaac Bronson, Mrs. Loise Clark, — Clinton, Mrs. Joel Granniss; Hester, wife of Jerry Moulthrop; Cretia, wife of John Talmage; Ruth, wife of Elisha Horton.

1796 — Charles Frisbie and wife.

1798 — John Frisbie.

Of persons who united with the church from 1798 to 1811, I find no record. In a list written on the inside of the cover of the old book, probably by Rev. Mr. Keys, several names occur that I find in no other place. They are the following:

Preserve Carter, Prince Duplax, Lud Lindsley, Mrs. Lud Lindsley, Mrs. Preserve Carter, Stephen Carter, Mrs. Stephen Carter; Lowly Carter, widow; Jesse Upson, Mrs. Jesse Upson, Mrs. Moses Byington, Jeremiah Scarritt, Washington Upson, Mrs. Washington Upson, Abigail Pardee, Asaph Hotchkiss, Mrs. Asaph Hotchkiss, John Potter, Mrs. John Potter, Joseph Parker, Mrs. Joseph Parker, Joseph M. Parker and Hannah, his wife; Henry Upson, Mrs. Henry Upson, Mrs. Selah Upson, Mrs. Manly Upson, Gates Upson, Mrs. Gates Upson, Isaac Upson, Mrs.

MEMBERS OF THE CHURCH.

Isaac Upson; Lydia Frisbie, Zeruiah Sutliff, Mrs. Ozias Norton, Mrs. John Thomas, Mrs. John Hotchkiss, Mrs. Bildad Hotchkiss; Martha Thomas, widow; Mrs. Joshua Minor, Daniel Rose, Mrs. Erastus L. Hart, Widow Sandford, Nathaniel Lane, Mrs. Laura Upson.

1811—Eldad Parker; Ruth, wife of Lewis Wakelee; Jonathan Case.

1812—Esther Harrison, widow; Lydia Alcox, Maria Wakelee, Lewis H. Wakelee, Pitman Stowe and his wife, Mrs. Elisha Horton, jr.

1813—Abner Hotchkiss and his wife, Mrs. Ira Hough, Lydia Rogers, Julia Upson, Delight Carter.

1814—Abiather Sutliff and Clarissa his wife, Manly Upson, Harvey Norton, Hannah Beach.

1815—Fanny Knight, widow; Beda Goodyear; Mary, wife of Reuben Carter; Mary, wife of Bela Row; Abigail Royce, Sarah Churchill, Luther Roper, Mrs. Luther Hotchkiss, Mrs. Ziba Norton, Mrs. David Frisbie.

1816—Daniel Holt and Abby his wife, Reuben Carter, Bildad Hotchkiss; Hannah, wife of Orrin Jackson; Sarah, wife of Jerry Moulthrop; Hannah, wife of William Bartholomew; Phebe, wife of Irad Bronson; Sarah Bronson; Lucette, wife of Obed Doolittle; Zechariah Hitchcock, Lois L. Doolittle, Mrs. Orrin Plumb.

1817—Luna, wife of Amos Pierson; Irad Bronson; Amy Tuttle, widow; Lucy Upson.

1821—Mrs. Higgins, Jonathan Bement and Hannah his wife, Anne M. Bailey, Lucius Tuttle, Rebecca Tuttle; Hannah, wife of John Bronson, jr.; Sarah, wife of Titus Brackett; Lucy, wife of Uri Carter; Betsey, wife of Almond Alcox; Thomas Upson and Jerusha his wife.

1827—Sally M. Upson, Laura Munson.

1828—Moses Pond, Samuel W. Upson, Clark Bronson and Experience his wife, Sophia R. Alcox, Orlinda Thomas, Selah Upson, Martha Tuttle, Wealthy Moulthrop, Hannah Norton, Fitch A. Higgins, Amanda Higgins, William Bartholomew, Lowman Upson, John S. Atkins, Esther Atkins, Ira Frisbie, Sarah Frisbie, Marilla Lindsley, Hannah M. Lindsley, Rachel Lindsley, Henrietta M. Bailey, Sylvia Thomas, Chloe Alcox, Bennet W. Parker, Marcus Upson, Mary Harrison, Clarissa Upson, Theda M. Carter, Laura A. Bement.

1829 — Elizabeth Alcox, Sarah Plumb, Lois Alcox, Benjamin A. Lindsley, Lucas H. Carter, Eunice Hotchkiss, Salina D. Carter, Asa Boardman, Louisa Boardman, Timothy H. Hotchkiss, Mary A. Hotchkiss, Mabel Downs, Sarah Scarritt.

1830 — Desire Bunnel, Charles Welton.

1833 — Polly Upson, Harriet Norton, Mary H. Upson, Charlotte R. Lindsley, Parlia A. Perkins, Sarah Upson.

1834 — Ruth Johnson; Lydia, wife of Moses Pond; Nancy, wife of Zenas Tolles; Parlia, wife of Leonard Beecher; Mary, wife of Josiah Thomas; Amanda Perkins; Lucy, wife of Lowman Upson; Luther Hotchkiss, Ansel H. Plumb, Luther Bailey, John B. Alcox, Russel Rowe, Cyrus Upson, Orrin Hall and Nancy his wife, Albert A. Boardman and Mary his wife; Ephraim Hall and Mary, his wife, Matthew S. Norton and Betsy M. his wife, David S. Bailey and Sarah L. his wife, Miles S. Hotchkiss and Abigail his wife, Jenette Upson, Mary A. H. Holt, Phebe L. Bronson, Thankful B. Bartholomew, Sarah Hotchkiss, Almira Norton, Rosanna L. Perkins, Lois A. Johnson, Lucy A. Bement, Sarah Jane Bartholomew, Rachel Pond, William R. Higgins, Lorin C. Holt, Stiles L. Hotchkiss, Hendric Norton, Polly Alcott, Esther R. Atkins, Harriet Alcott, Russel Upson, Adeline Upson, Roxanna Hall, Florilla Hickox, Isaac Upson.

1838 — Timothy U. Carter; Lois M., wife of Lucas Sutliff; Hannah V., wife of Carolus Byington; Bertha Bartholomew, Joel Alcott, Samuel Lindsley, Daniel H. Holt, Mrs. Luther Bailey, George A. Duran, Lucius Tuttle, jr.; Sylvia, wife of Eldad Parker; Polly, wife of Willard Plumb; Vina, wife of John Beecher; Henry D. Upson, Jarvis R. Bronson, Mary P. Smith, Lucius Upson, Anson Sutliff, Ezra Stiles Hough and Lucy his wife, Deidamia Minor.

1842 — Marietta Bradley, Mary A. Hough; Harriet, wife of Henry Beecher.

1843 — Lucy Ann, wife of Aaron C. Beech; Adah Finch, Stillman Bronson, Henry Beecher, Rollin W. Plumb; Lois A., wife of Ansel H. Plumb; Esther P., wife of Jarvis R. Bronson; Eliza A. Norton, George W. Carter, Rufus Norton, Mrs. Harriet

MEMBERS OF THE CHURCH.   153

E. Norton, Narcissa Sperry, Esther Alcott, Royce Lewis and Fanny his wife.

1844— Mrs. Rachel Upson, Hannah Tuttle, Esther Atkins, Charles Kirk, Benjamin A. Lindsley and Lucina his wife.

1846 — Sarah Ann, wife of Geo. W. Carter ; Matthew S. Norton and Betsey his wife.

1848 — Mercy Gaylord Alcott.

1849 — Emoret A. Bartholomew, Sarah Plumb.

1850— Lois S., wife of David M. Sanford ; Amos Roberts and Rebecca his wife, Miles M. Upson, Burritt W. Beecher, Newell B. Churchill, Lyman B. Bronson.

1853— Dudley H. Abbott ; Jenette, wife of Seth Wiard.

1854— Martha Tuttle, John Wickliffe Beach, Mary R. Hotchkiss, David F. Beach, Jane Beach.

1858 — Augusta E. Markland, James Alcott, Salina Alcott, Harriet Ann Alcott, Emily Alcott, Ardelia M. Tuttle, Mary A. Hough, Ann A. Hough, Ira H. Hough, Ezra S. Hough, Harriet E. Hough, Emma J. Odell, Sarah E. Bartholomew, Augustus E. Brackett, Joel W. Upson and Eleanor his wife, Lucian Upson, Leroy Upson, Saphrona Upson, William A. Munson, Julia A. Munson, Mary E. Hitchcock, Henry B. Carter, John H. Beecher, Joseph A. Beecher, S. Dwight Beecher, James B. Bailey, Elmer Hotchkiss, Mary E. Atkins, Lucy S. Bronson, John Frisbie, Francis G. Churchill, Esther E. Hough, Harriet L. Bronson, Emogene E. Minor, Laura Ann Hough, Amelia E. Rose, Rufus A. Sandford.

1859 — Mrs. Sarah Whitlock, Albert N. Lane and Esther Melissa his wife, Mary Harrison, Emma A. Upson, Edward H. Allen, Rev. Stephen Rogers and Jerusha his wife, Hannah Bement, Esther A. Beecher.

1860 — Andrew R. Rowe, David A. Sandford.

1861 — Mrs. Betsey Sperry.

1862 — Helen M. Rogers, Abigail Brooks.

1863 — Rev. Lent S. Hough, Hannah S. Hough, Leonard Blakeslee, Emma C. Hitchcock, Maria S. W. Hough, Mary E. Hough, Martha R. Hough.

1864— Sarah M. Moulthrop, Annis E. Hotchkiss, Emily M. Upson, Luther W. Plumb, Eliza A. Plumb, Emeline Thomas,

Sarah U. Hall, Helen R. Thomas, Harriet S. Norton, Omer C. Norton.

1865 — Mary E. Upson.

1866 — Helen R. Hall.

1867 — Mahlon Hotchkiss, Heman W. Hall, George W. Atwood, Huldah Atwood, Leverette A. Sandford, Harriet J. Hall, Amelia C. Hitchcock, Sarah J. Johnson, Augustus Rose, Mary Rose, Ella J. Rose, Arthur Terrill, James P. Alcott, Benjamin L. Bronson, Henry Fields. John T. Harrison, Evelin M. Upson, Frank C. Munson, Inez E. Munson, Mary Alcott, Mary W. Harrison, Anna C. Downs, Emilyette Upson, Isaac Hough, George Atkins, Cora A. Atkins, Elliot Bronson, Lydia J. Norton, Lydia S. Downs, Alice S. Lewis, Charles E. E. Somers, Sarah Terrill, Lucilla M. Upson.

1868 — Martha A. Brooks, Mary A. Richardson.

1869 — Rufus J. Lyman, Rev. W. C. Fiske and H. M. his wife, James P. Fiske, Sarah L. Fiske, William W. Fiske, Orrin Yemmans, Rebecca Yemmans.

1871 — Mary P. Carter, Sarah G. Thomas.

1872 — Persis H. Atwood, Frank G. Mansfield.

THE EPISCOPAL CHURCH.

CHAPTER I.

THE EPISCOPAL CHURCH.

This church, though never large, has performed an important work in this part of the great vineyard,—a work of which it need not be ashamed in any respect. It has suffered more by removal of its members than the other church, and as a consequence, it is reduced to a handful compared to its former numbers, and has not held regular service for several years.

Among the earliest settlers in Wolcott were Episcopalians, and when the First Society was organized and a "tax laid" for the support of the gospel, the Episcopalians were taxed the same as others, but their tax was appropriated, according to law, for the support of their church in Waterbury. The First Society being the legal one, assessed the ecclesiastical taxes on all persons within its bounds, and appointed special collectors to gather the tax of Episcopalians, and hence we find as early as 1772, Ensign Oliver Welton and Eliakim Welton, jr., "chosen to collect Rev. Mr. Scovill's rate," and this arrangement continued many years afterward, and therefore the Episcopalians paid, by tax, for the support of the gospel as regularly as the Congregationalists.

In 1779 the Episcopalians were so numerous as to petition the General Assembly to be made a distinct Society, as appears from the following record in the proceedings of the First Society : " Voted, to remonstrate against the memorial whereby we are cited to give reason, if any, at the General Assembly, why Josiah Cowles and others should not be made a distinct Ecclesiastical Society, and that Thomas Upson, Daniel Alcox, Daniel Byington and Jared Harrison be agents for the same purpose," and in consequence of this remonstrance, probably, this petition was not granted.

Soon after Mr. Woodward's settlement, persons began to withdraw from the First Society, in favor of other churches, and from 1791 to 1822, twenty-six families withdrew and joined the Baptist Societies in Bristol, Southington, and Waterbury; twenty withdrew in favor of no Society, and the following in favor of the Episcopal church :

1793 — Barna Powers.
1806 — Timothy Hotchkiss.
1808 — Daniel Byington, Streat Richards, Joseph Minor, Lewis Loveland, David Wakelee, Reuben Lewis, Jesse Alcox, jr., Nathaniel G. Lewis, David Alcox, jr., Joseph C. Alcox, Phineas Deming, Levi Brown, James Scarritt, David M. Beach, Isaac Downs, Elkanah Smith.*

1809 — John Norton, Caleb Merrills, Marvin Beckwith, jr.
1811 — Jairus Alcox, Titus Hotchkiss, John J. Kenea.
1812 — Levi Hall, Zephana Parker, Amon Bradley.
1813 — Joseph Twitchell, Richmond Hall, Samuel Upson, jr., Lyman Higgins, Jerry Todd, Levi Parker, Ambrose Ives, Archibald Minor.
1816 — Marcus Minor, Jeremiah Sperry, Harpin Hotchkiss.
1820 — Salmon Johnson.
1821 — Orrin Plumb.
1822 — William Parker.†

About the year 1805, the Episcopal people began to hold service at the house of Daniel Byington at the Mill

---

* And two others, whose names were afterwards erased, making eighteen at one time.

† We have the certificates of over ninety families that withdrew from the First Society, between the years 1791 and 1822.

CALL FOR THE FIRST SOCIETY MEETING. 159

Place, where they continued to hold it, most of the time, for a number of years.

The Episcopal Society was organized January 26th, 1811, at the house of Mr. Titus Hotchkiss, who then resided on the Twitchell place.

CALL FOR THE FIRST SOCIETY MEETING.

We, the subscribers, inhabitants of the town of Wolcott, being of the order of Christians denominated Episcopalians, and being desirous to form ourselves into a Society for the purpose of exercising all the privileges which by law are granted to the several Societies, being of the aforesaid order of Christians, do hereby agree to meet on the 26th day of instant November, at the dwelling house of Mr. Titus Hotchkiss, in said Wolcott, at one o'clock in the afternoon of said day, for the purpose of choosing a moderator and clerk of said meeting, which clerk, when chosen, shall be sworn as the law directs; and also to choose all other officers which shall then be thought necessary and proper for the good of said Society, and also to tax ourselves for the purpose of procuring such proportion of preaching as shall by the Society be thought best, being at all times governed and directed by a majority of said meeting, in the doing and performing of all which, as above written, will ever hereafter consider ourselves a Society; and to be guided by the same laws and in the same manner as other Societies of the same denomination, belonging to this State, are.

WOLCOTT, November 21, 1811.

John Welton, Moses Welton, Levi Hall, William Parker, William Hotchkiss, Ambrose Ives, Eliakim Welton, Timothy Hotchkiss, Streat Todd, Phineas Deming, Joseph Minor, John Norton, Zephana Parker, Bildad Hotchkiss, John J. Kenea, Asaph Finch, Levi Brown, Erastus Welton, Joseph Welton, Eliakim Welton, 2d, Titus Hotchkiss, Thomas Welton, Daniel Langdon, Hezekiah Bradley, Daniel Byington, David Wakelee, Joseph C. Alcox, Eleazer Finch.

MINUTES OF THE FIRST SOCIETY MEETING.

WOLCOTT, Nov. 26, 1811.

At a legal meeting this day holden at the dwelling house of

Mr. Titus Hotchkiss, by the members of the Episcopal Society, the following votes were passed by the members of said meeting: That Daniel Langdon be moderator of said meeting, and that Erastus Welton be clerk for the year ensuing; that Moses Welton be treasurer; that Moses Welton, Bildad Hotchkiss, and Irad Wakelee be Society's Committee for the year; Daniel Langdon and Thomas Welton, Wardens. Voted that a tax of one cent on a dollar be laid on the list 1811, and made payable to the Treasurer the first day of March, 1812, and that Irad Wakelee be Collector of said Tax. Voted that the annual society meeting be hereafter holden the last Monday in November, annually. That the society committee receive the money at the hands of the Treasurer, and at their discretion apply it for preaching the ensuing year."

For two years after the formation of the Society, the Rev. Mr. Prindle, then of Naugatuck, supplied the Society with preaching once a month during the summer season, six or seven months, at $6 per Sabbath, as the Treasurer's book shows. In 1815 Rev. Tillotson Bronson preached for them. After this, names of ministers are not mentioned for some years, yet the amount spent for preaching seems to have been most of the time nearly fifty dollars a year.

Services were conducted by laymen regularly in the absence of a minister, and the following committees were appointed from year to year to " read the prayers of the church," and also to read sermons.

1812 — Thomas Welton, Moses Welton, Elias Welton.

1813 — Thomas Welton, Moses Welton, Elias Welton, Erastus Welton. To read sermons — Elias Welton, Ambrose Ives, Levi Parker, Erastus Welton, Jarius Alcox, Joseph Welton.

1814 — To read prayers — Thomas Welton, Moses Welton, Eliakim Welton, Erastus Welton, Elias Welton. To read sermons — Ambrose Ives, John Kenea, Levi Parker.

1815 — To read prayers — Thomas Welton, Moses Welton, Erastus Welton, Elias Welton, Eliakim Welton, Eben Welton.

To read sermons — John J. Kenea, Levi Parker, Ambrose Ives, Elias Welton.

1816 — To read prayers — Thomas Welton, Moses Welton, Eliakim Welton, jr., Erastus Welton. To read sermons — Ambrose Ives, Levi Parker, William Alcox, Amos B. Alcox, Elias Welton, Erastus Welton.

1817 — To read prayers — Thomas Welton, Moses Welton, Eben Welton, Erastus Welton, Eliakim Welton. To read sermons — Ambrose Ives, William Alcox, Levi Parker, Erastus Welton, Ziba Welton, Amos B. Alcox.

1818 — To read prayers — Eben Welton, Moses Welton, Erastus Welton, Thomas Welton. To read sermons — Ambrose Ives, Erastus Welton, William Alcox, Levi Parker, Elias Welton.

1819 — To read prayers — Eben Welton, Thomas Welton, Erastus Welton, Moses Welton, Archibald Minor. To read sermons — Erastus Welton, Archibald Minor, William Alcox, Levi Parker.

1820 — To read prayers — Eben Welton, Moses Welton, Thomas Welton, Erastus Welton. To read sermons — Ambrose Ives, Archibald Minor, Erastus Welton, Elias Welton, William Alcox.

1821 — To read prayers — Thomas Welton, Moses Welton, Eben Welton, Erastus Welton, Archibald Minor, William Alcox. To read sermons — Archibald Minor, Erastus Welton, William Alcox, Levi Parker, Elias Welton, Willard Plumb.

1822 — To read prayers — Thomas Welton, Eben Welton, Moses Welton, Erastus Welton, Archibald Minor, William A. Alcox. To read sermons — Archibald Minor, Orrin Plumb, Elias Welton, Willard Plumb, William A. Alcox, Levi Parker, Erastus Welton, Levi Hall, Ambrose Ives.

This list of names for ten years exhibits the working force of the church without a minister. In contrast with the other church in Wolcott, it shows that as the Episcopal Society and church grew strong, the Congregational grew weak, and hence, in 1822 and 1823, when the Episcopal Society began to make arrangements to build a house of worship, the Congregational Society dismissed Mr. Keys for want of ability to support him, and entered upon the plan of lay preaching, by Isaac Bronson, which continued a number of years after. There seems to be no occasion for censure, but if the whole people could have consented to worship as one body, the result would have been, apparently, more happy and advantageous to the community and to the world.

BUILDING A HOUSE OF WORSHIP.

In 1817 the Society voted that "we meet at the house of Mr. Daniel Byington the winter coming," and at this house they probably had met during the winters, most of the time, from the commencement of holding services separate from Waterbury, and during the summer meeting in the school houses.

On April 10th, 1820, the Society, at an adjourned meeting, took into consideration the subject of building a house of worship, and "voted that we appoint an agent to consult the minds of gentlemen on the expediency of petitioning the Legislature for a grant of a lottery for the purpose of building a house of public worship." At an adjourned meeting held in the same month, April 24th, they "voted that we will build a house of public worship, provided that we can agree upon a spot for that purpose." Also "voted that we will build a house in the Centre, provided we can be accommodated with a place to set it, and that Levi Hall, Ambrose Ives, and Erastus Welton, be a committee to look out a spot to build a house."

At an adjourned meeting, held December 31st, 1821, they "voted that we will build a church in case we can get money enough subscribed, and that we will build it in the centre of the town, near the Meeting house, and that Archibald Minor, Levi Hall, Moses Welton, Eben Welton, Willard Plumb, and Ambrose Ives, be a committee to circulate subscription papers for the purpose of building a house."

On January 21st, three weeks later, they "voted to

ascertain the probable expense of a house from 40 by 30 to 46 by 36 feet, and also to get a plan of the frame." One week later they "voted to build a church 30 by 40 feet, that it be two stories high, with 20 feet posts and a cupola suitable for hanging a bell." At the same meeting they directed the Society Committee to "agree with Moses Pond for a room in his chamber to meet in for one year, if in their opinion they can get it reasonable." Moses Pond's house was at this time the public house at the Centre. In the Autumn of the same year they circulated subscriptions to raise money to defray expenses for hiring a house in which to hold public worship the year ensuing, and it is probable it was this chamber in Mr. Pond's hotel.

In December, 1823, they accepted the report of their committee on a place to build a house, and fixed a site and appointed a committee to forward the enterprise. Between the years 1822 and 1830, the Society met frequently, discussed the whole subject of building and appointed committees to forward the same, but the house did not appear in its place as desired. The Society was not able to build a church that would accommodate even its small congregation, and during the same time the Congregational Society was unable to "hire preaching." The "revival" in the Spring of 1828 in the Congregational Society under the Rev. Mr. Scranton had revived the religious energies of the whole community, and the Episcopal Society shared in its benefits. In February of 1830, they changed the size of the house to 24 by 36 feet, and proceeded to gather materials for the building.

A SITE GIVEN BY THE TOWN.

WOLCOTT, April 5th, 1830.

Then met according to adjournment, and at said meeting, upon the petition of a number of the members of the Episcopal Society in said town in the form following :

Whereas, the Episcopal Society in the town of Wolcott are

about to erect a house of public worship in said Wolcott, and being desirous to set the same somewhere near the Congregational Meeting house in said Wolcott, or as near as a suitable spot of ground can be obtained for that purpose, we, therefore, whose names are underwritten, petition the inhabitants of said Wolcott, in legal town meeting this day assembled, for leave to erect said house on the most eligible spot of ground belonging to said town of Wolcott on the south part of the public green.

Signed by JOHN J. KENEA and others.

WOLCOTT, April 5, 1830.

Voted to grant the prayer of the petition.

During the summer of 1830 the frame was raised, and in December the outside of the church was covered. The only record of expense of the Society is a paper-covered book, found in possession of Mr. Orrin Hall, having been left by Mr. Levi Hall at his death, containing Mr. Erastus Welton's account with the Society as treasurer from 1811 to 1823, and containing Mr. Levi Hall's account with the same from 1835 to 1839. These items give us no account of the cost of the church, nor when it was completed. It is probable that the church was not finished till some time during the year 1832, from the fact that a meeting of the Society was held on the first Monday of April, 1833, and they "voted to discharge Levi Hall, Archibald Minor, Thomas H. Welton, and Orrin Plumb, building committee for the church, from any further services as committee aforesaid, and from all liabilities in said capacity," which indicates the work of building completed at that time.

In 1836 a stove was put into the church, as appears from a subscription paper for that purpose, still preserved.

CHAPTER II.

ORGANIZATION OF THE CHURCH.

The early records of the church were destroyed, purposely, as we are informed, by Rev. Collis I. Potter, who was minister to this parish in 1850; but from a minute made in the transactions of the Society, we learn quite clearly that the church was organized on or about Easter, 1834, for the meetings are called "Meetings of the Episcopal Society" till October, 1833, when they adjourned to the first Monday after the next Easter, and on that date the record made is of "All Saints' Parish in Wolcott." I have no doubt, therefore, of the date of the organization.

The records destroyed contained the list of the members and families of the church, and their destruction left the Book of Records in an unseemly condition, such as we should think no one would tolerate,— especially for the reason given, that some few things objectionable had been written therein. Hence, as to the records of the church, we are carried forward to the year 1850, when the Rev. Mr. Potter, then minister of "All Saints' Church," makes the following minute: "The old register is exceedingly imperfect, partly from the negligence of former ministers, and partly from the fact that it has been judged expedient to destroy several pages containing matter which was inappropriate for a register of the church, and which gave offence to some." After thus giving reasons for the destruction of the records, he enters on an earnest exhortation to future ministers and wardens to keep the register fully and faithfully, and in a "proper manner;" but he himself makes no record whatever of past historical items, except this one of the destruction of the register. Instead of giving reasons why a register should be kept, it would have been better to copy such parts of the old register as were "proper" for a church record. Five years after Mr. Potter's reign of destruction in records, we come to some account of the members and families of the church, which was made by Rev. Ximenus Alanson Welton, who "took charge of the parish under the supervision of the Bishop," in 1855.

During the years 1836 and 1837, the church was supplied with preaching by Rev. Peter G. Clark, residing in Cheshire. Several receipts for moneys paid are preserved, but they are not explicit as to the amount of yearly salary; only from one receipt it might be concluded that he received $200 a year. In 1838 and 1839, Rev. Mr. Covill is mentioned as preaching to this church "half of the time."

In 1840 and 1841, and possibly longer, the church was supplied with preaching by Rev. Servilius Stocking, who resided in Wolcott, and may have been the first resident minister of this church. The salary seems to have been $300 a year, which was equal to the amount raised by the other Society at the same time.

From Easter, 1843, for one year, the Rev. Mr. Gregor supplied the pulpit, and the Rev. Wm. G. French the year following; and following him, in 1845 to 1846, the Rev. David Sandford was engaged, and after him Rev. John D. Smith, for three years. The Rev. Collis Ira Potter was employed as minister from the Spring of 1850 to that of 1855. He entered in a new register a list of communicants and families then belonging to the church, and continued a faithful registry of baptisms, confirmations, and deaths, during his stay in the parish. The Rev. Ximenus Alanson Welton followed Mr. Potter in

1855 and 1856, and showed equal faithfulness in regard to the records.

MINISTERS WHO PREACHED FOR THE EPISCOPAL PEOPLE IN WOLCOTT.

Rev. Mr. Prindle, of Naugatuck, two years once in six weeks, from 1811 to 1813.

Rev. Tillotson Bronson, of Cheshire, preached a short time.

From 1817 money was raised nearly or quite every year till 1835, to procure preaching, but the ministers' names are not mentioned in the records.

1836 and 1837 — Rev. Peter G. Clark of Cheshire.

1838 and 1839 — Rev. Mr. Covell, of Bristol.

1840 and 1841, and perhaps longer — Rev. Servilius Stocking, resident minister.

1843 — Rev. Mr. Gregor.

1844 — Rev. Wm. G. French.

1845 and 1846 — Rev. David Sandford.

1847 — Rev. John D. Smith, of Seymour, three years.

1850 to 1855 — Rev. Collis Ira Potter, four years.

1855 and 1856 — Rev. Ximenus Alanson Welton.

1858 — Rev. Samuel A. Appleton, assistant to Rev. Dr. Clark, of Waterbury.

1859 — Rev. James Morton, of Harwinton preached most of the year as supply on Sabbath.

1860 — Rev. J. M. Willey, assistant of Rev. Dr. Clark, of Waterbury. He is said to have been a "smart man," and enjoyed preaching at Wolcott very much.

Since Mr. Willey, Rev. Prof. Russell, of Waterbury, has preached a few times.

CLERKS.

1811 to 1823 — Erastus Welton.
1824 to 1835 — Orrin Plumb.
1836 to 1839 — Seth Horton.
1840 to 1841 — Orrin Plumb.
1842 to 1864 — Ezra L. Todd.
1865 to 1873 — Dennis Pritchard.

HISTORY OF WOLCOTT.

TREASURERS.

1811 to 1823 — Erastus Welton.
1824 to 1834 — Orrin Plumb.
1835 to 1841 — Levi Hall.
1842 to 1844 — Heman Hall.
1845 to 1847 — Levi Hall.
1848 to 1859 — Geo. G. Alcott.
1860 to 1873 — Dennis Pritchard.

SOCIETY COMMITTEES.

1811 — Moses Welton, Bildad Hotchkiss, Irad Wakelee.
1812 — Moses Welton, Irad Wakelee, Elias Wakelee.
1813 — Moses Welton, Ambrose Ives, Levi Parker.
1814 — Ambrose Ives, Levi Hall, Moses Welton.
1815 — Levi Hall, Ambrose Ives, Eliakim Welton.
1816 — Ambrose Ives, Levi Hall, Eliakim Welton.
1817 — Joseph Minor, Jeremiah Todd, Jared Welton.
1818 — Eben Welton, Joseph C. Alcox, Streat Todd.
1819 — Eben Welton, Streat Todd, Marcus Minor.
1820 — Streat Todd, Levi Hall, Eldad Alcox.
1821 — Levi Hall, William Plumb, Eldad Alcox.
1822 — Eldad Alcox, William Plumb, Archibald Minor.
1823 — Archibald Minor, Hezekiah Bradley, Erastus Welton.
1824 — Hezekiah Bradley, Archibard Minor, Levi Hall.
No record of election from 1825 until 1829.
1829 — Lyman Higgins, Orrin Plumb, Eldad Alcox.
1830 — Lyman Higgins, Levi Hall, Orrin Plumb.
1831 — Levi Hall, Eldad Alcox, Lyman Higgins.
1832 — John J. Kenea, Lyman Higgins, Marcus A. Minor.
1833 — Martin Upson, Marcus Minor, Seth Horton.
1834 — No record.
1835 — Marcus Minor, Chester Hotchkiss, Seth Horton.
1836 — Seth Horton, Jesse Nichols, Martin Upson.
1837 — Martin Upson, Heman Hall, Thomas H. Welton.
1838 — No record.
1839 — Marcus Minor, Moses Pond, Sammy Finch.
1840 — Moses Pond, Heman Hall, Willis Merrill.
1841 — Martin Upson, Levi Hall, James Alcott.

WARDENS OF THE SOCIETY. 169

1842 — Martin Upson, Lyman Higgins, Levi Hall.
1843 — Martin Upson, Harvey G. Plumb, Upson Higgins.
1844 — Upson Higgins, Hezekiah Todd, Thomas H. Welton.

WARDENS.

1811 — Daniel Langton, Thomas Welton.
1812 — Eliakim Welton, Thomas Welton.
1813 — Eliakim Welton, Thomas Welton.
1814 — Eliakim Welton, Thomas Welton.
1815 — Eliakim Welton, Thomas Welton.
1816 — Thomas Welton, Eliakim Welton, jr.
1817 — Eben Welton, Erastus Welton.
1818 — Eben Welton, Erastus Welton.
1819 — Thomas Welton, Moses Welton.
1820 — Thomas Welton, Moses Welton.
1821 — Erastus Welton, Moses Welton.
1822 — Erastus Welton, Eben Welton.
1823 — Moses Welton, Thomas Welton.
1824 — Hezekiah Bradley, Moses Welton.
No record of any elections from 1824 to 1829.
1829 — Levi Hall, Lyman Higgins.
1830 — Sammy Nichols, Hezekiah Bradley.
1831 — Sammy Nichols, Hezekiah Bradley.
1832 — Hezekiah Bradley, Sammy Nichols.
1833 — Lyman Higgins, Levi Hall.
1834 — No record.
1835 — Sammy Nichols, Heman Hall.
1836 — Lyman Higgins, Heman Hall.
1837 — Heman Hall, Lyman Higgins.
1838 — No record.
1839 — Lyman Higgins, Heman Hall.
1840 — Heman Hall, Lyman Higgins.
1841 — Heman Hall, Lyman Higgins.
1842 — Lyman Higgins, Moses Pond, Martin Upson.
1843 — Lyman Higgins, Moses Pond.
1844 — Lyman Higgins, Moses Pond.
No record until 1848.
1848 — Levi Hall, Martin Upson.

1849 — Lyman Higgins, Levi Hall.
1850 — Martin Upson, George G. Alcott.
1851 — Martin Upson, George G. Alcott.
1852 — Martin Upson, George G. Alcott.
1853 — Martin Upson, George G. Alcott.
1854 — Martin Upson, George G. Alcott.
1855 — Martin Upson, George G. Alcott.
1856 — Martin Upson, George G. Alcott.
1857 — Martin Upson, George G. Alcott.
1858 — Martin Upson, George G. Alcott.
1859 — Martin Upson, George G. Alcott.
1860 — Martin Upson, Willis Merrill.
1861 — Martin Upson, Willis Merrill.
1862 — Martin Upson, Willis Merrill.
1863 — Martin Upson, Willis Merrill.
1864 — Martin Upson, Willis Merrill.

VESTRYMEN.

1845 — Moses Pond, Martin Upson, Heman Hall, Marcus Minor, Levi Hall, Lyman Higgins, Hezekiah Todd.

1846 — Moses Pond, Chester Hotchkiss, Levi Hall, Lyman Higgins, George G. Alcott, Hezekiah Todd, Marcus Minor.

1847 — Lyman Higgins, Martin Upson, Hezekiah Todd, Moses Pond, Levi Hall, Willis Merrill, Geo. G. Alcott, Marcus Minor, Eldad Alcott.

1848 — Moses Pond, Chester Hotchkiss, Orrin Hotchkiss, Luther M. Pond, Geo. G. Alcott, Hezekiah Todd, Ezra L. Todd, David S. Bailey, Marcus Minor, Willis Merrill.

1849 — Moses Pond, Willis Merrill, Hezekiah Todd, Marcus Minor, George G. Alcott.

1850 — Ezra L. Todd, Marcus Minor, David S. Bailey, Willis Merrill, Bennet Upson, Luthur M. Pond, Wells Plumb.

1851 — Marcus Minor, Dennis Pritchard, Hezekiah Todd, Ezra L. Todd, Luther M. Pond.

1852 — Dennis Pritchard, Marcus Minor, Willis Merrill, Hezekiah Todd, Moses Pond.

1853 — Dennis Pritchard, Moses Pond, Marcus Minor.
1854 — Willis Merrill, Hezekiah Todd, Dennis Pritchard.
1855 — Marcus Minor, Willis Merrill, Dennis Pritchard.

1856 — Dennis Pritchard, Willis Merrill, Marcus Minor.
1857 — Dennis Pritchard, Marcus Miner, Willis Merrill.
1858 — Marcus Miner, Dennis Pritchard, Willis Merrill.
1859 — Dennis Pritchard, Willis Merrill, Marcus Minor.
1860 — George G. Alcott, Marcus Minor, Dennis Pritchard.
1861 — Dennis Pritchard, Ezra L. Todd, Marcus Minor.
1862 — Dennis Pritchard, Ezra L. Todd, Marcus Minor.
1863 — Dennis Pritchard, Ezra L. Todd, Marcus Minor.
1864 — Marcus Minor, Ezra L. Todd.

CIVIL HISTORY OF WOLCOTT.

CHAPTER I.

TOWN INCORPORATED.

The Ecclesiastical Society of Farmingbury, at a Society meeting held December 7th, 1787, passed the following votes respecting the privileges of a town : "Voted that we are willing and desirous to be incorporated into a town. The negative was called, and not a hand up. Voted that it is our mind when made a town to be connected to New Haven County. Voted that Deacon Joseph Atkins, Capt. Nathaniel Lewis, Capt. Charles Upson, Deacon Justus Peck, Streat Richards, Mark Harrison, be a committee, or agents, to treat or confer with the towns of Southington and Waterbury respecting our becoming incorporated into a town, and likewise to carry a memorial to the General Assembly in May next. Voted that we prepare a petition to the Hon. General Assembly for privileges of a town, at their session in May next."

At an adjourned meeting on the second Monday of January, 1788, the Society " Voted that we will choose a committee to treat with the Waterbury committee respecting our having town privileges, and that Captain Charles Upson, Daniel Byington, Streat Richards, Simeon Hopkins, Abraham Norton, Amos Seward, and Capt. Samuel Upson be the committee ; and said committee are desired to make their report to this meeting as soon as an agreement may be made ; and it is understood that the agreement of said committee is not binding on said Society until agreed to by said Society."

From Bronson's History of Waterbury we learn the opinion of that town respecting this movement:

In December, 1787, the inhabitants of Farmingbury presented a memorial, in town meeting, giving reasons why they should be incorporated into a distinct town, and asking the consent of the meeting. A committee was appointed to take the matter into consideration, and hear the proposals that might be made "concerning public moneys, bridges, and town's poor," &c., and report make. Josiah Bronson, Stephen Ives, Aaron Benedict, Ezra Bronson, John Welton, and Samuel Lewis were the committee. "It is rather a doubt in our minds," they reported, "of the expediency of granting them their request, on any consideration whatever, but more especially upon the offers and proposals in several articles by them made." *

On the 14th day of next April the Society "voted to reconsider the vote that was taken to send agents to the General Assembly in May next, to try to obtain priviliges of a town."

In a Society meeting, held on the 13th day of February, 1792, this subject was again taken up. It was at the same meeting that voted the settlement of Mr. Israel B. Woodward. "Voted that we prepare a petition to the Hon. General Assembly, at their session in May next, for town privileges; and Dr. John Potter, Lieut. Streat Richards, Mark Harrison, Esq., Capt. Charles Upson, Jonathan Carter, Lieut. James Bailey, Daniel Byington, Calvin Cowles, Capt. Nathaniel Lewis, Mr. Amos Seward, were chosen a committee, or agents, to treat with the towns of Southington and Waterbury respecting the above petition to the Assembly." We learn from the Waterbury History that this petition was not presented in the Spring, but in the Autumn session of the Assembly.

On the 8th of October, 1792, Farmingbury applied to the Legislature for the desired act of incorporation. The town of Waterbury " voted that if the memorialists would

---

* History of Waterbury, p. 282.

within eight days give up all right to the ministerial and school moneys, pay twenty pounds in consideration of being released from supporting the great bridge on the Woodbury road, bind themselves to take care of their portion, according to the grand list, of the town poor, and to pay their share of the town debts; then, in that case, the town would not oppose the object of the memorial."* We find no report of the Farmingbury committee.

In the fore part of December, 1793, the Society again voted to present a petition to the General Assembly, and appointed the following committee to attend to this business: Capt. Charles Upson, Mark Harrison, Esq., Lieut. Streat Richards, Dr. John Potter, Capt. Samuel Upson, Lieut. Charles Frisbie, Capt. Walter Beecher, Ensign Jonathan Carter, Simeon Plumb, Joseph Beecher, Jr., Daniel Byington, and Samuel Byington. Of this committee we hear nothing, except that in a Society meeting on the 5th day of February, 1795, the Society voted that "the committee heretofore appointed to prepare a petition to the General Assembly for town privileges, prepare the same." Hence it is probable they had done nothing about it.

On the 25th day of April, 1796, another committee was appointed, and this application was successful. The committee consisted of Mark Harrison, Esq., Captain Charles Upson, Capt. Streat Richards, Mr. Jacob Carter, Mr. Eliakim Welton, and Mr. Elijah Frisbie.

ACT OF THE GENERAL ASSEMBLY.

At a General Assembly of the State of Connecticut, holden at Hartford, on the second Thursday of May, 1796:

Upon the petition of the inhabitants of the Society of Farmingbury, in the towns of Waterbury and Southington,† in the coun-

---

* Waterbury History, p. 282.

† When Southington was incorporated a town, from Farmington, in October, 1779, the eastern part of Farmingbury was included within the boundaries of Southington, and belonged to that town until the above act took effect.

ties of Hartford and New Haven, showing to this Assembly that some years since said Society was formed by the extreme parts of said towns of Waterbury and Southington, with the dividing line of said towns and counties running from north to south through the centre of said Society, upon which line their Meeting house was erected and stands; that their local situation is such, being obstructed in their travel eastwardly by a mountain, and other natural impediments, that great inconveniencies arise in their attending upon public meetings, and other public services and duties, and various other disadvantages are attached to them under their present circumstances; praying to be incorporated into a distinct town, with usual town privileges, and to be added to the said county of New Haven, as per petition dated May 9th, 1796, on file; and the said towns of Waterbury and Southington having withdrawn all objections against the prayer of said petition,

Resolved, That all the land lying and being in said Society of Farmingbury, and according to the established lines and limits of said Society, be and the same hereby is incorporated into a town by the name of Wolcott,* and that it shall have and retain, and enjoy all the privileges incident and belonging to any other town in the State; except, only, that said town shall hereafter send but one representative to the General Assembly of this State, and that the said town of Wolcott shall hereafter support their proportion of the present town poor, according to their list in said towns of Waterbury and Southington, on the said 9th day of May; provided that all debts and taxes due on said 9th of May from the inhabitants of said Wolcott shall be paid and discharged, as the same then or now remains due and owing; and that all debts and credits of said petitioners with said towns of Waterbury and Southington (except those appropriated for schooling in said Southington) shall be according to their respective lists of the year 1795. And it is further ordered that the inhabitants of said town of Wolcott shall hold a town meeting on the 13th day of June next, for the purpose of appointing town officers, and the meeting

---

* The name of the town would have been Farmingbury, but for the fact that Lieutenant Governor Oliver Wolcott, presiding in the Assembly when the bill was voted on, and there being a tie vote, he gave the "casting vote," which made it a town, and in honor of this fact it was called Wolcott

shall be warned by a warrant signed by Mark Harrison, Esq., and posted on the public sign-post in said town at least five days before holding said meeting; and Mr. Aaron Harrison shall be moderator of said meeting, and said town shall then and there proceed to appoint a town clerk, and other town officers for said town, who shall continue in office until the second Monday of December next, or until others are chosen in their places and stead.

And it is further Resolved that said town of Wolcott be and the same is hereby annexed to the county of New Haven, and shall be and remain within and part thereof.

A true copy of record.
Examined by SAMUEL WYLLIS, *Secretary*.

A true entry of the bill in form of the Town of Wolcott.
Test. ISAAC BRONSON, *Regr*.

The following is the agreement of the towns named concerning the poor :

Know all men by these presents, that whereas the General Assembly, at their session in May last, incorporated the parish of Farmingbury into a distinct town from a part of the towns of Southington and Waterbury, by the name of Wolcott, said Wolcott to support their proportion of the town poor, and the town of Southington having appointed Asa Barnes, Ashbel Cowles, Elizur Andrews, Samuel Hart, and Daniel Langton, jr., and the said town of Wolcott having appointed Jacob Carter, Nathaniel Lewis, Calvin Cowles, and Mark Harrison, a committee to divide said poor, which dividend is this day concluded and made mutually by us the said committee, viz.: The said town of Wolcott do agree to take Elizabeth Bailey, and Susannah Bailey and her child, on the 13th day of December next, and Abraham Pierson and wife on or about the first day of said December, into their care as their proportion of the poor of said town of Southington, and said Southington does agree to take into their care as their proportion of the poor of said towns of Southington and Wolcott, viz: Amos Parsons, his wife and child, Rebecca Hitchcock, Amos Nicholson, Mary ———, and Eunice Buck ; said Wolcott to have no demand, of any name or nature, on said Southington; neither shall said Southington have any demand, of any name or nature, on said town of Wolcott, except a note of —— dollars, which note is to be delivered unto the selectmen of Southington as soon as said selectmen of Southington shall execute the said deed unto the said selectmen of Wolcott of the land deeded to said Southington selectmen by Philemon Barnes, now deceased, and each of said towns are hereby forever discharged from any demands on each other up until this date, except the above deed and note.

In testimony of the aforesaid agreement and settlement, we have hereunto set our hands, in Southington, this 25th day of November, A. D., 1796.

Ashbel Cowles, Asa Barnes, Jacob Carter, Nathaniel Lewis, Calvin Cowles, Mark Harrison, Samuel Hart, Daniel Langton, jr., committee.

A true copy. ISAAC BRONSON, *Reg'r.*

THE FIRST TOWN MEETING.

At a meeting of the inhabitants of the town of Wolcott, legally warned and holden according to appointment of the Hon. General Assembly, on the 13th day of June, 1796, Deacon Aaron Harrison, being appointed Moderator, proceeded to choose the following gentlemen to the several offices to which their respective names are annexed, viz:

Town Clerk — Isaac Bronson.

Selectmen — Mark Harrison, Streat Richards, Jacob Carter.

Treasurer — Mark Harrison.

Constables — John Potter, Streat Richards.

Surveyors of Highways — Daniel Dean, John Potter, Elnathan Thrasher, Simeon Plumb, Eliakim Welton, Joel Granniss, Charles Upson, Samuel Upson, jr., Nathaniel Lane, Jeremiah Scarritt, Nathan Barnes, Joseph Twitchell, Ebenezer Johnson, Truman Smith, Dan Tuttle, Streat Richards.

Listers — Daniel Byington, John Potter, Isaac Bronson.

Collector — Samuel Plumb.

Leather Sealer — Farrington Barnes.

Grand Jurors — Mark Barnes, Ashbel Upson, Walter Beecher.

Tything Men — John Frisbie, David Harrison, Solomon Plumb, William Bailey.

Gauger — Isaac Bronson.

Packer — William Bailey.

Sealer of Weights and Measures — William Stevens.

Key Keepers — Calvin Cowles, Dan Tuttle, Amos Upson.

Fence Viewers — Silas Hine, David Norton, Samuel Clinton, Amos Brockett.

At the same meeting, it was voted "that Messrs. Samuel Upson, Charles Upson, Streat Richards, Jacob Carter, Mark Harrison, Calvin Cowles, Nathaniel Lewis, and Daniel Byington, be a committee to reckon and settle all accounts, whether by book, note, or bond, that are or may be open with this and the towns of Waterbury and Southington, at or before the 9th day of May last ; to divide the town poor (if any be) according to list, and to compromise and settle all claims and demands, that are or may arise between this and said towns of Waterbury and Southington previous to said 9th day of May last, and, if possible, to effect such settlement, and make a true and just report of their doings to this town, at their annual meeting in December next. Voted, that the annual town meeting in this town be holden on the second Monday in December annually, and that the same — and all other ordinary town meetings — be warned by notification, set upon the sign-post eight days previous to said meeting, by the selectmen of the town for the time being."

Thus were the people of Farmingbury constituted a distinct town, by the name of Wolcott, after petitioning nine years, and after being an Ecclesiastical Society twenty six years ; and the only evil we could wish to Wolcott, when its century of town history shall be completed, is that its prosperity may be much greater than ever before, and that the celebration of that event may witness a population tenfold more than at any time in its past history.

THE HILLS OF WOLCOTT.

The town of Wolcott is situated on hills, there being only one valley of any extent within its territory, and that the one coming up from Waterbury to within half a mile of the centre of the town. The stream of water called Mad River, rising in the extreme northern portion of the town, runs down this valley to Waterbury.* West of Mad River, and in the northwesterly part of the town, is Spindle Hill. A little to the north, on the western boundary of the town, and rising higher than Spindle Hill, is Clinton Hill, for a time called New Canaan. This is the highest point of land in the town, and from it may be seen nearly a dozen church spires, in as many villages, and from it also may be seen Long Island Sound and Long Island. A little east of Clinton Hill is a large and nearly barren rock, called Rattlesnake Rock. A little distance northeast of this rock is Becar Hill, which is nearly as elevated as Clinton Hill, but does not afford so extensive a view as the latter. South of Spindle Hill is Chestnut Hill, extending south to the valley of Mad River, where the valley is half a mile wide. Between Chestnut Hill and Spindle Hill is Potucco's Ring.† The hill which is now Wolcott centre was known as Benson Hill, until it was called Farmingbury, and contained a settlement of but few families. A small hill south of the centre was called Hogfields. Woodtick‡ is in the southern part of the town, at the head of the valley that continues westward to the city of Waterbury. A little south of Woodtick is a hill with which has been connected a legend from which it derives the name of Tame Buck, and west of this is Bald Hill, and west of the Woodtick pond is Wolf Hill. East of the bound line, and situated near Mr. Shelton T. Hitchcock's present dwelling, is Judd's Hill, probably so called from the fact that Deacon

---

* This stream, near Waterbury, was called in early times Mill River.

† Potucco's Ring, written also Petucker's Ring, derived its name from an Indian who kindled a fire in a circle around the hill in order to shoot deer. Potucco himself, remaining within the ring was burned to death.

‡ So called from a story told of a man who, having laid aside his coat during the day while at work, found it at night in the possession of an innumerable number of insects called woodticks.

Thomas Judd, of Waterbury, father-in-law to Mr. Thomas Upson, was among the first land owners on or near it. The hill extending northwardly from Judd's Hill was sometimes spoken of as a part of Southington Mountain. That part of it, especially, where Captain Nathaniel Lewis and Mr. Thomas Upson resided, was called Southington Mountain by Waterbury people before Wolcott territory was settled. Southington Mountain, so called by Wolcott people, begins at the south-east burying ground, and extends northward about two miles. The land next to the highest in the town is in the north-east, and was called for many years Pike's Hill, and after that Rose Hill, and still later has been known as the Lindsley Hill. This hill, for some time supposed to be the highest in the town, is lower than Clinton Hill, is also a little lower than East Mountain, near Meriden, and a very little lower than the highest land near Long Island Sound, west of New Haven.

The hills of Wolcott are composed of ledges of gray rock, and in many parts the rock is near the surface, or rising above it; and where the rock is covered to a considerable depth, much of the soil is so filled with stones and small rocks that the cultivation of it is a difficult and laborious work. Some fields now under cultivation show nearly as great an area of stone as of soil, yet there are many acres of arable land. The greater part of the land under cultivation is at present devoted to grazing. If as much money was devoted to fertilizing the soil as in many other parts of the country, the trade of Wolcott would consist of exports more largely than imports. The rule governing most of the farmers at present seems to be, to get as much from the soil as possible and put nothing on it, which rule would bring barrenness to any land on the planet called Earth. One reason why the rule is in good favor, is because of the burdens laid upon the men left in the town, the young and strong men having gone away to engage in manufacturing and mercantile enterprises elsewhere, and there is not force sufficient remaining to cultivate the land. Many of those who have emigrated from Wolcott have been remarkably successful, and this success abroad has been an injury, in one respect, for the impression seems to prevail that young men can make money faster and enjoy it more in any place other than in Wolcott.

Those farmers who cultivate the land with energy, by hiring "help" and buying fertilizers, reap harvests as large as the average throughout the eastern portion of the nation. One thing sure to grow if the soil is left to itself, is white birch, chestnut, oak, and swamp maple trees. The average yearly export of wood is about four thousand cords, while the amount standing does not appear to be diminished. There are many acres of land now called woodland that were under thorough cultivation from thirty to fifty years ago. Mr. Levi Atkins has land where once he mowed an abundant crop of hay from which he has taken one crop of wood, some of the trees being from twelve to fifteen inches in diameter, and the second growth of wood on the same land is now of considerable value. Others have valuable timber land where they mowed large quantities of hay less than twenty-five years ago. Land with a full crop of wood standing is worth two-thirds more than without the wood, and when a farmer removes five or ten acres of wood, he applies to the assessors to lessen, proportionately, the assessment on his farm ; so that the amount of the "grand list" is diminishing every year, for the growth of the wood is slow compared with the time required for the removal of it. On the other hand, the increase of the assessment list in proportion to the growth of wood is a very difficult matter, and one against which the people seem to have strong prejudices. The area of woodland is increasing every year, because the trees are springing up on grazing land in many parts with great rapidity. Without considerable effort to subdue these growing bushes they will soon become trees, and the present pastures will become forests. From the fact of this rapid growth of wood on land which had been under cultivation from forty to seventy years, it may be properly concluded that the strength of the soil has not been exhausted, and hence with labor and fertilizers Wolcott soil could be made to produce as abundantly as ever.

STREAMS IN WOLCOTT.

Mad River is the largest stream within the limits of the town. It rises at the northern boundary and flows south and southwest into the Naugatuck River. Several streams flow into Mad River. One from Spindle Hill, called Stony Brook, enters the river from the west above the Great Falls, or the Mill Place; another from the east, north of the center, enters below the Great Falls, and is the one on which was situated the tannery of Mr. Ira Hough. Another stream from Buck's Hill enters the river in the Big Plains, and is the one on which Mr. Jonathan Bement built a tannery, near Gehula Grilley's residence, where Mr. Isaac Hough now resides. A small stream east of Capt. John Alcox's residence was called East Misery Brook. Another from the north-eastern part of the town enters Mad River a little north of Woodtick, while another from the south-east part, called Lily Brook, enters a little below Woodtick.

Three reservoirs are now constructed in this town in connection with Mad River, to supply the manufactories of Waterbury,— one in the northern portion of the town, covering Cedar Swamp; another in the south-eastern, adjoining Judd's Hill, and the other at the north end of Chestnut Hill. The last named, which is not yet completed, has been constructed at a much greater expense than the others; and all of them have been built by Waterbury manufacturing companies. In the north-east part of the town is Roaring Brook, running in a southeastern direction down Southington Mountain, on which is, at present, a saw mill of considerable power. There was another mill on the same stream further up, but nothing remains of it except the dam and the foundation walls.

CHAPTER II.

THE FIRST SETTLERS.

The land in Wolcott, belonging as it did originally to the towns of Farmington and Waterbury, was "taken up" largely by the inhabitants of those towns some years before any persons made their residence on these lands, and hence the Waterbury part of Wolcott was, much of it, owned by Waterbury people, and was settled largely by the people of that town, while the Farmington part was "taken up" by the people of that place, and many of the early residents were from that town, including Southington, a few coming from Wallingford. The Farmington part was laid into "long lots," being in three tiers, of one mile each. The first tier joined the Waterbury, or the "bound line," the second lay east of the first, and the third east of the second, extending to the foot of Southington Mountain. The whole length of each "long lot" is said (in some of the deeds) to have been three miles. The lots were numbered from north to south, and must have commenced near the northern boundary of Wolcott.

The earliest record of the purchase of land in this part of Wolcott that I have seen, except that of Mr. Thomas Upson, in 1732, is that by Lieutenant Heman Hall, on March 12th, 1750, on the long lot, number fifty-six; but on this farm was then a dwelling house, in which Mr. Joseph Preston was probably residing. This house stood on the "twenty-rod highway" running north and south on Southington Mountain, directly east from the present gamble-roofed house which he or his son, Captain Heman Hall, afterwards built. Mr. Hall sold this farm to Mr. Preston, of whom he purchased it, and the deeds are dated on the same day. On the 19th of the same month, Mr. Hall purchased another farm on lot fifty-six, of a Mr. Jonathan Mott, fifty acres, "with a dwelling house on it and a road across it," for two hundred and ten pounds. He purchased other land near this in 1754, but was then residing in Wallingford, and did not make his residence here until after this date. In 1753, Mr. James Pike, and his two sons, Samuel and David, were residing on or near Pike's Hill. Mr. Samuel Pike bought eighty-five acres on lot thirty-eight, of Mr. Robert Porter, of Farmington, for two hundred and fifty pounds, in 1753, which land "butted on Waterbury line." Mr. Cogswell purchased of Asa Cowles a part of lot 38, "middle tier," in 1754. Mr. David Pike sold land to Mr. Daniel Mix, in 1753, it being a "part of the lot his father owned." Mr. Benjamin Barnes owned land near that purchased by Lieut. Heman Hall, in 1753, and may have resided on it.

The earliest record I have seen of Mr. John Bronson in Wolcott, is that of 1762, but whether he was then residing here or not I am not able to say, certainly, but think he was. Mr. Justus Peck, afterwards Deacon, was in Wolcott as early as January 18th, 1762. Captain Nathaniel Lewis, probably, made his residence on the farm still known by his name, about 1760 to 1765, and Mr. David Frost near the same time, perhaps a few years later, and the Carters about 1770. The Beechers may have been here before 1765, as also the Brockets, Hortons, and some others who settled in the north-east portion of the town ; still, I am of the opinion that they had not been here long when the Society was organized, in 1770.

In Waterbury part, Mr. John Alcox, of New Haven, was the first resident, removing hither in March, 1731.

THE FIRST SETTLERS.

In the autumn of the same year Mr. Isaac Hopkins purchased the farm in the valley east of Chestnut Hill, and probably made it his residence the next year, 1732, the year that he was married, and on this farm he resided until his death. Mr. Benjamin Harrison was living on Benson Hill, now Wolcott Center, in 1739, when he purchased land adjoining "his own land," according to the reading of the deeds. He purchased one hundred and eleven acres of land of Stephen Hopkins, jr., of Waterbury, deeded July 2, 1737, which land joined on Isaac Hopkins' land. By the reading of some of Mr. Harrison's deeds it appears that other families had resided or were residing in that portion of the town before he removed there. After Mr. Isaac Hopkins and Mr. Benjamin Harrison, the following families became settlers in the valley south-west of Benson Hill: Elijah Frisbie, Roger Prichard, Eldad Mix, and a few others, before 1760; and Joseph Parker, Joseph Sutliff, Gehulah Grilley and Timothy Scott,* before 1770. On Spindle Hill, Thomas Welton and Eliakim Welton, and Shadrick Benham settled soon after John Alcox. Mr. Amos Seward was residing east

---

* Inhabitants of Waterbury subject to pay taxes in 1760, residing in East Branch (afterwards Wolcott), three miles or more from the Meeting house, as given in Bronson's History of Waterbury.

Thomas Welton,	£83	Isaac Cleveland,	£29
Benjamin Nichols,	34	Joseph Sutliff,	86
John Alcox, jr.,	54	Shadrick Benham,	26
John Alcox,	81	Josiah Adkins,	35
Benjamin Benham,	40	William Hickox,	52
Seth Bartholomew,	52	Abial Roberts, jr.,	2
Joseph Sutliff, jr.,	7	William Monson,	13
Conrad Johnson,	45	Daniel Alcox,	48
Eldad Mix,	22	James Alcox,	42
Edward Rogers,	21	William Woodward,	6
William Cole,	9	Isaac Hopkins,	151
Roger Prichard,	96	Barnabas Lewis,	36
James Bassett,	55	Abial Roberts,	73
Joseph Beach,	54	Josiah Rogers,	49
Whole No. 28.		Total,	£1,261

of Woodtick in 1770, and had been there some years, probably, and south of him were settled at that time several of the sons of Thomas Upson. Wait Hotchkiss came to Wolcott in 1765, and Abel Curtiss, Isaac Twitchell, and Joseph Beach, near the same time ; probably a little before. David Norton came about 1760. Josiah Rogers had been here but a short time before 1770, though his father, Deacon Rogers, of North Branford, purchased land here in 1724. Solomon Hotchkiss was an early settler on Spindle Hill, east of Mr. John Alcock's, but very few particulars concerning him and his family have been seen. Joseph Atkins removed here about 1758. In 1770 there were residing at the Center, then called Farmingbury, Aaron Harrison and the family of his brother Benjamin Harrison, Abraham Woster, John Barrett and the family of James Barrett, Joseph Atkins, and Josiah Talmage, and soon after were added Daniel Tuttle, Samuel Byington, and possibly a few others ; yet of this I am not certain.

WOLCOTT CENTER IN 1800.

The Center, soon after the town was incorporated, was a place of considerable mercantile business and land speculations, the land sales being stimulated by the expectation that a turnpike would be constructed from Torrington to New Haven, and that Wolcott would be an important station on that road. In 1796, Mr. Samuel Byington sold his farm and hotel, west of the Green, and a little southwest of the Meeting house, to Moses Todd, Bani Bishop, of Southington, and Hezekiah Todd, of Cheshire, for four hundred and eighty-four pounds. This farm contained forty-seven acres, the hotel and wheelwright shop, and was bounded on the north by Joseph Atkin's land, on the west by Mad River, on the south by David Norton's land and the highway. In February, 1797, this farm was purchased by Abijah Fenn, of Watertown, who built in the following year, 1798, the store near the corner of the lot towards the Meeting house, which he built on contract for Truman Woodward and Amos Baldwin, said to be of Wolcott, but who, probably, came from Watertown, previously. In 1800 Moses Todd purchased this store, and soon after sold it to Benham and Tuttle, who continued the store with great enterprise for a number of years. Mr. Fenn sold his hotel and farm in January, 1799, to Mark Harrison, Esquire, "for the consideration of eighteen hundred and thirty-three dollars." Mr. Dan Tuttle sold his place, containing ninety-three acres, at the south-west corner of the green, in 1797, to Moses Todd, for seven hundred and fifty pounds. This farm, Mr. Asaph Hotchkiss afterwards purchased, and resided on it some years, and gave some of it, lying west of the old bound line, for a public green. Mr. Asaph Hopkins came from East Haven to Woodtick and then to the Center, and was engaged largely in buying and selling land.

Rev. Mr. Woodward sold the Gillet place, March 4, 1799, to Charles Upson, Esquire, for five hundred and fifty pounds, and on the 26th of the same month he purchased of Mr. Bani Bishop "a certain piece of land about fifteen rods east of the Meeting house, containing about one acre of land, together with a large dwelling thereon standing, and store and horse shed near and adjoining the same," for eleven hundred and thirty dollars. In April following, he purchased of Elijah Birge thirty-five acres, with buildings, lying north of and adjoining the one acre. These buildings, including a dwelling house, stood opposite the burying ground, and was the house where a fatal accident occurred.* Mr. Woodward con-

---

* Some military officers came to the house early in the morning to "wake up" their fellow officer, and went into the house ; upon which, the resident officer arose quickly and said in a joke, "Go out of my house, or I will shoot you," he, supposing his gun was not loaded, and suiting his action to his words, fired, and the gun being loaded with a wad, the firing proved fatal in a few hours.

tinued to reside in the house east of the Meeting house until his death.

The old dwelling house now standing on the corner opposite the house Rev. Mr. Woodward resided in, was sold by Jabez Harrison, in January, 1799, to Moses Todd and Bani Bishop. Jabez Harrison was the son of Benjamin, the only brother of Deacon Aaron Harrison, and may have resided in this house a number of years. Todd and Bishop sold it to Aaron Harrison, jr., the land containing about half an acre. Mr. Harrison sold the south part, or about a quarter of an acre, to Darius Wiard, and then sold the house and lot in April, 1800, to Hezekiah Todd and Caleb Todd, who sold it in October of the same year to Matthew Wiard. In December 1801, Rev. Mr. Woodward purchased this dwelling, and the boundaries are thus designated: "a certain lot of land lying in said Wolcott, about fifteen rods Southeast of the Meeting house, and is butted North on highway, East on Lucius Tuttle, South on Darius Wiard, and West on said Town's land, containing about twenty-six rods of land, be the same more or less, with a dwelling thereon standing." This dwelling Mr. Woodward sold to Isaac Benham, of Waterbury, and Samuel Benham, of Wolcott, in 1802, the latter residing in it many years.

The house now the residence of Mrs. Johnson Alcott, was built by Darius Wiard, about the year 1800, and was the residence for a number of years afterward of Dr. John Potter. The house at the south-west corner of the Green was the residence of Mr. Daniel Tuttle for several years before 1797, and after that was the residence of Messrs. Asaph Hotchkiss, Isaac Hough, and for the last twenty years of Erastus W. Warner. I am of the opinion that the old cellar wall standing south-west of Mr. Erastus M. Warner's, near a large rock on east side of the present road, marks the place of the residence of Mr. John Barrett, the grave digger at the Center for many years.

The second house on the south side of the road going

east from the green appears, by a certain deed, to have been built by a Mr. Bishop in the summer of 1800, and it was afterward purchased by Mr. Lucius Tuttle, and possibly enlarged by him. The house next this on the east was built by Mr. Pitman Stowe, and was kept by him as a hotel for a number of years, after which Rev. Mr. Keys resided in it, and it is frequently spoken of at the present day as Mr. Keys' house. By some of the deeds it seems that there must have been a house here before the one Mr. Stowe built.

On the opposite side of the road from Mr. Keys' house, and a little east, was the residence, for some years, of Deacon Aaron Harrison. It was afterward the residence of Deacon Isaac Bronson for a number of years, and then of his son, Irad Bronson. East of the site of this house, and within a quarter of a mile of it, are remaining parts of the foundation walls of three other houses that were probably standing in 1820.

The house of Abraham Woster, in 1770, stood about three rods west of the present Meeting house; the committee who fixed the stake for the site of the first Meeting house said it was placed "a little north of Abraham Woster's house," but it must have been a little east instead of north.

THE PUBLIC GREEN.

The land given to the Ecclesiastical Society was located on the north side of the highway running east and west in front of the Meeting house, and all the Green south of this highway belongs to the town. The east part of this Green was given to the town by Charles Upson, Esq., in 1801, and is described in the deed as "a certain piece of land being and lying in said town of Wolcott, about ten rods southeast of the Meeting house, butting north on highway, east on Matthew Wiard and Darius Wiard, south on William Robinson, west on highway, or the bound line. The west part of this Green was given to the town by two individuals; the northwest corner, containing about a quarter of an acre, by Michael Harrison, in 1800, and the remaining part by Asaph Hotchkiss, in 1808.

THE MILL PLACE.

There was "Laid out to Benjamin Harrison," father of Deacon Aaron Harrison, "December 5, 1748, five acres of land in the Northeast quarter of the bounds at the Great Falls of the Mad River," on which he probably built a saw mill, for he sold the same with a saw mill on it, deeded November 19, 1751, to John Alcox and Abiel Roberts. This property, with a clothing mill then standing below and adjoining the saw mill, was purchased of John, David, and Joseph Alcox, by Abraham Norton, in 1787, and at this place was erected afterwards a grist mill, one half of which was deeded on purchase, to John Norton by John Alcox, James Alcox, Daniel and David Alcox, November 1, 1793. John Norton received by gift from his father, Abraham Norton, one fourth part of this mill property in 1791, and in 1793 a dwelling house and one acre of land. Abraham Norton removed to Litchfield, in 1796, at which time his son John purchased sixty-four acres of his land at the mill place. The year following he sold to his son John thirteen acres more, it being, probably, all he owned in that part of the town. This grist mill was owned for many years by John Norton, and known far and near by his name. There is now standing at these Great Falls only a saw mill and cider mill which are owned by Mr. Dennis Pritchard.

ATKINS' MILL.

Joseph Atkins built a grist mill on Mad River, some twenty rods below the Great Falls, about the year 1760, which he continued as the only grist mill in the parish for twenty years or more.

Mr. Atkins died in 1782, and in 1783 his son, Deacon

Joseph Atkins, sold half of this mill property to Thomas Upson, father of Charles Upson, and afterward Streat Richards owned the whole property for a number of years, deeding it in 1800 to Isaac Upson, with "about one quarter of an acre of land a few rods northeast of said mill, with a dwelling house standing on the same." Some years after this, the mill was removed to Woodtick, where it was operated as a grist mill. There is now a building known as the "old carding mill" standing on the site of Atkins' grist mill, but no work is done in it, and the indications are that it will soon go down the river. There are two mills on this river a few rods below the "old carding mill," one a saw mill, now doing yearly a large amount of work. It is said that Seth Thomas made an agreement about the year 1800 or a little after, for some mill property, owned by Daniel Byington at this mill place, proposing to engage in the manufacture of clocks, and that by some peculiar requisitions afterwards made by Mr. Byington, and because of the want of encouragement from the people of the town in constructing a road from the mill place to Cheshire so that he could reach the market conveniently with his merchandise, he gave up the project, and went to Plymouth Hollow, and entered upon the same plan there, and the result has been the establishing of that enterprising village now known as Thomaston, Connecticut.

WOODTICK.

Mr. Judah Frisbie was the first settler in Woodtick, as far as I have learned, and he purchased his first land here in the autumn of 1773, but did not reside on it until some years afterward. His account book shows that he boarded at Mr. Amos Seward's before he was married, and while, probably, he was working on his land and attending to business of various kinds (for he was a busy man). The same book shows that he was engaged in building, probably a house, in 1776. His brother-in-law, Elnathan Thrasher, was married in 1778, and probably settled on the farm now owned by Deacon Orrin Hall, the same year, where he resided until about 1800. Judah Frisbie mentions the saw mill as early as 1776, and as he sold lumber at different times and frequently from that time forward until 1790, it is probable that he owned a part or all of the mill. Abraham Norton sold one half of this saw mill in 1801 to Harvey Upson, the other half being "owned by Capt. Samuel Upson and Samuel Upson, jr."

The Atkins grist mill at the mill place was taken down (after 1800) and removed to Woodtick, and used for a grist mill for a time, and then changed into a paper mill, which has been greatly enlarged and improved by machinery, so that, at present, it is producing, yearly, a large amount of paper. It is now owned by Mr. Emerson M. Hotchkiss, late of Southington.

HOTELS.

The first hotel was that of Samuel Byington, on the west side of the Green, where he also had a wheelwright shop. Joseph Twitchell kept the same house after the year 1800, for a short time. Pitman Stowe kept a hotel a few years in the house that Rev. Mr. Keys afterwards occupied. Col. Moses Pond kept a hotel in the house previously occupied (about twenty-five years) by Mr. Lucius Tuttle. Daniel Alcox kept hotel for a time at the Center, probably in a house that stood near the corner of the roads east of the Center; one of the roads going east toward John Bronson's, the other toward Cheshire. Thomas Wiard had a hotel, but in what house I know not.

HIGHWAYS.

One hundred years before Farmingbury parish was organized, the hunters from Farmington followed the Indian trail, or path, that passed through what is now the towns of Bristol and Wolcott, to the valley of the Naugatuck and to Woodbury. After the settlement of Waterbury, this path became the traveled road between

Farmington and Waterbury, passing from Bristol over the hills in a direction a little south of west, through what is now the northwest corner of Wolcott, into the valley near the present village of Waterville, thence down the stream to Waterbury. Tradition says this road passed Mr. Levi Atkins' present dwelling, and that the Indian trail at that point passed a little further north, near a large shelving rock called "Jack's Cave."* This road continued to be, as I judge, the principal road between Farmington and Waterbury more than seventy years, until after the settlement of Spindle Hill. In 1750, nineteen years after Mr. John Alcock settled on Spindle Hill, a road was laid out from Mr. Eliakim Welton's running east of north until it reached the road above described, then east to the Farmington line at the Scarritt place,† it being a continuance of the road from Waterbury to Buck's Hill. We learn from the records that in 1754 another road was laid out from Waterbury to "Farmington bounds." This came up the Mad River, passing Mr. Isaac Hopkin's dwelling, the Abel Curtiss place, the mill place south of the great falls, thence east through land now inclosed in the Center burying ground, to the bound line, thence north on that line to the Scarritt place. This road was called the East Farmington road, the one passing Mr. Alcox's being the west.

When Mr. Thomas Upson settled on Southington Mountain there was probably no road from Waterbury to Southington, except a path for persons on foot and on horseback. The old "twenty rod highway" was the first laid out highway near his farm, as far as ascertained, and began south of Mr. Upson's dwelling (I know not how far), going north past Capt. Nathaniel Lewis' and David

---

* The Indians encamped under this rock nights in passing between Farmington and Woodbury. It was near this cave that the large chestnut tree stood from which Mr. Timothy Bradley said he cut two hundred bullets, which were shot into the tree by the Indians while shooting at a mark.

† See Waterbury Records.

Frost's dwelling, thence east across the brook to the present burying ground, thence north on the mountain to the northern boundary of present Wolcott, at least, but more probably to New Cambridge, now Bristol. The deeds recorded in Farmington that I have seen mention this twenty rod highway as far north as the "tenth long lot," making it certain that the road continued north as far as the first of the long lots at least. The date when the road was laid out I have not seen, but it was there twenty rods wide in 1750.

A few years after the incorporation of the town, there was considerable effort made by individuals and by the town, in town meetings, to secure a turnpike through the town from Torrington to New Haven. The town appointed committees at different times to meet other committees of the Legislature, to forward this object, and the town did considerable work on the road, but the project did not succeed.

About the time (near 1812-15) the New Haven turnpike was given up, the road on the southern boundary of the town running from Waterbury to Marion was made a turnpike, a large part of the stock being owned by the Upson families of Wolcott.

CHAPTER III.

PUBLIC SCHOOLS.

As early as 1763 the people of Farmingbury winter parish had their own schools and were exempted from paying tax for schools outside of the parish, and this privilege was granted them until the parish was organized. At the first Society meeting, in Nov., 1770, a committee of six was appointed to divide the Society into Districts, and that committee made report to the adjourned meeting in the same month, which report was accepted by the Society, but what the report was is not stated in the records, and hence the difficulty of ascertaining how many Districts were established. There are, however indications that from the first, and for several years afterwards, there were nine districts, for they appointed nine men as committeemen, and passed the following vote : " Each school committee shall collect their poll rate, each one in his district." The words "each one in his district," are quite definite information that one man only was appointed to a district. The names of the several committees indicate where these districts were located. Joseph Sutliff, jr., for the Southwest district ; Joseph Atkins for the one at the Mill place, for which district no name has been seen ; John Alcox for the West district ; Capt. Aaron Harrison at the Center; Jedediah Minor for the East district, near John Bronson's ; Nathaniel Lewis for the Southeast district ; Amos Seward for the South district ; Simeon Plumb for the North district, and Daniel Finch for the Northeast district. All these districts are mentioned by name as given above except the one at the Mill place, or at Daniel Byington's. It is probable that the schools in some of these districts were kept in private houses, and perhaps most of them at first, but when school houses were erected the Southeast district and the one at the Mill place were discontinued, as we learn of no school-house sites in these parts of the town. The East district continued many years; the school-house standing at the corner of the roads a litle east of Mr. Mark Tuttle's present dwelling house. This was the house in which Mr. David Harrison taught school much of the time for many years. The other districts, six in number, still continue.

EXPENSES OF THE SCHOOLS.

The expenses were paid "by the poll," that is, parents paid for their children, for each in proportion to the whole number of pupils and the number of days in attendance. Under this system it was often quite difficult for some parents to pay their school bills, and because of this many children were educated very little. Until the town was organized, the number of months the schools should be kept was decided by parish vote, and usually was voted to be according to law, but sometimes the vote was to "keep eleven months school." Wages were, for a man, from six to ten dollars a month, for a woman one dollar a week, and a school bill of eighty-eight dollars for the year was a great amount to be paid by the district, and was in reality a much greater burden then than any tax for schooling at the present time.

It is a matter of great congratulation to the people of this town that nearly three-fourths of the expenses of the schools are now paid by receipts other than taxes on the property of the town. The fund of $8,500 left to this town by the late Addin Lewis, of New Haven, a native of Wolcott, is of very great value in sustaining the schools. The income from this fund amounts to five hundred dollars per year, and with the fidelity continued that has characterized its administration hitherto, it will be hereafter a benefit incalculably great. That part of the will of Mr. Lewis which relates to Wolcott is given.

THE WILL OF ADDIN LEWIS AS IT RELATES TO THE TOWN OF WOLCOTT.

Section 8. If my said daughter shall die without disposing by her will of the estate mentioned in the foregoing article, I do give, devise, and bequeath all said estate (so not disposed of by her) to her lineal descendants who shall be living at the time of her death, in the same manner and proportions as the same would have descended and been distributed to them if she had owned the same as her own proper estate, and had died intestate and solvent; and if there should be no lineal descendants of my said daughter living at the time of her death, I give, devise, and bequeath ten thousand dollars of said estate to the School Society of the town of Wolcott, in Connecticut, for the purposes hereinafter expressed; and fifteen thousand dollars of said estate to the School Society of the town of Southington, in Connecticut, for the purposes hereinafter expressed; and five thousand dollars of said estate to " The President and Fellows of Yale College, in New Haven," for the purposes hereinafter expressed; and the balance of said estate shall go to increase proportionally the devises and legacies given in the following articles of this will.

And as to the said ten thousand dollars given as aforesaid to the School Society of the town of Wolcott, I direct that said Society shall hold the same as a permanent fund for the encouragement of the district schools in said town, and said Society shall annually pay the net income of said fund to the different school districts in said town in proportion to the number of children as ascertained by law; but every school district shall raise and expend for the support of district schools in such district during the year a sum equal to the sum to be paid to such district from the income of this fund, otherwise such district shall not for such year receive any part of said income, but the proportion of such district shall go to increase proportionally the sums to be paid for such year to the other districts as aforesaid; and if all the school districts in the said town of Wolcott shall neglect for any year to comply with the conditions aforesaid, then the whole of the net income of said fund for such year shall be paid to the different school districts in the town of Southington for the purposes and on the conditions aforesaid; and if all the school districts in the town of Southington shall neglect for any year to comply with the conditions aforesaid, then the whole of the net income of said fund for such year shall go to increase proportionally the devises and legacies given in the following articles of this will:

And whenever any persons or corporation shall have in their hands money to be invested in execution of any part of this will, I do expressly direct that said money shall in all cases be invested in mortgage security of unencumbered real estate of double the value of the amount of the loan secured thereon; and all loans may be varied from time to time on similar security.

In regard to the Southington Academy, for the erection and maintaining of which Mr. Lewis gave fifteen thousand dollars, he made this provision: "And all pupils from the town of Wolcott, not exceeding ten at any one time, who may wish to receive instruction in said institution, shall receive the same without any charge for tuition."

The income from this Lewis Fund of Wolcott, was five hundred dollars for the year 1873. In the same year were received from the School Fund and State appropriation two hundred and twenty dollars; from the Town Deposit Fund, one hundred and thirty dollars; in all eight hundred and fifty dollars. The actual expenses of all the schools for the same year were about twelve hundred dollars.

THE WHIPPING POST.

The whipping post stood east of the present Meeting house at the Center, near the southeast corner of the present horse sheds. Besides the three persons mentioned below, it is said, there were one man and a colored woman whipped at this post for stealing.

About the year 1815, Dr. George Williams (so he titled

himself), traveling through Wolcott, stayed over night at the house of Mark Upson, where he stole a shawl, and for which after trial, the court ordered seven lashes on the bare back. His hands were tied to the post a little higher than his head, and Capt. Levi Hall, constable, struck three blows when the lash came off, when some one said to the constable, "I am afraid the old man will not stand the blows quite so hard." The remaining blows were given lighter, the old man trembling greatly under the punishment. He was then taken to the store and his back washed with rum, upon which the old man said: "O my God, that is worse than the stripes, I think I will have a little inside," which was not denied him.

Pond and Granniss were convicted of stealing a cow about the year 1817, for which, after trial, the court ordered seven lashes each. Their hands were tied as in the case of Williams, and Levi Parker, constable, laid the blows on Granniss with considerable severity, he remaining stubborn and making no complaint. Pond was very penitent, and while they were tying his hands to the post he prayed God to have mercy on him, the tears falling from the eyes of many who witnessed the unpleasant scene. The blows were given lightly, and while putting on his coat, Pond said: "It is just that it was done." It is thought that this was the last whipping done at the whipping post in the town.

LAW IN WOLCOTT.

Besides the above described whipping I have heard of no criminal proceedings in the courts of the town, nor in the county, concerning the inhabitants of Wolcott, of any special importance, except that which was instituted in regard to the burning of the first Meeting house. There were some old " stocks" for fastening the feet of criminals, laid up many years in the horse sheds which stood west of the Meeting house, but no one remembers to have heard of any use to which they were ever put except to look at. The real facts I apprehend to have been these: There have existed in natural character and disposition of the people too much musical talent and good nature to allow disturbances of any serious kind to obtain a place of recognition among the people, and therefore they have worked hard, given much time and attention to singing, played the fife and drum, encouraged cheerfulness by pleasant associations, kept out of mischief, out of gaol, and off the gallows, and given as earnest adherence to religion as the average of country towns.

SMALL POX.

This disease was a great terror to the people and had made sad desolation in several families in the town before the year 1800. The following record indicates the conservatism of the people of those days in regard to the introduction of any new practice in medicine.

"At a special Town meeting held in Wolcott on the 27th day of October, 1800, Dr. John Potter prayed for liberty to set up or introduce the small pox by inocculation, into said town under the care, superintendence, and direction of the civil authority and selectmen of said town for the time being, or their successors in office, until said civil authority and selectmen, or the town at large by vote in legal meeting assembled, shall discontinue or suspend said liberty at the same meeting.

Voted to grant the prayer of the above petition, two-thirds of the members [voters] present being in the affirmative."

BURYING GROUNDS—THE CENTER BURYING GROUND.

In the Waterbury town records we learn the following action was taken in a town meeting held on December 10th, 1764: "At the same meeting Capt. George Nichols, and Capt. Stephen Upson, jr., were chosen a committee to go out eastward near Joseph Atkins', to view and purchase half an acre of land, upon the town cost, in that neighborhood where they shall think it most convenient for a burying ground."*

The earliest record on monuments is that of Lieut. Heman Hall, bearing date 1769.

In the Wolcott town records are found the following entries :

December 11, 1797. Voted that Messrs. Mark Harrison, Charles Upson, Streat Richards, and Moses Todd, be a committee to confer with William Stevens to investigate and search into the circumstances of the Center Burying Ground, to see if it is the property of said Stevens, as is by him asserted, and also to settle and compromise the matter with said Stevens if it appears to be his property, by exchanging a certain quantum of highway now in the enclosure of said Stevens therefor, and also to draw upon the treasurer for a small sum in order to enlarge said burying ground to three-fourths of an acre; provided they think proper, and cannot obtain it without.

On the 9th day of April next the town meeting appointed another committee "to negotiate with William Stevens concerning the Center Burying Ground, to enlarge the same to three-fourths of an acre, to exchange the highway now enclosed in said Stevens' lot as part payment, etc., and make report of their doings at the annual meeting in December next." At the annual meeting in next December the report of the committee was accepted, and the selectmen were authorized to attend to the execution of the deeds.

The three-quarters of an acre became too small, and about 1870 the ground was again enlarged, so as to include nearly two acres.

---

* Mr. Bronson, in the History of Waterbury, page 229, in a note, makes a mistake in supposing this ground to be the one at East Farms, for it was to be "near Joseph Atkins'," and he never resided at East Farms. Besides, the East Farms ground was laid out since the memory of some persons now living. He says this burying ground, near Atkins', was on Farmington road, which was true ; but Farmington road, instead of going direct to Southington, turned up Mad River, and through New Cambridge to Farmington.

PIKE'S HILL BURYING GROUND.

This ground was laid out about 1774, by a committee of the Society appointed to "fix a place or places for burying grounds." The ground is located on the north declivity of the hill adjoining the Alcox road, in a most picturesque place. Here but few graves were made, some of which were afterwards removed to the ground east at the foot of the same hill, about fifteen yet remaining. Graves continued to be made in this ground until 1805, when the one east was constructed, and all burying ceased in the old yard, it having been used but thirty years. Some five or six monuments remain having inscriptions on them; the other graves are indicated by small field stones. The inscriptions below are given precisely as they are written on the head stones:

In Memory of Mrs.
RACHEL BRACKITT, who
Died October ye 17th, 1776, in
Y^E 22D YEAR OF HER AGE.

While you are blooming young and spry
Perhaps you think you ne'er shall die;
But here's a witness of the truth,
That you may die when in your youth.

Here Lieth Interred
THE BODY OF MR.
MATHEW BLAKSLEE.
HE DEPARTED THIS
LIFE MAY Y^E 28, A. D.
1776, in ye 61st year
of his age.

In Memory of
THE WIDOW RHODA
BLAKSLEE, THE WIFE OF
MR. MATHEW BLAKSLEE.
SHE DEPARTED THIS
LIFE MARCH 12TH, A. D.
1781, in the 63rd year
of her age.

The foregoing inscriptions are on brown stone. The following are on blue stone:

In Memory of
MR. ABNER BLAKS-
LY. HE DIED NOV.
27th, A. D., 1791, In
the 51 year of
his age.

Ithamer,
SON TO
JESSE and PATIENCE ALCOX,
Died Aug. 9th, 1778,
Æ. 3 ys.

Lyman,
SON TO
JESSE and PATIENCE ALCOX,
Died Nov. 17th, 1781,
Æ. 16.

The foregoing are all the inscriptions that remain in the old ground.

THE NEW NORTHEAST BURYING GROUND.

At a Town meeting held April 8, 1805, the meeting voted, "That the selectmen be authorized to purchase at the expense of the town such quantity of land and in such place as they in their discretion think proper and best, to be appropriated as a burying ground in the northeast quarter of the town ; and that one rod in width be taken from the south side of the highway running east and west by the proposed burying ground the whole length of said ground and appropriated as a part thereof."

This new ground is on a gravel knoll at the foot of the hill east of the old ground, and is the one now in use as the northeast burying ground.

THE SOUTHEAST BURYING GROUND.

In March, 1772, the Society appointed a committee to "fix a place or places for burying grounds," and in 1776 it appointed three grave diggers, which indicates the existence of three graveyards, and their location defined by the residence of the three men — Mr. John Barrett at the Center, where he had filled the same office several previous years ; Mr. Zadoc Bronson at the northeast, and Mr. David Frost at the southeast. The earliest inscription on any monument in the Pike's Hill yard is dated May 28, 1776 ; the earliest date in the southeast yard is January 1, 1782, and is the grave of Archibald Upson, who died with small-pox.

THE SOUTHWEST BURYING GROUND.

At a Town meeting held Nov. 20, 1807, the meeting voted, "That Isaac Bronson, Mark Harrison, and Isaac Upson be a committee to view the circumstances of the southwest part of the town, and if they judge proper, lay out and purchase a burying ground in such place as they judge most convenient, and that the committee be authorized to draw on the town treasurer for payment of the sum which they shall agree to give for said ground, and take a deed thereof to the town." This is the present Woodtick burying ground.

THE YANKEE PEDDLERS.

The Yankee peddler has been a celebrated character in the Middle and Southern States more than in the Eastern, yet the origin of this kind of merchant was in the New England States, particularly in Connecticut. Wolcott raised from thirty to forty men who engaged at different times quite largely in this business, traveling through all the Middle States, and most of the Southern during the years from 1810 to 1840. Among the first who went out were Samuel Horton, Timothy Hotchkiss, Lyman Higgins, and Chester Hotchkiss. These sold "tin ware and Yankee notions;" beginning about 1810 and continuing for a number of years in the employment of a firm in Southington, and traveling mostly in Virginia, North Carolina, and South Carolina.

When Mr. Eli Terry,* then of Plymouth, completed in the year 1810, the first great contract of four thousand clocks, for a Waterbury company, the Yankee peddler was wanted to sell these clocks, and Wolcott not only furnished an important man, in the person of Seth Thomas to make these clocks, but also men to sell them. Mr. Terry's shop was on Hancock River, at a place known since as Hoadleyville, being about a mile west of the boundary of Wolcott. The cords for these clocks were spun by Wolcott women from flax raised in Wolcott, and much of the inside woodwork of these clocks was made of Wolcott "ivy" or "laurel," of which there is still an abundance. For many years this work occupied the attention of Wolcott people, and furnished them extra work in winter and some additional comforts of life. For

---

* See History of "American Clock Making" by Henry Terry, of Waterbury; and also the Biography of Mr. Seth Thomas, in this book.

a few years the clock peddling was confined mostly to the New England and Middle states, and was a different work from the selling of Yankee notions. The clocks were sold on "trial," the agent calling for the money six or more months after the delivery of the clocks, but the regular Yankee peddler sold for cash, if (as we have often heard him announce), he sold "two shillings worth for a six pence," at which ruinous prices his wife and babies certainly would starve.

About 1820 the spirit of enterprise called out a new and more numerous company of young men in the work of selling tin ware and Yankee notions, in the Southern States. Among these were Ephraim Hall, Seth Horton, Holt Hotchkiss, A. Bronson Alcott, Thomas Alcott, Jason Hotchkiss, Leverette Kenea, William Cowles, Levi Frisbie, and many others. Some went out with a horse and peddler's wagon, selling tin ware, razors, pins, needles, patent medicines, peppermint essence, suspenders, and a large number of such like things, called "Yankee notions;" others sold dry goods only, carrying them in two large trunks made for that purpose. Some of these men went in this employment one or two winters, while others continued until near the time of the late rebellion. Mr. Thomas Alcott was one of these, but the articles which he sold in later years consisted of carriages of various kinds, which he sold frequently on time, and hence lost considerable money by the war. The effect of this work on the young men, was to introduce them into mercantile life, which many of them continued, in one form or another, in different parts of the country, most of them making their homes and establishing themselves in business elsewhere, rather than in Wolcott.

TAXES.

The grand list was in 1860, $291,827; in 1865, $297,891; in 1870, $248,677; in 1871, $243,640; in 1872, $236,545; in 1873, $241,100. The tax collected in 1872 was eleven

TAX ASSESSMENT.

mills on the dollar, and that for 1873 is ten mills. The decrease of the grand list, as appears above, is mostly in consequence of the decrease of cattle and money at interest, considerable money having been placed in United States bonds, and other untaxable property.

The following is a town rate made on the list of 1789, of two pence half-penny on the pound, on the inhabitants of Farmingbury, in Waterbury.*

	s.	d.		s.	d.
John Alcox,	12	10	John Frisbie,	3	9½
James Alcox,	13	9	Gehulah Grilley,	1	7
David Alcox,	9	11	Cyrus Grilley,	4	8½
Solomon Alcox,	7	11½	Isaac Hopkins,	14	0
Samuel Alcox,	8	10	Wait Hotchkiss,	8	2½
John B. Alcox,	6	8	Simeon Hopkins,	10	5½
Daniel Alcox (Southington).	0	2	Joel Hotchkiss,	2	5½
Sarah Atkins,		9½	Daniel Johnson,	1	2½
Joseph Atkins,	3	4½	John Kenea,	4	2½
Samuel Bartholomew,	9	10	Daniel Lane,	1	10½
Samuel Byington,	19	3	Nathaniel Lane,	5	0½
Warner Barnes,	6	6½	Asahel Lane,	5	5
Isaac Blakeslee (N. Haven),	1	1½	Joseph Mallery,	4	9
Amos Beecher,	0	10	Jedediah Minor,	0	9
Ezekiel Barnes,	1	6½	Joseph Minor (Southington),	0	11
Josiah Barnes,	4	9½	Caleb Minor,	6	1½
Abel Baldwin (Watertown),	0	6½	Abraham Norton,	17	0
Daniel Byington,	10	5	Ozias Norton,	7	8
Jonah Byington,	3	9	Noah U. Norton,	7	1½
David Beckwith,	3	7½	Ruth Norton,	0	8½
Thaddeus Barnes,	0	1½	Joseph Noyce (Stratford),	5	1
Moses Byington,	4	0½	Joseph M. Parker,	1	4
Sturges Burr (N. Haven),	0	7	Streat Richards,	11	2
Abel Curtiss,	8	4½	Timothy Scott,	1	4
Joseph Curtiss (Stratford),	0	7½	William Stephens,	0	3½
Jonathan Carter,	0	7½	Ephraim Smith,	4	3½
Daniel Dean,	5	8½	Ephraim Smith, jr.,	8	9
Elijah Frisbie,	4	0	Joseph Sutliff,	4	4
Judah Frisbie,	9	1	Joseph Sutliff, jr.,	5	9
Charles Frisbie,	7	9	Nathan Stephens,	8	9½

---

* The original copy of this paper is in the possession of Mr. Silas B. Terry, of Waterbury, and was brought to light at the Centenary meeting.

	s.	d.		s.	d
Nathaniel Sutliff,	12	5½	Samuel Upson,	14	7
Amos Seward,	7	10	Ashbel Upson,	6	0
Justus Scott,	4	10½	Ezekiel Upson,	2	10
Josiah Talmage,	5	9	Charles Upson,	10	8½
John Talmage,	2	5	Eliakim Welton,	3	7
Jacob Talmage,	5	11½	Eliakim Welton, jr.	10	6½
Moses Todd (N. Haven),	0	5½	Benjamin Welton,	7	1
Joseph Twitchell,	4	6	Thomas Welton,	9	8
Elnathan Thrasher.	6	5	David Wakelee.	7	4
James Thomas,	10	8½	Eliakim Welton, 3d,	5	4½
Amos Upson (Southington),	0	7	Eben Welton,	6	2½
Josiah Upson, do	0	3	Philemon Wilcox,	4	1½

The sum total is found to be, errors excepted, £24 7 9½

The foregoing rate, made this 9th day of February, 1790, by us.

      EZRA BRONSON,
      SAMUEL JUDD,
      EPHRAIM WARNER,
      SIMEON HOPKINS,
      EBENEZER HOADLEY,
        Selectmen of Waterbury.

The order of the court to collect was made to Capt. Charles Upson, collector of the town rate in the town of Waterbury, in New Haven county, and signed by "Ezra Bronson, Justice Peace."

CHAPTER IV.

ROLL OF HONOR.

The following lists are believed to be complete, except that of the Revolutionary soldiers, which, probably, contains about two-thirds of those who were engaged in that war :

LIST OF FREEMEN IN THE TOWN OF WOLCOTT.

September, 1800 — Isaac Hopkins, Joseph Beecher, Joseph Smith, Aaron Harrison, David Norton, Joseph Sutliff, Rev. Israel B. Woodward, Ebenezer Johnson, Abel Curtiss, Jeremiah Scarritt, Nathaniel Sutliff, Moses Pond, Streat Richards, Mark Harrison, Charles Upson, Elisha Horton, Jacob Carter, Stephen Carter, Thomas Upson, Walter Beecher, Charles Frisbie, John Potter, David Harrison, Joseph M. Parker, Farrington Barnes, Daniel Johnson, Moses Todd, William Stephens, John Frisbie, Wait Hotchkiss, Preserve Carter, Samuel Upson, jr., Amos Upson, Mark Barnes, Joseph Beecher, jr., John Bronson, Elijah Perkins, Samuel Clinton, James Bailey, Philemon Wilcox, Philo Thomas, Isaac Bronson, Gideon Finch, Titus Sutliff, David Pardee, John Sutliff, Harvey Upson, David Frost, Darius Wiard, Jacob Talmage, Daniel Deane, Richmond Hall, Abner Hotchkiss, Nathaniel Lewis, Justus Peck, Calvin Cowles, Judah Frisbie, Simeon Plumb, Amos Brockett, Joseph Minor, Samuel Horton, Isaac Upson, Abel Beecher, David Wakelee, Joel Hotchkiss, Zephana Parker, Nathaniel Lane, John Norton, Jared Welton, Benoni Gillet, Zuar Brockett, Aaron Wiard, John J. Kenea, Eliakim Welton, Jesse Alcox, Joseph Twitchell, Justus Scott, Nathan Barnes, Bani Bishop, David Alcox, Ashbel Upson, John Hitchcock, Enos Beecher, Luther Atkins, Nathan Scarritt, John Clark, Samuel

Plumb, Solomon Plumb, Jesse Alcox, jr., Solomon Alcox, Heman Hall, David Talmage, Jesse Pardee, James Scarritt, Moses Byington, Timothy Bradley, Selah Steadman, Washington Upson, Michael Harrison, James Alcox, jr., Seymour Welton, Williams Bailey, Amos Baldwin, Philenor Bronson, Appleton Lewis, Samuel Horton, jr., Reuben Lewis, Levi Johnson, Truman Woodward, Abijah Fenn, Cyrus Clark, Josiah B. Morse, John B. Alcox, Mark Alcox, Joseph C. Alcox, Royce Lewis, Joseph Sutliff, jr., Michael Sutliff, Aaron Harrison, jr., Andrew Jerome, Lee Upson, Elijah Royce.

April, 1801 — Nathan Johnson, Shubael Upson, John Thomas, Luther Hotchkiss, James J. Truesdel, Levi Atkins, Joseph Plumb, Amasa Bradley. September, 1801 — Elijah Rowe, Nathaniel Sutliff, jr., Lucius Tuttle.

April, 1802 — Joel Alcox, Ebenezer Beecher, John Bronson, jr., Ashbel Atkins, John Dean. September, 1802 — Gates Upson, Thomas Wiard, Caleb Minor, Joshua Minor, Mark Welton, Gideon Finch, jr., Moses Bradley, Manly Upson, David Alcox, jr., Obed Alcox.

April, 1803 — Josiah Thomas, Silas Weed, Elijah Lane, Isaac Downes, Ransom Frisbie, Timothy Hotchkiss. September, 1803 — John Wiard, Stephen Carter, jr., Truman Smith, David Bailey, Rollin Harrison, Ephraim Smith, jr., Eleazer Finch, Marvin Beckwith.

April, 1804 — Jesse Silkriggs, Richard O. Hopkins, Elihu Moulthrop, Josiah Lane, Elias Welton, Gamaliel Plumb, Nathan Sutliff, Miles H. Richards, Leonard Harrison, David Scarritt, Prince Duplex. September, 1804 — Levi Hall, Miles Hotchkiss, Abiathar Sutliff, Joseph Welton, Jesse Dutton, Aaron Wiard.

April, 1805 — Moses Welton, Eldad Alcox. September, 1805 — Amos Parsons, Adonijah Moulthrop, Archibald Minor, David Frisbie, Amasa Mix, Titus Brockett, Asahel Bradley, Solomon Wiard, Levi Brown, Truman Sandford, James Bartholomew, Harvey Hopkins.

April 1806 — Silas Hine, Seth Thomas, William Hotchkiss. September, 1806 — David Churchill, Lester Scarritt, David M. Beach.

April, 1807 — Zephana Potter, Thomas Upson, Loammi Carter,.

LIST OF FREEMEN.

Luther A. Richards, Jared Harrison. September, 1807 — Isaac Curtiss, Sylvester Beecher, Isaac Frisbie, Asahel Brockitt, Joseph Minor, jr.

April, 1808 — Orrin Rice, Ira Hough, Nathaniel Barnes, Nathaniel G. Lewis, Bildad Hotchkiss, Aaron Pond, Clark Bronson. September, 1808 — Eldad Parker, Miles Harrison, Daniel Byington, jr., John Curtiss, Asa Granniss.

April, 1809 — Lyman Higgins. September, 1809 — Irad Bronson, Aaron Harrison, jr., Justus L. Peck.

April, 1810 — Archibald Barnes. September, 1810 — William Bartholomew, Samuel Bartholomew, Allen Upson.

April, 1811 — Jairus Alcox. September, 1811 — Uri Carter, Elisha M. Pomeroy, David S. Grillee.

April, 1812 — Mark Upson, Alpheus Pond. September, 1812 — William Parker, Irad Wakelee, Orrin Plumb, Amon Bradley.

April, 1813 — Orrin Jackson, Ziba Norton, Levi Parker. September, 1813 — Simeon N. Norton.

April, 1814 — Hezekiah Bradley, Aaron Finch, Thomas Horton. September, 1814 — Reuben Carter.

April, 1815 — Stephen Harrison. September, 1815 — Bartholomew Curtiss, Ransel Brockitt.

April, 1816 — Jerry Todd, Streat Todd, David R. Upson, Levi B. Frost, Abel Truesdell, Thomas H. Welton. September, 1816 — Eben S. Bartholomew, Seth Horton, Marvin Minor, Harpin Hotchkiss, Marcus Minor.

April, 1817 — Rev. John Keys, Sheldon Frisbie, Jeremiah Sperry. September, 1817 — Alpheus Bradley, Green Perkins, Harvey Norton, Miles Loveland, Willard Plumb.

April, 1818 — Asahel Lewis, Irad Harrison. July, 1818 — Bela Rose, Samuel Merriman, Milo G. Hotchkiss, Luther Roper, Leveret Kinnea, Jedediah G. Alcox. September, 1818 — Chauncey Royce, Almond Alcox, John Beecher, jr., William Smith, James Frisbie, Joseph P. Sandford, Anson G. Lane, Osmon Norton.

April, 1819 — Luther W. Plumb, Bazilla Bradley, John A. Potter, Salmon Johnson.

April, 1820 — Amos Bradley, Orrin Hall, Samuel W. Upson, William A. Alcox, William P. Tuttle.

April, 1821 — Leonard Horton, Marcus H. Upson, Wells Plumb, Leonard Beecher, John S. Atkins, Jesse Barnes.

April, 1822 — Osee Talmage, Robert A. Hickox, Cyrus C. Upson, Albert R. Potter, Shelden Welton, Garry Atkins, Chester Andrews.

April, 1823 — Jonathan Bement, Jerry Upson, William Munson, Almus Wakelee, Fitch A. Higgins, Anson Upson, Timothy Bradley, 2d, Jonas Hickox.

April, 1824 — Edward Lewis, Jacob Talmage, jr.

April, 1825 — Amos B. Alcox, Abraham Norton, Asaph Hotchkiss, Lucius Alcox, Ira Frisbie.

April, 1826 — Mark Tuttle, Ansel H. Plumb, William R. Bradley, Marshall Upson, James Bailey, jr.

April, 1827 — Ephraim Hall, John A. Bradley, Lucius Tuttle, jr.

April, 1828 — Ard Welton, George G. Alcox, Luther Bailey.

April, 1829 — Martin Upson, Wyllis Merrils, Prosper Hull, Erastus Nichols, Erastus Atkins.

April, 1830 — George Griswold, Hezekiah T. Upson, David Beecher, Harley Downs, Alben Alcox, Jesse L. Nichols, Albert Boardman, Orrin Byington, Asa Boardman, Alfred Lewis.

April, 1831 — David Bailey, Addison Alcox, Alfred Churchill, Loman Upson, Orestus Welton, Ezra L. Todd, Henry Minor, Marcus Upson, Northrop Jackson, Kneeland S. Hall, Charles H. Upson, Salmon Upson, James Alcox, jr.

April, 1832 — Jarvis B. Bronson, David Scarritt, jr., Russel Rowe, Levi Moulthrop, Shelden Smith, Isaac Alcox, William Blakeslee, Russel Upson.

April, 1833 — Abraham Tuttle, Rollin Tuttle, Lloyd Lewis, Thomas J. Lewis, Anson H. Smith, Joel Alcox, Sylvester Frost, Henry Harrison, Selah Upson, Henry D. Upson.

April, 1834 — Chester Hotchkiss, Stillman Bronson, Matthew S. Norton, Ives Lewis, Geo. W. Carter, Geo. Mansfield, Edward Welton, Selim Doolittle, Eri Welton, Chauncey Woodbridge.

April, 1835 — Johnson Alcox, Thomas Alcox, Sylvester Bradley, Isaac Hough, Levi Atkins, jr., Simeon H. Norton, Daniel T. Todd, Lucian E. Hickox, Levant D. Johnson, George Plumb, Martin L. Andrews, Thomas Upson, jr., Jeremiah S. Plumb, Henry Beecher, Newel Minor, Dennis Lewis.

LIST OF FREEMEN.

April, 1836 — Lucien Upson, Sherman Moulthrop, William Johnson, Ezra S. Hough, Seth Wiard, Upson Higgins, David B. Frisbie, Romeo Upson, Timothy N. Upson.

April, 1837 — Lewis Churchill, Ransom S. Todd, Harvey Thomas, Elihu Moulthrop, jr.

April, 1838 — Stiles L. Hotchkiss, Hendrick Norton, Lucius Upson.

April, 1839 — Edward W. Thomas, Rollin Harrison, Levi Frisbie, Lucius B. Welton, James Scarritt.

April, 1840 — Joel Brown, by certificate; Ira H. Hough, Isaac Hotchkiss, Harvey G. Plumb, John Hummiston, Jason Hotchkiss, Moses Pond, Charles Byington, Rufus Norton, Isaac Pardee; Elias Mix, by certificate; Dagget Barnes, by certificate. November, 1840 — Hezekiah Brown, by certificate; Mahlon Hotchkiss; Miles B. Ford, by certificate; David Warner, by certificate; Lewis Johnson, by certificate; Lynde Preston, by certificate; Merritt Welton, by certificate; Philip A. Cowles, by certificate; Algernon Newcomb, by certificate; Rufus Hotchkiss, by certificate; Sellock J. Nichols, by certificate.

March, 1841 — Charles Rose, Daniel Holt; Lucius Tuttle, by certificate; Harrison Welton. April, 1841 — Henry G. Hotchkiss, by certificate; Frederick J. Bunnell.

March, 1842 — Samuel Downs, by certificate. April, 1842 — Augustus Minor, Miles S. Upson, Eli Alcott, Asaph H. Upson; Francis Wood, by certificate; James Seeley, by certificate.

March, 1843 — John Dorman. April, 1843 — William Wiard, Andrew J. Plumb, Benjamin F. Finch; Julius A. Sandford, by certificate; Ambrose I. Downs, by certificate; Asahel Lane, by certificate. October, 1843 — Jabez Hard, by certificate.

April, 1844 — Joel W. Upson, Hezekiah Todd; Willis Upson, by certificate; Charles Kirk, by certificate; William Welton, by certificate; Norris Clark, by certificate; Elias Brooks, by certificate. October, 1844 — David F. Welton, Robert C. Todd, George C. Nichols, Samuel Nichols; Lucius Tuttle, by certificate; David Nichols, by certificate; Levi Norton, by certificate; Albert W. Hubbard, by certificate.

March, 1845 — Richard Mansfield, Noble Baldwin; Joseph Guernsey, by certificate; Algernon S. Plumb, by certificate; Hermon Woodin, by certificate.

April, 1846 — Uriah S. Tompkins, by certificate; Alva Andrews, by certificate; Levi Barnes, by certificate; Isaac Bates, Leroy O. Phillips, John H. Holt, Marshall Minor, Herrick Payne, by certificate; Isaac B. Baxter, by certificate; Cyrus Barnes, by certificate; Heman W. Hall, Cyrus Beach.

March, 1847 — John L. Beach, James M. Scarritt, Samuel Butler, Robert Hoadley, John Welton, John M. Beecher, Orlando Plumb, Chauncey P. Welton, David A. Sandford. April, 1847 — Orrin F. Hotchkiss, Luther M. Pond, William B. Barnes; Daniel Lane, by certificate; Edward J. Hall; Charles Dean, by certificate; Linus Barber, by certificate; Bennett Upson, by certificate; Bennett J. Wakelee.

November, 1848 — James L. Kenea, Samuel Brooks, Willis Bunnell; William Henry, by certificate; Nelson Thorp, by certificate.

April, 1849 — Noah H. Byington, Peter Brockett, Jesse Brockett.

April, 1850 — Sherman E. Welton, Asahel Brockett, Henry Todd, Charles A. Welton; Ira H. Smith, by certificate; Joel Johnson, by certificate; David F. Johnson, by certificate; Smith B. Pritchard, by certificate; Friend C. Eggleston.

April, 1851 — Asahel Brockett, by certificate; Stephen L. Norton, by certificate; Amos Brockett, by certificate; George W. Royce, by certificate; Asa Farrel, by certificate; Zadoc B. Bassett, by certificate; Willis Jerome, John L. Bradley.

April, 1852 — Lyman G. Bradley, by certificate; William Peckham, by certificate; George W. Winchell, Richard A. Lane, Charles W. Beach. October, 1852 — Sheldon B. Welton, Charles Allen, Albert N. Lane, Chester A. Andrews. November, 1852 — Erastus W. Warner, by certificate; David S. Smith, by certificate; Silas Pardee, by certificate; Merrit Beach, by certificate; Joseph H. Hull, by certificate; William C. Pluymut, by certificate; Bunville A. Bradley, Henry Lum, David H. Frost, Linus Thorp, Martin L. Hine.

April, 1853 — Dwight L. Kenea, by certificate; Daniel Riggs, by certificate; John Hurd.

April, 1854 — Andrew J. Slater, Orimel S. Webber, Albert P. Hitchcock, Samuel E. Davis, Erastus Todd, Roswell Pardee, Jeremiah S. Thomas, by certificate; Horace P. Leonard, by certificate; Liberty C. Palmer, Luther W. Plumb. October, 1854 — Samuel M. Tuttle; Hiram Chipman, by certificate.

April, 1855 — Frederick C. Slade, George F. Gates, Moses Bradley, Henry C. Walker, Ezra A. Pierpont, Burritt W. Beecher, Frederick L. Nichols, Samuel N. Sperry, Wallace H. Lee, Abiram S. Atwood, Aaron C. Beach, by certificate; Samuel M. Bailey, by certificate; Benjamin P. Downs, David H. Nichols, by certificate; Luther Higgins, William Waldon, by certificate.

April, 1856 — Darius Hummaston, Hiram Welton, William McNeil, by certificate; Shelton T. Hitchcock, by certificate; Wheaton S. Plumb, by certificate. October, 1856 — George L. Marks. November, 1856 — James B. Norton, Martin V. B. Hotchkiss, Frederick M. Upson, Lucien S. White, Henry A. Johnson, Horace R. Roberts, by certificate; Edwin Hough, by certificate; John D. Lane, by certificate; Elmon E. Smith, John J. Gaylord, by certificate; Robert Atkins, by certificate.

April, 1857 — Lucien Alcott.

April, 1858 — Henry D. Todd, Theodore Moulthrop, Daniel S. Rowe, James Foley, Patrick Foley, Joseph N. Millard, by certificate; John D. Pritchard, Levi W. Plumb, George S. Marks, Henry Aldrich, Lyman B. Bronson, Ozias S. Webster.

April, 1859 — Linas Lane, by certificate; Joseph Fairclough, jr., Adna Andrews, Homer F. Bassett, William B. Rase; Nelson Thorp, by certificate; Henry Chatfield, William Sherwood, Rodney F. Norton, Clark Wright, Sidney W. Alcott, by certificate.

April, 1860 — Amos M. Alcott, Theron Minor, George E. Alcott; Edwin Perkins, by certificate; Henry Rose. Andrew A. Norton, Berlin J. Pritchard, Emerson C. Bradley, John P. Butler; James W. Hough, by certificate. October, 1860 — David E. Downs, Lucius F. Norton; Philo Andrews, by certificate; Hobart Smith, by certificate.

March, 1861 — Newel Moulthrop; Henry L. Lane, by certificate; Henry B. Carter, Leroy Upson.

March, 1862 — Timothy Root; Arthur Byington, by certificate; William Shipley, by certificate; Ezra E. Bassett, by certificate; Edward Johnson, by certificate. April, 1862 — John E. Wiard; Elmer W. Hitchcock, by certificate.

March, 1863 — George Atkins, Rufus A. Sandford, Charles A.

Plumb; Leverette A. Sandford, by certificate; Seldon S. Norton, by certificate. April, 1863 — Richard Morrow, Theron S. Johnson; Leonard Blakeslee, by certificate; George S. Atwood, George E. Todd.

March, 1864 — Eugene Lane; Lyman C. Bradley, by certificate. November, 1864 — Lent S. Hough, by certificate; Charles S. Galpin, by certificate; James F. Robbins, by certificate; Leander Norton, by certificate; William F. Wiard, by certificate; Theron A. Sandford, by certificate; Charles F. Robbins.

March, 1865 — George N. Dingwell, by certificate.

March, 1866 — Benjamin F. Chipman; Joseph H. Somers, by certificate; Elijah H Warner, Mark H. Harrison, Lowry S. Richardson; Jesse Gaylord, by certificate; Edwin A. Welton, by certificate; Julius D. Beecher.

March, 1867 — Frederick W. Carter, John R. S. Todd, Elmer L. Andrews, Calvin B. Brockett, John H. Beecher, William McLaughlin, by certificate; J. Henry Garrigus, by certificate; Joseph Porter, by certificate.

March, 1868 — Chauncey F. Chipman, Joseph Fairclough, by certificate; Corald D. Blakeslee, by certificate; Elmer Hotchkiss, Reuben J. Lewis. April, 1868 — George W. Walker, James P. Alcott, Huber Birdsey, Oliver J. Norton. October, 1868 — Horace Garrigus, Benjamin F. Somers, Oliver L. Baldwin, Thomas Slade, Patrick Walsh. October, 1868 — Philo B. Lewis.

March, 1869 — George Bridgman, Patrick Donovan, Benjamin A. Pratt, George Sellew, Arthur W. Andrews, Edgar S. Moulthrop, Lester A. Hotchkiss.

March, 1871 — Henry Hall, Henry Tompkins, Rufus J. Lyman, Dewitt Todd, James A. Wakelee, Cornelius F. Munson, Benjamin L. Bronson, Charles E. S. Hall, Ransom Strong, Lavallette Upson; Michael Kelly, by certificate; John I. Ambler, by certificate.

March, 1872 — Fordyce D. Loomis, James Burns, Eri L. Lane, F. Albert Helmischkist, Charles E. Somers, Homer L. Atkins, Samuel L. S. Porter, Martin L. Andrews, jr., Bement D. Wakelee, Michael Kelly. October, 1872 — Elliot Bronson, Alfred M. Northrop, William H. Brown.

TOWN OFFICERS.

March, 1873 — Benjamin F. Brooks. April, 1873 — William Farrall.

March, 1874 — Anson O. Sanford, William E. Andrews, Emerson M. Hotchkiss, Ransom B. Hall, Alonzo Hart, Overton Jerome, Frank G. Mansfield. Nathan C. Prince, Horatio B. Strong, John M. Stevens, William Glynn, Evelyn M. Upson, Charles G. Yeomans, Samuel Orcutt.

TOWN OFFICERS.

Moderators — 1796, June : Deacon Aaron Harrison. 1796, December : Charles Upson. 1797-8 : Mark Harrison. 1799-1800 : Charles Upson. 1801-3 : Mark Harrison. 1804 : Deacon Joseph Atkins. 1805 : Daniel Byington. 1806 : Charles Upson. 1807 : Daniel Byington. 1808 : Nathaniel Lewis. 1809 : Streat Richards. 1810-11 : Mark Harrison. 1812 : Asaph Hotchkiss. 1813-17 : Mark Harrison. 1818-26 : Ambrose Ives. 1827-8 : David Frisbie. 1829-30 : Capt. Gates Upson. 1831 : Gates Upson. 1832-4 : David Frisbie. 1835-8 : Gates Upson. 1839 : Orrin Plumb. 1840 : Gates Upson. 1841 : Mark Tuttle. 1842 : Noah H. Byington. 1843-44 : Gates Upson. 1845 : Ira Frisbie. 1846 : Orrin Plumb. 1847-48 : Noah H. Byington. 1849 : Orrin Plumb. 1850 : Gates Upson. 1851 : Orrin Plumb. 1852-4 : Joseph N. Sperry. 1855 : Orrin Plumb. 1856 : George W. Carter. 1857-63 : Orrin Plumb. 1864 : George W. Carter. 1865 : Orrin Plumb. 1866 : Joseph N. Sperry. 1867-8 : George W. Carter. 1869-72 : Dennis Pritchard. 1873 : Elihu Moulthrop.

Town Clerks — Isaac Bronson, from 1796 to 1814, 17 years. Archibald Minor, from 1815 to 1838, 23 years. 1839-40 : Levi Moulthrop. 1841 : Isaac Hough. 1842 : Ezra S. Hough. 1843-44 : Joseph N. Sperry. 1845 : Elihu Moulthrop. 1846-47 : Joseph Sperry. Henry Minor from 1848 to 1873, 25 years.

Selectmen — June 13, 1796 : Mark Harrison, Streat Richards, Jacob Carter. December, 1796 : Jacob Carter, Charles Upson, Streat Richards. December, 11, 1797 : Streat Richards, Charles Upson, Amos Brockett. 1798 : Streat Richards, Amos Brockett, Elijah Perkins. 1799 : Streat Richards, Amos Brockett, Samuel Clinton. 1800 : Streat Richards, Amos Brocket, Joseph Minor.

1801 : Streat Richards, Amos Brockett, Stephen Carter. 1802 : Streat Richards, Nathaniel Lewis, Joseph Minor. 1803 : Isaac Bronson, Stephen Carter, David Harrison. 1804 : Isaac Bronson, Stephen Carter, David Harrison, Eliakim Welton, Joseph Atkins. 1805 : Nathaniel Lewis, Streat Richards, Joseph Minor, Titus Hotchkiss, Hezekiah Beecher. 1806 : Isaac Bronson, Hezekiah Beecher, Asaph Hotchkiss, John Potter, Isaac Upson. 1807 : Nathaniel Lewis, Streat Richards, Joseph Minor. 1808 : Streat Richards, Joseph Minor, Isaac Upson. 1809 : Streat Richards, David Wakelee, Joseph Minor. 1810 : Heman Hall, David Frisbie, Daniel Langdon. 1811 : Heman Hall, David Frisbie, Erastus Welton. 1812 : Heman Hall, David Frisbie, Erastus Welton. 1813 : Heman Hall, David Frisbie, Solomon Plumb. 1814 : Heman Hall, David Frisbie, Luther Andrews. 1815 : Solomon Pumb, Ambrose Ives, Levi Hall. 1816 : Levi Hall, Ambrose Ives, Titus Brockett. 1817 : Titus Brockett, Luther Andrews, Archibald Minor. 1818 : Titus Brockett, Luther Andrews, Luther Hotchkiss. 1819 : Luther Andrews, Luther Hotchkiss, Erastus Welton. 1820 : Levi Hall, Jerry Todd, Thomas Upson. 1821 : Levi Hall, Jerry Todd, Obed Alcox. 1822 : Obed Alcox,, David Frisbie, Thomas Upson. 1823 : Luther Andrews, David Frisbie, Obed Alcox. 1824 : Orrin Plumb, William A. Finch, Gates Upson. 1825 : Orrin Plumb, Luther Andrews, Obed Alcox. 1826 : Orrin Plumb, David Frisbie, Levi Hall. 1827 : Heman Hall, Titus Brockett, Luther Hotchkiss. 1828 : Luther Hotchkiss, David Frisbie, Orrin Plumb. 1829 : Orrin Plumb, Luther Andrews, Levi Hall. 1830 : Orrin Plumb, Moses Pond, Ira Hough. 1831 : Orrin Plumb, Ira Hough, Moses Pond. 1832 : Moses Pond, Luther Andrews, Ephraim Hall. 1833 : Moses Pond, Levi Hall, Orrin Hall. 1834 : Moses Pond, Orrin Hall, Mark Tuttle. 1835 : Orrin Plumb, Seth Horton, Mark Tuttle. 1836 : Orrin Plumb, Levi Hall, Leonard Beecher. 1837 : Orrin Plumb, Heman Hall, Ira Frisbie. 1838 : Ira Frisbie, Isaac Hough, Moses Pond. 1839 : Ira Frisbie, Moses Pond, Isaac Hough. 1840 : Ira Frisbie, Willard Plumb, Marvin Minor. 1841 : Luther Hotchkiss, Levi Hall, Mark Tuttle. 1842 : Willard Plumb, Carolus R. Byington, Marvin Minor. 1843 : Orrin Plumb, Dennis Pritchard. 1844 : Dennis Pritchard, Mark Tuttle, Isaac Hough. 1845 : Moses Pond, Carolus R. By-

TOWN OFFICERS.

ington. 1846-47: Dennis Pritchard, Orrin Plumb. 1848-49: Dennis Pritchard, Orrin Plumb, Joseph N. Sperry. 1850: Mark Tuttle, Seth Wiard: 1851-53: Isaac Hough, George G. Alcott. 1854: Isaac Hough, Orrin Plumb. 1855: Dennis Pritchard, James Alcott, jr. 1856: Henry Minor, Erastus W. Warner. 1857-60: Henry Minor, Levi Atkins. 1861-63: Henry Minor, Willis Merrill. 1864-69: Henry Minor, Shelton T. Hitchcock. 1870: Henry Minor, Augustus Minor. 1871-73: Henry Minor, Shelton T. Hitchcock.

Justices of the Peace — 1796-1804: Mark Harrison, Charles Upson.

1805-8: Mark Harrison, Charles Upson Isaac Bronson.

1809: Mark Harrison, Isaac Bronson, William Durand.

1810-16: Mark Harrison, Isaac Bronson.

1817-18: Mark Harrison, Isaac Bronson, Ambrose Ives.

1819: Mark Harrison, Ambrose Ives.

1820: Mark Harrison Ambrose Ives, Moses A. Street.

1821-4: Ambrose Ives, Archibald Minor.

1825: Ambrose Ives, Archibald Minor. David Frisbie.

1826: Ambrose Ives, Archibald Minor, Lyman Prindle, Samuel Wise.

1827: Archibald Minor, Levi Hall, Orrin Plumb, William A. Alcott.

1828: Archibald Minor, Orrin Plumb, William A. Alcott, David Frisbie, T. Upson.

1829-30: Archibald Minor, Orrin Plumb, David Frisbie.

1831-32: Archibald Minor, Orrin Plumb, David Frisbie, Luther Pritchard.

1833-34: Archibald Minor, Orrin Plumb, David Frisbie.

1835: Archibald Minor, David Frisbie, Orrin Plumb, Mark H. Byington.

1836: Archibald Minor, Orrin Plumb, Noah H. Byington, Levi Hall.

1837; Archibald Minor, Orrin Plumb, Noah H. Byington, Moses Pond.

1838; Archibald Minor, Mark Tuttle, William Bartholomew, George G. Alcott.

1839: Archibald Minor, Mark Tuttle, William Bartholomew,

Lucius Tuttle, jr., Carolus R. Byington, Orrin Plumb, Mark H. Byington.

1840: Archibald Minor, William Bartholomew, Carolus R. Byington, Mark Tuttle, Leverett Kinney, Orrin Plumb, George G. Alcott.

1841: Archibald Minor, Mark Tuttle, William Bartholomew, Carolus R. Byington, George G. Alcott, Isaac Hough.

1842: Gates Upson, William Plumb, Carolus R. Byington, Ezra S. Hough, Elihu Moulthrop, jr., Timothy Bradley, Marvin Minor, Mark Tuttle.

1843: Elihu Moulthrop, jr., Timothy Bradley, Carolus R. Byington, Willard Plumb, Leverett Kinney, Orrin Plumb.

1844: Carolus R. Byington, Archibald Minor, Orrin Plumb William Bartholomew, Mark Tuttle, Gates Upson.

1845: Gates Upson, Carolus R. Byington, Mark Tuttle, G. W. Carter, James Alcott, jr., Orrin Plumb.

1846: Gates Upson, Orrin Plumb, Carolus R. Byington, Willard Plumb, Elihu Moulthrop, jr., Joseph N. Sperry.

1847: Carolus R. Byington, Mark Tuttle, Orrin Plumb, George W. Carter, Stiles L. Hotchkiss.

1848: William Bartholomew, Carolus R. Byington, George W. Carter, Henry Minor, Mark Tuttle, Gates Upson.

1849: William Bartholomew, Henry Minor, Orrin Plumb, Willard Plumb, Joseph N. Sperry, Mark Tuttle.

1850: Ansel H. Plumb, Willard Plumb, Dennis Pritchard, Joseph N. Sperry, Mark Tuttle.

1851: George W. Carter, Henry Minor, Orrin Plumb, Willard Plumb, Joseph N. Sperry, Mark Tuttle.

1852–53: Carolus R. Byington, George W. Carter, Willis Merrill, Henry Minor, Dennis Pritchard, Joseph N. Sperry.

1854–55: Henry Minor, Ansel H. Plumb, Orrin Plumb, Willard Plumb, Joseph N. Sperry, Mark Tuttle.

1856–57: George W. Carter, Henry Minor, Orrin Plumb, Dennis Pritchard, Joseph N. Sperry, Erastus W. Warner.

1858–59: Carolus R. Byington, Henry Minor, Orrin Plumb, Dennis Pritchard, Joseph N. Sperry, Erastus W. Warner.

1860–61: James Alcott, jr., Isaac Hough, Henry Minor, Orrin Plumb, Dennis Pritchard, Joseph N. Sperry.

TOWN OFFICERS.

1862: Joseph N. Sperry, Dennis Pritchard, Henry Minor, Isaac Hough, Seth Wiard, James L. Kenea.

1863-4: Joseph N. Sperry, Dennis Pritchard, Henry Minor, James L. Kenea.

1865-7: Joseph N. Sperry, Dennis Pritchard, Henry Minor.

1868: Joseph N. Sperry, Dennis Pritchard, Henry Minor, Benjamin F. Finch, Isaac Hough, Seth Wiard.

1869: Joseph N. Sperry, Dennis Pritchard, Henry Minor.

1870-2: Dennis Pritchard, Henry Minor.

1873: Henry Minor, Amos M. Johnson, Dennis Pritchard.

1874: Henry Minor, Dennis Pritchard, Albert N. Lane, Amos M. Johnson, Frederick L. Nichols, Lucien Upson.

Representatives — October, 1796: Mark Harrison. May, 1797: Mark Harrison. October, 1797: Charles Upson. May, 1798: Charles Upson. October, 1798: Streat Richards. May, 1799: Mark Harrison. October, 1799: Charles Upson. May, 1800, to October, 1802: Isaac Bronson. October, 1802: Streat Richards. May, 1803, to October, 1805: Mark Harrison. October, 1805, to May, 1806: Streat Richards. May and October, 1807: Nathaniel Lewis. May, 1808: Isaac Bronson. October and May, 1809: Nathaniel Lewis. October, 1809: Streat Richards. May, 1810: Nathaniel Lewis. October, 1810: Joseph Minor. May, 1811, to May, 1815, including special session in August, 1812, and in January, 1815: Isaac Bronson. May, 1815: Ambrose Ives. October, 1815: Isaac Bronson. May, 1816, to October, 1817: Ambrose Ives. October, 1817, to May, 1818: Erastus Welton. May, 1819: Luther Andrews. 1820: Erastus Welton. 1821-2: Heman Hall. 1823: Levi Hall. 1824-5: David Frisbie. 1826-7: Archibald Minor.* 1828-9: David Frisbie. 1830: Archibald Minor. 1831: Luther Hotchkiss. 1832: Orrin Plumb. 1833-4: Archibald Minor. 1835: Orrin Plumb. 1836: Daniel Holt. 1837: Moses Pond. 1838: Salmon Upson. 1839: Noah H. Byington. 1840: Ira Hough. 1841: Ira Frisbie. 1842: Levi Moulthrop. 1843-4: Moses Pond. 1845: Sheldon Welton. 1846: Willard Plumb. 1847-8: Henry Minor. 1849: Marvin Minor. 1850: Dennis Pritchard. 1851:

---

* Mr. Minor is still living, and at the time of this writing is in the ninetieth year of his age.

Willis Merrill.   1852 : Isaac Hough.   1853 : Joseph N. Sperry.
1854 : Lyman Manvill.   1855 : Moses Pond.   1856 : Erastus W.
Warner.   1857 : George W. Winchell.   1858 : Henry Minor.
1859 : Shelton T. Hitchcock.   1860 : Erastus W. Warner.   1861 :
William McNeill.   1862 : E. W. Warner.   1863 : Seth Wiard.
1864 : James Alcott.   1865 : Orrin Plumb.   1866 : Henry Minor.
1867 : Augustus Minor.   1868 : Elihu Moulthrop.   1869 : Isaac
Hough.   1870 : Berlin J. Pritchard.   1871–2 : Shelton T. Hitchcock.   1873 : George W. Carter.   1874 : Shelton T. Hitchcock.
Senators — Orrin Plumb, George W. Carter.

REVOLUTIONARY SOLDIERS.

John B. Alcox,
Samuel Alcox,
Solomon Alcox,
Joseph Atkins, jr.,
Samuel Atkins,
Josiah Atkins,
Deacon Isaac Bronson,
Stephen Carter,
John Dean,
Judah Frisbie,

Benoni Gillet,
John Harrison,
Joel Hotchkiss,
Levi Johnson,
John J. Kenea,
Nathaniel Lane,
Dan Minor,
Joseph Minor,
Elijah Royce,
Captain Lucius Tuttle.

SOLDIERS IN THE LATE REBELLION.

The following list is very nearly complete of all Wolcott born citizens, and of all substitutes for such citizens, who entered the army in the "great American conflict :"

James P. Alcott,
Henry Alcott,
Newton Alcott,
Eugene Atwood,
Albert A. Andrews,
Martin L. Andrews,
Philo Andrews,
James B. Bailey,
Samuel M. Bailey,
Pliny Bartholomew,
Moses Bradley,
John P. Butler,

Charles E. Byington,
Dwight Beecher,
Francis Churchill,
Benjamin F. Chipman,
David L. Frisbie,
Frederick Harrison,
Mark H. Harrison,
Orrin Harrison,
Theron S. Johnston,
Elihu Moulthrop,
Evelyn E. Moulthrop,
Sherman Moulthrop,

SOLDIERS FROM WOLCOTT.

Newell Moulthrop,
David M. Manning,
Samuel A. Merriman,
John Mahon,
John Milligan,
Amon L. Norton,
Luzern T. Norton,
Burritt M. Norton,
Lucius F. Norton,
John Owens,
Charles H. Robbins,
William B. Rose,
Henry Rose,
Joseph H. Somers,
Samuel N. Sperry,
John Smith,
James Sweeney,
Alvah P. Tolman,
Thomas P. Tompkins,
Orrin Taylor,
George E. Todd,
Henry Todd,
Rev. Henry E. F. Upson,
Lucian Upson,
Leroy Upson,
George S. Wiard,
William Wiard,
William Wray.

The following are the names of some of the sons of former residents of Wolcott who were in the army in the late war:

Lucern, son of Simeon H. Norton, of Plantsville, died in battle.

Edgar, son of Jerry Upson, of Cheshire, died of disease contracted in the army.

David Frame, son of Rev. Aaron C. Beach, mortally wounded at Louisville, Kentucky, May 2d, 1862, aged 21 years.

Rev. Joseph H. Twitchell, chaplain, son of Deacon Edward Twitchell, of Plantsville.

Manton D. and Theron, sons of Russell Upson, of New Haven.

Hobart V., son of Luther Bailey.

Charles, son of Lucius Upson, of Plantsville.

BIOGRAPHY.

JOHN ALCOCK.

John Alcock, son of John, and grand-son of Phillip, was born in New Haven, where his father resided at that time, January 14, 1705. He married Deborah, daughter of Isaac Blakeslee, of North Haven, on the twenty-fourth anniversary of his birth, and settled in Wolcott in the spring of 1731, on a farm of 117½ acres of land, which he had purchased of Deacon Josiah Rogers, of Branford. He continued to add to his landed estate until he was the possessor of about one thousand acres. He purchased more than twelve hundred acres, but had given some to his children previous to the later purchases. He gave to each of five or six children a farm of about one hundred acres of land, in the immediate vicinity of his home, retaining his homestead for himself as long as he lived. He was a man of great energy and endurance, for without these qualities no man would or could have accomplished what he did in a wilderness country in the short space of time of forty-seven years. When he made his residence on this farm, coming up from Waterbury, he passed a little beyond the bounds of civilization into the territory of panthers, bears, wild-cats, and immense forests. Here he built his log house and introduced his bride of fifteen months as "queen of the realm," to the privations and severe toil which the circumstances must have imposed in following years. Before his strong arm the wilderness gave way, and in a few years neighbors were on every side. Prosperity was his lot until his acres numbered a thousand, and his sons and daughters a dozen, and his log house, being too strait, gave place to the more comfortable framed house.

He was a man of considerable public spirit, serving the town of Waterbury in different capacities, but especially as surveyor of lands and highways — the old records now showing his name connected with much work of this kind. His name is not prominent in the doings of the Ecclesiastical Society, for when it was organized he was sixty-six years of age, and had performed a large amount of hard labor, and was very properly allowed to rest on the retired list of prominent men of the community. He lived to see his children comfortably settled in life, most of them near him, and some of them highly honored as public citizens; and if a consciousness of having performed successfully the work of life can give satisfaction at its close, he must have enjoyed a larger share than is common among men.

He departed this life January 6th, 1777, within eight days of his seventy-second birth-day, and a little over forty-six years after his settlement on territory that became Wolcott nineteen years after his death; and had all the inhabitants of the town since his day been as energetic and diligent in the work of life as he, Wolcott would bloom as a garden, and would be the pride of the State. As the first settler of the town, every citizen must feel to honor his name, and congratulate his descendants, scattered in many parts of this great nation.

His wife, she that was Deborah Blakeslee, of North Haven, and became the queen bride of Wolcott, by being the first bride residing within its limits, survived her husband twelve years, departing this life January 7th, 1789, in the seventy-eighth year of her age.

CAPT. JOHN ALCOX.

Capt. John Alcox was the eldest son of Mr. John Alcock, the first settler in Wolcott, and was born December 28, 1731, and was, without doubt, the first child born in the territory of present Wolcott. He married, August 28, 1755, Mary Chatfield, daughter of Solomon Chatfield, of Derby, Connecticut, and settled on a farm, a little east of his father's residence, where his grandson, Almon, still resides, he being in the eighty-fifth year of his age. Captain Alcox was appointed one of the first prudential committee, at the organization of the first Ecclesiastical Society, and he and his wife Mary were among the number of forty-one persons who united in the formation of the first church in Farmingbury parish. He was a man of stability and honor, but his energy of character fitted him for military service more than ecclesiastical, and hence he was distinguished in the former more than the latter, though in the church he was a leading and substantial member.

All his commissions in the military service are preserved, though that of Sargeant is not at hand. That of Ensign was addressed, dated, and signed as follows: "To John Alcox, Ensign of the new erected company or trainband in Waterbury [Farmingbury] Winter Parish so called. Given under my hand and the seal of this colony, in New Haven, the 19th day of October in the 9th year of the Reign of our Sovereign, Lord George the Third, King of Great Britain, &c., A. D., 1769. By His Honor's Command, Jonathan Trumbull. George Wyllys, Secretary."

CAPTAIN'S COMMISSION.

Jonathan Trumbull, Esquire, Captain-General and Commander-in-Chief of His Majesty's Colony of Connecticut, in New England.

To John Alcox, Gent., Greeting : You being, by the General Assembly of this Colony, accepted to be Captain of the Thirteenth Company, or Trainband, in the 15th Regiment in this Colony, — reposing special trust and confidence in your loyalty, courage, and good conduct, I do, by virtue of the letters-patent from the crown of England to this corporation, me thereunto enabling, appoint and impower you to take the said Company into your care and charge, as their Captain, carefully and diligently to discharge that trust ; exercising your inferior officers and soldiers in the use of their arms, according to the discipline of war; keeping them in good order and government, and commanding them to obey you as their Captain for His Majesty's service. And you are to observe all such orders and directions as from time to time you shall receive, either from me or from other your superior officer, pursuant to the trust hereby reposed in you.

Given under my hand and the seal of this Colony, in Hartford, the 18th day of May, in the fourteenth year of the reign of our Sovereign Lord, George the Third, King of Great Britain, etc. Annoque Domini 1774.

By His Honor's Command, JONTH. TRUMBULL.
GEORGE WYLLYS, *Sec'y*.

In the Autumn after Mr. Alcox received his Captain's commission, and when Colonial matters were taking on a serious attitude toward the mother country, in consequence of the warlike preparations of Governor Gage, of Massachusetts, he received the following paper, apparently in General Putnam's hand-writing and signature, and signed by other persons :

PUTNAM'S ORDER.

POMPHRET, Sept. 3, 1774.
CAPT. HOPKINS : *

Mr. Keys this moment brought news that the men of war and

---

* Isaac Hopkins had been Captain previous to the appointment of John Alcox, and hence when he received the above notice, he not then being

troops began to fire on the people last night at sunset at Boston, when a post was sent immediately to inform the country; he informs the artillery played all night. The people are universally for Boston as far as here, and desire all the assistance possible;—it was occasioned by the country's being robbed of their powder as far as Framingham, and when found out, people went to take them and were immediately fired upon; six of our people were killed the first shot, a number more were wounded; and [I] beg you would rally all the forces and be upon the march immediately for the relief of Boston and the people that way.

ISRAEL PUTNAM.

A copy compared, etc.   WOLCOTT.
Per JAMES HUNTINGTON.   (Probably Governor.)

Ten days later, the Colonel of the Regiment sent the following paper:

To Captain John Alcox, Captain of the 13th Company in the 15th Regiment of the Colony of Connecticut:

These lines are to desire you to call forth the company under your command as soon as may be, and see that they and each of them are furnished with arms and ammunition according to law, and see that they hold themselves in readiness to march at an hour's warning, if need be.

Dated at Farmington, this 13th day of Sept., A D., 1774.

JOHN STRONG, *Colonel.*

The following paper is also preserved in Capt. Alcox's handwriting, except the name of Abraham Woster, and is now, 1874, ninety-nine years old:

To the Honorable Assembly to be holden at Hartford on the Second Thursday of May, A. D., 1775:

These may serve to inform your honors, that being required by a statute of law passed in your session in October last requiring all captains of military companies in the government to call out their companies twelve half days before the first day of May next

---

captain, passed the order to Mr. Alcox, who preserved it. It is now in possession of Mr. A. Bronson Alcott.

then ensuing, and to cause them to be taught in the art of military discipline, encouraging all that would faithfully attend, with a premium of one dollar for their service, whereupon I have warned out my company to said twelve half days within said act limited, and under me there have attended faithfully the said twelve and a half days, fifty-eight of those to draw pay. Eleven that have attended eleven half days, eight that have attended ten half days, two that have attended nine, two that have attended eight, and one that attended seven, on which I exhibit this account before your honor, requiring the aforementioned premium.

Dated Waterbury, May 9th, A. D., 1775.

JOHN ALCOX,
Capt. of the 13th Company in the Fifteenth Regiment.

The above is a true account of the proceedings of the above said half-day trainings.

ABRAHAM WOSTER,
Clerk of said Company.

On the reverse side of this paper is the following receipt and autographs :

FARMINGTON, June 24.

We, the subscribers, have received of Capt. John Alcox in full for our half-day training.

Ezekiel Upson,	Samuel Atkins,
Joseph Benham,	Abraham Tuttle,
Amos Hall,	Joseph Beecher,
James Thomas,	Wait Hotchkiss,
David Alcox,	John Bronson,
Aaron Welton,	Jacob Carter, jr.,
Elkanah Smith,	Noah Neal,
Eliakim Welton, jr.,	Abel Collins,
John Talmage,	Jared Harrison,
Abel Curtiss, sen.,	Charles Upson,
Heman Hall,	Jeremiah Smith,
James Alcox,	Mark Harrison,
Johnson Cleaveland,	Cyrus Norton,
Stephen Miles, jr.,	Abraham Woster,
Daniel Alcox,	Nathan Seward,

Samuel Harrison,	Nathaniel Sutliff,
Dan Tuttle,	Philemon Bradley,
Aaron How,	John Greely,
Curtiss Hall,	Isaac Newell,
John Miles,	Moses Pond,
Jeremiah Selkrigs,	

James Alcox received the wages for Phillip Barrett and David Alcox, jr., and receipted accordingly. Daniel Lane received "six shillings" for Joel Lane.

Captain Alcox espoused the cause of his country in the revolutionary war with great spirit and energy. It is said of him that on hearing some report, about the time of the commencement of the war, he buckled on his Captain's sword and walked to New Haven, twenty-five miles, to see if his services were needed as a soldier. Three of his sons, Solomon, Samuel, and John B., served in that war.

His wife, Mary, departed this life, February 28, 1807, and Mr. Alcox died September 27, 1808, wanting one day of being seventy-seven years of age.

A. BRONSON ALCOTT.*

The first settler of Wolcott, John Alcock, of New Haven, left a son, Captain John Alcock, who lived on Spindle Hill, along with his brothers, each possessed of a good farm. At his house his grand-son, Amos Bronson Alcott, now of Concord, Mass., was born November 29, 1799, being the eldest of eight children of Joseph Chatfield Alcox and Anna Bronson, his wife. The homestead of Joseph C. Alcox was near his father's, and it was there that Mr. Alcott spent his boyhood. The present house, built in 1819, is that from which Mr. Alcott set forth for Boston in 1828, when he began his active career in the great world. It stood near the fork of the road, where in former times was the district school house in which Mr. Alcott and his cousin, Dr. William A. Alcott, commenced their education, in the fashion described by Dr. Alcott many years ago. This school house has now disappeared, and the house and farm of Joseph C. Alcox have suffered from neglect since his death in 1829.

He was a skillful farmer and country mechanic, making farming tools and household utensils for his townsfolks, and having the best tilled and best fenced farm (of nearly 100 acres) in the Spindle Hill district. Two of his brothers had built log cabins on their clearings and lived in

---

* This biographical sketch was prepared by request of the author of this book, by F. B. Sanborn, Esq., of Concord, Mass., and is extended for the purpose of giving some account of the experiences of the young men of Wolcott in their southern tours, and of Mr. Alcott's efforts in education, for which the author extends to Mr. Sanborn his most cordial thanks.

them in the early part of this century, but he always occupied a frame house, and lived with comfort, though with frugality. He was a diffident, retiring man, and kept much at home, content with his simple lot ; industrious, temperate, conscientious, honorable in all his dealings, and fortunate in his domestic life.

His wife, the mother of Mr. Bronson Alcott, deserves special mention, since from her he inherited his name, his early religious training, and the general turn of his mind. Anna Bronson was the daughter of Captain Amos Bronson, of Plymouth : a man of property, influence, and decided theological opinions, somewhat at variance with those of the majority of Connecticut farmers at that time. She was the sister of an eminent clergyman and scholar, — Dr. Tillotson Bronson, for some years at the head of the Episcopal Academy in Cheshire, and previously rector of St. John's Church, in Waterbury. She had some advantages of culture not so common in Wolcott at that time, and at her marriage brought to the Spindle Hill neighborhood a refinement of disposition and a grace of deportment that gave a more polite tone to the little community. In course of time her husband and children joined her in the Episcopal form of worship, when introduced in their neighborhood, where the service was read (at the Spindle Hill school house), until in course of time a church was gathered. She united steadfastness and persistency of purpose with uncommon delicacy and sweetness of spirit, and was truly, as her son declares her, "meek, forgiving, patient, generous, and self-sustained, the best of wives and mothers." She lived to a great age, surviving her husband more than thirty years.

From his earliest years Mr. Alcott was fond of books, and read eagerly all that he could find. He went to school in the Spindle Hill district until he was thirteen years old, and at the age of twelve began to keep a diary, a practice which he has continued the greater part of the time since. Still earlier he had read Bunyan's Pilgrim's

Progress, the book of all others which had the greatest influence on his mind. He learned to write by practising with chalk on his mother's kitchen floor, and became in his boyhood a skillful penman, so that his first essay in teaching was as master of a writing school. He was mainly self-taught, in the higher studies, although he was for a time a pupil of his uncle, Dr. Bronson, at Cheshire, in 1813, and in 1815 of Rev. John Keys, of Wolcott Hill.

He worked during boyhood on the farm and in the shop with his father and brothers, and was dextrous at mechanical tasks. At the age of fourteen he worked for a while at clock making, in Plymouth, and in the same year went on an excursion into northern Connecticut and western Massachusetts, selling a few articles as he went, to meet the expenses of his journey. At the age of fifteen he was confirmed, along with his father, as a member of the Episcopal church, the ceremony being performed in Waterbury, by Bishop Brownell, after which young Alcott, with his cousin, the late Dr. Alcott, used to read the church service on Sundays at the school house in their neighborhood. The two cousins also carried on a correspondence at this time, and founded a small library for their mutual improvement. A few years later they visited Virginia and the Carolinas together, on one of those peddling pilgrimages which make such a romantic feature of Mr. Alcott's early life. Of one of these journeys Dr. Alcott has printed an extended account.

His first visit to New Haven was in 1813, when he went to a book store and sighed for a place in it, for the sake of reading all the books. And he turned his rambles in Virginia and North Carolina to good account in the way of reading; gaining access to the libraries of the great houses as he went along.

The beginning of these rambles was in the autumn and winter of 1818, when the youth was almost nineteen years old. At the age of sixteen he had played the part of a subscription book agent, selling copies of Flavel's "Keeping the Heart." His earnings were spent in New Haven for a prayer book for his mother, another for himself, a dictionary, and a supply of paper for his diaries. These short journeys in Connecticut, Massachusetts, and New York, had worn off his natural bashfulness somewhat, and had increased his longing to see more of the great world. His father and mother would fain have retained him at home, but he resolved to go to Norfolk in one of the coasting vessels from New Haven, and had a dream that he could easily, in Virginia, find a place as a teacher. Accordingly he sailed from New Haven, October 13th, 1818, in the good sloop "Three Sisters," Captain Sperry, skipper, with fifteen other passengers, chiefly peddlers from Connecticut and workmen going in the employ of the Tisdales, Connecticut tinmen, who had a shop at Norfolk. The voyage lasted about a week, and young Alcott landed in Virginia, October 20th. His passage money seems to have been ten dollars. For a few days after arriving at Norfolk he continued to board with Captain Sperry, but soon went to live at Tisdale's, the tinman, and was urged by him to enter his service. At first Mr. Alcott was bent on teaching, but having tried from the 24th of October to the 12th of November, without success, to get a school, and being then somewhat in debt, the youth accepted his offer, and began to peddle for him about the city. This continued until some time in December, but apparently without much pecuniary result, for just before the Christmas holidays we find Mr. Alcott buying a small stock of Virginia almanacs, and selling them to the citizens of Norfolk at a profit of two hundred per cent. Each almanac cost threepence, and was sold for ninepence, and the young merchant easily earned a dollar or two a day so long as the holidays lasted. Then it occurred to him to enlarge his stock, and to sell trinkets and silks to the families in the surrounding country. He went, therefore, to a dealer in "fancy goods" in Norfolk, and bought goods costing nearly three hundred dollars, which he bestowed in two small tin trunks, to be carried in the hand, as the peddler journeyed on foot from house to house. There were tortoise shell combs, thimbles, scissors, various articles of ornament for ladies, puzzles and picture books for children, spectacles, razors, and many other wares for the men, besides needles, buttons, sewing-silk, and much more that was not then a part of a peddler's stock in Eastern Virginia.

The first trip was made in January, 1819, and was a circuit from Norfolk, by way of Hampton, along the James River for awhile, then across the country to Yorktown, and by the York county plantations back to Hampton and Norfolk again. It proved profitable, and both goods and merchant found unexpected favor in the eyes of the Virginians. An American foot-peddler, a bashful Yankee, neither impertinent nor stingy, was a novelty in those regions, and, it soon appeared, an agreeable novelty. He was kindly received at the great houses of the planters, where he generally spent the night, accepting courteously their customary hospitality, though sometimes sleeping in the slave quarters. On Sundays and rainy days, when his trade could not be pursued, this diffident and bookish Autolycus remained in the planters' houses, and had permission to read in their libraries, where he found many books he had never seen or heard of before. In that part of Virginia there lived some of the oldest and best descended families of the Old Dominion, with large and choice libraries, which they allowed the young man from Connecticut to explore for himself. Biography was his favorite reading, then poems and tales, and he had a keen appetite — not so common among lads of nineteen — for metaphysics and books of devotion. Cowper's Life and Letters, Locke's Conduct of the Understanding, and Lavater's Physiognomy, were among the books thus read; nor was his favorite, Pilgrim's Progress, forgotten, which he found in fine editions among the Virginians.

A word may here be said of the style of life and of reading, schooling, etc., which had up to this time been familiar to Mr. Alcott. The region where he lived was one of the most primitive parts of Connecticut at the opening of the century, and, though it was so near to those centers of culture, Hartford and New Haven, was but scantily supplied with books. There were not a hundred volumes in the parish library, and it had fallen into disuse when Mr. Alcott was a lad in his teens. He used to get permission from his father on Saturday afternoons to go round to the houses of the farmers in Wolcott for several miles about to examine their libraries and read their books, which included the Bible, and perhaps half a dozen other books, among them Bunyan's Pilgrim's Progress, Hervey's Meditations, Young's Night Thoughts, and Burgh's Dignity of Human Nature, a book then in much vogue among the country people of New England. These volumes would be kept on a shelf in a corner of the family room, and young Alcott readily got leave to borrow them.

It was his custom for years to borrow and read the Pilgrim's Progress once a year; and this book, more than any other, gave direction to his fancies and visions of life. Wolcott, indeed, might pass either for the Hill Difficulty or for the Delectable Mountains, according to the mood of the inhabitant of its uplands. The township lay high, and Spindle Hill, or "New Connecticut," was at the summit of the range of Wolcott hills, commanding a wide prospect on all sides. Seven parish steeples were in sight, and from an oak-top the young Christian could see the glittering waters of Long Island Sound.

Books were always his solace and delight, and he read constantly of evenings, and while resting from work at noon, during his father's nap or pull at the tobacco-pipe, in which he indulged himself moderately. Sometimes, too, the barefoot boy took his book afield with him, and read under the wall or by some tree, while the oxen rested in the furrow.

To a youth thus bred, the comparatively elegant and courtly life of the wealthy Virginians was a graceful and impressive revelation,—the first school of fine manners which he had entered. An English gentleman, hearing the story of Mr. Alcott's early years—his farm life and his progress as a peddler—could scarcely believe it true. "Why," said he, "your friend has the most distinguished manners—the manners of a very great peer." He would have been still more surprised to learn that it was during the years of peddling that this polish of manner began to be acquired by contact with a class then esteemed the first gentlemen in America.

During these first months of 1819 he visited the Virginian towns of Portsmouth, Smithfield, Williamsburg, the old capitol of the colony, Gloucester, and others in that region, and traversed the surrounding districts, without anxiety or misadventure, and with something to show at the beginning of April as the profits of the winter's trade. Something more than one hundred dollars was the net income, after all debts were paid, and travelling homeward with this, Mr. Alcott put it into the hands of his father, as the price of the six month's time he had taken from the work of farm and shop. The money went into the new house which the father was then building (in 1819), and which is still standing.

In November, 1819, Mr. Alcott and his brother Chatfield went to Virginia and both engaged in peddling. They succeeded well, and carried home their earnings to their father in the summer of 1820. The following autumn, when Bronson Alcott was one-and-twenty, he went South again, this time as far as South Carolina, and with his cousin, afterwards Dr. Alcott, for a companion. Their plan was to teach school in the Carolinas, but that failed, and after making the journey on foot, from Charleston to Norfolk, they betook themselves, in the winter of 1820-21, to peddling again. During this winter Bronson Alcott suffered from a severe typhus fever, and William Alcott took care of him. The profits of the season were not so much as before, owing to this illness and other unfavorable circumstances. On his way home in June, Mr. Alcott, visited for the first time, Washington, Baltimore, Philadelphia, and New York. In the following September, the now experienced adventurer set forth from home, and after settling his affairs in Norfolk, he gave up merchandise and began teaching. His first school was a writing class in Warrenton, N. C. With the money thus earned he paid his way back to Wolcott in June, walking most of the distance. Not quite willing to abandon the hope of retrieving his fortune, he set forth again for the South with his cousin, Thomas Alcox, in October, 1822, and spent the winter in North Carolina, among the Quakers of Chowan and Perquimons counties, returning in the spring of 1823. Here he saw much of the Quakers and read their books, such as William Penn's No Cross, no Crown; Barclay's Apology; Fox's Journal; and other works of like spirit. The moral sentiment, as Mr. Alcott has since said, now superceded peddling, clearly and finally.

The next stage in his career was school keeping,— an occupation that he pursued for more than fifteen years, after once taking it up. His first school was in a district of Bristol, the adjoining town, and only three miles from Spindle Hill. Here he taught for three months, his wages being $10 a month besides board, and was so good a teacher as to make the school-committee desirous to engage him again. He did indeed teach school in Bristol the next winter (1824-5), but not in the same district, and for a part of the year he gave writing lessons at Wolcott. In the spring and summer of 1825 he resided in Cheshire with his uncle, Dr. Bronson, who then edited the *Churchmans Magazine*, for which Mr. Alcott procured subscribers and copied his uncle's manuscript for the printer. While residing with Dr. Bronson this season he read Butler's Analogy, Reid and Stewart's Metaphysics, Watts's Logic, Vattel's Law of Nations, and Dwight's Theology, his readings being to some extent directed by his uncle, with whom he continued to live after beginning to teach school in Cheshire, in November, 1825. This school occupied Mr. Alcott from that time until June, 1827, nearly two years, when he closed it and returned to Wolcott. He wrote a brief account of it and of his method in it, which was published in Mr. William Russell's "Journal of Education," in January, 1828, and attracted much notice, as the school itself had done. It was in Cheshire, in fact, that Mr. Alcott began to develope his peculiar system of instruction, which afterwards received so much praise and blame in Boston. He continued this system in a similar school in Bristol in the winter of 1827-8, and then removed to Boston to take charge of an infant school in Salem street, in June, 1828. In the following April, he opened a private school near St. Paul's church on Tremont street, in which he remained until November 5, 1830, when he gave it up to open a school in Germantown, near Philadelphia, where with his associate, Mr. W. Russell, he remained a little more than two years. On the 22d of April, 1833, he opened a school in Philadelphia, which continued until July, 1834, soon after which, September 22, 1834, Mr. Alcott returned to Boston and there began his famous Temple school, concerning which so much has been written and published. This was nearly eleven years after his first winter's school keeping in Bristol. Mr. Alcott had now reached the 35th year of his life, and the fifth of his married life.

Concerning the Cheshire school-keeping, which Mr. Alcott has always regarded as one of the most fruitful of his experiences, his brother-in-law, Rev. Samuel J. May, himself distinguished as a teacher and friend of education, says in his autobiography, under the year 1827: " Dr. William A. Alcott, then living in Wolcott, a philosopher and a philanthropist, wrote to give us some account of a remarkable school, kept on a very original plan, in the adjoining town of Cheshire, by his kinsman, Mr. A. B. Alcott. His account excited so much my curiosity to know more of the American Pestalozzi, as he has since been called, that I wrote immediately to Mr. Alcott, begging him to send me a detailed statement of his principles and method of training children. In due time came to me a full account of the school of Cheshire, which revealed such a depth of insight into the nature of man, such a true sympathy with children, such profound appreciation of the work of education, and was, withal, so philosophically arranged and exquisitely written, that I at once felt assured the man must be a genius, and that I must know him more intimately. So I wrote, inviting him urgently to visit me (in Brooklyn, Connecticut, where Mr. May then had a parish). He came and passed a week with me before the end of the summer. , I have never, but in one instance, been so immediately taken possession of by any man I have ever met in life. He seemed to me like a born sage and saint. He was a radical in all matters of reform ; went to the root of all theories, especially the subjects of education, mental and moral culture."*

At this time the Cheshire school was just coming to an end, in consequence, partly in opposition to the radical ideas of its teacher, who had now reached that point in his experience as a teacher where he had confidence in his own ideas and methods, and began to make them distinctly felt, not only by pupils, but by their parents, and by the community. Previous to 1827 the district schools of Connecticut, and of all New England, were at a low degree of discipline, instruction, and comfort, and in all these matters Mr. Alcott set the example of improve-

---
* Life of Samuel J. May, pp. 121-2. Boston : Roberts Brothers. 1873.

ment. He first gave his pupils single desks, now so common, instead of the long benches and double or three-seated desks, still in use in some sections. He gave his youthful pupils slates and pencils, and blackboards. He established a school library, and taught them to enjoy the benefits of careful reading ; he broke away from the old rule of severe and indiscriminate punishments, and substituted therefor appeals to the affections and the moral sentiment of children, so that he was able almost wholly to dispense with corporeal punishment. He introduced, also, light gymnastic exercises, evening amusements at the school-room, the keeping of diaries by young children, and, in general, an affectionate and reverent mode of drawing out the child's mind towards knowledge, rather than the pouring in of instruction by mechanical or compulsory processes. Familiar as this natural method of teaching has since become, it was an innovation five and forty years ago, — as much so as Pestalozzi's method had been in Europe when he began the instruction of poor children in Switzerland a hundred years ago. Mr. Alcott followed in the course pointed out by Pestalozzi, and may be said to have been his immediate successor and continuator, for Pestalozzi died, (February 1827) while Mr. Alcott was in the midst of his Cheshire school. It has been remarked that the plan of communicating all instruction by immediate address to the child's sensations and conceptions, and effecting the formation of his mind by constantly calling his powers into exercise, instead of making him a mere passive recipient, was original with Pestalozzi,— and so it was with Mr. Alcott. Our townsman added also a Platonic and mystic tinge to his system, which, although found in Pestalozzi's was not so marked. The most devoted of Pestalozzi's personal friends and followers in England, Mr. James Pierrpont Greaves, who first learned of Mr. Alcott's experiments in education from Miss Harriet Martineau, after her return from America in 1837, at once recognized the right of our townsman to the mantle of Pestalozzi. Afterwards, in founding a school near London, on the principles of his beloved master Pestalozzi, he gave it the name of "Alcott House." He was even meditating a voyage to Boston for the sake of making Mr. Alcott's acquaintance, when he was prevented by the illness which preceded his death in 1842. Mr. Alcott's own visit to England happening later in the same year, he never met Mr. Greaves.

The principles which guided Mr. Alcott in his long course of school-teaching, in so many places, being fully set forth in the "Record of a School," lately republished in Boston, need not here be dwelt upon in detail. They were Pathagorean, Platonic, Pestalozzian, and we may add, Christian; for though the forms of belief which he for sometime held varied widely from the standard of doctrine most commonly upheld in Connecticut, the spirit in which he acted was always that of reverent and self-sacrificing love,—the true spirit of Christianity. He was in advance of his age, and his ideas in education, now almost universally received, were slow in making their way among the plain and practical people of New England. Like Pestalozzi, he was continually at a disadvantage in dealing with affairs, and he was not so fortunate as to find a coadjutor in his schools who could supply the practical ability to match and complete his own idealism. Hence the brief period of his success in each place where he taught, and his frequent removals from town to town, and city to city. Everywhere he impressed the best men and women with the depth and worth of his character, the fervor of his philanthropy, the delicacy and penetration of his genius, and they spoke of him as Mr. May did, in the passage quoted above. They sought his fellowship, aided his plans, rejoiced in his successes, and knew how to pardon his failures. During the period from 1826 to 1836 he made the acquaintance and enjoyed the friendship of some of the most eminent persons in Connecticut, Massachusetts, New York and Pennsylvania; among them Drs. Gallaudet and Henry Barnard, of Hartford, Dr. Channing and Mr. Garrison, of Boston, Mr. R. W. Emerson, of Concord, Messrs. Matthew Carey, Roberts Vaux, and Dr. Furness, of Philadelphia; and many of the most esteemed Boston families,—the Mays, Phillipses, Savages, Shaws, Quincys, etc. Among the eminent women who took an interest in his school may be named, (besides Miss Martineau), Miss Margaret Fuller, Miss Elizabeth Peabody, her sister, the late Mrs. Hawthorne, Miss Elizabeth Hoar, and others. Both Miss Fuller and Miss Peabody were assistant teachers in the Temple school at Boston, and Miss Peabody compiled the accounts of it which were published under the title of "Record of a School," and "Conversations with Children on the Gospels." Mr. Emerson, who had become intimate with Mr. Alcott in 1835, saluted him with high expectation in this part of his career and said to him what Burke said to John Howard, "Your plan is original, and as full of genius as of humanity; so do not let it sleep or stop a day." To his friend at Concord Mr. Alcott seemed in his work as a teacher, a man in earnest, and of rare power to awaken the highest faculties,— "to awaken the apprehension of the Absolute," as he said. And this was the general verdict of those persons who visited the Boston school in the Masonic Temple, on Tremont Street, during the years 1834-5-6. The conversation with pupils on the New Testament, in the winter of 1835-6, excited some opposition, however, and the lectures of Dr. Graham, the vegetarian, in 1836, also gave offense. The publication of the "Conversations" in the winter of 1836-7 was the occasion of a fierce attack in the newspapers of 1837.

The hostile criticism poured out upon Mr. Alcott and his school after the publication of this book was singularly varied in its nature. The Boston Advertiser complained that "on the most important and difficult questions this teacher, while he endeavors to extract from his pupils every thought which may come uppermost in their minds, takes care studiously to conceal his own opinions." But this was not all : "In some cases he gives opinions, and sometimes opinions of very questionable soundness." He supposes, we are told, "that a new era in philosophy is dawning upon us in the discovery that childhood is a type of the divinity ; and the Advertiser sneeringly adds that "these conversations appear to be the first fruits of the new attempt to draw wisdom from babes and sucklings,"—as if, forsooth, there were anything unchristian or unscriptural in such an attempt. The Courier, a paper justly celebrated afterwards for standing firmly by the unpopular cause, was more abusive than the Advertiser, —compared Mr. A. with Kneeland, who had been indicted for blasphemy, and suggested that this teacher also should be brought before the "honorable judge of our municipal court." The indignation of Mr. Emerson was aroused at this injustice, and he wrote a note which was published in the Courier, the Advertiser having declined to publish it. It appeared in March or April, 1837, and said, among other things : " In behalf of this book I have but one plea to make — this, namely : Let it be read. Any reasonable man will perceive that fragments out of a new theory of Christian instruction are not quite in the best place for examination betwixt the price current and the shipping list. Try the effect of a passage from Plato's Phædo, or the Confessions of St. Augustine, in the same place. Mr. Alcott has given proof of a strong mind and a pure heart. A practical teacher, he has dedicated for years his rare gifts to the science of education. He aims to make children think, and, in every question of a moral nature, to send them back on themselves for an answer. He is making an experiment in which all the friends of education are interested. I ask whether it be wise or just to add to the anxieties of his enterprise a a public clamor against some detached sentences of a book which, as a whole, is pervaded with original thought and sincere piety?" But this protest had no effect on Mr. Buckingham, who soon after quoted in his Courier the opinion of a distinguished professor of Harvard College, to the effect that "one-third of Mr. Alcott's book was absurd, one-third was blasphemous, and one-third was obscene." "Such," remarked Mr. Buckingham, "will be the deliberate opinion of those who diligently read and soberly reflect."

To one who reads the two volumes thus severely condemned, after the changes of the last thirty or forty years, such bitterness only provokes a smile. They would now be admitted with little hesitation to Sunday School libraries, and to use in the Sunday Schools of most Protestant churches. But the effect of such denunciation then was crushing. The school at the Temple, which began in 1834 with thirty pupils, and had received as many as forty, fell to ten pupils in the spring of 1837, and after lingering along for a year or two, with one or two changes of place, was finally given up in 1839. The immediate occasion of closing it then was the unwillingness of Mr. Alcott's patrons to have their children educated in the same room with a colored child whom he had admitted, and when the protesting parents found Mr. Alcott determined not to dismiss the colored child, they withdrew their own children—leaving him with only five pupils,—his own three daughters, a child of Mr. William Russell, and young Robinson, the cause of offense. Up to this time (June, 1839) the receipts of Mr. Alcott for tuition since he began his school at the Temple, five years before, had been $5,730; namely, in the first year, $1,794, the second, $1,649, the third $1,395, the fourth, (after the attack in the newspapers), $549, and in the last year only $343. The expenses of rent, furniture, assistant teachers, and the maintenance of family had been much more than this,—and in April, 1837, the costly furniture, school library, and other apparatus of the Temple school were sold at auction. The city press and the city mob had their way with Mr. Alcott's school, just as two years before they had their way with Mr. Garrison's anti-slavery meeting. The poor and unpopular schoolmaster from Connecticut was hooted down, and his generous experiments in education were frustrated in Boston, in spite of the protests and appeals of such champions as Dr. Alcott, Mr. Emerson, Mr. Russell, James Freeman Clarke, Rev. Chandler Robbins, Miss Fuller, Dr. Furness, Dr. Hedge, and other friends of culture and philosophy.

During this period, as at all times since his marriage in 1830, Mr. Alcott found great sympathy and encouragement at his own fireside. Mrs. Alcott was a daughter of Col. Joseph May, of Boston, and was born in that city, October 8, 1800. The Rev. Samuel J. May, of Syracuse, whose memoir has been quoted, was her elder brother, born in 1793. It was at his parsonage house in Brooklyn that she first met Mr. Alcott, in 1827, when he was teaching school in Cheshire, and it was largely on her account and through the efforts of her family and friends that he went to Boston, in 1828, and took charge of the Salem street infant school. They were married May 23, 1830, and resided in Boston until their removal to Germantown in the following winter. Their oldest daughter Anna Bronson, now Mrs. Pratt, (the mother of Miss Alcott's "Little Men") was born at Germantown, March 16, 1831, and Miss Alcott herself (Louisa May) was born at Germantown, Nov. 29, 1832. A third daughter, Elizabeth Sewall, was born in Boston, June 24, 1835, and died in Concord, March 14, 1858. Miss May Alcott, the youngest of the four daughters, now a well-known artist, was born in Concord, July 26, 1840. The eldest of the four, Anna Bronson Alcott, named for her grandmother, was married May 23, 1860, the anniversary of her mother's wedding day, to Mr. John B. Pratt, of Concord, a son of Minot Pratt, one of the Brook Farm community in former years, and of late an esteemed citizen of Concord.

Their children are the famous "Little Men,"— Frederick Alcott Pratt, born March 28, 1863, and John Sewall Pratt, born June 24, 1866. Mrs. Pratt was left a widow by the sudden death of her husband Nov. 27, 1870, and has since resided much of the time, with her two sons, at her father's house in Concord.

It will be seen then that Miss Alcott, the authoress, was old enough to be a pupil, and in fact she was a pupil in her father's Boston school. She received her education mainly at home, after work, from her father and mother, both very competent to instruct her, and to lay the foundation of mind and character that her books display. Mrs. Alcott inherited from her ancestors, the Mays, Sewals, Quincys, of Boston, a vigorous constitution, a robust mind, and the kindliest and most comprehensive affections. In a domestic life interrupted by frequent changes of residence and of fortune, she was the stay of the household, a model wife and mother, and had a reserve force of philanthropy which expended itself freely on the good works of her husband, of her friends, or such as naturally fell to her own share. Many of her marked traits reappear, it is said, in her daughter Louisa, in whose books, also, much of the fireside history of the Alcott, May, Sewall, and Pratt families reappears in the guise of fiction.

From birth to 1823, a period of twenty-four years, we may consider Mr. Alcott as preparing himself for the work of life. From 1823 to 1839, nearly sixteen years, he was zealously occupied in the business of education. For the last thirty years and more he has stood forth as an ideal reformer, and the representative of a school of thought and ethics, of which he was one of the founders in New England. During the years from 1834 to 1840, the so-called Transcendental Movement was making progress among the New England people, and particularly in the neighborhood of Boston. Dr. Channing was one of its originators, and so, less directly, were Coleridge, Carlyle, and the Germans whom they make known to the

English-speaking races. Mr. Alcott was a Transcendentalist by birth, and early imbibed a relish for speculation and sentiments such as the Transcendentalists were familiar with. He first heard Dr. Channing preach (on the "Dignity of the Intellect") in April, 1828, and in October of the same year he listened to a sermon from R. W. Emerson, at the Chauncey Place church, Boston, on "The Universality of the Notion of a Deity." In Philadelphia, between the years 1830 and 1834, he read many metaphysical and mystical books, and speculated deeply on the nature of the soul and on human perfectability, so that he was well prepared, upon his return to New England in the autumn of 1834, to join in the then nascent Transcendental movement, which went forward rapidly to its culmination about 1840, after which it ebbed away, and gave its strength to other and more special agitations. In 1837, when the Philistines were in full cry against the Temple School and its heretical teacher, Mr. Alcott was spoken of as the leader of the Transcendentalists,—a distinction now generally given to his friend Mr. Emerson, with whom he became intimate in 1835-6. They joined in many activities of the time ; were members and originators of the somewhat famous Transcendental club, which met under various names, from 1836 to 1850. It was first called "The Symposium," and met originally on the 19th of September, 1836, at the house of George Ripley, then a minister in Boston. In the October following, it met at Mr. Alcott's house (26 Front street), and there were present Mr. Emerson, George Ripley, Frederic H. Hedge, O. A. Brownson, James Freeman Clarke, and C. A. Bartol. The subject of conversation that day was "American genius ; causes which hinder its growth." Two years' later, in 1838, we find it meeting at Dr. Bartol's, in Chestnut street, Boston, where of late years the "Radical Club" has often gathered ; there were then present Mr. Emerson, Mr. Alcott, Dr. Follan, Dr. C. Francis, Theodore Parker, Caleb Stetson, William Russell, James Freeman Clarke, and John S. Dwight, the famous musical critic. The topic discussed was "Pantheism." In September, 1839, there is record of a meeting at the house of Dr. Francis, in Watertown, where, besides those already mentioned, Margaret Fuller, William Henry Channing, Robert Bartlett, and Samuel J. May, were present. In December, 1839, at George Ripley's, Dr. Channing, George Bancroft, the sculptor Clevenger, the artist-poet C. P. Cranch, and Samuel G. Ward, were among the company. These names will give some notion of the nature of the club, and the attraction it had for thinking and aspiring persons. In October, 1840, we find Mr. Alcott in consultation with George Ripley and Margaret Fuller, at Mr. Emerson's house, in Concord, concerning the proposed community, which was afterwards established at Brook Farm. In 1848, the Transcendental club became the "Town and County Club," on a wider basis, and in a year or two came to an end, having done its work.

During this period of Transcendental agitation, from 1835 to 1850, Mr. Alcott gradually passed through the various degrees of his progress as a reformer. In 1835, he gave up the use of animal food, and the next year wanted Dr. Sylvester Graham to lecture in his school. Still earlier he had joined the anti-slavery society, when founded by William Lloyd Garrison, and he was present at many of the celebrated gatherings of abolitionists,—for instance at the Lovejoy meeting in Faneuil Hall, in 1837, when Wendell Phillips made his first appearance as an anti-slavery orator. In 1840, he met at Chardon Street chapel, with the "Friends of Universal Reform," among whom were Garrison, Edmund Quincy, Henry C. Wright, Theodore Parker, W. H. Channing, Mrs. Maria Chapman, Abby Kelly, Christopher Greene, and others of the same school of thought. Soon after this, plans for life in communities began to be much talked about, and Mr. Alcott indulged in the hope that something might thus be done to reform the evils of the time. He was invited to join the Brook Farm community, and that of Adin Ballou at Hopedale in Milford, but declined and instead, fell back for a while on plain living and manual labor at Concord, where he worked in field and garden, and in the winter of 1840-1 chopped wood in the woodlands of that village.

Speaking of this period in Mr. Alcott's life, Dr. Channing said in a letter to one of his friends, written in July, 1841:—"Mr. Alcott little suspects how my heart goes out to him. One of my dearest ideas and hopes is the union of *labor* and *culture*. I wish to see labor honored, and united with the free development of the intellect and heart. Mr. Alcott, hiring himself out for day labor, and at the same time living in a region of high thought, is, perhaps, the most interesting object in our Commonwealth. I do not care much for Orpheus in 'The Dial;' but Orpheus at the plough is after my own heart. There he teaches a grand lesson; more than most of us teach by the pen."

Sailing for England in May, 1842, his experience there confirmed Mr. Alcott in his dream of an ideal community, and on his return in October, he began to prepare for founding such a paradise. Meanwhile he refused to comply with the requirements of civil society, and for declining to pay his tax was lodged in the Concord jail, January 16, 1843. The late Samuel Hoar, father of Judge Hoar, and Hon. George F. Hoar, paid the tax without Mr. Alcott's consent, and he was released the same day. During the following spring, in company with one of his English friends, Charles Lane, he examined estates with a view to purchase one for the proposed community, and finally Lane bought the "Wyman Farm, in Harvard, consisting of 90 acres, with an old farm-house upon it, where Mr. Alcott and his family, with Mr. Lane and a few others, took up their abode in June, 1843, calling the new home "Fruitlands."

This place, a picturesque farm, lying now along the Worcester and Nashua railroad, and bordering the Nashua river in Harvard, Mass., was not well adapted for such an experiment as Mr. Alcott and his friends undertook; nor did their hopes and plans agree with the condition of things in the world. Their way of life was to be cheerful and religious, free from the falsehood and the cares that infested society; it became, in fact, hard and dismal, and ended in bringing Mr. Alcott, almost with despair in his heart, to give up his hopes of initiating a better life among mankind by the example of such communities as he had planned Fruitlands to be. He finally abandoned the farm, in poverty and disappointment, about the middle of January, 1844. The lesson thus taught, was a severe one, but Mr. Alcott looks back upon it as one of the turning points in his life. From that day forward, he has had less desire to change the outward condition of men upon earth than to modify and enlighten their inward life. He soon after returned to Concord, and in 1845 bought a small farm there with an old house upon it, which he rebuilt and christened "Hillside." A few years later when it passed into the hands of Nathaniel Hawthorne, he changed the name to "Wayside." It is the estate next east of that where Mr. Alcott now resides, in Concord. At "Hillside" Mr. Alcott gardened and gave conversations, and in the year 1847, while living there, he built in Mr. Emerson's garden, not far off, the unique summer house which ornamented the grounds until within ten years past, when it decayed and fell into ruin. In 1848 he removed from Concord to Boston, and did not return until 1857. Since then he has lived constantly in that town.

It was a favorite theory of Mr. Alcott's, through all this period of agitation and outward activity, that he could propagate his ideas best by conversations. Accordingly, from 1839 to the present time, a quarter of a century, he has held conversations on his chosen subjects, and in many and widely separated parts of the country. He has not valued, as many reformers do, the opportunity of moving great numbers of people, at conventions and in churches, but has preferred the more quiet, and, as he esteems it, the more natural method of conversing. This period of his life may perhaps then be best described as the period of conversation; although of later years he has often spoken from pulpits and platforms, on the same topics with which his conversations have to do. It is to be remembered, also, that Mr. Alcott was the first person in America, at least in modern times, to develop conversation as a means of public instruction, for which it was much employed in the period of Greek philosophy. An ingenious critic, Mr. Harris, of St. Louis, has lately argued that the philosophy of Mr. Alcott is rather that of Aristotle than of Plato; but however this may be, it is certain that his conversational methods are more like those which Plato has made so familiar than like the sententious disquisitions of Aristotle. In spirit, it must be said that from what we know of Pythagoras, he was more nearly the prototype of Mr. Alcott in philosophy than either Plato or Aristotle.

The literary period of Mr. Alcott's life has been subsequent to his greatest activity as a teacher by conversation, and it is only of late years that he has appeared as the author of volumes. The "Record of a School," and the "Conversations on the Gospels," were compiled by other persons, reporting what was said. During the publication of the Dial, from 1840 to 1844, when it was the organ of the Transcendentalists, Mr. Alcott contributed some pages, among them his "Orphic Sayings," which attracted much notice, not always of the most respectful kind. Other writings of that period and earlier, for the most part, remained in manuscript. After a long period in which he published little or nothing, Mr. Alcott, about 1858, became the superintendent of schools in Concord, and in this capacity printed several long reports, which are noticeable publications. He published some essays, poems, and conversations in the Boston

Commonwealth and The Radical, between 1863 and 1868, and in the last-named year brought out a modest volume of essays entitled "Tablets." This was followed, in 1872, by another volume styled "Concord Days," and still other volumes are said to be in preparation. Mr. Alcott has been pressed to write his autobiography, for which his journals and other collections would give him ample material, and it is to be hoped he will apply himself to this task. Should the work include his correspondence with contemporaries, it would be of ample bulk and of great value.

At all times he was enamored of rural pursuits, and has practiced gardening with zeal and success. His present Concord estate, of a few acres only, was laid out and for years cultivated by himself. His connection with the public schools of Concord continued for some years and was of much service to them. In later times he has visited and spoken in the schools wherever he happened to be lecturing or conversing, particularly at the West, where he has been warmly welcomed in his annual tours. His home has been at all times a center of hospitality, and a resort for persons with ideas and aspirations. Not unfrequently his formal conversations have been held there; at other times in the parlors of his friends, at public halls or college rooms, or in the chambers of some club. A list of the towns and cities in which these conversations have taken place, with the names of those who have had part in them, would indicate how wide has been the influence, for thought and culture, exercised by Mr. Alcott in this peculiar manner.

Mr. Alcott is in person tall and fair, of kindly and dignified bearing, resembling somewhat the portraits of Wordsworth, but of a more elegant mien and a more polished manner than Wordsworth seems to have possessed. There are several portraits of Mr. Alcott, at different ages,— one a crayon sketch by Mrs. Richard Hildreth, taken in 1855, and another by Seth Cheney the Con-

necticut-born crayon artist, taken about 1855. This is
not a crayon, however, but a medallion in plaster, and
perhaps the best representation of Mr. Alcott's features
yet made. A bust modelled by the sculptor, Thomas
R. Gould, in the autumn of 1873, when cut in marble, will
give his features and expression at the age of seventy-
four. At this period, though touched by time, he is still
youthful in spirit and capable of much travel and fatigue
and of assiduous mental labor. It is not, however, so
much by intellectual efforts that he has distinguished
himself, as by a "wise passivity," and a natural intuition,
or as Mr. Emerson has said of him, in the sketch which
the New American Cyclopedia contains, by "subtle and
deep science of that which actually passes in thought."
Mr. Emerson adds: "Thought is ever seen by him in its
relation to life and morals. Those persons who are best
prepared by their own habit of thought set the highest
value on his subtle perception and facile generalization."
No person of our time seems to have valued them more
highly than Mr. Emerson himself, and the long and constant friendship between these two founders of a school
of philosophy in New England deserves mention in any
memoir of either. Mr. Alcott has sought to pay a tribute
to his friend by the writing of an essay concerning his
genius, which was privately printed in Cambridge in 1865.

Some of the other writings of Mr. Alcott have already
been mentioned, and all of them will be found in the
Wolcott Centenary Library. They are compiled in
part from the journals which he has been in the habit
of keeping for many years, and which, along with his
"Autobiographical Collections" now form a long series of
volumes in his library, of great personal and historical
interest. They have been freely used in the preparation
of this sketch. But however much or little he may write
in the serene years of age which still remain to him, he
will probably point to his children, as the old poet did
to his early lost son, —

"Ben Jonson, his best piece of poetry."

MISS LOUISA M. ALCOTT.

Miss Louisa May Alcott, the popular writer of humorous and pathetic tales, owes her training, and thus her success in writing, to her father and mother more than to all the world beside. Her instruction for many years came almost wholly from them, and though her genius has taken a direction quite other than that of Mr. Alcott (guided strongly by her mother's social humor and practical benevolence), it still has many traits of resemblance ; while the material on which it works is largely drawn from the idyllic actual life of the Alcott family. It can scarcely be remembered when Louisa Alcott did not display the story-telling talent, either with her voice or with her pen. Her first book was published nineteen years ago, and had been written several years before that. For a long period afterward she contributed copiously to newspapers and periodicals of no permanent renown, though some of the pieces then written have since appeared in her collection of tales. Her first great success as a writer was in 1863, when, after a brief experience as an army nurse, followed by a long and almost fatal illness, she contributed to the Boston Commonwealth those remarkable papers called "Hospital Sketches." These were made up from her letters written home during her army life, and bore the stamp of reality so strongly upon them, that they caught at once the popular heart. They were re-printed in many newspapers, and in a small volume, and made her name known and beloved all over the North. From that time forward she has been a popular writer for the periodicals, but her great success as an author of books did not begin until she found a publisher of the right quality in Mr. Thomas Niles, of the Boston firm of Roberts Brothers, who have now published all her works for six years. Within that time the "Little Women" and their successors have been published, and the sale of all her books has exceeded a quarter of a million copies. Her earliest novel, "Moods," published in 1864, by A. K. Loring, of Boston, did not at first command much attention, but has since sold many thousand copies. Her second novel, "Work," was published by Roberts, in the summer of 1873, and at once had a great sale, both in America and in Europe. Many of her books have been translated into French and German, and there are now few living authors whose works are so universally read.

MISS MAY ALCOTT.

Mr. Alcott's youngest daughter, now pursuing her art in England, has been known for some years as a graceful artist, and art teacher. She has studied in London and in Rome, as well as in her own New England, and though she has attempted few original pictures or sketches, she has shown an appreciation for drawing and modelling and coloring, which give promise of excellent work hereafter. It is interesting to know that the best portraits of her mother in existence are the work of her hands—one a crayon sketch, and the other a medallion modelled by Miss May Alcott quite early in her course as an art student. She has also had some practice of late, as a writer, and several of her letters from Europe have been published in the journals of the day.

The town of Wolcott can point with pride to the career of the Alcott family in all its branches, as one of its glories. Those who have remained within the town limits have been diligent and virtuous citizens, while of those who have gone forth into the great world, more than one have distinguished themselves and become illustrious without wandering from the ancestral path of virtue and fidelity. Mr. Bronson Alcott has held opinions and engaged in enterprises, during his lifetime, which would not have commanded the entire approbation of his townsmen, had they been called to pass judgment upon them ; but with the general result of his long and varied life, neither they nor he can have reason to be dissatisfied. He has not accumulated riches, nor attained political power, nor made labor superfluous and comfort cheaper by ingenious mechanical inventions. But he has maintained, at all times and amid many discouragements, the Christian doctrine that the life is more than meat, and that the perishing things of this world are of small moment compared with things spiritual and eternal. He has devoted himself, in youth with ardor, in mature and advancing years with serene benevolence, to the task of improving the hearts and lives of men, by drawing their attention to the sweetness of philosophy and the charms of a religion at once contemplative and practical. There is no higher work than this, and none that leaves so plainly its impress on the character and aspect of him who spends a lifetime in it. Those who had the pleasure of seeing and hearing Mr. Alcott, at the Centenary gathering will remember how much his words and his presence added to the interest of that occasion. And we are confident the reader will not regret the space allotted to his biography in this collection.

DR. WILLIAM A. ALCOTT.

Dr. William A. Alcott was born in Wolcott, Connecticut, on the 6th of August, 1798. His father was a hard working farmer, in moderate circumstances, being a lineal descendant of the third generation of Mr. John Alcock, the first settler in the territory which became Wolcott. His mother, Anna Andrus Alcott, was descended from Abraham Andrus, one of the original settlers of Waterbury, and was a woman of practical good sense, having been a teacher in the public schools, which was regarded, in those days, as more than an ordinary accomplishment. His opportunites for education were confined to the district school, for three or four months in the summer, and four months in the winter, until he was eight years old, and after that age, to the winter term for four or five years. After this he attended for about six months the select school taught by Rev. Mr. Keys, the minister of the parish, in which school he acted frequently as tutor, and where he first began to develop a genius and pleasure in teaching, which afterwards formed a large part of his life work. He possessed from his early years a taste for the reading of books, which was probably inculcated by his mother, and continued to be fostered by his associations with his cousin, A. Bronson Alcott, who was also of the same mind. In addition to the books in his father's house, and those which he could borrow from the neighbors, he had access to the parish library, after he was fourteen years of age, which library, though not in a flourishing condition, furnished a number of very valuable books, and some of them exerted a most marked influence upon his character in after years.

When a little more than eighteen years of age he commenced teaching school in his native district, the school house standing but a few rods west of his father's dwelling house, and in the district where the larger part of the pupils and inhabitants were his relatives. The wages were ten dollars per month for three months, and seemed doubtless quite a sum for a lad to bring into his father's treasury, even though the father boarded him during the time; especially when the work performed out of school hours was equal in value to the board. In those days the son had no right to money for his labor while under twenty-one years of age, for the law said the son should serve the father until twenty-one, and to obey the law was one part of Christian life, whether the law was Christian or not. His labor in the school and that for his father consumed every moment not occupied in sleep, and divided his efforts to such an extent that the success of the school was not what it would have been if the time out of school could have been given to plans and appliances for the forwarding of the work of teaching.

We make the following extracts from a Memoir of Dr. Alcott, published in Barnard's Journal of Education, for March, 1858:

For six successive winters, with the single interruption of one year (when he went to teach), he continued to be employed in different parts of Hartford and Litchfield counties, with a gradually increasing compensation. By a few he was valued because they thought him a smart master, who would make the pupils know their places; by others, for his reputation as a scholar; and by others still, because he was valued highly by the children. It was in those days very much as it is now; parents would not visit schools where their children were if they could help it; and what they knew about the school they had to take at second-hand. Two things he certainly did as a teacher: he labored incessantly, "both in season and out of season." No man was ever more punctual or more faithful to his employers. And then he governed his school with that kind of martial law which secured a silence, that in the common schools of that day had been little known, which fact secured for him one species of reputation that extended far and wide, so that his services were by a particular class much sought after.

In a teacher's life under the influences, and surrounded by the difficulties that existed in those days, it could not be expected but that some mistakes would be made, yet with all these, he was pre-eminently a successful teacher and was very greatly attached to his employment, and began to entertain the hope that he could one day make teaching his one permanent occupation though there were serious difficulties in the way. The scanty wages, twelve dollars a month, gave little encouragement to such an object, besides male teachers were usually hired for only three or four months in the year, and if he concluded on this life work his chosen profession, that of a printer, must be abandoned, which he was not fully reconciled to do.

In the spring of 1822, when he was nearly twenty-four years of age, after he had closed his sixth annual winter term, he engaged in a school for one year. It was a new thing in the place, but relying on his fame, which had long since reached them, and anxious to obtain his services, even at extra cost, it was agreed to employ him for the time above mentioned, including a vacation of one month, at nine dollars a month, or ninety-nine dollars a year and his board. To this was added, by a liberal individual, one dollar, making the sum one hundred dollars, upon which the offer was accepted, and he began his school early in May. He boarded in the families, which, to a person of a missionary spirit, such as he possessed, had its advantages, and Dr. Alcott endeavored to improve these opportunities to raise the standard of education among the people. One of the first things he urged upon the attention of his employers was an improvement of the school-room, and after much effort and patience in urging upon parents the physical benefits of some reforms, he secured seats in the schoolroom with backs to them in the place of the old slab benches. Heating and ventilating came next, but the most he could accomplish in this respect was to open the doors and windows at every recess, and let the pure air of heaven sweep through for a few moments. His largest improvements, however, were in regard to methods of teaching, particularly for the youngest pupils, and for these he substituted the employment of drawing on slates as an amusement as well as improvement, which was a new idea in the schools of those days. He procured a dozen or two of small slates and one large one, which latter answered for a blackboard, upon which were pictured birds, dogs, cats, houses, trees, and many other things, and proceeding from these to the making of letters in the printed form, then to words and their arrangement into sentences, and compositions. He delighted, also, to get around him a group of children, and by telling stories of history thus secured their cheerful and punctual attendance rather than by way of flogging. To these exercises he added some extra recitations out of school hours which he was not allowed to hear in the formal six hours. His zeal and labors were as untiring as they were unheard of before in that region, for he not only gave up his mornings and evenings to the children and their parents, but he would not permit himself to sit in the school room, and was literally on his feet from morning until night, or, as more commonly expressed, was "always on the jump."

The severities of his self-denials and exertions, joined to other causes, especially a feeble and delicate constitution, brought on him, toward the end of the summer, a violent attack of erysipelas, from the effects of which, though he escaped with his life, he never entirely recovered.

At the close of the year for which he had engaged, although the district did not feel able to continue him by the year, they unanimously engaged him for the term of six months the ensuing winter, at the price of thirteen dollars a month. This was deemed a compensation quite in advance of those times, and was accepted as entirely satisfactory." During the winter of 1824-5, Mr. A. Bronson Alcott succeeded him in this district while Dr. Alcott was engaged in the central school of Bristol, a district adjoining the scene of his former labors. Here he took upon himself the additional work of the study of medicine, restricting himself to four hours of sleep, which brought on him a severe illness, from which causes he did not add to his reputation as a teacher. In studying medicine he had no intention to relinquish teaching but the better to prepare himself for this profession, and also, should his health fail, of which there were increasing signs, he might have another method of doing good and securing a competency for life.

During the winter of 1825-6, he attended a regular course of medical lectures at New Haven, and in the following March received a Diploma to practice medicine and surgery. At this time his health was far from good and he began to have apprehensions of fatal results of lung difficulty.

Leaving the college at a season of the year when it was not customary to hire male teachers, he, after some hesitation made application for the central school in his native town at a dollar and a half a week and " board around," that being the usual rate paid to female teachers. This offer, though unexpected and not a little mysterious, was accepted by the district; and in May, 1826, he commenced his work.

It was his settled determination, and he did not hesitate to make it fully known, to have a model school, on his own favorite plan, although the pecuniary means were wanting. He had not ten dollars in the world. All his resources, after paying for his medical education and a few books, and after remunerating his father, as he was proud to believe he did, for the expense of bringing him up, were soon exhausted in fitting up his schoolroom, — in the purchase of maps, designs, vessels for flowers and plants, and such fixtures as in his judgment would conduce to the proper cultivation of the mind and heart and taste of his pupils. He rightly judged that a plain and unpretentious people, who knew him well, would not seriously object to innovations which cost them nothing in dollars and cents. He was, indeed, regarded as a little visionary, but was allowed to go on uninterrupted in his plans; and in his missionary life, going from house to house for his board, he had opportunity for making, from time to time, such explanations as were quite satisfactory.

Besides carrying out and perfecting the approved method of

teaching the elementary branches, which he had for several years been applying with so much success, he added to them several others, particularly in defining grammar and geography. He introduced, also, what he called his silent, or Quaker, exercises. This consisted in requiring his pupils, at a certain time every morning, usually immediately after the opening of the school and devotional exercises, to lay aside everything else, and give themselves up to reflection on the events, duties, and privileges of the twenty-four hours next preceding. At the close of this unbroken silence, which usually lasted five minutes, any pupil was liable to be called upon to relate the recitations and events of the preceding day, in their proper order and sequence.

In commencing this school in his native town, Dr. Alcott had other and very exalted ulterior aims. His warm heart embraced no less than the whole of his townsmen. These he meant to enlighten, elevate, and change, until Wolcott should become a miniature Switzerland. But his pulmonary difficulties, which had been for ten years increasing upon him, aggravated, no doubt, by hard study, improper diet, and other irregularities of the preceding winter, now became threatening in the extreme. Besides a severe cough and great emaciation, he was followed by hectic fever, and the most exhausting and discouraging perspirations. He fought bravely to the last moment, but was compelled to quit the field and relinquish for the present all hopes of accomplishing his mission.

For a short time he followed the soundest medical advice he could obtain; keeping quiet, taking a little medicine, eating nutritious food, and when his strength would permit, breathing pure air. This course was at length changed for one of greater activity, and less stimulous. He abandoned medicine, adopted for a time, the "starvation system," or nearly that, and threw himself by such aids as he could obtain, into the fields and woods, and wandered among the hills and mountains. In the autumn he was evidently better and was able to perform light horticultural labors a few hours of the day, and to ride on horseback. For six months he continued the horseback exercise, almost daily, as a sort of journeyman physician; at the end of which period he commenced the practice of medicine on his own responsibility, at

Wolcott Centre, continuing to make his professional visits on horseback. His hopes of inspiring the people of his native town with a spirit of improvement now revived. He not only practiced medicine but took a deep interest in the moral and intellectual condition of the people. He superintended a Sabbath school; aided in the examination of the public school teachers, and held teachers meetings in his own hired house. Not Oberlin himself, in his beloved Ban de La Roche, had purer or more benevolent or more exalted purposes."

Dr. Alcott's application to become a member of the Congregational Society is still preserved among the papers of the Society, and corroborates the above extracts.

Dr. Alcott's Letter.

" *Clerk of the Congregational Society in Wolcott :*

Sir :—Believing that regular public preaching of the Gospel useful to Society in general and a means of training up children in the way they should go, as well as of affording instruction to the ignorant and those that are out of the way even in later life;— and furthermore despairing of seeing any other Society in town do any thing at present, I have come to a conclusion to make request that my name be entered among the names of those who belong to your Society, until such a state of things shall arise as may seem to justify the withdrawing of my support. Should a tax be laid *this day* suffer me to be considered a member of the Society and taxed accordingly. Yours, &c.

WM. A. ALCOTT.

Wolcott, April 16, 1827.

The Sabbath school which the Doctor inaugurated was the first one in the parish superintended by a layman, and was a successful school, being remembered with great pleasure by a number of people still living.* One feature of the school was the books which the superintendent contrived (some way, no one knows how,) to obtain for the children to read. It was a marvel of joy

---

* See page 109 of this History.

then, and as such is still very distinctly remembered. Not content with this effort to furnish books for the Sabbath School, "he began to collect a library for the town." These volumes were loaned from time to time, but the plan was so troublesome that he abandoned it, and prevailed with his friends and townsmen to establish a public town library on the ruins of the old one, to which reference has been made. This library continued a few years, and then was distributed among the original contributors.

He had already begun to write for the newspapers, on various subjects, particularly on common school education. A series of papers had been contributed and published in the Columbian Register, of New Haven, as early as 1823, and several shorter series on the same subject appeared in this and other papers during the years 1826 and 1827. Another series appeared from his pen between the years 1826 and 1829, in the Boston Journal of Education, then under the care of William Russell.

These papers brought him into association with the best minds in his native State, on the subject of educational improvement, particularly the Rev. Samuel J. May, of Brooklyn, Conn., and others in Hartford.

Dr. Alcott's labors in Wolcott, in his profession as physician and his connection with the Sabbath school and the Ecclesiastical Society, are spoken of in the highest terms of praise, though it is acknowledged that his opinions and ideas were regarded at the time, by some of the people, as radical and a little visionary. To-day his memory is honored by all the people, and at the late Centenary meeting no descendant of Wolcott's sons was received with greater cordiality by the people than Rev. William P. Alcott, the only son of the Doctor.

In the Autumn of the year 1829, he resigned his medical practice and engaged in teaching a school in the town of Southington. In this school he followed successfully some of his new ideas of teaching, so far that a decided impression was made by them, but the effort impaired his health so that he gave up for a time all hope of teaching and concluded to labor on a farm near New Haven. Just as he was settling on the farm he had occasion to be in Hartford, where, to his surprise, he met Rev. Wm. C. Woodbridge, who had returned from Europe, and, though in feeble health, was endeavoring to rouse the attention of a few friends of education to the necessity of forming a school for teachers, on the plan of Mr. Fellenberg's school, in Hofwyl, which he had been studying for some time. Mr. Woodbridge inquired of Dr. Alcott what he considered the capital error of modern education. "The custom of pushing the cultivation of the intellect at the expense of health and morals," was the reply. This question and reply laid the foundation for an acquaintance and friendship that was as lasting as the life of the parties. He engaged as an assistant to Mr. Woodbridge in a "miniature Fellenberg school" in the vicinity of Hartford, for the moderate compensation of twelve dollars a month, and such was his enthusiasm in trying to elevate the common schools, that when offered three hundred dollars a year as teacher he only required Mr. Woodbridge to raise his wages to fifteen dollars a month.

During this engagement with Mr. Woodbridge the press teemed with his articles; especially the Connecticut Observer and Hartford Courant. One very substantial and elaborate review of a report on the Manual Labor School of Pennsylvania, the product of his pen, appeared and met with much favor, and was quoted by foreign writers. At this time he conceived the idea of establishing a journal of education, but for several reasons was under the necessity of delaying the enterprise.

It was during the years 1830 and 1831 that he prepared, and on several occasions delivered, his essay on the construction of school houses, to which the American Institute of Instruction, in the Autumn of 1831, awarded a premium, and which led the way to that large and thorough improvement in this department, which is now going on in this country and elsewhere.

At this time, also, he engaged with Mr. Gallaudet, Hon. Roger W. Sherman, Hon. Hawley Olmstead, Mr. Woodbridge, and others in forming a state society for the improvement of common schools, and he did much to sustain it.

A History of the first public school of Hartford, in which some recent advances had been made, a volume of a hundred pages or more, was written by him about this time, and also a volume of nearly the same size, entitled " A Word to Teachers." It is believed that his essays, in conjunction with the labors of others, had much influence, not only in New England, but throughout the United States. The most important of all his numerous labors at this period was his travels for the purpose of collecting facts concerning schools. Reports of these travels were made in various ways, and enlisted much interest and tended to awaken the public mind to the subject of common schools. In 1831, Mr. Woodbridge removed to Boston to edit the Journal of Education, and induced the Doctor to follow him. On his arrival in Boston, through a severe storm, he was attacked with a pulmonary difficulty, from which he but slowly recovered, but from which difficulty, thereafter, for nearly twenty-five years, he was surprisingly free ; nor did he often have so much as a common cold.

Doctor Alcott had formed many valuable acquaintances in Connecticut ; among them were Dr. John L. Comstock, Rev. Horace Hooker, Rev. C. A. Goodrich, Noah Webster, A. F. Wilcox, and Josiah Holbrook, and therefore he left the state with regret.

Besides assisting Mr. Woodbridge in conducting the Journal of Education, by writing a large proportion of the articles on physical education, methods of instruction, and book notices, he was for two years, 1832 and 1833, the practical editor of a children's weekly paper, started by Mr. Woodbridge and his aged father. The paper was called the "Juvenile Rambler," and was perhaps the first paper of the kind ever issued in this country. He also engaged in labors in various forms in the cause of education, never losing sight for a moment of the public schools. During 1832 and 1833 he wrote "The Young Man's Guide," a book which found an extensive sale, and proved remunerative to its author, as well as accomplishing a great amount of good. At the end of the year 1833, he was engaged by S. G. Goodrich as the editor of a monthly journal entitled "Parley's Magazine," which he edited four successive years, continuing his relation with the "Annals of Education," which he did to the end of his career, sometimes with pay, and sometimes without. His contributions to the periodical press, many of them to the Recorder, Watchman, and Traveler, of Boston, and to the Boston Medical and Surgical Journal, have been almost innumerable. He preserved copies of more than a thousand. Probably no individual up to his time ever devoted more hours during forty years to education, especially that of the common school and the family, than Doctor Alcott. It is difficult to imagine any mode in which more beneficial results could be secured to the schools than by the varied and instructive lectures which he delivered to schools, teachers, parents, and pupils, during many years of travel for this purpose, and the innumerable hints and suggestions which his conversation would supply, on the subjects of hygiene, elementary instruction, and physical and moral training, to all, whether old or young. The labor of such a life is not easily summed up or described, but one conclusion is inevitable: it was a life of immense work, and is very fittingly represented by a remark written by the sister of the Doctor's wife, in a letter to the author of this book: "He was an earnest worker for humanity; the great purpose and aim of his life being to make men better,— to raise them physically, intellectually, and morally."

Dr. Alcott married (January 14th, 1836,) Miss Phebe L. Bronson, daughter of Deacon Irad Bronson, of Bristol, and grand-daughter of Deacon Isaac Bronson, of Wolcott, who still survives him. His children are William P., now a successful Congregational minister, and Phebe A., married and residing in Alabama.

Dr. Alcott's home, for the last fifteen years of his life, was in the town of Newton near Boston, and the last seven on a place of his own in Auburndale, a village of that town, where he died of pleurisy, March 29, 1859. His remains were buried in the Newton cemetery. His last illness lasted but one week, and he seemed to be convalescent on the day before his death, so much so that he dictated several letters, and as a member of the School Committee gave some directions concerning the grading of the school grounds. During the night his suffering returned in great severity, he being unable to lie down. He was conscious that his end was near, and made such final arrangements as were necessary. In the morning his pain was less but his breath grew shorter and he became unable to speak. Towards noon, while sitting in an easy chair, he suddenly looked up, extending his hands in the same direction, while an expression of delight passed over his face, as if he beheld a vision of glory, and fell asleep. His wife and daughter were with him in his last sickness and received his last expressions of confidence and devotion, and to his son, then in college and for whom it was thought unnecessary to send until it was too late, he sent this message: "Tell William to live for others, not for himself." He died, as he had always hoped to die, "with his harness on." It was his desire that a post mortem examination should be made, which revealed such a variety of morbid conditions of the lungs as to make it surprising that he had lived so long. He was accustomed to say that "through the Divine blessings on his simple diet and healthful modes of living, his life had been lengthened twice as long as King Hezekiah's."

DR. WILLIAM A. ALCOTT.

In the life and labors of Dr. Alcott, as well as in many others, the people of Wolcott have much reason to feel greatly honored.

Dr. Alcott's published volumes are classified as follows:

I. Works designed particularly for schools and teachers, and friends of education,—nineteen volumes,—nine of them containing over three hundred pages each.

II. Physiology, physical education, and health,—thirty-one volumes,—twelve of which contain over three hundred pages; several of which had passed through twelve editions each, two fifteen, and one twenty-one, in 1858.

III. Books for the family and school library,—fourteen volumes,—one of which had passed through twelve editions, one through seventeen, and one through twenty-two editions in 1858.

IV. Books for Sabbath School library,—forty-four volumes.

Whole number of volumes, one hundred and eight.

REV. WILLIAM P. ALCOTT.

Rev. William P. Alcott, son of Dr. William A. Alcott, was born in Dorchester, Mass., July 11th, 1842. He graduated at Williams College in 1861, and at Andover Theological Seminary in 1865. After preaching for a short time in Heath and Cohasset, Mass., and giving a course of lectures on chemistry in Williams College, he was settled over the Congregational church, in North Greenwich, Conn., Feb. 18, 1868, where he still remains. He was married Aug. 26, 1868, to Sarah Jane, daughter of the late Rev. David Merrill, of Peacham, Vt. He has been very successful in his parish and is rising in influence and esteem in his own denomination, and wherever known. He was moderator this year (1873) of Fairfield West Consociation. His intellectual character is of the scientific-philosophic type, yet he holds firmly to revealed truths as such, and is reliable in his convictions and judgments. His mother being a Bronson (grand-daughter of Dea. Isaac) he has an inheritance of ancestry in which many would find great satisfaction.

While in college he accompanied, by appointment, a scientific expedition to Greenland,—an honor and an advantage quite important. He has given much attention to science, and especially to botany. As might be expected, he cherishes many of the thoughts and principles of moral and physical culture, so forcibly and practically given to the world by his honored father.

JOSEPH ATKINS.

Joseph Atkins came from Hartford to Bristol about 1752, where he owned a dwelling and several pieces of land, and the half of a grist mill. He removed to Wolcott in 1758 or 1759, where he purchased several pieces of land. Not long after his settlement here, he built a grist mill on Mad River, a little below the Great Falls. He afterwards owned a saw mill near his grist mill. In 1770 he resided with his son Joseph, and it is thought that the house in which they lived stood half a mile east of the mill, on a lot lying south of the highway, a little east of Mr. Ira H. Hough's present dwelling house, but it possibly may have stood near the mill. Mr. Atkins was a very energetic, successful business man, and was an important man in the organization of Farmingbury Society, and in building the first Meeting house. He gave two acres of earth surface for the use of the Society for a church site, and other purposes. It could not be said to be land, for much of it is rock, but yet it is very good upon which to build a church, and has served that end as well as any portion of the town could. His name, and that of his wife, Abigail, stand seventh and eighth on the list among the first members of the church. He died in 1782, as given on the church record,— there being no inscription on grave stones to mark his grave. He was seventy-one years of age. His wife, Abigail, died in 1796, and was probably over eighty years of age.

DEACON JOSEPH ATKINS.

Deacon Joseph Atkins, the son of Joseph, senior, who came from Bristol, was elected second deacon of the church April 19, 1786, or four years after the death of his father, and when the church was prosperous, and had a large number of men that, we should judge, might have served acceptably as deacons. He is said to have been a polemical deacon, always ready to go through with the argument of the decrees without hesitancy, and without a shadow of doubt as to the interpretation of the Scriptures thereby given. He was a very faithful, diligent Christian man, always at his place in church, and in visiting and comforting the flock, as an under shepherd. On a Sabbath, once, a bear came from the wood and took a pig from the deacon's pen and made a dinner of him, but it is not asserted that the reason of his taking the *deacon's* pig was that he was sure the deacon would be at church on that day; nor do we learn that the deacon staid at home on Sunday afterward in order to shoot that old bruin; but we are quite certain that if the people at church in those days had heard the report of a gun on Sunday (a thing we do not mind now-a-days), they would have rallied to a man for a fight with the Indians, not dreaming that any other occurrence could be sufficient cause for such a desecration of that day.

Faith ran in grooves in those days, and one groove was politics (not allowable now-a-days), and when Mr. Thomas Jefferson came up in politics against the great Washington, it is said the deacon was terrible on poor

Thomas. The argument ran thus: "If Jefferson (supposed to be an infidel) were made President of the United States, the Meeting houses would be burned to the ground, and Christians would be burned at the stake." To us this is amusing, knowing as we do how perfectly innocent Mr. Jefferson was of all this kind of argument. However, it shows how diligent the deacon was to watch over the faith and liberty of the church, even though he might not watch the bears of the woods sufficiently on Sunday to save his pigs. After the death of the deacon's father, in 1782, he resided near the mill, east side of the river, in a house built, perhaps, by his father, or by Mr. James Barrett, who resided in that vicinity as one of the first settlers in that part of the town. It was near this house that the deacon's great apple tree stood, from which he is said to have taken apples in such quantity that he made nineteen barrels of cider from one harvesting. The tree was cut down by Mr. Ira H. Hough a few years since, it being over four feet in diameter at the place where it was cut off. The Deacon maintained his integrity of character and faithfulness to the church until 1805, when he resigned his office of deacon and removed west, being among the first settlers (it is said) in the town of Smyrna, Chenango county, N. Y., where he died.

REV. AARON C. BEACH.

Rev. Aaron C. Beach was born in South Orange, N. J., and was graduated at Yale College, in 1835, and in the autumn of the same year entered Yale Theological Seminary, with greatly impaired health. He was licensed to preach by the New Haven West Association, at Waterbury, in 1838, and continued in the seminary about two years after. Late in the year 1841, while visiting in Southington, he was invited to preach in Wolcott, accepted the invitation, and preached in the school-house December 19th, the Meeting house not being completed. He then engaged to preach for the people of Wolcott six months, at the end of which time he received a unanimous call to become their pastor, accepted it, and was ordained to that office June 22d, 1842. It was no small work to engage as pastor of a church and parish where there had been so much division and violent feeling as had been in Wolcott during three years previous to 1841; but Mr. Beach was, as far as now can be seen, "the right man in the right place." The house of worship was completed during the fall and winter, and dedicated January 19th, 1843, when the old difficulties seem to have been buried forever, and the people with one heart followed their leader into the harvest-field to gather the harvest. During his fifteen years of labor here forty-four were added to the membership of the church, twenty-seven of whom by profession; and the dwelling-house (now the parsonage) was built by himself, as his house, and was afterwards sold to the Society. His labors seem to have been of the quiet, steady, every-day-life sort, without great excitement, and without days of complaining and discouragement. Such a life-work of faithfulness is not always appreciated by those to whom it is devoted. In a letter, received from Mr. Beach since this book was commenced, he speaks, as also he did at the Centenary meeting, in the highest terms, of the kindness and sympathy which he received during the whole time of his labors in the parish, and the feeling of kindness is reciprocated from this parish toward him.

Mr. Beach married Lucy Walkley, of Southington, December 28th, 1840. She died in Wolcott, April 2d, 1853. He married, 2d, Jane Talcott, of Portland, Conn., May 6th, 1856. His children are as follows:

David Frame, born in Southington, Conn., October 5th, 1841, and was in the army against the late rebellion, and died of a mortal wound in Louisville, Ky., May 2d, 1862, aged 21.

John Wickliffe, born in Wolcott, January 5th, 1843, and is now settled pastor of the Congregational church at Windsor Locks, Conn.

Lucinda Clark, born in Wolcott, May 1st, 1845, and died in Portland, Conn., May 2d, 1860, aged 15 years, and was buried in Wolcott.

Olive Huldah, born in Wolcott, October 9th, 1847, and died in New Jersey, October 3d, 1848, and was buried there.

Roger Sherman, born in Wolcott, January 5th, 1850, and died in Wolcott, January 30th, 1852.

Since leaving Wolcott two daughters have been added to his family; Laura, the latter of which, died September 28th, 1873, in the sixteenth year of her age.

It will be seen by this record that Wolcott was a place of trial and many sorrows, as well as patient toil, to this good minister of the Lord, and that the graveyard at Wolcott Center has some monuments upon which, when he looks, there will come thrilling remembrances of the past.

And how peculiar the fact that, after having visited Wolcott at the Centenary meeting, and seeing many familiar and friendly faces, and visiting the beautiful little monument in the graveyard that marks the sleeping dust of those once treasured ones of his own household, he should find the waves of sorrow flowing over his home again within fifteen days.

After leaving Wolcott, as pastor, he preached a short time in Marlborough, Conn., receiving a call to become settled pastor, but did not accept it. Soon after this he was installed pastor in Millington parish, East Haddam, Conn., where he is still diligently laboring for the good of men.

REV. JOHN WICKLIFFE BEACH.

Rev. John Wickliffe Beach was born in Wolcott, Conn., January 5th, 1843, and was the second son of Rev. Aaron C. and Lucy Walkley Beach, of Wolcott. A severe illness (scarlet fever) in early childhood left him in delicate health, from which he did not recover for many years, and from this fact his attention was directed to study more than it might otherwise have been under the circumstances of life in which he was placed. His father's limited salary as pastor in Wolcott would have driven him into other pursuits of life but for the habit of early culture and a natural love of learning, and as it was, there was much doubt for years of accomplishing his great desire of collegiate education. But by encouragement and some assistance from kind and considerate friends, and by persevering efforts on his part, he was graduated at Yale College in 1864. His religious life, in definite form, began while in Wolcott, at eleven years of age, when, under his father's ministry, he united with the church. When, therefore, he was graduated, his early and careful Christian life gave a balancing influence in the choice he made as to his future life, to make the preaching of the gospel his life-work. In preparing for this work he spent five years, some of the time teaching, and the balance of the time in Yale Divinity School, in New Haven. None but those who have the trial of such a protracted effort of preparation to commence the work of life, can understand the severe tax of courage and endurance, mental and moral as well as physical, of such a preparation, and especially when the end of such preparation promises, as to this world, small remuneration and limited comforts. Nine years of mercantile life in the place of nine years of college and seminary studies, would have brought this young man, with ordinary success, to a comfortable establishment in a successful, independent business, whereas, as it was, he was only prepared to begin his profession.

His is not an isolated case, but that of many of the successful ministers of the gospel in this country. When, therefore, a young man has run such a race at the beginning of life, and enters upon his life-work, he is worthy of much confidence and encouragement from his parish and friends.

In 1869, John Wickliffe Beach received the degree of Bachelor of Divinity from Yale Divinity School, and the same year began his pastoral labors for the Congregational church at Windsor Locks, Conn., and after preaching there one year was ordained pastor, September 28th, 1870, in which place he is still successfully prosecuting his pastoral labors, and the prospect is that he will honor the name of Wickliffe.

DEACON ISAAC BRONSON.

Deacon Isaac Bronson was born July 19th, 1761. His father, John Bronson, was a native of Southington, and was descended from the Waterbury Bronson family, through John, the son of John Bronson, one of the original thirty subscribers in 1674, in the settlement of Waterbury. Deacon Isaac inherited the characteristics of the Waterbury Bronson families,— strength and decision of intellectual and moral qualities,— and upon these his whole life career was built. Being the son of a plain farmer, in a new country, his early years were passed under disadvantages as to his intellectual aspirations. His life was introduced almost at first to calamity. He says in his journal : "At the age of sixteen months I lost my left eye, and schools not being kept much in those days in the out parts of society, I had not the benefit of one until half way in my sixth year, when I attended one for about three months. When I began in this school I did not know my letters, but soon learned them, and went from class to class until I arrived to the first, during that term ; and before I was eight years old, I had read the Bible through in course, and every other book I could lay my hands on, and so unbounded was my desire after reading, that if I could get hold of a book that I had not read, it was not in the power of my brothers and other mates, either by frowns or flatteries, to persuade me to leave it for the sake of play."

This taste for literature and knowledge so entirely occupied his mind as he grew up to manhood, that when he saw no way to attain a collegiate education, he became greatly discouraged as to life, and fell into a state of indifference and bashfulness that nearly proved his ruin. He says that "it proved my ruin as to this world;" meaning, probably, that he, but for this, could have devoted himself to ordinary work with satisfaction and success. He says also of this thirst for improvement of intellect: "My days were spent in fruitless wishes, and my nights in dreams of books, and of college, and of learning, for years together, until I lost all hopes; although I believe that my living in such an obscure place, and being kept so exceedingly under, and always at home, served to crush me more entirely, and increase my bashfulness until I dare not speak to a person, or I should have attempted, by some means or other, to obtain, and should have persevered in the attempt until I should have forced my way to the attainment of, such a degree of literature as would have enabled me to have spent my life in its delightful researches."

This was written soon after his conversion, and before he was twenty-five years old, and illustrates the manner of training children in those days by good Christian parents; the "keeping them under," and making them bashful as a sign of humility.

Of his religious exercises in early years, he says: "The first workings of conscience which I recollect was when about eight years old, on the occasion of my mother's reading the sufferings of Christ, which made me weep bitterly. When I was about twelve years old, the disease called 'canker' made great ravages in the neighborhood where I lived,— great numbers died. This gave me a violent shock, so that for several months I was in the case of the wicked man mentioned in Job; a dreadful sound was in my ears, for death appeared to be at hand; but it soon wore off. Again, when about half way in my fifteenth year, I set up a new resolution, and partly from awakenings of conscience, and partly from my being debarred from learning, I fell into a kind of melancholy, so that I scarcely smiled for a long time. I sometimes thought of enlisting in the service (revolutionary war), on purpose to get where my life was in constant danger, in hope that it would make me in continual fear of death, and thereby induce me to prepare for it. At last I enlisted, particularly with this view. Alas! how different did it prove!" His description of the reaction of his mind from religion during his soldier life is startling, though to a philosophical mind nothing otherwise would be expected. After returning from the war he continued in this reactionary state of mind several years.

When about half way in his twenty-second year he married Thankful Clark, probably the daughter of Israel Clark, who resided a little north or north-west of Capt. Heman Hall's, and a few months after, was attracted to church by the "extraordinary eloquence," as he says, of the preaching of Rev. Edmond Mills, who was filling Mr. Gillet's pulpit, Mr. Gillet being unable to preach. During the revival which occurred in the summer of 1783, under the preaching of Mr. Mills and Mr. Miller, he entered into the Christian life with great exercises of mind, and also with great decision and earnestness. This new life revived a thirst for knowledge, but brought with it encouragement instead of despondency, and being in his own family, with a noble-spirited wife to cheer him in every good work, his mind was relieved from its many years of morbid reflections and distrust, and his rejoicing was very great. He dates the commencement of his Christian life on the ninth day of August, 1783, and on the 27th of the same month he entered into a "covenant of self-dedication to God," as directed by Dr. Doddridge, of which act he says: "Then, if I know my own heart, on full consideration and serious reflection, I came to this happy resolution,— that whatever others might do, I would serve the Lord, and as I humbly hope, sincerely entered into the following covenant."* This he copied on paper, and signed. On the 21st day of August, 1786, he renewed this covenant, with great confessions of unfaithfulness, and renewing of consecrations to the Lord. At the end of his name on this paper he made a circle, nearly one inch in diameter, and within the circle he made the form of a heart. Inside of the heart he wrote, "May all my heart be thine, my God," and outside the heart, but within the circle, he wrote, "Sealed for eternity, I hope. Amen, and amen." In the year 1788 he united with the church, having hesitated to do it previously because of a feeling of unfitness. His religious life, as indicated in his journal, was characteristic of the age in which he lived; more self-condemnatory than hopeful, yet it was the life of hope to him.

His health was, much of the time, for a number of years, quite poor. He wrote: "May, 1790. Having sustained great loss of blood by bleeding at the nose, which brought on great weakness, and having continual pain at my stomach and in my head for about two months, being troubled with influenza, and continuing to bleed several times a day, I began to conclude my stay here would be but short." As to this prospect of the great change, he expressed resignation to the Divine will, and writes: "But I wished to bring up my children, if it might be, though the greatest attachment I have to this world, by far, is one of the most prudent, kind, and affectionate wives the world ever produced, who spared no pains to render my life comfortable and agreeable, and who was very anxious to have me recover, and would be up and taking care of me when she ought to have been in bed, and to have had a nurse herself." And the result was, that soon after this care for him, his wife was very ill, so that her life seemed about to end here, which weighed heavily on his mind; but she recovered.

---

* See Dr. Philip Doddridge's "Rise and Progress," published by American Tract Society, page 242.

The following is taken from his journal :

WOLCOTT, October 13th, 1802.
After twelve years interregnum I again sit down to write, in the bitterness of my soul, a few words respecting the hand of God at this time lying heavy upon my poor broken, desponding heart. Alas! alas! I have just now closed the eyes of my first-born,— my Isaac, the son in whom I greatly delighted; always faithful, dutiful, and obedient; apt to learn, delighted with reading, of a retentive memory, reflecting mind, and penetrating judgment, and acute discernment for one of his age in the characters and dispositions of all whom he beheld. He was scrupulously fond of truth at all times; sober and temperate in his deportment at all seasons, particularly upon the Sabbath; modest and diffident of himself, he was to me, I had well nigh said, every way agreeable; but O, my God, how hast thou, in a sudden and distressing manner, torn him from me at the age of eighteen years. Assist me, O blessed Jesus, thou who when on earth didst weep at the grave of a friend thyself; thou who knowest all the tender emotions, all the heart-rending sorrows which harrow up the soul of a fond father in my distressed situation. O, may that almighty power of thine that supports the falling universe sustain me in this trying moment."

The following stanzas were composed by himself, soon after the burial of the body of his son, as he says, "On visiting the grave of my dear son on the morning after a violent storm."

> Heart-rending sight! how cruel was that storm,
>   That did not spare this loved, this hallowed mound;
> With wanton rage could Isaac's grave deform,
>   Tear it in twain and wash the earth around.
>
> But why this grief? these unavailing tears?
>   Isaac is safe from storm and tempests' rage;
> Terrestrial scenes no more excite his fears,
>   And worldly cares no more his mind engage.
>
> When solemn darkness veils the midnight skies,
>   And the huge tempest bellows o'er the plain,

Here in the dust, my once loved Isaac lies,
    Nor heeds the howling winds, nor drenching rain.

When driving snows and rattling hail storms sweep
    In fierce tornadoes o'er this hallowed ground,
Lashing his grave till my fond passions weep,
    He sleeps secure, nor hears the ungrateful sound.

Harsh thunders roar, red lightning's shafts are hurled,
    Volcanoes bellow, fiery comets blaze,
And rumbling earthquakes shake the solid world,—
    Silent he sleeps and no attention pays.

Yet fond affection draws me to this place;
    Pensive I leave my family and fire,
And, under covert of the evening shades,
    To Isaac's grave I secretly retire.

I find him not, but sit and weep alone;
    His name I call — his silence mocks my cries;
The most obedient, dutiful of sons,
    Regardless of a father's call now lies.

Oh, my fond heart, resign parental joys,
    Nor hope to see him till the final hour,
Since naught can move him but Jehovah's voice,
    Wait the sure efforts of Almighty power.

Soon will the moment come when Gabriel's voice
    Shall rouse the sleeping dust, bid Isaac rise;
Then may I have the bright, the ecstatic joy
    Of rising with him far above the skies.

May I so live that death may be no dread;
    And when I'm called to bid my last farewell
To earthly things, and make the grave my bed,
    May I ascend with God and saints to dwell.

There may I meet my son in realms of bliss,
    And hail him happy in those worlds of light,
No more to suffer such sad pangs as this
    From parting, but endless joys unite.

In trying to draw instruction from this afflicting Providence, he remarks:

I feel that for a long time I have been too much involved in the world and its cares. I have a large and chargable family to provide for, and no means to do it with scarcely, and ever since the incorporation of this town I have been crowded with a large weight of public business; some years eighteen or twenty different offices, and no years less than ten or twelve in the town, the society, the school society, and the like, which have engrossed a large proportion of my time and thoughts; and in the spring of eighteen hundred, and for four succeeding sessions, I was chosen to represent the town in the General Assembly. All these various avocations, but perhaps more than all the rest, my corrupt inclinations, have served to keep my heart at too great a distance from my God. Perhaps, though I have never allowed myself to be elated by any of these trifling considerations, yet I have undoubtedly been inclined to place my heart on, and to expect my happiness too much from the world, and the good opinion of my poor fellow worms. Perhaps I have set my heart too much upon my children, and especially upon the dear object I now lament.

His public labors were, probably, more than those of any other man in the town up to the present day. After the labors he speaks of as having been done previously to 1802, he was justice of the peace eight years, representative five years in succession, from 1811 to 1815. He was surveyor of lands so many years that it is said that he knew at once where to go to commence tracing any line in the town. He was deacon of the church from 1805 until his death, in 1845, and from 1822 to 1827 supplied the place of pastor in the church; attending many funerals, as well as reading sermons on the Sabbath, and making himself distinguished far and near in attendance on conferences of the churches and public meetings.

The few scraps of his writings that are preserved indicate extensive reading and much study, especially of the then authorities of the church. He mentions as particularly helpful to himself, "Watts' Logic," "Doddridge on

Education." Quoting the list of books of classic authors recommended by him, "Shuckford's Connections," D'Prideau's works, and J. Taylor's writings.

Near the close of his life he seemed to be determined to destroy his writings, and unfortunately succeeded, excepting his journal, and eight or ten other fragments, which his daughter, Mrs. Bartholomew, succeeded in literally pulling out of the fire while they were burning in the dooryard, where he had made a bonfire of them. The following are some of them:

The store keeper's wish, made and put up in Bani Bishop's store when I attended for him [before 1800] to prevent people having such noisy scrapes as they had done before, staying late Saturday nights, etc.

> May customers plenty now enter these doors,
> With a mind for to trade and their pockets well stored;
> May they chink down the cash, and the goods take away,
> Thus keep me employed throughout the whole day.
> And others, likewise, though they do not pay down,
> As many good people that can't may be found;
> If their credit is good and their residence steady,
> May they step in and trade and pay when they're ready.
> May those who are idle or knavish ne'er call,
> Nor ask to be trusted here any at all.
> May innocent mirth be a guest at the store,
> But the tongue of profaneness ne'er enter the door.
> May none ask for liquor to make them the worse,
> Or, if they should do it, may they meet a repulse.
> May each one retire before it is late,
> And the store never once be defiled with a scrape.
> May none be insulted while here they do business,
> Neither old men or boys, or maidens, or widows.
> May trading go brisk all the week at the store,
> And Saturday sunset fasten the door.

Hymn made out on the death of General Washington, February, 1700, on going into the Meeting house to commemorate his death:

[Tune of Friendship]

With solemn awe and humble dread
May we this sacred mansion tread,
   While every heart is filled with gloom.
For mighty God thine awful frown
Hath cast our glory to the ground,
   And veiled our honors in the tomb.

Our Father and our faithful guide,
Our Friend, our Trust, our Strength, our Pride,
   Whose presence gladdened every heart,
Lies cold and mouldering in the dust;
Great God we own the sentence just
   That bid him from this world depart.

For, while the blessing we enjoyed,
Our hearts and tongues were not employed,
   As such rich favors did demand,
In praising God whose goodness shone
In giving us great Washington
   To be the bulwark of our land.

Was not the man too highly prized,
And made an idol in our eyes?
   Did not our hopes on flesh rely,
Forgetting, while we him applaud,
He's but the instrument of God,
   And, like all other men, must die?

Yet gratitude to our great chief
Forbids us to conceal our grief,
   While rising sobs our bosoms swell;
In such amazing scenes of woe
Stern virtue bids our tears to flow,
   And bids us all our sorrows tell.

Permit us, Lord, to enter here,
In mourning clad, with grief sincere,

While waves of sorrow o'er us roll;
With due submission, mild and meek,
Our loss to mourn, thy blessing seek
    With humble fervency of soul.

Let us his deeds of fame relate,
And bless the God that made him great;
    Trace the bright road his feet have trod;
And while we grieve and mourn for him,
Get near the font that fed the stream,
    And rest our souls alone on God.

When treason's black infernal shades,
Or diplomatic skill invades,
    With all the cursed arts of hell;
When faction's hateful front appears,
Or war's fell trumpet grates our ears
    With cannon's roar and savage yell,

Though Washington in silence lie,
We have a greater Friend on high,
    Who governs with resistless might;
A sure support in all distress,
Superior to an arm of flesh,—
    Who dwells in uncreated light.

To Him we'll seek, to Him we'll go,
In all the scenes of death and woe;
    When tumults rise and nations roar,
We'll at his footstool prostrate fall,
And make our God our all in all,
    When this vain world shall be no more.

The deacon's real character was nearly the complete opposite of his usual manner and deportment. A warmer heart, probably, did not beat in Wolcott; yet this made him sensitive and reserved, and being naturally diffident, and made much more so by the early training he received, and failing to accomplish that degree of study he so much desired,—these, all combined, caused him to appear cold and unfriendly, except on extra occasions, when his true character shone out in grandeur and power. Hence in his addresses and prayers at funerals, he was captivating and moving in a remarkable degree. All now living, who have heard him, say they "never heard his equal at funerals." It is said that his address on the death of Washington, at the time he composed the preceding verses, was the most masterly production of the kind ever heard in Wolcott, and was talked of as such for years. The same is said of an address he gave at a conference of churches at Cheshire. It is not surprising, therefore, that he is spoken of as " The great man of Wolcott."

He died April 28th, 1845, aged eighty-four years. His wife, Thankful, died June 23d, 1847, aged ninety-three years. His children bear the impress of his character in modesty and decision to the present day.

TIMOTHY BRADLEY.

Timothy Bradley came from North Haven to Wolcott, and settled on a farm on the west side of Cedar Swamp, in the north part of the town. Nearly all of his descendants are now gone from the town. He was a good citizen, honest and industrious, and had, so far as known, but one exceptional quality of character, and that was the telling of such improbable stories that no one thought of believing them; though nothing disappointed him more than to have it suggested that any one doubted his narrations. It is said that his sons grew up with the same exceptionable habit,— one of them, at the age of twelve years, declaring that for a little extra birth-day dinner, at that age, he ate twelve dozen eggs, without the least injury.

SOME OF MR. BRADLEY'S STORIES.

A carpenter was at work on the steeple of the North Haven Meeting house with a heavy broad-axe. The axe came off the helve; he called to those below to get out of the way of the falling axe; a man below seeing it coming, and not having time to move out of the way, opened his mouth and caught the edge between his teeth, without injury.

He owned a broad-axe that was made of razors, which had a peculiar ring while being used. At the close of a day's work on the shore of Long Island Sound, he left his axe where he had been at work. The next morning it was gone. He went to work, and after some little time he thought he heard the axe ring, and, after giving attention to the direction whence the sound came, he discovered that the axe was being used on the shore of Long

Island, across the Sound, a distance of about twenty miles. He jumped on his faithful mare, a trusty beast, and she swam across the Sound, carrying him. He obtained his axe, and returned in the manner in which he went.

While at work in July, harvesting grain near the Sound, there came a change of weather, to freezing cold, and the change was so sudden that the frogs had not time to go under the water, but were frozen in the ice.

On a certain occasion, speaking of a superior cat which he had, he said he had no doubt but that the cat had caught a cart body full of "chipmunks" that summer.

In a certain year he had very wonderful potatoes; the tops grew twelve feet long, and the largest potatoes in the ground were not bigger than the head of a pin.

He said he once cut down four chestnut trees which stood near together, and a shower of rain coming on just then he went to the house, and when the rain was over he went back, and a flash of lightning, striking at the stumps, had split each of the four trees into quarters, from end to end.

His son Moses went to Ohio to visit an old neighbor who had removed there for the purpose of hunting. At the time of the visit, he said this neighbor had on hand three thousand pounds of deer tallow, which he was to use in greasing the patches he put around his rifle balls, and that this amount of tallow would last only two or three weeks.

REV. JAMES D. CHAPMAN.

Rev. James Dyer Chapman was born in Columbia, Conn., in November, 1799. He graduated at Yale College in 1826, and studied theology at Yale Divinity School from 1830 to 1833. He preached as supply at Prospect, Conn., one year,—from September, 1832, to September, 1833. He preached for the Wolcott church first in July, 1837, probably, and on August 4th, 1837, the Society instructed the Prudential Committee to hire him six weeks, "as a candidate for settlement," and at the end of that time the Society invited him to become their settled pastor, which invitation he accepted, and was ordained to that office October 25th, 1837. His salary was three hundred dollars paid by the Society, and whatever additional that might be obtained from the Connecticut Home Missionary Society, which amounted to fifty dollars a year during his three years' service. Under such circumstances it is not surprising that he purchased a farm, whereby to add a little to the comfort of his family. His labors in Wolcott were in peculiarly trying times, and through the whole he conducted himself in such a manner as to receive the unqualified expression of the confidence of the members of the church, in meeting assembled near the close of his labors, and without the slightest intimation, by the Consociation which dismissed him, of any want of discretion in regard to his ministerial life or preaching. That he was an honest man in his religious principles and in his practice, and was true to his convictions, is evident from the many things he suffered because of his anti-slavery sentiments. He was dismissed by Consociation November 9th, 1840, and it must have been one of the greatest days of joy of all his life when thus released from a position in which he had received the vilest treatment for preaching Bible truth according to the golden rule.

On June 12th, 1844, he was employed at Cummington, Mass., where he continued to preach ten years, and where he died, December 19th, 1854, aged 55 years.

REV. WARREN C. FISKE.

Rev. Warren C. Fiske preached in Wolcott three years as stated supply, and retired at his own pleasure to his present home in Charlton, Mass. A bronchial difficulty led him to retire from regular pastoral work.

He was born in Wales, Mass., September 21st, 1816, and experienced religion in his thirteenth year. He was fitted for college at Monson Academy, in Monson, Mass. He entered Amherst College in the fall of 1836, in the twentieth year of his age, and graduated in 1840. He then engaged in teaching at the Salem Academy, in New Jersey, and continued there two years, and then entered, in the fall of 1842, the East Windsor Theological Seminary (since removed to Hartford), and graduated in 1845.

He married Harriet M. Parsons, of East Haddam, Conn., May 19th, 1847, and in June following went to Wisconsin as home missionary, where he remained three years, returning East in June, 1850, and was settled in Marlborough, Conn., in November of the same year. After eight years' labor in this place he was dismissed, in January, 1858, and settled in Canton, Conn., the next month. Here he remained three years and a few months, being dismissed on July 1st, 1861. After this he was stated supply one year in Barkhamstead, Conn., and from that place he came to Wolcott, in May, 1869, where he was and is still much respected. His wife was also highly esteemed as a noble-hearted Christian woman, and friend to all the people, and their children are spoken of in the kindest and highest terms. They were all born in Marlborough, Conn., as follows : Isaac Parsons, born September 16th, 1852 ; Sarah Lyon, born November 4th, 1854; William Warren, born June 26th, 1857.

JUDAH FRISBIE.

Judah Frisbie was a man of great energy in work; a man of considerable influence in the Woodtick community and throughout the town; a man with peculiar traits of character,—for his account books containing full accounts of business transactions during forty years, *i. e.*, from 1762 until 1800, are still preserved, and this was a peculiarity for his day, the like of which the writer has not found concerning any other man in the town. He not only wrote the minute items of his own work, but the remarkable occurrences in the community, and hence we are indebted to his notes for many items of history. The account books he used were made by himself, of unruled paper, sewed together, and covered with brown or "pasteboard" paper, or leather. The one with earliest accounts was used by him before he enlisted in the Revolutionary army; the second is filled mostly with his journal in the war, and his family records; the third contains accounts after the war. From the first of these books we learn that his account with Ebenezer Warner, for board, began February 20th, 1763, and the board bill ran thus :

To 2 meals, to 4 meals, to 3 meals, 9 shillings. To four meals, 4 shillings. To 1 meal, one shilling. To 18 meals, 18 shillings.

In 1772, we find him working for various individuals, and some extracts will indicate the work and the wages.

JOSEPH SUTLIFF, DR.

	s.	d.
To riding to Abraham Hotchkiss',	0	10
To two horse journeys to said Hotchkiss',	1	6
To an axe,	1	10

	s.	d.
To a horse to mill,	0	6
To mowing two half days,	2	0
To cradling at hogfields,	1	7
To cradling oats and buckwheat,	2	6
To 6 dozen buttons,	0	6
To Lucy Scott's pole rate,	2	3
To a day's work, hoeing,	2	6
To three dozen of buttons,	1	0
To a day's work,	2	6
To two day's work,	5	0

EBENEZER WARNER, CREDIT.

	s.	d.
By one horse one week and one day,	1	1
By pasture for a colt one week and four days,	1	2
By horse to Judd's meadow,	0	10
By a day's work with oxen and cart,	2	0
By two quarts of rum,	2	0
By pulling flax a spell,	0	6
By a day's work with one yoke of oxen,	1	4
By eight pounds beef,	1	4
By carting lath,	2	0
By a tree which made 150 clapboards,	1	0
By a pair of oxen and cart to town,	1	3
By a team a day,	2	8

DANIEL BYINGTON, DR.

	s.	d.
To running buttons,	0	6
To running 4 dozen buttons,	0	13

1773. JOSEPH HOTCHKISS, CREDIT.

	s.	d.
By sawing 150 feet of boards,	2	3

1773. JOSEPH SUTLIFF, DEBTOR.

	s.	d.
To two quarts of metheglin,	1	6
To cradling buckwheat,	2	9
To one quart metheglin,	0	9
To two quarts metheglin,	1	6

In the spring of 1776, while at home on furlough from the army, he entered several items in the first book.

APRIL 23, 1776. TIMOTHY SCOTT, CREDIT.

	s.	d.
By 290 feet of boards,	8	10
By sawing 265 feet of boards,	3	10

JUDAH FRISBIE.

	s.	d.
By sawing 150 feet of plank,	3	0
By sawing 130 feet of boards,	2	0
By sawing 100 feet of boards,	1	6
By sawing 182 feet of plank,	3	8
By sawing 140 feet of plank,	2	10

1774. WILLIAM NICHOLS, DEBTOR.

To two thousand shingles, £1 10s.

HANNAH FRISBIE, DEBTOR.

To a quart of metheglin,	0	9
Credit by picking and breaking wool,	2	4

1776. WILLIAM WAKELEE, CREDIT.

By sawing 3 logs 8 feet in length,		
By sawing 60 feet of plank,	1	2
By sawing 230 feet of boards.	3	5

In December, 1773, there was "laid out to Judah Frisbie four acres and fifty-six rods of land in the north-east quarter of the bounds, at the Little Plain, a place east of the Great Plain, next to the bounds of Farmington." This was the first land he bought in the east part of Woodtick, and was surrounded by "common land," and hence was the first land taken up by actual residence in Woodtick, as far as is known. Another piece was laid out to him at the same time of two acres and a half, extending from the highway east to the bound line. The first house is said to have been a log house, or a very small framed house. It may have been built with the 785 feet of boards and the 472 feet of plank which his account book tells us Timothy Scott sawed for him in 1776. He was not married until 1779, and the account book items rather indicate that he had a house for his wife when he married her,— a fact not the fortune of every young man in those days, and possibly not of every one at the present day. He afterwards built another house, which was taken down in 1872, by his great-grandson, David L. Frisbie, and on the same site he has built a fine house, good for the next hundred years. The house he took down is said to have been eighty-nine years old.

Mr. Frisbie's journal is given in full, because of its connection with the war of the Revolution:

A REMARKABLE SEASON.

On the 24th day of April, in the year 1773, things were so remarkably forward as that rye began to ear, the buds and leaves in the woods began to be considerably thick, the buds of walnut and black oak began to part and shoot forth into leaves, and I saw one cherry sprig that had grown nine inches this season. It is to be noticed that on the 14th of May, apple trees were past the bloom.

June, the first part, 1773. Having occasion to travel into several towns, viz., Lenox, Richmond, and Norfolk, I saw on the 11th and 12th days of June, the biggest grass I ever saw, and on the 12th I saw grass mowed and the hay carried off. It is to be observed that on the night following the 11th of June there was a great frost, which much damaged Indian corn,— killed it to the ground in many places, cut off some pieces of wheat and rye, and much damaged others. And it is likewise to be noticed that we had a remarkable warm fall and fore part of winter, so that the whole summer was very long. But about the eight and twentieth day of December, there fell a snow, and by numbers of succeeding snows, the ground was deeply covered, and good sleighing and sledding held till the latter part of February. I would likewise remark that Mr. Alexander Gillet was ordained at Farmingbury, on the 29th day of December, in the year 1773.

JOURNAL AS A SOLDIER IN THE REVOLUTION.

WATERBURY, May 10th, 1776.

I, that is, Judah Frisbie, enlisted into the government service. Met our company the 31st of May, in Waterbury, and had a sermon by Rev. Mr. Leavenworth. June the first, we marched for New York, setting out at noon, and marched to the stores in Derby, being thirteen miles. June 2d,— marched from about five miles from above Derby town, through it, across Ripton to Stratford, being thirteen miles. June 3d, we marched through

JUDAH FRISBIE.

Poquonack to Old Fairfield, where we were stationed three weeks, keeping two guards, the one at the State house, the other at the battery. June 24th, we marched across Green's Farms to Norwalk, being thirteen miles. June 25th, marched to Stamford, where we attended meeting in the afternoon, and at night marched to Greenwich, the whole being fourteen miles. June 26th, we joined our regiment, which was General Woster's, and, Colonel Waterbury's regiment attending us, we set out for New York, and marched through Rye, about twelve miles, to New Rochelle. The 27th, setting out early, we met General Washington, who passed us in a genteel manner, and there followed him a band of music. June 28th, we marched to the Bowery, of the city of New York; it being very stormy, we got into barns. June 29th, we encamped a little back of New York, where we continued three weeks, keeping two guards,— the General's and the main guards; the rest of the time being spent in exercises and reviews. July 18th, we had general orders to decamp and go to Harlem, which we accordingly did, where we encamped in the manner we did at York. About the 24th of July, Colonel Waterbury's regiment had orders to embark for Albany, which they did, and were sent to Canada.

I myself about this time went back to take care of one of our company that was left sick at New York. After his recovery I again returned, and was sick myself, at a hospital. On the 8th of August our regiment, as many as were able, embarked for Long Island in pursuit of the regulars that were robbing the inhabitants of their cattle, sheep, etc. They were there about three weeks, after which they returned, and informed that they — a few of them — had been fired on by an armed schooner belonging to the regular fleet that was lying off in the Sound, who gave them chase as they were in a small boat. A barge also chased them swiftly, and ordering them to strike, which they refused, gave fire on the barge and caused her to withdraw. They lost no lives, but supposed they killed three regulars. They had their stations during their stay in several places, separately or in parties,— as Plumb's Island, Shelter Island, East Hampton, etc. It should have been noticed that while they were gone, on Thursday night, 24th of August, the people of York were removing from the Battery some cannon, of their own property, the Asia, man-of-war, lying in the harbor, took occasion to fire on the city, which much alarmed the city, and many of its inhabitants moved back to the country. September 28th, we had general orders for a march to Canada. We embarked in six vessels, but while we were getting on board, a sergeant was drowned in the North River, which was the first man we lost in the regiment after we joined them. The said sergeant's name was Peck, belonging to Captain Porter's company.

September 29th, we sailed for Albany, and arrived the first day of October; landed and went into the barracks, but, by being frightened through fear of the small-pox, we removed to Greenbush, where we tarried till the 9th, when we again crossed the river, and the 10th we took our way through Albany, thence across the Mohawk river to the Half Moon. October 11th, we went along the still waters to Saratoga. October 12th, we marched to Fort Edward, across Harris' Ferry. October 13th, we marched to Lake George. October 14th, 15th, and 16th, we crossed Lake George to Fort Ticonderoga, where we tarried until the 22d of October, when we set out to go up Lake Champlain. The same day we landed at Crown Point, but went about six miles above and lodged on the east side of the lake in the woods. The 23d we went about forty miles up the lake, and lodged on an island. October 24th, we went up the lake about thirty-five miles and lodged the west side the lake, in the woods. The 25th, we went to the island of "Oxnawix." October 26th, we went to a battery two miles below St. Johns. October 27th, we went across the lake, east, a little below St. Johns, and were fired upon from the fort, but had no man killed; only one wounded, and that slightly. We then traveled through miry woods, in which we got bewildered, till most night, having heavy pieces, when we came in sight of an encampment, which was our design. This encampment, lying two miles north of St. Johns, and on the west side of the river Sorell, we being to the east, were helped across the river by the French, and accordingly we pitched our encampment by the other. The 28th of October, at night, we began a battery within about sixty rods of the fort, which we were two days and three nights in building, during which time we had a considerable number of bombs, cannon balls, and grape-shot fired at us from the fort; but it was remarkable that we had not a man killed, and only a few slight wounds. The first day of November we opened our battery in the morning, and continued a hot fire from it, and from a battery the east side of the lake, till near night, when the fort was forced to a capitulation, which held till the third day of November, and then the regulars marched out with their arms, the artillerymen coming out first, with a field piece, and the train following them. They paraded and laid down their arms, our people taking possession of them. Our officers marched their soldiery into the fort, taking possession of the same. It is to be noted that on the first of November we had two men killed and another wounded. The sixth day of November we marched for Montreal, and though the traveling was extremely bad, yet we arrived at Laparary, where we tarried awhile, and I was sent on a guard of prisoners, and it fell to my lot to take care of a sick man, at the Half-way House, until our men had been to Montreal and returned for home.

The 18th of November they came to where I was, and I marched with them to St. Johns. The 19th, we got five brass cannon and six "hoits" out of St. Johns. The 20th, we set out from St. Johns, rowing about twenty-four miles, and lay the west side of the lake, among the French. The 21st, we rowed about thirty miles, and lay in the woods, and on the 22d we rowed about thirty-two miles, and lodged on the west side of the lake, among the English settlements. The 23d, we rode about thirty miles, and lodged the east side of the lake, among the English settlements. The 24th, we were forced to leave the lake, by reason of ice, and take our baggage on our backs and, marching, we arrived at Ticonderoga. The 25th, we crossed Lake Champlain, eastward, and lay in the woods. The 26th, we marched for Otter Creek Road, but it being stormy, we got lost, being bewildered the most of that day. The 27th, we marched about ten miles, from Shoreham to Sudbury, and the 28th we came to Huberton, being about ten miles. The 29th, we came through Castletown to Poultney, about fifteen miles, and the 30th we came about eleven miles, to Wellstown. December 1st, we came through Paulet, thence through Rueport to Dorset, about seventeen miles. December 2d, we came through Manchester, thence through Sunderland, thence through Allington to Shaftsbury, about twenty-two miles. December 3d, we traveled to Bennington, about twelve miles, and December 4th we came through Poundwell to East Hoosack, about sixteen miles, to Captain Jones'. December 5th, we came about three miles, to Mr. Todd's. December 6th, we came to Lansingburg, about fourteen miles, and the 7th we came through Pittsfield, thence through Lenox to Stockbridge, about twenty miles. December 8th, we came through Barrington to New Marlboro, twenty miles. December 9th, we came to Norfolk, where I stayed with my cousin till the 13th, when I traveled through Colebrook, thence across a part of Winchester and Barkhamstead, thence across New Hartford, thence through West Simsbury, thence through Farmington to Farmingbury.

JOURNAL BEGINNING AUGUST 12TH, 1776.

Marched with Ensign Gaylord from Farmingbury, with twelve men, to Wallingford. August 13th, Lieutenant Peck joining us, we marched to East Guilford. August 14th, Captain Meigs, with his company, sailed from New York. We arrived at New York the 15th, and tarried there until the 20th of August, when we marched up and crossed the North river about ten miles above the city, and were stationed at Fort Lee. September 5th, died one Lyman, of Captain Denny's company, with camp distemper. September 8th, died Sergeant Mosley, of Captain Denny's company, with camp distemper.

Here suddenly ends the journal of the war life of Judah Frisbie. The little book in which this is written by himself is 16 mo., covered with thin "pasteboard," written in a very plain hand, and almost elegant style, and the composition indicates an unusual aptness in writing a journal. It is here copied almost word for word.

The following extracts from Judah Frisbie's account-book show the prices of several articles as sold in a farming community:

1767 TO 1774. CAPTAIN GEORGE NICHOLS, DEBTOR.

	£	s.	d.
To a month's work,	1	10	0
To 1 bushel of wheat,	0	4	0

JUDAH FRISBIE.

	s.	d.
To a bushel and a half of wheat,	0	6	0
To two bushels Indian corn,	0	4	0
To one day's mowing,	0	3	0
To a day's work cradling,	0	3	0
To a day's mowing,	0	3	0
To two day's reaping,	0	6	0
To five shillings cash,	0	5	0
To paying by Ebenezer Wakelee,	0	8	0
To a day's mowing,	0	3	0
To two day's mowing,	0	6	0

1785 TO 1789. CHARGES TO DIFFERENT INDIVIDUALS.

	s.	d.
To a pair of oxen half a day,	0	8
To a yoke of oxen two-thirds of a day,	1	0
To a horse to Farmingbury and to Southingt'n,	0	4
To a pair of women's soles,	1	6
To five pounds and four ounces of pork,	2	9
To two bushels of rye.	7	0
To half bushel of potatoes,	0	9
To one and a half pounds of fat,	0	9
To half pound of butter,	0	5
To ten pounds seven ounces of pork,	6	1
To a quart of rum,	1	3
To a pound of butter,	0	10

As balancing in part some of the above charges, we find credit:—

	s.	d.
By a day's work,	2	0
By two days' work,	4	0
By a day's farming,	2	0
By two days,	4	0
By half a day,	1	0

ELNATHAN THRASHER, DEBTOR.

	s.	d.
To a live sheep weighing ninety pounds, at a penny a pound,	7	6
Credit (in part) by cash,	1	4
By seven pounds of mutton,	1	0

NATHANIEL SUTLIFF, DEBTOR.

To a bushel of flaxseed, 6s.

NATHANIEL BARNES, THE SMITH, DEBTOR.

	£	s.	d.
To seven hundred boards,	1	1	0
To five pounds and fourteen ounces of steel, at eight pence per pound,	0	3	11
To four pounds three ounces of flax,	0	1	9
To five pounds of flax,	0	2	1
To six pounds of flax,	0	2	6

MR. GILLET, DEBTOR.

	s.	d.
To eight pounds of mutton,	2	0
To four pence over pay in grain the last year's rate, the above to go on March, 1790, rate,	0	4
To a bushel of rye,	3	0
To twenty-eight pounds of beef,	4	8
To six pounds of tallow,	3	0
To a pound of hog suet,	0	6
To a pound of beef suet,	0	6
To a bushel of rye.	3	0
To over pay on last rate bill.	2	5
To a bushel of wheat.	5	0

REV. ALEXANDER GILLET.

Rev. Alexander Gillet was ordained first pastor of the Church and Society of Farmingbury December 29th, 1773, as we learn from the diary of Mr. Judah Frisbie, for though the church book that Mr. Gillet kept is dated December 29th, 1773, yet he does not say in it that he was ordained that day. He had preached for the Society previously to the installation, five months or more, and it was during this service, on November 18th, 1773, and after he had received a call from the Society to become its pastor, that the church was organized. He served the parish with great devotedness under many difficulties, nearly eighteen years, being honorably dismissed by a conference of churches, and highly commended by the conference, and was soon after installed pastor of the church in Torrington, Conn., where he continued many years. The description of him and his labors published in Sprague's Annals, vol. 2, and taken in part from the funeral sermon preached at his death, and in part furnished by Rev. Mr. Marsh, will be interesting to many, and is given in full.

The poem annexed is certified to be the production of Mr. Gillet by very reliable persons of the parish. It was printed in a public journal many years since, and cut from the paper and preserved with great care to the present time; and it is so much like Mr. Gillet's cast of mind, and like the style of religious thought of those days, that it is here given in full.

"Alexander Gillet, son of Zaccheus and Ruth Gillet, was born in Granby (Turkey Hills), Conn., August 14th

(O. S.), 1749. He early discovered a great fondness for books, and especially for history. At the age of thirteen he was the subject of serious impressions during a revival which then prevailed in several towns in Hartford county; and these impressions, though they seem subsequently to have greatly declined, never entirely left him. At the age of fourteen he began his preparation for college, under the Rev. Nehemiah Strong, his pastor, and completed it under the Rev. Roger Viets, an Episcopal clergyman, and a missionary of the society for propagating the gospel in foreign parts. He was admitted a member of Yale College, in June, 1767, at an advanced standing, and was graduated in September, 1770. It was not till the summer of 1769 that his mind seems to have become fully settled in regard to the doctrines of the gospel, and not until about the close of 1770 that he was the subject of any religious experience that he himself believed to be genuine. In May, 1771, he united with the church in Turkey Hills (Granby), though owing, probably, to there being no settled minister in the place, he had no opportunity of joining in the celebration of the Lord's Supper until December following. After leaving college he taught a school for a year or more at Farmington, and it is supposed that he may have studied theology during that time, under the direction of the Rev. Timothy Pitkin. He was licensed to preach by the Hartford Association, at Northington, on the 2d of June, 1773. On December 29th of the same year he was ordained the first pastor of the church in Farmingbury (now Wolcott), where he remained almost eighteen years, diligently employed in the duties of his office. Owing to a difficulty which arose in his parish, involving no delinquency on his part, his pastoral relation to them was dissolved in November, 1791, and in May following he was installed pastor of the First Church, Torrington, with very promising prospects of usefulness. Here he continued to labor during the rest of his life.

Mr. Gillet's ministry was attended with much more than the ordinary degree of visible success. At Wolcott he was privileged to see large numbers added to his church, as the fruit of several revivals that occurred in connection with his labors. During the period of his ministry at Torrington there were three seasons of deep religious interest among his people, the results of which are equally benign and extensive. Of one of these last-mentioned revivals he published a detailed and interesting account in an early volume of the Connecticut Evangelical Magazine.

Mr. Gillet had much of the missionary spirit, and several times volunteered to perform missionary labor. Long before the Connecticut Missionary Society was formed, he performed good service in some of the destitute portions of the counties of New London and Windham. In 1789, or 1790, he made a missionary tour of several months in the new settlements of Vermont, under the approbation of the Association of New Haven County, and almost entirely at his own expense; his pulpit being supplied a part of the time by his brethren in the vicinity. And at a later period he went, several times, by appointment from the Connecticut Missionary Society, into those destitute regions, on the same errand of good will to men.

During a few of his last years, Mr. Gillet, on account of the advancing infirmities of age, was unable to perform the same amount of ministerial labor to which he had been accustomed; and yet there was scarcely any perceptable waning of his intellectual faculties, with the exception only of his memory, till near the close of his life. On being informed of some small mistakes which he had made in the pulpit, in consequence of the failure of his recollection, he proposed to his people, in the Autumn of 1824, to release him from his public duties till the following Spring, and to employ some other preacher in his stead; at the same time voluntarily relinquishing his salary during that period. He resumed his labors after having devoted a few months to rest and relaxation, and thenceforward continued to supply his pulpit, with few exceptions, as long as he lived. He officiated on the last Sabbath of his life with his usual correctness and fervor. On the following Tuesday, January 19, 1826, he entered into rest. During the greater part of the day there was nothing to indicate to himself or others the approaching change; for though he complained, about noon, of a shooting pain in his breast, it was supposed to be only a rheumatic affection, to which he had before occasionally been subject. About four o'clock in the afternoon, his wife, having occasion to go into his study to ask him a question, observed that he made no reply. Upon her repeating the question, and still receiving no answer, she hastened to him and found him unable to speak. He was immediately laid upon the bed, and after uttering, with difficulty, a few broken sentences, ceased to breathe, being in the seventy-second year of his age, and the fifty-third of his ministry. His funeral was attended on the succeeding Sabbath, and an appropriate sermon preached by the Rev. Luther Hart, of Plymouth, which was published.

Mr. Gillet was married, in December, 1779, to Adah, third daughter of Deacon Josiah Rogers, of Farmingbury, a descendant of John Rogers, the martyr. They had six children, one of whom, Timothy Phelps, was graduated at Williams College, in 1804, and has been for many years pastor of the Congregational church in Branford, Conn. Mrs. Gillet died in May, 1839, aged seventy-seven.

Mr. Gillet published a sermon in a volume entitled "Sermons on Important Subjects," 1797, and a sermon at the ordination of his son, 1808. He was a contributor to the Connecticut Evangelical Magazine, and to the Christian Spectator.

FROM THE REV. FREDERICK MARSH.

WINCHESTER, CONN., May 27th, 1856.

DEAR SIR:—My first knowledge of the Rev. Alexander Gillet was in New Hartford, during the great revival, 1798 and 1799, when he occasionally came there with Mr. Mills, Mr. Miller, and others, to assist Dr. Griffin. My particular acquaintance with him commenced soon after coming to this place, in 1808. From that time (as our parishes were contiguous) till his decease in 1826, our relations became more and more intimate, and I can truly say that he ever treated me with paternal kindness. Besides the ordinary ministerial exchanges and intercourse, he used to visit us and preach in seasons of special religious interest.

In his person, Mr. Gillet was rather above the medium stature and size, of a full habit, broad shoulders, short neck, and large head. His position was erect, except a slight forward inclination of the head. His face was broad, and unusually square and full, illumined by large, prominent blue eyes, the whole indicating more of intellect than vivacity. His ordinary movements were grave and thoughtful. In his manner he was plain, unostentatious, and at the greatest possible distance from all that is obtrusive. He was courteous and kind, swift to hear and slow to speak, apparently esteeming others better than himself, and in all his intercourse exhibiting a delicate sense of propriety.

As a man of intellect he held a decidedly high rank. He had an aversion to everything superficial. Ever fond of study, he went thoroughly and deeply into the investigation of his subject, whatever it might be. He was an admirable linguist, and above all excelled in the knowledge of the Bible,— not merely in his own language, but in the original. As a scholar, he was characterized by great accuracy. I have heard an eminent minister, who fitted for college under his instructions, say that he never found any tutor so accurate and thorough in the languages as Mr. Gillet. He was also very familiarly and extensively acquainted with history; and he studied history especially as an exposition of prophecy.

But the crowning attribute of his character was his devoted piety and high moral excellence. While great simplicity and godly sincerity characterized his habitual deportment, it was still only by an intimate and extended acquaintance with him, and by observing his spirit and conduct in trying circumstances, that one could gain anything like a full view of this part of his character. During seventeen years of familiar intercourse with him, my mind became constantly more impressed with the depth of his piety,— his unreserved consecration to God, his self-sacrificing devotedness to the cause of Christ and the highest interests of his fellow men. Among the most striking elements of his religious character were meekness, humility, and a conscientious and apparently immutable regard to truth and duty.

In social life, Mr. Gillet's constitutional reserve, and defect of conversational powers, rendered him less interesting and useful than might have been expected from such resources of mind and heart as he possessed. Ordinarily he said little in ecclesiastical meetings. Patiently listening to all the younger members choose to say, he would remain silent, unless some gordian knot was to be untied, or some latent error to be detected; and then he would show his opinion to good purpose. With individuals and in private circles, where religious or other important topics became matter of conversation, he would often talk with much freedom and interest.

In his ministeral character and relations there was much to be admired and loved, and some things to be regretted. It may readily be inferred from what I have already said in respect to his intellectual powers and attainments, his piety, his studious habits and devotedness to his appropriate work, that his sermons were of no ordinary stamp. And thus it really was. He presented Divine truth with great clearness and point. Hence his preaching took strong hold of congregations in times of revival. Often in closing his discourse by an extemporary effusion, he would turn to some one class of hearers, and urge upon them his subject in its practical bearings with a tenderness and earnestness that were quite overpowering.

But as his delivery was rendered laborious and difficult by an impediment in his speech, he could not be called a popular preacher. Those who regarded the manner more than the matter of a discourse would pronounce him dull. But he was a skillful and faithful guide to souls; and his labors were abundantly blessed not only to the people to whom he ministered but to others.

Of pastoral labor Mr. Gillet performed less than many of his brethren. His constitutional diffidence, his incapacity for entering into free and familiar intercourse with people generally, and his love for study, probably all combined to produce in him a conviction that he could accomplish the greatest good by making thorough preparation for the pulpit, for occasional meetings, and seasons of prayer, rather than devoting much of his time to pastoral visits.

On the whole, he was an able, laborious, faithful and successful minister — ever bringing out of his treasure things new and old, edifying the body of Christ, enjoying the confidence and affectionate regard of his brethren, and exhibiting uniformly such an example of consistency with his profession as to leave no room to doubt either his sincerity or his piety.

I remain, dear sir, fraternally and truly yours,

FREDERICK MARSH.

GLOOM OF AUTUMN.

[Said to have been composed by Alex. Gillet.]

Hail! ye sighing sons of sorrow,
   View with me the Autumnal gloom;
Learn from hence your fate to-morrow —
   Dead perhaps — laid in the tomb.

See all nature, fading, dying!
   Silent all things seem to mourn;
Life from vegetation flying,
   Calls to mind my mouldering urn.

Oft an Autumn's tempest rising,
   Makes the lofty forest nod;
Scenes of nature, how surprising!
   Read in nature, nature's God.

See our Sovereign, sole Creator,
   Lives eternal in the skies;
While we mortals yield to nature,
   Bloom awhile, then fade and die.

Nations die by dread Belona,
    Through the tyranny of kings;
Just like plants by pale Pamona
    Fall to rise in future springs.

Mournful scenes, when vegetation
    Dies by frost, or worms devour;
Doubly mournful when a nation
    Falls by neighboring nation's power.

Death my anxious mind depresses,
    Autumn shows me my decay;
Calls to mind my past distresses,
    Warns me of my dying day.

Autumn makes me melancholy,
    Strikes dejection through my soul;
While I mourn my former folly
    Waves of sorrow o'er me roll.

Lo! I hear the air resounding
    With expiring insect cries:
Ah! to me their moans how wounding —
    Emblem of my own demise.

Hollow winds about me roaring;
    Noisy waters round me rise;
While I sit my fate deploring,
    Tears are flowing from my eyes.

What to me are Autumn's treasures,
    Since I know no earthly joy?
Long I've lost all youthful pleasure'—
    Time must youth and health destroy.

Pleasure once I fondly courted,
    Shared each bliss that youth bestows;
But to see where then I sported
    Now embitters all my woes.

Age and sorrow since have blasted
    Every youthful, pleasing dream;
Quivering age with youth contrasted:
    Oh, how short their glories seem.

As the annual frosts are cropping
    Leaves and tendrils from the trees,
So my friends are yearly dropping
    Through old age or dire desease.

Former friends, oh, how I've sought them!
    Just to cheer my drooping mind;
But they're gone, like leaves in Autumn,
    Driven before the dreary wind.

Spring and Summer, Fall and Winter,
    Each in swift succession roll —
So my friends in death do enter
    Bringing sadness to my soul.

Death has laid them down to slumber;
    Solemn thought — to think that I
Soon must be one of their number—
    Soon, so soon with them to lie.

When a few more years are wasted;
    When a few more suns are o'er;
When a few more griefs I've tasted
    I shall fall to rise no more.

Fast my sun of life's declining,
    Soon 'twill set in endless night;
But my hopes are past repining;
    Rest in future life and light.

Cease this fearing, trembling, sighing;
    Death will break the awful gloom —
Soon my spirit fluttering, flying,
    Must be borne beyond the tomb.

REV. TIMOTHY P. GILLET.

The following biographical sketch is taken from the funeral sermon of Rev. T. P. Gillet, preached by Rev. W. P. Eustis, jr., pastor of Chapel Street church, New Haven, at Branford, November 7th, 1866:

Timothy Phelps Gillet was born June 15, 1780, in Farmingbury, now Wolcott, being the eldest child of Alexander and Adah Gillet. His father was, at the time of his birth, pastor of the church in Farmingbury, and after a settlement of eighteen years, was dismissed November, 1791, and in the following May was installed pastor of the First Church in Torrington, where he died, January 19, 1826, in the seventy-seventh year of his age, and the fifty-third of his ministry. His wife was the third daughter of Deacon Josiah Rogers, of Farmingbury, Conn., and a descendant of the famous John Rogers.* Rev. Alexander Gillet was the child of pious parents, who lived in a part of Simsbury, Conn., now Granby, and was trained in the knowledge of divine truth by his devout grandmother.

The father of Timothy was a man of uncommon ability, and was, in his day, among the leading preachers in Connecticut. Graduating at Yale College, in 1770, he retained his familiarity with classical literature, and after the meridian of life commenced the study of Hebrew, and modestly acknowledged, in later years, that he had read through the Hebrew bible three times. He had a large library for that day, and in theology claimed to be a disciple of Edwards. His ministry was abundantly blessed, and one of the early volumes of the "Connecticut Evangelical

---

* Deacon Rogers belonged to the family of Thomas Rogers, who came over in the Mayflower.

Magazine" contains his narrative of a great revival of religion in Torrington, where his son Timothy was hopefully converted. This son, the eldest of six children, two of whom survive, inherited many of his father's characteristics, and we trace a family likeness between the pastor at Torringford and the pastor at Branford, in the portrait of the former, by his friend, Rev. Luther Hart.

The following sentences of this brief memoir might be applied to the venerable son, as well as to the honored father : " It was one of the most prominent traits of his character that he made all of his literary pursuits subservient to the momentous business of his holy calling. He daily consecrated his time and talents to the service of Christ. Scarcely has any person, in any station, uttered fewer words at random. Possessing a wonderful command over his passions, provocations rarely betrayed him into expressions which demanded regret ; and carefully guarding against all undue animal excitement, even if others in his company were facetious, it is not recollected that he ever uttered a sentence inconsistent with the dignity and sobriety becoming the gospel. His eldest son has observed, 'Though he frequently smiled, I never heard him laugh.'"

Alluding to his personal habits and characteristics, the writer adds :

Upon him whose character is attempted to be delineated in these pages, no defect, on the score of economy, could be charged. Without patrimony, and receiving, till within a few years of his death, a small salary, he yet, by the assistance of his frugal and industrious companion, brought up six children ; assisted one of them in procuring a collegiate education, and left his family in possession of a valuable farm.

Another leading trait in his character was, that he did everything methodically, and in season. At a particular hour he retired at night, and at a particular hour he rose in the morning. He was distinguished for his punctuality in the fulfillment of his public and private engagements.

These quotations indicate the origin of those characteristics in which the son closely resembled the father, whom he revered. Timothy P. Gillet entered Williams College in 1800, when he was twenty years of age, and graduated in 1804. After graduation, Mr. Gillet taught for one year at Cornwall, and then in the academy at Williamstown, until, in 1806, he was appointed tutor, and retained that office for a year and a half. Gordon Hall, Samuel J. Mills, and James Richards, were then under-graduates in that college, and Mr. Gillet has stated to members of his congregation that they were accustomed to hold a prayer-meeting in his room, and to consult in regard to the duty of carrying the gospel to the heathen. He never lost the interest thus awakened in foreign missions, but was an earnest advocate of the cause, and a warm friend of the American Board. During his tutorship he studied theology under President Fitch, and was licensed as a candidate for the gospel ministry, by the Litchfield North Association, September 30th, 1806. In the winter of 1807-8, having resigned his tutorship, Mr. Gillet supplied the pulpit, for two Sundays, at East Haven, and was then invited to preach in the vacant pulpit of the church at Branford. He received, shortly after, a call to settle with them in the gospel ministry, on a salary of five hundred dollars, and the privilege of cutting fire-wood on the Society's lands, until, from continued ill health or infirmity, he should be no longer able to perform the duties of a gospel minister among them. This invitation was accepted, and June 15th, 1808, on his twenty-eighth birth-day, he was ordained to the work of the gospel ministry as pastor of this church.

Mr. Gillet was married, November 29th, 1808, to Sallie Hodges, who, after nearly sixty years of a happy and peaceful wedlock, survives him to mourn his absence, tarrying for the summons which will reunite them in the heavenly society.

He died at his residence in Branford, November 5th, 1866, in the eighty-seventh year of his age, and the fifty-ninth of his ministry.

DEACON AARON HARRISON.

Aaron Harrison was born May 3d, 1726, in East Haven, where his great-grandfather settled after emigrating from England. His father, Benjamin, removed from East Haven to Wolcott, in 1738, and settled on Benson Hill, now Wolcott Center, where Aaron resided until near the close of life, when he removed half a mile south-east, where he died. Coming to Wolcott at the age of twelve years, where there were no schools within six miles, he in some way attained to a proficiency of scholarship more than ordinary, under the circumstances, as appears in his writings and the prominent relations to the community which he sustained through life.

He married, October 26th, 1748, Jerusha, daughter of Obadiah Warner. His brother Benjamin and sister Abigail married a daughter and son of Dr. Benjamin Warner, the brother of Obadiah.

In the organization of the Ecclesiastical Society and Church of Farmingbury, Aaron bore a responsible and honorable part, and on the fourth of January, 1774, he was chosen first deacon of the church, when in his forty-eighth year. He was chosen moderator of the first Society meeting, a position of special honor at that time, and served in many offices of the society and church many years thereafter. He was the first captain of the military company of Farmingbury Winter parish,— Isaac Hopkins, probably, being the second, and John Alcox the third. The deacon's kindly disposition, his intelligence and faithfulness to the public good, were such that the people reposed in him the fullest confidence and trust, as indicated by Deacon Isaac Bronson, who felt at liberty to talk with "that good man, Deacon Aaron Harrison," when he was afraid to speak to any one else on the subject of religion. He was, indeed, the under shepherd in the church during the labors of Revs. Gillet, Woodward, Hart, and Keys,—a term of nearly fifty years, being at the time of his death a father to all "Israel" in this parish. The first public prayer offered in the first Meeting house was by Deacon Aaron Harrison, and in that house he worshiped forty seven years, hearing in his latter days the remarkable voice of his grand-son, Stephen, leading the hosts of Israel in the songs of the sanctuary.

The following extracts are taken from that part of his journal which is still preserved:

OCTOBER 21, 1797, IN THE SEVENTY-SECOND YEAR OF MY AGE.

When I look upon a life of sin and iniquity, through the course of the age of man, it seemeth impossible that such a creature should ever be saved. I am a stupid creature and dead in sin, and a faithless hypocrite, but not in utter despair, because the grace of God is infinite. But O that I could overcome my lusts and get into the liberty of Christ Jesus. O that I could act and conduct right towards God and men! O that I could keep a conscience void of offense towards God and men!

October 14.—Melancholy apprehensions concerning my state and situation, looking on myself to be on the brink of eternity and so unconcerned and unmoved that I wonder at my own stupidity.

May 29, 1798.—I have lived to see seventy-two years this present month. There has not been a sermon preached in Wolcott Meeting house since Mr. Woodward preached his first sermon on probation, but that I have heard, except a few Sabbaths when I was sick with the pere-pneumonia, which I look upon as strange, considering my age and infirmities.

It is a poor sign for people to rejoice more in their good frames and good feelings than in the perfections of the blessed God.

Man lives a fool, a fool he cannot die.

May 1, [or 3] 1799.—I have lived seventy-three years this day, but am dead while I live.

May 23, 1799.—Yesterday Mr. Curtiss Hall fell from a tree that was already down, as he was standing upon the body of the tree, about six feet from the ground, was immediately struck senseless and died the next morning, without speaking a word.

July 24, 1802.— Mr. David Norton, aged seventy-one, sitting near the fire, was struck with lightning which came down the chimney, and instantly expired. He was a constant attendant on public worship and religious conferences; improved in church, and was approved in society as a useful member; frequently visiting and helping and praying with the sick. Labor and care, misfortune and wearisomeness were his constant attendants through life, and he has left an infirm and almost helpless widow to mourn her loss in briny tears.

January 20, 1803.— Departed this life, by the fall of a tree, which instantly killed him, Mr. Nathan Johnson, a man of profession and example, and in the prime of life, leaving a widow and a young child.

Take the alarm, O my soul!

July 8, 1812.— Taken into church—Esther Harrison, Freelove Upson, Maria Wakelee, and Lydia Alcox, in younger life. May they live and adorn the Christian profession.

He died Sept. 5, 1819, aged 93, and his wife died eight days later, Sept. 13, 1819, aged 92; they having been married more than seventy years. The following record was made by Rev. Mr. Keys, concerning the funeral: "He had been a man highly useful and highly esteemed in this place. He was one of those through whose exertions a located society was first established in this place. He aided in procuring the town charter; moderated the first town meeting; was the first captain of a military company; was the first deacon of the church, and offered up the first public prayer in the first Meeting-house. He was buried on the sixth, and his bier was followed by a large concourse of people. It being the day of a semi-annual military review,— the militia being then under arms,—

the procession was met by the company and escorted to the Meeting house where the Throne of Grace was addressed, and a short address made to the congregation; thence to the grave-yard, where the remains were deposited in the tomb, followed by the tender sympathies of many relatives and friends."

Some of the people now living remember that funeral procession; the long concourse of people; the military men with their reversed arms; the slow, solemn tread of the company, while the band played the funeral dirge (Pleyel's Hymn), thrilling every heart with sadness by the peculiar strains of minor music, as rendered by the old style instruments.

Well might the people sorrow, for a good man of Israel had fallen. Not many men live so long and do as much public service, and go down to their last sleep so generally respected, loved, and honored as he. His life is a worthy pattern for the church for ages to come. The church had trials and difficulties severe, but in the midst of them stood, always, Deacon Harrison, firm to justice, full of mercy, true to God, and large-hearted towards all men. He had seen the wilderness give place to a prosperous, fruitful land. The church from a feeble band had become numerous and strong, though many had gone before him to the church triumphant. His children, grandchildren, and great-grandchildren, had grown up around him, to give him only honor and gladness in the closing years of life,

Eight days after his departure his wife Jerusha followed him to that land for which they had been striving for many years, and where he was scarcely introduced to the angelic throng before she joined him in the melody and harmony in that land of life.

REV. LUCAS HART.

Rev. Lucas Hart was a descendant of Deacon Simeon Hart, one of the pioneers of what is now Burlington, then Farming West Woods, and subsequently West Briton. Deacon Hart was the first deacon of the church organized at the ordination of its first pastor, Rev. Jonathan Miller. The father of Lucas was the third son of Deacon Simeon, and was a prominent man in the town in civil, military, and ecclesiastical matters. His name was Simeon. Lucas was born at West Briton, June 5th, 1784. When quite young he was employed as a school teacher in the winter season, studying at the same time, until he commenced fitting for college. When nineteen years old he united with the church in his native place, under the pastoral care of the Rev. Jonathan Miller. From this time he bent all his energies to get an education, teaching in the winter, and working on the farm with his father in the summer, until the spring previous to his arriving at the age of twenty-one. At this time he commenced in earnest to fit for college. He went to Morris Academy, then in South Farms, now the town of Morris, in Litchfield county, to prosecute his studies, and by too close application to study, injured his health, which he never afterwards regained. Unwilling to give up the idea of becoming a minister, he applied himself, as he was able, to theological studies, his pastor being his instructor; at the same time writing largely on theological subjects, as he had been accustomed to do for several years. When twenty-six years old he was licensed by the Litchfield

North Association, September 25th, 1810. He was employed by the Missionary Society of Connecticut, part of the time, until he commenced preaching for the church in Wolcott, in August, 1811. He was ordained pastor in Wolcott December 4th, 1811. He married Harriet, daughter of Deacon Amos Harris, of East Haven, on Thanksgiving evening, November, 1811, about a week before his ordination. He was a good minister and pastor, and successful in his work a year and ten months. In the fall of 1813, he went with his wife and child to East Haven, to his wife's father's, on a visit, where he and his little son were sick with dysentery. His son died October 11th, and he October 16th. His son, Edward Lucas, was born after his father's decease. This son is now a successful teacher, resides in Farmington, and has in his care two Chinamen and one Spanish lady as his pupils. The widow died in New Haven, February 23d, 1853.

LUCAS C. HOTCHKISS.

Mr. Lucas Curtiss Hotchkiss, the son of Major Luther Hotchkiss, was born in Wolcott, October 14, 1807, and resided with his father, on the farm, until he was eighteen years of age, during which time he attended the District school in the winters after he was of sufficient age to attend school. In 1825, he went to that part of Southington called Plantsville, where he engaged as a mechanic for Messrs. Merriman and Copps, manufacturers of lasts and many kinds of handles used in making boots and shoes. Here he continued three years, making some intellectual improvement by attending school in the winters. In the spring of 1828, he removed to Meriden, and was in the employ of Messrs. Lauren, Merriman, & Co., making ivory and wooden combs, and machinery for the manufacturing of the same. After a few years this firm dissolved, and Mr. Hotchkiss became partner in the same business with Messrs. Walter Webb and Philo Pratt. He was afterwards partner with Mr. Oliver Snow in the manufacture of hardware and general machinery.

In 1829, he united with the First Congregational church in Meriden, where he still holds his membership, and in which church he was leader of the choir for a number of years. To him music has lost none of its charms, especially when in the order of the "old tunes." Like many others, when prosperity began to favor his labors in worldly goods, he returned to his native town, and won for his bride Miss Rufina Hall, daughter of Captain Levi Hall, in October, 1831. He has four children. His daughter, Sarah Ann, married Mr. Edward P. Yale, a successful merchant of New Haven; his daughter, Olive, married Mr. L. W. Curtiss, of New Britain; and his son, Levi H., married Miss Mary Marshall, of Hartford. His wife, Rufina, died in 1850, aged forty years. About two years afterwards he married Mary Ann Raymond, of New Haven, and the son of this marriage, Arthur R., resides in Providence, R. I.

Mr. Hotchkiss has a very pleasant home in West Meriden, where he now resides, striving to accomplish good for humanity in various ways, as opportunity affords. He has been a man of thought, taking notice of passing events around him in all his life, and hence many items of history are incorporated in this book which will add much to the pleasure of the reader, for they are all of the pleasant and cheerful kind.

He has furnished the following interesting reminiscences:

Some of the school teachers in the Center district from 1812 to 1825, were these: Thomas Upson, Mark Upson, Irad Bronson, William Bartholomew, Clark Bronson, Luther Roper, Levi Parker, William A. Alcott, John Potter son of Dr. Potter. Mr. John Clark of Waterbury taught a select school in the winter of 1826, in the house where Rev. Mr. Keys had lived. The old school house stood very near the present one. The writing tables extended around on three sides of the room, and were placed against the wall, so that the writers sat with their backs to the teacher. Long benches, made of oak slabs, extended around the room in front of the writing tables. Benches were made for small children, in the same style, with no backs. Bible reading, without opposition, was the custom in the morning. Columbian Orator, American Preceptor, and Webster's Spelling Book, were text books. Writing and spelling were leading studies every day, and on Saturday the Old Assembly Catechism, in the Congregational order and the Episcopal order, were regularly repeated. Daily exercises were required in the Moral Catechism, in Webster's spelling book, and the sounds of the letters of the alphabet, viz: b has one sound, as in bite, etc.

When David Harrison taught school in the East district, he had a nephew by the name of Beebe, living with him and attending school. Mr. Harrison composed some verses, which the boy repeated, and for which he received hundreds of pennies:

"Alvin Miles Beebe is my name,
I am a lad of little fame;
Yet I can read, and spell, and play,
Which is my business every day.
Before I lived, my father died;
Three orphans left and me beside —
And here I stand, a squint-eyed lad,
Pray, give me a cent — I will be glad."

This Mr. Beebe now resides in West Haven, and has a family grown to manhood.

One of the members of the military company, a good, honest man, but very odd, was chosen a corporal, and when the choice was announced by the captain, he stepped in front of the company and spoke as follows: "Gentlemen, officers, and fellow-soldiers — I am greatly surprised at the choice you have made, when there are such men as the Plumbs and the Beechers, who are not afraid of the woods full of Indians, nor a hell full of devils. I thank you for the respect you have shown me, but I cannot accept." Then making a low bow, took his place in the ranks.

This same person went to spend an evening with a young lady, in the West district, and she refused his company by saying she was sick. "Well," said he, "if you are sick, you must be prayed for," and he wrote a notice (giving the name as was the custom) and gave it to the minister the next Sabbath, who read it, and prayers were offered in the presence of the young lady, but she did not rise as was the custom.

Daniel Munson married Maranda Selcriggs, the daughter of widow Molly Selcriggs. The next day Mr. Jared Welton's daughter told Dinah, a negro woman, what had happened. Said Dinah: "Law me, du tell; Daniel Munson smart man, married Randa Selcriggs; how it does seem; what a happy choice it is to Mrs. Molly — git all Mrs. Molly's wood. Did oor pappa and mamma do to wedding?"

Praying for the sick was a custom regularly observed. When

any members of the congregation were sick, the following notice was read from the pulpit: Elijah Royce and wife request the prayers of God's people in behalf of their son, who is dangerously ill; friends and neighbors joining with them in this request." Any members of the family present at the reading, would rise in their seats. If the sick recovered, thanks were returned, the form of rising in the audience being observed. If the person died, another notice would be read, as follows: "Elijah Royce and wife having lost a beloved son, by death, ask the prayers of God's people that this severe affliction may be sanctified to their spiritual and everlasting good." I speak of Mr. Royce's family, as they were often sick. This was in Mr. Keys' time.

Mr. Keys once preached from the text: "Ephraim is joined to his idols; let him alone." Ephraim Hall was present, and was young enough to smile, then, as did many others; they are too old now to smile.

Mr. Keys exchanged pulpits with the minister at Northfield. In those days it was the custom for the leader of the choir to name the tune so loud that the singers and the congregation could hear. The minister from Northfield, in opening the service, read the hymn commencing:—

"Lord, what a wretched land is this
That yields us no supplies."

The chorister named the tune Northfield, at which many smiled; the catch of the word indicating that the minister had come from such a wretched land.

Mr. Keys, while preaching a sermon, told of a man who, while riding over a bridge, the bridge gave way, and he exclaimed, as he went down, "Devil take all!" at which the young people smiled, which was a rare occurrence in those days, for many were so superstitious as to think it sinful to smile in church.

REV. LENT S. HOUGH.

Rev. Lent S. Hough was born in Wallingford, January 21st, 1804, of worthy parents, and was the second child of a family of nine children. His childhood and youth were spent in his father's home, on the farm, where he received a good common school and academical education. He taught a district school one winter in Meriden, and afterwards taught a select school two years, summer and winter, in Freehold, Monmouth county, New Jersey. His classical, and part of his theological education, was obtained in Bangor, Maine. He graduated, theologically, at Yale Divinity School, in 1831. During his last years in Yale he preached frequently as supply of vacant churches, and in aiding neighboring pastors. Under his preaching, in his native town, in aid of an aged pastor, a revival commenced, in which there were many conversions.

About the time of graduating he was ordained pastor of the church in Chaplain, where he remained five years and a half, when his health became poor, causing his dismission. He afterwards preached as stated supply three years in North Madison, and one year in Bethel. He then preached in Middletown, Westfield Society, as stated supply, nine months, and was then installed pastor of the same Society, where he remained seventeen years. He came from Westfield to Wolcott, as stated supply, where he preached six years. Here he labored with success, though considerable of the time with poor health. The letter of commendation of him as their pastor, from

Westfield to the church in Wolcott, is preserved, and is of the highest honor to him as a successful pastor and minister. While in Wolcott, there were considerable repairs done upon the Meeting house, and furnishing inside, which were creditable both to him and the people. From Wolcott he went to Salem sixteen months, and from Salem to East Lyme, where he has labored with much success three years, and where he still resides, receiving the greatest kindness from his people, while deeply afflicted in his family.

CAPT. HEMAN HALL.

Captain Heman Hall was the son of Lieutenant Heman Hall, the first of the name who settled in Wolcott, and was born in Wallingford, in the year 1750. His father purchased land in Wolcott as early as 1754, but removed hither some years after, and resided near the present, so-called, "gamble-roofed house" on the road from Wolcott Centre to Marion. Captain Heman, it is thought, built this gamble-roofed house, and resided in it with his mother until 1800, when they exchanged this farm for the one then owned by Elnathan Thrasher, in Woodtick, where his grandson Orrin now resides. He married Rebecca Finch about the year 1770, by whom he had eight children, three of whom are recorded as being baptised at the same time, October 20th, 1776.

He was entrusted with the military authority of "Ensign of the Ninth company or train-band, in the Fifteenth regiment in this State," on the 27th day of May, 1785, and subsequently was made captain of the same company, and has been known as Captain Heman Hall ever since. His son Heman was made corporal in 1795, and sargeant in 1797. His son Levi has been designated as Captain Levi, and is still so called.

Captain Heman Hall was near relative to the Hon. Lyman Hall, of Georgia. This Lyman was the son of Hon. John Hall, and was graduated at Yale College in 1747; studied medicine and located at Midway, Ga. Having earnestly espoused the cause of his country in the Revolution, his efforts contributed much to induce the people of Georgia to join the Confederacy. He was in May, 1775, elected to Congress, and as a member of which, he signed the Declaration of Independence, and continued in that body until the close of the year 1780. In 1783 he was elected Governor of Georgia. He died in February, 1791, aged sixty-six. Captain Heman was a man of prominence and responsibility in Farmingbury Society from its first organization until his death in 1795, at the age of forty-five.

EPHRAIM HALL.

Ephraim Hall was the son of Sargent Heman, and grandson of Captain Heman, and great-grandson of Lieutenant Hall, the first of the name in Wolcott. He was born September 15th, 1799. In the autumn, when twenty-two years of age, he went to South Carolina to work on the Broad and Saluda rivers in constructing canals and locks around the falls in those rivers. Early the next spring, an opportunity presenting itself, he engaged two or three months in peddling, traveling on foot. After this he spent six or seven winters in peddling in the Southern States, and working on a farm at the north during the summer. He first engaged in selling tin-ware for the Yale Brothers, of Wallingford, they having a depot in Richmond, Virginia, where their peddlers obtained their goods, transporting them through the country with a horse and wagon. He peddled by license, taking license for a county or two, and remaining all winter within the prescribed circuit. At first he found this business wearisome and discouraging, but when he became acquainted he fared well and did well in the business. He learned to fall in with the notions and prejudices of the people, and let them talk as they pleased, and then everything went well. He usually paid for the privilege of staying over night, and sometimes traded to the amount of thirty dollars, sometimes forty, sometimes over a hundred. He would seldom go away without trading, for the people learned to expect him at a certain time, and prepare for his coming; especially was this the case in the later years when he sold dry goods.

For several summers he worked for Rev. Wm. Robinson, of Southington ; the good minister saying in the autumn when he closed work : "Well, Ephraim, when you get back in the spring, come over and see me, and if I am living I shall want you again to work for me."

He married, September 9th, 1824, Mary Minor, daughter of Archibald Minor, Esq., with whom he lived until her death, July 19th, 1870. He had three children, only one of whom survives him. His farm in Wolcott was that now owned by C. Frank Munson ; the large maple trees now standing by the roadside at that place he set there soon after he purchased the farm. This farm he gave to his grandson a few years since, and made his residence at Wolcott Center.

When the anti-slavery cause began to move the public mind, Mr. Hall was found on the side of the oppressed, and calmly, but decidedly, he maintained their cause as long as he lived. In his anti-slavery sentiments, as in all other things, he was not violent, but calm and decided, firm and true, at any cost. In 1839, his horse, with those of a few other men, was sheared because of his anti-slavery principles ; and when the Meeting house was burned, through this excitement, and there seemed to be no prospect of peace in the old Society, he, with several others of the most reliable members of the church, withdrew, and formed a second Society. Through the high and honorable decision of the Consociation held on the subject, the rights of the church were guaranteed, and then the new Society dissolved and returned to help the old in building the new Meeting house, and in settling a pastor.

His regular subscription to the American Missionary Society in behalf of the Freedmen has been, for several years, one hundred dollars a year, and in his will he left to that society the sum of fifteen hundred dollars. He was a true man to the church and humanity, and was greatly respected by the citizens of his native town. He died June 7th, 1874, in the seventy-fifth year of his age.

DR. AMBROSE IVES.

Dr. Ambrose Ives was the son of Abijah, and grandson of Abraham Ives, and was born in Wallingford, December 20th, 1786. He studied medicine with Dr. Cornwall, of Cheshire, and settled in Wolcott about the year 1808, at which time Dr. Potter was enjoying a good degree of confidence from the people of the community. The young physician was regarded by some as intrusive in coming into the field where one physician could attend all the sick, and by others as a welcome friend, who might, possibly, be helpful in turning aside the death messenger. Dr. Ives identified himself with the interests of the community to such a degree, and gave such diligent attention to his profession, that he soon secured an extensive practice, and an important standing as a citizen. On the 30th day of March, 1817, he married Wealthy Hopkins, daughter of Charles Upson, Esq., and thereafter continued his professional labors until 1827, when he removed to Wallingford to look after his deceased father's estate. Dr. Ives was celebrated in Wolcott for careful living, diligence in his profession, and not particularly enterprising in the town and local interests. He identified himself with the Episcopal church and did good service therein. From Wallingford he removed to Plymouth, where he resumed his profession, and soon obtained a large practice. In 1834 he became interested in the manufacture of gilt buttons at Waterville and took charge of the business. In 1837 he removed his residence to Waterbury, and in 1839 sold his interest at

Waterville and became a stock owner in the company of Brown & Elton, and continued in this connection until his decease. He died in Waterbury, January 31st, 1852, having accumulated quite a fortune.

His wife, Wealthy H., survived him a few years, always manifesting much interest in the people of her native town, and made a present of a very choice Communion Set to the Congregational church a short time before her decease.

REV. JOHN KEYS.

Rev. John Keys was a Presbyterian minister, and came from the Albany Presbytery, State of New York, and hence of his early history we have no knowledge. He was settled in Wolcott in the days of its greatest prosperity. The inhabitants numbered about eleven hundred. The old Meeting house was crowded with hearers, and among them were as fine a class of men and women, young people and children, as could be found in any rural congregation in the land. The money credit of the town of Wolcott is said to have been at this time as high as any town in the State. Its fame for schools and education was noted. The commercial business of the town rivaled that of Waterbury, Southington, and Bristol. The salary ($500 and twenty-five cords of wood) was liberal for those days, and the circumstances under which he was introduced into his office and work were most favorable. The installation sermon, preached by Dr. Lyman Beecher, was sufficient to inspire a man and a congregation a lifetime. The ceremonies of that installation were imposing, and have been referred to by many out of Wolcott, as well as in it.

The council met at the house of Mr. Keys, a little east of the church, for examination. When the hour came for services at the church, the members of the council formed in procession, two by two, then the gentlemen and ladies of the choir, and following them, in the same manner, the members of the church, all walking to the church. Miss Abigail Hall, now (1873) residing in Meriden, says, the Meeting house was full. The singers sat in the gallery, nearly filling the front seats on three sides. The ladies sang with their bonnets off in those days,— and they were bonnets, not hats. "Mr. Henderson, who had been employed to teach a singing-school, took charge of the singing at the installation. The bass singers sat on the west side of the gallery, David Harrison, with bass viol, in the center ; the tenor and counter on south side, and Stephen Harrison, with tenor viol, in the center; first treble on east side, and Doct. Harvey Norton, with violin, in the center." Such was the choir in 1814, and such were the encouraging facts around Mr. Keys as a minister. He was a laborious, diligent, good man, careful of all, and a true man. All those who remember him speak kindly of him, without a word of reproach. Eight years he toiled for this people, as though they were his own children, and when the separation came it was a heavy trial to him. His letter to the church is the saddest of the kind I have ever read. He commences that letter with the following words : "The painful hour seems now arrived, in the sovereign dispensations of Providence, when we must part." He was endeared to many young men who had attended his school, by influences arising in such labor, which are not easily severed, and can never be forgotten. He closed his labors in December, 1822, at a time of the year when a church should hesitate to dismiss a faithful servant. Without house, or home, or work, with a large family, in the dead of winter, is rather a sad picture concerning one who gave up all secular pursuits to preach the gospel !

Mr. Keys moved to Ohio, and other western States, where he resided forty-six years, and died at Dover, Ohio, in 1868, aged eighty-six. His wife, Mary, died at Peoria, Illinois, in 1850, aged sixty-six. Their children were Mary O. (Kingsbury), now living in Toledo, Ohio ; John A., now living in Visalia, California ; William M., now living in Saltillo, Nebraska ; Richard M., now living in California ; David C., died in 1867, in Oakland, California ; Catharine S. (Moore), living in Dover, Ohio ; Lucy H. (Abbott), living in Cleveland, Ohio ; Charles F., died in 1837, in Alabama ; Luther H., living in Greeley, Iowa. This record dates in 1873.

SIMEON H. NORTON.

Simeon H. Norton, son of Simeon N., and great-grandson of David Norton, was born in Wolcott, August 11th, 1813. He began attendance in the district school at the Center, when but two years and nine months old, and continued to attend the same until twelve years of age, during which time he acquired, besides the regular studies of the school in that day, some knowledge of geography, arithmetic, and English grammar. At the age of thirteen he engaged in a manufactory in Meriden, Conn., where he continued two years, at which time, being at the age of fifteen, he accepted an invitation to teach the north district school of his native town, one term, in which being quite successful, he accepted an invitation to teach the north-east school the following summer and winter terms; and while engaged in teaching he was pursuing a course of study preparatory to the teaching of a high school, the accomplishment of which was of great consideration in his own mind. In order to perfect this desire, he attended the Episcopal Academy at Cheshire, where he became an Episcopalian. At the age of nineteen he engaged as teacher in the largest district school in Bristol, where he continued teaching, summer and winter, three years,— at the same time teaching singing school in the winter season, and taking charge of the choir of the Episcopal church. During his last term in Bristol he wrote to Dr. William A. Alcott, then in Boston, to assist him in obtaining the place of assistant in some high school in that city, to which the Doctor responded cordially, expressing great pleasure in the aspirations of the young men of Wolcott. Before any arrangement of this kind could be made, Mr. Norton was urgently requested to engage as clerk in the store of Messrs. Benham and Tuttle, in Wolcott, which invitation he accepted, and notified his friend the doctor, in Boston, accordingly. He was in the store at Wolcott one year, and during that time served as acting school-visitor for the town, that being the first office he ever held by the votes of the people. From Wolcott he went to Bristol, and engaged as clerk in a store in the same portion of the town where he had taught school, and where he accepted his old place in the Episcopal choir. At the end of four years he left Bristol, and entered, as clerk, the store of Messrs. H. M. Welch & Co., in Plainville, the largest store at that time in that part of the country, and continued there about four years, during which time, there being no Episcopal church in the place, he attended regularly the Congregational church, and served, by invitation, as leader of the choir during the time of his residence there.

In the spring of 1843, he was urged to go into partnership with an old merchant at Plymouth, which offer he declined, but engaged with him as clerk in the store. Not being well pleased with the business of selling liquors as connected with this store, he left as soon as the time of his engagement expired, and, collecting all his capital, located himself in a store at a place now known as Hitchcock's Station, in Southington, where he remained three years, and then removed to Plantsville, where he still resides. He engaged in this place as a merchant, keeping a temperance store, until 1869, when, having been quite successful in business, he retired from the same, to pass the remaining years in quietness and rest.

While in his store, he held the office of postmaster fifteen years, from 1853, and has since received a good share of honor in various offices in the town,—standing several years as first selectman, going once to the legislature, and has been for several years, and is now, a justice of the peace. He has been called on to serve as administrator of estates, drawing deeds and wills, and other like documents, to a large extent, and continues to receive a high degree of confidence from his fellow-citizens.

When twenty-three years of age he married Sarah Ann, daughter of Capt. Levi Hall, of Wolcott, with whom he spent thirty-five years of happy wedded life, until her death, in 1872. Of his wife's Christian life and death he speaks in the highest terms.

In politics, Mr. Norton has been a Democrat, though not a strong partizan, and at the breaking out of the late war, he took the ground that the rebels, having taken up arms against the government, should be put down by force of arms, and sustained the efforts of the United States for the accomplishment of that end. His only son, twenty-one years of age, enlisted, and fell at his post, May 3d, 1863, in the terrible battle of Chancellorsville, where several of his Wolcott friends also fell.

DR. JOHN POTTER.

Dr. John Potter came to Wolcott and established himself as a physician about the year 1780, and was trusted and respected many years as a physician and citizen. He was active in the Ecclesiastical Society, and sustained a large share of the responsibilities of the offices of the same; and so far as the records show, or the friends remember, he acquitted himself in all things as a faithful man in his profession, and a worthy citizen. He married Lydia, the daughter of Deacon Aaron Harrison, than which family there was none more honorable in the community.

His children grew up around him in honorable, and active employments, but when the glory of Wolcott began to decline, they removed west, and last of all, the Doctor went, also, saying he went "west to die, not to live," for his days were nearly run. He was of the progressive kind of physicians, for when it was noised abroad that inoculation by kine-pox would secure the community from the dreadful ravages of small-pox, he at once petitioned the town for the privilege of introducing the practice of vaccination. His children and family are very kindly remembered by some of the older people of the town at the present time.

REV. NATHAN SHAW.

Rev. Nathan Shaw, son of Solomon and Betsy (Dilingham) Shaw, was born in Abington, Mass., June 3d, 1788. In 1796 his father removed to Cummington, Mass., where, under the instruction of Rev. James Briggs he prepared for college. He studied theology one year at Andover Theological Seminary, and with Rev. Alvan Hyde, D. D., of Lee, Mass. Having performed, for a year, missionary labor in Berkshire County, Mass., he was ordained, in 1820, over the Congregational church in West Stockbridge, Mass. In 1826 he was settled over, or served the church as stated supply, in Curtisville, Stockbridge, Mass. He subsequently supplied various churches in Massachusetts and Connecticut. In 1831, on the fourth of July, the Society in Wolcott voted to hire him four months, and before that time expired they voted to hire him one year. The probability is that he preached here nine or ten months only. After leaving Wolcott he was engaged among the Osage Indians, under the American Board of Commissioners for Foreign Missions. He died in 1865.

SETH THOMAS.

Seth Thomas was the son of James Thomas, who married Maria Ward, of West Haven or Orange, Conn., and removed to Wolcott. James came from Scotland to this country. Seth Thomas is said to have been born in Wolcott, where he lived until about the year 1810. He was a man of few words, but of great energy and perseverance in any employment in which he engaged. His father was a cooper, but he turned somewhat naturally to the trade of a carpenter, in connection with which, probably, he obtained some knowledge of mill property and manufacturing interests. He was apprenticed to Mr. Daniel Tuttle, of Plymouth, and in consequence of his quiet attention to his duties, and want of boyish vanities, he was called, by some of the wild lads of Wolcott, "Daniel Tuttle's fool." As in many cases, so in this — history shows who are wise and who are fools.

Mr. Thomas engaged in the manufacture of clocks in the firm of Terry, Thomas & Hoadley, at Hoadleyville, in about the year 1810, where he continued three years. It is said that previous to this engagement he made an offer for the purchase of the mill property of Mr. Daniel Byington, at Wolcott, and desired the town to open a road direct to Cheshire for the export of goods that might be manufactured by him. But the spirit of enterprise had not come upon the people of Wolcott, and Mr. Thomas being discouraged as to the location, went to Hoadleyville and thence to Plymouth Hollow, now Thomaston. It is possible that this proposition to come to Wolcott was made just before going to Thomaston. Had he received suitable encouragement, the enterprising village of Thomaston might have been in Wolcott instead of Plymouth, for the water power in Wolcott is pronounced by competent judges to be superior to that of Thomaston. About the year 1813, Mr. Thomas purchased some property of Mr. Heman Clark, in Plymouth Hollow, containing a small manufactory of some kind, and here commenced, on his individual responsibility, the making of clocks. In this business he had great success; and about 1830, he built a cotton manufactory, which, after some years, was reconstructed into the clock making business. Such was the prosperity of his enterprises that about 1850 a joint stock company was formed, which resulted in the enlargement of the business so as to establish depots for the sale of goods in different parts of the world. The present capital stock in use is half a million of dollars. The branch depots are located in New York, Chicago, San Francisco, and London.

Thomaston now numbers two thousand inhabitants, and is an enterprising, thriving village. Such has Wolcott lost, and such has Plymouth gained, and such are the results of the energy of one man.

REV. BENONI UPSON, D. D.

Dr. Benoni Upson was born in "Farmington Part" of what is now Wolcott, Conn., February 14th, 1750. His father was Thomas Upson, who resided one mile north of the Meeting house in Wolcott. His mother was Hannah Hopkins, of Waterbury, sister of the celebrated Dr. Samuel Hopkins, of Newport, R. I. He graduated at Yale College in 1776, and was ordained pastor of the church in Kensington April 21st, 1779. August, 1778, he was married to Livia Hopkins, daughter of Joseph Hopkins, Esq., of Waterbury. Their children were eight, viz: Gustavus, Laura, Henry, Livia, Laura, Sophia, Sally, William. Of these but one was living in 1863. Dr. Upson was for fourteen years fellow of Yale College, from which in 1817 he received the honorary degree of Doctor of Divinity.

Rev. Royal Robbins in his notes upon the history of the church in Kensington, as given in "Contributions to the Ecclesiastical History of Connecticut," p. 412, speaks of him as a "wise and benevolent man, a lover of peace, and a peacemaker, and distinguished, with his family, for hospitality. In the sermon preached by Mr. Robbins at the funeral of Dr. Upson, he describes him as "in social intercourse highly agreeable,— courteous and attentive to all, his address at once dignified and easy, agreeable and cheerful in his feelings, companionable and conciliating, tender and gentle." He says, also, that he was "a valuable friend and counsellor; in his intellectual character, possessing a clear understanding and ready wit; a man of information and of great native sagacity, admirably acquainted with human nature, and cautious and wary, prudent and discreet."

Rev. Mr. Hillard, in a letter, speaks of him as "a most accomplished gentleman. He was regular in his attendance upon the ministry and ordinances of religion, after as well as before giving up his ministerial labors,— being for several of the last years of his life the oldest man usually seen in the congregation. He was buried in the East burying ground, Kensington. The inscription on his monument is as follows : " Rev. Benoni Upson, D. D., native of Waterbury, Conn.; Graduate and Fellow of Yale College ; Pastor of the Church of Christ in Berlin ; Ordained April 21, 1779; Died Nov. 13, 1826, aged 76 years."

REV. HENRY E. L. UPSON.

Rev. Henry E. L. Upson was born in Wolcott, May 21, 1831, and was a twin brother to Harriet Arabella Frances Upson. He was baptized by the name of Henry Eugene Loomis, and was the son of Thomas and Jerusha Upson, and grandson of Esquire Charles and Mary (Moulthrop) Upson. His early school days were spent at the Centre District school of Wolcott, of which he gave some reminiscenses at the Centenary meeting. He was fitted for college at Lewis Academy, in Southington, and entered Yale college in 1855, from which he graduated with honors in 1859. He was one year in the Andover Theological Seminary, and two years, nearly, in Yale Theological Seminary, at New Haven. While in the Seminary at New Haven he was appointed, August 7, 1862, chaplain of the Thirteenth Regiment of Connecticut Volunteers, by Governor Buckingham, and was ordained June 22d, and joined his regiment in New Orleans, where he remained to the fall of Fort Hudson. He distinguished himself by gallant conduct on several occasions, and received special commendation from his superior officers for efficient efforts for the physical comfort of the soldiers, while earnestly exercising his office as a minister among them.

He resigned his chaplaincy and left the service of the United States August 7, 1863, to become the pastor of the Congregational church in New Preston, Conn., where he was installed September 23, 1863, in which place his labors have been ordinarily successful, and where he still continues to preach.

He married Miss Abbie A. Platt, daughter of Prof. Merritt and Abigail (Merwin) Platt, of Milford, Conn., October 13, 1863. He is the only Upson, descended from Wolcott, who is now in the ministry, so far as we know. Dr. Benoni Upson was great-uncle to Henry, and spent a long and successful life in the ministry. Rev. A. J. Upson, D. D., of Albany, N. Y., professor in Union College, being a descendant of the Waterbury Upsons, and of the same original family with the Wolcott Upsons.

REV. ISRAEL B. WOODWARD.

Rev. Israel Beard Woodward was born in Watertown, Conn., December 4th, 1767. He was the son of Israel and Abigail (Stoddard) Woodward, and great-grandson, on his mother's side, of Rev. Anthony Stoddard, the settled Congregational minister of Woodbury, Conn., for sixty years. He was graduated at Yale College in 1789, at the age of twenty-two, and was ordained pastor of the church in Wolcott in June, 1792. From the time of graduation to his settlement, he had three years for theological studies, but where he pursued these, or whether he did or not, regularly, we have not learned; but we have no doubt that one of his cast of mind would avail himself of such advantageous preparation for so great a work. From the first the majority of the people of Wolcott were greatly pleased with Mr. Woodward, for his style of preaching was quite the opposite of his predecessor, Mr. Gillet. Mr. Gillet never indulged in remarks that would create a smile, but Mr. Woodward was a man of cheerful spirit, and his natural turn of mind would make a pleasing reply or remark, in little matters in conversation, which was relieving and agreeable to most persons, and the aptness and appropriateness of his illustrations in the pulpit would sometimes create a smile in the audience; yet he was sedate and quite serious, and this sharpness of perception and application of truth in a cheerful way made him an acceptable preacher to most persons. It was, I apprehend, the pleasant witicisms of ordinary times, turned into sarcasms in the exciting political times of Mr. Thomas Jefferson, that offended some of Mr. Woodward's parishioners who withdrew from the support of the church at that time ; and yet there are indications that Mr. Woodward's most earnest church members, who became very zealous in politics, influenced more persons to leave the Society than he did ; for they declared their belief, that if Mr. Jefferson was elected president, the religious liberties of this country would be at once annulled, and persecution would reign instead ; and there are those living now who have heard their fathers repeat these sayings as given by Mr. Woodward's strongest church members. There can be no doubt of the honesty and uprightness of these men who opposed Jefferson, for Jefferson was commonly reported an infidel, and infidelity was a great enemy and persecutor of the Christian church in the sixteenth and seventeenth centuries, both in England and in America. And the political excitements immediately following the revolution were nearly as effective on the minds of the people as was the revolution itself, and Wolcott, which had suffered severely in the loss of its men in the war, could not forget how dearly it had bought Freedom. And had not Mr. Woodward endeared himself to the people by dignity of character, and a cultivated mind, and also by a hearty sympathy with them in all their trials and privations, the loss of support to the church would doubtless have been far greater than it was. Mr. Woodward was the strong band of union in those days, though the people knew it not ; yet he could not maintain his position without saying something on the political questions of the day,— for a large majority of the people were Federalists, and opposed to Mr. Jefferson's politics. And this may have been the reason why he sent to the Society's annual meeting in November, 1800, a proposition to be dismissed. He may have found it so hard to harmonize the conflicting elements, that he was greatly discouraged, and preferred to be relieved from the distressing situation. When he requested to be dismissed, the parish meeting voted a committee to go to him and "inform him that the Society, for various reasons, wish not to act upon the proposition by him made as to a dismission; particularly as they are well pleased with his performances as their minister, and are by no means willing for a dissolution of the pastoral connection between him and them." These words, "by no means," tell no more than the truth for the men of the Society.

One of the present parishioners relates that he has heard his mother say, many times, that Mr. Woodward was the best man she ever knew. Mrs. Woodward is said to have been a kind and noble woman, much esteemed by the people. A colored girl was employed in the family. A short time after Mr. Woodward's death she became displeased at some request of her mistress, and retorted by saying, "I wish you had died instead of Mr. Woodward." This girl, living in New Haven some five years since, told the fact to a person who was at the late Centenary meeting, and as she told it she repeated the good qualities of her late master with much interest and feeling. Yet such a man and minister, so kind-hearted, sympathetic and feeling in religious life, and in regard to the sorrows of men, was, in the common expression used, "full of his jokes." The old superstition that a Christian should never laugh, is one of the darkest errors of the Roman Catholic Church, and found no countenance in the life of this good man.

SOME OF MR. WOODWARD'S JOKES.

A man with a pig under his arm passing Mr. Woodward's house one morning, saw Mr. Woodward in the yard, and addressed him with "Good-morning." Mr. Woodward's ready reply was: "Good-morning, gentlemen, both of you."

It was customary in those days for minister and people, all, to use intoxicating drinks, and Mr. Woodward and his church members kept up this custom, not discerning the fearful consequences of such a practice. On one occasion Mr. Woodward sent his work boy to the store for a bottle of whisky. The boy returned with the bottle, when Mr. Woodward asked him what kind of liquor he had brought. He replied the store keeper said it was whisky. "Have you not tasted it?" said Mr. W. "No," said the boy. "Then," said Mr. W., "you shall have none of it, to pay you for not tasting it."

The next time he sent him on a like errand he asked him the same question,— "What have you?" "Rum," said the boy. "How do you know?" "I drank some, and treated the company at the store,"— and the half empty bottle indicated that the company was rather numerous.

Mr. Woodward being so ready at repartee, the people learned to reply to him in the same way, and were much pleased when they could catch him with a pleasant word. He hired a man to work for him, and the man came to engage in the work about ten o'clock in the morning. Mr. Woodward said: "Rather late, Mr. H——, to begin a day's work." Mr. H. replied: "It is about the time you usually begin work for me," referring to Mr. Woodward's preaching on Sabbath.

He was very fond of children, taking them on his knee and kissing them. There is a woman now in the parish whose mother, when a little girl, hid from Mr. Woodward many times, when he came to her father's home, so as not to be kissed.

The students in his school enjoyed his pleasant ways very much, and hence they came to look upon him as a father, as well as a teacher, and the tenderness with which the poet, Mr. Maxwell, speaks of him is seldom equaled. Mr. Woodward wore a cue in the old style on the back part of his head. One Sabbath this cue was left at home and observed by the students. Mr. Woodward's little dog, that would follow him anywhere, if allowed, was at home; the students put the cue or "switch of hair" on the dog's head, and let him out the door. The dog went direct to church, mounted the pulpit stairs, in presence of the audience, sat down at the pulpit door, facing the audience, and there remained until the benediction. The children of the audience, big and little, had hard work to keep sober faces during that service. Notwithstanding the pleasant witicisms and cheerful manner of life of Mr. Woodward, he is said to have been a man of much dignity of character, and highly respected in his parish and by all who knew him in neighboring parishes.

Of his students no list can be obtained, and but few persons now living remember the names of any of them. Mr. Stephen Upson, of Waterbury, who became one of the most celebrated lawyers of the State of Georgia, "pursued his classical studies for a time with Mr. Woodward."

Mr. J. G. Percival,* the poet of considerable celebrity, pursued his studies, for a time, with Mr. Woodward. A Mr. Peck, from New Haven, was here, and cut the initials of his name and the date on Mr. Woodward's " doorstone," in 1803, where they still remain.

Mr. William Maxwell, of Virginia, attended school at Mr. Woodward's, and on hearing of his death, composed an elegy of great pathos and beauty, on Wolcott and Mr. Woodward. This poem was read at the late Centenary meeting, and might properly be placed as one of the papers of that occasion, but I place it in connection with Mr. Woodward's name because of its beautiful memorial character, and the appropriate honor it does his memory.

This poem is secured by the very great favor of the

---

*James Gates Percival, the poet, was born in Berlin. near Hartford, Conn., on the 15th of September, 1795. He entered Yale College, when fifteen years of age, and graduated in 1815, with the reputation of being the first scholar of his class. He received the degree of Doctor of Medicine from Yale Medical school, in 1820. He published several volumes of poems and miscellaneous prose writings. He was appointed assistant surgeon in the U. S. army, in 1824, and acted as professor of chemistry in the Military Academy at West Point. This position he resigned, and for two years subsequently he superintended the printing of the first quarto-edition of Dr. Webster's American Dictionary. Few men possessed higher poetical qualities than Percival. He died in 1856. See National Fifth Reader, p. 238.

Hon. L. W. Cutler and Judge Curtiss, of Watertown, Conn.

Mr. Woodward owned land in several parts of the town besides his home at the Centre. He owned a considerable part of a distillery that was constructed in the old mill where Mr. Ira Hough ground bark for tanning purposes; but very little is known of this distillery, except the fact of its short existence.

Mr. Woodward belonged to the militia of the county in some office, probably that of chaplain, and the following letter explains itself somewhat, while it furnishes some characteristics of the man.*

WOLCOTT, Sept. 7, 1803.

MR. STANLEY:

I send you by the bearer, Mr. Lucius Tuttle, my old beaver. I want you to display upon it a little military skill. I have no use for it except on brigade or regimental reviews. That old despot, *Poverty*, sternly forbids me to lay out ten or twelve dollars for a hat to be used but once a year.

Now, sir, I am little acquainted with the mechanical operation of furs, nevertheless, I will presume to give you my ideas. The hat you will find torn about one inch and a half directly in front, and a small breach made on the left wing. I have supposed that a surgical operation need first be performed, and perhaps a piece taken out in front, which would make the angle more obtuse and in less danger of pricking people on public occasions. It is my wish, not to have my hat drawn directly perpendicular in front, nor to have the point of the cock sunk to a horizontal direction, ending in abstract sharpness. But I wish it to incline about thirty degrees from a perpendicular, and terminate half way between the form of a *cap-a-pie* military hat and what its name is. To speak in plain English, I want it made decent for a chaplain, remote from either extreme.

As to the looping, binding, or trimming the hat, you will act your own judgment, and indeed, in all you do to it. All I would

---

* The letter in Mr. Woodward's own hand writing is still in the possession of Mrs. Mark Tuttle, of Wolcott.

do, is to express my wishes, believing you will wish to gratify them. It doubtless wants a thorough dressing, and if you can do it so as to make the hat answer, I should be glad you would undertake it, if not, to return it by the bearer.

I should be glad to have it done so that I might obtain it within fifteen or sixteen days. By complying with the above request, you will much oblige me, and shall receive a just compensation.

From, sir, your humble servant,

Mr. W. Stanley.   Israel B. Woodward.

The address on the outside of the letter is,

MR. WHITING STANLEY,
Hatter,
Cheshire.

Mr. Woodward married about the time of his settlement, "Sally," the daughter of the Rev. John Smalley, D. D., of New Britain, Conn., an accomplished woman, of whom we hear no complaints, and who survived her husband some years, and on whom the parishioners of Wolcott used to call with pleasure, years after she left Wolcott, and while she lived in New Haven or East Haven.

In the summer and fall of 1810 the typhoid fever prevailed fearfully in Wolcott, beginning in the family of Mark Harrison, Esq. The disease was so uncontrolable by the physicians that the people of the community feared to go near a house where it prevailed. Mr. Woodward, true to his pastoral relations and his natural kindness of heart, visited the sick and bereaved, administering comfort as best he could in such a trying time. As a consequence, the fever "set in," and on the 17th of September, 1810, he closed his labors and sufferings on earth, and entered the, to us, great unrealized future. He was forty-three years of age, and left no family besides his wife.

His death made a great vacancy in the community,

nearly or quite all lamenting him as their great and true friend, and feeling that his place could not easily be filled in the sacred office of minister and pastor.

WOLCOTT.* AN ELEGY.

In these green shades where soft Eliza † flows
To soothe her own dear poet in his woes;
While ev'ning gales from yonder willows breathe
The balmy sighs that dying flow'rs bequeath,
Thus let me rove, forgotten and alone,
To muse on sorrows that are all my own.
Alas! the guardian of my early days,
The fond inspirer of my tuneful lays,
Long cherished object of my filial love,—
My Woodward leaves me for the realms above!
And I am left, thro' long succeeding years,
To mourn my loss with unavailing tears.
Then come, sweet muse, resume the lyre again,
And teach my heart a sad lamenting strain;
Some soothing air to whisper soft relief,—
At once indulge, and tranquilize my grief.
And thou, sad memory, to sorrow true,
Restore the scenes my happy childhood knew;
Those faded scenes thou only canst restore,
Now past forever, and beloved the more.
High on a mountain all unknown to Fame,
Tho' grac'd with Wolcott's venerable name,
The village bloom'd in her serene retreat,
And smil'd to see the clouds beneath her feet.
Such scenes of old the saintly hermit sought,—
Retreat for Penitence, and pious Thought;
Where Faith might love to breathe a parting sigh,

---

* Here the author, William Maxwell, Esq., lived for some time, when a boy, under the care of the Rev. Israel B. Woodward, pastor of the place, pursuing his preparatory studies for admission into Yale College. The death of that gentleman, communicated in the letter of a friend, first suggested the idea of this poem.

† Elizabeth river, Virginia.

And hope a shorter passage to the sky.
Mild were the virtues of the village train,
The rural virgin, and the faithful swain;
Hid from the world, unconscious of its arts,
While Peace and Innocence possessed their hearts.
Virtue beheld them with approving eye,
And vice confessed her homage by her sigh.
There Woodward reign'd the genius of the place,
The friend and guardian of the simple race.
And well the pastor led his little flock,
Thro' peaceful meadows to the gushing Rock;
Himself before, lest they should go astray,
His only care to help them on their way,—
Fulfill his office, and approve his love
To the great Shepherd of the fold above.

'Twas on a hill just rescued from the wood,
The Preacher's hospitable mansion stood,
Where oft the taper, with inviting ray,
Allur'd the stranger from his weary way,
And oft the cheerful table spread its best
To win the smile of some unbidden guest.
Beside the fence bloom'd many a graceful vine,
The blushing rose, and sweeter eglantine;
Before the door, the green sward, trim and gay,
Entic'd the lamb and little child to play.
Spring set her flow'rs, too beautiful to last,
And Winter nipp'd them with unwilling blast.

Here, led by Heav'n, a happy child I grew,
Fresh as the wild rose in the morning dew;
The bird that carol'd on the hawthorn by,
Less gay, and scarce more volatile than I.
Then oft the groves and solitudes around
Bore witness to my lyre's unskillful sound;
So soon I felt the darling passion strong,
And lisp'd the feelings of my heart in song.
I knew the merry mock bird's fav'rite tree,
And dear enough his wildwood notes to me;

I aim'd no death against the robin's breast,
The sparrow twitter'd fearless on her nest:
Young as I was, a visionary boy,
I felt a sympathy with Nature's joy;
And Woodward, happy as myself the while,
Look'd on, and owned my pleasure with a smile.
Not his the brow of dark, forbidding frown;
With graceful ease his spirit would come down
To share my childhood's inoffensive play.
With useful freedom, profitably gay;
Pleased from his graver studies to unbend,
And lose awhile the master in the friend;
To win and guide me still his constant view,
At once my teacher and my playmate too.
Thus, all unknown the anxious cares of man,
How fair the morning of my life began!
My head unburdened with Ambition's schemes,
Light all my slumbers, innocent my dreams;
Too sweet the scenes my playful fancy drew,
And Hope half whisper'd, "You may find them true."
Stay, rude Experience, hear my pleading sigh,
Nor bid these visions of Remembrance fly.
Why wake the dreamer from his smiling sleep?
Why wake the dreamer to be wise and weep?

Each season then in her successive reign,
Brought some peculiar blessing in her train.
'Twas sweet when Spring renew'd the faded scene,
And dress'd the landscape in her cheerful green;
When little birds on ev'ry conscious tree,
Renew'd their songs of simple melody;
And many a tender, many a merry lay,
All sweet, came mingled from the budding spray:
All sweet, but sweeter sung the happy swain,
While smiling Beauty listen'd to his strain.

Next Summer came with soft luxurious sweets,
And lur'd our footsteps to her green retreats.
Now sweet to ramble thro' those waving trees,

And breathe the fragrance of the ev'ning's breeze !
The moon looks down with chaste and tender beam,
And smiles to see her image in the stream.
In silent joy we gaze upon the sky,
Till the sweet pleasure melts into a sigh.
Or let me pause upon the mountain's brow
(Where oft the Muses listen to my vow),
And view with eyes that fondly overflow,
The various beauties of the scene below —
Lawns, mountains, villages, in fair display,
All soften'd by the sun's descending ray.
Thy steeple, Southington, that high in air,
Invites the rustic to the house of pray'r :
And spread around it, many a smiling plain,
Waving with harvests of the golden grain.
The farmer's mansion, fair in modest pride,
With barns of plenty rising at its side ;
Bright running streams that shine between the hills,
While fancy hears the music of their rills ;
And, far retreating into fading blue,
Old Carmel mountain closing in the view.
O lovely scenes so dear to me before !
O lovely scenes that I shall see no more !
Still may thy wilds bloom ever undecay'd,
A grateful shelter to the mountain maid !
Still may thy charms in all their beauty shine !
For other eyes — but never more for mine.

And now, with all his shining honors crown'd,
Rich Autumn strews his treasures all around —
And sweet it is to snuff the swelling gale,
That steals its fragrance from yon bending vale,
Where lusty Labor makes his toil a play,
And smiling bears his yellow spoils away :
Or here I wander o'er the custom'd hill,
Where lovely Nature smiles to see me still,
Viewing the foliage of her lively trees,
That gayly rustle in the passing breeze ;
Too vain to gratify admiring eyes

With all the fancy of their various dyes —
Ah! soon to vanish, when the falling leaf
Suggests its moral to the heart of grief.

Last, Winter comes with all his dear delights,
His cheerful days, and still more cheerful nights;
His songs and pastimes that can never tire,
And charming tales around the sparkling fire;
While storms without, tho' terrible their din,
Endear the silence of the calm within.
The sun has set behind yon dusky trees;
Shut close the door upon the whistling breeze,
Now heap the fire, and trim the cheerful light,
To welcome in the pleasures of the night;
While Phebe carols to her humming wheel,
Or little Mary turns the winding reel,
Perhaps the merry doctor sings his song,
Or tells a story to the list'ning throng;
While Woodward, still with gay, good natured mirth,
As playful as the kitten on the hearth,
Improves the joy with charms that never fail,
And draws a moral from each harmless tale.
Shut close the door, — winds whistle as ye will, —
The storm may come, but we'll be happy still.

So passed the joys that charm'd my early youth, —
Dear fleeting joys of innocence and truth;
As roses die upon the summer wind,
And leave a sad sweet memory behind.

Fair was the scene, when Sunday's smiling day
Call'd the good villagers to praise and pray;
When up the hill in order they repair,
To join their pastor in the house of prayer:
The sober matron, in her russet best,
Her little infant smiling at her breast;
The blooming maid, — her eyes are raised above, —
Her bosom sighs, — but not with earthly love;
The swain, unconscious of his resting plow,

And free to seek a nobler service now,
Forget alike their labors and their sports;
They meet their Maker in his earthly courts.
Away with earth! I see the Preacher rise!
And hark! he speaks! a message from the skies!
No poor ambition, void of grace and sense,
Betrays his tongue to gaudy eloquence;
He scorns the tricks of vain theatric art,
That catch the eye, but cannot cheat the heart.
Warm, but yet prudent, is his temper'd zeal;
He feels himself, and makes his hearers feel.
How sweet the accents of that silver tongue,
That wins the old, and fascinates the young!
The scoffer hears at last, and, undeceiv'd,
Wonders to find how much he had believ'd.
Ev'n children listen to the simple style,
And half divine the doctrine by his smile.

Where yonder locust overhangs the stream,
And contemplation loves to sit and dream;
Those parting trees the village school disclose,
Where little children, rang'd in shining rows.
Whisper their tasks as busy as you please,
And murmurs rise, like hum of hiving bees;
All trim and shining in their best attire,
They wait with awe the coming of the Squire;
But Woodward most their beating hearts attend,—
Well known by all to be their dearest friend.
This quarter day they feel resolved to shew
Quite all they know, and something over too.
And see, he comes! the whisper flies around:
Now all is still, and silence rules the ground.
On him alone their eyes intently gaze,
And little bosoms tremble for his praise;
For he shall mark where bashful merit lies,
Tho' half conceal'd by modesty's disguise,
And crown the petty candidate for fame,
Who lifts an artless blessing on his name.
And soon the tale thro' all the village flies,

How little Reuben won the letter'd prize.
The mother, too, with fond and simple joy,
Tells how the Pastor call'd her son "good boy,"
And how he said — she never can forget —
"He'll be a man before his mother yet."
O tender scenes of innocent delight!
But ah! no more! — they vanish from my sight —
Like colors melting in the ev'ning skies.
What shades of darkness gather on my eyes!
See! there they move, yon sad funereal train!
Wind round the hill, and seek the lowly plain.
They bear him off upon that gloomy bier:
They bear him off and leave me weeping here,
And now they hide him in the narrow grave!
My sorrows flow — alas! they could not save!

O Wolcott! all thy pleasant days are fled!
Thy friend, thy father, rests among the dead!
The hand of Death has wither'd all thy flowers,
And Winter howls along thy leafless bowers.
Thy hills that echo'd to the lowing kine,
Thy plains where golden harvest us'd to shine,
The tuneful groves — all, all, have felt the wound;
And all is still, and desolate around.

Now let me seek that silent scene once more,
And trace the path so often trod before;
Move o'er the vale, a silent shade of woe,
While sorrow wakes, and bids my eyes o'erflow;
Gaze at the spot, seen dimly thro' my tears,
The peaceful nest of early happy years,
And drink once more the murmurs of the grove,
Where oft together we were wont to rove —
Then turn, and pause on that forsaken hill,
Beneath the moon's pale beam, when all is still;
And O! yet dearer to my mourning breast,
Steal to the grave where Woodward takes his rest;
Bedew with faithful tears the grassy mound,
And mix my sighs with those that breathe around.

I reach the hill, but tremble to ascend.
I fear to meet my dear departed friend.
These mossy tresses floating from the trees,
Too sadly murmur on the passing breeze;
Unearthly voices whisper in the air,
And all is dark, and changed, to my despair.
There stands the house of God! I know not how—
It looks not as it did—how silent now!
Is this the meadow so loved before?
Alas! how faded! it shall bloom no more!
Yon drooping elm, that dear familiar tree—
It hangs its head—it is to weep with me!
And the sweet green on which my childhood play'd—
Ev'n the sweet green, is wither'd and decay'd!
I seek the house, my dear abode so late:
He comes not now to meet me at the gate.
How still and mournful is the silent hearth,
Once the dear scene of Nature's simple mirth!
No more the doctor, or the cheerful Squire,
Shall crack their nuts and jests around the fire;
No more the maid her humming wheel suspend,
To hear the tale of sorrows without end;
Nor I, the least of all the harmless train,
Shall taste those joys of innocence again.

But where is she, the partner of his heart?
Perhaps in some recess she mourns apart.
Ah! no! she would not linger here alone;
Spoil'd is the nest, the wounded dove has flown,
And whither, whither will the mourners fly?
Who now will kiss the sorrow from her eye?
Her father's hospitable home is near,
And friends and kindred shall embrace her there;
And she shall feel the solace of their love,—
But sigh for him whose spirit soars above.

I too must leave this sad deserted scene;
It soothes no more to be where I have been.
Lost all the charms my bosom held so dear.

Alas! I feel I have no business here.
O gentle stream, whose melancholy flow
Now bears a sympathy in all my woe!
Ye trees, whose sorrow-soothing branches wave
In mournful murmurs o'er my Woodward's grave!
Ye groves, where Silence and Despondence dwell!
Ye rocks, still vocal with his funeral knell!
One parting look — one sad, one final view —
One look — and now — eternally adieu!

'Tis past! the vision leaves me like a dream!
Again I rove beside my native stream,
And see! the colors of departing day
Are fading slowly, silently away;
While yon bright star, the herald of the night,
Comes smiling forth, and sparkles with delight.
So would I steal from life's tumultuous throng,
And leave a world where I have liv'd too long;
So pass away, unseen by human eyes,
And melt serenely in my native skies;
Yet not extinct — the soul that God has given,
Shall shine forever, as a star, in heaven!

THE CENTENARY MEETING.

THE CENTENARY MEETING.

FIRST DAY.

September 10th and 11th, 1873, will long be memorable days in the town of Wolcott,—they being devoted to the first centennial celebration of the Congregational Church and Society of that town*. The day opened with clear sky and promise of good weather, though a little cool. Precisely at sun rise the church bell began to ring, and the effect was thrilling to the ear, while the imagination ran over the hundred years past, contrasting it with the present, and calling up the changes and onward march of events during these years.

At ten o'clock the bell rang again, for the assembling of the people in the large tent constructed for the occasion in the center of the green.

After a little delay from the coldness of the morning air, the audience gathered at the call of the drum band, the old honored band of Wolcott, playing an old fashioned tune, in charming style. Then followed the singing of a hymn from the collection printed for the occasion. The hymn begins : —

> Oh, 'twas a joyful sound to hear
> Our tribe devoutly say,
> "Up, Israel, to the temple haste,
> And keep our festal day."

It was sang to the old tune "Mear." In the singing, the

---

* The meeting would have taken place on the 18th of November, but for the fact that the coldness of the weather would have rendered it impracticable at that time of the year.

choir were accompanied by a cabinet organ, bass viol, violin, and silver flute, all played with skill and power. In the choir were skilled singers, old and young, natives of Wolcott, mostly, and residents here and from abroad. These, with the large audience, who were supplied with the hymns, sang with gladness and spirit. The one hundred and forty-seventh Psalm was read, and seemed peculiarly appropriate. A prayer, offered by Rev. A. C. Beach, a former pastor, touched all hearts, and very happily opened the meeting in the right spirit. The singing of the next hymn,—

Oh, for a thousand tongues to sing,

to the old tune of "Exhortation," added to the interest of the meeting.

The acting pastor, Rev. S. Orcutt, made a brief and pertinent address of welcome. He alluded to the nature of the occasion, and the auspicious circumstances of the day, and announced that the exercises had been arranged to cover two days, and would consist of historical addresses, old fashioned music, and off hand remarks by former residents and other friends of the town.

After the welcome the Rev. A. C. Beach was introduced, and began his remarks by avowing his deep interest in the occasion. As he reviewed the hundred years, he found his own pastorate covered one-seventh of that period. While lamenting that he had done so little, he yet rejoiced in his work, and was grateful to God for sparing him to witness this hour. There came to his mind mingled memories,— pleasant and sad. The monuments in the grave yard reminded him of loved ones gone before, to a better land. His only surviving son was born here, and this son he was glad to speak of to-day as a minister of Christ. He made a playful allusion to the fact that some thought that the son excelled the father, and for his part, he half believed it.

After another hymn, a paper prepared for the occasion,

on the settlement of the town and organization of the First Society was read by Rev. H. R. Timlow, of Southington. This paper consisted in part of extracts from the first chapters of the History of Wolcott.

After the reading of this paper, Mr. A. Bronson Alcott, of Concord, Mass., was introduced. He said he was proud to stand there as the descendant of John Alcock, the first settler. He alluded to the name as being Alcock, originally, but that it had been changed to Alcox, and also to Alcott. John Alcock was a surveyor, and owned about twelve hundred acres of land. He had four sons and four daughters. To each son he gave a farm, and to each daughter, as she was married, he gave an endowment. Two settled at North Haven, and one each at Bristol and Plymouth, Conn. He spoke of the graveyard as containing the dust of the past generations, and was happy to-day to do honor to the memory of the good who had lived here. He was ready to praise them for what they did and suffered. Living, as they did, quite a mile apart, there was but little social intercourse, except on the Sabbath. Nor were there roads, as now,— only paths. Neither had they many horses, and they went chiefly on foot. He humorously gave his recollection of old-time ministers and usages. Human nature was the same then as now, and about as unimpressible. He was taught the catechism — both Westminster and that of the Episcopal church. These two streams he thought about satisfied the wants of his nature. Boys and girls carried their shoes in their hand until near the church, when they would put them on. The tithing-men were around to keep order. His description of the big hats and ill-fitting garments that clothed the boys, was laughable. He thought that, on the whole, the young people behaved better in church than they do now. The first preaching he remembered was that of Rev. John Keys, pastor from 1814 to 1822. Mr. Keys was highly educated, and conducted a school, which was flourishing, and of great use to the town. It was the custom then for children to repeat the text at home, giving chapter and verse, and often the whole chapter was read in the family. Mr. Alcott said he early began to take notes of the sermon, a fact that was a discipline to him of great service in after life. After sunset, on the Sabbath, there was great liberty, and then the "courting" was done. He spoke of the farmers going to church in warm weather with the coat upon the arm. The clothing of both sexes was home-spun. He told of his first appearance in broadcloth, and how he earned the money to buy the suit,— his pride when going to church, and how he was "taken down" by the remarks of bystanders. He spoke of his early thirst for knowledge,— how he gathered, from the neighborhood, old almanacs and papers, and finally coming across a copy of "Pilgrim's Progress," how he devoured it. This book he commended to the young before him as a priceless treasure.

No report can do Mr. Alcott's remarks justice, for his mirthfulness cannot be transferred to paper.

There were exhibited at this time a number of articles over a hundred years old. A dozen or more chairs on the platform, each of which indicated a hundred years of use; a table, also of the same description, covered with a home-spun linen table-cloth, that was more than a hundred and twenty-five years old, yet perfectly white, and good as new; a large, elegant book, over two hundred years old, imported from England by the Pritchard family, and a number of other articles of smaller value.

Rev. W. W. Belden was introduced, and made remarks of interest concerning the Governors Wolcott, after the younger of whom this town was named. He also gave some account of the historical occurrences on the tenth of September,— the day on which the meeting was being held.

At twelve o'clock a recess was taken for two hours, during which time the large company partook of a collation on the green; the ministers and speakers, their wives and families, being invited to the parsonage for dinner and rest. During this recess many old friends shook hands and talked over old times, and "seemed young again." The weather being the most delightful possible, all were glad as in the days of youth; though the remembrances spoken of brought tears to many eyes.

Re-assembling at two o'clock, at the call of the drum band, a hymn was sung, and prayer offered by Rev. Mr. Belden. A paper containing the names of the ministers of the town, and the length of their services, was read by Rev. J. Wickliffe Beach, from which it appeared that the settled pastors have been seven; the whole number of years they served were seventy, an average of nearly ten years. In one hundred years the church has had ninety years of preaching services,— or 4,680 Sabbaths, or 9,360 sermons. The expense of hiring ministers eighty-five years amounted to $42,500, $3,000 of which had been paid by the Connecticut Home Missionary Society.

Another paper containing a short account of the organization of the Congregational church in Wolcott, was read by Rev. William P. Alcott.

Mr. A. Bronson Alcott, by desire, then read the following address from the pen of Edward Bronson Cooke, Esq., editor of the Waterbury American:

FRIENDS AND CITIZENS OF WOLCOTT: — Having been invited on behalf of the committee, to furnish some reminiscenses of my youthful days, in regard to the town and people of Wolcott, on this great occasion, I most cheerfully comply, hoping that the facts and incidents will interest many of my hearers, and meet their approbation and acceptance. Though not a native born citizen, yet I am no stranger here, having a family relationship through the medium of the Wolcott Upsons, the grandmother of the writer being Jemima, the daughter of Joseph Upson, who married my grandfather, Moses Cooke, of Waterbury, in 1766, a lineal descendant of Thomas Upson, the ancestor of the Wolcott and

Waterbury Upsons, all original proprietors and first settlers, who came from Farmington and Hartford in the company of the Rev. Mr. Hooker, all of Puritan stock and lineage. The writer also has the honor to claim his descent from the Bronsons, Judds, Porters, Scotts, and others, all of whom were original proprietors of Waterbury, including Wolcott, Middlebury, Watertown and Plymouth.

Thus having defined my position, I claim the undisputed right to an eligible seat in this august assemblage, both by propinquity of blood and courtesy, and to all I cordially extend the right hand of fellowship. Now, having passed the eightieth mile stone of one hundred years, I am here to answer to the long centennial roll call, the oldest survivor of whom probably being present, although unknown to the writer, but whoever he may be, I congratulate him upon having lived to the present period, and witnessed the grand march of events as they have rolled onward, introducing new ideas and modern inventions in the industrial world,— on the farm, in the workshop, the manufactory, and the warehouse. Within the last century, the steam engine, steamboats, canals, railroads, and, to crown all, the genius of a Morse has invented the lightning telegraph, followed by the lightning printing press, revolutionizing time and space, and uniting together the whole universe by a girdle around the world, making the most distant inhabitants next door neighbors.

Among my earliest impressions of Wolcott, the names of Gates Upson, Col. Streat Richards, and the Rev. Israel B. Woodward, were the most familiar I can call to remembrance. The former, Mr. Upson, came to Waterbury about 1802-3, and taught the Waterbury Center District School, consisting at the time of about one hundred scholars, ranging from five to eighteen years, of both sexes,— at that time being deemed one of the hardest schools in the country. Fortunately, however, for all parties concerned, he was equal to the position, both as a teacher and disciplinarian, having but on two occasions to administer corporeal punishment during the whole term, proving himself a most thorough and competent instructor, and an honor to his profession, acquitting himself to the entire satisfaction of his patrons. A model man in all respects, leaving behind him a reputation and influence which was felt for many years after he left the town and district, whom we did not again meet until the installation of Rev. Mr. Keys, in 1814.

The first time I ever saw Wolcott, was at a General Training held there about 1803, the regiment of which at that time being commanded by Col. Streat Richards, who, by the virtue of his office, ordered the regiment to parade at Wolcott,— the only time that Wolcott was ever honored by that distinction. The Colonel was then in his prime and glory; a man of wit, of strong impulses, of a gay disposition, well calculated for a popular officer, having that pride and ambition which constitutes the essentials of a military profession, but not averse to show, or "fuss and feathers," when having an opportunity to show himself off upon a well trained charger, clad in the old colonial or revolutionary uniform, with well powdered wig, ruffles on his bosom and at the wrists, high white-topped boots, three-cornered plumed hat, *a la mode*,— the old regime of the Baron Steuben school, forming an imposing picture of the olden time. The Colonel felt his station, and casually observed to a brother officer, that on Sunday the Lord commanded, but to-day (Monday), his day, *he* was in command,— and the troops found it out during the day. Waterbury being so near at hand, all the boys from eight to fifteen were bound to attend, and although wheel conveyances were scarce at that time, they organized a company, and resolved to foot it over the hills to the town center, starting from home an hour or two before daylight, arriving there just as the glorious sun gilded the eastern horizon, in time to see the out-of-town companies enter the village, and headed by martial music and colors flying, were conducted by the adjutant to the station for inspection. Captain John Kingsbury, of the old light infantry, being brigade inspector, and Garret Smith adjutant. This occupied the forenoon till dinner, which was taken under the shade trees on the green, the boys participating in a shilling cut, after which the regiment took up the line of march to an open field, about a mile east of the center, where the parade and review took place, with all the pomp and circumstance of the old time General Training. Wolcott bore off the palm, as she always did, by her soldier-like bearing, neat and tidy uniforms, and her splendid military band,— the nucleus of the celebrated drum band still existing in spirit to the present time. The day was unusually fine, the display grand and without accident, an honor to the town and its intelligent people; the only drawback being for those spectators condemned to foot their return after the fatigues of the day.

The second time I saw Wolcott was in the year 1813, at the installation of the Rev. Mr. Keys, the successor of the Rev. Mr. Woodward, though on a very different occasion, but which brought together a concourse of people filling the church to its utmost capacity, and the town with strangers. The leading minister on that occasion was the Rev. Dr. Lyman Beecher, of Litchfield (father of Henry Ward), then in his prime, who preached the sermon, in the course of which he paid a warm eulogium upon the life and character of the deceased pastor as an impressive preacher, a kindly and able instructor of youth, and one of the most useful and enterprising of citizens,— a great loss to the church and its people by his death. The deceased was one of the most popular of men; by his amiable manners, his fine sociable qualities, and a great favorite with young people; and particularly at weddings, parish gatherings for religious and benevolent purposes. The singing by the Wolcott choir received the highest praise from those present. After the exercises in the church were concluded, the writer dined at the village tavern then kept by Gates Upson, our old teacher, who provided an excellent entertainment for all who were present.

And now, in conclusion, at the time of the installation of Mr. Keys, in the autumn of 1813, Wolcott had evidently reached its maximum, in points of population, business, and prosperity. The census of 1810, as published by authority, gave Wolcott a population of 952 souls,— at that time a flourishing town, supporting two well stocked stores with a large home trade, and three public houses,— one in the center, one at Shrub Oak, and the other known as Lewis', on the mountain, all apparently doing a fair business. A wonderful change, indeed, as we contrast the population of 1810 with that of 1873, as follows, viz.: 1810, 952; 1830, 843; 1850, 603; 1860, 574, and in 1870, 491 — a decline of fifty per cent. in the last sixty years. These figures exhibit the two extremes of 1810 and 1870, showing the instability and vicissitudes of human calculation, which governs the times and its people. This decline, however, must not be attributed to any fault or deficiency on their part, as lacking in industry or enterprise over circumstances beyond their control, while such an imputation would be wrong and unjust. The reasons are manifold; and first the western emigration fever entered Wolcott early in the present century, sowing the seeds of discontent, and bearing off some of her best and most enterprising citizens, giving up their farms and moving to the new Eldorado,—many of whom would afterwards gladly have returned had they the adequate means. But the greatest obstacle to its increase has been the establishment and multiplication of manufactories in the neighboring towns, by drawing off the young men as they became of age, to enter the factories, induced by the offer of higher wages, they leaving the old homesteads to take care of themselves, and their fathers in their old age. This is the solution which explains itself. But Wolcott has reached bottom at last, the real hard pan, and must rise again, and with her present staid population, with her renewed energies, by putting the shoulder to the wheel in earnest, must show to those of the next century, that her sons have not degenerated, or we are no prophet.

Thus we have known Wolcott and its people for sixty years, as industrious, intelligent, and upright a community as is to be found in the State; as we have met them at their fireside, their fairs, cattle shows, and other public gatherings, where a welcome hospitality was always extended, as the editor of the American is ready to testify, a large number of whom have been its steady patrons for nearly thirty years, to whom we tender our most hearty compliments, hoping they may live to see Wolcott what she was in her most prosperous days, before the next century expires.

Another paper, containing an account of the district and select schools of Wolcott was read, and was followed by remarks by Hon. B. G. Northrop, Secretary of the State Board of Education. He said he did not appear as a native, but as a visitor. He presented words of congratulation to the people on the joyfulness of this meeting, and the honor reflected from the past, as exhibited in the papers read, but urged upon the people the propriety of considering the defects as well as the glory of the past. He noticed that, according to the statistics, the present state of education was defective, and should receive the earnest attention of the people. He proceeded to show that all of our country towns were suffering, and traced the causes by referring to the effect of the want of education in some of the European nations. The absorption of capital in the railroads, and in the cities, was depopulating the rural districts. These districts should be beautified and magnified as the best place for the training of the young. The youth rush to the city to find employment and entertainment, but he would have them cultivate industries that they can pursue in the country. He proposed a town library, to be commenced at this time, the setting of trees along the streets, and other improvements. His remarks were received with pleasure, and were very appropriate and encouraging.

He was followed by Mr. A. Bronson Alcott, on the subject of a town library, and he proposed a present of the books of the Concord authors to start the enterprise.

Remarks by Rev. William H. Moore, Secretary of the Connecticut Home Missionary Society :

The public worship of God has been a central idea in our Connecticut towns from the first. In the early days the general court would not incorporate a community as a town until the people showed their ability and readiness to support a minister; and not unfrequently one of the first votes passed after the organization of the town, was to provide for the preaching of the gospel. It was in this spirit that twenty-one men and twenty women, accustomed to go from five to seven miles to worship with the churches of which they were members, took letters, and were constituted the church in Farmingbury, November 18th, 1773; the parish lying then partly in the town of Farmington, and partly in the town of Waterbury; and the church being the third of the nine springing from the Waterbury First,— formed in 1687;

and the eighth of the twenty-two springing from the Farmington First,—formed in 1652. Southington, the south parish in Farmington, became a town in 1779, and the parish of Farmingbury became the town of Wolcott in 1796. The church has had seven pastors, averaging ten years each, and five stated preachers, averaging three years each, and has been no long time without a minister. Its ministers have been good men, in doctrine and in life. The discipline of the church has been conducted with firmness and wisdom. There have been eight years of spiritual refreshing, in which the church has received the following numbers on profession: 1774, 13; 1784, 18; 1815, 10; 1816, 10; 1828, 30; 1843, 10; 1858, 37; 1867, 33,—in all, 161. It reported in 1840, 116 members, probably the largest number it has ever attained; in 1852, 66; and in January, 1873, 93.

A noticeable fact in the history of this place, is the steady decline of the population. The town first appeared in the census in 1800, when the population was 948. In 1810, it was 952. Since 1810 it has gone down with every census, and in 1870 was only 491. It lost in 1810 to 1820, 9; in 1820 to 1830, 100; in 1830 to 1840, 210; in 1840 to 1850, 30; in 1850 to 1860, 18; in 1860 to 1870, 94. The only other town in the State which has declined at each census from 1810 to 1870 is Hartland, which, in this period, has lost 39 per cent. But Wolcott has in this time lost 48 per cent. In 1870, only two towns in Connecticut had fewer inhabitants than Wolcott, namely: Marlborough, 476, and Andover, 461.

This fact is, naturally enough, discouraging. But what can be said for your comfort? You have reason to be proud of the migration which has gone forth from you, even as the old folks lingering at the hearth-stone where they have trained a family now scattered by the ways of Providence to bless the world. Your case is not desperate. Your estates, tenements, and families, have an aspect of thrift. You are not poor. The tax list of 1872 was $252,789, or an average of $512 for each person, and $2,022 for each of the one hundred and twenty-five families reported in 1870,—in which respect you are better off than many of us ministers. Your young people, as they grow up, move away; but you are not past fruitfulness, nor blighted with barrenness, and had in January, 1873, 100 school children, and an average of $2,348 of taxable property for each of these children, while Waterbury had only $2,067, and Southington only $1,817 for each school child. In this comparison only fifty towns in the State are above you, and 113 are below you. In this order, Wolcott is numbered 51; Waterbury, 87; and Southington, 114.

Religion has not waned among you. The spiritual condition of the place is certainly better than in 1800, and better than in 1850. The ratio of the members of this church to the population (nineteen per cent.) is larger now than then. Probably no equal period in the history of the church has been more fruitful than the last fifteen years,— 1857 to 1872. In this time you have raised up two ministers of the gospel,— the only two ever raised here. In this time, while 94 have been removed from the church—a number larger than it now contains—namely: 3 by discipline, 40 by death, and 51 by letter, you have added 115, namely: 24 by letter, and 91 by profession, including the fruits of the two most extensive revivals ever enjoyed here. These additions by profession have averaged one for each communion season in the whole fifteen years. You have a good Meeting house and parsonage, and the Society is free from debt. You have a fine choir, a flourishing Sabbath school, embracing all ages, and a stable and intelligent congregation, attending church all day. You have made a commendable advance in the salary of the minister,— from $500 in 1861, to $950 in 1873. In addition to the local support of the gospel, you have given in the last fourteen years, for charities, $2,066.25,— or an average of about $150 a year. You have the aid of the Connecticut Home Missionary Society, which has voted you in 1832 to 1873, $3,335, and will not fail to stand by you so long as you are needy and worthy of its assistance. You are not the weakest, nor the most irresolute of the aided churches. Only three of those assisted this year have more taxable property than you. In January, 1873, the resident members of this church had $49,691 of taxable property, on which they pledged for the expenses of the year $575, or a per centage of .01157, and an average of $17.42 for each of the thirty-three male members of the church.

And while the town stands so well in property as compared

with other towns, it is to be noted and remembered that we have seventy-six Congregational churches in this State,— or more than one-quarter of our whole number,— which are smaller than this church.

In this condition of things you have reason to respect your history, your church, and yourselves, and to be hopeful. With a right spirit in yourselves, you have a right to expect the aid, if need be, of prosperous sons who have gone out from you, the help of the abler churches, and the blessing of God securing you an eligible future for the life that now is, and for that which is to come.

Rev. J. Wickliffe Beach followed in remarks explanatory of the statistical representation of the town, as contrasted with former years.

Another paper was read containing a sketch of the formation of the Episcopal Society and church in Wolcott.

Remarks by Simeon H. Norton, Esq., of Plantsville :

MR. CHAIRMAN:— It is always pleasant to be kindly greeted by friends, but to-day I am extremely happy to meet you and these my fellow citizens in this great meeting. The associations are delightful, and I feel their magnetic influence in every fibre of my system, while standing in my old native town surrounded by the friends of my youth. You may not attach any great importance to anything I shall say, since you have a large amount of speaking talent here to-day; yet while they build the substantial superstructure I may fill in the chinking. Now, ladies and gentlemen, being a native Wolcott man, I beg your patient consideration for a short time while I indulge in some personal reminiscences. The scenes of my childhood and youth are vividly brought to my mind this day. My rambles over these hills, and through these valleys,— my early admiration of the vast extent and unfathomable depth of the mill pond in yonder hollow,— all recur to me with great clearness. In my early youth I looked with amazement at the magnificent machinery of Norton's carding machine and grist mill, and wondered where all the money came from to build such enormously great works. Having been to the mill one day, upon returning home, I asked my mother if there was another mill in the world as large as Uncle John's grist mill. Benham and Tuttle's store I considered the greatest emporium of trade in the universe, and doubted if there were any other men in the world rich enough to buy as many fine things as they exhibited in their store. And, oh! how my mouth did water for the candies in their jars,—but alas! I had no money with which to buy them. On one training day I had five cents, and only five, for spending money, and with this I intended to buy at least two rolls of candy, and a few peanuts. As soon as I arrived upon the ground Mr. Manly Upson tempted me to give the whole of my money for a little foolish picture book. Presently the boys came around me eating their candies, and asked me why I did not buy some. Then my joy and courage all fled, and bursting into tears said: "I have paid all my money for a darned, little, foolish, picture book." At that time a very kind hearted but eccentric man came along, whose name was Richard Hopkins, *alias* Dick Brady. Perhaps it may be interesting to our Southington friends who are here, to be informed that this man was a brother of Mrs. Elihu Carter, who was the mother of our respected townsmen, Messrs. Hopkins and Asahel Carter. Well, Uncle Dick asked me what was the matter. I told him I had paid Mr. Manly Upson all my money for a darned little picture book, and had none to buy candy with. He said he would go with me to Mr. Upson, and get him to take the book and give me the money; but this Mr. Upson peremptorily declined, and was inexorable. Upon this Uncle Dick gave me five cents from his own pocket, after talking rather harshly to the man who sold me the book. Oh, what a sense of thankfulness filled my young heart towards that kind man. I thought Uncle Dick would surely go to heaven, and that the other man would as surely go in the opposite direction. Since arriving to the years of manhood, I have received many favors from distinguished men, but they all dwindle into insignificance compared with that of my kind old Uncle, Dick Brady.

Now, my friends, that was a great lesson to me, and may be to my young friends present. Whenever I am tempted to buy anything I do not really need, I think of the little, darned, foolish picture book. The moral of the lesson is, that when we see a poor, destitute, crying boy among many happy children, we may accomplish a great good by helping such a boy.

Another remembrance is peculiarly pleasant to me,— it is that of the singing I used to hear in Wolcott. I thought there was no tenor vocalist in the world equal to Stephen Harrison; and in all candor I must say that I never heard a sweeter or more natural voice for singing tenor than his.

My early school teachers, too,— Mr. Bartholomew, Capt. Gates Upson, Mr. Isaac Bronson, and others,— I regarded as the very embodiment of learning. I used to sit on the little slab bench with four legs and eagerly imbibe their marvelous teachings. And our school committee I considered the most august body in the world. I had no idea that any other body of men could be found who could be half as dignified, half as consequential, half as magnanimous, as they were.

Another item. I never felt as rich in my life, or so much like a millionaire, as when I received twenty-five cents from Mr. Ira Hough, for two long days' work, gathering apples.

The first clergyman of whom I have any recollection was the Rev. John Keys. Oh, how dignified, how holy, how awfully sublime, he appeared to me. I regarded him as belonging to a superior order of beings. I was afraid of him. His name was Keys, and I had the superstitious notion that he held in his hands the keys of the bottomless pit into which he would put all naughty boys. Many a time, when I saw him coming in the distance, I have run back or turned into the fields to avoid meeting him.

On Saturday afternoons, in the public schools, we always recited the Westminster Catechism, all through, from "What is the chief end of man?" to "What doth the conclusion of the Lord's Prayer teach us?" After the recitation the teacher would talk to us on religious subjects, and then allow the school to ask questions. I was very diffident, but on one occasion I mustered courage to ask the question : "Mr. Bartholomew, who made God?" The teacher smiled, and asked me what I thought of the question. I could not tell. Upon which one boy in the school, by the name of Ezra S. Hough, jumped up and said, "I know who made God." The teacher gave him liberty to tell, when he said,

"I don't know *certain*, but I *guess* Mr. Keys did." In those days it was considered very impious to smile when the Catechism was under consideration, but on this occasion Mr. Bartholomew laughed outright, and said to the little boy, "You had better go and ask Mr. Keys."

In the old church, on one occasion, when we had a long prosy sermon, a young man, by the name of Timothy Hotchkiss, who occupied one of the old-fashioned pews alone, lay down on the seat, and fell asleep. The meeting ended, the congregation retired, the house was closed, and the young man left asleep. After sleeping about two hours, he awoke and succeeded in creeping out of one of the windows. Upon arriving home, his mother said, "Timothy, why are you so late from meeting?" He replied, "I tell you what it is, mother, we had a long-winded preacher to-day."

While on reminiscences I must not omit to say that three of the most important, interesting, and solemn scenes of my life were enacted on this very ground. The old Meeting house was used for the conveniences of town meetings, as well as religious services, and in it I took the Freeman's oath, and solemnly swore to be true and faithful to my State and to my country, and always to cast my vote as should conduce to the best good of the same, according to the dictates of my own conscience; and, allow me to add, that every freeman should have this oath written upon the tablets of his heart, and be governed by it in all his political actions.

In yonder little church, I took the vows of God upon me, and before God, angels, and men, solemnly promised, that by God's help, I would obediently keep His holy commandments, and walk in the same all the days of my life.

In that same church I stood before the altar, on the 16th day of October, 1836, and held one by the hand, whom I promised to love, comfort, honor and keep, in sickness and in health, so long as we both should live.

My friends, this town is the place of my birth, the home of my early years, and though in the providence of God I have been absent from it most of my years, yet I have always cherished a lively remembrance of it, and have always had great respect for the general character of my native townsmen, and whenever I hear anything said of them derogatory, it stirs within me a feeling of resentment. Wherever my residence has been, it has been in the midst of Wolcott men, and I have seen them greatly respected and occupying places of trust and responsibility. After leaving Wolcott my residence, for different periods of time, was in the following places: Meriden, Bristol, Plainville, and Plymouth. In 1844 I alighted in the town of Southington, where I now reside. I first struck on the banks of the "raging canal," when there was no railroad in Southington. The first two men who greeted me were Mr. Isaac Burritt, who will speak to you at this meeting, and his brother, the world-renowned Elihu Burritt, who will also address you. I found then in Southington a population of fifteen hundred, it has increased to five thousand. I am much attached to my adopted town, and desire gratefully to acknowledge that the people of the town have bestowed upon your poor, diffident Wolcott boy a large amount of patronage and confidence.

One word to my Episcopal brethren and friends. Allow me to earnestly advise you to unite with the Congregationalists, here, and help support their organization. And, although you will miss some of the solemn, impressive, and distinctive features of our church service, yet we all have the same holy bible for the foundation of our faith and practice. During the last illness of my dear wife, the Rev. Mr. Eastman frequently called on her, and it was her dying request that he should attend her funeral with an Episcopalian clergyman, and it has always been my practice to worship with Christians of other denominations in the absence of the service of the church of my choice.

In looking around me to-day the sad reflection involuntarily comes to my mind that many of my former friends and acquaintances are not here. Where are they? Some have gone to distant lands; others have passed that bourne from whence no traveler returns. My father and mother, and sisters Jennette and Justina, lie in yonder grave yard. My sister Hannah Higgins lies in the yard in the south part of this town. My sister Julina Bail lies in one of the cemeteries in New Haven. My brothers, Levi and Samuel, remain with me in the land of the living—the former in Plantsville, the latter in Sacramento, Cal.

Many of the companions of my earlier years are gone. Where is Colonel Tuttle? Where is Ezra S. Hough, and where are many, many others? We call them, but they answer not! A messenger has taken them hence and they come not again nor answer the call of their friends. And it is the impression of this hour that whither they have gone we are all rapidly hastening.

Now, my friends, one reminiscence of a more modern date and I shall have done. The last time that I had the pleasure of addressing a public meeting in this town was on the Fourth of July, 1863. At that time a dark cloud, like a pall, hung over our beloved country. But two months previous my only son had fallen in the terrible battle of Chancellorville. The storm of civil war was upon us; its lightnings were flashing and its thunders roaring! At that meeting you passed a resolution by acclamation that the rebellion must be crushed at whatever hazard or cost. It was a dark day for our country. At that meeting the people of this town assembled *en masse*, in yonder grove, re-enforced by many from the adjacent towns, and over all floated our national flag. I notice that the same flag now waves over this bower.

My fellow citizens, there is to my mind overwhelming inspiration in the "Old Flag of our Union," which now floats triumphantly over all the people of this great nation. But a few years ago that sacred emblem of national honor was insulted, torn down and trampled in the dust by those who had sworn to protect it. The people of the loyal states solemnly resolved to raise and protect it to their utmost, and it is now the flag of all the people. Republicans and Democrats; old line Whigs and Abolitionists; Christians and sinners; all, with rare exceptions, rushed to the support of the flag. For *it* the people sacrificed their sons and brothers, their fathers and husbands, upon the altar of their country. When our good old ship of state was on the breakers; when the storm of civil war was periling all our cherished hopes, then these brave kindred went out to the rescue, and, blessed be God, they saved the old ship! And now the glorious constellated banner of the United States floats over all this vast expanse of country,— from Maine to the Rio Grande, from the Atlantic to the Pacific. Our national sun does not seem destined to set in the dark night of chaos, but bids fair to culminate in the meridian sky.

Rev. Mr. Hillard, of Plymouth, followed in remarks in the highest style of anecdote and illustration, which greatly animated the audience, and prepared them to come up to the second day's meeting with the greater intellectual appetite for what might be in store. Thus ended the first day of the great meeting at Wolcott.

THE CENTENARY MEETING.

SECOND DAY.

The morning opened cloudy, but about ten o'clock brightened up, with a soft south wind, and most delightful weather. The audience was nearly the same as the day before,—about one thousand,—and but for the threatening of the weather in the morning, would have been much larger. The memorial meeting of the morning opened with affecting remembrances of the past, and passed into inspiring hopes of the future. The first paper read contained the names of the inhabitants who settled in Wolcott before the year 1770, as fully as had been obtained. The second paper contained the names and ages of persons who had lived to be over seventy years of age, as follows:

John Alcott, first settler, aged 71; his widow Deborah, 77; Obed Alcox, 71; his widow Anna, 87; Eldad Alcox, 71; Capt. John Alcox, 77; his wife Mary, 71; James Alcox, 1st, 74; his widow Hannah, 92; James Alcott, 2d, 87; his wife Esther, 85; Jesse Alcox, 74; his widow Patience, 97; David Alcox, 81; John B. Alcox, 73; his widow Lois, 70; Mark Alcott, 74; widow Lydia Alcott, 82; Jedediah G. Alcott, 79; widow Elizabeth Alcott, 84; Thomas Alcott, 73; Anna Bronson Alcott, widow of Joseph C., 91; Joseph Atkins, sen., 71; his widow Abigail, 80; Luther Atkins, 71; Esther Atkins, 74; Levi Atkins, sen., 81; his widow Eunice, 91; Abel Beecher, 74; Capt. Joseph Beecher, 90; his wife Esther, 75; John Beecher, 74; Luther Andrews, 77; widow Martha Andrews, 89; Israel Baldwin, 87; his wife, 80; Deacon James Bailey, 78; widow Thede Bailey, 91; Benjamin

THE CENTENARY MEETING. 397

Bement, 88; Jonathan Bement, 72; Zealous Blakeslee, 73; his wife Sarah, 72 — both died on the same day; Hezekiah Bradley, 82; widow Anna Bradley, 79; Moses Bradley, 71; Titus Brackett, 77; Sarah, wife of Titus Brackett, 71; Zuar Brackett, 87; his wife Eunice, 81; widow Semantha Brooks, 84; Daniel Byington, jr., 86; his widow Elizabeth, 87; John Bronson, 103; his wife Hannah, 72; John Bronson, jr., 91; Deacon Isaac Bronson, 84; his widow Thankful, 93; Hannah Bronson, 88; Clark Bronson, 82; his wife Experience, 72; Samuel Downes, 73; Obed Doolittle, 90; Stephen Carter, 88; widow Lucy S. Carter, 76; Mary Chatterton, 95; widow Sarah Churchill, 92; widow Sarah Finch, 85; widow Ruth Finch, 86; Adah Finch, 77; Eleazer Finch, 83; his wife Hannah, 76; Jerusha Finch, 77; Judah Frisbie, 73; his widow Hannah, 83; John Frisbie, 84; Reuben Frisbie, 78; Elijah Frisbie, 82; David Frost, 83; Mr. Gridley, 91; widow Naomi Guernsey, 87; Asa Hall, 76; Capt. Heman Hall, 73; Capt. Levi Hall, 80; Lydia, widow of Heman Hall, 79; widow Betsey A. Hall, 86; Mary, wife of Ephraim Hall, 70; Nancy, wife of Orrin Hall, 74; Deacon Aaron Harrison, 93; his widow Jerusha, 92; widow Lydia Harrison, 76; Samuel Horton, 84; Elisha Horton, 81; Mary, wife of Ira Hough, 83; Betsey, wife of Lyman Higgins, 74; Timothy Higgins, 75; his widow, 75; Isaac Hopkins, 96; Harvey Hopkins, 76; Titus Hotchkiss, 81; Timothy Hotchkiss, 77; Isaac Hotchkiss, 83; Milo G. Hotchkiss, 75; his wife Abigail, 73; Major Luther Hotchkiss, 84; his widow Anna, 83; Abner Hotchkiss, 75; his widow Mary, 72; widow Patience Hitchcock, 97; John J. Kenea, 76; his widow Obedience, 88; Levi Johnson, 72; his widow Ruth, 80; Nathaniel Lane, 76; widow Melicent Lane, 88; Daniel Lane, 86; his widow Keziah, 87; Royce Lewis, 73; Lud Lindsley, 75; Nathaniel Lewis, 90; Lois, widow of Appleton Lewis, 83; Joseph Minor, 89; his wife Mary, 82; Joshua Minor, 83; Marcus Minor, 80; Elihu Moulthrop, 75; Mrs. Mills, 74; David Norton, 71; Ozias Norton, 87; widow Hannah Norton, 87; widow Viah Norton, 73; widow Abigail Norton, 73; Samuel Nichols, 95; Joseph M. Parker, 77; Eldad Parker, 85; his wife Sylvia, 74; Mary Parker, 99; David Pardee, 84; Elizabeth Pardee, 77; Deacon Justus Peck, 75; Col. Moses Pond, 87; Solo-

398   HISTORY OF WOLCOTT.

mon Plumb, 79; his wife Lydia, 76; widow Mary Rowe, 83; widow Phebe Rich, 85; Orrin Plumb, 75; Samuel Plumb, 74; widow Lucretia Plumb, 85; Willard Plumb, 70; William C. Pluymert, 74; widow Pluymert, 83; Amos Roberts, 76; widow Eunice Smith, 83; David Scarritt, 81; his wife Hannah, 73; Joseph N. Sperry, 71; Josiah Thomas, 73; his widow Mary, 88; Martha, widow of James Thomas, 79; widow Jemima Thomas, 85; John Thomas, 75; Jerry Todd, 73; widow Amy Todd, 98; Capt. Lucius Tuttle, 97; widow Rebecca Tuttle, 86; widow Amy Tuttle, 76; Lucius Tuttle, 89; Abraham Tuttle, 89; widow Eunice Tyler, 84; widow Sarah Truesdell, 94; Rhoda, widow of Washington Upson, 72; Capt. Samuel Upson, 79; his wife Ruth, 70; Gates Upson, 72; Selah Upson, 78; his widow Martha, 83; Deacon Harvey Upson, 88; his wife Rachel, 76; Ashbel Upson, 71; Martin Upson, 77; his wife Phebe, 73; widow Margaret Warner, 84; Eliakim Welton, 1st, 79; Eliakim Welton, 2d, 95; his wife Amy, 87; Vodicia Welton, 73; widow Julia A. Welton, 71; widow Hannah Welton, 88; Bronson Welton, 79; Elias Welton, 77; Aaron Wiard, 74; Olive Wiard, 77; Philomela, widow of Jared Welton, 85; Joseph Smith, 75.

In all, 177 who lived over 70 years. Of these, 97 lived over 80 years, 24 lived to be over 90 years old, and 10 lived to be over 95 years old. John Bronson lived to be 103 years old. When he was one hundred years old a a centenary meeting was held in Wolcott to celebrate his one hundredth anniversary, at which time a sermon was preached and a pleasant time enjoyed.

The Mother of David Norton lived in Wolcott several years, and returned to Guilford, Conn., when she was 105 years old, and she lived to be 110 years old.

Remarks were made by the acting pastor, appreciative of the great service the clerks of the church and society had rendered in keeping the records so fully and carefully. But for want of time in preparing it, a list of these officers would have been read on this occasion. A list of the deacons of the church was then read, and some remarks made by the present minister in regard to them, and particularly Deacon Aaron Harrison, and Deacon Isaac Bronson. Of Deacon Harrison, it was said he was the first deacon of the church, the first captain of the first military company in Wolcott, and made the first prayer in the first Meeting house. At his burial the military were in review, and marched to the grave, following the corpse, the band playing with muffled drums a funeral dirge. This dirge was performed by the band present, and gave great satisfaction to all, and was so peculiarly appropriate that it was called for again in the afternoon. Following this was a funeral hymn : —

> "Why do we mourn departing friends,
> Or shake at death's alarms?"

sung to the tune China, C. M., in the old style,— slow and pathetic. This was followed by remarks memorial, by Rev. A. C. Beach, who remembered with great satisfaction Deacon Isaac Bronson. Mr. Isaac Bronson, son of Deacon Irad Bronson, of Bristol, and grandson of Isaac, made some appropriate remarks, and to these were added remarks by Mr. A. B. Alcott, in the same cheerful yet kindly remembrances of the good man now gone.

THE CENTENARY POEM.

Inscribed to the Congregational Church and Society of Wolcott, Conn.

BY WILLIAM ELLERY CHANNING.

> The Ages pass, their heroes live and fade,
> And mythic pens prose to a future shade;
> Again the Trojan plains refresh our sight,
> The flashing plumes Astyanax delight,
> Again to us,— again his Sabine farm
> That Roman Horace sends us with a charm,
> And silver Virgil slowly tunes his lay,—
> Time was and is,— let us implore to-day!
>
> In these plain fields, upon old Spindle Hill,
> Not vainly Wolcott looks nor turns its mill,
> Mad River,— child of the deep and moss-clad swamp,
> Around whose spruce our wandering thoughts encamp;

For sweet renew the fading dreams of old,
When the fleet Indian here was hunting bold ;
Not merely savage, but possessed with sense,
Social and kind, shrewd in his eloquence.
No mere destructive, formed to mash and slay,
He loved to see the softening light delay
On Wolcott's height and touch her shadowy vales ;
Child of mysterious thought and Nature's ails.
His altar was the sunshine on the hills,
The bird's quick song, the woodland or the rills,
And where to-day we greet the Hundred Years,
Since first this church allayed uncivil fears,
Tolled on dark centuries a moldering knell,
Trees were their pillars, winds were all the bell.

To us, this hundred years more than a line
Of tawny sachems comes, a thought divine ;
It, in our human nature has its dates,
And more to *us*, than outward things relates.
The Father's home, Wolcott the dear, the good ;
The hills, the vales a crowning multitude,
Eyeing afar the steeples where they shine ;
From Spindle Hill we touch the blue sea brine,
And Farmingbury names the simple truth.
As now, so in the pastime of her youth,
They ploughed the shining glebe, they stocked the mill,
Rising from homelier attributes to skill.
Our virtuous Fathers, strong and steady folk,
Slow in their motion, not divest of joke ;
On "proxing day" they voted for the best,
To guide the impulse of the busy nest.
They brewed the vintage oft from mellow grain,
Saw rich Pomona load the joyous wain,
Bearing great tributes from the orchards fair,
In sparkling cups desiderable cheer.
Pleased with sobriety our yoemen held
Feasts of the farming genius, not impelled
By thoughtless fashion's quite unfeeling sway,
A spendthrift worm that eats its web away.
The husking frolic made the barn aloud,
The ruddy corn sent laughter through the crowd,
While the coy virgin held the blackened ear,
Half mischief bent, she still reserved its fear ;
And gay *Philander marching* chose his love,—
His *choice forever*, let us hope to prove.
No word profane then sullied house or street ;

The time was innocent, its moral sweet.

So lived the Fathers ; natural men were they,
Whate'er they held, the youth should swift obey.
They did not spare the law, the child to spoil ;
They cherished industry, nor thought it toil.
Duly each Sabbath to this church they came,
Devoutly pious in salvation's flame ;
Good counsels got, that brought the week in view ;
Here might one think, and here his thought renew.

An English race, an English tint may prize ;
The Saxon blonde that shines from friendly eyes.
Light waves the tress across yon Parian brow ;
Blue are those tender orbs as violets grow,—
Those pleasant glances of the English maid,
Stealing along the barnside, by the glade.
Such blood shows temperate, such in virtue grows ;
Loves the old homestead, where the sires repose ;
The modest field along the gentle height ;
They rest from all their labors, from the fight.
The silent hermits of the peaceful cell,
"After life's fitful fever they sleep well."
So sang a poet once, and yet *this* race,
After life's earnest action, seek for grace.
Softly that watchful sky bends patient down,
And winds and waters smooth their burial-town.

And must we ask for monuments more high
Than these plain stones, and should this church defy,
With pillared arches or o'er-fretting spire,
Time's deepest dents or the last judgment-fire ?
A glittering abbey but a sty of monks,
Dull contributions piled o'er filthy trunks ?
Our *people* are the church, its virtues shine
Of theirs, in eminence, the work divine ;
If they control their thoughts, their passion stay,
Seek generous acts, and truth and love obey,—
Strive for unhappy souls, who strewn about,
Need home and friends, wrecked on the rabble rout ;
The pallid widow left her mate to mourn,—
The narrow orphan by remonstrance shorn.

We build this church of justice, carve the right
Along her battlements, whose heaven-born flight
Defies the patience of the loftiest tower,
Spurns history and dates from Virtue's hour ;

Something that never feels the chill of death,
No moth, no rust, that draws its lovely breath
From groves of Palm, by Rivers of the Cross,
Deliverance from alarm, beyond all loss.
Such are our altars, these our flamens wear
Across their hearts : Be good and true, be fair ! —
Like some cold fountain to a traveler's taste,
In his hot summer toil across the waste.

Nor all unknown, for from this mount may flow
Pure streams of thought, such as the gods allow.
The youthful pilgrim with his pack unslung.
From far Virginia's vales, unbind his tongue,
And prove how love and beauty yet are clear
In Wolcott's skies as to the Athenian year.
And many a mirthful child shall eager hold
The cheerful sermons from this pulpit rolled ;
Tales that in all the households of the land
Call up their "Little Women" to be grand.
Let us *believe*, yea, may we oft declare,
That round us lies a scene as rich, as fair,
As that Boccacio dreamt, and Milton caught,
When on its wings upsprung the verduous thought
Of Paradise ; rare, because innocent,
Fair, because true,— pledge of a people bent
To make their problem clear,— self-government.
No gilded King betrays his hollow fate,
The tattered symbol of a treacherous date ;
No tax-built church compels us here to sign
Thirty-six articles, or life resign.
Here every man be, to himself, a state,—
His own prerogative, his own debate.
This land *is ours*, those heavens are our own,
The race here blossoms more maturely grown ;
We may not seek to live a down-trod life,
Bring back mad Rome, or whet Napoleon's knife.
Enough the grassy fields that round us lie,
Enough the cheerful hill, dear Wolcott's eye,
That by its lifting purifies the air,
And shows us blither to both sun and star.

Child of the ancient Race ! who sailed with fate,
Across cold ocean's vault not desolate,—
Child of the blue-eyed Saxon ! here thy sire
Built his warm hearth-stone, here lit up its fire.
Never let us forget from whence we came,—

THE CENTENARY MEETING. 403

From Shakespeare's fields, fanned by an English flame ;
United by the past, yet one to-day,
Fused in humanity's o'ermastering ray.
Then may the people lift the song of praise,
And ask the Lord to grant them length of days,
To screen our church from madness and deceit,
In virtue's strength each virtuous soul entreat.
And in those future hours, when future years
Build up, by hundreds, o'er our smiles and tears,
Must never sin nor stain pollute this soil,
Of peace the faithfulest, of love the oil!

When, in reading, Mr. Alcott came to the passage about Philander, he recited the old-fashioned ditty, "Come, Philander, let's be marching," to the great glee of the audience, many of whom had never heard it. There was great regret that Miss Alcott could not be present on such an interesting occasion, which was enjoyed to the utmost by those who participated in it.

Names of persons who removed from Wolcott to Meriden, Conn., prepared by Mr. L. C. Hotchkiss.

John Sutliff, in 1819. Lucas C. Hotchkiss, in 1828. James H. Williams, in 1844. Junius Norton, Phineas Bradley, Abigail Hall, Levia Davidson, Esther E., wife of James Hough, in 1860. Anson Sutliff, in 1817 ; removed in 1857, and died in Minnesota, aged 59. Isaac Hotchkiss, in 1810; died in Bristol, aged 83, and was buried in Wolcott. Mary Hotchkiss, died in 1840, and was buried in Wolcott. Olive Ann Webb, in 1825; died in November, 1855, aged 84. Emily Welton, in 1824; died in 1825; buried in Wolcott. Rufina Hotchkiss, in 1831; died September, 1850, aged 40. Lucy Hough, married T. T. Hubbard, in 1846, and died February 9th, 1855. Cornelia Hough, died 1856. Caroline Hough, married George Parker, and died in 1864. Statira Williams, in 1835; died August 18th, 1870, aged 73. Richmond Hall, jr., in 1840; died 1848, aged 45. Thomas Hotchkiss, in 1832; died in 1866, aged 56. Albert R. Potter, in 1830. Anson Williams, in 1842. Newell Minor, died 1861. Leonora Downs, in 1864; died in 1870, aged 65; buried in Wolcott. Mary Ann Norton, in 1833; married Joel T. Butler in 1835; died in Alabama in 1837.

After recess, the meeting again assembled at two o'clock, and after opening exercises, Mr. Isaac Burritt, of Plantsville, was introduced, and spoke as follows concerning the inhabitants of Southington who were natives of Wolcott:

There was a handful of corn planted on the top of Wolcott Mountain, which after a brief growth was transplanted upon the sands of Southington. Of that seed and its fruitage I am to speak on this occasion. A man's birth-place, with all its ineradicable impressions upon both mind and heart, is an essential element in his history and character, and is recognized as such by the Lord, who says that "He shall count when he writeth up the people that this and that man was born there." The history of the world shows that the average man grows better upon the hills than the plains, and better still upon the mountains than the hills. As the springs gush out of the mountains and hillsides, with their pure and health-giving waters, to find their way down to the valleys, so there are continuous streams of people, with their pure morals, systematic economy, thrift, and well developed physical constitutions, flowing from the mountainous and hill countries to the cities to recover from corruption and degeneration the cities, without which "they would become like Sodom and be made like unto Gomorrah."

The mountains have been in all ages the refuge and stronghold of liberty and religion among men. The temple of the Lord, and the city of His chosen people, were builded upon a mountain, while the metropolis of sin and Satan was upon the plains. And in the future, as in the past, it is divinely declared, "The mountain of the Lord's house (the concentration of holy influences) shall be established upon the top of the mountains, and all people shall flow unto it." This (Wolcott) undoubtedly is the place, for it answers the description. There is also confirmatory evidence as strong as holy writ, for it is written, "The last shall be first;" and as Wolcott is the last town in the State, or will be, if emigration goes on, this must be the place so far as Connecticut is concerned. This being the case, it ought to increase the value of real estate here.

The first name on the roll of honor, of grateful remembrance and obligation of the town of Southington to Wolcott, is that of Addin Lewis, who gave fifteen thousand dollars to found the Lewis Academy in that town, which has been a high school to a large part of its youth, including seven young men of the place now in the ministry.

Statira Alcott, widow of Amos Shepherd, and three other young women of the age of nineteen, were married, removed to Southington, and each had a son during the same year. Their husbands were accused, humorously, of stealing sheep in Wolcott,—and taking their pick, at that.* The progeny of these lambs are here to-day in large numbers, and I do not think they will "go back on" their fathers for that. Samuel Shepherd, Statira's son, is the owner of the extensive greenhouse and grounds at Plantsville; furnishing Southington and neighboring towns with flowers, plants, and shrubbery. Amos Shepherd, her son also, has fine mechanical genius, and is superintendent of the Peck, Stow, and Wilcox Company. James Shepherd, of Bristol, a third son, is an expert solicitor of patents at Washington.

Rev. Henry E. Barnes, son of Ida Alcott, wife of Selah Barnes, an eloquent and able minister, and pastor of the Congregational church at Moline, Illinois.

Romantha Carter, of gigantic frame, at present an invalid, but formerly of great physical power, "lifting up his axe against the thick trees." Theda Carter, wife of Salmon F. Clark, of large personal power and executive ability; distinguished and valued for uniting puritanical convictions of religious duty with great geniality of spirit and manner, and for moulding her sons in the same likeness. James Clark, her son, has demonstrated the possession of mechanical talents of a superior order. His massive machines reverse the Yankee maxim of thrift; instead of "strike while the iron is hot," make it hot by striking. Delight Carter, wife of Deacon Edward Twitchell, in Jewish fashion, named by a forecast

---

*It was stated by the author of this book, at the Hitchcock picnic, in 1873, that it was not certain that the character of the young men of Southington was above reproach, for some of them did carry away, by night visits, some of the finest lambs of the Rev. Israel B. Woodward's flock, *i.e.*, some of the young ladies of his parish, in about the year 1800. And the Rev. Mr. Keys, and other ministers, in after years, suffered in like manner.

of her spirit and character, and of sweet and precious memory to all who knew her.

Eleazor Finch, his present countenance so indicative of suffering long endured. His bent form, and shrunken limbs, show but little of that athletic power which distinguished him in prime of life. Thirty-nine years he was in the Peck Smith Manufacturing Company. Dennis B. Finch, his son, has long been deputy sheriff of Hartford County. Annie Finch, his daughter, has greatly distinguished herself by rare gifts and culture as a vocalist and "sweet singer in Israel." At present she is in the West Meriden choir, at a salary of eight hundred dollars a year.

Sylvester Frost. — Herrick Frost, his son, is an attractive and successful wholesale merchant in New Haven, of the firm of Tyler & Frost. Henry Frost is a rising merchant of Plainville. Patty Frost, widow of Herrick Payne, genial and sensible in her old age. She writes of Wolcot: "I attended Sabbath school, the first known in my childhood, at the old church, fifty-six years ago, — *i. e.* in 1817,— under Mr. Keys. I walked two miles, and when near the church, I took off my stockings,— if they had become soiled,— and put on a clean pair, which I carried for that purpose, hiding the soiled ones by the roadside until my return. We had no question or library books, but learned a chapter from the Bible during the week, and recited it on the Sabbath. We had no fire or warmth but our clothing, from our starting until our return home. There were square pews in the old church; the young people sat up in the gallery, the boys on one side, the girls on the other; but we could see each other. There was a tything man to keep us staid."

Levi B. Frost established himself in what is now called Marion, as a blacksmith; his sole capital being his brawny hands, stout heart, and resolute will, with unmitigated application to labor, striking when his iron was hot, sixteen hours a day in the shoeing season. He built up a large estate as a farmer and manufacturer, and put up buildings for his sons. He was long a pillar in the Baptist church, of public spirit and usefulness, member of the legislature, and selectman of the town.

Widow of Ira Frost, daughter of Col. Pond, was possessed of a spirit and countenance that never grew sharp under the greatest provocations. Her husband and children all gone, "she looks like patience on a monument, smiling at grief."

Deacon Timothy Higgins, when a young man, went down Wolcott mountain to Southington, with his worldly effects tied up in a cotton handkerchief, to work for Asa Barnes. He stipulated to have steady work, as he wanted no "nick days," and to have fifty cents a day when not on job work. Of quick perception, great executive ability, and systematic economy; working in his tanyard fifteen hours a day. By these forces, with the Divine favor, he was greatly successful, as to this world's goods, until 1833, when his life was turned from Mammon unto God. Since that time, in the language of Oak Ames, but not in its spirit, he has put his money "where it would do the most good." Since which period, also, he has filled a large place in the religious labors of church and society. His right hand knows what his left does not, for he is a man who gives fifteen hundred dollars a year in charities, out of an income of twenty-five hundred. His son, Lucius Higgins, is a useful minister in Sanark, Ill.

Susan Hall, wife of Lewis Woodruff, and deaconess in the Baptist church; of excellent judgment, executive ability, and taste; the principal milliner in the town for the godly women. What she says is fit and proper for them, they wear, asking no questions for fashion sake.

Lucy Hall, widow of Judge Merriman. Her son, Mansfield Merriman, has exhibited from childhood the possession of talents and scholarship superior to any native of the town. When a small boy, he milked his father's cows with one hand, and studied Latin out of a book held with the other, and did the churning in the kitchen in a similar manner. He carried his books to the field to get snatches of study while at work; earned and put into the bank four hundred dollars, and ran away to college in his teens; took the second prize of Yale College in his Freshman year; received the offer of the presidency of a college in Tennessee during his third term, by the recommendation of the faculty; received the highest commendation from the general government for his report of the survey of the Delaware River. He has lately returned from Germany with the colloquial poetry of the language fully his own.

Luman Lewis has been for forty years the principal stone mason and mover of buildings in the town. He has raised up a large family of children of robust development. Two of his sons were volunteers in the late war.

Ives Lewis has long been a blacksmith in the town.

Bennet J. Lewis, son of Nathaniel Lewis, is postmaster in Marion.

Simeon H. Norton, esq., was for ten years the first merchant and the first postmaster in Plantsville. For several years he was first selectman of the town; has been member of the legislature, and for many years the acting magistrate of the place. He has performed the difficult duties of that office in such a manner as to secure the confidence and approval of all classes. He is withal a clear and forcible writer.

Julina Norton, wife of Prof. Bailey, of Yale College, had great literary ability.

Levi P. Norton has long been a leading merchant in Plantsville; has very good taste and judgment in dress and dry goods, and, being childless, has built his monument, better than marble, in a neat settlement of residences, west of the cemetery of Plantsville, now numbering eighteen, called Pine Park.

Deacon Edward Twitchell learned his trade of Deacon Higgins. In active, protracted labor, and executive ability the master and apprentice were alike. Edward Twitchell had a well-balanced mind. He devoted his leisure hours to reading, obtaining much practical knowledge, of which he made good use in conversation and address. His habits were to work from twelve to fourteen hours a day in his tanyard, and to spend his evenings in visiting the sick and poor, and watching with them, and attending religious meetings. Soon after his apprenticeship, conversing with the speaker, he said: "I have looked over the fields of enterprise in life and concluded that the best way for me to serve God and be useful to my fellow men is to 'tan hides.'" His life of great usefulness and earnest godliness demonstrated the wisdom of his judgment. Joseph Twitchell, his son, fired with patriotism, left his studies, at the breaking out of the war, and was long a chaplain in the army. His fervid appeals did more to fill the quota of volunteers from Southington than any other agency. He is at present the well-known pastor of the Asylum Hill Church, of Hartford. Edward Twitchell, jr., inherited his father's name, business, and spirit — the last his best legacy. The business firm consists of Hon. H. D. Smith, son-in-law of Deacon Higgins, Edward Twitchell, and George Smith. It is but just to say of the firm, as it is of Wolcott parentage, that it gave ten thousand dollars toward the building of the Plantsville Congregational church. Sarah Jane Twitchell, his daughter, has long been a devoted and distinguished teacher of the children of the Freedmen of Atlanta, Ga.

Dwight Twitchell, brother of Deacon Edward, learned his trade also of Deacon Higgins, and was long a member and jobber of the Stowe Manufacturing Company; now in a green old age of leisure, residing in a house lately erected, contrasting widely with his Wolcott origin. Mrs. Jennie Twitchell (Pultz), his daughter, is the gifted singer in the Plantsville choir.

Burritt Parker, a cabinet and coffin maker by trade, and such a man ought to have many serious thoughts.

Lucas Upson, long the leading merchant of Southington; honest and genial, and sagacious in business; selectman, a great politician, and the most popular candidate of his party.

Jerry Upson. He does not belong to that class of so vinegar an aspect as would not deign to show their teeth by the semblance of a smile, though Nestor himself should say the jest were laughable. Jerry has a "merry heart, which doeth good like a medicine." The spirit is not catching, the more the pity. His only son gave his young life for the life of the country.

Parlia Perkins, wife of Dr. Noah H. Byington, whose husband is a leading physician in Southington; she is very highly respected; of pleasant disposition, and good judgment.

Lucius Sutliff is a prominent joiner of the town; is highly esteemed, as also his sons, who occupy important positions in the community.

Hopkins Upson, a merchant in partnership with his uncle several years, and an honorable citizen.

Deacon Lucius Upson, of Plantsville church, has been school teacher, mechanic, clerk, and farmer. In him is illustrated how the mind can hold the body up, by genial love, Christian zeal, and ceaseless labor for the good of others. Elijah was a man of like passion and prayer, who shut up heaven by the space of three years and six months.

"The place from whence such virtuous things proceed, is honored by the doers' deeds."

May the Lord bless this old church and the town of Wolcott, while the sun and moon endure, for the sons and daughters they have given to Southington.

The Hon. Elihu Burritt, of New Britain, made the following remarks:

I am happy to be here to-day to enjoy the fellowship of all the interesting memories which this occasion revives. These commemorations are full of deep and varied interest. And there is one circumstance about them that we are entitled to speak of with just complacency. These commemorations are, as far as I know, exclusively New England institutions. They show the best characteristics of the New England mind. They show that our hard-soiled and hilly towns have a history far longer than the lives of their oldest inhabitants — a history that we revere, a history reaching back in some cases to those perilous years when the red Indians of the country outnumbered the whites — a history of hardship, privation, of faith, patience, and patriotism — one long battle of life, in which our forefathers and foremothers acted their parts with a Christian heroism that makes us love their memories. There are a hundred small towns and villages in New England in which you may read the continuous record of a century or more on the grave-stones in their church-yards. Many of these church-yards are divided in the middle by a kind of equatorial line. On the one side you will see the old red sandstone monuments that tell us that the men and women beneath lived and died subjects of the British crown, and called England "home," just as naturally, proudly, and fondly as Canadians and Australians now call our common motherland by that pleasant Saxon name. Then, side by side with these colonial graves, sometimes on the same stone, we may read the names of the first men of the village who died in the full right and title of citizens of a new-born nation. Both English fathers and their American sons were happy and true in their lives, and in their deaths they

were not divided. No volume ever written unfolds the history of
the two Englands — of the mother and daughter — so fully and
impressively as any one of our grave-yards a hundred years old.
And no stones in them should be more tenderly watched and
cared for than those erected before the American Revolution.
For what pages of our New England history are dearer to us than
those that record the lives and characters of our pre-Revolutionary
fathers and mothers.

Now it is these foot-prints of our history, hidden by a brook,
but seen on either side, that give these New England centenaries
their peculiar interest. No one of our smallest towns, in all the
centuries it is yet to see, will, I am sure, ever erase the foot-prints
on the farther side of that brook, or seek to break or tarnish the
hasp that connects its history with the history of that noble mother
country which has begotten and nursed more free and glorious
nations than all the other kingdoms of the world. And it is a fact
worthy of mention on an occasion like this. There is not a town
or village like this in New England which does not resemble Old
England more fully than any great commonwealth or nation can
do. The children that England has sent abroad to people all
latitudes and climates with young and growing nations, far out-
number, with their offspring, all her population at home. Not
one of these young and scattered communities but remembers
her and speaks of her with filial pride and affection. Now, is not
this goodly old town, set upon these eternal hills, just such another Old England in these pleasant maternal relations? Has
not Wolcott sent out as many families into the broad territory of
this great Union as England has sent colonies into the distant
continents and islands of the globe? Do not her children and her
children's children, thus scattered abroad in widely sundered
families, think of her and speak of her with the same filial sentiments?

This, then, to my mind, is the aspect and appreciation in which
we should view the life and relations of any New England town
as old as this, or younger still. It is not what it is and has been
at home, but what it is, has been, and does abroad; what elements of social, moral, and political life it has contributed to
other communities far and near; what men and women it has

sent out to impart the vitality of their characters to other towns, and States, and to the nation at large. Its history, without including this vital department of its being and influence, would be like the play of Hamlet with Hamlet left out. Certainly this whole history of a town, the whole of its home life and outside life, should be passed in review on an occasion like this. And we have had some of these facts and aspects presented to us to-day.

It is both a necessity and custom for great commercial and manufacturing corporations to take stock of their establishments at the end of the year, to see what they have sold or produced in that period, what they have gained, and what material they have on hand to begin a new year with. Well, it is equally fitting that every town, at the end of its century, should take stock — an inventory of its being, faculties, and influence; of the men and women it has produced, in the hundred years, who have made their mark at home or abroad; of the institutions it has established and sustained, and of the working material, the faculty, and the will it has for beginning a new century. I am sure that all the people of this town, and all who claim kindred with it, have good reason to be proud and happy at the inventory it presents the world at the end of its first century. I am equally sure that the young generation here, who are to inherit the coming century, will remember this occasion, and resolve to make a history in their day which their children's children will review with pride and gladness at the next centenary which Wolcott will celebrate.

I think that not one of our New England towns could make a contribution to the history of the country at large which would be so interesting, instructive, and valuable as the simple record of its men and women; of the life it has lived at home, and the life and character it has sent abroad in a hundred years. I remember well how deeply I was impressed with a few facts stated of another small, stony, hard-soiled Connecticut town. A distinguished native of old Lebanon told me that that town had produced five governors, and had given a full college education to seventy-two men for the ministry, and other learned professions, since its incorporation. What a record that to present to the world! What faith and patience, what tireless industry and self-sacrificing frugality, are represented by these simple facts! Think of a little community of farmers toiling on small and stony farms, and making them yield not only comfortable sustenance, clothing, and schooling for their children at home, but the means of giving a full classical education to seventy-two graduates of Yale College in the life-time of their town! How instructive and useful would the history of such New England towns be to the rich and fertile townships of our great West, who send agents to Lebanon and other small communities in New England, to solicit contributions for the support of Western Colleges!

We have seen what a record Wolcott has contributed to the history of our good old Connecticut, and the whole State may truly and proudly say, "well done!"

The following lines, written for the occasion by Amos M. Johnson, esq., of Wolcott, were sung to the tune "New Jerusalem," C. M.:

ONE HUNDRED YEARS.

One hundred years have passed away,
 And memory now revives ;
One hundred years are passed and gone !
 This Church,— it still survives.

One hundred years,— the greatest age
 That mortals ever knew !
One hundred years,— the wisest sage
 Will ever keep in view.

What scenes the memory brings to view !
 What wonders have been wrought !
How many souls been born anew,—
 Their God and Saviour sought.

The fathers of this Church now rest,—
 In yonder graveyard lie ;
Their spirits dwell among the blest,
 In bliss, beyond the sky.

One hundred years,— how great the sum,
 And yet how quickly sped !
One hundred years, the next to come,
 Will find us with the dead.

> Then let us live with Heaven and Hell
> And Death before our eyes!
> One Hundred years,— we then shall dwell
> In glory 'bove the skies.

Mr. Orcutt again exhibited "antiquities." Among them was a pair of high-heeled slippers worn by a Wolcott lady at the commencement ball of Yale College. The sword of Captain John Allcock, presented to him by George III, and now in the hands of a grandson, was shown by A. Bronson Alcott, who gave an interesting account of the high uses to which it had been put by his patriot ancestor. A large fan over one hundred years old was exhibited, which, in size and appearance, resembles the fans just coming into use. A musket made in London, and carried in the French war by David Welton, of Wolcott, was exhibited. Mr. George Pratt, of Southington, stated a family tradition that this musket was once so skillfully used that it "brought down" in succession three British officers.

The Rev. Mr. Upson read a list of the deacons of the church in Wolcott from the beginning. Mr. Isaac Bronson, of Bristol, a descendant of one of the first deacons of the church, followed with some remarks. He gave interesting traditions of the Bronson family. A diary of Deacon Isaac Bronson, which had been preserved, was shown and extracts from it read by Deacon Samuel Holmes. Deacon Holmes read a hymn composed by Deacon Bronson on the death of Washington, and which was sung in the church at the time. Rev. A. C. Beach added some recollections of Deacon Bronson, who was an old man when he was pastor here, and he pronounced him one of the noblest men he ever knew. These allusions to Deacon Bronson brought A. Bronson Alcott to his feet again, who referred to the Deacon's efficiency as a church officer at a time the church was without a pastor. He was peculiarly gifted in prayer, and impressed every one with his deep sincerity and nearness to God. His counsels and prayers were sought by the sick and afflicted. No man ever lived in Wolcott with such natural gifts as he, and had he been favored with a liberal education, he would have equaled any of the great men this State has produced.

Judge W. E. Curtis, of New York, was introduced, and very tenderly alluded to a former pastor, Rev. Mr. Woodward. He held in his hand a small volume of poems by William Maxwell, esq., of Norfolk, Va. Mr. Maxwell, seventy years ago, was an inmate of Mr. Woodward's family, and by him prepared for college. Upon hearing of his instructor's death, he composed a poem upon "Wolcott," which is contained in this volume. Judge Curtis read extracts from the poem. A general desire was expressed to have the poem published in an account of the proceedings.

A. Bronson Alcott was again called for to give an account of his cousin Wm. A. Alcott, M. D., and widely known in our country as a teacher and author. He said that although cousins, they were more like brothers. They were much together in younger years, and helped one another in their literary course. Dr. Alcott has done more for primary education than any other person. He was very successful as a teacher and author. It is said that he wrote over one hundred books, and also edited three different journals. He was a "vegetarian," and for many years tasted no meat. Mr. Alcott, before closing, alluded very modestly to his own family, among whom is the celebrated authoress of "Little Women." This allusion awakened the people, who listened with "erect ears" to all that was said of their favorite authoress.

The Rev. Wm. P. Alcott, of Greenwich, and son of Dr. W. A. Alcott, having been called for, arose and gave some facts concerning the family. His grandfather, John Bronson, was a man of extraordinary strength and endurance. At eighty he challenged the young men of Wolcott to engage in a "mowing match" with him for a day, but none of the young yeomanry were bold enough to accept the challege. The lesson that Mr. Alcott would impress, was what could be accomplished by work. The sons of Wolcott had achieved all honor and influence by hard work. He mentioned that his father learned arithmetic at night, holding the slate on his left arm and candle (the candlestick being a potato) in his left hand. Under great difficulties he attained his final eminence.

The next speaker was George W. Seward, esq., of New York, only surviving brother of the late Secretary Seward. A branch of the Seward family lived in Wolcott, and among the earliest settlers was Amos Seward, who is held in fragrant memory. Mr. Seward began by thanking the good people of Wolcott for the generous hospitality that had been extended to him since he came among them. He entered into some of the details of the family history. Without speaking of his immediate family, he related some facts concerning his ancestors who were prominent in the revolutionary war. His grandfather was Col. John Seward, of Morristown, N. J. Col. Seward was not only a patriot, but one of the most active of patriots. He made himself felt as a power on the side of the colonies, and feared by tories. Several anecdotes of his skill as a marksman, and acts as a soldier, were given.

As a general desire had been expressed to hear something about his brother, the late Secretary Seward, he gave two interesting facts. When Mr. Seward was Governor of New York, in 1839, he was invited, in connection with President Van Buren, to attend a Sabbath school celebration on Staten Island. He addressed them, and in the course of his remarks said, that great wealth, education, and talents, even in this country, tended to aristocratical views and feelings, and were prejudicial to the interests and well being of the masses. And the counteracting agency was to be found in the Sunday schools of the day. These are the great leveling agencies which are to educate the masses and fit them for citizens and voters, and to hold the institutions of the country and a free government in perpetuity. By some these sentiments were considered the noblest the Governor ever uttered during his long and eventful career. Another fact. The ex-Secretary, seated in the parlor with some friends, and talking of incidents during the war, stated that shortly after the Mason and Slidell arrest, he received a confidential communication from Louis Napoleon, in which was expressed personal respect for the Secretary, as a statesman, but that he (the Emperor) must bow to the will of the French people, and recognize the confederacy, and declare war in its behalf. The same day this letter was received, a reply was sent to the Emperor, telling him, in substance, to keep hands off,—that we neither asked for nor would permit interference on the part of any European government,—and should he recognize the Confederacy, and send troops to this country, we would emancipate the slaves, and before this Union would submit to a slave government, we would put arms into the hands of the slaves, and doom the Southern States to devastation and ruin. Some friends were at once sent to England and France to maintain our cause, and it only cost us $7,000.

The Rev. Henry Upson was the next speaker, and gave recollections of his childhood here.

Deacon Samuel Holmes, of Montclair, N. J., was now called out, and before he took his seat showed himself what all before knew,—that he was a prince among deacons. He urged with great practical effect that the people should at once establish a town library, and offered fifty dollars for the purpose. This generous offer was at once responded to by others, until two hundred and fifty dollars were subscribed.

While the subscription to the library was in progress,

Rev. Mr. Hillard, of Plymouth Center, was called on and spoke as follows :

MR. CHAIRMAN: — I consent to speak on one condition only, and that is that the subscription to the library shall go forward without interruption. That is of more consequence than talk. The library ought to be secured, and now is the time to secure it. So much butter at least ought to come of this two day's stirring of the cream. So let the subscription go right on. My estimate of that is about what the boy's was, on a certain occasion, of a collection. Three boys, the story goes, not much accustomed to religious services, strolled, one day, into a meeting, where, besides the usual exercises of prayer and song, a collection was taken up. On leaving the meeting they went off sailing together, and a squall coming up, and the case looking desperate, Jim, the leader of the crew, felt that they must have help. Turning to his companions, who were shivering with fright, he inquired, "John, can you pray?" "No," was the answer, "not here." "Joe, can you sing?" "No, not now." "Well," was Jim's conclusion, "something religious has got to be done right off; we'll take up a collection." So, in my opinion, one of the most religious things that we can do just here and now is to take up a collection.

I have been greatly interested in the exercises of this centennial. My heart has gone out in thorough sympathy with all your pride and joy. It has almost seemed to me that I had a personal share in it. You remember the affecting passage in Mark Twain's "Innocents Abroad," in which he describes his feelings on being shown, in his travels, the grave of Adam. It overwhelmed him, he says, with emotion, to come, in that far off land, upon the grave of a blood relation. So, though not myself born here, I somehow feel as though those who have been born here were my blood relatives, and so have been interested in their histories. [Question from the crowd, "Don't you wish you had been born here?"] Some one asks if I do not wish I had been born here. No, I do not; for I do not believe in a man's going back on his mother, and so I am not going back on old Preston, the town where I was born, even for the sake of being born in Wolcott. But I will tell you how near I come to wishing I had been born

THE CENTENARY MEETING. 419

in Wolcott. You recollect that Mrs. Jarley in the exhibition, in her wax works, of those miracles of art, the Siamese Twins, informs her audience that they were born, one on Cape Cod, and the other on the Island of Borneo. Now, since being here these two days, and listening to all that Wolcott has been and done, though glad that I myself was born in Preston, I have wished that instead of being born a single child, and so limited to a single birth-place, I had been born a twin, and that my twin brother had been born in Wolcott.

But though missing thus myself the honor of being born in Wolcott, I have become convinced that it must have been here that a certain distinguished character of history was born. I refer to the Roman Emperor Marcus Antoninus. I am not quite sure in my dates — this always was a weakness with me — but if I get muddled some one of the learned gentlemen here present can set me right. I am not sure about the dates, but I am confident, from internal evidence, that Antoninus, the Roman Emperor, was born on Wolcott Hill. And the ground of my confidence is this: In a passage in his "Meditations," weary of the littleness and meanness of life around him, and challenging to life high and noble, he exclaims, "Live as on a mountain;" and while listening to Mr. Alcott and others as they have entertained and instructed and inspired us with reminiscences of the fathers of Wolcott, I have said to myself, "It was from life here on Wolcott Hill that Marcus Antoninus got his idea." I am confident of it, and if those inveterate liars, the dates, deny this, I have only to say that if he wasn't born here, it would have been wisdom in his head if he had been.

But soberly, it seems to me a grand thing to have been born in Wolcott. We do not, in our fast and pretentious time, appreciate as we should these old hill-towns of New England. Why, here are the head-springs of all her greatness. Just as the streams which furnish the power in the valleys head on these hills, so the intelligence and strength and energy of manhood, which makes the villages and cities, come from these hill-parishes. Not more is the rich soil that forms the valley meadows washed from these rocky hills, than is the society which constitutes the valley communities the contributions of these hill-towns. Without this

supply those communities would soon become extinct. As
physicians tell us that were it not for the ever fresh supply of
healthy men and women from the country, the cities would soon
become depopulated, and a desert waste,—so were it not for the
fresh supplies of intelligence and character and energy trained
on these hills, the valley communities would soon lose their
importance and power. When I was down at Block Island this
Summer, a government vessel was at work there clearing out the
rocks from the harbor bottom. The man who did the work, or
seemed to, was the diver, who, in his armor, went down into the
water and made fast the grappling chains. On him was concentrated all the attention. But there was another man, not much
noticed, who attracted my attention. He remained on deck and
steadily turned a crank. That crank worked an air-pump, and
from that pump a tube went down into the water and supplied
the diver with fresh air for his work. How long do you think the
diver down there under water would have gone on with his work
if the man at the air-pump had ceased to turn the crank? So,
though the valley communities seem to do the work, and so get
the credit of it, it is these hill-parishes that pump down the fresh
air to them, and keep them alive. Very quickly would come the
end of their history if you were to stop turning the crank. It is
with the hill-parishes of New England as it was with the hill-
fortresses of Palestine. You recollect the passage in the Old
Testament which records the discomfiture of the Syrians in their
attack on one of those forts; and you recollect the explanation
of that discomfiture by the Syrians: "Their gods are gods of the
hills; therefore they were stronger than we, but let us fight against
them on the plain, and surely we shall be stronger than they."
So the gods of New England's strength and greatness have ever
been gods of the hills,—and this of spiritual as of physical strength.
Here, in these hill-parishes, have headed the spiritual streams that
in their flowing forth have blessed the world. From Torringford
Hill, from the parsonage of old Father Mills, flowed the stream
of American missions. So take any chapter of New England's
spiritual greatness and power, and you will find the sources of it
largely here. Here head the rivers, the streams whereof make
glad the city of God.

You, then, whose lot is cast here in Wolcott, whose destiny it is to remain here, count it no mean destiny. You may so improve it that there shall be none nobler. Remember the answer of the Down-East Yankee to the contemptuous inquiry suggested by the rocks and ice, "What they raised there;" "We raise men!" It is a good place, a grand place, here on these rocky hills to raise men. Here, bless God, this has not yet come to be one of the lost arts. In these old parishes children are yet born, and of all crops this is the noblest. Given the man, and you have given all things. Raise the children, then; train them up for manhood and womanhood; train them up for God; send them out healthy, strong, noble, pure, upright, God-fearing, and God-serving, to bless the world, and you will not have lived in vain. Remember the decision of David in the case of the brook Besor. Part of the company, you remember, did not cross the brook; were too faint to pursue and "tarried by the stuff." Their pursuing and victorious companions, returned from the victory, refused them a share in the spoils. But David reversed their decision, and made it a law forever, "As his part is that goeth down to the battle, so shall his part be that tarrieth by the stuff; they shall part alike." It is the law of God's Kingdom. Be faithful, and you shall find it the law of your reward. "They also serve who only stand and wait."

Then, next to the children, there are the aged. Towards these hill-parishes our hearts are ever turning, because "here's where the old folks stay." The old folks, God bless them!—the old fathers and mothers, and grandfathers and grandmothers, here is where they stay,—sending their children out to influence, and wealth, and power, while they remain, quiet and unknown. Boys, girls, count it not a hardship to stay by the old folks. Count not life so devoted lost. God has a blessing for those who honor father and mother when they are old. Again I say, God bless them! we owe all to them. Boys, you will never lose anything by staying by them while they stay here below; and you, girls, when somebody, one of these days, asks you if he may have you, tell him, "Yes, if he'll take the old folks with you."

And now these festivities are at an end and we must disperse. You, people of Wolcott, who are to remain, life may seem to you lonely when the occasion is over and the friends from abroad whom you are proud of, and whose presence has given you joy are gone, and you settle back to the old, plain, common life of Wolcott. But suffer no reaction of sadness. Rather look on to the higher festival, the heavenly home-coming, of which this is but a symbol, when all the history of your lives with all their outcome shall be made up before God. The morning succeeding the night of the Transfiguration seemed, doubtless, to the disciples who had been with Jesus on the mount, plain and lonely with its contrast of earthly plainness with the heavenly glory. But beyond was the Mount of Ascension, and to it, across the intervening valley, the Mount of Transfiguration looked. So, across your remaining life on earth, plain and lonely though to the earthly view it may be, there waits for you the glory of your eternal reward, when the King shall say, "Come, ye blessed of my Father, you have been faithful in a few things, enter into the joy of your Lord." Keep this prospect clear by faith before you, and may it ever strengthen your hearts.

After one or two more brief addresses, a vote of thanks to the citizens for hospitality was passed, and the hymn

>"Blessed be the tie that binds
>   Our hearts in Christian love;
> The fellowship of kindred minds
>   Is like to that above,"

was sung, with the sense as well as the sound, and the benediction pronounced by Rev. A. C. Beach. At the close a number of persons came to the platform to obtain each one flower from the beautiful collection placed there by Mr Shepherd, of Southington. They wanted "just *one flower*," to carry to their distant homes,— Kansas and elsewhere,— as a memento of this centenary meeting.

GENEALOGIES.

ALCOTT.

ALCOCKE, ALCOCK, ALCOCKS, ALCOX.

This name is spelled Alcock in English history. As a surname it was established, by authority of the king, about the year 1616, by the granting of a "coat of arms," and according to the law established by King Henry Third, about 1250, was inherited by all descendants of the family. The full development of the "Science of Arms" occurred during the "Holy Wars," or the "Crusades," and hence most of these insignia, date back, only, to that period, and from this fact, these signs bear a decidedly religious character. On the Alcock shield is "Fesse; emblematic of the military girdle worn around the body, over the armour;" three heads of the cock, emblematic of watchfulness. From this shield and crest we learn that the peculiar characteristic for which this family was honored as soldiers, was watchfulness.

The name was spelled Alcock in this country, until about 1770, when the spelling was changed to Alcox, and also Allcox. This was the spelling on all records, as well as in the family, until 1820 to 1825, when by the proposition of Dr. William A., and A. Bronson Alcott, it was, by common consent, not by legislative enactment, changed to Alcott, and in this form has become world-renowned.*

1 THOMAS.†— FIRST GENERATION.

THOMAS ALCOCK, the progenitor of all bearing the name in Connecticut, came from England in Winthrop's company, in 1630,

---

* Mr. Savage tells us that this name was written Alcott by some of the family in the early records of Massachusetts.

† John Alcock was born at Beverly, Yorkshire, England, and was Bishop of Rochester, Worcester, and Ely, in the time of Henry VII.; also Lord Chancellor of England. He founded Jesus College, Cambridge, and was distinguished in his day for learning and piety. He died October 1, 1500, and was buried in a sumptuous tomb of his own designing in Ely Cathedral.

with his brother George.* In the covenant of the First church of Boston, dated at Charlestown, August 27, 1638, Thomas Alcock stands forty-sixth on the list of original members. "Ano. 8: 7: 1639, our brother Thomas Alcock and sister Margary were recommended to Dedham," where he settled. He afterwards removed to Boston, where he died, September 14, 1657. His widow, Margary, married John Benham, of New Haven, to which place she removed about 1660, where she died.

Children: 2 *Mary*, bapt Nov. 3, 1635, d 1644; 3 *Elizabeth*, bapt Dec. 10, 1637, d same year; 4 *Elizabeth*, b Oct. 4, 1638, m May 6, 1656, Joseph Soper of Boston; 5 *Sarah*, b Dec. 28, 1639; 6 *Hannah*, b May 25, 1642; 7 *Mary*, b June 8, 1644, m Sept. 27, 1664, James Robinson of Dorchester, d March 13, 1718; 8 *Rebecca*, b 1646; 9 *Phillip*, b 1648; 10 *John*, b in Boston, May 6, 1651, m Constance, daughter of Humphrey Milam of Boston, where he died before 1712. He had two sons and six daughters.

9 PHILLIP.— SECOND GENERATION.

PHILLIP ALCOCK, son of Thomas and Margary Alcock, was born in Dedham, Mass, and removed to New Haven with his mother. He married, Dec. 5, 1672, Elizabeth, only daughter of Thomas Mitchell. He married at Wethersfield his second wife, April 4, 1699, Sarah, widow of Nathaniel Butler. He had large landed estates, besides his home lot in New Haven, on the North side of what is now George Street, between College and Temple streets, adjoining the Beecher family property. He died in 1716, ae. 68.

Children: 11 *John*, b July 14, 1675; 12 *Thomas*, b 1677, m Mary Gedney, and a second wife Abigail Austin; 13 *Elizabeth*, b Feb. 6, 1679, m —— Gray; 14 *Phillip*, b Nov. 19, 1681; 15 *Agnes*, b 1683, m —— Harrison.

11 JOHN.—THIRD GENERATION.

JOHN ALCOCK, son of Phillip and Elizabeth [Mitchell] Alcock, of New Haven, married Susanna ———, and lived on the paternal estate in New Haven, owning land at East Haven, Walling-

---

*George Alcock settled at Roxbury, Mass., where he was a deacon of the church, and an important man in the colony.

ford, and elsewhere. He died March, 1722, ae. 47 ; his wife died in 1737.

Children: 16 *Abigail,* who married, Jan. 6, 1736, Caleb Thomas of New Haven, d Feb. 23, 1793, ae. 73; 17 *John,* b Jan. 14, 1705, settled in Waterbury; 18 *Elizabeth,* b July 13, 1708, m Samuel Humiston of New Haven; 19 *Sarah,* b Aug. 12, 1711, m John Alling of New Haven; 20 *Stephen,* b Aug. 10, 1714, m Abigail Humiston of New Haven, and lived at Amity, now Woodbridge ; 21 *Mary,* b Aug. 10, 1717, m Daniel Lines of New Haven.

17 JOHN.— FOURTH GENERATION.

JOHN ALCOCK, son of John and Susanna Alcock of New Haven, was married, Jan. 14, 1729 or 30, by Rev. Isaac Stiles of North Haven, to Deborah, daughter of Isaac Blakeslee of North Haven. In 1731 he removed to Waterbury, bringing his wife and infant child, Lydia, and settled on Spindle Hill, Wolcott. He died Jan. 6, 1777, ae. 71 ; his wife died Jan. 7, 1789, ae. 77. (See Biog. p. 231.)

Children: 22 *Lydia,* b Nov. 24, 1730, m Isaac Blakeslee of North Haven, where she resided, d Nov. 15, 1796, ae. 66 ; 23 *John,* b Dec. 28, 1731 ; 24 *James,* b June 1, 1734 ; 25 *Jesse,* b March 23, 1736; 26 *Daniel,* b March 25, 1738; 27 *David,* b Jan. 12, 1740; 28 *Deborah,* b 1741, married 1st, Isaac Twitchell, 2d, Wait Hotchkiss, and settled near the " Mill Place " in Wolcott, d June 18, 1831, ae. 89 ; 29 *Mary,* b 1744, m June 28, 1763, Obed Bradley of North Haven, where she settled. She d March 1825, ae. 81; 50 *Thankful,* b 1748, m Thaddeus Baldwin of Plymouth, Conn., where she lived, and d March 1, 1839, ae. 90; 31 *Hannah,* b 1751, m Joel Norton of Bristol, where she lived, and d March 1, 1821, ae. 70; 32 *Anna,* m Abel Curtiss of Wolcott, lived near the "Mill Place," d Feb. 5, 1822 ; 33 *Stephen,* d young.

23 JOHN, JR.— FIFTH GENERATION.

CAPT. JOHN ALCOX, son of John and Deborah (Blakeslee) Alcock, was born in Waterbury (Wolcott), in the year his father settled on Spindle Hill. He married, Aug. 28, 1755, Mary, the daughter of Solomon Chatfield of Derby, Conn. He built a house on Spindle Hill, near his father's, where Almon Alcott now

(1873) resides; and where he (John) died Sept. 27, 1808, ae. 77; Mary, his wife, died Feb. 28, 1807, ae. 71. (See Biog. p. 233.)

Children: 34 *Lydia*, b Dec. 8, 1756, m 1st, Charles Frisbie, 2d, Capt. Nathaniel Lewis, both of Wolcott, d Sept. 23, 1831, ae. 74; 35 *Solomon*, b May 8, 1759; 36 *Samuel*, b Nov. 29, 1761; 37 *John Blakeslee*, b June 24, 1764; 38 *Mary*, b Sept. 8, 1766, d Feb. 18, 1770; 39 *Isaac*, b April 12, 1769; 40 *Joseph Chatfield*, b May 7, 1771; 41 *Mark*, b May 11, 1773; 42 *Thomas*, b Oct. 16, 1775, d April 27, 1778.

24 JAMES, 1ST.

JAMES ALCOX, son of John and Deborah (Blakeslee) Alcock, married Hannah Barnes, and settled a mile northeast of the old homestead, where his grandson, James, now (1873) resides. His house was built in the Autumn of 1774, and he moved into it while the carpenters were at work upon it. On the 5th of December following, his son James was born. Three weeks from that day the house took fire in the night and was consumed. Strangled by the smoke, he awoke, and began some efforts to save the house. His wife, who had not been out of the house during her illness, tried to raise the window, but this could not be done, it being new. She then broke the window with her hands, and gave the baby to his sister outside, and she crept out, the window consisting of only four panes of glass, and went to the neighbors, with no apparel except her night clothes, her hands bleeding by the way from cuts by the glass. Nothing was saved from the house but the members of the family. In nine days the frame of a new one was raised, and it is still standing. People came from far and near to help build this house; some coming over fifteen miles. He resided in this house until his death, Aug. 9, 1806, ae. 72.

Children: 43 *Obedience*, m John J. Kenea; 44 *Rosanna*, m John Frisbie, d Aug. 18, 1830; 45 *Meliscent*, m Nathaniel Lane, 1793, d in Wolcott, ae. 88; 46 *James*, b Dec. 5, 1774; 47 *Mehitable* m James Bradley; 48 *Lois*, bapt April 2, 1780, m John Smith; 49 *Diadama*, bapt July 14, 1782, m Joshua Minor of Wolcott; 50 *Hannah*, m Osman Norton; 51 *Livia*, bapt Oct. 29, 1786, m Edward Goodyear; 52 *Rhoda*, bapt Dec. 6, 1789, m Lewis Sanford.

GENEALOGIES. 429

25 JESSE.

JESSE ALCOX, son of John and Deborah (Blakeslee) Alcock, married Patience Blakeslee, and settled in the northeast part of Wolcott. He died October 29, 1829, ae. 74. His widow, Patience, married Zechariah Hitchcock, and died 1840, ae. 97.

Children: 53 *Sarah*, m David Churchill; 54 *Lyman*, d Nov. 17, 1781, ae. 16; 55 *Susan*, m John Beecher, and d Nov. 3, 1836, ae. 69; 56 *Jesse*, m Lucy Minor, June 16, 1791, d July 6, 1814; 57 *Joel*, m Elizabeth Johnson; 58 *Hannah*, m Daniel Byington; 59 *Chloe*, bapt Dec. 7, 1783, m Salmon Shelley; 60 *Ithamer*, d Aug. 9, 1798, ae. 3.

26 DANIEL.

DANIEL ALCOX, son of John and Deborah (Blakeslee) Alcock, married Elizabeth Dutton. He settled first, in Wolcott Center; and afterwards removed to Colebrook, where he died, May 24, 1805, ae. 67.

Children: 61 *Asa*, m Sabra Plumb; 62 *Daniel;* 63 *Samuel;* 64 *Joseph;* 65 *Benjamin*, m Chloe Norton; 66 *Elizabeth;* 67 *Mary*, m —— Darrow; 68 *Benoni;* 69 *Susanna*, m Abram Tuttle; 70 *Urana*, m William Burr.

27 DAVID.

DAVID ALCOX, son of John and Deborah (Blakeslee) Alcock, married, July 5, 1767, Abigail Johnson. She died Feb. 5, 1793, ae. 53. He married 2d, Sarah Pratt, Feb. 5, 1795. He lived on the old homestead, and died there Jan. 29, 1821, ae. 81.

Children: 71 *Amy*, b Sept. 16, 1768, d May 5, 1830, ae. 62; 72 *Abigail*, b Dec. 14, 1770, m Aug. 26, 1793, Asahel Lane; 73 *David*, b April 10, 1774, m Anna Fenn; 74 *Obed*, b Sept. 8, 1776, m July 13, 1797, Abigail Andrews, d Aug. 8, 1847, ae. 71; 75 *Eldad*, and 76 *Medad*, twins, b Sept. 14, 1779; 77 *Eunice*, b Oct. 17, 1782, m April 24, 1806, Archibald Mosher; 78 *Deborah*, b Nov. 25, 1784, m 1st, Feb. 18, 1808, Isaac Minor, 2d, Lorin Fancher, March 4, 1820.

35 SOLOMON.— SIXTH GENERATION.

SOLOMON ALCOX, son of Capt. John and Mary (Chatfield) Alcox, married 1st, Pamelia Roberts, 2d, widow Abigail Goodyear, both of Wolcott. He lived near "Potucco's Ring," near his father's, and died May 21, 1818, ae. 59; his wife, Pamelia, died Aug. 20, 1810, ae. 49.

Children: 79 *Lydia*, m and d in Ohio; 80 *Hannah*, m 1st, Richard Withington of Bucks Hill, and 2d, Capt. Gates Upson of Wolcott; 81 *Seth*, d in Ohio; 82 *Solomon*, d in childhood; 83 *Leonard*, d near Cleveland, O., where Seth resided in 1857.

36 SAMUEL.

SAMUEL ALCOX, son of Capt. John and Mary (Chatfield) Alcox, married Lydia Warner of Bucks Hill. He died at the Mill Place, on Mad River, June 9, 1819, ae. 49; his wife, Lydia, died May 2, 1848, ae. 82.

Children: 84 *Jairus*, m Sarah W. Warner of Waterbury and d in Western New York; 85 *Mary*, m Isaac Hotchkiss of Wolcott, d Dec., 1840; 86 *Cleora*, d Feb. 16, 1826, ae. 33; 87 *Statira*, m Oct. 4, 1819, Amos Shepherd of Southington; 88 *Candace*, m George Griswold, and moved to Iowa, thence to Washington Territory, where she now resides.

37 JOHN BLAKESLEE.

JOHN B. ALCOX, son of Capt. John and Mary (Chatfield) Alcox, married Lois Gaylord of Wolcott, and resided near his father's homestead, on Clinton Hill. He died Sept. 17, 1837, ae. 73; Lois, his wife, died April 7, 1839, ae. 70.

Children: 89 *Riley*, m 1st, Ruth Frisbie, 2d, Olive Warner, settled in Waterbury, and d there, May 21, 1857, ae. 74; 90 *Almon*, b Feb. 22, 1790, and is still living; 91 *Jedediah G.*, b June 24, 1793; d May, 1872.

39 ISAAC.

ISAAC ALCOX, son of Capt. John and Mary (Chatfield) Alcox, married Isabel Lane of Wolcott, sister to Mary, the wife of Mark Alcox, his brother. He lived at East Church Parish, near Terryville, in Plymouth, where he died Sept. 12, 1809, ae. 40.

Child: 92, he had an only child which died an infant.

40 JOSEPH CHATFIELD.

JOSEPH C. ALCOX, son of Capt. John and Mary (Chatfield) Alcox, married, Oct. 13, 1796, Anna, daughter of Capt. Amos

Bronson of Plymouth, and sister of Rev. Tillotson Bronson, D. D., Rector of St. John's church in Waterbury. Joseph first lived near "Potucco's Ring," but in 1805 he settled near his brother, John Blakeslee, at Clinton Hill, or New Connecticut, the highest land in Spindle Hill district. He died April 3, 1829, ae. 58; his widow, Anna, died at West Edmeston, N. Y., Aug. 15, 1863, ae. 90.

Children: 93 *Betsey*, b April 4, 1798, d Nov. 5, 1798; 94 *Amos Bronson*, b Nov. 29, 1799; 95 *Chatfield*, b Oct. 23, 1801; 96 *Pamelia, and* 97 *Pamila*, b Feb. 4, 1805. Pamelia m James Bailey of Wolcott, moved to Pennsylvania, and d Feb. 11, 1849. Pamila m Ransom Gaylord of Bristol, went to Stockbridge, N. Y., and d June 14, 1833; 98 *Betsey*, b Feb. 14, 1808, m Linus Pardee of Wolcott, and removed to West Edmeston, near Oriskany Falls, N. Y.; 99 *Phebe*, b Feb. 18, 1810, m William Norton of Wolcott, lived on the family homestead, where she d July 28, 1844, ae. 34; 100 *George*, b March 26, 1812, d July 10, 1812; 101 *Junius*, b July 6, 1818, m Nancy Jane Pritchard of Litchfield, Conn., lived at Oriskany Falls, N. Y., and d April 16, 1852, ae. 34; 102 *Ambrose*, b Sept, 10, 1820, m Anna V. Upson of Wolcott, and resided at Plantsville, in Southington, and removed thence to Fair Haven.

41 MARK.

MARK ALCOX, son of Capt. John and Mary (Chatfield) Alcox, married Mary Lane of Wolcott, in 1795. He lived on his father's homestead several years, then settled near James Alcott's, where his son Thomas resided many years. In winter he engaged largely in the manufacturing of clock cords. He d Nov. 21, 1846, ae. 74; she d Oct. 8, 1834, ae. 61.

Children: 103 *Alma, and* 104 *Amanda*, twins, d in infancy; 105 *Thomas*, never married. He lived on his father's homestead and died at his sister Salina's home, Oct. 30, 1872, ae. 73. He traveled in the Southern States, mostly in Virginia and the Carolinas, over twenty years, selling various articles of merchandise. It was Thomas and Amos B. Alcott who bought broadcloth suits with ruffled shirts, in Broadway, New York, on their first return from the south. This was the last fancy "rig" Thomas ever put on. 106 *Emily*, m Amos Newton; 107 *Albin*, m Chloe Finch, d December, 1871; 108 *Salina*, b Aug. 12, 1807, m James Alcott, 3d, of Wolcott; 109 *Isaac*, m 1st, Mary Farnesworth, 2d, Clarissa Higby, and lived at Plainville, Conn.; 110 *Almira*, m Thomas Matthews, and resides in Hopeville, Waterbury, and has sons, George and Isaac.

46 JAMES, 2D.

JAMES ALCOX, son of James and Hannah (Barnes) Alcox, married Esther Castle, Jan. 8, 1800. She died March 6, 1861, ae. 85; he died May 30, 1862, ae. 87.

Children: 111 *Lucius*, b Jan. 24, 1801; 112 *Lois*, b July 9, 1805, m Ansel H. Plumb; 113 *Infant*, b Feb. 27, 1807, d young; 114 *James*, b May 18, 1809; 115 *Phineas C.*, b Dec. 2, 1817; 116 *Leverett*, b Dec. 5, 1820.

73 DAVID, JR.

DAVID ALCOX, son of David and Abigail (Johnson) Alcox, married Anna Fenn of Plymouth.

Children: 117 *Fenn*, b Feb. 3, 1804, m Susan Taylor; 118 *Eli*, b April 21, 1810; 119 *Irena*, b Oct. 4, 1817; all removed west.

74 OBED.

OBED ALCOX, son of David and Abigail (Johnson) Alcox, married, July 13, 1797, Anna, daughter of William Andrus, a soldier of the Revolution, and descendant of Abraham Andrus, one of the original settlers of Waterbury. She was born at Watertown, Sept. 1, 1777. His home and farm were about half a mile north of his father's, on the road going east. He engaged largely in the manufacture of clock cord and clock pinions for Terry, Thomas, and Hoadley. He died Aug. 5, 1847; Anna, his wife, died Sept. 2, 1864.

Children: 120 *William A.*, b Aug. 6, 1798; 121 *Lovina*, b Jan. 17, 1801, m William Knowles of Haddam, Feb. 8, 1820, d March 1, 1821; 122 *Florenna*, b Aug. 9, 1804; d Dec. 18, 1856; 123 *George G.*, b March 25, 1807.

75 ELDAD.

ELDAD ALCOX, son of David and Abigail (Johnson) Alcox, married widow Sybil Bartholomew, Jan. 29, 1817. He died June 5, 1850, ae. 71.

GENEALOGIES. 433

Children: 124 *Sarah Ann*, b Jan. 9, 1818; 125 *Newell*, b Dec. 23, 1820.

76 MEDAD.

MEDAD ALCOX, son of David and Abigail (Johnson) Alcox, married, April 30, 1801, Sylvia Bronson of Plymouth. She was born Nov. 22, 1776. He resided in Plymouth, and died Jan. 13, 1829; his widow, Sylvia, died Sept. 18, 1855, ae. 79.

Children: 126 *Dennison*, b Nov. 8, 1801; 127 *Rosetta*, b Aug. 3, 1803, m Alfred Churchill; 128 *Johnson*, b Dec. 19, 1804; 129 *Julia*, b Oct. 12, 1806, m Willis Merrill, Oct. 18, 1827; 130 *Addison*, b Sept. 6, 1808; 131 *Sylvia Ann*, b July 14, 1810, d Feb. 10, 1811; 132 *Lucy Maria*, b Aug. 10, 1817.

89 RILEY.—SEVENTH GENERATION.

RILEY ALCOTT, son of John B. and Lois (Gaylord) Alcott, married 1st, Olive Warner, 2d, Ruth Frisbie, April 13, 1820. His residence was in Waterbury, near Wolcott, where his son Gaylord now resides. He died May 21, 1857, ae. 74; his wife, Olive, died March 14, 1819, ae. 28; his widow, Ruth, is now in her 88th year.

Children by first wife: 133 *Isaac*, d Nov. 19, 1826, ae. 14. By second wife: 134 *Jane*, b Sept. 1, 1821, m Abel Beardsley of Plymouth, where she resides and has children, Charles H., William G., Arthur S., Ella, Samuel, Mary, Jennie, Rodolph, and Franklin; 135 *Gaylord*.

90 ALMON.

ALMON ALCOTT, son of John B. and Lois (Gaylord) Alcox, married 1st, Betsey Cleveland, April 4, 1816; she died Oct. 18, 1827, ae. 32. He married, 2d, Polly Cleveland, Dec. 7, 1829; she died Oct. 12, 1838.

Children: 136 *Lois G.*, b March 22, 1817, d Oct. 5, 1827; 137 *Clarissa*, b Sept. 29, 1822, m George M. Hard, and has children, Estella C., George W., and John A.; 138 *Sidney W.*, b Sept. 6, 1827, d June 29, 1829. By second wife: 139 *Sidney W.*, b Aug. 1, 1831; 140 *Rufus C.*, b Feb. 28, 1833; 141 *Lucian*, b July 11, 1835; 142 *Infant*, d.

91 JEDEDIAH G.

JEDEDIAH G. ALCOTT, son of John B. and Lois (Gaylord) Alcox, married 1st, Sophia Roper, she died Jan. 19, 1833. He married 2d, Mercy Gaylord of Harpersfield, N. Y. His residence was on Clinton Hill. He died in New Haven, April 22, 1872, ae. 79.

Children: 143 *Mary;* 144 *Olive;* 145 *John;* 146 *Charles;* 147 *Egbert.*

94 AMOS BRONSON.

AMOS B. ALCOTT, son of Joseph C. and Anna (Bronson) Alcott, married Abigail May, May 23, 1830, at King's Chapel, Boston. She was born Oct. 8, 1800. They reside in Concord, Mass. (See Biog. p. 238.)

Children: 148 *Anna Bronson*, b March 16, 1831, at Germantown, Penn., m John B. Pratt, May 23, 1860, and has sons, Frederick A., b March 28, 1863, and John Sewall, b June 24, 1866. Mr. Pratt d Nov. 27, 1870. 149 *Louisa May*, b Nov. 29, 1832, at Germantown, Penn.; 150 *Elizabeth Sewall*, b June 24, 1835, at Boston, d March 14, 1858, at Concord Mass.; 151 *May*, b July 26, 1840, at Concord.

95 CHATFIELD.

CHATFIELD ALCOTT, son of Joseph C. and Anna (Bronson) Alcott, married 1st, Nancy Comstock of Paris, N. Y., 2d, Miranda Bailey, and lived at Oriskany Falls, N. Y.

107 ALBIN.

ALBIN ALCOTT, son of Mark and Mary (Lane) Alcott, married Chloe Finch of Wolcott, June 24, 1807. He died Dec. 11, 1871. His wife died Sept. 24, 1870.

Children: 152 *Emeline*, b Sept. 7, 1829; 153 *Henry Gilbert*, b Feb. 27, 1832; 154 *Mariette*, b March 10, 1834; 155 *Sarah Jane*, b April 19, 1836; 156 *Amos Newton*, b Oct. 17, 1838; *James P.*

111 LUCIUS.

LUCIUS ALCOTT, son of James and Esther (Castle) Alcott, married Emily Roberts of Burlington, and removed to Plymouth Hollow, where he died Oct. 14, 1856, ae. 56.

Children: 157 *Robert C.*, m Mary Trowbridge; 158 *John*, m Frances Knowles, and has a son Charles.

GENEALOGIES.

114 JAMES, 3D.

JAMES ALCOTT, son of James and Esther (Castle) Alcott, married Salina, daughter of Mark Alcott, Aug. 27, 1833, and resides on the homestead of his father and grandfather.

Children: 159 *Esther Melissa*, b April 9, 1835, m Albert N. Lane, Nov. 17, 1855; 160 *Harriet Ann*, b Dec. 15, 1837, m William F. Grilley, Jan. 8, 1860, and has daughter, Eva Melissa, b Oct. 16, 1866; 161 *Emily*, b March 15, 1841, m 1st, Berlin Pritchard, Nov. 1, 1860, and has a son, Evelin James, b Dec. 16, 1866; 162 *Mary* b Sept. 12, 1842, m Coral D. Blakeslee, May 31, 1868.

115 PHINEAS C.

PHINEAS C. ALCOTT, son of James and Esther (Castle) Alcott, married 1st, Emily Horton, and removed to Medina, O., 2d, Sarah Welton of Ohio.

Children: 163 *Esther;* 164 *Mary;* 165 *Lois;* 166 *Eva*.

116 LEVERETT.

LEVERETT ALCOTT, son of James and Esther (Castle) Alcott, married Mary Williams of Ohio. After some experience in selling goods in Southern States, while quite young, he engaged with the Suspender Co., of Waterbury, for a time, in selling their goods in Ohio. After his engagement with this company expired he engaged in the mercantile business for himself. His first store was in Medina, O., and from that place he removed to Cleveland, where he has had large success.

Children: 167 *Eddie*, d young; 168 *Willie;* 169 *Frankie*.

120 WILLIAM ANDRUS.

DR. WILLIAM A. ALCOTT, son of Obed and Anna (Andrus) Alcox, married Phebe L., daughter of Deacon Irad Bronson June 14, 1836. He died March 28, 1859. (See Biog. p. 265.)

Children; 170 *William Penn*, b July 11, 1838; 171 *Phebe Ann*, b Oct. 17, 1840, m Walter Crafts, resides in Alabama, and has a son, Walter Nathan, and daughter, Phebe R., b Nov. 17, 1873.

123 GEORGE GARY.

GEORGE G. ALCOTT, son of Obed and Anna (Andrus) Alcox, married Harriet Nichols, Oct. 25, 1835. He died June 27, 1869.

Children: 172 *Lovina A.*, b Dec. 29, 1836, m H. F. Bassett, April 8, 1855, and has children, Sarah Antoinette, b May 23, 1857, and Frank Alcott, b April 19, 1867. 173 *George Edwin*, b Oct. 1, 1838; 174 *Antoinette*, b April 24, 1840, m O. E. Smith, May 14, 1863, resides in Massachusetts, and has children, Hattie, b June 6, 1864, d March 8, 1867; Annie Alcott, b Oct. 19, 1866; Mabel, b March 23, 1870, d Dec. 19, 1872; Olive, b Dec. 15, 1872. 175 *Anna*, b May 29, 1843, m Edward W. Peck, Sept. 13, 1865, resides in Birmingham, Conn., and has children, Lewis A., b Jan. 17, 1866; Beulah, b May 29, 1868; Lovina, b Jan. 14, 1870, Archibald A., b Sept. 24, 1872. 176 *Elmer*, b March 4, 1848, m Adeline Johnson.

126 DENNISON.

DENNISON ALCOTT, son of Medad and Sylvia (Bronson) Alcox, married Emily Blakeslee, June 24, 1825, at Paris, N. Y., resides, now, in Wisconsin.

Children: 177 *Amelia*, b May 4, 1826; 178 *Maria*, b Oct. 31, 1827; 179 *William*, b July 31, 1833.

128 JOHNSON.

JOHNSON ALCOTT, son of Medad and Sylvia (Bronson) Alcox, married Harriet, daughter of Silas Merrill of Wolcott, June 21, 1830. He died Jan. 23, 1872.

Children: 180 *Adeline*, b April 18, 1831, d July 22, 1848; 181 *Martha*, b March 21, 1833, m John Howd, April 5, 1855, and has a daughter, Hattie, b June 23, 1861; 182 *Emily*, b Jan. 3, 1837, d Aug. 10, 1840; 183 *Burritt*, b May 3, 1839, d May 12, 1863; 184 *Emma*, b Aug. 4, 1844, m Frederick C. Neal of Southington, and has sons, Charlie and Frank.

130 ADDISON.

ADDISON ALCOTT, son of Medad and Sylvia (Bronson) Alcox, married Almira Norton of Wolcott, Sept. 12, 1838, resides in Iowa.

Children: 185 *Amos Bronson*, b June 2, 1839; 186 *Emmerson C.*, b Sept. 22, 1843; 187 *Mary Elizabeth*, b March 12, 1847; 188 *Hannah Jane*, b Aug. 22, 1849; 189 *Celia Maria*, b June 9, 1852; 190 *Carrie Eugenia*, b May 16, 1855.

GENEALOGIES.

135 GAYLORD.— EIGHTH GENERATION.

GAYLORD ALCOTT, son of Riley and Ruth (Frisbie) Alcott, married Caroline E. Blackman of Roxbury, May 20, 1850. She died Feb. 10, 1862. He married 2d, Elizabeth Bronson of Southington, April 18, 1870.

Children by first wife: 191 *Hubert Gaylord*, b June 25, 1851, d Sept. 6, 1851; 192 *Abel Seward*, b Nov. 6, 1852; 193 *Morris Blackman*, b March 13, 1854; 194 *James Lorenzo*, b Feb. 27, 1856; 195 *Edmund Gaylord*, b May 27, 1858, d Sept. 22, 1865; 196 *Carrie E.*, b March 20, 1861, d May 11, 1862.

139 SIDNEY W.

SIDNEY W. ALCOTT, son of Almon and Polly (Cleveland) Alcott, married Mariette Alcott in 1854; resides in Waterbury.

Children: 197 *Clara E.*, b Sept., 1856; 198 *Rufus C.*

140 RUFUS C.

RUFUS C. ALCOTT, son of Almon and Polly (Cleveland) Alcott, married 1st, Mary B. Pinks of New Britain, May 8, 1853, 2d, Maria Hitchcock of Oxford, Sept. 30, 1858.

Children by first wife: 199 *Alice J. C.*, b June 27, 1854. By second wife: 200 *Frederick C.*, b April 8, 1860, d Feb. 4, 1868; 201 *Hubert*, b Sept. 28, 1861; 202 *George A.*, b Oct. 22, 1864; 203 *William R.*, b Feb. 21, 1867; 204 *John F.*, b April 25, 1868; 205 *Antoinette L.*, b July 28, 1871.

141 LUCIAN P.

LUCIAN P. ALCOTT, son of Almon and Polly (Cleveland) Alcott, married Maria E. Robinson of Goshen, March 22, 1859, and lives on his father's homestead.

Children: 206 *Bertha*, b June 7, 1861; 207 *Frances E.*, b May 10, 1864; 208 *Lois G.*, b Jan. 28, 1866; 209 *Eddie L.*, b April 20, 1867.

170 WILLIAM PENN.

REV. WILLIAM P. ALCOTT, son of Dr. William A. and Phebe (Bronson) Alcott, married Sarah Jane, daughter of Rev. David Merrill, of Vermont. (See Biog. p. 278.)

Children : 210 *William Bronson*, b Jan. 6, 1870, d Sept. 10, 1872; 211 *Mary Hunt*, b March 17, 1871; 212 *David Merrill*, b Aug. 25, 1873.

173 GEORGE EDWIN.

GEORGE E. ALCOTT, son of George G. and Harriet (Nichols) Alcott, married Sarah E., daughter of Willis Upson, March 4, 1861. They removed to Page Co., Iowa, November, 1868.

Children: 213 *Willis Upson*, b Jan. 7, 1867; 214 *Maria Antoinette*, b Aug. 18, 1869; 215 *Harriet Eliza*, b Aug. 28, 1871.

ATKINS.

ADKINS, ATKINS.

This name was written on Hartford and Waterbury records Adkins until near 1770, and after that time it uniformly appears on the Waterbury records as Atkins. Adkins is an English name, the heraldic signs indicating that the family were in the Crusades, and received special honor for faithfulness in the defence of fortifications.

JOSIAH.

JOSIAH ADKINS, of Middletown, Conn., married Elizabeth Wetmore, Oct. 8, 1673; died Sept. 12, 1690, leaving seven children minors, and three older, probably by a former wife.

Children: 1 *Thomas;* 2 *Samuel;* 3 *Elizabeth.* Minors: 4 *Sarah*, ae. 16; 5 *Abigail*, 14; 6 *Solomon*, 12; 7 *Josiah*, 10; 8 *Benjamin*, 8; 9 *Ephraim*, 6; 10 *Elizabeth*, 3.

7 JOSIAH, JR.— SECOND GENERATION.

JOSIAH ADKINS, son of Josiah and Elizabeth (Wetmore) Adkins, married Mary Wheeler of Stratford, Dec. 16, 1708, and resided in Middletown. He died Nov. 1, 1724.

Children: 11 *Joseph*, b Sept., 1709; 12 *Mary*, b Oct. 14, 1710; 13 *Elizabeth*, b Feb., 1712; 14 *Abigail*, b Aug. 14, 1713; 15 *Josiah*, b Oct. 11, 1715; 16 *John*, b Oct. 14, 1717, d Nov. 1, 1724.

11 JOSEPH.— THIRD GENERATION.

JOSEPH ADKINS,[*] son of Josiah and Mary (Wheeler) Adkins, married Abigail Rich, and removed to Bristol, Conn., where he purchased seventeen acres of land, the deed being dated, "March

---

[*] See Biog. p. 279. See also pp. 18 and 20.

6, in the 23d year of the reign of King George, 1749-50." He was a miller, and sold, in 1753, eighty acres of land with a corn mill, to Samuel Thompson of Kensington. He removed to Wolcott about 1759, where he had purchased land a year or two before. He was a very important and highly esteemed man in Farmingbury parish. He died in 1782; his wife, Abigail, died in the Autumn of 1796.

Children: 17 *Sarah*, m Isaac Cleveland of Wolcott, and removed to "Cherries Brook" parish, in East Simsbury, Conn. She had two sons and two daughters. 18 *Mary*, m Simeon Plumb of Wolcott; 19 *Joseph*, b about 1743; 20 *Rebecca*, m Heman Wooster, and died in the Eastern part of Massachusetts, leaving two sons and two daughters; 21 *Samuel*, b 1753; 22 *Abigail*, b Aug. 19, 1745, m Gideon Finch of Wolcott; 23 *Elizabeth*, m Joel Lane of Wolcott, May 22, 1776; 24 *Josiah*.

19 JOSEPH, JR.— FOURTH GENERATION.

Deacon Joseph Atkins, son of Joseph and Abigail (Rich) Adkins, married Phebe Hall, and was a respected and reliable citizen, and was deacon of the church nineteen years. He removed to Chenango Co., N. Y., in 1805, and died there April 5, 1820, ae. about 77; his wife, Phebe, died in the Summer of 1828. (See Biog. p. 280.)

Children: 25 *Rosannah*, b March 5, 1768, m Jonas Heacock of Waterbury, Conn., d Jan. 11, 1790; 26 *Sylvia*, b Nov. 3, 1769, d Jan. 11, 1790; 27 *Asahel*, b Feb. 20, 1772; 28 *Samuel*, b Jan. 1, 1774, of whom we have no account; 29 *Xenia*,† b June 30, 1776, d Jan. 8, 1777; 30 *Adah*, b Jan. 9, 1778, d Oct., 1778; 31 *Phebe*, b May 26, 1780, m Joseph Twitchell of Wolcott; 32 *Abigail*, b June 7, 1783, m Ziba Norton of Wolcott; 33 *Joseph*, and 34 *Joel*, twins, b Feb. 10, 1786.

21 SAMUEL.

Samuel Atkins, son of Joseph and Abigail (Rich) Adkins, married Esther, daughter of Jedediah Minor of Wolcott, May 19, 1774; lived and died in Wolcott, July 13, 1788, ae. 35.

Children: 35 *Levi*, bapt Feb. 20, 1785; 36 *Ashbel*, bapt Feb.

---

† Xenia, on church book.

GENEALOGIES. 441

20, 1785; 37 *Betsey*, bapt Feb. 20, 1785, m Reuben Chatfield of Waterbury, removed to Colbrook, Conn., where she died; 38 *Esther*, bapt Sept. 4, 1785, d unmarried; 39 *Samuel*, bapt June 16, 1788.

24 JOSIAH.

JOSIAH ATKINS, son of Joseph and Abigail (Rich) Adkins, married Sarah, daughter of Deacon Josiah Rogers. He left Wolcott in 1802 or 3, and settled in Ashtabula Co., O., sixty miles east of Cleveland. Josiah Atkins was a remarkably strong man, being about six feet in height and very muscular, and of great ambition in work. He is said to have walked seven miles in November and chopped seven cords of coal wood (seven feet long) in one day, and walked home before dark. Charles Upson, Esq., measured off one acre of grass for him, and he mowed it in four hours, then took his place with the other mowers and worked with them all day. There was at least three tons of hay on the acre he mowed. Capt. Nathaniel Lewis said of him, "that he would mow or reap or chop more in one day, or any number of days, than any man in the town."

Children: 40 *Paulina;* 41 *Flaminius;* 42 *Lucinda;* 43 *Philintus*, who d March 19, 1801, by a flood which carried away the grist mill he was in, at Canton, Hartford Co., Conn.; 44 *Diana;* 45 *Josiah;* 46 *Albertus;* 47 *Philintus*.

27 ASAHEL.— FIFTH GENERATION.

ASAHEL ATKINS, son of Deacon Joseph and Phebe (Hall) Atkins, married 1st, —— Warner, 2d, Widow Prudence Metcalf. He resided in Chenango Co., N. Y., where he died April 6, 1857, ae. 85.

Children by first wife: 48 *Fardice W.*, b May 19, 1797, m Pleuma Judson of Connecticut, and lives in the western States; 49 *Selma*, b May 3, 1799, m Robert Ames, Nov. 13, 1818, had sons Fardice, Robert, and two others, and daughter Sallie; 50 *Loverna*, b March 6, 1802, m Jira Fish, has sons Asahel J. and Luke M., and daughters Pleuma, Vienna, and Alvira; 51 *Aaron G.*, b Feb. 12, 1804; 52 *William S.*, b Dec. 8, 1805; 53 *James T.*, b in 1808, m Matilda Cash, had three or four children. Children by second wife: 54 *Sarah Ann*, b Dec. 22, 1814, m

John D. Truman, and has children, Charles E., b March 4, 1835; Arsenith, b Sept. 8, 1836; Sarah M., b Aug. 21, 1838; Mariette A., b March 19, 1841; Marcus H., b June 4, 1844; Harriet C., b July 6, 1846, d Feb. 8, 1847; Harriet L., b May 21, 1849.   55 *Alvira Malinda*, b in 1817, m Ludington Frink, March 18, 1835, had children, Rosina, b Jan. 18, 1836; Frances A., b Sept. 24, 1837; Billings C., b Dec. 30, 1839; Philo L., b May 7, 1842; Marvin A., b Oct. 27, 1845; Mary E., b March 17, 1847.   56 *Mary S.*, b March 26, 1820, m Benjamin Ingersoll, had three sons; 57 *Eliza D.*, b Nov. 6, 1822, m James Becker, has one son; 58 *George;* 59 *Charles D.*, b Dec. 8, 1811.

33 JOSEPH, 3D.

Joseph Atkins, son of Deacon Joseph and Phebe (Hall) Atkins, married Elizabeth Cutting.

Children: 60 *Rumin;* 61 *Cemantha;* 62 *Harriet;* 63 *Lois;* 64 *Norman.*

34 JOEL.

Joel Atkins, son of Deacon Joseph and Phebe (Hall) Atkins, married Esther Burrows of Connecticut. He was skilled as a joiner. He built the first Presbyterian Meeting house in Norwich village, the county seat of Chenango Co., N. Y., and also the first Meeting house in the village of Smyrna of the same county, besides much other work of a superior kind. He left Chenango county many years ago, and has not been heard of since.

Children: 65 *Emily*, d June, 1874; 66 *Julia;* 67 *Adaline;* 68 *Leander*, m Eunice Chapman, and has a son, Irvin; 69 *William;* 70 *Riley.*

35 LEVI.

Levi Atkins, son of Samuel and Esther (Minor) Atkins, served seven years as apprentice to Deacon Elisha Stevens of Naugatuck, as shoemaker and tanner. He married Eunice Smith of Naugatuck, and removed to Middlebury, Conn., where he built a house near the brick-yard, and afterwards removed to Wolcott, where Dennis Pritchard now resides. He afterwards removed to Bucks Hill and thence back to Wolcott, where his son Levi now resides. Here he took care of his grandfather, Jedediah Minor,

GENEALOGIES.

while he lived, and here, also, he died, April 4, 1856, ae. 81; his wife, Eunice, died July 29, 1869, ae. 91.

Children: 71 *Julia*, b 1797, d Oct. 29, 1835, unmarried; 72 *John S.*, b Aug., 1798; 73 *Garry*, born May, 1800; 74 *Harriet*, b 1802, m Asaph Hotchkiss of Wolcott, removed to Medina, O., and died there, leaving one daughter, Caroline; 75 *Erastus*, b 1804; 76 *Betsey*, b 1808, m Prosper Hull of Tolland, Mass., d Oct. 30, 1847, leaving no children; 77 *Esther*, b 1810, m Anson H. Smith of Wolcott; 78 *Levi and* 79 *Leva*, twins, b Nov. 5, 1813; Leva m William Johnson of Wolcott, her children were Henry, b 1835, and Theron, b 1841. 80 *Vina*, b June 13, 1816, d June 10, 1832.

36 ASHBEL.

ASHBEL ATKINS, son of Samuel and Esther (Minor) Atkins, married —— Cowles of Southington, removed to Genesee, N. Y., and died there.

39 SAMUEL, JR.

SAMUEL ATKINS, son of Samuel and Esther (Minor) Atkins, married a daughter of Philo Bronson, and lived and died in Waterbury.

Children: 81 *Edwin ;* 82 *Ellen.*

41 FLAMINIUS.

FLAMINIUS ATKINS, son of Josiah and Sarah (Rogers) Atkins, went to Ohio with his father in 1802-3. He carried the first mail from Buffalo to Detroit, on foot, through the wilderness. He had with him a large dog, two rifles, and an axe. He continued to carry the mail, when he went only half way and met the mail from Detroit and returned to Buffalo. On one occasion he waited for the mail two days and three nights, in a shanty he had put up for the purpose, and while there the old dog drove a large panther up a tree, in the night, and in the morning the long rifle despatched him, to the great relief of the master of the shanty. Mr. Atkins, it is said, was over six feet in height, and chopped, in Ohio, an acre of heavy forest timber as a fallow, for one dollar and a half.

51 AARON G.—SIXTH GENERATION.

AARON G. ATKINS, son of Asahel and —— (Warner) Atkins,

married Maria P. Garton, Feb. 22, 1826. He resides in North Norwich, Chenango Co., N. Y., and is seventy years old, being a grandson of Deacon Joseph Atkins.

Children: 83 *David H.*, b Sept. 17, 1829, m Margaret Cratsonbury, Oct. 25, 1854; 84 *Mary M.*, b Oct. 15, 1831, m David E. Williams, Dec, 15, 1852, d May 31, 1855; 85 *Sally G.*, b Oct. 21, 1839, m David E. Williams, March 31, 1858, d Feb. 2, 1866; 86 *James T.*, b Aug. 7, 1841.

52 WILLIAM S.

WILLIAM S. ATKINS, son of Asahel and —— (Warner) Atkins, married Eunice C. Babcock, Jan. 6, 1839.

Children: 87 *George H.;* 88 *Delos L.*, a lawyer of ten years' standing, now residing in Sherborne, N. Y.; 89 *Carlos;* 90 *Pluma.*

72 JOHN SMITH.

JOHN S. ATKINS, son of Levi and Eunice (Smith) Atkins, married Esther, daughter of Rollin Harrison of Wolcott. He removed to Berlin, Conn., where he died Oct. 25, 1864, ae. 64.

Children: 91 *Wealthy*, m Charles Higgins of Berlin, Conn; 92 *Rollin*, d young; 93 *Adaline*, m Joseph Eggleston, resides in Winsted, Conn.; 94 *Juliette*, d young.

73 GARRY.

GARRY ATKINS, son of Levi and Eunice (Smith) Atkins, married, 1st, Melvina Welton of Plymouth, Conn., and removed to Medina, Ohio, in 1829.

Children: 95 *Ellen W.*; 96 *Harriet A.*; these were born in Wolcott. He has a daughter, 97 *Elizabeth*, by his fifth wife.

78 LEVI, JR.

LEVI ATKINS, son of Levi and Eunice (Smith) Atkins, married 1st, Dec. 11, 1836, Emily Buckingham, of Roxbury, Conn. She died May 1, 1847, and he married, 2d, widow Eunice A. Grilley, Feb. 6, 1848. He is professionally a farmer and shoemaker, but practically a musician. His drum band has long been celebrated through the State, and especially so during the late war. With the violin he is quite at home, as is also his son Homer with the piccolo, and Atkins' Quadrille Band is well and favorably known throughout the county. The one peculiarity about his music is a little preference for the "old-fashioned tunes." He lives comparatively at his ease, but retains the characteristic of his great and first ancestor in Wolcott,— " whatever he undertakes must be carried to completion."

Children by first wife: 98 *Infant*, b 1837, died young; 99 *Mary Emily*, b Nov. 7, 1839, m Leverett Sandford of Wolcott, d Feb. 6, 1873, leaving one son, Leverett, b July 7, 1862; 100 *George*, b Jan. 26, 1842; 101 *Stiles H.*, b Sept. 29, 1844, d March 28, 1871, not married. Children by second wife: 102 *Homer L.*, b Oct. 23, 1850.

100 GEORGE.

GEORGE ATKINS, son of Levi and Emily (Buckingham) Atkins, married Cora Sandford, Oct., 1866.

Children: 103 *Emma*, b March, 1869.

BARNES.

1 STEPHEN, 1ST.

STEPHEN BARNES, said to have come from Long Island, resided a short time in Branford and married Mary ———.
Children: 2 *Benjamin*, b Dec. 13, 1702 ; 3 *Stephen*, b Jan. 2, 1704 or 5; 4 *Sarah*, b May 17, 1708; 5 *Experience*, b Dec. 4, 1710.

2 BENJAMIN.

BENJAMIN BARNES, son of Stephen, 1st, married, Dec. 7, 1727, Hannah Abbott, and settled in the eastern part of Southington.
Children : 6 *Lydia*, b Oct. 22, 1728; 7 *Mary*, b June 17, 1730, m Noah Woodruff, Dec. 5, 1752; 8 *Sarah*, b Sept. 29, 1732, m John Bronson, March 30, 1750; 9 *Deborah*, b Nov. 10, 1734; m Luke Hart, March, 1764; 10 *Eunice*, b Nov. 8, 1737, m Joseph Mallory, 1774, and settled in Wolcott, d Nov. 22, 1793.

3 STEPHEN, 2D.

STEPHEN BARNES, son of Stephen and Mary Barnes, married, Jan. 5, 1725 or 6, Martha Wheadon of Branford, and settled in the southwest part of Southington. He was a large land-holder, and a man of influence and respectability in the community. His wife, Martha, died March 18, 1773, ae. 65, and was buried in Plantsville burying-ground, and on her headstone is written: "I am the first brought here to turn to dust." He died March 27, 1777, ae. 73.
Children : 11 *Mary*, b Oct. 22, 1726, m Jacob Carter, Jr. ; 12 *Stephen*, b. Dec. 3, 1728, settled in Wolcott ; 13 *Jonathan*, b. Feb. 21, 1730 or 31 ; 14 *Martha*, b Aug. 22, 1734 ; 15 *William*, b Nov. 10, 1738; 16 *Nathan*, b Aug. 25, 1742; 17 *Asa*, b Aug. 24, 1745.

GENEALOGIES.

12 STEPHEN, 3D.

Sergeant STEPHEN BARNES, son of Stephen and Martha (Wheadon) Barnes, married Sarah Barnes Nov. 14, 1751, and settled in Wolcott on Southington mountain. He was an active and influential man in Farmingbury Society a number of years from its commencement in 1770, serving as Society's committee, school committee, and Society's collector, and in other offices. He is called Sergeant in 1772, and must have been one of the first officers in the first military company organized under the king, in Farmington part of Farmingbury. He died Aug. 26, 1784, ae. 50. His wife Sarah died March 4, 1798, ae. 69.

Children: 18 *Sarah*, b Aug. 13, 1754, d Nov. 6, 1784 (a few days after her father), ae. 31; 19 *Philemon*, b June 26, 1757, m Anna Scott of Waterbury, in 1779, d Jan. 29, 1795, ae. 38, and his wife, Anna, d Aug. 9, 1798, ae. 41; 20 *Farrington*, b Dec. 2, 1760; 21 *Mark*, b March 12, 1764; 22 *Martha*, b Jan. 29, 1768, m Samuel Poole of Bristol, June 24, 1788; 23 *Nathan*, b Jan. 8, 1771.

13 JONATHAN.

JONATHAN BARNES, son of Stephen and Martha (Wheadon) Barnes, married Elizabeth Woodruff, Aug. 4, 1757, and lived in Southington. He died Jan. 7, 1807, ae. 76. She died Feb. 8, 1814, ae. 76.

Children: 24 *Jonathan*, b March 13, 1763, m Rachel Steel, Feb. 19, 1789; 25 *Elizabeth*, b Oct. 21, 1764, m Rufus Ward, Oct, 10, 1787, went to Ohio; 26 *Mary*, b Mar. 4, 1767, d July 6, 1772; 27 *Stephen*, b Feb. 12, 1769, m Sally Andrews; 28 *Sylvia*, b Aug. 7, 1771, m Roswell Hart, d March 21, 1857; 29 *Lois*, b 1772, m Gideon L. Smith, Nov. 15, 1793; 30 *Levi*, b June 28, 1777, m Hezekiah Woodruff, Oct. 28, 1800; 31 *Joel*, b 1779, m Rebecca Stevens; 32 *Truman*, bapt July 6, 1783, m Lowly Barrett, Jan. 3, 1815.

15 WILLIAM.

WILLIAM BARNES, son of Stephen and Martha (Wheadon) Barnes, married Martha, daughter of John and Elizabeth (Judd) Upson, of Waterbury. He removed from Southington to Southampton, Mass., in March, 1800.

Children: 33 *Hannah*, b Aug. 8, 1757; 34, *Azuba*, b Feb. 27,

1759; 35 *Benjamin*, b Oct. 6, 1761; 36 *Experience*, b Sept. 17, 1763; 37 *William*, b Feb. 2, 1767; 38 *Elijah*, b July 22, 1771.

16 NATHAN.

NATHAN BARNES, son of Stephen and Martha (Wheadon) Barnes, married Sarah Byington, Dec. 1, 1763, and lived and died in the west part of Southington. No children.

17 ASA.

ASA BARNES, son of Stephen and Martha (Wheadon) Barnes, married Phebe Barnes, and lived in what is now called Marion, in Southington. He died Feb. 13, 1819, ae. 73. Sarah, his widow, died Jan., 1811.

Children: 39 *Naomi*, b April 27, 1766; 40, *Allen*, b July 15, 1767, d Sept. 27, 1809; 41 *Selah*, b March 4, 1769; 42 *Ruth*, b Dec. 21, 1771; 43 *Martin*, b June 17, 1773, d Sept. 29, 1776; 44 *Eli*, b May 21, 1775; 45 *Asa*, b July 22, 1777; 46 *Martin*, b March, 1779, d Sept., 1780; 47 *Ira*, b Nov. 15, 1781; 48 *Philo*, b March 2, 1783; 49 *Dennis*, who died Sept., 1811.

20 FARRINGTON.

FARRINGTON BARNES, son of Stephen and Sarah (Barnes) Barnes, married Sally Talmage of Wolcott, Dec. 25, 1783, and resided a little north of David Frost, on Southington Mountain. He afterwards removed to Northampton, Mass.

Children: 50 *Archibald;* 51 *Nathan.*

21 MARK.

MARK BARNES, son of Stephen and Sarah (Barnes) Barnes, married Sarah Roberts of Wolcott, Nov. 16, 1786.

Children: 52 *Abigail*, b March 11, 1789; 53 *Sarah*, b April 26, 1791; 54 *Mark*, b Dec. 13, 1795; 55 *Sylvia*, b Aug. 11, 1798; 56 *Martha*, b Nov. 18, 1800; 57 *Moses Roberts*, b June 18, 1803.

23 NATHAN.

NATHAN BARNES, son of Stephen and Sarah (Barnes) Barnes, married Elizabeth ———

Children: 58 *Nathan Whiting*, b Sept. 18, 1797; 59 *Eliza*, b Dec. 14, 1798.*

---

* There have been other families of this name (Barnes) in Wolcott, some of whom came from Waterbury.

BARTHOLOMEW.

WILLIAM BARTHOLOMEW was born in Northford, Conn., Nov. 13, 1783. He married Hannah C., daughter of Dea. Isaac Bronson, Nov. 13, 1811, and lived in Wolcott, nearly a mile south of the center. He united with the church in 1828, under the labors of Mr. Scranton, and was a valuable man to the church and community, serving both in various offices. He died March 22, 1850, aged 66. His wife, Hannah, is still living (1873).

Children: 1 *Thankful Bronson*, b Sept. 22, 1812; 2 *Israel Beard Woodward*, b June 23, 1814; 3 *Bertha*, b Sept. 3, 1816, m David Gaylord, of Wallingford, Oct. 4, 1841; 4 *John Milton*, b Feb. 3, 1818, d Feb. 4, 1818; 5 *Sarah Jane*, b Nov. 28, 1819, m Ira H. Smith of North Haven, Feb. 27, 1846; 6 *Emeret Amelia*, b Oct. 12, 1832, m Julius Morse of Cheshire, June, 1855.

2 ISRAEL B. W.

ISRAEL B. W. BARTHOLOMEW, son of William and Hannah (Bronson) Bartholomew, married Maria Theresa Byington of Southington, Sept., 1841. He died in Hannibal, Mo., Sept. 1, 1846, ae. 32. His wife, Maria Theresa, died in St. Louis, Mo., Jan. 26, 1844, ae. 21.

BEECHER.

1 JOHN.

JOHN BEECHER'S name appears very early in New Haven records.

Children recorded in New Haven: 2 *John*, b Aug. 9, 1671; 3 *Mary*, b Feb. 23, 1672; 4 *Johanna*, b July 21, 1677; 5 *Jemima*, b Feb. 11, 1681; 6 *Joseph*, b Feb. 13, 1683; 7 *Ebenezer*, b April 12, 1686.

6 JOSEPH, 1ST.

JOSEPH BEECHER, son of John the first, lived in New Haven.

Children: 8 *Allis*, b Jan. 28, 1695; 9 *Joseph*, b Nov. 22, 1698; 10 *Lidiah*, b Feb. 15, 1700; 11 *Hezekiah*, b June 14, 1703; 12 *Nathaniel*, b March 7, 1706; 13 *Eliphalet*, b May 31, 1711.

9 JOSEPH, 2D.

JOSEPH BEECHER, 2d, married Sarah Ford, May 15, 1729, and lived in New Haven.

Children: 14 *Joseph*, b Feb. 9, 1731; 15 *Moses*, b Feb. 2, 1733; 16 *Timothy*, b Feb. 8, 1735; 17 *Abell*, b Nov. 17, 1737; 18 *Titus*, b July 5, 1740; 19 *Amos*, b June 10, 1743.

14 JOSEPH, 3D.

Capt. JOSEPH BEECHER, son of Joseph and Sarah (Ford) Beecher, married Esther Potter, and settled in northeastern part of Wolcott, before the year 1770. He was a reliable, active man in the Society and church many years. He is called captain in 1778, in the records of the Society, and must have been among the first officers of the first military company in Farmington part of Farmingbury. He is said to have been first cousin to Rev. Dr. Lyman Beecher.

GENEALOGIES. 451

Children: 20 *John*, b Jan, 10, 1756; 21 *Nathan*, bapt June 16, 1774, m Lucy, daughter of Dea. Peck (probably); 22 *Sybil*, bapt June 16, 1774, m (probably) Jesse Potter of New Haven; 23 *Joseph*, bapt June 16, 1774; 24 *Hezekiah L.*, bapt June 16, 1774; 25 *Esther*, bapt Aug. 7, 1774; 26 *Sylvester*, bapt April 15, 1781.

17 ABELL.

ABEL BEECHER lived in Wolcott, and died Oct. 27, 1811, and his son, 27 *Abel*, died in 1813.

19 AMOS.

CAPT. AMOS BEECHER was in Wolcott some years, his name not being as prominent on the records of the Society as his brother Joseph's.

Children: 28 *Samuel;* 29 *Lucy;* 30 *Amos;* 31 *Rebecca;* 32 *Salmon I.*, all bapt July 29, 1781.

20 JOHN.

JOHN BEECHER son of Joseph and Esther (Potter) Beecher, married Susanna Alcox, and lived on or near the homestead of his father. She died Nov. 3, 1836, ae. 68. He died Aug. 4, 1829, ae. 75.

Children: 33 *Lyman*, b Aug. 19, 1793, and was killed by the falling of a tree, Jan. 17, 1805; 34 *John*, b May 5, 1795; 35 *Julia*, b March 27, 1797, d Nov. 5, 1846; 36 *Leonard*, b Nov. 27, 1798; 37 *Delight*, b May 17, 1801, m Marcus H. Upson, Jan. 13, 1830, removed to Burlington, Conn.; 38 *Jesse Lyman*, b Oct. 16, 1803, d Nov. 22, 1841; 39 *Esther Potter*, b March 1, 1806, m Jarvis R. Bronson, June 24, 1835; 40 *Henry*, b Jan. 4, 1809.

34 JOHN.

JOHN BEECHER, son of John and Susannah (Alcox) Beecher, married widow Vina Smith, July 26, 1826. She was born May 11, 1800. He resides on his father's homestead.

Children: 41 *Ellen Augusta*, b June 12, 1827, m Rufus Norton, April 15, 1845; 42 *Angeline Minerva*, b Sept. 6, 1829, d July 15, 1846; 43 *Burritt William*, b Aug. 1, 1832, d Jan. 6, 1859; 44 *Infant*, d young.

36 LEONARD.

LEONARD BEECHER, son of John and Susannah (Alcox) Beecher, married Polly, daughter of John Frisbie, built a fine house near his father.

Children: 45 *John Merritt*, b 1825 ; 46 *Noble Leonard*, b Jan., 1838.

40 HENRY.

HENRY BEECHER, son of John and Susannah (Alcox) Beecher, married Harriet Barnes, and lives in Bristol.

Children: 47 *John*, lives in Brookline, N. Y. ; 48 *Joseph*, lives in New Jersey ; 49 *Dwight*, lives in Bristol, Conn.

43 BURRITT WILLIAM.

BURRITT W. BEECHER, son of John and Vina (Smith) Beecher, married Esther A., daughter of Dea. A. H. Plumb, July 8, 1855.

Children : 50 *Arthur F.*, b Aug. 29, 1856, d Sept. 13, 1858; 51 *Helen A.*, b June 28, 1858.

BRADLEY.*

1 TIMOTHY.

TIMOTHY BRADLEY came from North Haven to Wolcott about the year 1769 and resided first in a small log house. In 1772 he built a frame house which is still occupied by some of his descendants. He was a member of the Congregational church, a good citizen, and kind neighbor. (See Biog., p. 298.)

Children: 3 *Asahel;* 4 *Timothy;* 5 *Ziba;* 6 *Moses;* 7 *Amasa;* 8 *Amon;* 9 *Chloe;* 10 *Lydia;* 11 *Phebe.*

2 ABEL.

ABEL BRADLEY was a brother of Timothy and came from North Haven to Wolcott and lived near his brother in the northern part of the town, on the west side of Cedar Swamp.

Children: 12 *Abigail;* 13 *Rosanna;* 14 *John,* who weighed three hundred pounds and was strong in proportion to his unusual weight.

3 ASAHEL.

ASAHEL BRADLEY, son of Timothy, lived in Wolcott.

Children: 15 *Asahel;* 16 *Rosetta;* 17 *Alpheus;* 18 *Barzilla;* 19 *Timothy;* 20 *Melinda;* 21 *Stephen,* who had three children.

4 TIMOTHY, JR.

TIMOTHY BRADLEY, son of Timothy, lived in Wolcott.

Children: 22 *Amasa;* 23 *Ziba;* 24 *Amon;* 25 *Lydia;* 26 *Phebe;* 27 *Chloe.*

5 ZIBA.

ZIBA BARDLEY, son of Timothy, Senr., lived in Wolcott.

Children: 28 *Harry;* 29 *Lovinia;* 30 *Nancy.*

---

* A number of the Bradley families removed to Ohio as pioneers.

6 MOSES.

MOSES BRADLEY, son of Timothy, 1st, lived in Wolcott.
Children : 31 *Lue ;* 32 *Sylvester;* 33 *Riley ;* 34 *Cynthia.*

7 AMASA.

AMASA BRADLEY, son of Timothy, 1st, lived in Wolcott.
Children : 35 *Rachel ;* 36 *Harry ;* 37 *Jemima ;* 38 *Chloe.*

8 AMON.

AMON BRADLEY, son of Timothy, 1st, lived in Wolcott.
Children : 39 *Maria ;* 40 *Albert,* had three children ; 41 *Lewis,* had three daughters and one son ; 42 *Sally.*

15 ASAHEL, JR.

ASAHEL BRADLEY, son of Asahel, 15th.
Children : 43 *Alpheus ;* 44 *Orange ;* 45 *Lyman ;* 46 *Orlando.*

18 BARZILLA.

BARZILLA BRADLEY, son of Asahel, Senr.
Children : 47 *Asahel ;* 48 *Herman ;* 49 *Stephen,* and two more.

19 TIMOTHY.

TIMOTHY BRADLEY, son of Asahel, Senr.
Children : 50 *Mariette ;* 51 *Burwell ;* 52 *Emmerson.*

22 AMASA.

AMASA BRADLEY, son of Timothy, Jr.
Children : 53 *Harry ;* 54 *Levi ;* 55 *Rachel ;* 56 *Jemima ;* 57 *Diadama.*

23 ZIBA.

ZIBA BRADLEY, son of Timothy, Jr.
Children : 58 *Harry* ; 59 *Lovinia* ; 60 *Nancy.*

24 AMON.

AMON BRADLEY, son of Timothy, Jr.
Children : 61 *Harry* ; 62 *Alpheus* ; 63 *Volney.*

33 RILEY.

RILEY BRADLEY, son of Moses, and grandson of Timothy, 1st.

GENEALOGIES.

Children : 64 *Charles*; 65 *Eliza*; 66 *Edward Burdett*; 67 *Moses*; 68 *Mary*; 69 *George Adelbert*; 70 *Nancy*; 71 *Jennette*; 72 *Harriet*; 73 *Virginia*.

51 BURWELL.

BURWELL BRADLEY, son of Timothy, 19th.
Children: 74 *Augusta*; 75 *Frances*; 76 *Jesse*; 77 *Nellie*.

52 EMMERSON.

EMMERSON BRADLEY, son of Timothy, 19th.
Children: 78 *Wallace*; 79 *Winslow*; 80 *Bertie*.

66 EDWARD BURDETT.

EDWARD B. BRADLEY. son of Riley, 33.
Children: 81 *Lilla*; 82 *Edward*; 83 *Hattie*; 84 *Harry*; 85 *William*.

69 GEORGE ADELBERT.

GEORGE A. BRADLEY, son of Riley, 33.
Children : 86 *John*; 87 *Ralph*.

BROCKETT.

1 SAMUEL.

SAMUEL BROCKETT removed from Wallingford to Wolcott, having several children who were born in Wallingford. His wife, Ruth, died in Wolcott, April 14, 1780.

Children: 2 *Eunice*, b Jan. 15, 1744; 3 *Zuer*, b March 24, 1746; 4 *Joel*, b June 14, 1739; 5 *Joel*, b July 28, 1760; 6 *Zenas*, b July 12, 1752; 7 *Benjamin*, b Oct. 1, 1760; 8 *Rachel*, d in Wolcott, Oct. 17, 1776.

3 ZUER.

ZUER BROCKETT, son of Samuel and Ruth Brockett, married Eunice ———, and lived in the northeastern part of the town, his name being found on parish records very early. His wife, Eunice, died March 11, 1833, ae. 81. He died Sept. 17, 1834, ae. 87.

Children: 9 *Ramel;* 10 *Titus*, m Sarah, daughter of Dea. Justus Peck, and d Feb. 21, 1857, ae. 77. His wife, Sarah, d April 23, 1850, ae. 71.

AMOS.

AMOS BROCKETT, born April 10, 1756, married Lucy Dutton, March 27, 1783, and lived in northeast part of Wolcott.

Children: 1 *Zephna*, b June 21, 1784; 2 *Eli*, b Sept. 11, 1786; 3 *Amos*, b April 16, 1789; 4 *Alva*, b Jan. 20, 1792; 5 *Lucy*, b Dec. 8, 1793; 6 *Joel*, b Sept. 9, 1795; 7 *Rhoda*, b March 8, 1798; 8 *Rebecca*, b Oct. 9, 1799; 9 *Rachel*, b Sept. 22, 1801. By second wife, Rachel: 10 *Benjamin D.*, b Oct. 14, 1803; 11 *Zenas*, b May 4, 1806; 12 *Timothy D.*, b Dec. 31, 1808.

BROOKS.

1 HENRY.

HENRY BROOKS, Sen., of Cheshire, had eight children : 2 *Henry;* 3 *Mary;* 4 *Nabby;* 5 *Stephen;* 6 *Jerusha;* 7 *Phebe;* 8 *Sarah;* 9 *Joel.*

2 HENRY.

HENRY BROOKS, Jr., lived in Cheshire, and had eleven children : 10 *Henry;* 11 *Allen;* 12 *Enos;* 13 *Tenna;* 14 *Betsey;* 15 *Mary;* 16 *Jesse;* 17 *Aaron;* 18 *John;* 19 *Elias,* b May 2, 1796; 20 *Simeon.*

19 ELIAS.

ELIAS BROOKS, son of Henry, Jr., married, 1st, Juliana Ives of Cheshire, May 26, 1824. She was born April 19, 1806, died Jan. 14, 1840. He married, 2d, Abigail Austin, Nov. 23, 1840.

Children by first wife : 21 *Joel,* b June 20, 1825, d June, 1861 ; 22 *Samuel,* b June 8, 1827, d Nov., 1850 ; 23 *Levi,* b Oct. 6, 1828, d April 28, 1857 ; 24 *Aaron,* b Sept. 5, 1831, d Nov. 14, 1853 ; 25 *Julia Ann,* b June 3, 1834. Children by second wife : 26 *Martha Adaline,* b Nov. 1, 1842 ; 27 *Esther A.,* b Oct. 6, 1846, d June, 1850 ; 28 *Benjamin Franklin,* b March 17, 1852; 29 *Henry Elias,* d an infant.

BRONSON *

1 JOHN.

JOHN BRONSON, believed to have been one of the company who came with Mr. Hooker to Hartford, in 1636, was in the bloody Pequot battle of 1637. He removed to Tunxis (Farmington) about 1641, and was one of the seven pillars at the organization of the Farmington church in 1652. He died Nov. 28, 1680. His estate was £312.

Children: 2 *Jacob*, b Jan., 1841, m Mary —— and lived in Farmington, in the Society of Kensington; 3 *John*, b Jan., 1644; 4 *Isaac*, b Nov., 1645; 5 *Mary*, m —— Ellis; 6 *Abraham*, removed to Lyme, where he died at an advanced age, leaving descendants; 7 *Dorcas*, m Stephen Hopkins of Hartford; 8 *Sarah*.

3 JOHN.

JOHN BRONSON, son of the first of the name in Farmington, was an early settler in Mattatuck (Waterbury) where he died.

Children: 9 *John*, b 1670; 10 *Sarah*, b 1672; 11 *Dorothy*, b 1675; 12 *Ebenezer*, b 1677; 13 *William*, b 1682; 14 *Moses*, b 1686; 15 *Grace*, b 1689.

9 JOHN.

JOHN BRONSON, son of John of Waterbury, removed from Waterbury to Southington, and married Rachel Buck of Weathersfield, Jan., 1697.

Children: 16 *John*, b Nov. 21, 1698, d 1716; 17 *David*, b Aug. 9, 1704; 18 *Jonathan*, b May 14, 1706; 19 *Joseph*, b June 15, 1708; 20 *Rachel*, b July 6, 1710; 21 *Mary*, b Jan. 30, 1712; 22 *James*, b Nov. 29, 1713.

* This name is often spelled Brownson in the early records.

GENEALOGIES.

18 JONATHAN.

JONATHAN BRONSON, son of John and Rachel (Buck) Bronson, married Abigail Clark, May 17, 1732, lived in Southington, and died Aug. 20, 1751, ae. 45.

Children: 23 *Asahel*, b Oct. 25, 1733; 24 *John*, bapt July 6, 1735; 25 *Ann*, b March 30, 1737; 26 *Abigail*, b Feb. 18, 1739; 27 *Jonathan*, b Dec. 24, 1740; 28 *Son* b Jan. 20, 1743, d; 29 *Zadoc*, b Aug. 7, 1745; 30 *Huldah*, b April 18, 1747; 31 *Lois*, b Jan. 6, 1749; 32 *Isaac*, b June 20, 1751.

24 JOHN.

JOHN BRONSON, son of Jonathan and Abigail (Clark) Bronson, married, March 30, 1758, Sarah Barnes. She was born Sept. 27, 1732, and died Dec. 17, 1804, ae. 73. Mr. Bronson settled in Wolcott soon after his marriage, probably. The earliest deed of his that I have seen is dated 1762. He owned but one farm, so far as known, that being the one now owned by Dea. George W. Carter. He was a man of rigid intellectual qualities and vigorous physical nature. Being reared in the days of Calvinistic theology he was a Calvinist of the strictest sort, and having had but little advantages of education, he entertained, like many of his day, a decided prejudice against the higher departments of education, as disqualifying men for the more honest employments of life. Hence when his son Isaac desired to go to college the father was most decidedly opposed to it. He was a very hard worker, and retained marvelous strength after he was eighty years old. He was considerably active in the parish Society for a number of years after its organization. After the death of his first wife he married the widow of Curtiss Hall. He died Nov. 10, 1838, ae. 103 years, 3 months, and 25 days, thereby living to be the oldest of any person in the town except the mother of David Norton.

Children: 33 *Joel*, b March 9, 1759, lived in Burlington, Ct.; his son was the well known Dr. Bronson of that place. 34 *Isaac*, b July 19, 1761; 35 *Benjamin Barnes*, b Aug. 19, 1763, lived and died in Southington; 36 *Philenor*, bapt in Southington, April 27, 1766; 37 *Hannah;* 38 *John*, b Jan. 31, 1776.

29 ZADOC.

ZADOC BRONSON, son of Jonathan and Abigail (Clark) Bronson,

married Eunice Dutton Nov. 19, 1766, and settled in Wolcott, where he was an active man some years in the parish Society, serving particularly as grave digger and school committee in the North East District.

Children : 39 *Abigail Dutton*, bapt Dec. 4, 1774; 40 *Zadoc*, bapt Oct. 6, 1776; 41 *Zenas*, bapt April 23, 1780; 42 *Rhoda*, bapt Oct. 16, 1785 ; 43 *Eunice*, bapt May 10, 1789. These were all baptized in Farmingbury parish ; there may have been others baptized in Southington.

33 JOEL.

JOEL BRONSON, son of John and Sarah (Barnes) Bronson, married ———, and resided in Burlington, Conn.

Children : 44 *Ira*, who married a Frisbie; 45 *Samuel*, m Ursula Humphrey ; 46 *Avis*, m Simeon Woodruff of Burlington, and was the mother of Dr. Woodruff of New Britain ; 47 *Mary*, m Pettibone of Burlington; 48 *Nancy*, m Woodruff; 49 *Joel ;* 50 *Cynthia*, m Bull of Plymouth.

34 ISAAC.

Deacon ISAAC BRONSON, son of John and Sarah (Barnes) Bronson, married, Feb. 10, 1773, Thankful Clark (probably), the daughter of Israel Clark of Wolcott, who, I think, lived where Ransom Hall now (1874) resides. He resided much of his life at Wolcott Center, being one of the most active and highly esteemed men in the Society, church, and town, that ever lived in it. He died April 28, 1845, ae. 84. His widow, Thankful, died June 23, 1847, ae. 93. (See Biog. p. 287.)

Children : 51 *Isaac*, b Aug. 18, 1784, d Oct. 13, 1802, ae. 18 ; 52 *Clark*, b Dec. 6, 1786; 53 *Irad*, b Aug. 27, 1788; 54 *Hannah C.*, b Aug. 25, 1790, m William Bartholomew of Northford, Conn., lived in Wolcott ; 55 *Thankful*, b Oct. 28, 1792, d May 4, 1808 ; 56 *Sarah*, and 57 *Mary*, twins, b July 28, 1795. *Sarah* married Samuel Atwater of Hamden, and removed to Windham, N. Y., and d 1866, and *Mary*, m Harry Tuttle, and lived in Cheshire, d Dec. 12, 1854, ae. 59 ; 58 *Urania*, b Dec. 10, 1799, m Sheldon Frisbie, removed to Ohio, and thence to Illinois, where she d July, 1854, ae. 54.

38 JOHN, JR.

JOHN BRONSON, son of John and Sarah (Barnes) Bronson, married Hannah Root of Farmington. She was born Feb. 14, 1781, and died Feb. 24, 1853, ae. 72. He lived in Wolcott, on his father's homestead, and died Nov. 25, 1866, ae. 91.

Children : 59 *Jarvis Root*, b April 5, 1808 ; 60 *Sarah Ann*, b April 1, 1711, m George W. Carter ; 61 *Stillman*, b Sept. 11, 1812 ; 62 *Pitkin*, b May 2, 1815 ; 63 *Sarah Maria*, b June 18, 1823, d Sept. 5, 1827.

52 CLARK.

CLARK BRONSON, son of Isaac and Thankful (Clark) Bronson, married, May 24, 1813, Experience Hart of Burlington, Conn. She was born July 9, 1792, and died in Wolcott, Jan. 13, 1864. He resided in Wolcott the greater part of his life, and was an active and honored man in the church and community. He died in Hartford, Jan. 20, 1868, ae. 82.

Children : 64 *Isaac H.*, b April 28, 1814, d Dec, 29, 1814 ; 65 *Oliver H.*, b Jan. 24, 1816 ; 66 *Sylvia M.*, b Feb. 5, 1818, d Feb. 19, 1819 ; 67 *Sylvia M.*, b March 13, 1820, d March 3, 1829 ; 68 *Robert Clark*, b March 29, 1825, d March 12, 1850 ; 69 *Betsey B. Tuttle*, adopted daughter, b Sept. 1, 1835, resides in Litchfield.

53 IRAD.

Deacon IRAD BRONSON, son of Isaac and Thankful (Clark) Bronson, married Phebe Norton of Bristol, Nov. 6, 1811. He was deacon of the church in Wolcott nine years, and was highly esteemed. He removed to Southington, thence to Bristol, where he still resides, being in his 86th year.

Children : 70 *Phebe L.*, b Nov. 8, 1812, m Dr. William A. Alcott, June 14, 1836 ; 71 *Isaac*, b May 15, 1815, is married, and resides in Bristol, no children ; 72 *Elizabeth T.*, b Jan. 27, 1818, not married.

59 JARVIS ROOT.

JARVIS R. BRONSON, son of John and Hannah (Root) Bronson, married Esther P., daughter of John Beecher of Wolcott, June 24, 1835, and resides in the northeast part of the town, retaining distinctly some of the characteristics of the Bronson family.

Children : 73 *Lyman B.*, b Oct. 7, 1836 ; 74 *Son*, b Nov. 6, 1843, d ; 75 *Martha Elton*, an adopted daughter, b Oct. 2, 1838.

61 STILLMAN.

STILLMAN BRONSON, son of John and Hannah (Root) Bronson, married Charlotte R. Lindsley of Wolcott, March 29, 1840, and resides in the northeast part of the town.

Children : 76 *Emerson R.*, b March 21, 1841, d Feb. 21, 1846 ; 77 *Lucy S.*, b June 26, 1843, m Benjamin C. Lum, Oct. 31, 1867, and resides in New Haven, having a son, William S., b Aug. 2, 1868, and daughter, Charlotte C., b Nov. 6, 1871 ; 78 *Harriet L.*, b Dec. 7, 1844, d Nov. 10, 1869 ; 79 *E. Bruce*, b Feb. 23, 1847, d Oct. 7, 1862; 80 *Benjamin L.*, b July 16, 1849; 81 *Elliott*, b May 13, 1851 ; 82 *Esther L. M.*, b July 16, 1853, d Oct. 25, 1869 ; 83 *Edith M.*, b Nov. 1, 1860.

62 PITKIN.

PITKIN BRONSON, son of John and Hannah (Root) Bronson, married Sarah Merriam, and lives in Waterbury.

Children : 84 *John T.;* 85 *Edward P.;* 86 *Nellie ;* 87 *Willie.*

65 OLIVER HART.

OLIVER H. BRONSON, son of Clark and Experience (Hart) Bronson, married Emily Munson of Wallingford, Ct., Nov. 14, 1840. He learned the trade of carriage making of Chauncy Munson of Wallingford, and afterwards married his eldest daughter. He resided a short time in Meriden and removed thence to Waterbury where, in 1841, he established a carriage business which he carried on successfully until about 1852 when he engaged in the Waterbury Lumber and Coal Co., where he remained until 1863. He then removed to Hartford and opened a coal yard, in which business he continued until his death, Nov. 28, 1867. His widow still resides in Hartford.

Children: 88 *Henry Trumbull*, b Sept. 18, 1842 ; 89 *Alice Emily*, b April 21, 1848 ; 90 *Lillie Martha*, b March 6, 1859, d May 31, 1862; 91 *Arthur Hart*, b May 14, 1865.

73 LYMAN B.

Deacon LYMAN B. BRONSON, son of Jarvis R. and Esther P. (Beecher) Bronson married Martha A., daughter of Mark Tuttle, Jan. 1, 1859. He united with the church when thirteen years of age, and was active and very successful in his church relations.

At the time of his death he was deacon of the church, superintendent of the Sunday school, and one of the most reliable and valuable young men of the community, and many persons remarked concerning him, that "Any one could be more easily spared than he." After a few days sickness with diphtheria he closed his earthly life May 27, 1866.

Children: 92 *Edward L.*, b May 18, 1860; 93 *Esther Ardelia*, b Aug. 27, 1862, d June 23, 1866.

88 HENRY TRUMBULL.

HENRY T. BRONSON, son of Oliver H. and Emily (Munson) Bronson, married Ellen Amelia Philips of New York, June 10, 1869, and resides in Hartford, Ct. He enlisted, in Aug., 1862, in the 23d Connecticut Volunteers, and served as 1st Sergeant of Co. A, one year, about New Orleans, under Gen. Banks, and a part of the time in erecting fortifications under Gen. Weitzel.

Children: 94 *Oliver Hart*, b March 26, 1870; 95 *William Henry*, b Sept. 28, 1871; 96 *Helen Chauncey*, b Jan. 3, 1873.

BROWN.

WILLIAM H. BROWN, born March 5, 1828, in Boston; married Mary A. E. Richards, April 11, 1871. Resides half a mile south of Wolcott Center.
Child: *Willie*, b Jan. 16, 1872, d Oct. 17, 1872.

1 JOHN.

JOHN BROWN was born July 4, 1844, in Maryland. He married, August 13, 1866, Sarah Ann Pratt of Cheshire, born Jan. 1, 1848. They reside near Mr. Isaac Hough's, on the road from Wolcott to Waterbury.
Children: 2 *George Winfield*, b July 14, 1868; 3 *Nellie Ann*, b May 10, 1870.

BYINGTON.

1 DANIEL.

DANIEL BYINGTON, Senr., born Sept. 18, 1711, was son of Jonathan of Branford, came to Wolcott, and was one of the leading men in organizing the parish of Farmingbury, and lived at the "mill place." He was chosen clerk of the Society at its first meeting, and held that office one year, after which his son accepted it. He and his wife Sarah united with the church in May after its organization. He appears to have been a mechanic, and to have had a shop for the construction and repairing of various wooden articles of use in those days. He died Nov. 11, 1781, but no grave-stone with an inscription marks his resting-place, for at most of the graves constructed in those early times there were only small field-stones placed without any inscriptions.

Children: 2 *Daniel;* 3 *Samuel.*

2 DANIEL, JR.

DANIEL BYINGTON, Jr., married Elizabeth Hall, daughter of the first settler of that name in Wolcott. He was clerk of the Society twenty-six or seven years, and was on committees of various kinds for many years. His mechanical skill, and that of his son Daniel, was celebrated for years for the making of the "great wheels" for spinning wool, and the "little wheels" for spinning flax. (See note, page 71.)

Children: 4 *Moses;* 5 *Jared;* 6 *Jonah;* 7 *Heman;* 8 *Daniel;* 9 *Anne,* all baptized March 20, 1774; 10 *Elizabeth,* bapt July 30, 1775; 11 *Rufus,* bapt June 14, 1778; 12 *Lydia,* bapt June 10, 1781; 13 *Zebulon,* bapt Feb. 13, 1785; 14 *Active,* bapt Oct. 26, 1788.

3 SAMUEL.

SAMUEL BYINGTON, son of Daniel Byington, Senr., married Olive ——, and had a farm and "tavern," or public house, at Wolcott Center. Many of the business meetings of the Society were held at his house.

Children: 15 *Abraham*, bapt July 19, 1789; 16 *Adnah*, bapt Nov. 27, 1791.

8 DANIEL, 3D.

DANIEL BYINGTON, son of Daniel and Elizabeth (Hall) Byington, married Susy ——, and lived at the mill place, and was a mechanic with his father.

Children: 17 *Zina*, b July 20, 1795; 18 *Amy*, b Oct. 28, 1797; 19 *Hiram*, b Aug. 19, 1800. By second wife: 20 *Polly*, b Sept. 3, 1805; 21 *Randal*, b Sept. 15, 1806; 22 *Wells*, b Nov. 8, 1808; 23 *Coral*, b June 12, 1811; 24 *Ambrose Ives*, b Feb. 18, 1813; 25 *William Robinson*, b July 25, 1814.

CARTER.

1 JACOB, 1ST.

JACOB CARTER came from Southold, L. I., to Branford, Conn., and married Dorcas Tyler, Dec. 4, 1712. She died 1735 or 6.

Children: 2 *Sarah*, b Feb. 4, 1714; 3 *Jacob*, 2d, b Nov. 26, 1716; 4 *Abel*, b June 4, 1718.

3 JACOB, 2D.

JACOB CARTER, son of Jacob and Dorcas (Tyler) Carter, married Mary, daughter of Stephen Barnes, 2d, and settled in the south part of Southington, where he died July 6, 1796. Mary, his wife, died Oct. 23, 1788, ae.62.

Children: 5 *Jacob*, b May 1, 1745; 6 *Sarah*, b Sept. 16, 1747; 7 *Stephen*, b July 11, 1749; 8 *Jonathan*, b May 20, 1751; 9 *Ithiel*, b Aug. 1, 1753, lived in Warren, and later in Torrington and other parts; 10 *Isaac*, b May 12, 1757; 11 *Levi*, b Sept. 23, 1762. These all settled in Wolcott. 12 *Elihu*, bapt March 18, 1759, lived in Southington.*

4 ABEL.

ABEL CARTER, son of Jacob and Dorcas (Tyler) Carter, married Mary Coach April 17, 1739.

Children: 13 *Dorcas*, b June 28, 1739; 14 *John*, b Nov. 20, 1741; 15 *Daniel*, b May 29, 1744; 16 *Abel*, b March 21, 1747.

5 JACOB, 3D.

JACOB CARTER, son of Jacob and Mary (Barnes) Carter, married Mary Hitchcock, and settled on East Mountain, Wolcott. His wife, Mary, was killed by being thrown from a wagon in

---

* For these names see Town Records of Branford and Southington.

Becket, Mass., in 1818. After her death he lived with his children in the latter place.

Children: 17 *Preserve*, b Feb. 24, 1773; 18 *Marcus*, b July 28, 1774, removed to Massachusetts, thence to New York and Michigan; 19 *Rhoda*, b Nov. 6, 1775, m Washington Upson; 20 *Mary*, b Feb. 16, 7781; 21 *Uri*, b June 15, 1782; 22 *Gaius*, and 23 *Loami*, twins, b Dec. 2, 1785.

7 STEPHEN.

STEPHEN CARTER, son of Jacob and Mary (Barnes) Carter, married Triphena Upson, June 2d, 1779, and lived for a time where Dea. Miles S. Upson does, and afterward he lived near Mahlon Hotchkiss' present dwelling. They are all removed from Wolcott.

Children: 24 *Stephen*, bapt Jan. 15, 1786; 25 *Reuben*, bapt Jan. 15, 1786.

8 JONATHAN.

JONATHAN CARTER, son of Jacob and Mary (Barnes) Carter, married Abigail Moulthrop, Jan. 10, 1776, and lived in Wolcott.

Children: 26 *Joel*, b Dec. 5, 1778; 27 *Ira*, b May 4, 1781; 28 *Asa*, bapt July 4, 1784; 29 *Eli*, b Oct. 5, 1786.

10 ISAAC.

ISAAC CARTER, son of Jacob and Mary (Barnes) Carter, married ——.

Children: 30 *Seth*, b March 17, 1783; 31 *Sybil*, b Jan. 8, 1785; 32 *Zera*, b April 17, 1787; 33 *Salmon*, and 34 *Salma*, twins, b April 20, 1789.

12 ELIHU.

ELIHU CARTER, son of Jacob and Mary (Barnes) Carter, married Mercy Scott, Jan. 29, 1789. She died Nov. 10, 1789. He married, 2d, Sarah Hopkins, Nov. 2d, 1790.

Children by first wife: 35 *Polly*, m Nathan Lewis. Children by second wife: 36 *Mary*, b Oct. 24, 1789; 37 *Mercy*, b Dec. 22, 1791, m John Howd; 38 *Hopkins*, b Dec. 11, 1794, married Phila Frisbie; 39 *Asahel*, m Aurelia Pond; 40 *Janette*, b Sept. 5, 1803, m Timothy Higgins, Nov. 4, 1824.

GENEALOGIES.

17 PRESERVE.

Major PRESERVE CARTER, son of Jacob and Mary (Hitchcock) Carter, married Polly Wood, of Bristol, and resided in Wolcott. He was a man of considerable influence in the church, Society, and town, and maintained the dignity and honor characteristic in the Carter family.

Children: 41 *Preserve W.*, who died in Waterbury; 42 *Polly W.*, m —— Crofts, of Waterbury, has children Edward, Margaret, and Mrs. Frederick Norton; 43 *C—— H——*.

21 URI.

URI CARTER, son of Jacob and Mary (Hitchcock) Carter, married L. S. Baxter, of Wolcott, died Feb. 6, 1835. She died March 17, 1867.

Children: 44 *George W.*, b Jan. 18, 1811; 45 *Henry J.*, b Feb. 17, 1813; 46 *John M.*, b Oct. 2, 1815; 47 *Mary E.*, b March 12, 1818, married William W. Steel, and has children Fannie and Truman; 48 *L. Salina*, b Feb. 25, 1820; 49 *Cyrus H.*, b Oct. 19, 1822.

22 GAIUS.

GAIUS CARTER, son of Jacob and Mary (Hitchcock) Carter, married Hannah Perkins of Wolcott, and removed to Becket, Mass.

Children: 50 *Mark;* 51 *Stephen;* 52 *Mary;* 53 *Lydia*.

23 LOAMI.

LOAMI CARTER, son of Jacob and Mary (Hitchcock) Carter, married Marcia, daughter of David Harrison, of Wolcott.

Children: 54 *Ezra;* 55 *Esther;* 56 *Joel;* 57 *Irad;* 58 *Ami*.

44 GEORGE WILLIS.

Deacon GEORGE W. CARTER, son of Uri and L. S. (Baxter) Carter, married Sarah A. Bronson, who died March 12, 1868. Married, 2d, Mary P. Baldwin, May 10, 1871. She was born March 27, 1823. He is deacon of the church, and has served the Society continuously, as clerk and treasurer, over twenty years. Has been a senator and representative in the State Legislature.

Children: 59 *Henry B.*, b Dec. 2, 1839; 60 *Mary M.*, b May

23d, 1842, m George W. Walker; 61 *Sarah S.*, b May 23, 1842, d Aug. 24, 1866; 62 *Hannah J.*, b Jan. 26, 1844, m Elmer Hotchkiss; 63 *Frederick W.*, b Oct. 27, 1845; 64 *Walter S.*, b Dec. 3, 1853, d May 8, 1855.

45 HENRY J.

HENRY J. CARTER, son of Uri and L. S. (Baxter) Carter, married Mary Elton, of Burlington, and removed to Michigan, in 1840; has three children.

46 JOHN M.

JOHN M. CARTER, son of Uri and L. S. (Baxter) Carter, married, removed to New Madrid, Missouri, and died Feb., 1865, leaving three children. His wife's death occurred previous to his.

59 HENRY B.

HENRY B. CARTER, son of George W. and Sarah A. (Bronson) Carter, married Mary R., daughter of Stiles L. Hotchkiss, Feb. 1, 1860, and resides near his father-in-law's home.

Child: 65 *Charles H.*

CHURCHILL.

1 DAVID.

DAVID CHURCHILL married Sarah, daughter of Jesse Alcox, Senr., and lived near Amos Seward's.

Children : 2 *Ruth*, b Aug. 31, 1787; 3 *Clara*, b Jan. 8, 1789; 4 *Ithimar*, b May 18, 1790; 5 *Milton*, b Nov. 15, 1791 ; 6 *Lewis*, b Oct. 8, 1793; 7 *Polly*, b Aug. 29, 1795, d Sept. 5, 1795; 8 *Polly*, b Jan. 28, 1797; 9 *Sally*, b July 3, 1798; 10 *Alma*, 11 *Albert*, 12 *Alfred*, triplets, b May 28, 1804; *Albert* d Aug. 16, 1804. This is the only case of triplets I have found on Wolcott records.

12 ALFRED.

ALFRED CHURCHILL, son of David and Sarah (Alcox) Churchill, married.

Children: 13 *Eveline*, b Oct. 3, 1830; 14 *Newell B.*, b July 11, 1833; 15 *Dennis A.*, b Feb. 5, 1837.

CURTISS.

ABEL.

ABEL CURTISS married Anne Alcox, and lived on a farm a little west of the "mill place," where he died.

Children: 1 *Deborah*, b Dec. 31, 1771, m Zephaniah Parker; 2 *Abel*, b Nov. 29, 1773; 3 *John*, b Dec. 7, 1775; 4 *Anna*, b Nov. 23, 1778, m Truman Sanford, and had children Pamelia, Triphena, Maria, Curtiss, Rhoda, Marilla, Ruel, Rufus; 5 *Sylvia*, b Dec. 9, 1780, m Silas Merrill of Wolcott; 6 *Isaac*, b Feb. 11, 1783, removed to New York; 7 *Joel*, b Sept. 21, 1786; 8 *Bartholomew*, b April 19, 1788, m —— Brockett, and removed; 9 *Roxanna*, b April 28, 1790, m William Parker, March 22, 1808, lived a time in Wolcott.

3 JOHN.

JOHN CURTISS, son of Abel and Anne (Alcox) Curtiss, married, and lived on the old homestead, where he died.

Children: 10 *Carlos;* 11 *Augustus;* 12 one other.

7 JOEL.

JOEL CURTISS, son of Abel and Anne (Alcox) Curtiss, married Hannah, daughter of David Pardee, and removed to Cairo, N. Y., where he died. His wife died in Illinois.

Children: 13 *Polly;* 14 *Harriet;* 15 *George;* 16 *Elmira;* 17 *Anson;* 18 *Ann Eliza*.

FAIRCLOUGH.

JOSEPH FAIRCLOUGH was born in Birmingham, England, Feb. 16, 1792, and married Elizabeth Mills, Oct. 1, 1817. They came to New York early in 1828. He died, Nov., 1865, in Waterbury.

Children: 1 *John*, b in England, July 10, 1818; 2 *Mary*, b in England, Jan. 28, 1820, married, 1st, Laurin Russell, March 19, 1841; 2d, Edward de Bellefonds, Aug. 7, 1848; 3 *Charles*, b in England, Jan. 19, 1822, d Jan. 20, 1822; 4 *Susanna*, b in England, Jan. 24, 1825, m Thomas Royce, Feb. 18, 1844; 5 *Charles S.*, b Feb. 17, 1828, in New York; 6 *Thomas*, b Feb. 11, 1831; 7 *Joseph*, b Sept. 6, 1833; 8 *Matthew*, b March 13, 1834, d Sept. 25, 1836; 9 *James*, b March 11, 1837, d July 4, 1863, not married; 10 *Peter*, b Nov. 4, 1841, d Nov. 11, 1841.

1 JOHN.

JOHN FAIRCLOUGH, son of Joseph and Elizabeth (Mills) Fairclough, m Lavinia Merrill, Feb. 17, 1844, and resides in Waterbury.

5 CHARLES S.

CHARLES S. FAIRCLOUGH, son of Joseph and Elizabeth (Mills) Fairclough, married Eliza Brodrick.

6 THOMAS.

THOMAS FAIRCLOUGH, son of Joseph and Elizabeth (Mills) Fairclough, married Elizabeth Ann Kahoe, April 4, 1859, in New York; now resides in Wolcott.

7 JOSEPH.

JOSEPH FAIRCLOUGH, son of Joseph and Elizabeth (Mills) Fairclough, married Catharine A. Baldwin, July 2, 1857; lives in Wolcott.

Children: 11 *Mary E.*, b March 26, 1859, d May 25, 1864; 12 *Charles S.*, b March 24, 1861; 13 *Harriet E.*, b May 3, 1863; 14 *Benjamin F.*, b Oct. 8, 1865; 15 *Henry H.*, b March 15, 1868; 16 *Emma J.*, b Sept. 17, 1870; 17 *Laura E.*, b Nov. 15, 1872.

FINCH.

1 GIDEON.

GIDEON FINCH was born Oct. 23, 1743, and married, in Wolcott, Abigail, daughter of Joseph Atkins, Senr., and settled in Wolcott. She was born Aug. 19, 1745.

Children: 2 *Isaac*, b Feb. 6, 1769; 3 *Samuel*, b 1771, d young; 4 *Gideon*, b Jan. 6, 1775, removed to Ohio; 5 *Abigail*, b Feb. 16, 1778, m Daniel Hall of Waterbury; 6 *Samuel*, b Dec. 2, 1780; 7 *Joel*, b June 21, 1783, d in Wolcott, not married; 8 *Jerusha*, b Feb. 5, 1786, d in Wolcott, not married; 9 *Adah*, b Dec. 16, 1789, d in Wolcott, not married.

6 SAMUEL.

SAMUEL FINCH, son of Gideon and Abigail (Atkins) Finch, married Sarah Barnes of Waterbury, and lived on a farm half a mile west of the "mill place." He died April 22, 1841, ae. 60. His wife, Sarah, was born May 5, 1786, died Dec. 26, 1870, ae. 84.

Children: 10 *Sarah E.*, b Dec. 29, 1804, m 1st, William Blakeslee, 2d, Munson Wilcox; 11 *Chloe B.*, b June 24, 1807, m Albin Alcott; 12 *Samuel G.*, b Aug. 23, 1810, d Aug. 10, 1827; 13 *Lucian R.*, b March 19, 1813, resides in New Haven; 14 *Eliza A.*, b Dec. 18, 1818, m Hendrick Norton; 15 *Benjamin F.*, b Sept. 24, 1821; 16 *George S.*, b Jan. 30, 1827, d Jan. 12, 1828.

13 LUCIAN R.

LUCIAN R. FINCH, son of Samuel and Sarah (Barnes) Finch, married, Feb. 18, 1837, Charlotte, daughter of Chauncey Turner, of Susquehannah Co., Penn. She was born Sept. 28, 1816. He resides in New Haven, and is a commission merchant in New York city.

Children: 17 *Leroy W.*, b Jan. 18, 1839; 18 *Henry T.* b June 24, 1843, m Sarah Barker of Glens Falls, N. Y., July 2, 1873: 19 *Edward L.*, b May 31, 1845; 20 *George Chauncey*, b Nov. 1, 1852, d July 28, 1854, at New Haven, Conn.

15 BENJAMIN FRANKLIN.

BENJAMIN F. FINCH, son of Samuel and Sarah (Barnes) Finch, married Janette Hall of Plymouth, daughter of Sherman Hall, and grand-daughter of Jonathan Hall, of Wallingford. He resides on his father's homestead.

17 LEROY W.

LEROY W. FINCH, son of Lucian R. and Charlotte (Turner) Finch, married, Oct. 14, 1862, Martha H. Hunter of Montgomery Co., Md. She died Aug. 15, 1870. He died July 19, 1872.

Child: 21 *Lucian J.*, b April 5, 1867, living with his grandparents.

19 EDWARD L.

EDWARD L. FINCH, son of Lucian R. and Charlotte (Turner) Finch, married Anna R. Crane, of New York City, Feb. 12, 1873.

Child: 22 *Edward Ridley*, b Nov. 15, 1873.

FRISBIE.

1 JOHN.

JOHN FRISBIE, and Abigail Culpepper, his wife, came from Wales, and settled in Branford, Conn.

2 ELIJAH.

ELIJAH FRISBIE, son of John and Abigail (Culpepper) Frisbie, married, 1st, Abigail Culver, who died April 19, 1771; 2d, Elizabeth Ives, who died Oct. 11, 1776. He married, 3d, Lydia Redfield. He came from Branford to Wolcott, in 1759, and lived on the road to Waterbury, near John Frisbie's present residence. He died Feb. 15, 1800, ae. 81.

Children: 3 *Esther*, b 1743, d 1795; 4 *Judah*, b Sept. 12, (o. s.) 1744; 5 *Reuben*, b 1746; 6 *Abigail*, m Dan Tuttle; 7 *Charles*, b 1752; 8 *Hannah*, m Elnathan Thrasher, and lived in Woodtick, on the farm now owned by Orrin Hall, and had children, John, Abigail, Betsey, Hannah, and Elnathan; 9 *Sarah*, m Ichabod Merrill; 10 *John*, b 1762.

4 JUDAH.

JUDAH FRISBIE, son of Elijah and Abigail (Culver) Frisbie, married Hannah, daughter of Israel Baldwin of Buck's Hill, Aug. 12, 1779, and settled in Woodtick. (See Biog., p 303.)

Children: 11 *Mary*, b 1780, m Abner Hotchkiss; 12 *David*, b Jan. 12 (o. s.), 1782; 13 *Hannah*, b Nov. 10, 1783, m Orrin Jackson, and had children, Northrop, Mary M., Andrew B., Frisbie J., Eliza, Orrin H., Hannah J.; 14 *Judah*, d 1829.

5 REUBEN.

REUBEN FRISBIE, son of Elijah and Abigail (Culver) Frisbie,

married, 1st, Hannah Wakelee, born 1751, d 1778; 2d, Ruth, daughter of Amos Seward, June 3d, 1779. She died 1833. He died 1824.

Children by first wife: 15 *Elizabeth*, m Mark Warner; 16 *Daniel*, m Eunice Hill; 17 *Ebenezer*, m Deborah Twitchell: 18 *Abigail*, m —— Sanford. By second wife: 19 *Polly*, m Daniel Jackson; 20 *Samuel*, m 1st, Isabella Barnes, 2d, Margaret Conner; 21, *Ruth*, m Riley Alcott; 22 *Sally*, m Zara Warden.

7 CHARLES.

CHARLES FRISBIE, son of Elijah and Abigail (Culver) Frisbie, married Lydia Alcott. He died 1799, ae. 47. His widow married Capt. Nathaniel Lewis.

Children: 23 *Ransom ;* 24 *Polly ;* 25 *Isaac ;* 26 *Sheldon*, 1st, d in infancy; 27 *Sheldon*, 2d; 28 *Charles*.

10 JOHN.

JOHN FRISBIE, son of Elijah and Abigail (Culver) Frisbie, married Rosanna Alcott, Jan. 4, 1787. He died in 1846, ae. 84.

Children: 29 *Levi*, d Nov. 14, 1852; 30 *Amanda*, m Green Perkins, had children, Rosanna, Mark, Parley, m Dr. Byington of Wolcott, and later of Southington; 31 *Esther*, m Salmon Johnson, had children, Charlotte, John F., Charles; 32 *James*, d Dec., 1862; 33 *Parley*, m Leonard Beecher, had children, Merritt, Noble; 34 *Ira*.

12 DAVID.

DAVID FRISBIE, son of Judah and Hannah (Baldwin) Frisbie, married Leva Hall, Feb., 1805. He lived on his father's homestead.

Children: 35 *Samira*, b Aug. 10, 1806, m Joel Johnson, Aug. 11, 1825, and removed to California, where both died, leaving three sons: 36 *Hannah V.*, b Nov. 15, 1810, m Oct. 10, 1829, Carlos R. Byington of Southington, d Nov. 10, 1870, leaving three sons; 37 *Almira*, b Nov. 17, 1812, m David Somers, Oct. 16, 1830; 38 *David B.*, b July 19, 1814.

27 SHELDON.

SHELDON FRISBIE, son of Charles and Lydia (Alcott) Frisbie, married Urana Bronson.

GENEALOGIES.   479

Children : 39 *Isaac ;* 40 *Bronson ;* 41 *Sheldon.*

34 IRA.

IRA FRISBIE, son of John and Rosanna (Alcott) Frisbie, married Sarah E. Hotchkiss, Dec. 20, 1826. He died July 6, 1863.

Children : 42 *John,* d in infancy ; 43 *Emogene ;* 44 *Elizabeth*, b Jan. 21, 1832; 45 *John*, b Oct. 1, 1838.

38 DAVID B.

DAVID B. FRISBIE, son of David and Leva (Hall) Frisbie, married Charlotte Hall of Cheshire, and lived on his father's homestead.

Children: 46 *David L.*, b March 15, 1841.

46 DAVID L.

DAVID L. FRISBIE, son of David B. and Charlotte (Hall) Frisbie, married Ann Downes of Waterbury, Oct. 8, 1868, and lives on the old homestead.

Children: 47 *Frank David,* b Dec. 30, 1870; 48 *Berkley Levi*, b March 8, 1874.

FROST.

1 DAVID, SENR.

DAVID FROST, Senr., was born Sept. 5, 1742, and married Mary ——, born Dec. 22, 1740. They lived three miles east of Waterbury, on Southington road, at a place now called East Farms. He died Dec. 15, 1812. His wife, Mary, died Feb. 6, 1819, ae. 79.

Children : 2 *Jesse*, b Oct. 18, 1762, became a Baptist minister, living not far from his father's home ; is well and favorably remembered by the old people now living ; 3 *Enoch*, b Jan. 8, 1765, lived in town of Waterbury; 4 *David*, b March 1, 1767, settled on Southington mountain; 5 *Naomi*, b July 1, 1770; 6 *Mary*, b March 24, 1775, d Sept. 14, 1778 ; 7 *Mary*, b March 11, 1780.

4 DAVID, JR.

DAVID FROST, son of David and Mary Frost, married Mary Ann, daughter of David Hitchcock of Southington. He settled on Southington mountain, a little north of Capt. Nathaniel Lewis, and was a man of considerable responsibility and influence in the town. He died March, 18, 1850, ae. 83. His wife, Mary Ann, was born June 14, 1770, and died Nov. 24, 1832, ae. 62.

Children: 8 *Naomi*, b Aug. 10, 1792, m —— Neal; 9 *Levi Brown*, b Aug. 21, 1794; 10 *Lucy*, b March 29, 1797, m Seth Alcox ; 11 *David Hitchcock*, b Oct. 16, 1799; 12 *Martha*, b Feb. 14, 1803, d Aug. 16, 1803 ; 13 *Patty*, b Nov. 4, 1804, m Herrick Payne ; 14 *Sylvester*, b May 8, 1807 ; 15 *Polly Ann*, b Aug. 31, 1809.

9 LEVI BROWN.

LEVI B. FROST, son of David and Mary Ann (Hitchcock) Frost,

GENEALOGIES.   481

married Sylvia, daughter of Capt. Nathaniel Lewis, and lived in Marion, Southington.

Children: 16 *Ira Sylvester*, b Aug. 20, 1820; 17 *James L.*, b Aug. 15, 1823, d Sept. 24, 1843; 18 *Lewis Hall*, b March 10, 1826; 19 *Levi Dwight*, b Oct. 10, 1830; 20 *Reuben Thomas*, b Aug. 20, 1835; 21 *Mary Ann*, b July 17, 1841, m Lewis Dailey of Watertown, Conn.

18 LEWIS HALL.

LEWIS H. FROST, son of Levi B. and Sylvia (Lewis) Frost, married Adaline Lewis; resides in Marion.

Children: 22 *Lewis E.*; 23 *James*.

19 LEVI DWIGHT.

LEVI D. FROST, son of Levi B. and Sylvia (Lewis) Frost, married Cornelia Thorp; resides in Marion.

Children: 24 *Cora M.*, b June 4, 1859; 25 *Edson L.*, b April 11, 1862; 26 *Edgar W.*, b June 9, 1864; 27 *Cornelia C.*, b Sept. 26, 1866, d Aug. 5, 1868; 28 *Cornelia G.*, b Jan. 22, 1869.

20 REUBEN THOMAS.

REUBEN T. FROST, son of Levi B. and Sylvia (Lewis) Frost, married Helen Stever of Bristol; lives in Marion.

Child: 29 *Helen J.*, b May 22, 1874.

GILLET.

Nathan and Jonathan came from England to Dorchester, Mass., in 1630. Nathan was admitted freeman in Dorchester in 1634, and removed to Windsor in 1635, and afterward removed to Simsbury where his wife died Feb. 21, 1670.

Children: 1 *Elizabeth*, b Oct. 6, 1639; 2 *Abia*, b Aug. 22, 1641; 3 *Rebecca*, b June 14, 1646, d July 13, 1647; 4 *Elias*, bapt July 1, 1649; 5 *Sarah*, bapt July 13, 1651; 6 *Benjamin*, b Aug. 29, 1653; 7 *Nathan*, b Aug., 1655; 8 *Rebecca*, b Dec. 8, 1657.

7 NATHAN, JR.

NATHAN GILLET, Jr., son of Nathan the emigrant, married, 1st, Rebecca Owen, June 13, 1692; 2d, Hannah Buckland.

Children by first wife: 9 *Isaac*, b Aug. 2, 1693; 10 *Dinah*, b Oct. 18, 1696. By second wife: 11 *Azariah*, b March 28, 1705; 12 *Ann*, b April 3, 1707; 13 *Zabed*, b April 6, 1710; 14 *Hannah*, b Aug. 11, 1712; 15 *Gothiniel*, b Jan. 7, 1714; 16 *Gideon*, b Aug. 12, 1717.

9 ISAAC.

ISAAC GILLET, son of Nathan and Rebecca (Owen) Gillet, married Elizabeth Griswold Oct. 29, 1719. His will was dated Dec. 24, 1762.

Children: 17 *Isaac*, b May 16, 1720, married Honora Stephens Dec. 28, 1742; 18 *Zaccheus*, b Dec. 18, 1724; 19 *Jacob*, b Jan. 29, 1726; 20 *Elizabeth*, b Feb. 2, 1728; 21 *Ava*, b Dec. 28, 1731, d Dec. 28, 1736; 22 *Ava*, b Dec. 10, 1739.

18 ZACCHEUS.

ZACCHEUS GILLET, son of Isaac and Elizabeth (Griswold) Gillet, married, 1st, Ruth Phelps, Dec. 15, 1743; 2d, widow Sarah Dean of Wolcott, Dec. 17, 1778. He resided in Granby until 1773 or 1774, when he removed to Wolcott. He died Jan. 7, 1793.

Children: 23 *Zaccheus*, b Nov. 11, 1745; 24 *Ava*, b Oct. 4, 1747, d Sept. 3, 1748; 25 *Alexander*, b Aug. 14, 1749; 26 *Ruth*, b Sept. 29, 1751; 27 *Mary*, b Aug. 4, 1753, m Josiah Atkins, of Wolcott, Nov. 25, 1779; 28 *Nathan*, b Sept. 29, 1755; 29 *Elizabeth*, b March 30, 1758, m Elkanah Smith of Wolcott, July 26, 1781; 30 *Benoni*, b July 23, 1760; 31 *Anne*, b Jan. 3, 1763, m George Cornish, d March 13, 1793; 32 *Rachel*, b Nov. 28, 1764, m Noah Uzza Norton, April 22, 1784; 33 *Timothy*, b July 21, 1770, d April 22, 1780.

25 ALEXANDER.

Rev. ALEXANDER GILLET, son of Zaccheus and Ruth (Phelps) Gillet, married Adah, daughter of Deacon Josiah Rogers, Dec. 3, 1778. He died Jan. 19, 1826, in the 77th year of his age and the fifty-third of his ministry. His wife, Adah, died May 10, 1839, aged 77. (See Biog., p. 313).

Children: 34 *Timothy Phelps*, b June 15, 1780, d Nov. 5, 1866, ae. 86. (See Biog., p. 322.) 35 *Asaph*, b Oct. 15, 1782, d Aug. 21, 1846, ae. 64; 36 *Esther*, b May 26, 1785, d Dec. 30, 1834, ae. 50; 37 *Adah*, b Oct. 10, 1787, still living, being in her 87th year; 38 *Elias*, b June 11, 1792, d Oct. 26, 1871, ae. 79; 39 *Marianna*, b Jan. 13, 1796, d Nov. 4, 1815, ae. nearly 20.

23 ZACCHEUS.

ZACCHEUS GILLET, son of Zaccheus and Ruth (Phelps) Gillet, married Elizabeth ——, and lived in Wolcott, where five of his children were baptized.

Children: 40 *Zaccheus Phelps*, bapt May 8, 1777; 41 *Sarah Thrasher*, bapt Oct. 14, 1781; 42 *Dinah Holcomb*, bapt Oct. 3, 1784; 43 *Selina*, bapt July 15, 1787; 44 *Rachel*, bapt Oct. 28, 1790.

28 NATHAN.

NATHAN GILLET, son of Zaccheus and Ruth (Phelps) Gillet, married Lucy, daughter of Dea. Aaron Harrison of Wolcott, April 16, 1779.

30 BENONI.

BENONI GILLET, son of Zaccheus and Ruth (Phelps) Gillet,

married Phebe Dean, daughter of his father's second wife, Oct. 16, 1783, and, after some years settled in Fair Haven, Conn., where he died.

Children : 45 *Theophilus*, and 46 another brother, went to St. Augustine, Florida, one being captain and the other an officer on a vessel. They were invited to tea, and the next day they died, having been poisoned. 47 *John* was a merchant in Dublin, 120 miles west of Savannah, Ga., where he became wealthy, and then returned to Fair Haven, Conn. He was afterward one of a firm called "Gillet, Hotchkiss, & Tuttle." They purchased a large tract of land at Nauvoo, Ill., to which place Mr. Gillet removed. 48 *Merritt* lived awhile in Georgia. 49 *Marcus* went to Florida, and was a successful merchant, and died there leaving children.

HALL.

Lieut. HEMAN HALL, the first of the Halls in Wolcott, was the son of Nathan Hall of Wallingford, and Nathan was the son of John Hall of New Haven, and this John was the son of John Hall of Boston, New Haven, and Wallingford, who was an emigrant, having come to America before 1660. The emigrant's sons, John, Thomas, and Samuel, settled in Wallingford before their father.

1 JOHN.

JOHN HALL, of England, married Jane Woolen. He was freed from training in 1665, being then in his 60th year, and was most certainly in New Haven as early as 1639, and at Wallingford about the year 1670. He died early in the year 1676, ae. 71.

Children: 2 *John*, bapt Aug. 9, 1646; 3 *Sarah*, bapt Aug. 9, 1646, at New Haven; 4 *Richard*, b July 11, 1645; 5 *Samuel*, b May 21, 1646, d March 5, 1725; 6 *Thomas*, b March 25, 1649; 7 *Jonathan*, b April 5, 1651; 8 *David*, b March 8, 1652, d July 17, 1727, ae. 75.

2 JOHN, JR.

JOHN HALL, son of John and Jane Hall, married Mary, daughter of Edward Parker, at New Haven, Dec. 6, 1666, and settled in Wallingford with the first planters in 1670. He died Sept. 2, 1721, ae. 86. She died Sept. 22, 1725.

Children: 9 *Elizabeth*, b Aug. 11, 1670, in New Haven; 10 *Daniel*, b July 26, 1672, m Thankful Lyman, March 15, 1693; 11 *Mary*, b June 23, 1675; 12 *Nathaniel*, b Feb. 8, 1677; 13 *John* b March 14, 1681, m Elizabeth Royce; 14 *Lydia*, b Jan. 21, 1683; 15 *Samuel*, b Dec. 24, 1686, d Nov. 1, 1689; 16 *Esther*, b Aug. 30, 1693; 17 *Caleb*, b Sept. 14, 1697.

12 NATHANIEL.

NATHANIEL HALL, son of John and Mary (Parker) Hall, married Elizabeth Curtiss, May, 1699. She died Sept. 30, 1735, and he married, 2d, Lydia Johnson, Sept. 15, 1736. He died Aug. 16, 1757.

Children : 18 *Amos*, b Jan. 24, 1700, m Ruth Royce ; 19 *Margaretta*, b Dec. 21, 1701, d Oct. 30, 1707 ; 20 *Caleb*, b Jan. 3, 1703, d May 11, 1766, ae. 62 ; 21 *Moses*, b June 6, 1706, d Feb. 15, 1765, ae. 59 ; 22 *Mary*, b Oct. 30, 1707 ; 23 *Nathaniel*, b April 17, 1711, d Dec. 18, 1727 ; 24 *James*, b April 23, 1713 ; 25 *Elizabeth*, b Sept. 22, 1715 ; 26 *Desire*, b June 19, 1719 ; 27 *Heman*, b Oct. 17, 1720.

27 HEMAN.*

Lieut. HEMAN HALL, son of Nathaniel and Elizabeth (Curtiss) Hall, married Elizabeth ———, and was among the early settlers in Wolcott. He died in 1769, and the date on his grave-stone is the earliest in the Center grave-yard in Wolcott. Elizabeth, his wife, married, 2d, Mr. Lee, who came to Wolcott with Mr. Hall and his family. She died about 1804.

Children : 28 *Curtiss*, b 1746 ; 29 *Heman*, b 1750 ; 30 *Phebe*, m Dea. Joseph Atkins ; 31 *Elizabeth*, m Daniel Byington, Jr.

28 CURTISS.

CURTISS HALL, son of Heman and Elizabeth (Curtiss) Hall, married Rachel Beecher, said to have been first cousin to Rev. Dr. Lyman Beecher. Mr. Hall was killed "by falling from a tree which was already down," in 1799, ae. 53. His widow married, John Bronson.

Children : 32 *Moses*, bapt Nov. 2, 1788 ; 33 *Richmond*, b March 23, 1773 ; 34 *Mary*, bapt Nov. 2, 1788, m Reuben Lewis ; 35 *Anne*, bapt Nov. 2, 1788, m Luther Hotchkiss, Nov. 24, 1800 ; 36 *Leva*, bapt Nov. 2, 1788, m David Frisbie ; 37 *Amos*, bapt Nov. 2, 1788 ; 38 *Sukey*, d 1778 ; 39 *Sukey*, bapt Nov. 2, 1788, m Thomas Wiard, removed to Massachusetts ; 40 *Rachel*, bapt Nov. 2, 1788, d Nov. 3, 1788 ; 41 *Infant*, d Aug. 23, 1785 ; 42 *Infant*,

---

* This name is written Harmon in the Wallingford History, but is Heman on Wallingford Town Records.

GENEALOGIES. 487

d 1786 ; 43 *Infant*, d July 27, 1787 ; 44 *Sylvia Curtiss*, bapt May 1, 1789; 45 *Infant*, d March 9, 1790; 46 *Infant*, d 1795; 47 *Child*, d 1797.

29 HEMAN.

Capt. HEMAN HALL, son of Heman and Elizabeth Hall, married Rebecca Finch of Wolcott, and lived on the homestead, where he died, 1795, ae. 45. His wife, Rebecca, was born in 1746, and died June 3, 1805, aged 59. (See Biog., p 338.)

Children : 48 *Sally ;* 49 *Rebecca*, m Osee Bronson, and removed to Madison Co., N. Y., where they both died. Their son, Miles Bronson, has been a missionary in India about thirty years. 50 *Heman*, b 1775 ; 51 *Levi*, bapt Sept. 18, 1778 ; 52 *Sally*, bapt April 30, 1780 ; 53 *Ursula*, bapt Aug. 18, 1782, m Noah Walker, and removed to Saybrook; 54 *Sarah*, b 1780, m Willsey, d July 19, 1860, ae. 80 ; 55 *Lizzie E.*, m Daniel Byington.

32 MOSES.

MOSES HALL, son of Curtiss and Rachel (Beecher) Hall, married Olive Porter, and removed to Waterbury.

Children: 56 *Nelson ;* 57 *Hopkins ;* 58 *Samuel ;* 59 *Olive*, m John P. Elton.

33 RICHMOND.

RICHMOND HALL, son of Curtiss and Rachel (Beecher) Hall, married Lucy Dudley, July 3, 1795, lived in Wolcott, and died Nov. 12, 1825. His wife, Lucy, was born Jan. 22, 1774, and died Nov. 14, 1842.

Children : 60 *Rachel Beecher*, b Feb. 16, 1796, m Stephen Merriman of Southington, d Jan. 30, 1839 ; 61 *John*, b Jan. 24, 1798, d April 7, 1844 ; 62 *Abigail*, b Oct. 25, 1799, now living in Meriden ; 63 *Curtiss*, b Oct. 8, 1801, settled in Susquehanna Co., Penn., d 1870 ; 64 *Richmond*, b July 27, 1803, d in Meriden, Conn., April 23, 1848 ; 65 *Lucy*, b Oct. 5, 1805, m Mansfield Merriman of Southington ; 66 *Emeline*, b Aug. 7, 1807, m ———— Richardson, removed to Slatersville, R. I. ; 67 *Susan*, b Nov. 24, 1809, m Lewis Woodruff, and resides in Southington ; 68 *Leva*, b June 5, 1812, m John Davidson, lives in South Meriden ; 69 *Eleanor*, b Nov. 22, 1814, m Jared Matthews, and removed to

New York, d July 26, 1854; 70 *Elizabeth*, b Sept. 1, 1818, m ------ Steel, and resides in Windham, N. Y.

50 HEMAN.

Sergt. HEMAN HALL, son of Heman and Rebecca (Finch) Hall, married, Dec. 12, 1796, Lydia, daughter of David Hitchcock of Southington. His commission as sergeant is dated at Farmington, 1797. He and his widowed mother changed the farm on the road towards Marion for the one owned by Elnathan Thrasher, in Woodtick, where he died, Feb. 4, 1848, ae. 73. Lydia, his wife, b Aug. 4, 1777, d Feb. 9, 1856, ae. 79.

Children: 71 *Orrin*, b Oct. 11, 1797; 72 *Ephraim*, b Sept. 5, 1799; 73 *Polly*, b Aug. 17, 1801, m Willard Plumb, Jan. 1, 1822; 74 *Lydia*, b June 21, 1804, m William Frost, June 24, 1823, and lived at East Farms in Waterbury; 75 *Rebecca F.*, b Aug., 1808, m William H. Payne, May 31, 1829, and settled in Waterbury; 76 *Roxanna*, b April 1, 1816, m Laurin L. Stevens, Sept. 30, Sept. 30, 1838, d Dec. 11, 1867, ae. 50.

51 LEVI.

Capt. LEVI HALL, son of Heman and Rebecca (Finch) Hall, married, 1st, Sarah Welton, who died Oct. 13, 1842, ae. 64; 2d, Miss Warner, of Plymouth. He was a leading man in the Episcopal Church a number of years. He died June 27, 1857, ae. 80.

Children: 77 *Kneeland T.*, not married, d April 6, 1859; 78 *Hector H.*, b July 30, 1808; 79 *Rufina*, b Oct. 9, 1810, m Lucius C. Hotchkiss; 80 *Sarah Ann*, b Oct. 26, 1813, m Simeon H. Norton.

71 ORRIN.

Dea. ORRIN HALL, son of Heman and Lydia (Hitchcock) Hall, married Nancy Minor, and lives in Woodtick, on his father's homestead, and is in his 77th year. His wife, Nancy, died Feb. 9, 1873.

Children: 81 *Heman W.*, b June 11, 1824; 82 *Harriet Julina*, b Nov. 6, 1834.

72 EPHRAIM.

EPHRAIM HALL, son of Heman and Lydia (Hitchcock) Hall,

GENEALOGIES. 489

married Mary Minor, Sept. 9, 1824. His wife, Mary, was born Nov. 23, 1800, d July 19, 1870, ae. 69. He died June 7, 1874. (See Biog., p. 340.)

Children: 83 *Lydia Ann*, b 1825, d Sept. 5, 1826; 84 *Charles Y.*, b March 6, 1827; 85 *Julia Ann*, b. Nov. 18, 1829, m Wm. A. Munson of Wolcott.

78 HECTOR H.

HECTOR H. HALL, son of Levi and —— (Warner) Hall, married Mary, daughter of Dr. Branch of South Carolina, but formerly of Vermont. He formed a partnership with Lucius Tuttle, Jr., in 1832, and went to South Carolina, where he engaged in the dry goods business, remaining until 1838. He then settled on a farm in Cumberland, Indiana, remaining there until 1870, when he sold his farm and invested his money in real estate in Indianapolis, and is one of the leading men in that city.

80 HEMAN WILLSEY.

HEMAN W. HALL, son of Orrin and Nancy (Minor) Hall, married Betsey Ann, daughter of Joseph N. Sperry, and lived on the old Curtiss Hall farm.

Children: 86 *Sarah Ursula*, b April 17, 1847, m Charles M. Potter, Oct. 20, 1866, and has a son Herbert L., b Dec. 3, 1871; 87 *Ransom B.*, b July 12, 1852; 88 *Hattie L.*, b Jan. 10, 1863.

84 CHARLES Y.

CHARLES Y. HALL, son of Ephraim and Mary (Minor) Hall, married Janette A. Smith, June 6, 1848. He died March 10, 1849, ae. 22.

Child: 89 *Charles E. S.*, b May 17, 1849.

87 RANSOM B.

RANSOM B. HALL, son of Heman W. and Betsey A. (Sperry) Hall, married Anna Root, Feb. 25, 1874.

89 CHARLES E. S.

CHARLES E. S. HALL, son of Charles Y. and Janette A. (Smith) Hall, married Emma A., daughter of Dea. Miles S. Upson, Sept. 25, 1869.

Child: 90 *Louis Charles*, b Dec. 7, 1872.

HARRISON.*

THOMAS HARRISON, from England, settled in New Haven, in that part now called East Haven. He took the oath of fidelity at New Haven, April 4, 1654. He had three brothers who came with him to this country, viz. : Richard, Benjamin, and Nathaniel. Richard was a few years at Branford, but removed to New Jersey. Nathaniel and Benjamin settled in Virginia. Benjamin, it is said, was grandfather of the late William Henry Harrison, President of the United States. Thomas married, 1st, the widow of John Thompson of New Haven, and, 2d, widow Elizabeth Stent, March 29, 1666.

Children: 1 *Thomas*, b March 1, 1657; 2 *Nathaniel*, b Dec. 13, 1658 : 3 *Elizabeth*, b Jan. 1667; 4 *John ;* 5 *Samuel ;* 6 *Isaac ;* 7 *Mary*.

1 THOMAS.

THOMAS HARRISON, son of Thomas Harrison and his first wife, married Margaret Stent, daughter of his step-mother.

Children: 8 *Lydia*, b 1690; 9 *Jemima*, b 1692; 10 *Thomas*, b Oct. 12, 1694, removed to Litchfield, Conn.; 11 *Abigail*, b Nov. 17, 1696; 12 *Benjamin*, b Aug. 7, 1698, settled in Waterbury, now Wolcott, about 1738 ; 13 *Joseph*, b May 25, 1700; 14 *David*, b Feb. 7, 1702 ; 15 *Aaron*, b March 4, 1704, d 1708 ; 16 *Jacob*, b Oct. 23, 1708, d 1748.

10 THOMAS.

THOMAS HARRISON, son of Thomas and Margaret (Stent) Harrison, married Elizabeth Sutliff, April 21, 1721, and lived for a time in the eastern part of North Branford. He purchased 1000 acres of land in Litchfield, Conn., in the eastern part of the

---

* See Bronson's History of Waterbury.

parish of South Farms, to which he removed in 1739. He gave 100 acres of land to each of nine sons, reserving only 100 for himself. He was chosen deacon of the First Church in Litchfield in 1755.

Children: 17 *Thomas;* 18 *Ephraim;* 19 *Gideon;* 20 *Titus;* 21 *Abel;* 22 *Jacob;* 23 *Lemuel;* 24 *Elihu;* 25 *Levi.*

12 BENJAMIN.

BENJAMIN HARRISON, son of Thomas and Margaret (Stent) Harrison, married Mary Sutliff, Oct. 19, 1720, and settled in that part of Waterbury now Wolcott, about 1738. He died in 1760, leaving his wife, Mary, and three children.

Children: 26 *Abigail*, m David Warner, son of "Dr. Ben," of Buck's Hill; 27 *Benjamin*, b 1722; 28 *Aaron*, b April 26, 1726.

27 BENJAMIN.

BENJAMIN HARRISON, son of Benjamin and Mary (Sutliff) Harrison, married Dinah, daughter of Dr. Benjamin Warner, of Buck's Hill, Dec, 24, 1741, and died March 13, 1760, in his 39th year.

Children : 29 *James*, b Oct., 1742, d 1760; 30 *Jabez*, b Oct., 1744; 31 *Lydia*, b Sept., 1747; 32 *Samuel*, b Sept., 1750, d 1750; 33 *Rozel*, b 1751; 34 *Daniel*, b July, 1754, m Phebe Blakeslee, Feb. 7, 1774, the first marriage performed by Rev. Alexander Gillet, and the first recorded in Farmingbury parish.

28 AARON.

Dea. AARON HARRISON, son of Benjamin and Mary (Sutliff) Harrison, married Jerusha, daughter of Obadiah Warner, and grand-daughter of Dr. Ephraim Warner of Waterbury. She was born Oct. 13, 1727. He was deacon of the church in Wolcott 45 years. He died Sept. 5, 1819, ae. 93. She died Sept. 13, 1819, five days after her husband, ae. 92.

Children : 35 *Jared*, b Oct. 13, 1749; 36 *Mark*, b Aug., 1751; 37 *Samuel*, b March 19, 1753; 38 *David*, b 1756 ; 39 *John*, b Dec. 3, 1758, went into the army of the revolution, and d Nov. 10, 1776, ae. 18; 40 *Aaron*, b (probably) 1760, was in the war of the revolution, d near New Haven, 1808 ; 41 *Lucy*, b March

1, 1762, m Nathan Gillet, brother of Rev. Alexander Gillet, April 16, 1779; 42 *Lydia*, b 1766, m Dr. John Potter of Wolcott, Sept. 27, 1783, d Sept. 27, 1796, ae. 30.

35 JARED.

JARED HARRISON, son of Aaron and Jerusha (Warner) Harrison, married Hannah ——, and resided in Wolcott some years; removed to Watertown, Conn., and was elected deacon of the church there in 1801; removed to Whitestown, N. Y., and died there, Jan. 21, 1810, ae. 61.

Children: 43 *Daniel Webster*, bapt March 25, 1777; 44 *Roswell*, bapt. May 25, 1777; 45 *Benjamin*, bapt May 25, 1777; 46 *John*, bapt Jan. 11, 1778; 47 *Ruth*, bapt June 18, 1780. All baptized in Wolcott.

36 MARK.

MARK HARRISON, Esq., son of Aaron and Jerusha (Warner) Harrison, married Rebecca Miles of Wolcott, March 30, 1775. He was a man of prominence and influence, and of a more progressive mind than many of his fellow-townsmen; and if the town records indicate the truth, Wolcott would have been much more of a town now than it is if it had followed his advice, for he seems to have been in favor of helping Seth Thomas in establishing his clock manufactory in Wolcott, and was a leader in several other improvements which the people were slow to adopt. His wife, Rebecca, died Aug. 20, 1810, ae. 59. He married, 2d, widow Hannah Beach, Feb. 24, 1811. He died July 15, 1822, ae. 71.

Children: 48 *Michael*, b Jan. 17, 1776; 49 *Abigail*, b Oct. 5, 1777, m Reuben Beebe, and d Feb. 10, 1862, leaving a son, Miles Beebe, in West Haven. Reuben Beebe d Sept. 26, 1810. 50 *Susannah*, b Sept. 27, 1779, m —— Clinton, and removed to Ohio; 51 *Rollin*, b March 14, 1782; 52 *Rebecca*, b Aug. 5, 1784, m Lucius Tuttle of Wolcott; 53 *Miles*, b July 9, 1787, m —— Hotchkiss of Wolcott, d in Ohio, leaving several children; 54 *Sarah*, b May 1, 1790, d April 21, 1791; 55 *Stephen*, b Sept. 20, 1792.

37 SAMUEL.

SAMUEL HARRISON, son of Aaron and Jerusha (Warner) Harrison, married Phebe ——.

GENEALOGIES.   493

Children: 56 *Olive*, bapt Sept. 1, 1784; 57 *Deliverance*, bapt Sept. 1, 1784; 58 *Lucy*, bapt Sept. 1, 1784; 59 *Lydia*, bapt Sept. 1, 1784; 60 *Josiah*, bapt Sept. 1, 1784; 61 *Palmyra*, bapt March 12, 1786.

38 DAVID.

DAVID HARRISON, son of Aaron and Jerusha (Warner) Harrison, married, 1st, Hepzibah Roberts of Wolcott, Dec. 10, 1778. She died Aug. 28, 1793. He married, 2d, Lydia, daughter of Wait Hotchkiss, and she died July 25, 1838, ae. 76. He died April 5, 1820, ae. 64.

Children: 62 *Laura*, b Aug. 1, 1779; 63 *Leonard*, b Sept. 27, 1781; 64 *Marcia*, b Oct. 17, 1783; 65 *Jared*, b March 10, 1786; 66 *Aaron*, b July 30, 1788; *Mary*, b Oct. 22, 1790; 68 *Joseph*, and 69 *Benjamin*, twins, b Aug. 27, 1793. By second wife: 70 *Lowly*, b 1795, d Sept. 26, 1826, ae. 31; 71 *Irad*, b 1796, d Nov. 30, 1826, ae. 30; 72 *Lyman*, d young.

48 MICHAEL.

MICHAEL HARRISON, son of Mark and Rebecca (Miles) Harrison, married Cynthia Rosanna Welton, and lived in New Haven, and died there with the same fever with which Rev. Mr. Woodward died in Wolcott. Mr. Harrison died Aug. 22, 1810, two days after his mother died in Wolcott, he having watched with his father's family in Wolcott. His wife, Cynthia R., died in Waterbury, 1867 or 8.

Children: 73, *Sarah*, m Hiram Upson, lived in Waterbury; 74 *Maria*, m Meigs Allen, lived in Plymouth, Conn.; 75 *Rebecca*, m James Somers of Milford.

51 ROLLIN.

ROLLIN HARRISON, son of Mark and Rebecca (Miles) Harrison, married Esther Moulthrop, and died July 22, 1810, with the great fever that prevailed at that time.

Child: 76 *Esther*, m John S. Atkins of Wolcott, and lives in New Haven.

55 STEPHEN.

STEPHEN HARRISON, son of Mark and Rebecca (Miles) Harrison, married Lois ———. He was celebrated for having the most remarkable tenor voice in singing that was ever heard in Wolcott. That voice he used cheerfully and constantly for many years in aid of public worship in both churches. His wife, Lois, died Sept. 14, 1859, ae. 66. He died July 11, 1866, ae. 73.

Children: 77 *Henry*, b March 9, 1810; 78 *Michael*, and 79 *Rollin*, twins, b Oct. 3, 1811, *Michael* d Dec. 21, 1811; 80 *Charlotte*, b Oct. 17, 1813, m Ferdinand Cadwell, May 12, 1831, had children, Ferdinand G., b Aug. 5, 1832, Solomon F., b May 12, 1834, George D., b May 16, 1837, Mortimer H., b Oct. 1, 1839, was a soldier in the late war, and died in hospital at Washington, Birdsey A., b Feb. 10, 1843, Charles G., b June 1, 1845, John W. and James W., twins, b Jan. 9, 1847, Laura Jane, b April 1, 1853; 81 *Michael*, b July 29, 1815; 82 *Isaac*, b June 4, 1817; 83 *Orrin*, b March 1, 1819; 84 *Mark*, b April 10, 1821, d March 24, 1841; 85 *William Franklin*, b Feb. 8, 1823; 86 *Alma Jane*, b May 7, 1825, m James M. Cadwell, May 22, 1846; 87 *Caroline Miles*, b May 16, 1827, m Milo M. Gilbert, June 1, 1835, and had children, Adaline, b April 8, 1846, Ella Jane, b Sept. 6, 1853, Charles H., b Sept. 28, 1858, Milo M., d April 10, 1873; 88 *Jennet*, b Jan. 20, 1829, d Sept. 20, 1831; 89 *Emily*, b Nov. 11, 1830, d Oct. 2, 1831; 90 *Emily Jennet*, b July 4, 1832, m Emerson B. Thomas, Jan. 3, 1853, and had children, Elsie J., b Feb. 5, 1856, Carrie J., b July 16, 1859, Emerson B., d June 20, 1863, in his country's service, at New Orleans; 91 *Frederick*, b July 2, 1834, d July 8, 1864, in his country's service; 92 *Eliza Ann*, b May 27, 1836, m Luther W. Plumb of Wolcott.

77 HENRY.

HENRY HARRISON, son of Stephen and Lois Harrison, married Wealthy H., daughter of Gates Upson, Nov. 29, 1832. She was born Nov. 25, 1812, and died July 7, 1848. He married, 2d, Mary H. Goodrich, July 2, 1859. He lives half a mile east of Wolcott Center.

Children: 93 *Henry Upson*, b April 27, 1839, d April 28, 1842; 94 *Mark Hotchkiss*, b June 30, 1843; 95 *Mary Wealthy*, b Nov. 29, 1846, m Sidney B. Ruggles of Southington, and d Feb. 18, 1873.

79 ROLLIN.

ROLLIN HARRISON, son of Stephen and Lois Harrison, married

GENEALOGIES.

H. F. Mesherel of Southington, April 12, 1833. He died in New Britain, March 24, 1866, ae. 55.

Children: 96 *Martha E.*, b Feb. 1834; 97 *William H.*, b Feb. 19, 1836, d Oct. 26, 1862, in the United States service, in South Carolina; 98 *Charles E.*, b Jan. 26, 1843, d Sept. 11, 1847.

81 MICHAEL.

MICHAEL HARRISON, son of Stephen and Lois Harrison, married Eliza J. Hayes, Sept. 26, 1837.

Children: 99 *Harriet*, b April 28, 1838, m Charles Noble; 100 *Charles*, b June 15, 1840; 101 *Franklin*, b April 11, 1850.

82 ISAAC.

ISAAC HARRISON, son of Stephen and Lois Harrison, married Elizabeth Small, Oct. 15, 1836.

Children: 102 *William B.*, b Sept. 21, 1837, and was killed at the battle of Bull Run, Aug. 30, 1862; 103 *James H.*, b Sept. 6, 1839, d Dec. 30, 1843; 104 *Stephen E.*, b Aug. 19, 1840, m Etta Shepherd, July 9, 1870; 105 *Susan E.*, b June 3, 1844, m Theodore Olive, Aug. 7, 1862; 106 *James H.*, b Sept. 20, 1845, m Deborah Walker, June 28, 1871; 107 *Edward*, b July 20, 1847, d Aug. 27, 1847; 108 *Washington R.*, b Sept. 16, 1848; 109 *Matilda*, b Feb. 10, 1852, d Feb. 11, 1852; 110 *Caroline H.*, b June 30, 1853; 111 *Martha O.*, b April 12, 1858.

83 ORRIN.

ORRIN HARRISON, son of Stephen and Lois Harrison, married Emily Harrison, Jan. 28, 1840.

Children: 112 *Theodore F.*, b March 14, 1842; 113 *Mary A.*, b Jan. 22, 1846, m John A. Parker, June 30, 1867, has children, Charles Motley, b Aug. 14, 1868, Lena Violetta, b July 7, 1870; 114 *Henry Franklin*, b Nov. 12, 1849, m Nancy Reed, May 17, 1868; 115 *Adalena*, b July 14, 1852, m William A. Benedict, Nov. 30, 1871; 116 *Caroline*, b June 9, 1857, d March 1, 1864; 117 *Jessie E.*, b March 14, 1863.

85 WILLIAM FRANKLIN.

WILLIAM F. HARRISON, son of Stephen and Lois Harrison, married Harriet A. Bradley, Jan. 20, 1844.

Children: 118 *James F.*, b March 16, 1846 ; 119 *John T.*, b Feb. 8, 1848 ; 120 *Edwin M.*, b May 25, 1851 ; 121 *Wilbur E.*, b May 22, 1854.

94 MARK HOTCHKISS.

MARK H. HARRISON, son of Henry and Wealthy H. (Upson) Harrison, married Mary Palmer, who was born April 9, 1843.

Children: 122 *George W.*, b May 26, 1864; 123 *Josephine Wilbur*, b Aug. 18, 1866.

100 CHARLES.

CHARLES HARRISON, son of Michael and Eliza J. (Hayes) Harrison, married

Children: 124 *Abel*, b April, 1869 ; 125 *Eva*, b Dec. 31, 1872.

112 THEODORE F.

THEODORE F. HARRISON, son of Orrin and Emily (Harrison) Harrison, married Charlotte Corbin, Nov. 12, 1864.

Children : 126 *Frederick*, b March 14, 1866 ; 127 *Frank Arthur*, b Feb. 29, 1868; 128 *Eugene Corbin*, b 1870.

118 JOHN T.

JOHN T. HARRISON, son of William F. and Harriet A. (Bradley) Harrison, married Harriet E. Hough of Wolcott, Oct. 3, 1869.

Children : 129 *Walter Stiles*, b Feb. 1, 1871; 130 *Frederick James*, b Feb. 26, 1874.

HIGGINS.

1 TIMOTHY, SENR.

TIMOTHY HIGGINS was born in Milford where his father then resided. He married Hannah Allen and lived in Milford until about 1803 when he removed to Middlebury, Conn. In Milford he was engaged as a shipping merchant. He remained in Middlebury until 1819 when he removed to Wolcott, whither his son Fitch and his son-in-law, Jonathan Bement, had preceded him.

Children: 2 *Allen*, died young; 3 *Harriet*, m Beers Bradford, lived in Middlebury; 4 *Lyman;* 5 *Laura*, m Elias Tibbles of Milford; 6 *Hannah*, m Jonathan Bement, resided in Wolcott and had children, Eliza, Laura, Ann, Lucy, Louisa; 7 *Fitch;* 8 *Lucy*, m Adolphus Baldwin of Milford; 9 *Luther* and another child, twins; 10 *Timothy*, b Dec. 8, 1800.

4 LYMAN.

LYMAN HIGGINS, son of Timothy and Hannah (Allen) Higgins, married Betsey, daughter of Samuel Upson of Wolcott, Jan. 25, 1808, lived near the mill in Woodtick. She died Nov. 15, 1853. He died July 31, 1866, ae. 83.

Children: 11 *Emily*, b July 26, 1809, m Lucius Frisbie Jan. 31, 1828, d May 12, 1830; 12 *Upson*, b Jan. 27, 1815; 13 *Sally*, b Sept. 28, 1818, m Harvey Plumb of Wolcott, May 3, 1840.

7 FITCH.

FITCH HIGGINS, son of Timothy and Hannah (Allen) Higgins, married Amanda Royce and lived on the Parker farm, now owned by Augustus Rose. He took an active part in sustaining the Society and church, and was a citizen of honor and good report. He removed to Wisconsin as a pioneer and was engaged, to a considerable extent in buying and selling real estate. His first wife died about 1840. He married again.

Children: 14 *Emeline*, m Rollin Tuttle, of Wolcott, and removed to Wisconsin, and had children, Mary Ann, Eliza, Amanda; 15 *William*, m in Wisconsin and has a family of several children. Children by second wife: 16 *Charles;* 17 *Frederick*.

9 LUTHER.

LUTHER HIGGINS, son of Timothy and Hannah (Allen) Higgins, married widow Lambert of Waterbury, lived a time in Wolcott, and removed to Cheshire.

Children: 18 *Henry;* 19 *Mary;* 20 *Stephen*, who died in the late war.

10 TIMOTHY, JR.

TIMOTHY HIGGINS, son of Timothy and Hannah (Allen) Higgins, married Janette Carter of Southington, Nov. 4, 1824, and settled in Southington as a tanner in which business he was successful. He has been deacon, and an active man in the Congregational church in Southington for a number of years.

Children: 21 *Laura A.*, b Aug 31, 1828, m, April 2, 1852, Joseph B. Beadle and resides in New Jersey, and has children, Emma, Charles, John; 22 *Janette C.*, b Jan. 31, 1830, m H. D. Smith of Plantsville, April 24, 1850, and had children, William, Charles D., Janette; 23 *Lucius H.*, b July 4, 1832; 24 *Mary*, b April 8, 1834, m E. P. Hotchkiss, Dec. 5, 1855; 25 *Harriet*, b March 21, 1836; 26 *Infant*, b April 8, 1838, d April 16, 1838; 27 *Edwin*, b June 19, 1841, d Sept. 30, 1861; 28 *Augusta*, b May 31, 1843, d Oct. 16, 1852; 29 *Julia*, b Dec. 15, 1845, d Feb. 19, 1847; 30 *Julia W.*, b Jan. 31, 1843, d July 25, 1852.

12 UPSON.

UPSON HIGGINS, son of Lyman and Betsey (Upson) Higgins, married, 1st, Hannah M. Norton, June 7, 1840. She died Jan. 16, 1842. He married, 2d, Mary Upson, Sept. 18, 1842, and she died Jan. 25, 1862. He resides on the homestead of his father.

Children: 31 *Amelia M.* and 32 *Hannah A.*, twins, b Jan. 15, 1842, Amelia M. d Aug. 15, 1843. By second wife: 33 *Amelia*

J., b Feb. 22, 1844, m Sidney B. Ruggles of Plantsville, Feb. 25, 1874; 34 *Ann C.*, b Oct. 29, 1848, d Jan. 4, 1864; 35 *Frederick U.*, b Aug. 7, 1853.

HITCHCOCK.

SHELTON T. HITCHCOCK was born in Waterbury, Conn., Dec. 13, 1822, and married Cornelia C. Andrews of Wolcott, Oct. 6, 1855. She was born Aug. 22, 1833. Mr. Hitchcock resides on the old turnpike road, near Judd's Hill, in Wolcott. He has been representative and selectman a number of terms each.

Children: 1 *Jennie J.*, b March 26, 1857; 2 *Nettie C.*, b Aug. 22, 1860; 3 *Eva M.*, b Sept. 1, 1862, d Sept. 8, 1862; 4 *Elbert S.*, b Nov. 7, 1867.

HOPKINS.

JOHN HOPKINS, of Hartford, Conn., left a widow, Jane, and two children: 1 *Stephen;* 2 *Bethia*, m Samuel Stocking of Middletown.

1 STEPHEN.

STEPHEN HOPKINS, son of John and Jane Hopkins, married Dorcas, daughter of John Bronson, 1st, of Farmington, and lived at Hartford.

Children: 3 *John;* 4 *Stephen;* 5 *Ebeneezr;* 6 *Joseph;* 7 *Dorcas;* 8 *Mary.*

5 EBENEZER.

EBENEZER HOPKINS, son of Stephen and Dorcas (Bronson) Hopkins, resided at Hartford.

Children: 9 *Ebenezer*, bapt Nov. 19, 1693, d young; 10 *Jonathan*, bapt June 28, 1696; 11 *Ebenezer*, b June 25, 1700; 12 *Mary*, b Jan. 30, 1705; 13 *Stephen*, b Aug. 8, 1707, settled in Waterbury; 14 *Isaac*, b Nov. 28, 1708, and settled in that part of Waterbury now Wolcott; 15 *Sarah*, b June 25, 1710.*

14 ISAAC.

Capt. ISAAC HOPKINS, son of Ebenezer of Hartford, came to Waterbury (Wolcott), and married Mercy, daughter of Thomas Hickox, Sept. 21, 1732. She died May 27, 1790. Mr. Hopkins died Jan. 13, 1805, ae. 96. His house stood on the road from Wolcott to Waterbury, at the corner of the roads, a little north of Mr. W. A. Munson's present dwelling. He was one of the most valuable men of the Society and church of Farmingbury.

Children: 16 *Obedience*, b Sept. 1, 1733, d 1736; 17 *Simeon*,

---

* See Bronson's History of Waterbury.

b April 30, 1735, d 1736; 18 *Bede*, b Nov. 21, 1737, m Samuel Judd; 19 *Simeon*, b Nov. 19, 1740; 20 *Irene*, b 1742 or 3; 21 *Ruth*, b Dec. 26, 1745, d 1752; 22 *Ore*, b June 18, 1748, d 1749; 23 *Mittee*, b Dec. 14, 1750, d Nov., 1806; 24 *Mary*, b Dec. 4, 1753; 25 *Wealthy*, b June 2, 1756; 26 *Ruth*, b Dec. 10, 1759, m 1st, Ziba Norton, 2d, Thomas Welton.

19 SIMEON.

Capt. SIMEON HOPKINS, son of Isaac and Mary (Hickox) Hopkins, married Lois, daughter of Obadiah Richards, Nov. 15, 1764, and died May 4, 1793. He was an influential man in the society and church, and was actively engaged in their support while he lived. Besides being a farmer he pursued the business of making leather.

Children: 27 *Hannah*, b Aug. 5, 1765, m Joseph M. Parker, Feb. 28, 1787, and resided in Wolcott; 28 *Sarah*, b June 2, 1767, m Elihu Carter; 29 *Electa*, b July 8, 1770, m Joseph Twitchell, April 16, 1793; 30 *Isaac*, b Jan. 11, 1773; 31 *Lois*, b July 21, 1775, m Samuel Upson, son of Capt. Samuel Upson; 32 *Richards Obadiah*, b Jan. 11, 1778, never married, d in Massachusetts; 33 *Polly*, b Sept. 19, 1779, m Salmon Tuttle of Sheffield, Mass.; 34 *Harvey*, b June 9, 1782.

HOTCHKISS.

HODGKIS, HOTCHKISS.*

SAMUEL HODGKIS came from Essex, England, and was in New Haven as early as 1641. He married Elizabeth Cleverly, Sept. 7, 1642, and died at New Haven, Dec. 28, 1663. The name is spelled at first Hodgkis, but the third generation spelled it, nearly uniformly, Hotchkiss.

Children: 1 *John*, b 1643; 2 *Samuel*, b 1645; 3 *James*, b 1647; 4 *Joshua*, b Sept. 16, 1651; 5 *Thomas*, b Nov. 31, 1654; 6 *David*, b March 9, 1657.

1 JOHN.

JOHN HODGKIS, son of Samuel and Elizabeth (Cleverly) Hodgkiss, married Elizabeth, daughter of Henry Peck of New Haven, Dec. 5, 1672. His will was proved in New Haven, Sept. 23, 1689.

Children: 7 *John*, b Oct. 11, 1673; 8 *Joshua*, b 1675; 9 *Joseph*, b June 3, 1678, went to Guilford; 10 *Josiah*, b July 24, 1680; 11 *Caleb*, b Oct. 18, 1684; 12 *Elizabeth*, b July 18, 1686.

9 JOSEPH.

JOSEPH HODGKIS, son of John and Elizabeth (Peck) Hodgkis, went to Guilford, married Hannah, daughter of Isaac Cruttenden of Guilford, April, 1699, and was a weaver in Guilford. His tax in 1716 was for £50 11s, and for weaving £2 0s 3d. He died July 31, 1740. His wife, Hannah, died March 27, 1756.

Children: 13 *Joseph*, b Sept. 3, 1700; 14 *Isaac*, b Dec. 25,

---

* For collateral branches see Bronson's History of Waterbury; C. H. S. Davis' History of Wallingford; Dodd's History of East Haven.

GENEALOGIES. 503

1702; 15 *Wait*, b Jan. 18, 1704; 16 *Hannah*, b Sept. 13, 1707; 17 *Deborah*, b Jan. 18, 1710, d young; 18 *Miles*, b July 28, 1712, died young; 19 *Mark*, b July 1, 1714.

15 WAIT.

WAIT HOTCHKISS, third son of Joseph and Hannah (Cruttenden) Hodgkis, married Sarah Bishop, Nov. 2, 1731. She died in Guilford, April 24, 1761. He removed to Wolcott in 1777, where he died July 30, 1778.

Children: 20 *Wait*, b Nov. 18, 1733; 21 *Lois*, b Oct. 5, 1735, d May 9, 1818; 22 *Sarah*, b June 5, 1738, d Feb. 5, 1746; 23 *Selah*, b Dec. 24, 1742.

20 WAIT.

WAIT HOTCHKISS, son of Wait and Sarah (Bishop) Hotchkiss, married Lydia Webster of Bolton, Conn., Oct. 16, 1759, and settled in Wolcott in 1764 or 5. His wife, Lydia, died April 12, 1776. He married, 2d, widow Deborah Twitchell, Oct. 10, 1776. He died 1799, ae. 66. His widow, Deborah, died June 18, 1831, ae. 89.

Children: 24 *Joel*, b in Guilford, Aug. 8, 1760; 24 *Lydia*, b in Guilford, Aug. 28, 1762; 25 *Sarah*, b in Wolcott, March 27, 1765, never married; 26 and 27 *Abner*, and a twin sister that lived but a short time, b May 24, 1771. Children by second wife: 28 *Luther*, b Dec. 9, 1778; 29 *Miles*, b July 23d, 1783; 30 *Isaac*, b Oct. 16, 1787.

23 SELAH.

SELAH HOTCHKISS, son of Wait and Sarah (Bishop) Hotchkiss, married Rebecca ———, and may have lived in Wolcott a short time.

Children: 31 *Lucy*, b Oct. 3, 1771; 32 *Jesse*, b Jan. 17, 1777, who resided in Wolcott a short time and went "west."

24 JOEL.

JOEL HOTCHKISS, son of Wait and Lydia (Webster) Hotchkiss, married Mary, daughter of Dea. Josiah Rogers of Wolcott, Feb. 6, 1785, and died in 1798, ae. 38.

Child: 33 *Asenath*, m Ira Hough.

26 ABNER.

ABNER HOTCHKISS, son of Wait and Lydia (Webster) Hotchkiss, married Mary Frisbie, Nov. 19, 1805. She was born 1780, and died Feb. 3, 1852, ae. 71. He lived where his son Mahlon now does, and died March 21, 1846, ae. 75.

Children: 34 *Joel* b March 25, 1807, d Aug. 27, 1852, ae. 37 ; 35 *Sarah*, b April 8, 1809; 36 *Joel Arba*, b Oct. 26, 1814, d Aug. 27, 1852 ; 37 *Mahlon*, b Aug. 3, 1819.

28 LUTHER.

Major LUTHER HOTCHKISS, son of Wait and Deborah (Twitchell) Hotchkiss, married Anne, daughter of Curtiss Hall, Nov. 24, 1800. He lived half a mile south of Wolcott Center, and his farm included most of a piece of land called "Hog-Fields," and contained some of the most tillable land in the town. He was a good and highly respected citizen, and a faithful supporter of the church. He died April 14, 1863, ae. 84. His wife, Anna, died March 3, 1864, ae. 83.

Children : 38 *Olive Ann*, b Nov. 22, 1801, m Walter Webb, and removed to Meriden, where she died Nov., 1855. Her husband now (1873) resides in La Crosse, Wis. They had four children, Luther E., Walter W., John B., Mary A. ; 39 *Sarah Elizabeth*, b Sept. 24, 1805, m Ira Frisbie; 40 *Lucas Curtiss*, b Oct. 14, 1807; 41 *Thomas Goldson*, b Feb. 6, 1811 ; 42 *Stiles Luther*, b March 25, 1817.

40 LUCAS CURTISS.

LUCAS C. HOTCHKISS, son of Luther and Anne (Hall) Hotchkiss, married, 1st, Rufina, daughter of Capt. Levi Hall, Oct. 13, 1831. She died Sept. 19, 1850. He married, 2d, Mary Ann Raymond of New Haven, Dec. 2, 1851.

Children by first wife : 43 *Sarah A.*, b Sept. 29, 1832, m Edw. P. Yale, and has children, Flora R., b Aug. 22, 1855, Anna M., b May 29, 1858, Charles F., b Jan. 15, 1871 ; 44 *Olive W.*, b Jan. 24, 1836, m Lucius W. Curtiss of Bristol, Dec. 15, 1857, and has children, Nettie B., b Aug. 26, 1860, Bertha Olive, b April 13, 1863, d Sept. 11, 1863 ; 45 *Levi H.*, b April 25, 1844. By second wife : 46 *Arthur R.*, b March 18, 1854.

GENEALOGIES.

41 THOMAS GOLDSON.

THOMAS G. HOTCHKISS, son of Luther and Anne (Hall) Hotchkiss, married Sarah L. Pratt of Meriden, in 1837. He died in Meriden, Dec. 22, 1866.

Children: 47 *Philo P.*, b 1838; 48 *Luther*, b 1840, lives in Detroit, Mich; 49 *Addie*, b May, 1844, m —— Curry of New York.

42 STILES LUTHER.

STILES L. HOTCHKISS, son of Luther and Anne (Hall) Hotchkiss, married, 1st, Mary Ann Holt, Oct. 12, 1836. She died Sept. 9, 1863, ae. 46. He married, 2d, Annis E. Bassett of Plymouth, Conn., March 31, 1864.

Children by first wife: 50 *Martha Anna*, b July 1, 1827, d Sept. 9, 1842; 51 *Mary Rufina*, b March 29, 1840, m Henry Carter, Feb. 1, 1860, has son, Charles H., b Oct. 31, 1862; 52 *Elmar*, b March 17, 1846.

45 LEVI H.

LEVI H. HOTCHKISS, son of Lucas C. and Rufina (Hall) Hotchkiss, married Mary B. Marshall of Hartford, Conn., Oct. 18, 1870.

Child: 53 *Marshall*, b Oct. 18, 1871.

47 PHILO P.

PHILO P. HOTCHKISS, son of Thomas G. and Sarah L. (Pratt) Hotchkiss, married Miss Imley of Hartford, and has two children residing in Brooklyn, N. Y.

52 ELMAR.

ELMAR HOTCHKISS, son of Stiles L. and Mary A. (Holt) Hotchkiss, married Hannah Jane, daughter of Deacon Geo. W. Carter, May 2, 1866.

HOUGH.*

JOEL.

JOEL HOUGH, son of Joseph and Catharine Hough of Wallingford, settled in Hamden, Mount Carmel Society, where he died. He was a shoemaker and farmer.

Children: 1 *Ira*, b March 7, 1784, settled in Wolcott, Conn.; 2 *Joseph*, settled in Cheshire, Conn., m —— Moss, daughter of Bowers Moss of that place; 3° —— went to western New York; 4 *Amos*, m Nancy daughter of Nehemiah Rice of Wallingford, d at Hamden in 1869; 5 *Joel*, went to state of New York.

1 IRA.

IRA HOUGH, son of Joel and Catharine Hough, came to Wolcott about 1805. He married Asenath, daughter of Joel Hotchkiss, Nov. 15, 1808. She died Aug. 31, 1810. He married, 2d, Mary Hubbard of Meriden, Conn., Jan. 1, 1812. He was a shoemaker and tanner and resided by the little brook west of Wolcott Center. He was an active man in the Society and town for some years. He died June 13, 1851, and Mary, his wife, died March 6, 1869.

Children by second wife: 6 *Isaac*, b Nov. 23, 1812; 7 *Ezra Stiles*, b Aug. 9, 1814; 8 *Ira Hotchkiss*, b May 4, 1818; 9 *Mary Asenath*, b Oct. 2, 1822, m Miles S. Upson, April 20, 1845; 10 *Sally*, b Jan. 17, 1830, d April 9, 1849.

6 ISAAC.

ISAAC HOUGH, son of Ira and Mary (Hubbard) Hough, married Laura Ann Johnson of Wolcott, April 6, 1835, and resides on road towards Waterbury on the Gehula Grilley farm.

---

* See History of Wallingford.

Children: 11 *Mary Aurelia*, b June 9, 1839, m William Upson, Feb. 23, 1874; 12 *Anne Amelia*, b May 8, 1843, m J. H. Beecher, April 6, 1863, and had daughter, Carolina Amelia, b July 21, 1865, d March 3, 1873. She obtained a divorce and the custody of her daughter some time before the daughter died; 13 *Hobart Isaac*, b Oct. 1, 1850, d Oct. 1, 1861.

7 EZRA STILES.

EZRA S. HOUGH, son of Ira and Mary (Hubbard) Hough, married Lucy Minor of Wolcott, April, 1836. He died Jan. 1, 1843, and his wife, Lucy, died Feb. 9, 1855. He was clerk of the First Society in Wolcott the last three years of his life, and was an active and highly respected young man.

Children: 14 *Cornelia*, b Sept. 21, 1836, d June 1, 1856; 15 *Caroline*, b May 14, 1838, m George T. Parker, Feb., 1865, d July 17, 1865.

8 IRA HOTCHKISS.

IRA H. HOUGH, son of Ira and Mary (Hubbard) Hough, married, 1st, Mary P. Smith of Wolcott, April 9, 1841. She died Oct. 2, 1867, and he married, 2d, widow Martha A. Bronson, daughter of Mark Tuttle, June 1, 1868.

Children by first wife: 16 *Ezra Stiles*, b June 12, 1842, d Feb. 28, 1862; 17 *Harriet Eliza*, b June 26, 1845, m John T. Harrison, Oct. 3, 1869; 18 *Emily Smith*, b Aug. 29, 1849, d April 19, 1861. By second wife: 19 *Mary Rebecca*, b May 13, 1870.

JOHNSON.

AMOS M.

AMOS M. JOHNSON was born Oct. 1, 1816, and was the son of William and Anne (Mitchell) Johnson, who were descended from the first settlers of ancient Woodbury. He married Sarah, youngest daughter of Hon. Orrin Plumb of Wolcott, May, 1854, and lives in the north part of Wolcott.

Children: 1 *Sarah Jane*, b Nov. 12, 1855; 2 *Hannah Maria*, b Sept. 5, 1858.

WILLIAM.

WILLIAM JOHNSON, of Bristol, married Leva, daughter of Levi Atkins, Senr., and lived in the north part of Wolcott.

Children: 1 *Henry Atkins*, b 1835; 2 *Theron Smith*, b 1841.

1 HENRY A.

HENRY A. JOHNSON, son of William and Leva (Atkins) Johnson, married Alphia Sanford, and lives in Plymouth.

Children: 3 *Hattie;* 4 *Willie;* 5 *Carrie;* 6 *Nettie;* 7 *Freddie.*

2 THERON.

THERON JOHNSON, son of William and Leva (Atkins) Johnson, married Sarah J. Alcott.

Child: 8 *Josephine Lillian.*

EDWARD.

EDWARD JOHNSON was born in New Hartford, N. Y., and married widow Laura Scovill, Sept. 21, 1850, in Vienna, N. Y., and came into Wolcott in 1856.

Children: 1 *Ellen Amelia*, b Nov. 17, 1853, m Willie E. Somers, Jan. 15, 1874; 2 *Infant,* died.

KENEA.

JOHN JORDAN.

JOHN J. KENEA was born in that part of Stratford now called Huntington, March 21, 1763. Little is known of his father, except that he was a Scotchman and a sea captain. His mother's name was Jordan. At the age of 15 he enlisted and served in the revolutionary war. At its close he came to Wolcott, and learned the cooper's trade of James Alcox, and married his eldest daughter, Obedience, May 5, 1785. He died Jan., 1840, ae. 77. His widow, Obedience, died in 1855, ae. 88.

Children: 1 *Huldah*, b Feb. 5, 1788, m Isaac Hunt, Sept., 1811, and d Nov. 2, 1813, leaving a daughter Huldah; 2 *Leverette*, b Jan. 10 1791; 3 *Sophia*, b Dec. 15, 1798, m Dec. 18, 1836, Horace Stevens, of Plymouth, and married, 2d, Daniel Baldwin of the same place; 4 *Hilah*, b May 26, 1802, m Jan. 8, 1822, Wells Plumb of Wolcott, and had children, Salome, Orlando, Henry; 5 *Bede*, b June 4, 1805, m Abial Canfield of Oxford, in 1831, and had children, John, Leverette, Henry, Walter, Alice; 6 *John Henry*, b May 14, 1809.

2 LEVERETTE.

LEVERETTE KENEA, son of John J. and Obedience (Alcott) Kenea, married Laura L. Fuller of Barkhamstead, Sept. 28, 1826. He died March 10, 1846.

Children: 7 *James L.*, b July 10, 1827; 8 *Lauriette*, b April 6, 1829, m Henry Sage of Berlin, April, 1852, and has children, Florence and George H.; 9 *Leverette D.*, b Aug. 21, 1831, m Harriet M. Welton of Waterbury, April, 1864, and has children, Hattie W. and Edith Lee; 10 *Harriet E.*, b April 11, 1834, m James E. Smith of Plymouth, March 13, 1854. She died Jan. 23, 1866; 11 *Henry W.*, b July 14, 1836, d Oct. 23, 1849.

6 JOHN HENRY.

JOHN H. KENEA, son of John J. and Obedience (Alcott) Kenea, married, Oct. 22, 1837, Mehitabel H. Phelps of New York. He died in Madison, Wis., June 3, 1863.

Children: 12 *Emily Barton*, b July 31, 1838, m Lucius C. Cary of Madison, Wis., March 21, 1857, and has sons Harry and Freddie.

LANE.

1 DANIEL.

DANIEL LANE married in Killingly, his native place, Mary Griswold, and removed to Wolcott His wife, Mary, died in Wolcott, Aug. 29, 1789, and he married, 2d, Sarah Seward, April 6, 1791. He died in 1794.

Children: 2 *Mabel*, m David Beckwith, Dec. 18, 1786, and removed to Camden, N. Y.; 3 *Nathaniel*, and 4 *Isabel*, twins; Isabel m Isaac Alcox, and removed to Plymouth; 5 *Asahel;* 6 *Mary*, m Mark Alcox; 7 *Daniel*.

3 NATHANIEL.

NATHANIEL LANE, son of Daniel and Mary (Griswold) Lane, married Millicent Alcox, and lived a little north of the James Alcox place.

Child: 8 *Anson Griswold*, b 1796.

5 ASAHEL.

ASAHEL LANE, son of Daniel and Mary (Griswold) Lane, married Abigail, daughter of David Alcox, and removed to Camden, New York, having children.

7 DANIEL, JR.

DANIEL LANE, son of Daniel and Mary (Griswold) Lane, married Keziah Norton, of Wolcott, and lived in Plymouth, Conn.

Children: 9 *Linus*, m —— Jewell, and removed to Cornwall, Conn.; 10 *Lucas*, m ——Jewell, lives in Plymouth, and has children; 11 *Lucia*, m Erastus Todd, removed to Southington; 12 *Elizabeth*, m Joel Barnes, and removed to Plymouth; 13 *Leonard;* 14 *Asahel*.

8 ANSON GRISWOLD.

ANSON G. LANE, son of Nathaniel and Millicent (Alcox) Lane, married Lydia Ann, daughter of Richard F. Welton, and lived on his father's homestead.

Children: 15 *Richard Anson,* b Aug. 19, 1829; 16 *Albert N.,* b July 22, 1831; 17 *Edward Ephraim,* b July 29, 1836, went to Warsaw, Ill., and m Carrie Rosevelt.

13 LEONARD.

LEONARD LANE, son of Daniel and Keziah (Norton) Lane, married Lucy Jewell, and lived in Plymouth. He was found dead on the Waterbury and Southington turnpike, on Southington mountain, in Wolcott,— supposed to have been murdered.

15 RICHARD ANSON.

RICHARD A. LANE, son of Anson G. and Lydia Ann (Welton) Lane, married Elizabeth Hawkins, and removed to Kankakee, Illinois.

Children: 18 *Willie,* d young; 19 *Edward;* 20 *Charles Albert;* 21 *Ida.*

16 ALBERT NATHANIEL.

ALBERT N. LANE, son of Anson G. and Lydia A. (Welton) Lane, married Esther Millicent, daughter of James Alcott, Nov. 17, 1855, and lives on the Lane homestead.

Child: 22 *Elsie Salina,* b Aug. 18, 1856.

LEWIS.

1 WILLIAM.

WILLIAM LEWIS came from England in the ship "Lion," which arrived at Boston Sept. 16, 1632. He was admitted freeman Nov. 6, 1632, and belonged to the Braintree company which removed from Braintree August, 1632, to Cambridge. He was one of the earliest settlers of Hartford in 1636, and was juryman and selectman in 1641. He afterwards became one of the first settlers of Hadley in 1653; was representative for Hadley in 1662 and for Northampton in 1665. His wife's name was Felix, who died in Hadley April 17, 1671. Soon after, he removed to Farmington, where he died Aug. 2, 1683.

Child: 2 *William*, the only child, was born in England.

2 WILLIAM, JR.

WILLIAM LEWIS, son of William and Felix Lewis, married, 1644, Mary Hopkins, said to have been a daughter of William Hopkins of Stratford; 2d, Mary Cheever, daughter of the celebrated school teacher, Ezekiel Cheever, of New Haven. He was an important man in Farmington, being first registrar.

Children by first wife: 3 *Mary*, b May 6, 1645, m Benjamin Judd, son of Thomas; 4 *Lewis Philip*, bapt Dec. 13, 1646; 5 *Samuel*, b Aug. 18, 1648; 6 *Sarah*, b 1652, m Daniel Boltwood; 7 *Hannah;* 8 *William;* 9 *Felix;* 10 *Ebenezer;* 11 *John;* 12 *James*. By second wife: 13 *Elizabeth*, b Oct. 20, 1672, d 1674; 14 *Ezekiel*, b Nov. 7, 1674; 15 *Nathaniel*, b Oct. 1, 1676; 16 *Abigail*, b Sept. 19, 1678; 17 *Joseph*, b March 15, 1679 or 80; 18 *Daniel*, b July 16, 1681.

5 SAMUEL.

SAMUEL LEWIS, son of William and Mary (Hopkins) Lewis,

married Elizabeth —— and was made freeman, 1676. He held the rank of Sergeant and died Nov., 1725.

Children: 19 *Hannah*, bapt Oct. 4, 1691; 20 *Samuel*, b March 29, 1692; 21 *John*, b Sept. 28, 1703; 22 *Nehemiah*, b May 3, 1705; 23 *Nathan*, b Jan. 23, 1707; 24 *Hester*, b Nov. 8, 1708; 25 *Josiah*, b Dec. 31, 1709; 26 *Job*, b Jan. 13, 1713.

23 NATHAN.

NATHAN LEWIS, son of Samuel and Elizabeth Lewis, married Mary Gridley, July 28, 1730, and settled in Southington where he died Sept. 7, 1799.

Children: 27 *Job*, b April 20, 1731, m Hannah Curtiss; 28 *Rhoda*, b 1733; 29 *Nathan*, b Dec. 15, 1734; 30 *Lemuel*, b 1735; 31 *Timothy*, b April 18, 1740; 32 *Mary*, b Dec. 31, 1743; 33 *Asahel*, b Feb. 25, 1744 or 5; 34 *Nathaniel*, b Dec., 1747, settled in Wolcott; 35 *Hannah*, b 1753.

30 LEMUEL.

LEMUEL LEWIS, son of Nathan and Mary (Gridley) Lewis, married —— Royce, lived in Southington. He died in 1821, ae. 86.

Children: 36 *Ebenezer;* 37 *Elisha;* 38 *Royce*, b Feb. 1, 1784; 39 *Merab*, m Dr. Root; 40 *Sally*, m Arnold Atwater, and had children Orrin, Charles, John, Heman, Laura, Emeline, Belinda, Maria; 41 ——, who m —— Newell.

34 NATHANIEL.

CAPT. NATHANIEL LEWIS, son of Nathan and Mary (Gridley) Lewis, married Sarah Gridley, Feb. 15, 1769, and settled on Southington mountain, on what is still known as the Capt. Lewis place. He held the rank of Captain, and was, otherwise, one of the most efficient men in the Society and in the town of Wolcott. His wife Sarah died Aug. 11, 1809, ae. 68. He married, 2d, widow Lydia Frisbie. He died Feb. 24, 1839, ae. 90, and on his gravestone is written: "He was one of the first settlers of this town. An honest man."

Children: 42 *Sylvia*, b Dec. 31, 1770, m Isaac Upson of Wolcott; 43 *Reuben*, b Aug. 16, 1772; 44 *Appleton*, b Aug. 18, 1774; 45 *Addin*, b Nov. 18, 1776, d, being scalded, Nov. 1, 1779; 46

Addin, b Jan. 14, —; 47 *Roxanna*, b Nov. 28, —, m Lee Upson; 48 *Salome*, m Seth Peck; 49 *Nathaniel G.*; 50 *Sarah*.

38 ROYCE.

ROYCE LEWIS, son of Lemuel and ——— (Royce) Lewis, married Electa, daughter of Pomeroy Newell, and settled in Wolcott in 1798. His wife was born Feb. 2, 1783, d 1808. He married 2d, widow Fanny Smith, in 1809. He died in 1848, ae. 64.

Children by first wife : 51 *Lucy*, b 1799, m Romeo Warren, settled in South Norwich, Chenango Co., N. Y., and had children, Andrew, Mary, Sophia, Edward; 52 *Charles*, b June 1803; 53 *Lemuel*, and 54 *Edwin Newell*, twins, b Nov. 7, 1806; 55 *Pomeroy*, b June 1808. By second wife: 56 *Electa*, b 1810, m Ely Sanford, lives in Binghampton, N. Y., had children, Edwin and Emerson; 57 *Ann*, b 1812, m Edward Terry, and died in Waterbury, leaving one son, George E., b Sept. 15, 1836; 58 *Harvey*, b 1813; 59 *Laura*, b 1816, m Lewis Wilmot, lived and died in New Haven, had children, Mordant, John, Lewis; 60 *Fanny*, b 1818, m Orrin L. Botsford, lives in Plainville, and had children, Thomas, Lucy J., Catharine; 61 *Martha*, b 1826.

43 REUBEN.

REUBEN LEWIS, son of Nathaniel and Sarah (Gridley) Lewis, married Mary Hall of Wolcott.

Children : 62 *Nathaniel C.*, b Dec. 16, 1797; 63 *Sylvia*, m Levi B. Frost; 64 *Ira G.*, m Fanny Tully of Southington; 65 *Luman;* 66 *Thomas Z.*; 67 *Ives A.*; 68 *Sarah G.*, m Henry A. Pond of Bristol, Conn., and had children, Robert H. and Ellen S.

44 APPLETON.

APPLETON LEWIS, son of Nathaniel and Sarah (Gridley) Lewis, married widow Lois Hall, Nov. 15, 1797, and lived near his father's home. He died July 29, 1820, ae. 46. His wife, Lois, died March 23, 1860, ae. 83.

Children : 69 *Rufus*, b Oct. 29, 1798; 70 *Mille Ann*, b Sept. 7, 1800, m Joel Wightman of Southington; 71 *Edward*, b June 27, 1802, m Janette Wightman of Southington; 72 *Alfred*, b June 20, 1804, m Rosanna Barnes of Southington; 73 *Julina*, b Oct. 22, 1807, m Truman Dailey of Watertown; 74 *Lloyd*, b Jan.

15, 1810, m Dama Phinney of Southington; 75 *Dennis*, b Feb. 16, 1812, m Lucinda Phinney of Southington; 76 *Lois Melissa*, b Nov. 28, 1814; 77 *Jared Appleton*, b Jan. 9, 1818, d Aug. 17, 1825.

46 ADDIN.

ADDIN LEWIS, son of Nathaniel and Sarah (Gridley) Lewis, married Fanny Lewis of Southington, and had three children, all of whom died young. He was a merchant, and while pursuing this business in Mobile, Ala., he was elected mayor of the city, and was highly respected. He became quite wealthy, and returned to New Haven, where he died, leaving, by bequest, $8,500 to the town of Wolcott, the interest to be used for the support of public schools. He left, also, nearly $15,000 for an academy in Southington. In these gifts he has left monumental honors more lasting than granite or marble, and conferred the greatest possible benefit upon his native town and its half-mother town, Southington. (See remarks on p. 200, and the will of Mr. Lewis, on p. 201.)

49 NATHANIEL G.

NATHANIEL G. LEWIS, son of Nathaniel and Sarah (Gridley) Lewis, married Amanda Truesdel of Bristol.

Children: 78 *Sophia*, m Russel Judson of Bristol, Conn.; 79 *Maria*, died; 80 *Amanda*, m Jeremiah Ely of Hartford.

52 CHARLES.

CHARLES LEWIS, son of Royce and Electa (Newell) Lewis, married Emeline Bartholomew, and lives in Plainville, Conn.

Children: 81 *Henry;* 82 *Romeo;* 83 *Gustavus;* 84 *Marion;* 85 *Nellie;* 86 *Josephine.*

53 LEMUEL.

LEMUEL LEWIS, son of Royce and Electa (Newell) Lewis, married Eliza Tubbs, and lives in Oxford, Chenango Co., N. Y.

Children: 87 *Electa;* 88 *Lucy;* 89 *Elizabeth;* 90 *Charles.*

54 EDWIN NEWELL.

Dea. EDWIN N. LEWIS, son of Royce and Electa (Newell) Lewis, married Lucinda Curtiss, Nov. 27, 1833, and lives in Plainville, Conn.

GENEALOGIES. 517

Children: 91 *Rudett A.*, b May, 1836; 92 *Charles C.*, b April 6, 1840; 93 *Ella F.*, b Sept. 22, 1848, m Henry T. Gibson of Woodbury, Conn.

55 POMEROY.

POMEROY LEWIS, son of Royce and Electa (Newell) Lewis, married ——, and lives in California.

Children: 94 *Thomas;* 95 *Charles;* and others.

58 HARVEY.

HARVEY LEWIS, son of Royce and Fanny (Smith) Lewis, married Elizabeth Bassett, and lives in Salem Center, Indiana.

Children: 96 *Hiram;* 97 *Laura A.;* 98 *Newell;* 99 *Dwight;* 100 *Frank.*

62 NATHANIEL C.

NATHANIEL C. LEWIS, son of Reuben and Mary (Hall) Lewis, married Lucy N. Adams of Bristol, March 19, 1823, and died Aug. 19, 1849, ae. 52. His wife died Feb. 19, 1855.

Children: 101 *Reuben Bennet*, b Jan. 18, 1824; 102 *Anna Lucina*, b Feb. 10, 1827, d Oct. 16, 1828.

65 LUMAN.

LUMAN LEWIS, son of Reuben and Mary (Hall) Lewis, married Maria Foot of Southington.

Children: 103 *Addin*, m Eliza Goldsmith of Torrington; 104 *George F.*, m Emma A. Cowles of Southington; 105 *Emma*, m Bernard Kennedy of New York; 106 *James*, m Alice Riley of Southington; 107 *Sarah*, m Joseph Long of Southington; 108 *Dwight H.*, m Julia Johnson of Southington.

66 THOMAS Z.

THOMAS Z. LEWIS, son of Reuben and Mary (Hall) Lewis, married Samantha Seeley of Waterbury.

Children: 109 *Mary Z.*, m Bennett Merchant of Waterbury; 110 *Reuben T.;* 111 *Alice.*

67 IVES A.

IVES A. LEWIS, son of Reuben and Mary (Hall) Lewis, married, 1st, Almira Hall of Waterbury, and, 2d, Harriet N. Thompson of Southington.

HISTORY OF WOLCOTT.

Children: 112 *Oliver R.*, m Sarah Thorp of Long Branch, J. By second wife: 113 *Arvilla;* 114 *Ida H.*

91 BURDETT A.

BURDETT A. LEWIS, son of Edwin A. and Lucinda (Curtiss) Lewis, married Anna Westover of New Britain, and lives in Plantsville.

Children: 115 *Burton W.;* 116 *Brayton;* 117 *Helen.*

101 REUBEN BENNETT.

REUBEN B. LEWIS, son of Nathaniel C. and Lucy (Adams) Lewis, married Eunice Osborn of Oxford, Conn., Jan. 29, 1851, and lives in Marion, Southington.

Children: 118 *Rosena Theresa,* b Nov. 18, 1851; 119 *Emma Lucina,* b July 21, 1854; 120 *Emerson Wellesley,* b Jan. 31, 1856; 121 *Warren Fremont,* b Sept. 5, 1862.

LINDSLEY.

BENJAMIN.

BENJAMIN LINDSLEY was born, tradition says, in Branford, Conn., in 1743. He married Keturah Auger, who was born in 1748. He settled in Bristol in 1773 or 4, his first deed being dated 1774. He died in 1784, and his wife died in 1824.

Children: 1 *Sarah*, b Feb. 5, 1766; 2 *Keturah*, b Feb. 2, 1768; 3 *Lud*, b Sept. 24, 1770; 4 *Rachel*, b Oct. 24, 1772; 5 *Jared*, b Dec. 5, 1774; 6 *Lucretia*, b March 17, 1777; 7 *Dorcas*, b April 12, 1779; 8 *Benjamin*, b Nov. 10, 1782; 9 *Eldad*, b June 19, 1784. All of these children married and removed to central part of New York State except the third, Lud.

3 LUD.

LUD LINDSLEY, son of Benjamin and Keturah (Auger) Lindsley, married Hannah Gaylord of Bristol and settled in Wolcott, in the Spring of 1801, on Rose Hill, afterward called Lindsley Hill.

Children: 10 *Rebecca A.*, b March 8, 1798, d June 2, 1814; 11 *Murilla*, b Jan. 7, 1800; 12 *Hannah M.*, b Sept. 16, 1802, m Gad Lewis of Bristol; 13 *Rachel*, b Jan. 2, 1805, d Feb. 12, 1841; 14 *Benjamin A.*, b July 31, 1809; 15 *Samuel*, b Dec. 2, 1811, d Nov. 14, 1855; 16 *Charlotte R.*, b Dec. 21, 1816, m Stillman Bronson of Wolcott.

14 BENJAMIN A.

BENJAMIN A. LINDSLEY, son of Lud and Hannah (Gaylord) Lindsley, married Lucina, daughter of Selah Upson, May 16, 1844, and lived on his father's homestead. He was a good citizen, an industrious farmer, and is said to have had the best cultivated farm in the town. He was an active, reliable member of the Society and church, and is spoken of throughout the community, with respect and honor. He died Feb. 22, 1867, leaving no children.

MERRILL.

1 SILAS.

SILAS MERRILL married Sylvia, daughter of Abel Curtiss, and ved in Wolcott.

Children: 2 *Polly*, m Ashbel Allen and removed to Salisbury, onn.; 3 *Sheldon*, never married; 4 *Roxy;* 5 *Willis*, b Jan. 19, 803; 6 *Harriet*, m Johnson Alcott.

5 WILLIS.

WILLIS MERRILL, son of Silas and Sylvia (Curtiss) Merrill, mar- ed Julia Anna, daughter of Medad Alcott, Oct. 18, 1827. She as born Oct. 12, 1806.

Children: 7 *Harriet*, b Aug. 13, 1828, d Sept. 25, 1829; 8 *Lu- lia*, b March 30, 1831, m Timothy Root of Wolcott, April 18, 861; 9 *Sylvia Ann*, b March 3, 1836, d May 29, 1836; 10 *Juli- te*, b July 6, 1844, m Arthur W. Ashburn, June 7, 1866, and has iildren, Willis Merrill, b July 9, 1868, Addison Alcott, b March 5, 1870, Walter James, b Jan. 5, 1872.

MINOR.*

1 CLEMENT.

CLEMENT MINOR inherited the homestead of his father, William, in Somerset, England, and departed this life the 31st of March, 1640, and was interred in Chow Magna, in the county of Somerset.

Children: 2 *Clement;* 3 *Thomas;* 4 *Elizabeth;* 5 *Mary.*

3 THOMAS.

THOMAS MINOR, emigrated to "Connecticut Colony in New England" and was living at Stonington, Conn., in 1683.

His children were: 6 *John*, who removed to Stratford, then to Woodbury, Conn.; † 7 *Thomas*, of whom we find no record; 8 *Clement*, married and settled in New London, where some of his descendents now live, and from whom the Lyme Minors sprung; 9 *Ephraim*, settled in Stonington; 10 *Judah*, record says, went East; 11 *Manassah*, settled in Stonington, ancestor of the North Stonington Minors; 12 *Joseph;* 13 *Samuel;* 14 *Ann;* 15 *Maria;* 16 *Eunice;* 17 *Elizabeth;* 18 *Hannah.*

JEDEDIAH.

JEDEDIAH MINOR was born in Lyme, Conn., and married Elizabeth Marvin of that place, and settled in Wolcott about 1756, and lived, first, on the road going directly east from the Center towards Dea. Carter's present dwelling. He lived a little east of

---

* Cothren's History of Ancient Woodbury.

† Grace, daughter of Capt. John Minor of Stratford, and afterwards of Woodbury, married Samuel Grant, Jr., of Windsor, Conn., April 11, 1688, and thus became the ancestress of Gen. Ulysses S. Grant, the President of the United States.

the top of the hill, and afterwards moved to the top of the hill, north of Augustus Minor's present dwelling.

Children: 1 *Betsey*, m William Roberts of Bristol; 2 *Joseph*, who was about 12 years old when his father came to Wolcott; 3 *Esther*, m Samuel Atkins, who lived half a mile east of Levi Atkins' present dwelling; 4 *Dan*, enlisted in Revolutionary army and died with small pox; 5 *Caleb;* 6 *Lucretia*, m Michael Dayton of Watertown; 7 *Lucy*, m Jesse Alcox, June 16, 1791; 8 *Theda*, m William Barnes of Southington; 9 *Joshua;* 10 *Elizabeth*.

2 JOSEPH.

JOSEPH MINOR, son of Jedediah and Elizabeth (Marvin) Minor, married Mary, daughter of Capt. Samuel Upson. He lived and died on his father's homestead, a mile north of Wolcott Center.

Children: 11 *An Infant* that died May 3, 1783; 12 *Archibald*, b May 23, 1784; 13 *Joseph*, b April 22, 1786; 14 *Wealthy*, b Dec. 8, 1789, m Elihu Moulthrop; 15 *Marcus*, b July 17, 1790; 16 *Marvin*, b Aug., 1792; 17 *Nancy*, b July 12, 1798, m Orrin Hall; 18 *Mary*, b Nov. 23, 1800, m Ephraim Hall.

5 CALEB.

CALEB MINOR, son of Jedediah and Elizabeth (Marvin) Minor, married Jane Terrill of Naugatuck, and lived in Wolcott, for a time, then removed to Sheffield, Mass., where he died.

Children: 19 *Isaac;* 20 *Sally;* 21 *Theda;* 22 *Betsey;* 23 ——.

9 JOSHUA.

JOSHUA MINOR, son of Jedediah and Elizabeth (Marvin) Minor, married Diadama Alcox and lived in the northwestern part of the town.

Children: 24 *Selden;* 25 *Hiram;* 26 *Renselaer;* 27 *Newell;* 28 *Lucy*, m Ezra S. Hough; 29 *Diadama*, m George Plumb; 30 *Olive*.

12 ARCHIBALD.

ARCHIBALD MINOR, son of Joseph and Mary (Upson) Minor, married Betsey Tuttle of Plymouth, Oct. 27, 1808, and resides half a mile north of the Meeting house, being in his ninety-first year. He has been one of the most useful, respected, and hon-

GENEALOGIES. 523

ored citizens of Wolcott, having served the town in many offices for many years. Accomplished with the pen, his legible handwriting adorns many a page of town records. Gifted with a voice of great melody he aided, many years, divine worship with regularity and hearty earnestness, nor has his voice yet, though much broken, lost all its sweetness or power. His closing years seem tinted with a richer golden sunset than falls to the lot of many in this world.

Children: 31 *Henry*, b Dec. 17, 1809; 32 *Harriet*, b Dec. 8, 1811, m George W. Welton of Waterbury.

13 JOSEPH, JR.

JOSEPH MINOR, son of Joseph and Mary (Upson) Minor, married Charlotte Munson of Wolcott, lived a time on the David Norton farm, then removed to Ohio.

Children: 33 *Austin*; 34 *Marcus*; 35 ———.

15 MARCUS.

MARCUS MINOR, son of Joseph and Mary (Upson) Minor, married Harriet, daughter of Titus Hotchkiss, and lived a time on the old homestead, then on the old Squire Charles Upson place, and later he removed to Bristol, where he died Sept. 8, 1872, ae. 80.

Children: 36 *Maria*, b Oct. 29, 1813, m, Nov. 22, 1838, Willard Downs, lived in Wolcott and had children, Edson, b Sept. 10, 1839 (who m Josephine Upson and had children, Lizzie M. and George E.), Hattie E., b Aug. 14, 1842. She died April 25, 1872; 37 *Marshall* and 38 *Marcus*, twins, b June 16, 1824.

16 MARVIN.

MARVIN MINOR, son of Joseph and Mary (Upson) Minor, married Amanda Johnson of Bristol. She died June 22, 1851. He died Nov. 7, 1864.

Children: 39 *Caroline*, b April 29, 1819; 40 *Augustus*, b March 11, 1821; 41 *James W.*, b Feb. 11, 1828; 42 *Elvira*, b July 28, 1831.

31 HENRY.

HENRY MINOR, son of Archibald and Betsey (Tuttle) Minor, married Sarah J. Clark of Waterbury, and resides on the homestead of his father. He has served the town in various offices besides being Town Clerk twenty-five years.

Child: 43 *Theron C. A.*

37 MARSHALL.

MARSHALL MINOR, son of Marcus and Harriet (Hotchkiss) Minor, married Mary E. Downs.

Children: 43 *Marcus W.*, b July 29, 1852; 44 *George N.*, b July 9, 1854; 45 *Cornelius E.*, b July 29, 1856; 46 *Etta A.*, b May 15, 1859.

40 AUGUSTUS.

AUGUSTUS MINOR, son of Marvin and Amanda (Johnson) Minor, married Emogene E. Frisbie, and lives on his father's farm, in a new house built by himself.

Child: 47 *Charlie J.*, b Aug. 26, 1855.

43 THERON.

THERON C. A. MINOR, son of Henry and Sarah J. (Clark) Minor married, Dec. 1, 1861, Sarah Jane, daughter of Erastus W. Warner of Wolcott and resides in Waterbury.

Child: 48 *Myrtie D.*, b Oct. 6, 1862.

MOULTHROP.

MOULTHROPP, MOLTHROP, MOULTROP, MOULLTROP, MOLTROP, MOLTROUP, MOULTROUP, MOULTREP.

This is a Danish name and the first Matthew Moulthrop is said to have come from Denmark to New Haven. There are all of the above spellings on the records except the second, which is probably the original one, Moulthropp.

1 MATTHEW.

MATTHEW MOULTHROP, married Jane ———, was early in New Haven and removed to Stony River, East Haven, in 1662.

Children: 2 *Matthew*; 3 *Elizabeth*, m John Gregory, 1663; 4 *Mary*.

2 MATTHEW, JR.

MATTHEW MOULTHROP, son of Matthew and Jane Moulthrop, married Hannah Thomson in 1662, lived in East Haven.

Children: 5 *Hannah*, b Jan., 1663, d young; 6 *Hannah*, b April 20, 1665; 7 *John*, b Feb. 5, 1667; 8 *Matthew*, b July 18, 1670; 9 *Infant*, b 1673; 10 *Lydia*, b Aug. 8, 1674; 11 *Samuel*, b June 1677, d; 12 *Samuel*, b April 13, 1679; 13 *Keziah*, b April 12, 1682.

7 JOHN.

JOHN MOULTHROP, son of Matthew and Hannah (Thompson) Moulthrop, married Abigail Bradley, June 29, 1692, lived in East Haven.

Children: 14 *Abigail*, b Aug. 12, 1693; 15 *John*, b March 17, 1696; 16 *Mary*, b 1698, d; 17 *Sarah*, b 1701, m Adonijah Morris; 18 *Dan*, b Dec. 1, 1703; 19 *Israel*, b June 7, 1706; 20 *Joseph*; 21 *Timothy*.

20 JOSEPH.

JOSEPH MOULTHROP, son of John and Abigail (Bradley) Moulthrop, married Mary Wheadon, lived in East Haven.

Children : 22 *Joseph;* 23 *Elihu;* 24 *Jude;* 25 *Adonijah*, lost in the French war ; 26 *Hannah;* 27 *Rhoda;* 28 *Mary;* 29 *Lucretia;* 30 *Abigail.*

23 ELIHU.

ELIHU MOULTHROP, son of Joseph and Mary (Wheadon) Moulthrop, married Mary Hotchkiss, Nov. 21, 1770, lived in East Haven until after the birth of his children, when he removed to Wolcott.

Children : 31 *Jared;* 32 *Polly;* 33 *Adonijah;* 34 *Elihu;* 35 *Esther.*

34 ELIHU, 2D.

ELIHU MOULTHROP, son of Elihu and Mary (Hotchkiss) Moulthrop, married Wealthy, daughter of Joseph Minor, in 1807, and lived in Wolcott.

Children : 36 *Caroline*, b Aug. 21, 1808, d ; 37 *Levi*, b Jan. 5, 1811 ; 38 *Sherman*, b May 18, 1813 ; 39 *Elihu*, b March 16, 1816 ; 40 *Mary*, b Jan. 12, 1824, d 1826.

37 LEVI.

LEVI MOULTHROP, son of Elihu and Wealthy (Minor) Moulthrop, married Charlotte S. J. Stocking, Sept. 8, 1841. She was born June 9, 1825.

Children : 41 *Philura Phonora*, b Nov. 16, 1842, m, 1st, Moses S. Fuller, 2d, Joseph B. Fenn, had two children, both died young. She died July 1, 1872 ; 42 *John Rowe*, b Feb. 20, 1845 ; 43 *Henry Harwood*, b Feb. 6, 1849.

38 SHERMAN.

SHERMAN MOULTHROP, son of Elihu and Wealthy (Minor) Moulthrop married Sarah Ann, daughter of Eldad Alcott, April 23, 1835, and lives on the old David Alcox place.

Children : 44 *Theodore*, b Feb. 4, 1836 ; 45 *Augusta*, b March 19, 1838, m George Waters of Waterbury; 46 *Newell*, b Feb. 29, 1840; 47 *Frederick*, b Dec. 12, 1844, d March 5, 1853 ; 48 *Edgar S.*, b Nov. 10, 1847 ; 49 *Frederick C.*, b July 30, 1855.

39 ELIHU, 3D.

ELIHU MOULTHROP, son of Elihu and Wealthy (Minor) Moulthrop, married Sarah M., daughter of Lucius Tuttle, and lives in Wolcott.

Children: 50 *Antoinette M.*, b Sept. 4, 1839, m Robert Stevenson of Ansonia and has a daughter Jessie E.; 51 *Evelyn E.*, b July 12, 1841, enlisted in late war and died Aug. 30, 1864, in Georgia.

46 NEWELL.

NEWELL MOULTHROP, son of Sherman and Sarah A. (Alcott) Moulthrop, married Jennie E. Thompson of Bristol, July 5, 1868.
Child: *George*, b May 24, 1870.

48 EDGAR S.

EDGAR S. MOULTHROP, son of Sherman and Sarah A. (Alcott) Moulthrop, married Kate Rogers of Cornwall, Conn., April, 1870.

MUNSON.

1 WILLIAM A.

WILLIAM A. MUNSON was born in Waterbury Dec. 14, 1824, and married, Oct. 5, 1846, Julia A., daughter of Ephraim Hall.

Children: 2 *Cornelius F.*, b Dec. 28, 1849; 3 *Inez Yale*, b May 15, 1852, m John Thompson of East Haven, resides in Waterbury, and has children, Ella Mary, b Jan. 2, 1870, John, b Jan. 15, 1873: 4 *Eva Luella*, d young.

2 CORNELIUS F.

CORNELIUS F. MUNSON, son of William A. and Julia A. (Hall) Munson, married Eveline I., daughter of Merritt Frisbie of Southington.

Child: *Emma Fidelia*, b May 31, 1871.

NICHOLS.

The ancestor of the Waterbury Nicholses came from Long Island.

1 RICHARD.

Richard Nichols, son of George of Long Island, had

Children: 1 *Elijah;* 2 *Joseph;* 3 *Samme;* 4 *James;* 5 *Richard;* 6 *Sarah;* 7 *Marian,* m Bronson; 8 *Lydia;* 9 *Tamar.*

3 SAMME.

SAMME NICHOLS, son of Richard, married Abigail Landon, and lived in the western part of the town of Waterbury.

Children: 10 *Erastus,* d young; 11 *Charles;* 12 *Polly;* 13 *Almira;* 14 *Abigail;* 15 *Julia;* 16 *Erastus,* b June 8, 1798; 17 *Rhoda;* 18 *Richard;* 19 *Jessie;* 20 *Harriet,* d young; 21 *Harriet.*

16 ERASTUS.

ERASTUS NICHOLS, son of Samme and Abigail (Landon) Nichols, married Rachel Pardee, Feb. 25, 1819, and resides on the Pardee place, in Woodtick. She was born April 30, 1798.

Children: 22 *Phyletta,* b Feb. 1, 1820, m Frances Wood, and lives in Southington; 23 *George E.,* b June 8, 1821; 24 *Samuel,* b Sept. 3, 1823; 25 *Polly,* b Aug. 27, 1825, d Dec. 25, 1825; 26 *Polly,* b Nov. 6, 1826, m David T. Welton, d Sept. 8, 1845; 27 *Frederick L.,* b Nov. 1, 1832; 28 *Emma E.,* b April 24, 1838, d Aug. 22, 1863.

23 GEORGE.

GEORGE NICHOLS, son of Erastus and Rachel (Pardee) Nichols, married Eliza O. Marsh of Brookfield, Madison Co., N. Y.

Child: 29 *Mary Henrietta,* b Oct. 31, 1845, m Luther S. Hall, of Middletown, Conn.

24 SAMUEL.

SAMUEL NICHOLS, son of Erastus and Rachel (Pardee) Nichols, married Charlotte Wells, Jan. 18, 1851. She was born July 12, 1830.

Children: 30 *Eugene Ellison*, b Jan. 18, 1854; 31 *Emma Eliza*, b Sept. 12, 1861, d Jan. 29, 1865; 32 *Samuel*, b Sept. 16, 1872.

27 FREDERICK L.

FREDERICK L. NICHOLS, son of Erastus and Rachel (Pardee) Nichols, married Helena Ann Stevens of Wolcott, Nov. 2, 1854. She died June 24, 1864.

Children: 33 *Helen E.*, b Nov. 27, 1857; 34 *Susan R.*, b. Sept. 2, 1861; 35 *Charlotte E. Joslin*, an adopted daughter, b Feb. 13, 1853, m, June, 1872, Henry Carnett, resides in New York Mills, N. Y.

30 EUGENE ELLISON.

EUGENE E. NICHOLS, son of Samuel and Charlotte (Wells) Nichols, married Emma A. Smith of New London, Sept. 20, 1873.

NORTON.

THOMAS NORTON, emigrated from Ackley in Surrey, England, to Guilford, Conn., in 1639, having a wife and three daughters at that time. He married Grace Wells some fourteen years before he came to America.

Children: 1 *Anne*, b about 1625, and m John Warner of Saybrook and Hartford; 2 *Grace*, b 1627, m William Seward, April 2, 1651, of New Haven and Guilford, and d May 29, 1689; 3 *Mary*, b 1635, m Samuel Rockwell, son of William of Windsor, April 9, 1660; 4 *John*, b 1640; 5 *Abigail*, b 1642, m Ananias Tryon of Killingworth, Aug. 6, 1667; 6 *Thomas*, b 1646, m Elizabeth Mason, May 8, 1671.

4 JOHN.

JOHN NORTON, son of Thomas and Grace (Wells) Norton, married, 1st, Hannah Stone, 2d, Elizabeth Hubbard. He was a miller of Guilford, and died May 5th, 1704.

Children: 7 *John*, b Nov. 18, 1666, d Jan. 10, 1667; 8 *John*, b May 29, 1668; 9 *Susannah*, b Oct. 4, 1672; 10 *Mary*, b 1680; 11 *Thomas*, b May 4, 1675; 12 *Hannah*, b Feb. 4, 1677 or 8, m Ebenezer Stone, Jan. 16, 1702.

8 JOHN, JR.

JOHN NORTON, Jr., son of John the miller of Guilford, married Hannah, daughter of Emanuel Peck of Wethersfield, Nov. 14, 1694. He died March 15, 1711. She died Oct. 22, 1739.

Children: 13 *Anna*, b Oct. 16, 1695, d Oct., 1721; 14 *Mary*, b Dec. 6, 1697; 15 *John*, b Dec. 23, 1699; 16 *Sarah*, b Feb. 26, 1702; 17 *Joseph*, b Oct. 10, 1704: 18 *Elizabeth*, b Oct. 6, 1706, m David Benton, Aug. 8, 1728, of Guilford, d Aug. 25, 1756; 19 *Hannah*, b March 4, 1710, d 1724.

15 JOHN, 3D.

JOHN NORTON, son of John and Hannah (Peck) Norton, married, 1st, Elizabeth Robinson, and, 2d, Mary Morgan, daughter of John of Groton. He lived in Guilford and died Jan. 11, 1798, ae. 99.

Children: 20 *Hannah;* 21 *John;* 22 *Ruth,* m Nathan Chittenden, Oct. 23, 1756, of Guilford; 23 *Zebulon,* m Naomi Booth, moved to Wolcott, and afterwards to Bloomfield, N. J.; 24 *Abraham,* m —— Doolittle, removed to Wolcott, had 4 sons and 9 daughters; 25 *Mary,* m I. Pierce of Southbury, Conn.; 26 *Nathan;* 27 *Andrew;* 28 *Huldah;* 29 *Elizabeth,* b 1732, d single, Oct. 21, 1788.

17 JOSEPH.

JOSEPH NORTON, son of John and Hannah (Peck) Norton, married Mary Champion of Lyme, April 11, 1728. He died in Guilford, May 9, 1781. His widow, Mary, resided several years in Wolcott with her son David and is said to have been 105 years old when she left Wolcott and went to Guilford to live with a son there. She died, July 13, 1800, ae. 110 years.

Children: 30 *Simeon,* b May 3, 1729, lived in Guilford and d Dec. 22, 1772; 31 *David,* b Oct. 21, 1730; 32 *William,* b Jan. 22, 1732, d June 17, 1760; 33 *Hannah,* b Oct. 1, 1734; 34 *Philamon,* b June 24, 1736, d Oct. (?), 1736; 35 *Noah,* b Jan. 27, 1740, d May 31, 1763; 36 *Beniah,* b 1742, d Nov. 10, 1803.

31 DAVID.

DAVID NORTON, son of Joseph and Mary (Champion) Norton, married, 1st, Submit Benton, Nov. 11, 1752. She died about 1755. He married, 2d, Suza Bishop. His home and farm were about half a mile south west from Wolcott Center. Dea. Aaron Harrison speaks of him, after his death, in the highest terms, both as a citizen and Christian. Abraham Norton, of considerable note in this town, was first cousin to this David.

Children: 37 *Ozias,* b Feb. 10, 1753; 38 *Cyrus,* b Jan. 14, 1755, m Jerusha Johnson of Wolcott and removed to N. Y.; 39 *Ziba,* bapt. June 20, 1757, m Ruth Hopkins, Nov. 26, 1778, had daughter, Philomela, m Jared Welton; 40 *Suza,* bapt. June 12, 1759; 41 *Zebul,* bapt. Sept. 22, 1761, m Rhoda Norton, his

GENEALOGIES.   533

cousin; 42 *Noah Uzza*, bapt. July 3, 1764, m Rachel Gillet, of Wolcott, April 18, 1784, settled in New York.

37 OZIAS.

OZIAS NORTON, son of David and Submit (Benton) Norton, married Maria Frisbie. He died Feb. 6, 1840, ae. 87.

Children: 43 *David*, m —— Welton and removed West; 44 *Keziah*, m Daniel Lane, of Wolcott; 45 *Susan* and 46 *Elizabeth*, twins, Susan m Daniel Byington, Elizabeth m Thomas Cook and settled in Ohio; 47 *Moses Frisbie*, m Percy Barber, removed to Ohio; 48 *Jonathan Fowler*, m Polly Smith, lived and died in Wolcott; 49 *Ziba;* 50 *Simeon Newton*, b March 28, 1791; 51 *Jedediah Harmon*, b May 11, 1788.

49 ZIBA.

ZIBA NORTON, son of Ozias and Maria (Frisbie) Norton, married Abigail Atkins of Wolcott.

Children: 52 *Adah*, b June 23, 1803, m, 1st, M. Doolittle, 2d, Geo. W. Royce, had children, Marcia, Cecilia, William; 53 *Talcott*, b Sept. 19, 1807, m Belinda Hall of Plymouth, had daughter Amelia; 54 *Leonora*, b March 12, 1805, m Harley Downs, had daughters, Esther Elvira, d, and Esther Elvira; 55 *Phebe*, b Dec., 1809, m George W. Winchel; 56 *Minerva*, b March, 1812, m Everest Norton, had children, Rutilla, Rufus, Sylvester; 57 *Hendric*, b Dec., 1817; 58 *Rufus*, b 1819; 59 *Manville*, b June 8, 1821; 60 *Rufinus*, b Sept., 1824.

50 SIMEON NEWTON.

SIMEON N. NORTON, son of Ozias and Maria (Frisbie) Norton, married Rebecca Parker of Wolcott, Nov. 11, 1812. He died in Wolcott, Feb. 5, 1847.

Children: 61 *Simeon Hopkins*, b Aug. 11, 1813; 62 *Levi Parker*, b Sept. 22, 1815; 63 *Hannah Miriam*, b Jan. 4, 1818, m Upson Higgins, of Wolcott; 64 *Janette*, b July 31, 1821, d young; 65 *Justina*, b Aug. 8, 1822, d young; 66 *Julina Janette*, b Jan. 28, 1825, m Prof. Louis Bail, of New Haven; 67 *Samuel Newton*, is in California.

51 JEDEDIAH HARMON.

JEDEDIAH H. NORTON, son of Ozias and Maria (Frisbie) Norton, married Hannah, daughter of Matthew Rowe of Fair Haven, Sept 4, 1805. She was born Sept. 21, 1782, died Sept. 9, 1873. He resides in Plymouth, in his 87th year.

Children: 68 *Ozias Rowe*, b June 12, 1806; 69 *Rodney Frisbie*, b Dec. 10, 1807, m Lucinda Blakeslee, of Bristol, and d Oct. 11, 1871; 70 *Stephen Ludington*, b July 23, 1810; 71 *Matthew Simeon*, b Aug. 19, 1812; 72 *Selden S.*, b Nov. 25, 1813; 73 *Eunice R.*, b Aug. 21, 1817, m Lewis Smith, and resides in Hartford; 74 *Hannah R.*, b Nov. 10, 1819, m Elliot Dawson, resides in Plymouth; 75 *Jedediah Roswell*, b June 28, 1822; 76 *Daniel Eli*, b Sept. 16, 1826.

57 HENDRICK.

HENDRICK NORTON, son of Ziba and Abigail (Atkins) Norton, married Eliza Finch.

Children: 77 *Lucius;* 78 *Mary;* 79 *Emeline;* 80 *George.*

58 RUFUS.

RUFUS NORTON, son of Ziba and Abigail (Atkins) Norton, married, 1st, Harriet Smith, 2d, Ellen Beecher.

Children: 81 *Harriet;* 82 *Omar;* 83 *Winfield;* 84 *Carrol;* 85 *Minnie.*

59 MANVILLE.

MANVILLE NORTON, son of Ziba and Abigail (Atkins) Norton, married Thankful Foss of Skaneatelas, N. Y., lives in town of Waterbury.

Children: 86 *Mary A.;* 87 *Harley D.;* 88 *Amos F.;* 89 *Adelbert H.*

60 RUFINUS.

RUFINUS NORTON, son of Ziba and Abigail (Atkins) Norton, married Mary Ann Brooks of Albany, N. Y.

Child: 90 *Charles.*

61 SIMEON HOPKINS.

SIMEON H. NORTON, son of Simeon N. and Rebecca (Parker) Norton, married Sarah Ann, daughter of Capt. Levi Hall, Oct. 16, 1836, settled in Southington. She was born Oct. 26, 1813, d Feb. 24, 1872.

Children: 91 *Luzern Townsend*, b July 22, 1841, died in the

Battle of Chancellorsville, May 3, 1863 ; 92 *Sarah Eveline*, b May 26, 1846, d March 29, 1849 ; 93 *Sarah Eveline*, b May 19, 1848, m Walter A. Cowles, Jan. 3, 1872.

68 OZIAS ROWE.

OZIAS R. NORTON, son of Jedediah H. and Hannah (Rowe) Norton, married Fanny Roper of Wolcott.

Children: 94 *Harriet* ; 95 *Maria* ; 96 *Charles* ; 97 *Martin*.

70 STEPHEN LUDINGTON.

STEPHEN L. NORTON, son of Jedediah H. and Hannah (Rowe) Norton, married Lucinda Bradley. He died June 7, 1867.

Children: 98 *Ammon ;* 99 *Lewis ;* 100 *Oliver ;* 101 *Andrew ;* 102 *Eunice;* 103 *Sarah ;* 104 *Turtius ;* 105 *Wallace ;* 106 *Addie*.

71 MATTHEW SIMEON.

MATTHEW S. NORTON, son of Jedediah H. and Hannah (Rowe) Norton, married Betsey Maria, daughter of John Thomas of Wolcott, Nov. 30, 1831. She was born Sept. 1, 1811. He died May 22, 1874.

Children : 107 *James R.*, b Aug. 21, 1833 ; 108 *Caroline E.*, b July 24, 1836, m George A. Dingwell, and had children, Nelson, Wesley, Freddie, Augustus and Infant ; 109 *Burrett M.*, b Jan. 30, 1848, d June 7, 1864, in the late war, aged 16 years.

72 SELDON S.

SELDON S. NORTON, son of Jedediah H. and Hannah (Rowe) Norton, married, 1st, Aury C. Nichols, 2d, Anna M., daughter of Arthur Decker of New York.

Children: 110 *Ellen Hannah*, b Oct. 20, 1851, m Lewis E. Dailey, 1868, and has children, Alfred and Jennie ; 111 *Lucius* and 112 *Lucian*, twins, b May 19, 1855 ; 113 *Emma Jane*, b June 26, 1857 ; 114 *Elmar*, b Feb. 26, 1862.

76 DANIEL ELI.

DANIEL E. NORTON, son of Jedediah H. and Hannah (Rowe) Norton, married, 1st, Mary Russell, 2d, Addie Russell, Dec. 10, 1867.

Children : 115 *Dwight Edward*, b Oct. 13, 1868 ; 116 *Jerrus Stephen*, b Nov. 21, 1871.

PARDEE.

ELIPHALET PARDEE married, 1st, —— Blakeslee and lived in North Haven. She died in North Haven and he married, 2d, widow Bishop, who died in Wolcott.

Children: 1 *David;* 2 *Jessie;* 3 *Mary*, m Solomon Barnes, lived and died in North Haven; 4 *Abigail;* 5 *Hannah*, m John Cooper of North Haven.

1 DAVID.

DAVID PARDEE, son of Eliphalet Pardee, married, 1st, Polly Spencer of North Haven, who died April 15, 1802. 2d, Philetta Neal, 1805. He settled in Wolcott, in Woodtick, where Erastus Nichols resides. He died Feb., 1844.

Children: 6 *Hannah*, b Jan. 2, 1786, m Joel Curtiss of Wolcott and removed to New York and died in Illinois; 7 *Rosel*, b Feb. 23, 1788; 8 *Heman*, b Feb. 17, 1791; 9 *Silas*, b Sept. 13, 1795; 10 *Rachel*, b April 30, 1798, m Erastus Nichols, Feb. 25, 1819, and lives on the Pardee homestead; 11 *Linus*, b Jan. 28, 1801.

7 ROSEL.

ROSEL PARDEE, son of David and Polly (Spencer) Pardee, married Polly Nichols of Waterbury.

Children: 12 *Mary Ann;* 13 *Esther;* 14 *Henry Spencer;* 15 *Jane;* 16 *Nancy.*

8 HEMAN.

HEMAN PARDEE, son of David and Polly (Spencer) Pardee, married, 1st, Almira Nichols, 2d, Sarah Brockett.

Children: 17 *Isaac;* 18 *Charles;* 19 *Emeline;* 20 *Isaac;* 21 *Abigail;* 22 *David;* 23 *Polly;* 24 *Charles;* 25 *Heman.* By second wife: 26 *Almira.*

GENEALOGIES.

9 SILAS.

SILAS PARDEE, son of David and Polly (Spencer) Pardee, married Polly Root.

Children : 27 *Lewis;* 28 *Eliza;* 29 *Olivia;* 30 *Silas;* 31 *Laura Ann;* 32 *Belinda;* 33 *Ruth M.;* 34 *Polly;* 35 *Rachel;* 36 *Maria.*

11 LINUS.

LINUS PARDEE, son of David and Polly (Spencer) Pardee, married Betsey Alcott and removed to New York State.

Children : 37 *Joseph Dwight;* 38 *Ann Delight;* 39 *Adelaide;* 40 *Emeliza.*

PARKER.

1 JOSEPH.

JOSEPH PARKER was among the early settlers in Wolcott. His house was on the bound line near Amos Seward's, south part of Wolcott. His wife Mary lived to be 99 years of age.

Children: 2 *Joseph M.;* 3 *Zephaniah,* called Zephna, or "Uncle Zeph"; 4 *Mary,* m David Wakelee.

2 JOSEPH MERRIAM.

JOSEPH M. PARKER, son of Joseph and Mary Parker, married Hannah, eldest daughter of Simeon Hopkins, Feb. 28, 1787. He was a prominent man in the Society, in his day.

Children: 5 *Eldad,* b July 24, 1787; 6 *Levi,* b March 26, 1791; 7 *Rebecca,* b Sept. 9, 1794, m Simeon N. Norton.

3 ZEPHANIAH.

ZEPHANIAH PARKER, son of Joseph and Mary Parker, married Deborah, eldest daughter of Abel Curtiss. He sold the Churchill place and bought that now owned by Augustus Rose.

Children: 8 *Alpha;* 9 *Roena,* m Selah Hall of Waterbury; 10 *Harvey;* 11 *Almira,* m Micah Ruggs of Southington; 12 *Almon;* 13 *William;* 14 *Joel;* 15 *Zephaniah;* 16 *Willard.*

5 ELDAD.

ELDAD PARKER, son of Joseph M. and Hannah (Hopkins) Parker, married Sylvia —— and lived some time at Wolcott Center. He was a man of remarkable intellect and physical endurance, but of poor judgment, uncultivated manners at times, and was led captive by old customs. He died aged 85.

Children: 17 *Bennet Woodward,* b May 12, 1808; 18 *Joseph*

GENEALOGIES. 539

Merriam, b Aug. 11, 1814, was a wild boy, left home in his teens and died young.

6 LEVI.

LEVI PARKER, son of Joseph M. and Hannah (Hopkins) Parker, married and lived considerable of his life in New Haven. He was a very fine man; was clerk in New Haven some years, then returned to his native town and died aged about forty years.

Children : 19 *George*, who was a successful clock manufacturer in Bristol. He went to California about 1860, where he resides, having accumulated a large property, and is much respected. 20 *Jane*, the wife of Noah M. Pomeroy, a clock manufacturer in Bristol. They now reside in Hartford, in affluent circumstances.

17 BENNET WOODWARD.

BENNET W. PARKER, son of Eldad and Sylvia Parker, was an ambitious, resolute boy. His father apprenticed him, against the wish of the boy, to Fitch A. Higgins, to learn shoemaking. He ran away; was advertised as a "Ragged boy, escaping, with a little patch on his back, and one cent reward, but no charges, paid for his recovery." A few years after, Bennet appeared in Yale College, where he graduated. He afterwards became a successful physician in the State of New Jersey, where he died in the meridian of life.

WILLIAM.

WILLIAM PARKER, supposed to be brother to Zephaniah (not certain) married Roxanna, daughter of Abel Curtiss, March 22, 1808.

Children : 1 *Bennet*, b March 12, 1809 ; 2 *Edward*, b Sept. 10, 1812 ; 3 *Sarah Ann*, b Feb. 23, 1815 ; 4 *George Wolcott*, b March 26, 1817 ; 5 *Stillman*, b June 7, 1819; 6 *Charlotte*, b June 16, 1821 ; 7 *Samuel Jackson*, b Sep. 25, 1829.

PECK.

DEACON JUSTUS PECK* was a descendant of Deacon Paul Peck of Hartford, and was the son of Zebulon Peck, who died in Bristol, Conn., Jan. 13, 1795. Justus was born Nov. 14, 1737, and married, Sept. 6, 1759, Lucy Frisbie and settled in Wolcott previous to 1762. He was Deacon twenty-eight years and his wife was one of the first members of the church. He died Nov. 23, 1813, ae. 76. His wife, Lucy, died Dec. 11, 1823, ae. 83.

Children: 1 *Lucy*, b March 10, 1761, m and d in New Hampshire, leaving children; 2 *Elisha*, b Sept. 9, 1763; 3 *Mary*, b Sept. 23, 1766, m Joshua Cook of Rutland, Vt., Jan. 20, 1789; 4 *Sarah*, b June 10, 1768, d March 30, 1773; 5 *Rachel*, b Nov. 13, 1771, m Rev. Asa Talmadge of Southington, Oct. 17, 1801, d June 5, 1845; 6 *Justus*, b June 28, 1774, d Sept. 2, 1777; 7 *Sarah*, b June 28, 1779, m Titus Brockett of Wolcott, d April 23, 1850, ae. 71; 8 *Lowly*, b Dec. 15, 1782, m Stephen Carter, Jr., Nov. 15, 1804, d Dec. 14, 1861, ae 79; 9 *Rhoda*, b Jan. 4, 1786, d March 30, 1792; 10 *Justus Lot*, b April 29, 1788, m Sarah Merriman of Southington, d April 15, 1812.

---

* See Peck Genealogy.

PLUMB.

1 SIMEON.

SIMEON PLUMB was among the early settlers in Wolcott, and married, about 1762, Mary, daughter of Joseph Atkins, Senior, and lived in the northern portion of the town ; the road is known as "Plumb Street." His wife, Mary, died in 1807, and he died in 1813.

Children: 2 *Solomon;* 3 *Samuel*, b July 13, 1766 ; 4 *Gamaliel;* 5 *Joseph*, bapt. Aug. 7, 1774 ; 6 *Sarah*, bapt. Dec. 10, 1775 ; 7 *Sylvia*, bapt. June 28, 1778, m James Scarritt, June 13, 1781 ; 8 *Azariah*, Amariah on church book, bapt. July 30, 1780 ; 9 *Sabra*, m Asa Alcox, May 18, 1780 ; 10 *Sibyl;* 11 *Susanna*, bapt. March 28, 1784.

2 SOLOMON.

SOLOMON PLUMB, son of Simeon and Mary (Atkins) Plumb, married Lucretia Scarritt, Jan. 28, 1790. He died in 1848.

Children : 12 *Orrin;* 13 *Amanda*, m Solomon Griggs ; 14 *Willard*, b July 29, 1796 ; 15 *Wells;* 16 *Romanthy*, m —— Gridley ; 17 *Jerry*.

3 SAMUEL.

SAMUEL PLUMB, son of Simeon and Mary (Atkins) Plumb, married, Sarah, daughter of Jeremiah Scarritt, Jan. 17, 1797. She was born Sept. 6, 1778, and married, 2d, —— Truesdel, and died Jan. 28, 1873, in her 95th year. Samuel Plumb died Oct. 25, 1840, ae. 74.

Children : 18 *Luther Wheaton*, b Oct. 2, 1797, d in South Carolina, July 9, 1822 ; 19 *Vina*, b May 11, 1800 ; 20 *Ansel Harvey*, b Jan. 6, 1803 ; 21 *Mary*, b Sept. 2, 1805, d 1806 ; 22 *Almon*, b Aug. 4, 1807 ; 23 *George Henry*, b Oct. 15, 1813 ; 24 *Rollin Wiard*, b Feb. 11, 1821.

5 JOSEPH.

JOSEPH PLUMB, son of Simeon and Mary (Atkins) Plumb, married Phebe Sutliff, Dec. 4, 1800. She died March 22, 1813.

Children: 25 *Sabra*, b Dec. 19, 1801; 26 *Harvey*, b Aug. 6, 1804; 27 *Triphena*, b Feb. 10, 1808; 28 *Hester*, b Oct. 19, 1810.

12 ORRIN.

ORRIN PLUMB, son of Solomon and Lucretia (Scarritt) Plumb, married, 1st, Diadama Gaylord, 2d, Hannah Beach, and was long known as Squire Plumb. He was the "Boss" politician of his party and received a large share of the honors of the same.

Children: 29 *Harvey;* 30 *Andrew*, is in the West; 31 *Jane;* 32 *Diadama;* 33 *Sidney;* 34 *Sarah*.

14 WILLARD.

WILLARD PLUMB, son of Solomon and Lucretia (Scarritt) Plumb, married Polly, daughter of Sergeant Heman Hall, Jan. 1, 1822. He lived within the North East School District, and died Feb. 18, 1867.

Children: 35 *William A.*, b April 4, 1825, d Nov. 29, 1834; 36 *Solomon W.*, b Jan. 3, 1829, lives in Southington; 37 *Loretta B.*, b Jan. 20, 1834, d June 21, 1837; 38 *Levi W.*, b Nov. 16, 1836, is living in Waterbury; 39 *Lydia Ann*, b Nov. 29, 1845, d Aug. 23, 1849.

15 WELLS.

WELLS PLUMB, son of Solomon and Lucretia (Scarritt) Plumb, married Highly Kenea, and lived in Wolcott, northeastern part.

Children: 40 *Salome*, m Edwin Hough; 41 *Orlando;* 42 *Henry;* 43 *Henry*.

20 ANSEL HARVEY.

Deacon ANSEL H. PLUMB, son of Samuel and Sarah (Scarritt) Plumb, married Jan. 9, 1828, Lois, daughter of James Alcott, 2d, and lived on the old homestead. He died Aug. 20, 1870, ae. 67, and is spoken of by all as a very good and reliable man, and a consistent, exemplary deacon.

Children: 44 *Luther W.*, b Sept. 16, 1832; 45 *Esther A.*, m Burritt W. Beecher.

GENEALOGIES. 543

23 GEORGE HENRY.

GEORGE H. PLUMB, son of Samuel and Sarah (Scarritt) Plumb, married Diadama, daughter of Joshua Minor, May 3, 1840. She was born Jan. 13, 1820. They reside in Terryville.

Children: 46 *Mary A.*, an adopted daughter, b May 25, 1846; 47 *Newell M.*, b Sept. 17, 1853; 48 *Wallace G.*, b Dec. 10, 1858; 49 *Elsie Jane*, b Dec. 15, 1861, d June 5, 1867.

24 ROLLIN WIARD.

ROLLIN W. PLUMB, son of Samuel and Sarah (Scarritt) Plumb, married, Sept. 1, 1844, Caroline N., daughter of Jesse Brooks of Cheshire, and lives in Terryville.

Children: 50 *Rollin Jesse*, b Sept. 13, 1853; 51 *Henry Brooks*, b Dec. 24, 1857; 52 *Caroline Louisa*, b Oct. 13, 1862, d Jan. 10, 1873.

44 LUTHER W.

LUTHER W. PLUMB, son of Ansel H. and Lois (Alcott) Plumb, married Eliza A. Harrison, May 11, 1856.

Children: 53 *Frank;* 54 and 55 two daughters, twins.

ROLLIN JESSE.

ROLLIN JESSE, son of Rollin W. and Caroline N. (Brooks) Plumb, married Cora J. Rossiter, July 29, 1872, and lives in Terryville.

Child: 56 *Charles Wetmore*, b Dec. 28, 1873.

POTTER.

Dr. JOHN POTTER, son of Joel Potter of Southington, came to Wolcott and married Sept. 11, 1783, Lydia, the daughter of Dea. Aaron Harrison, and was a practicing physician many years. He identified himself fully with the religious, social, and political interests of the town and secured only a comfortable living. For many years the "brethren" used to go over to Dr. Potter's house, at intermission on Sunday and smoke the pipe of peace, and talk over the important events of the town and nation; events more important as then regarded than any that transpire in later days. (See Biog., page 35.) His wife Lydia died Sept. 26, 1796. He married, 2d, widow Highly Clark, March 30, 1797, and removed West about 1820.

Children: 1 *Zephna*, b Oct. 19, 1785, became a physician and went West; 2 *Samuel Young*, b Feb. 11, 1794. By second wife: 3 *John Adams*, b Feb. 25, 1798; 4 *Lydia Maria*, b Sept. 23, 1799, d Oct. 12, 1799; 5 *Albert Rodney*, b Nov. 29, 1800; 6 *Sarah Maria*, b March 5, 1803.

PRITCHARD.

1 ROGER.

ROGER PRITCHARD came from England and settled adjoining Wolcott territory in the Big Plains near Mark Warner's late residence, on the south road from Woodtick to Waterbury. He was a very stout, fearless man and was chosen leader to keep the Indians from committing depredations. He died Sept. 19, 1792, ae. 76, and was buried in the old burying ground in Waterbury city.

Children: 2 *Roger;* 3 *Amos;* 4 *Abraham.* All settled on Buck's Hill.

2 ROGER, JR.

ROGER PRITCHARD, son of Roger Pritchard the first settler, was a tailor by trade and had no children.

3 AMOS.

AMOS PRITCHARD, son of Roger Pritchard the first settler, was a farmer, and was called the "Old Trumpeter" on account of his strength of voice, which could be heard distinctly three miles. He was twice married.

Children : 5 *Amos;* 6 *Lydia,* m Eleazar Hall, had three children; 7 *Roger,* who died in infancy; 8 *Sabra,* m Isaac Alling, had children, Elvira, Norman; 9 *Roger;* 10 *Orry;* 11 *Elias;* 12 *Ruth,* never m, d Jan. 16, 1873, ae. 80.

4 ABRAHAM.

ABRAHAM PRITCHARD, son of Roger Pritchard the first settler, married Anna Hotchkiss and had children.

Children: 13 *Reuben;* 14 *Abigail,* m Lemuel Cleaveland and had children ; 15 *John;* 16 *Sarah;* 17 *Abraham.*

5 AMOS, JR.

AMOS PRITCHARD, eldest son of Amos, Senr., married Limera Lounsbury.

Children: 18 *Asahel;* 19 *Roxanna;* 20 *Harvey;* 21 *Marinda;* 22 *Erastus;* 23 *Marshall;* 24 *Lovicy;* 25 *Esther;* 26 *Betsey;* 27 *Isaac.*

9 ROGER.

ROGER PRITCHARD, son of Amos Pritchard, married Chloe Nichols.

Children: 28 *Gilbert;* 29 *Dennis;* 30 *Amy*, m Charles Seeley, Dec. 24, 1843, and had children, Chloe, George, Charles, Grace Dwight, Polly. She died May 3, 1870.

10 ORRY.

ORRY PRITCHARD, son of Amos, Senr., married Dyer Hotchkiss.

Children: 31 *Charles;* 32 *Henry;* 33 *Mary;* 34 *Amos;* 35 *Sarah.*

11 ELIAS.

ELIAS PRITCHARD, son of Amos, Senr., married Hannah Payne.

Children: 36 *Luman;* 37 *Minerva;* 38 *Emeline;* 39 *Rebecca;* 40 *Clarissa;* 41 *Roxanna;* 42 *George;* 43 *David;* 44 *Harvey;* 45 *Infant*, d.

13 REUBEN.

REUBEN PRITCHARD, son of Abraham and Anna (Hotchkiss) Pritchard, had

Children: 46 *Sarah*, m Arad Wakelee, and had children, David and Sarah; 47 *Amera*, m Henry Oaks.

15 JOHN.

JOHN PRITCHARD, son of Abraham and Anna (Hotchkiss) Pritchard had

Children: 48 *Eben;* 49 *Beza;* 50 *Celestia;* 51 *Buel;* 52 *Luther;* 53 *Mary Ann;* 54 *Abigail.*

28 GILBERT.

GILBERT PRITCHARD, son of Roger, grandson of Amos, Senr., married Julia Ann Sutton.

GENEALOGIES. 547

Children: 55 *Mary*, m John B. Downs and had child, Nellie; 56 *Candee;* 57 *Julia.*

29 DENNIS.

DENNIS PRITCHARD, son of Roger, and grandson of Amos, married, 1st, Julia A. Downs, Jan. 30, 1831. She died Dec. 16, 1868, ae. 57. 2d, Mrs. Polly (Welton) Minor, March 10, 1870. He owns the John Norton mill property and resides on a farm a little east of the mill.

Children: 58 *John D.*, b Sept. 25, 1834; 59 *Berlin*, b March 31, 1839.

58 JOHN D.

JOHN D. PRITCHARD, son of Dennis and Julia A. (Downs) Pritchard, married Caroline Norton and lived on the Thomas Upson place. He died Oct. 13, 1866, in the midst of prosperity.

Children: 60 *Harriet J.*, b Jan. 27, 1859, d April 17, 1874; 61 *Willey E.*, b Dec. 7, 1863; 62 *Esther C.*, b Aug. 30, 1866.

59 BERLIN.

BERLIN PRITCHARD, son of Dennis and Julia A. (Downs) Pritchard, married Emily, daughter of James Alcott, Nov. 1, 1860. He died Oct. 17, 1872.

Child: 63 *Evelyn*, b Dec. 16, 1866.

RICHARDS.

Col. STREAT RICHARDS, son of Abijah and Huldah (Hopkins) Richards of Waterbury, was born Dec. 12, 1750 and married Eunice Culver, and was among the early settlers in Wolcott, near Potucco's Ring. He became a prominent man in the parish Society about 1790, and for twenty years was a stirring, energetic citizen. He was ambitious of distinction in the way of usefulness to his fellow men, never shunning work or responsibility. As a farmer, he has left the marks that show his home to have been the scene of energy and thrift. The house, still standing, must have been equal to any in the town, in comfort, convenience and appearance, all of which cost energy and work. In the militia, and in the town offices, agencies, and enterprises, he was ready, always, to go to the front, with a helping hand, an open purse, and a resolute heart. And though at times, he may have used some large words with a little flourish, yet he was equal, under all circumstances, to the propositions he introduced. His was a useful life to the community and would have received higher consideration than it did but for a slight pretentiousness in performing the duties assigned him. He removed from Wolcott about 1815, to Westminster, Vt., where he died in July, 1835.

Children: 1 *Polly*, b June, 1778, d March, 1780; 2 *Miles Hopkins*, b 1779, d 1834, in Waterbury, never married; 3 *Achsa*, b May 30, 1783, m Nathaniel Lewis of Wolcott, and died in 1847; 4 *Luther Abijah*, b Sept. 25, 1785; 5 *Sally*, b in 1789, m Daniel Steel of Waterbury, 1813, d in Illinois, Feb. 1, 1853; 6 *Amanda*, b April 10, 1792, m Jasper Johnson, 1813, and after her sister's death, married Daniel Steel Feb., 1854, d in Waukegan, Ill., Aug. 29, 1868.

4 LUTHER ABIJAH.

LUTHER A. RICHARDS, son of Streat and Eunice (Culver) Richards, married in 1813, Mary Page of Vermont, and settled in Westminster, Vt., to which place he went in 1807 or 8. He died Jan. 29, 1840.

Children: 7 *Mary A.*, m Hobart V. Welton of Waterbury, Oct. 28, 1834, where she resided until her death in 1873, leaving four children; 8 *Roderick S.;* 9 *Abijah*, d an infant; 10 *Luther A.;* 11 *Sarah A.;* 12 *Amanda;* 13 *Harriet;* 14 *Huldah H.;* 15 *Mark;* 16 *Henry G.;* 17 *George A.;* 18 *Frances E.;* 19 *William E.*

ROGERS.

1 JOSIAH.

Deacon JOSIAH ROGERS, a descendant of John Rogers, the martyr of England, was a wealthy and influential man in North Branford, now Northford. He bore the rank of captain as well as deacon. He bought land in Wolcott, on which his son, Josiah, afterwards settled as early as 1724. His sons, Edward and Medad, owned lands in Wolcott. He died Oct. 5, 1784, ae. 76. Martha, his wife, died Dec. 17, 1794, ae. 85.

Children : 2 *Ruth*, b Oct. 8, 1728, m Amos Seward and d April 29. 1810, ae. 82 ; 3 *Rebecca*, b June 10, 1731, d 1809, ae. 76 ; 4 *Josiah*, b Sept. 16, 1733, settled in Wolcott ; 5 *Edward*, b Jan. 12, 1736 or 7, d Dec. 6, 1801 ; 6 *Gideon*, b Nov. 11, 1739, d Nov. 3, 1807, ae. 68 ; 7 *Martha*, b June 6, 1741, d Oct. 16, 1819, ae. 79 ; 8 *Mary*, b Oct. 13, 1743 ; 9 *Elihu*, b Jan. 28, 1745 ; 10 *Ebenezer*, b Jan. 29, 1747 ; 11 *Medad*, b 1750 ; 12 *Timothy*, b Dec. 24, 1752.

4 JOSIAH.

Deacon JOSIAH ROGERS, eldest son of Josiah and Martha Rogers of Branford, married, 1st, Sarah ――――, who died Sept. 17, 1779, ae. 40 ; 2d, Mary ――――, and settled in Wolcott, about 1760. He was elected Deacon of the church in Wolcott, Jan. 26, 1774, which office he held twenty-nine years, being one of the reliable and faithful men of the parish. All of his descendants have long since left Wolcott. Some of them are in the "Black river" country, near Oswego, N. Y. He died Oct. 1, 1803, ae. 70.

Children by first wife : 13 *Sarah*, b Nov. 22, 1756, m Josiah Atkins of Wolcott, 1777, and d Dec. 31, 1778, ae. 22. (Mr. Atkins married, 2d, Mary Gillet, Nov. 25, 1779, and had

GENEALOGIES. 551

children); 14 *Mary*, b Oct. 25, 1758, m Joel Hotchkiss; 15 *Adah*, b Sept. 5, 1762, m Rev. Alexander Gillet, Dec. 3, 1778, d May 10, 1839, ae. 77; 16 *Josiah*, b April 2, 1765, d July 16, 1815, ae. 50; 17 *Enoch*, b Sept. 28, 1769, d June 20, 1813, ae. 44; 18 *Joseph*, b Nov. 26, 1771, d Dec. 27, 1798, ae. 27; 19 *Jacob*, b July 3, 1774; 20 *Lydia*, b Nov. 19, 1777. By second wife: 21 *Samuel*, b April 11, 1781; 22 *Ruth*, b Jan. 1, 1783; 23 *Martha*, b Nov. 15, 1784.

11 MEDAD.

Rev. MEDAD ROGERS, son of Josiah and Martha Rogers of Branford, married Rachel Baldwin of Kent. He died Aug. 25, 1824, ae. 74.

Children: 24 *Flora*, m Ira Kellogg of New Fairfield, Conn.; 25 *Louisa*, m Seeley Barnum of New Fairfield; 26 *Amzi*.

12 TIMOTHY, M. D.

Dr. TIMOTHY ROGERS, son of Josiah and Martha Rogers of Branford, married, removed to Hamilton, Madison Co., N. Y., was a practicing physician for many years, and had several children.

27 MEDAD.

MEDAD ROGERS, son of Dr. Timothy, married Lydia Crosby, aunt to the author of this book. She was born May 23, 1789, and died Aug. 25, 1832, ae. 42. They resided in Hamilton, Madison Co., N. Y. He died Dec. 18, 1866, ae. 82.

Children: 28 *Amanda*, b May 23, 1808; 29 *Asahel Timothy*, b June 28, 1810; 30 *Hinkley*, b Feb. 1, 1812, d Oct. 8, 1815; 31 *Harriet*, b Sept. 22, 1814, m John R. Baldwin of Branford, Conn; 32 *Henry H.*, b Sept. 13, 1819, d Sept. 17, 1819; 33 *Lyman*, b Sept. 14, 1821.

ROOT.

TIMOTHY ROOT, son of Mark Root of Farmington, was born April 19, 1830, and married, Oct., 1852, Mary Jane Goodwin of Wolcottville. She was born Aug. 27, 1835, died May 18, 1860. He married, 2d, Lucelia Merrill of Wolcott, April 18, 1861, and lives a little north of Woodtick.

Children by first wife: 1 *Anna Elizabeth*, b July 19, 1853, m Ransom B. Hall, Feb. 25, 1874; 2 *Ellena Goodwin*, b Oct. 3, 1857, d March 22, 1858. By second wife : 3 *Jane Luetta*, b Feb. 20, 1863, d March 13, 1873 ; 4 *Julia Ellena*, b Aug. 29, 1864 ; 5 *Marguretta Burd*, b Nov. 8, 1867.

ROSE.

1 DANIEL.

DANIEL ROSE came from Branford to Wolcott, settled on "Pike's Hill," afterward "Rose Hill" where he died.

Children: 2 *Hannah*, b 1773, m, 1st, Capt. Page of North Branford and had one son, Andrew S. Page, who raised a large and respectable family, and died 1864, ae. 66. She married, 2d, Swayne Moulthrop and had two sons: Major, the eldest, has an Art Gallery in New Haven; and Lembert, who died in New Haven about 1864. 3 *Sally*, never married, died recently in Grand Isle, near Canada; 4 *Bela;* 5 *Daniel;* 6 *Chandler*, lived and died in Middlebury, Vt., leaving a family; 7 *Rensselaer*, lived and died in Berlin, Conn., leaving three daughters; 8 *Betsey*, b 1791, m Wm. Butler of Hartford, Conn., and died Oct. 30, 1867, leaving several children "well to do."

4 BELA.

BELA Rose, son of Daniel, married Mary Brockett, and lived and died in Wolcott. He lost both hands in a wool picking machine in Plymouth Hollow.

Children: 9 *Charles;* 10 *Augustus*, b May 28, 1812; 11 *Rebecca*, m Asahel Thomas; 12 *Mary*, m John Payne and lives in Straitsville, Conn.; 13 *Jessie B.*, b Jan. 10, 1821; 14 *Daniel*, married; 15 *Jane*, m —— Moses; 16 *Henry*, m Harriet Seeley; 17 *Bela*, m Amanda Todd.

10 AUGUSTUS.

AUGUSTUS ROSE, son of Bela and Mary (Brockett) Rose, married, 1st, Rachel, daughter of Moses Byington, 2d, Mrs. Charlotte Frisbie, 3d, Mary A. Comer, April 9, 1856, who was born Dec.

25, 1834. Children by first wife : 18 *William Bela*, b Feb. 19, 1838; 19 *Cornelia E.*, b July 22, 1842, m Sept. 1, 1862, Edwin L. Bolster of Waterbury and has a son, Elvin S., b July 17, 1863. By second wife : 20 *Edwin*, b Dec. 31, 1853. By third wife : 21 *Ella Jane*, b Jan. 1857; 22 *Everette E.*, b Jan. 5, 1862, d June 14, 1874.

13 JESSE B.

JESSE B. ROSE, son of Bela and Mary (Brockett) Rose, married, 1st, Perlina Hart of Bristol, 2d, May 7, 1867, Mrs. Harriet E. Griswold of Goshen. She was born Nov. 29, 1840. He learned his trade by six years apprenticeship in a Woolen Mill in Bristol, and settled in Wolcottville in 1850 as an overseer. He afterwards became partner in the Union Manufacturing Company, having a business employing $230,000 capital.

Children : 23 *Edwin C.*, b May 18, 1844; 24 *Wallace A.*, b Dec. 16, 1848, d Feb. 16, 1850; 25 *Willie A.*, b. Aug. 22, 1852. His second wife has a son, 26 *Frederick H. Griswold*, b May 4, 1862.

23 EDWIN C.

EDWIN C. ROSE, son of Jesse B. and Perlina (Hart) Rose, married Mattie E. Hamilton, Nov. 26, 1870. She was born in Cincinnati, Sept. 20, 1852.

Child : 27 *Edwin H.*, b April 19, 1872.

SCARRITT.

JEREMIAH SCARRITT was an important man in Wolcott, from 1790 to 1815, being engaged to considerable extent in buying and selling farms. His wife, Mary, united with the Congregational church, May 4, 1777, by letter, making it certain that they came into Wolcott before that time. He died March 21, 1825, aged 91. His wife, Mary, died Jan. 26, 1827, aged 92.

As near as I can ascertain some of their children were: 1 *Sarah*, b 1779 m, 1st, Samuel Plumb, Jan. 17, 1797, 2d, —— Truesdell, and d 1873, ae. 94; 2 *David*, b 1781, m Hannah —— and had a son David, who died April 25, 1870, aged 65; 3 *Jeremiah*, bapt. March 1, 1782.

JAMES SCARRITT married Sylvia Plumb June 13, 1871, and was probably brother to Jeremiah.

SEWARD.

1 AMOS.

AMOS SEWARD was born in Durham, Conn., and baptised March 27, 1726. He had two brothers and a sister; Salmon, bapt Jan. 21, 1721 or 2; Catharine, bapt. Dec. 31, 1727; Nathan, bapt. June 14, 1730, who removed to Cornwall, Conn., thence to Utica, N. Y. Amos Seward came to North Branford, where he married Ruth Rogers, sister to Deacon Josiah Rogers of Wolcott, and from that place he removed to Wolcott about 1760, and settled on a farm a mile southeast of Woodtick. He was one of the solid, respected men of the first Society, being appointed with Deacon Aaron Harrison for a number of years to lead the worship of the congregation, before they had a settled pastor. While various titles were applied to other persons, he was invariably honored with " Mr." apparently in a very respectful manner, so long as he lived. He died in Wolcott. His widow, Ruth, removed to New Hartford, near Utica, N. Y.

Children: 2 *Sarah*, m Daniel Lane; 3 *Ruth*, m Reuben Frisbie; 4 *Nathan*, m Martha Gridley of Wolcott, June 3, 1779; 5 *Lois*.

SLATER.

ANDREW J. SLATER, born Oct. 6, 1830, in Cairo, N. Y., married Lucy A. Robbins, daughter of Mrs. Edward Johnson of Wolcott, May 4, 1856. His wife, Lucy A., was born Feb. 7, 1838, in Cleveland, N. Y.

Children: 1 *William Henry*, b June 27, 1858; 2 *Sarah E.*, b June 14, 1862; 3 *Laura E.*, b April 26, 1866, d Sept. 10, 1868; 4 *Joseph W. C.*, b Aug. 25, 1869.

SMITH.*

JARED SMITH of Prospect, married Eunice Tyler of the same place, and settled in Wolcott.

Children: 1 *Isaac;* 2 *Jedediah;* 3 *Jeremiah;* 4 *Orrin;* 5 *William;* 6 *Franklin;* 7 *Philo;* 8 *Hiram;* 9 *A. Hector;* 10 *Alma;* 11 *Eunice;* 12 *Lois;* 13 *Emily.*

5 WILLIAM.

WILLIAM SMITH, son of Jared and Eunice (Tyler) Smith, married Vina Plumb, Sept. 25, 1818. He died Aug. 21, 1822.

Children: 14 *Mary*, b Aug. 11, 1819, m Ira Hough; 15 *Harriet*, b Sept. 13, 1821, m Rufus Norton, and died Aug. 20, 1844.

9 ANSON HECTOR.

A. HECTOR SMITH, son of Jared and Eunice (Tyler) Smith, married Esther, daughter of Levi Atkins, Senr., and lives in the northeastern part of Wolcott.

Children: 16 *Harriet C.*, b Nov. 28, 1827; 17 *Jenette A.*, b Aug 2, 1829, m, 1st, Charles Y. Hall, June 6, 1848, 2d, Robert Atkins.

---

* Ephraim Smith and Ephraim, Jr., were in Wolcott in 1799. They came from Derby. Jeremiah Smith married Betty Cleaveland, in Wolcott, in 1778. There was a Joseph Smith, also, of some prominence.

SOMERS.

DAVID SOMERS was born in Milford, Conn., Nov. 29, 1808. He married, Oct. 16, 1830, Almira, daughter of David Frisbie of Wolcott, and lived in Woodtick. He died Sept. 15, 1860.

Children: 2 *Dwight Leroy*, b in Waterbury, May 28, 1832 ; 3 *Augusta A. E.*, b April 15, 1834, m Heman Miller, Sept. 26, 1853, resides in Waterbury; 4 *Joseph Hill*, b June 24, 1836 ; 5 *Amelia Rebecca*, b Sept. 2, 1840, m Alfred Carpenter Dec. 25, 1858, d April 26, 1859; 6 *Christine Estelle*, b June 5, 1844, m Andrew W. Goldsmith, Jan. 1, 1868, has children: Jennie Augusta, b Nov. 19, 1868, George Edwin, b June 6, 1870, d Aug. 8, 1870, Annie Amelia, b Aug. 12, 1872, d Nov. 1, 1873 ; 7 *Benjamin Levi*, b April 15, 1847 ; 8 *Charlie Edward E.*, b March 6, 1850 ; *Willie Eldridge*, b Jan. 17, 1854.

2 DWIGHT LEROY.

DWIGHT L. SOMERS, son of David and Almira (Frisbie) Somers, married Emogene Chatfield, Aug. 2, 1862, resides in Waterbury.

Children: 10 *Lillie*, b Sept., 1868 ; 11 *Robbie Dwight*, b June, 1870.

4 JOSEPH HILL.

JOSEPH H. SOMERS, son of David and Almira (Frisbie) Somers, married Frances D. Woolworth of Naugatuck, July 30, 1861, resides a mile north of Wolcott Center.

Children: 12 *Lizzie Amelia*, b Oct. 12, 1864 ; 13 *David Chester*, b July 22, 1866 ; 14 *Josie H.*, b Jan. 3, 1868 ; 15 *Fannie* and 16 *Freddie*, twins, b Aug. 2, 1871, Fannie d July 16, 1872, Freddie d Feb. 14, 1874; 17 *Mira M.*, b Aug. 17, 1873.

SPERRY.

JOSEPH N. SPERRY, of Cheshire, came to Wolcott, and married Abigail, daughter of William Tuttle, who lived with her aunt, Mrs. Benham, in Wolcott. He took an active part in the Society and the Town, occupying various offices and acquiting himself honorably. He married for his second wife, Narcissa Kinney, and for the third —— Bristol. He died, May 9, 1871, ae. 70.

Children: 1 *Betsey Ann*, b June 29, 1827, m Heman W. Hall; 2 *Samuel N.*, b Dec. 17, 1833; 3 *Phebe L.*, b March 11, 1838.

2 SAMUEL.

SAMUEL N. SPERRY, son of Joseph N. and Abigail (Tuttle) Sperry, married, 1st, Rosanna Thorp of Southington, 2d, Sarah E. Norton, Feb., 1872.

Children: 4 *Jane L.*, b Aug, 31, 1859, d Dec. 10, 1865; 5 *Charles A.*, b Jan. 3, 1866.

STEVENS.

1 NEHEMIAH.

NEHEMIAH STEVENS, son of Elijah, was born in Guilford, Sept. 11, 1799.

Child : 2 *John M.*, b Aug. 8, 1829.

2 JOHN M.

JOHN M. STEVENS, son of Nehemiah Stevens, was born in Middletown, Conn., and married Oct. 11, 1852, Antoinette E. Goff, born in Middletown, June 7, 1835. He resides on the Seth Wiard farm, northeastern part of Wolcott.

Children : 3 *Justus N.*, b Nov. 17, 1857 ; 4 *John J.*, b Sept. 17, 1859; 5 *Alfred M.*, b Aug, 18, 1872.

SUTLIFF.

1 JOSEPH, SENR.

JOSEPH SUTLIFF was in Wolcott as early as 1765, his house being probably at the foot of Chestnut Hill, on the old road going directly up the hill. He was a tailor, one leg being defective, so that he walked with a cane or crutch. His wife died July 10, 1780. He afterwards married Catharine, sister to Amos Seward. She died Nov. 11, 1791. He died Nov. 11, 1801.

Children by first wife: 2 *Joseph;* 3 *Nathaniel;* 4 *Anne*, m Daniel Dean, May 16, 1776; 5 —— m —— Scott.

2 JOSEPH, JR.*

JOSEPH SUTLIFF, son of Joseph, the first in Wolcott, married, 1771, Zerviah Webster, sister to Lydia, the wife of Wait Hotchkiss. He lived on the farm afterwards owned by Ephraim Hall, a little east of Chestnut Hill.

Children: 6 *Zerviah*, b Jan. 29, 1772, m Gideon Curtiss; 7 *Joseph*, b Dec. 27, 1773, the second child baptized in Wolcott; 8 *Michael*, b Feb. 5, 1776; 9 *Lydia*, b Feb. 1, 1778; 10 *Abiathar*, b May 7, 1780, removed West and was killed by the fall of a tree; 11 *Nathan*, b April 4, 1782.

3 NATHANIEL.†

NATHANIEL SUTLIFF, son of Joseph, Senr., had

Children: 12 *John;* 13 *Nathaniel;* 14 *Titus;* 15 *Hannah;* 16 *Anne*, all bapt. April 19, 1774; 17 *Ruth*, bapt June 21, 1778; 18 *Elizabeth*, bapt Dec. 14, 1782.

---

* See Waterbury Town Records.
See Church Records.

12 JOHN.

JOHN SUTLIFF, son of Nathaniel, married —— Munson.

Children: 19 *Anson*, b 1798, went to Meriden in 1817, married Miss Cumstock of Deep River, Conn., and removed to Minnesota, in 1857, where he died, ae. 59. 20 *Statira*, b 1800, m Jerry Williams of Waterbury, settled in Meriden in 1835, d in 1873, ae. 73; 21 *John*, b 1802, went to Meriden in 1819, married, 1st, Mary Ann Dayton of North Haven, 2d, Rebecca Miles of Cheshire; 22 *Lucius*, b 1806, m Rachel Foot, lives in Southington; 23 *Lucas*, b 1808, m Maria Melissa Upson of Wolcott, who died in 1871, in Southington, ae. 66 years.

14 TITUS.

TITUS SUTLIFF, son of Nathaniel, married Roxanna (or Sally) Selcriggs.

Children: 24 *Garry ;* 25 *Eliza ;* 26 *Leicester;* 27 *Nancy ;* 28 *Fanny ;* 29 *Delevan.*

THOMAS.

JAMES THOMAS came from Scotland, married Martha Barnes, and settled near James Alcox on Spindle Hill.

Children: 1 *John;* 2 *Josiah;* 3 *Martha*, m Luther Andrews, had children, Chester, Luther, Randall, Harriet, Alma; 4 *Phebe*, m Truman Prince; 5 *Seth;* 6 *Sibyl*, m John Newton and lived in Naugatuck; 7 *James*, d young.

1 JOHN.

JOHN THOMAS, son of James and Martha (Barnes) Thomas, married Jemima Tomlinson.

Children: 8 *James:* 9 *Maria:* 10 *Maria:* 11 *Jenette*.

2 JOSIAH.

JOSIAH THOMAS, son of James and Martha (Barnes) Thomas, married Mary Bowen of Bristol.

Children: 12 *Nancy*, m Apollos Camp; 13 *Olinda*, m Samuel Sanford; 14 *Mary*, m Eli Norton; 15 *Edward Woodward*, b Dec. 25, 1817; 16 *Emeline*, b May 5, 1819.

5 SETH.

SETH THOMAS, son of James and Martha (Barnes) Thomas, married, 1st, Philinda Tuttle, 2d, Laura A. Andrews. (See Biog., page 352).

Children by first wife: 17 *Philinda*. By second wife: 18 *Seth;* 19 *Martha;* 20 *Amanda;* 21 *Edward;* 22 *Elizabeth;* 23 *Aaron*.

15 EDWARD WOODWARD.

EDWARD W. THOMAS, son of Josiah and Mary (Bowen) Thomas, married Sarah J. Warner of Plymouth, Feb. 15, 1854.

Children: 24 *Edward J.*, b Oct. 20, 1855; 25 *Lalah*, b July 3, 1857, d 1863; 26 *Hattie*, d 1863; 27 *Alice E.*, b July 20, 1863; 28 *Fanny*, b March 6, 1866; 29 *Clara*, b Nov. 16, 1849; 30 *Jennie*, b July 10, 1872.

TODD.

1 CHRISTOPHER.

CHRISTOPHER TODD was a son of William Todd of Pontefract, Yorkshire, England. He married Grace, daughter of Michael Middlebrook of Hold Mills, and came to this country as one of the original settlers of Davenport's New Haven Colony, in 1637. He owned the large lot on Elm street, between Church and Orange streets, subsequently known as the Blue Meeting-house Lot, where St. Thomas church now stands, and resided on it. The place remained in the family for a hundred years. He was a farmer, miller, and baker, having bought a mill which the town had erected.

Children: 2 *John;* 3 *Samuel*, b in 1645; 4 *Mercy;* 5 *Grace;* 6 *Michael;* 7 *Nancy*.

3 SAMUEL.

SAMUEL TODD, son of Christopher and Grace Todd, married Mary, daughter of William Bradley, Nov. 26, 1668. He succeeded his father in the mill, and died in 1714.

Children: 8 *Samuel*, b July 1, 1672; 9 *Joseph;* 10 *Mary;* 11 *Sarah;* 12 *Joseph;* 13 *Hannah;* 14 *Jonah;* 15 *Daniel;* 16 *Abigail;* 17 *Mercy;* 18 *James*.

8 SAMUEL, JR.

SAMUEL TODD, son of Samuel and Mary (Bradley) Todd, married, 1st, Susannah Tuttle, Sept., 1698, 2d, widow Esther Maltby. He was a farmer in North Haven, and a Deacon, and died Dec., 1741.

Children: 19 *Lydia*, m Rev. Benjamin Doolittle of Northfield, Mass., and had eleven children; 20 *Caleb;* 21 *Stephen*, settled in Northford and had nine children; 22 *Mehitable;* 23 *Christo-*

pher, m and had nine children ; 24 *Samuel*, was the first pastor in the North Parish, Waterbury, Conn., and had nine children ; 25 *Susannah*, m Rev. Caleb Humaston and had twelve children ; 26 *Elizabeth*, m Dea. Samuel Sackett.

20 CALEB.

CALEB TODD, son of Samuel and Susannah (Tuttle) Todd, was born Feb. 2, 1700, and married Mary, daughter of Samuel Ives, Dec. 15, 1725, and settled in North Haven. He died July 5, 1737.

Children: 27 *Phebe*, m David Blakeslee ; 28 *Hezekiah*, b May 2, 1728 ; 29 *Berthia*, m Matthew Gilbert.

28 HEZEKIAH.

HEZEKIAH TODD, of North Haven, married Lydia, daughter of Ebenezer Frost, Jan. 17, 1753, and settled in Cheshire, a little south of Judd's Hill in Wolcott.

Children : 30 *Caleb ;* 31 *Hezekiah*, b Nov. 5, 1755 ; 32 *Bethuel ;* 33 *Lydia*, m Joel Sackett of North Haven ; 34 *Moses ;* 35 *Oliver ;* 36 *Joel ;* 37 *Phebe*, m Parker Bates, d in Southington.

30 CALEB.

CALEB TODD, son of Hezekiah and Lydia (Frost) Todd, married and had children.

Children: 38 *Lyman ;* 39 *Farrington ;* 40 *Allen ;* 41 *Luther*.

31 HEZEKIAH.

HEZEKIAH TODD, son of Hezekiah and Lydia (Frost) Todd, married Mercy, daughter of Joseph and Hannah (Blakeslee) Holt, Jan., 1783. He settled in Cheshire, adjoining Wolcott, and died there, May 18, 1836, ae. 81. His farm is now occupied by Wm. Todd. Mercy, his wife, died Sept. 12, 1819.

Children : 42 *Hannah*, b April 13, 1784, m Freeman Upson ; 43 *Jerry*, b Dec. 3, 1785 ; 44 *Lydia*, b Dec. 7, 1789, m Joseph Holt of Waterbury, and died in Wisconsin ; 45 *Streat*, b Aug. 27, 1792 ; 46 *Mercy Melinda*, b June 11, 1794, never married, d Jan. 22, 1822 ; 47 *Lucina*, b March 7, 1796, m Samuel J. Holmes of Waterbury, May 2, 1822, and had children : Israel, b Aug. 10, 1823 ; Samuel, b Nov. 30, 1824 ; William B., b Dec. 16, 1826, d

May 2, 1828; Sarah, b July 6, 1829, m J. W. Hough of Homer, N. Y.; William B., b July 25, 1831; Hannah Adelia, b Nov. 8, 1834, d May 18, 1835; 48 *Polly Ann*, b May 12, 1800, m Timothy Porter of Waterbury, Dec., 1824.

32 BETHUEL.

BETHUEL TODD, son of Hezekiah and Lydia (Frost) Todd, married Esther Ives of North Haven, and settled in Waterbury. He married, 2d, widow Sarah Welton.

Children by first wife: 49 *Bethia*, m Reuben Bartholomew and removed to Chautauqua Co., New York; 50 *Lovisa*, m Levi Upson of Southington; 51 *Russell*, m Sarah Clark; 52 *Roxy*, m Daniel Scott; 53 *Leverett*, moved into New York; 54 *Phebe*, m Martin Upson of Wolcott; 55 *Sala*, m Salome Upson and moved to Ohio; 56 *Miles*, m Laura Hotchkiss and resides in Waterbury. By second wife: 57 *Esther* and 58 *Sarah*.

34 MOSES.

MOSES TODD, son of Hezekiah and Lydia (Frost) Todd, married Delight, daughter of Timothy Upson, and moved to Ohio.

Children: 59 *Sarah*, m Abijah Pardee of East Haven and moved to Ohio; 60 *Woodward;* 61 *Charlotte;* 62 *Isaac* and 63 *Kneeland*, twins.

35 OLIVER.

OLIVER TODD, son of Hezekiah and Lydia (Frost) Todd, married Betsey Smith and lived and died in North Haven.

Children: 64 *Zerah;* 65 *Deborah;* 66 *Roswell;* 67 *Maria;* 68 *Betsey;* 69 *Bede;* 70 *Emily;* 71 *Louisa*.

36 JOEL.

JOEL TODD, son of Hezekiah and Lydia (Frost) Todd, married Mabel Mansfield in North Haven.

Children: 72 *Dennis;* 73 *Orrin;* 74 *George;* 75 *Louisa;* 76 *Caleb*.

43 JERRY.

JERRY TODD, son of Hezekiah and Mercy (Holt) Todd, married Rebecca Tuttle of East Haven, in 1806.

Children: 77 *Daniel*, b July 31, 1807; 78 *Amy*, b April 10,

GENEALOGIES. 567

1809, m Sherman B. Chipman of Waterbury, d Nov., 1831; 79 *Hezekiah*, b Aug. 9, 1821.

45 STREAT.

STREAT TODD, son of Hezekiah and Mercy (Holt) Todd, married Ruth W. Welton, Feb. 16, 1815, d Oct. 25, 1860.

Children: 80 *Ransom S.*, b Jan. 18, 1816; 81 *Jenette*, b Aug. 17, 1817, m Harry Thomas, d May 9, 1836; 82 *Robert C.*, b April 21, 1820; 83 *Edwin*, b Jan. 30, 1823; 84 *James*, b Oct. 18, 1825; 85 *William S.* and 86 *Willis H.*, twins, b Jan. 19, 1828, William S., d Dec. 12, 1833, and Willis H., d Nov. 9, 1871; 87 *Franklin*, b Nov. 24, 1832, m Adaline Thomas, and settled in Ohio; 88 *Eveline*, b July 29, 1834, m Nelson Morris of Waterbury, and has daughter, Nellie J., b April 19, 1860; 89 *Jane*, b Aug 9, 1836; 90 *William S.*, b May 20, 1838, m Emogene Minor, Nov. 28, 1862, no children.

51 RUSSELL.

RUSSELL TODD, son of Bethuel and Esther (Ives) Todd, married, 1st, Sarah Clark, 2d, —— ——.

Children: 91 *Bennet*, b about 1820, m widow Ives of Cheshire; 92 *Rosaline*, m —— Scott.

56 MILES.

MILES TODD, son of Bethuel and Esther (Ives) Todd, married Laura Hotchkiss, and settled in Waterbury.

Children: 93 *Nelson*, m Mary Brooks; 94 *Sarah*, m John Clark.

77 DANIEL.

DANIEL TODD, son of Jerry and Rebecca (Tuttle) Todd, married Nancy Mansfield of Oxford, Conn., Jan. 3, 1830, and died Dec. 29, 1871.

Children: 95 *Emily*, b Oct. 21, 1831, d 1841; 96 *Henry*, b June 27, 1833, d May 20, 1837; 97 *George*, b Dec. 15, 1835; 98 *Henry*, b Feb. 14, 1837; 99 *Amy*, b Jan. 16, 1842, m George Sills of Wolcott; 100 *Emily*, b March 17, 1843, d Jan. 14, 1853.

79 HEZEKIAH.

HEZEKIAH TODD, son of Jerry and Rebecca (Tuttle) Todd, married Lucy Hotchkiss of Wolcott and moved to New Jersey.

Children: 101 *Leicester ;* 102 *Sherman ;* 103 *Chester Jerry ;* 104 *Eunice Rebecca :* 105 *Eugene :* 106 *Lucy.*

80 RANSOM S.

RANSOM S. TODD, son of Streat and Ruth (Welton) Todd, married Cornelia E. Sperry, Oct. 15, 1849, d June 24, 1857.

Children: 107 *Edson R.*, and 108 *Edgar A.*, twins, b Aug. 21, 1850, Edgar A. d in infancy.

82 ROBERT C.

ROBERT C. TODD, son of Streat and Ruth (Welton) Todd married Louisa Barnes of Cheshire, April 2, 1843, and resides in Wolcott.

Children: 109 *Ellen E.*, b April 2, 1844, d June 11, 1865; 110 *John R. S.*, b March 7, 1846; 111 *Emily J.*, b Feb. 26, 1848, d Oct. 14, 1856; 112 *James A.*, b Oct. 29, 1851; 113 *Edwin A.*, b Jan. 21, 1854.

83 EDWIN.

EDWIN TODD, son of Streat and Ruth (Welton) Todd, married, 1st, Salina Hall, Oct. 27, 1847. She died June 27, 1865. He married, 2d, Lucinda C. Barnes, Sept. 13, 1865. He died Oct. 30, 1868.

Children: 114 *William E.*, b Aug. 29, 1848; 115 *Andrew*, b Jan. 6, 1851, d in infancy.

84 JAMES.

JAMES TODD, son of Streat and Ruth (Welton) Todd, married Esther Hall, May 29, 1853, and lives in Cheshire.

Children: 116 *Lina E.*, b May 5, 1856; 117 *Hattie L.*, b Sept. 17, 1858; 118 *James I.*, b July 4, 1861, d Sept. 6, 1862; 119 *Lucy P.*, b May 14, 1864, d Jan. 8, 1873; 120 *Edna J.*, b June 10, 1867.

97 GEORGE.

GEORGE TODD, son of Daniel and Nancy (Mansfield) Todd, married Ann L. Lynch, July 4, 1858.

Children: 121 *Ellen Elizabeth*, b Aug. 27, 1859. Has in his care Ann Jane (Palmer) Todd.

98 HENRY.

HENRY TODD, son of Daniel and Nancy (Mansfield) Todd, married Emma Slade, Feb. 9, 1857.

Children: 122 *Arthur*, b Jan. 17, 1858; 123 *Bertha*, b Aug. 4, 1859.

114 WILLIAM E.

WILLIAM E. TODD, son of Edwin and Salina (Hall) Todd, married Emeline Barnes.

Children: 124 *Edwin S.*, b March 25, 1869; 125 *Eva L.*, b July 30, 1870.

TUTTLE.*

WILLIAM TUTTLE, Elizabeth his wife, and three children, John, Ann, and Thomas, sailed from London in the ship "Planter," in April, 1625. They landed in Boston the same year, and removed to New Haven in 1639. He had twelve children, from whom have descended a numerous and respectable race. It is said that this William had a brother John, who settled on Long Island, the ancestor of the Long Island "Tuthills."

Children: 1 *John*, b 1631, m Catharine Lane, lived in New Haven; 2 *Ann*, b 1633; 3 *Thomas*, b 1635, m Hannah Powell, lived in New Haven; 4 *Jonathan*, b 1637, m Rebecca Bell, removed to North Haven in 1670; 5 *David*, b 1639, d, leaving no children; 6 *Joseph*, b 1640, m Hannah Munson, settled in East Haven; 7 *Sarah*, b 1642, m John Slauson; 8 *Elizabeth*, b 1645, m Richard Edwards, and was the mother of Rev. Timothy Edwards, and grandmother of Jonathan Edwards, D. D., the celebrated theologian; 9 *Simon*, b 1647, m Abigail Beach; 10 *Benjamin*, b 1648, never married; 11 *Mercy*, b 1650; 12 *Nathaniel*, b Feb. 24, 1652, m Sarah Howe.

9 SIMON.

SIMON TUTTLE, son of William and Elizabeth Tuttle, married Miss Abigail, daughter of John Beach, and was among the first subscribers to the compact for the settlement of New Haven village (now Wallingford), in 1669-70, and settled there near his father Beach's land, perhaps on a portion of it. His house lot was No 13, east side Main street, with 8 acres of out land. He died April 16, 1719, ae. 72 years. Mrs. Abigail died Aug., 1722.

---

* A full history of the Tuttle family is to be published soon by George F. Tuttle, of New York.

GENEALOGIES. 571

Children: 13 *Daniel*, b Nov. 11, 1680, m Ruth Howe, Oct. 18, 1711; 14 *Timothy*, b 1681; 15 *Thankful*; 16 *Rebecca*, b April 30, 1698; 17 *Jonathan*, b Sept. 18, 1701; 18 *Isaiah*, b July 10, 1704; 19 *Elizabeth*, b Nov. 8, 1705; 20 *Deborah*, b Jan. 1, 1709; 21 *David*, b April 25, 1713.

14 TIMOTHY.

Dea. TIMOTHY TUTTLE, son of Simon and Abigail (Beach) Tuttle, married Thankful Doolittle, Nov. 2, 1706. She died Nov. 23, 1728. He married, 2d, Mary Howe of New Haven, June 9, 1729, and she died Jan. 22, 1747-8. He married, 3d, Sarah Humiston, June 28, 1749. He died at Cheshire, April 15, 1756, aged 76. He built the first frame house in Cheshire, in which house four generations of his descendants were born and lived.

Children: 22 *Rachel*, b April 10, 1706, m Nathan Tyler; 23 *Ebenezer*, b May 18, 1708, d Dec. 3, 1736, ae. 28; 24 *Ephraim*, b April 10, 1710; 25 *Mary*, b Oct. 3, 1712, m Miles Hull of Derby, Dec. 4, 1729; 26 *Gershom*, b Aug. 11, 1714, settled in Bristol, Conn., d ae. 74; 27 *Timothy*, b Dec. 4, 1716, m Hannah Wadhams of Goshen, Conn.; 28 *Abigail*, b April 11, 1719, m John Gaylord of Cheshire; 29 *Simon*, b June 12, 1721, settled in Bristol, Conn., 30 *Moses*, b Dec. 18, 1723, settled in Cheshire; 31 *Thankful*, b Nov. 15, 1826, d Dec. 9, 1747; 32 *Mehitable*, b Nov. 15, 1730, m Andrew Clark; 33 *Ichabod*, b July 2, 1732, d Jan. 9, 1747-8.

24 EPHRAIM.

EPHRAIM TUTTLE, son of Deacon Timothy and Thankful Tuttle, married Esther Hotchkiss, June 11, 1731. She died May, 1732, of small pox. He married, 2d, Hannah Payne, Jan. 16, 1734. She died May 22, 1756, ae. 42. He married, 3d, Thankful Preston, Dec. 16, 1761. He died in Cheshire, Feb. 2, 1775, ae. 64.

Children: 34 *Edmund*, M. D., b Nov. 26, 1733-4, d May 5, 1763, ae. 30; 35 *Esther*, b Feb. 10, 1736; 36 *Ebenezer*, b Oct. 15, 1737; 37 *Ephraim*, b March 20, 1739; 38 *Noah*, b June 30, 1741, d July 23, 1742; 39 *Timothy*, b July 1, 1743, d young; 40 *Noah*, b Dec. 18, 1744, d June 30, 1828, at Camden, N. Y., ae. 84; 41 *Timothy*, b May 17, 1745, went to Ohio; 42 *Hannah*, b

Jan. 4, 1746-7; 43 *Lucius*, b Dec. 4, 1749, d in Wolcott, June 27, 1846, ae. 97; 44 *Thankful*, b March 13, 1752. By second marriage: 45 *Ruth*, b Jan. 3, 1761-2; 46 *Edmund*, b Dec. 30, 1764, d Jan. 1, 1856, ae. 90.

43 LUCIUS.

Captain LUCIUS TUTTLE, son of Ephraim and Hannah (Payne) Tuttle, married Hannah, daughter of Andrew and Lowly Hull of Cheshire. He was a prominent man in Cheshire, for many years, and during the Revolution was under General Washington's command at Boston and Long Island, and himself had command of a company of his townsmen at the battle which resulted in the surrender of General Burgoyne and his army, at Saratoga, N. Y., in 1777. His wife died Aug. 11, 1800, ae. 46. He died at the house of his son Lucius, in Wolcott, June 27, 1846, ae. 97.

Children: 47 *Andrew Hull*, b Aug. 28, 1775, married and moved to South Carolina, where he died; 48 *Lucius*, b Aug. 7, 1776; 49 *Betsey Ann*, b April 8, 1778, m Samuel Benham of Cheshire. They settled in Wolcott, and died there, leaving no children; a pair of silk slippers is preserved, and was exhibited at the late Centenary meeting, which Miss Betsey Ann wore at a Commencement Ball, at Yale College, when she was 15 or 16 years old, *i. e.*, in 1793 or 4. She died April 8, 1864, ae. 86; 50 *Marcus*, b March 24, 1780; 51 *Anson*, b Dec. 22, 1781, had a family, and died at New Lisbon, N. Y., Feb. 19, 1863, ae. 82; 52 *William B.*, b Feb. 11, 1784, m, had a family, d Jan. 6, 1822, ae. 38; 53 *Gaius*, b July 5, 1786, m Bede Gaylord, d March 16, 1855, ae 68; 54 *Hannah*, b March 24, 1787, d June, 1846, ae. 59; 55 *Esther*, b Dec. 30, 1792, m Levi Doolittle of Cheshire, d March 20, 1855, ae. 62.

48 LUCIUS, JR.

LUCIUS TUTTLE, son of Capt. Lucius Tuttle and Hannah (Hull) Tuttle, came to Wolcott in the year 1800, and engaged in business with his brother-in-law, Samuel Benham, as a merchant. He married Rebecca, daughter of Mark Harrison, Esq., of Wolcott, Dec. 19, 1802. He died July 7, 1865, ae. 89. His wife, Rebecca, died Aug. 10, 1870, ae. 86. He was probably the most enterprising and energetic business man of whom Wolcott can boast. Soon after coming to Wolcott in 1800, he brought in the first wagon ever seen there, for the purpose of carrying away and bringing in merchandise, and for thirty years that wagon and others were kept on the road, much of the time, night and day. This made a better market than any other place within twenty miles, north or west, and hence all things flowed into it. "All sheep and oxen," and the forbidden swine; and all butter and grains, and gold well refined, as well as some "shin plasters." This made the town a thriving, prosperous one,—enterprising and energetic, and without a revival of this spirit the town will soon repose with "Rip Van Winkle."

Children: 56 *Mark*, b Oct. 21, 1803; 57 *Lucius*, b Sept. 17, 1805; 58 *Samuel Benham*, b Dec. 21, 1807; 59 *Rollin*, b May 28, 1810; 60 *Rebecca M.*, b May 31, 1812, m Orrin Byington of Wolcott, lived in Wisconsin, and had sons, Lucius, Charles E., killed at Bentonville, N. C., in the last battle of the late war; 61 *Adeline*, b Dec. 19, 1814, m Russell Upson of Wolcott, now of New Haven; 62 *Edward H.*, b July 28, 1819; 63 *Sarah M.*, b Feb. 10, 1820, m Elihu Moulthrop; 64 *William P.*, b March 18, 1824, d Jan. 13, 1825; 65 *William P.*, b Sept. 11, 1826, d Aug. 10, 1850, at Cleveland, Ohio, ae. 23.

56 MARK.

MARK TUTTLE, son of Lucius and Rebecca (Harrison) Tuttle, married Martha, daughter of Selah Upson, April 12, 1827, and resides half a mile southeast of Wolcott Center, on the Southington road.

Children: 66 *Samuel*, b Aug. 20, 1828, d July 7, 1830; 67 *Samuel Mark*, b March 29, 1832; 68 *Martha Ann*, b Feb. 17, 1839, m, 1st, Lyman B. Bronson, Jan. 1, 1859, 2d, Ira H. Hough, June 1, 1868; 69 *Ardelia Maria*, b May 7, 1843, m Leroy Upson, Nov. 26, 1862.

57 LUCIUS, 3D.

LUCIUS TUTTLE, son of Lucius and Rebecca (Harrison) Tuttle, married Laura A. Bement. He died April 13, 1858, ae. 52.

Children: 70 *Eugenia;* 71 *Lucius.*

58 SAMUEL BENHAM.

SAMUEL B. TUTTLE, son of Lucius and Rebecca (Harrison)

Tuttle, married, 1st, Sabrina Ives of Bristol, 2d, Lucretia Carlisle of Goshen.

Child: 72 *Carrie*.

59 ROLLIN.

ROLLIN TUTTLE, son of Lucius and Rebecca (Harrison) Tuttle, married Emeline Higgins of Wolcott, lives in Kenosha, Wis.

Children: 73 *Wallace M.;* 74 *Margaret;* 75 *William*.

62 EDWARD H.

EDWARD H. TUTTLE, son of Lucius and Rebecca (Harrison) Tuttle, married Louisa Bement of Wolcott, and resides in New Haven.

Children: 76 *William;* 77 *Edward*, d young; 78 *Eddie;* 79 *Louis*.

67 SAMUEL MARK.

SAMUEL M. TUTTLE, son of Mark and Martha (Upson) Tuttle married Susan E., daughter of Henry Walker of Saybrook, May 1st, 1856. She was born Aug. 7. 1835.

Child: 80 *Charles Samuel*, b April 28, 1860.

TWITCHELL.

ISAAC TWITCHELL, son of Joseph and Elizabeth (Thompson) Twitchell of Oxford, Conn., married Deborah Alcox of Wolcott, about 1767-8, and settled half a mile northwest of the "Mill Place," on a farm, afterwards owned by Moses Beach, and now known as the Beach place. He died Feb. 10, 1776, ae. 35. Deborah, his wife, m Wait Hotchkiss, and died Jan. 18, 1831, ae. 89.

Children: 1 *Joseph*, b July 15, 1769; 2 *Mary*, m John Norton of Wolcott; 3 *Deborah*, bapt Sept. 17, 1775, m Ebenezer Frisbie, and removed to Ohio.

1 JOSEPH.

JOSEPH TWITCHELL, son of Isaac and Deborah (Alcox) Twitchell, married Electa, daughter of Simeon Hopkins of Wolcott, April 16, 1793. She died Jan. 13, 1803. He married, 2d, Phebe, daughter of Dea. Atkins of Wolcott, Feb. 19, 1804. She died Dec. 5, 1823. He died in Wolcott, March 14, 1824.

Children: 4 *Isaac*, b Jan. 9, 1795, d March 31, 1799; 5 *Polly*, b Dec. 23, 1797, m, 1st, Orrin Hollinbeck, 2d, John Barnes, resides in Cheshire, Conn., had children, Orrin and Roxanna; 6 *Lois Electa*, b Jan. 27, 1800, m, 1st, Amos Beach, 1823, 2d, Friend Barnard, 1827; 7 *Isaac Hopkins*, b Jan. 10, 1803, d March 28, 1838, ae. 35, not married. By second wife: 8 *Joseph Atkins*, b Dec. 18, 1804; 9 *Stoddard Whitman*, b Dec. 27, 1806; 10 *Edward*, b Sept. 5, 1810; 11 *William Henry*, b Jan. 11, 1813; 12 *Dwight*, b Jan. 24, 1816; 14 *Hobart Amos*, b at Wolcott, Aug. 9, 1820.

8 JOSEPH ATKINS.

JOSEPH A. TWITCHELL, son of Joseph and Phebe (Atkins)

Twitchell, married Elizabeth Scales, and removed to City Point, Miss.

Children: 14 *Mary;* 15 *Emeline;* 16 *Rosamond;* 17 *Pleasant William;* 18 *Joseph;* 19 *Clark.*

9 STODDARD WHITMAN.

STODDARD W. TWITCHELL, son of Joseph and Phebe (Atkins) Twitchell, married Dorcas Matthewson, Oct. 31, 1833, resides at Hamburg, Mich. No children.

10 EDWARD.

Dea. EDWARD TWITCHELL, son of Joseph and Phebe (Atkins) Twitchell, married, 1st, Selina D. Carter, Sept. 3, 1835; 2d, Jane Walkley, May 16, 1850. He entered upon his life career in Southington, when about sixteen years of age, and, as remarked by Rev. E. C. Jones in the funeral discourse, he literally "Worked his way up to prominence, as a man of business, property, and high standing in society." In the same discourse, Mr. Jones said with emphasis: "How can we do without Deacon Twitchell." Also: "He was a man of remarkable industry," "a modest man," "a conscientious man," "a man of genuine practical piety." He died April 16, 1863.

Children: 20 *Joseph Hopkins,* b May 27, 1838; 21 *Edward William,* b Nov. 5, 1839; 22 *Upson Carter,* b Oct. 10, 1841, d Jan. 24, 1843; 23 *Sarah Jane,* b June 28, 1844, m Rev. Edmund A. Ware of Atlanta, Ga., Nov. 10, 1869, and has children, Katharine and Edward Twitchell; 24 *Mary Delight,* b Oct. 8, 1851; 25 *Sarah Ann Elton,* an adopted daughter, b Nov. 20, 1835, d Sept. 29, 1849; 26 *Olive Newell,* b Aug. 18, 1854; 27 *Timothy Dwight,* b Sept. 6, 1856, d Sept. 18, 1858; 28 *Julia Emeline,* b Dec. 25, 1859; 29 *Anna Walkley,* b Oct. 8, 1862, d June 27, 1863.

11 WILLIAM HENRY.

WILLIAM H. Twitchell, son of Joseph and Phebe (Atkins) Twitchell, married Margaret A. Hull, and resides in West Windsor, Mich.

Children: 30 *Edward B.;* 31 *Samantha.*

GENEALOGIES. 577

3 HOBART AMOS.

HOBART A. TWITCHELL, son of Joseph and Phebe (Atkins) Twitchell, married Hannah M. Wilner of Genesee, N. Y., Dec. 29, 1844, and resides in Hamburg, Mich.

Children: 32 *Alsena Phebe*, b June 2, 1846; 33 *Lois Selina*, b Sept. 25, 1847; 34 *Mortimer Hobart*, b Oct. 9, 1849; 35 *Gracia Maria*, b Sept. 14, 1851.

20 JOSEPH HOPKINS.

Rev. JOSEPH H. TWITCHELL, son of Edward and Selina D. (Carter) Twitchell, married Julia H. Cushman, of Orange, N. J., Nov. 1, 1865. He graduated at Yale College and Yale Divinity School, was a working Chaplain in the Army in the late war, and is now the Pastor of the Asylum street Congregational church, Hartford.

21 EDWARD WILLIAM.

EDWARD W. TWITCHELL, son of Edward and Selina D. (Carter) Twitchell, married Sarah L. Harrison of Southington, and is a successful business man in Plantsville.

Child: 46 *Alice Cary Moore*.

47

UPSON.

1 THOMAS.*

THOMAS UPSON was early in Hartford. He was one of those, not proprietors, enumerated in 1638, who had a privilege of getting wood and keeping cows on the common. He was an original proprietor and settler of Farmington, and married Elizabeth Fuller in 1646. He died July 19, 1655, and his widow married Edmund Scott.

Children: 2 *Thomas*, removed to Saybrook and died there, having no children; 3 *Stephen;* 4 *Mary;* 5 *Hannah;* 6 *Elizabeth*, d July 20, 1655.

3 STEPHEN.

STEPHEN UPSON, son of Thomas and Elizabeth (Fuller) Upson, married, Dec. 29, 1682, Mary, daughter of John Lee, Senr., of Farmington, and died in 1735, aged 85. His wife died Feb. 15, 1715 or 16. He removed to Waterbury before his marriage and became proprietor, Dec. 29, 1679, to the amount of fifty pounds. He signed the £60 agreement with Mr. Peck and was one of the committee to settle bounds with Woodbury in April, 1702. He was Surveyor, School Committee, Grand Juror, often Townsman, and three times Deputy to the General Court, in May, 1710, Oct., 1712, Oct., 1729. He was Sergeant in 1715, and in 1729 he had a seat with the veterans in the new meeting house.

Children: 7 *Mary*, b Nov. 5, 1683, m Richard Welton, son of John; 8 *Stephen*, b Sept. 30, 1686; 9 *Elizabeth*, b Feb. 14, 1689 or 90, m Thomas Bronson; 10 *Thomas*, b March 1, 1692 or 3; 11 *Hannah*, b about March 16, 1695, m, 1st, Thomas Richards, 2d, John Bronson, and was living a widow in 1751; 12 *Tabitha*,

---

* See History of Waterbury.

b March 11, 1698, m John Scovill, 2d; 13 *John*, b Dec. 13, 1702; 14 *Thankful*, b March 14, 1706 or 7, m James Blakeslee.

10 THOMAS.

THOMAS UPSON, son of Stephen and Mary (Lee) Upson, married Rachel, daughter of Dea. Thomas Judd, and "lived on Cole Street, near East Main," Waterbury. He sold this home and removed, in 1732 or 3, into Farmington, afterwards Southington, and now the southeastern corner of Wolcott, where he lived and died, respected and esteemed, leaving a numerous family, who have done great honor to his name. His wife, Rachel, died July 13, 1750, aged 56. He died Sept. 29, 1761, aged 68.

Children: 15 *Thomas*, b Dec. 20, 1719; 16 *Mary* and 17 *John*, twins, b Jan. 21, 1721, Mary m Josiah Newell of Southington, John d 1741; 18 *Josiah*, b Jan. 28, 1724 or 5; 19 *Asa*, b Nov. 30, 1728; 20 *Timothy*, b Oct. 8, 1731; 21 *Amos*, b March 17, 1734; 22 *Samuel*, b March 8, 1737; 23 *Freeman*, b July 24, 1739, d 1750.

15 THOMAS.

THOMAS UPSON, son of Thomas and Rachel (Judd) Upson, married Hannah, daughter of Capt. Timothy Hopkins of Waterbury, May 28, 1749. He settled one mile north of Wolcott Center, where his son, Squire Charles, afterward lived. He died in 1798, aged 79. His wife, Hannah, died June 6, 1757.

Children: 24 *Benoni*, b Feb. 14, 1750; 25 *Charles*, b March 8, 1752; 26 *Sylvia*, b June 7, 1756, d 1764.

18 JOSIAH.

JOSIAH UPSON, son of Thomas and Rachel (Judd) Upson, married Elizabeth ———, and settled in Marion, Southington. He died Dec. 21, 1806, aged 82. His widow, Elizabeth, died Aug. 9, 1823, aged 96.

Children: 27 *Ruth*, bapt Jan. 17, 1755; 28 *James*, bapt June 11, 1757; 29 *Simeon*, bapt March 15, 1761; 30 *Thomas*, bapt April 3, 1763; 31 *Josiah*, m March 5, 1789, Margaret Scott.

19 ASA.

Capt. ASA UPSON, son of Thomas and Rachel (Judd) Upson, married Mary Newell of Southington, Jan. 17, 1750. He held the military rank of Captain and died in Bristol, Feb. 5, 1807, aged 78. His widow died Nov. 17, 1816, aged 84.

Children: 32 *Truman*, b Dec. 20, 1751; 33 *Rachel*, b Dec. 26, 1753; 34 *Asa*, b 1755; 35 *Saul*, b Jan. 24, 1758; 36 *George*, b Feb. 4, 1760, d March 3, 1732, in Bristol, ae. 62; 37 *Mary*, b Jan. 28, 1762; 38 *Job*, b June 5, 1764, d July 11, 1764; 39 *Sylvia*, b Aug. 10, 1765; 40 *Lucy*, b Sept. 14, 1767; 41 *Adah*, b June 14, 1770.

20 TIMOTHY.

TIMOTHY UPSON, son of Thomas and Rachel (Judd) Upson, married Delight Norton, March 25, 1755, and lived on the homestead at the foot of the first hill, east from the top of Southington mountain, on the old road. He built, in 1775, a house a little further east, on the same road. He was a very exemplary, good man. He died Sept. 4, 1799, aged 68. His widow, Delight, died Feb. 24, 1828, aged 94.

Children: 42 *Tryphena*, b Sept. 1, 1756, m Stephen Carter; 43 *Freelove*, b March 22, 1759, m James Smith of Southington; 44 *Sarah*, b June 20, 1761, m Dr. Samuel Towner and removed to Vermont; 45 *Ashbel*, b March 19, 1764; 46 *Timothy*, b Sept. 21, 1866; 47 *Delight*, b March 11, 1869, m Moses Todd, removed to Vermillye, Ohio; 48 *Seth*, b June 21, 1771; 49 *Martin*, b March 29, 1774, d Feb. 7, 1777; 50 *Selah*, b May 20, 1776; 51 *Freeman*, b June 16, 1781.

21 AMOS.

AMOS UPSON, son of Thomas and Rachel (Judd) Upson, married Sarah Woodruff of Southington, Feb. 27, 1766, who died Feb. 13, 1797, aged 56. He married, 2d, April, 1798, widow Dorcas Alford of Kensington. He died July 8, 1819, being burned to death while clearing a piece of land, aged 85 years.

Children: 52 *Lucy*, b Nov. 19, 1766, m —— Bacon, removed to Mass.; 53 *Shubel*, b Nov. 15, 1767, d Aug. 20, 1773; 54 *Sarah*, b March 18, 1769, d Sept. 13, 1773; 55 *Amos*, b March 14, 1771, m, May 8, 1794, Keziah Root; 56 *Mark*, b Aug. 2, 1772; 57 *Shubel*, b 1774, m Roxanna Cowles; 58 *Levi*, b Jan. 2, 1777, d Aug. 12, 1779.

22 SAMUEL.

Capt. SAMUEL UPSON, son of Thomas and Rachel (Judd) Up-

GENEALOGIES. 581

son, married Ruth Cowles, April 5, 1759, and settled on the road about a mile west of his father's home. He was an active and influential man in the Parish Society many years. When the road was made into a turnpike he became largely interested in that enterprise. He died Feb. 25, 1816, aged 79.

Children: 59 *Mary*, b Feb., 1759, m Joseph Minor; 60 *Archibald*, b April 26, 1761, d 1782; 61 *Isaac*, b Dec. 22, 1763; 62 *Obed*, b Jan. 2, 1767; 63 *Harvey*, b Nov. 11, 1769; 64 *Samuel*, and 65 *Ruth*, twins, b Aug. 16, 1772, Ruth, m Moses Byington; 66 *Jerusha*, b June 27, 1775, d 1775; 67 *Manly*, b March 12, 1777; 68 *Betsey*, b Aug. 10, 1779, m Lyman Higgins.

24 BENONI.

BENONI UPSON, D. D., son of Thomas and Hannah (Hopkins) Upson, married Livia, daughter of Joseph Hopkins of Waterbury. He was pastor of the Congregational church in Kensington many years and died Nov. 13, 1826, aged 76. (See Biog., page 354.)

Children: 69 *Gustavus*; 70 *Laura*; 71 *Henry*; 72 *Livia*; 73 *Laura*; 74 *Sophia*; 75 *Sally*; 76 *William*.

25 CHARLES.

CHARLES UPSON, son of Thomas and Hannah (Hopkins) Upson, married, 1st, Wealthy Hopkins, May 26, 1773. She died Dec. 28, 1783. He married, 2d, widow Mary Moulthrop, Nov. 24, 1784. He resided on the homestead, and was a man of large influence in the community, and in 1805 had the largest tax list of any of the men in the Society. He subscribed the largest sum for the settlement of Rev. Mr. Woodward in 1792. He was Justice of the Peace so many years that he was spoken of mostly as "Squire Charles," and the farm where he lived is known at the present time as the place of "Squire Charles Upson." He was accidentally killed in New Haven by hitting his head against a beam while riding into a barn on a load of hay, April 29, 1809, aged 57. His widow, Mary, died March 30, 1826, aged 76.

Children by first wife: 77 *Washington*, b Sept. 2, 1775; 78 *Lee*, b May 7, 1778; 79 *Gates*, b July 18, 1780. By second wife: 80 *Thomas*, b Sept. 23, 1785; 81 *Charles Hopkins*, b July 19, 1788; 82 *Mark*, b Oct. 24, 1790; 83 *Wealthy H.*, b April

18, 1794, m, March 30, 1817, Dr. Ambrose Ives, and after some years removed to Waterbury.

28 JAMES.

JAMES UPSON, son of Josiah and Elizabeth Upson, married, Jan. 4, 1781, Mary, daughter of Josiah Cowles. He died in Southington, Jan. 22, 1803, aged 45. His widow died Sept. 2, 1842, aged 85.

Children: 84 *Asahel*, m Aug. 7, 1806, Lydia Webster; 85 *Salmon*, m Aug. 28, 1816, Belinda Lewis; 86 *Levia*, b 1786, d Oct. 22, 1801; 87 *Stanley*, b 1796, d March 20, 1797.

45 ASHBEL.

ASHBEL UPSON, son of Timothy and Delight (Norton) Upson, married Mehitable Castle of Waterbury, in 1787, and lived in Woodtick.

Children: 88 *Allen*, b Nov. 30, 1788; 89 *Freelove*, b Feb. 7, 1790, d Feb. 20, 1842; 90 *Julia*, b Dec. 21, 1793, d Nov. 20, 1813; 91 *Lucy*, b June 5, 1796, m Samuel W. Truesdell, removed to Pennsylvania; 92 *Ashbel*, b Sept. 5, 1798; 93 *Selah*, b Nov. 21, 1800; 94 *Salmon*, b Sept. 8, 1803; 95 *Loman*, b May 9, 1806; 96 *Clarissa E.*, b Sept. 9, 1809, d Jan. 27, 1830.

46 TIMOTHY.

TIMOTHY UPSON, son of Timothy and Delight (Norton) Upson, married Mary Johnson.

Children: 97 *Martin;* 98 *Amanda;* 99 *Joel;* 100 *Robinson;* 101 *Mary;* 102 *Salome;* 103 *Timothy;* 104 *Romeo.*

48 SETH.

SETH UPSON, son of Timothy and Delight (Norton) Upson, married Chloe Blakeslee of North Haven, Dec. 25, 1795, settled in Burlington and died there.

Children: 105 *Orrin*, b May 29, 1799; 106 *Theodosia*, b Oct. 19, 1799; 107 *Seth*, b July 14, 1801; 108 *Chloe*, b April 12, 1803.

50 SELAH.

SELAH UPSON, son of Timothy and Delight (Norton) Upson, married Martha Hitchcock, Oct. 18, 1802, and lived a mile and a

GENEALOGIES.

half south of Woodtick. He died June 3, 1854, aged 78. His wife, Martha, was born Oct. 29, 1780, and died Dec. 31, 1863, aged 83.

Children: 109 *Sabrina*, b Aug. 21, 1804, m Chester Thorp of Southington, Feb. 9, 1825; 110 *Martha*, b Aug. 28, 1807, m Mark Tuttle, April 12, 1827; 111 *Henry D.*, b Oct. 5, 1809; 112 *Emily*, b June 24, 1814, d June 28, 1815; 113 *Emily M.*, b April 16, 1817, d Sept. 13, 1865; 114 *Miles S.*, b Dec. 6, 1820; 115 *Joel W.*, b Jan. 10, 1823.

51 FREEMAN.

FREEMAN UPSON, son of Timothy and Delight (Norton) Upson, married Hannah Todd in 1802.

Children: 116 *Nancy*, b Feb. 21, 1803, m Joel Moss of Cheshire; 117 *Hezekiah T.*, b March 21, 1805; 118 *Julius*, b Feb. 15, 1807; 119 *Bennet*, b Feb. 21, 1809; 120 *Fidelia D.*, b July 6, 1811, m Lucius Odel, lived and died in Waterbury; 121 *Emma*, b June 12, 1813, d Jan. 19, 1833; 122 *Willis*, b Oct. 2, 1815, d Sept. 6, 1819; 123 *Julia*, b Nov. 19, 1817, m Joseph H. Rogers of East Haven; 124 *Willis*, b April 5, 1820; 125 *Lucina*, b May 2, 1822, m Benjamin A. Lindsley, May 16, 1844.

56 MARK.

MARK UPSON, son of Amos and Sarah (Woodruff) Upson, married, May 9, 1796, Mereb, daughter of Immer Judd of Southington, and settled in the south part of the same place, where he died Nov. 16, 1806, aged 33. After his death, his widow, Mereb, lived, with her daughter, Elpatia, near Boston, where she died.

Children: 126 *Dana Judd*, b 1797; 127 *Marcus*, b 1799, d July 11, 1831, ae. 32; 128 *Elpatia*.

61 ISAAC.

ISAAC UPSON, son of Samuel and Ruth (Cowles) Upson, married Sylvia, daughter of Capt. Nathaniel Lewis, lived in Woodtick and at the Mill place.

Children: 129 *Jerusha*, b May 22, 1789, m Thomas Upson; 130 *Ira Gridley*, b Oct. 11, 1791; 131 *Lucas*, b June 7, 1796; 132 *Harriet*, b Aug. 3, 1800, m Abel Hendrick, died in New Britain in 1869.

62 OBED.

OBED UPSON, son of Samuel and Ruth (Cowles) Upson, married Sybil Howe and lived in Waterbury.

Children: 133 *Laura;* 134 *Hiram;* 135 *Maria;* 136 *Garry;* 137 *Leva;* 138 *Charlotte.*

63 HARVEY.

Dea. HARVEY UPSON, son of Samuel and Ruth (Cowles) Upson, married Rachel Wheeler Nov. 28, 1796. She was born Aug. 25, 1775. He was deacon of the church twenty-five years. He bore the military rank of Captain, and is spoken of as a good man, faithful and true in all the relations of life. The blessings of a good man descend to his children.

Children: 139 *Samuel Wheeler,* b Oct. 8, 1798; 140 *Jerry,* b Nov. 16, 1800; 141 *Marshall,* b Feb. 22, 1803; 142 *Lois Melissa,* b Aug. 27, 1805, m Lucas Sutliff; 143 *Marcus,* b Aug. 20, 1807; 144 *Harvey Woodward,* b Nov. 22, 1810; 145 *Lucian,* and 146 *Lucius,* twins, b Feb. 13, 1815.

64 SAMUEL.

SAMUEL UPSON, son of Samuel and Ruth (Cowles) Upson, married Lois, daughter of Simeon Hopkins, and removed to Camden, N. Y.

Children: 147 *Wealthy,* b Dec. 24, 1793; 148 *Archibald,* b Feb. 11, 1796; 149 *Ruth,* b Feb. 2, 1798; 150 *John,* b March 19, 1801; 151 *Polly,* b Oct. 24, 1803; 152 *Alvin,* b Sept. 1, 1806; 153 *Salmon,* b May 29, 1809; 154 *Hopkins,* b Dec, 29, 1811; 155 *William,* b June 10, 1814; 156 *Major Isaac,* b May 10, 1817.

67 MANLY.

MANLY UPSON, son of Samuel and Ruth (Cowles) Upson, married Laura, daughter of David Harrison.

Children: 157 *David,* b Feb. 2, 1802; 158 *Betsey,* b June 27, 1803; 159 *Ira Cowles,* b April 21, 1805; 160 *Marcia,* b Dec. 2, 1806; 161 *Nelson,* b Nov. 14, 1808; 162 *Sophia,* b June 20, 1811; 163 *Caleb Strong,* b May 30, 1813; 164 *Lucas Hart,* b Aug. 15, 1815; 165 *Mary Maria,* b Nov. 10, 1818; 166 *Lucas Manly,* b April 30, 1821.

GENEALOGIES.

77 WASHINGTON.

WASHINGTON UPSON, son of Charles and Wealthy (Hopkins) Upson, married Rhoda Carter.

Children: 167 *Marcus;* 168 *Cyrus;* 169 *Charles*, lives in Pennsylvania.

78 LEE.

LEE UPSON, son of Charles and Wealthy (Hopkins) Upson, married Roxanna Lewis.

Children: 170 *Sarah;* 171 *Israel;* 172 ——; 173 ——.

79 GATES.

GATES UPSON, son of Charles and Wealthy (Hopkins) Upson, married, 1st, Polly Hotchkiss, June 25, 1809. She died March 21, 1830, aged 37. He married, 2d, Polly Smith of Wallingford, April 12, 1832, and she died Oct. 18, 1840, aged 54 years. He married, 3d, Rachel Hotchkiss, Sept. 8, 1842, who died Feb. 5, 1845. He married, 4th, Hannah Withington, May 21, 1846. He was a prominent man in the Society and Town for a number of years.

Children : 174 *Mary Hotchkiss*, b Feb. 15, 1811, d May 3, 1836; 175 *Wealthy Hopkins*, b Nov. 25, 1812; 176 *Asaph;* 177 *Hotchkiss*, b Oct. 1, 1820; 178 *Henry*, b June 10, 1829, d May 12, 1830.

80 THOMAS.

THOMAS UPSON, son of Charles and Mary (Moulthrop) Upson, married Jerusha, daughter of Isaac Upson, May 14, 1807. His house was half a mile north of the Center, where he lived some years, and where all of his children were born. He removed to Berlin about 1834, where he died March 8, 1848, aged 63. His wife, Jerusha, died Aug. 9, 1864, aged 75.

Children: 179 *Charles Hopkins*, b Jan. 28, 1808; 180 *Gustavus*, b Feb. 10, 1810; 181 *Russell*, b Jan. 31, 1811; 182 *Thomas*, b March 25, 1813; 183 *Jenette*, b June 28, 1815, m Renselaer Minor, son of Joshua, May 14, 1835, and has children, Robert, b April 18, 1837, and Ellen Jenette, b Sept. 3, 1839; 184 *Isaac*, b June 9, 1817 ; 185 *Samuel*, b Feb. 7, 1820; 186 *John*, b March 14, 1822; 187 *William*, b July 2, 1825; 188 *Ambrose Ives*, b April 18, 1827 ; 189 *Seth Peck*, b April 5, 1830, d July 30, 1865;

190 *Henry*, and 191 *Arabella H. F.*, twins, b May 21, 1831, Arabella died Jan. 11, 1857.

94 SALMON.

SALMON UPSON, son of Ashbel and Mehitable (Castle) Upson, married Maria Jackson Nov. 26, 1835, removed to Bristol, Wisconsin, in June, 1840.

Children: 192 *Julia*, b Dec. 6, 1836, m John C. Newberry of Pilot Point, Texas; 193 *Mary J.*, b Nov. 5, 1838, m J. R. Marsh, Kenosha, Wis.; 194 *Salmon E.*, b in Wisconsin; 195 *Hannah A.*, b Sept. 9, 1844, d 1845; 196 *Lucy M.*, b Aug. 9, 1846, m Alson Stonebreaker and lives in Racine, Wis.; 197 *Hannah A.*, b Sept. 18, 1850; 198 *Ellen E.*, b Oct. 5, 1852, d April 10, 1872.

97 MARTIN.

MARTIN UPSON, son of Timothy and Mary (Johnson) Upson, married Phebe Todd and lived in Woodtick.

Children: 199 *Mary*, b Aug. 26, 1824; 200 *Ann V.*, b Feb. 11, 1826; 201 *Julina*, b April 11, 1828; 202 *Clarissa C.*, b April 11, 1830; 203 *Lucy A.*, b May 19, 1832; 204 *Frederick M.*, b March 3, 1835; 205 *Salome*, b Jan. 22, 1839.

114 MILES S.

Dea. MILES S. UPSON, son of Selah and Martha (Hitchcock) Upson married Mary A., daughter of Ira Hough, April 20, 1845, resides a mile east of the Center and is a prosperous farmer.

Children: 206 *Emma A.*, b Feb. 9, 1846, m Charles E. S. Hall, Sept. 25, 1869; 207 *M. Elodine*, b May 3, 1850; 208 *Evelyn M.*, b May 7, 1852; 209 *Eugenia L.*, b Aug. 11, 1859; 210 *Martha A.*, b Nov. 27, 1864.

115 JOEL W.

JOEL W. UPSON, son of Selah and Martha (Hitchcock) Upson, married Eleanor Gaylord, Oct. 3, 1855, and resides on his father's homestead. His wife, Martha, was born Jan. 4, 1831.

Children: 211 *Evalena J.*, b July 30, 1856; 212 *a daughter*, b July 23, 1858, d same day; 213 *Ellen E.*, b July 23, 1860, d Aug. 9, 1862; 214 *Ella A.*, b April 11, 1863; 215 *Harriet A.*, b June 4, 1865, d Dec. 22, 1872; 216 *Carrie E.*, b July 17, 1868.

GENEALOGIES.

126 DANA JUDD.

DANA J. UPSON, son of Mark and Mereb (Judd) Upson, married Mary Clark of Utica, N. Y. He died in Southington, Aug. 27, 1829, aged 32. After his death his widow removed to Utica with her children.

Children: 217 *Elizabeth E.*, bapt Oct. 12, 1828, in Southington; 218 *Anson Judd*, is pastor of the Second Presbyterian church in Albany, N. Y.

134 HIRAM.

HIRAM UPSON, son of Obed and Sibyl (Howe) Upson, married Sarah, daughter of Michael Harrison, lives in Waterbury.

Children: 219 *Leva;* 220 *Laura;* 221 *Maria;* 222 *Garry;* 223 *Caroline;* 224 *Charlotte;* 225 *Luther.*

139 SAMUEL WHEELER.

SAMUEL W. UPSON, son of Harvey and Rachel (Wheeler) Upson, married Sally Maria Stevens of Columbus, Chenango Co., N. Y., March 28, 1820, and now resides in New Haven. They celebrated their Golden Wedding March 28, 1870, and have six children and eighteen grandchildren.

Children: 226 *Charles Dwight,* b Aug. 20, 1821; 227 *Albert S.,* b March 16, 1823; 228 *Emeline M.,* b Dec. 5, 1824, m Franklin Downs of Bristol; 229 *Clark W.,* b Nov. 6, 1826; 230 *M. Ashmun,* b Nov. 29, 1830, m Elbert McLendon of Alabama.

140 JERRY.

JERRY UPSON, son of Harvey and Rachel (Wheeler) Upson, married Rhoda Munn of Southbury, Nov. 24, 1829. She was born June 14, 1809. He lives in Marion, Southington.

Children: 231 *Ellen,* b Sept. 12, 1830, m Ira B. Andrews of Cheshire, d Oct. 16, 1850; 232 *Jane,* b Feb. 8, 1832, d April 4, 1848; 233 *Edgar,* b Sept. 24, 1840, d Aug. 1, 1864, having contracted sickness in the late war; 234 *Ella Jane,* b July 21, 1849, m Leonidas M. Camp of Rocky Hill, June 1, 1871.

141 MARSHALL.

MARSHALL UPSON, son of Harvey and Rachel (Wheeler) Upson, married Esther Jenette Barker of Bristol, lives in southern part of the Town.

Child: 235 *Lavallette*, b Sept. 27, 1849.

143 MARCUS.

MARCUS UPSON, son of Harvey and Rachel (Wheeler) Upson, removed to South Carolina.

Children: 236 *John Drenan;* 237 *Marcus;* 238 *Holly;* 239 *Rachel.*

144 HARVEY WOODWARD.

HARVEY W. UPSON, son of Harvey and Rachel (Wheeler) Upson, married Elizabeth Ransom of Oxford and lives in Cheshire.

Children: 240 *Charles*, a physician, and resides in Massachusetts; 241 *George*.

145 LUCIAN.

LUCIAN UPSON, son of Harvey and Rachel (Wheeler) Upson, married Lois A. Johnson, and lives on the homestead, south part of the Town.

Children: 242 *Leroy*, b Jan. 14, 1840; 243 *Sophronia E.*, b June 30, 1842, m J. H. Garrigus of New Jersey, Dec. 24, 1865, and had children, Ella May, b Oct. 28, 1866, d Nov. 13, 1866, Walter Henry, b March 10, 1869, Fannie E., b Oct. 29, 1871, Willie L., b Jan. 25, 1874; 244 *Lucella M.*, b Nov. 13, 1853, m James A. Todd, Oct. 29, 1874.

146 LUCIUS.

Dea. LUCIUS UPSON, son of Harvey and Rachel (Wheeler) Upson, married, Nov. 8, 1840, Lucy K. Bement, lives in Plantsville, Southington.

Children: 245 *Josephine L.*, b Aug. 6, 1841, m David E. Downs, May 24, 1865, and has children, Lizzie M., b May 17, 1869, George E., b Aug. 11, 1872; 246 *Charles B.*, b July 27, 1843; 247 *Augusta E.*, b April 26, 1845; 248 *Justina E.*, b Jan. 13, 1847; 249 *Bement W.*, b Jan. 19, 1849; 250 *Emma J.*, b Oct. 22, 1851; 251 *Edward L.*, b March 27, 1856; 252 *Arthur W.*, b July 13, 1858; 253 *Frank E.*, b May 17, 1861.

179 CHARLES HOPKINS.

CHARLES H. UPSON, son of Thomas and Jerusha (Upson) Upson, married Nancy S. Whittlesey of Southington. He was a merchant in that place.

Children : 254 *Mary Whittlesey*, b Feb. 2, 1843 ; 255 *Charles Hopkins*, b Dec. 17, 1849.

180 GUSTAVUS.

GUSTAVUS UPSON, son of Thomas and Jerusha (Upson) Upson, married Rachel C. Woodruff of Hartford, April 20, 1836, who died March 30, 1843. He married, 2d, Emily M. Woodruff, sister of 1st wife, July 1, 1844, who died Nov. 30, 1872. He is a farmer.

Children : 256 *Alice Rachel*, b Aug. 2, 1837 ; 257 *Francis Maria*, b Nov. 30, 1845; 258 *Royal Robbins*, b April 15, 1848 ; 259 *Amelia Elizabeth*, b July 18, 1850.

181 RUSSELL.

RUSSELL UPSON, son of Thomas and Jerusha (Upson) Upson, married Adeline, daughter of Lucius Tuttle, Senr., May 19, 1834. He lives in New Haven.

Children : 260 *Theron*, b Oct. 14, 1835; 261 *Emily*, b June 5, 1837; 262 *Eveline*, b Feb. 4, 1839; 263 *Martin*, b March 31, 1843, was in the army in the late war, d 1866 in Chicago; 264 *Fanny*, b Nov. 30, 1848 ; 265 *Charles*, b May 25, 1853.

182 THOMAS, JR.

THOMAS UPSON, son of Thomas and Jerusha (Upson) Upson, married, Sept. 13, 1841, Mrs. Mariette Smith of Berlin, whose maiden name was Robbins.

Children : 266 *Thomas* and 267 *William G.*, twins, b June 22, 1844; 268 *Minnie Francis*, b Oct. 29, 1855.

184 ISAAC.

ISAAC UPSON, son of Thomas and Jerusha (Upson) Upson, married Elizabeth D., daughter of Benjamin Allen of Berlin, Sept. 23, 1856. She died Oct. 13, 1866. He married, 2d, Mrs. Fidelia Buckley, whose maiden name was Roberts, April 18, 1867.

Children : 269 *Harriet Elizabeth*, b March 6, 1857 ; 270 *Benjamin Allen*, b Feb. 13, 1859; 271 *Ambrose Isaac*, b Sept. 11, 1860; 272 *George B. McLelland*, b Aug. 23, 1862 ; 273 *Henry Gridley*, b Dec. 6, 1863.

185 SAMUEL.

SAMUEL UPSON, son of Thomas and Jerusha (Upson) Upson, married Margaretta, daughter of Rollin Dickinson of Southington, Sept. 15, 1841. He was a merchant in that place and afterwards in Kensington. He was several times a member of the Legislature. His first wife died Nov. 29, 1844. He married, 2d, Ann Elizabeth, daughter of Henry Whittlesey of Southington, Nov. 5, 1845.

Children: 274 *Margaretta*, b March 17, 1843; 275 *Lovine*, b Sept. 17, 1847; 276 *Julia Whittlesey*, b March 29, 1851; 277 *Nellie Eveline*, b March 22, 1855; 278 *Grace*, b Aug. 21, 1863.

186 JOHN.

JOHN UPSON, son of Thomas and Jerusha (Upson) Upson, married Cornelia, daughter of Dr. Timothy Jones of Southington, July 29, 1856. She died June 21, 1861. He married, 2d, Mrs. Emily B. Humiston of New York City, daughter of Russell Barnes of Cheshire, Feb. 16, 1870. He was a merchant in Southington, Kensington, and New York City. He resides in New Haven.

187 WILLIAM.

WILLIAM UPSON, son of Thomas and Jerusha (Upson) Upson, married Mary, daughter of Samuel Hart of Berlin, Oct. 15, 1856, who died June 30, 1871. He married, 2d, M. Aurelia, daughter of Isaac Hough, and is a farmer in Kensington.

Children: 279 *William Henry*, b March 29, 1858; 280 *Lucy Jenette*, b March 26, 1860; 281 *Arthur William*, b June 25, 1863; 282 *Alice Cornelia*, b June 9, 1868; 283 *Mary Hart*, b April 15, 1871.

188 AMBROSE IVES.

AMBROSE I. UPSON, son of Thomas and Jerusha (Upson) Upson, married Mary Scovill, daughter of Rev. Dr. Clark of Waterbury, Nov. 2, 1864. He was a merchant in Michigan, some years, in which State he was member of the Senate two years. He afterwards removed to New York City, where he was engaged in business fifteen years. He now resides in Hartford.

Children: 284 *Ambrose Ives*, b in New York, Feb. 11, 1866; 285 *Mary Scovill Clark*, b in New York, March 1, 1871.

GENEALOGIES.

190 HENRY.

Rev. HENRY UPSON, son of Thomas and Jerusha (Upson) Upson, married Abbie A. Platt of Milford, Oct. 13, 1863. (See Biog., page 356.)

242 LEROY.

LEROY UPSON, son of Lucian and Lois J. (Johnson) Upson, married Ardelia M. Tuttle, Nov. 26, 1862, and resides in Waterbury.

Children : 286 *Walter Leroy*, b June 19, 1866, d July 7, 1866 ; 287 *Addie Maria*, b May 12, 1868; 288 *Herbert Manton*, b April 4, 1873.

246 CHARLES B.

CHARLES B. UPSON, son of Lucius and Lucy K. (Bement) Upson, married Hester L. Potter, June, 1866.

Children : 289 *Alice J.*, b Aug. 6, 1867 ; 290 *Emma L.*, b April 26, 1870.

WAKELEE.

1 EBENEZER.

EBENEZER WAKELEE was born in Stratford, Conn., where his father, James, resided. He came to Wolcott and married Elizabeth Nichols of Waterbury, and settled on land purchased by his father, it being several hundred acres. He was probably the first settler in that part of Wolcott, called, originally, the "Big Plains." The residence of the late Bement J. Wakelee is the old homestead.

Children: 2 *David;* 3 *Elizabeth*, m Reuben Frisbie; 4 *Sarah*, m Josiah Barnes of Waterbury, Nov. 20, 1777, resided in Wolcott; 5 ——

2 DAVID.

DAVID WAKELEE, son of Ebenezer and Elizabeth (Nichols) Wakelee, married Mary, daughter of Joseph Parker, Feb. 21, 1788, and lived on the homestead.

Children: 6 *Hannah*, m Allen Upson; 7 *Arad*, m Esther Pritchard; 8 *Mary*, m Julius Jones of Litchfield; 9 *Lovisa*, never married; 10 *Iram*, m Content Sabins and died in Southington; 11 *Sabrina*, m Rufus Smith of Pennsylvania; 12 *Almus*, b March 9, 1801; 13 *Miranda*, m Norton G. Smith of Pennsylvania; 14 *David*, m Clarinda Carrier of Susquehanna Co., Penn., in which place he settled.

12 ALMUS.

ALMUS WAKELEE, son of David and Mary (Parker) Wakelee, married Harriet E. Bement about 1824 and resided on the homestead.

Children: 15 *Hannah Eliza*, b March 20, 1826, m Willis Upson and had daughter Sarah, who married George E. Alcott; 16. *Bement J.*, b Oct. 25, 1828.

GENEALOGIES. 593

16 BEMENT J.

BEMENT J. WAKELEE, son of Almus and Harriet E. (Bement) Wakelee, married, Aug. 16, 1848, Salinda Hickox of Susquehanna Co., Penn., and lived on the homestead, and died Jan. 15, 1855.

Children: 17 *James Almus*, b July 21, 1849; 18 *Bement David*, b Oct. 28, 1859, d April 10, 1873; 19 *Edward Decosti*, b May 30, 1852, d Aug. 1, 1853; 20 *John Evelyn*, b March 12, 1854, d Jan. 12, 1855.

WARNER.*

JOHN WARNER was among the early settlers of Hartford and Farmington.
Children: 1 *John;* 2 *Daniel;* 3 *Thomas;* 4 *Sarah.*

1 JOHN, JR.

JOHN WARNER, son of John, was in Waterbury in 1703, and returned to Farmington, where he died soon after 1706.
Children: 5 *Ephraim;* 6 *John;* 7 *Robert* (see Cothren's History of Woodbury, p. 752); 8 *Ebenezer;* 9 *Lydia;* 10 *Thomas.*

5 EPHRAIM.

Doct. EPHRAIM WARNER, son of John, married Esther, daughter of Obediah Richards, Aug. 16, 1692, and died Aug. 1, 1753, aged 83. He practiced medicine a few years in Woodbury, and then returned to Waterbury, where he became a prominent man in the town. He was townsman, school committee, town collector, deputy to the general court, several years. He was the second captain of the "train band."
Children: 11 *Margaret*, b Feb. 16, 1693, d March, 1693; 12 *Ephraim*, b Oct. 29, 1695, d Dec. 28, 1704; 13 *Benjamin*, b Sept. 30, 1698; 14 *John*, b June 24, 1700; 15 *Obediah*, b Feb. 24, 1702 or 3; 16 *Esther;* 17 *Ephraim;* 18 *Ebenezer.*

13 BENJAMIN.

Doct. BENJAMIN WARNER, son of Ephraim, married Hannah, daughter of Josiah Strong of Colchester, March 17, 1720, and died April, 1772, aged 73. His widow, Hannah, died April, 1785, aged 85. He was a physician, and lived on Buck's Hill, where his father gave him a house and lands.
Children: 19 *Josiah*, b April 10, 1721, m Rebecca Brown; 20

---

* See History of Waterbury. Those parts of the Warner family who are connected with Wolcott families are given.

GENEALOGIES.   595

Dinah, b Feb. 11, 1723, m Benjamin Harrison, brother of Dea.
Aaron of Wolcott ; 21 *Reuben*, b Oct. 12, 1725, d March 28, 1727 ;
22 *Margaret*, b Nov. 9, 1727, m Oliver Welton ; 23 *Reuben*, b Sept.
21, 1729; 24 *David*, b Nov. 27, 1731 ; 25 *Benjamin*, b Jan. 26,
1734; 26 *Anna*, b Jan. 31, 1736, m John Hickox, jr.; 27 *Ephraim*,
b June 26, 1738, m Lydia Brown, March 30, 1760, d May 20,
1808, his widow died July 20, 1815 ; 27 *Eunice*, b Aug. 5, 1740,
m John Hickox, 3d ; 28 *Ard*, b Nov. 1, 1742, m Elizabeth Porter.

14 JOHN.

Dea. JOHN WARNER, son of Ephraim and Esther (Richards)
Warner, married Esther, daughter of David Scott, Dec. 17, 1724.
She died Feb. 18, 1726, and he married, 2d, Mary, daughter of
Thomas Hickox, Oct. 3, 1728, who died in 1784. He settled
first on Buck's Hill, where his father gave him twenty acres of
land, valuing it at "£60 money." He afterwards removed to
Northbury, and was the third deacon in the Northbury church,
appointed in 1746. He died Sept. 7, 1794, aged 94 years.

Children : 29 *Esther*, b Sept. 11, 1729, d Sept. 4, 1730; 30
Phebe, b Jan. 8, 1732 ; 31 *Annis*, b Jan. 3, 1735; 32 *James*, b
Dec. 11, 1739 ; 33 *Mary*, b Oct. 9, 1742, d April 21, 1745; 34
Elijah, b March 21, 1746 ; 35 *John*, b Oct. 14, 1749, m Anne
Sutliff.

19 JOSIAH.

JOSIAH WARNER, son of Benjamin and Hannah (Strong) Warner, married Rebecca, daughter of James Bronson, March 26,
1748, and died Aug. 26, 1750. His widow died Jan. 5, 1756.

Child : 36 *Ozias*, b Aug. 21, 1749, m Tamar Nichols.

24 DAVID.

DAVID WARNER, son of Benjamin and Hannah (Strong) Warner,
married Abigail Harrison, sister of Dea. Aaron of Wolcott, Dec.
11, 1753.

Children: 37 *Josiah*, b Oct. 6, 1754, m Anne Pritchard; 38
Aaron, b Nov. 24, 1756, m Lydia Welton ; 39 *Urania*, b Oct. 1,
1758 ; 40 *James H.*, b Dec. 18, 1760 ; 41 *Benjamin*, b Nov. 17,
1762.

28 ARD.

ARD WARNER, son of Benjamin and Hannah (Strong) Warner,

married Elizabeth, daughter of Doct. Daniel Porter, Jan. 12, 1764, and died April 30, 1824, aged 82. His widow died Aug. 21, 1835, aged 90.

Children: 42 *Johanna*, b 1764, m Samuel Gunn, had several children, and died in Ohio; 43 *Lydia*, b 1766, m Samuel Alcox, lived in Wolcott; 44 *Ephraim*, b 1768, was drowned in 1786; 45 *Elizabeth*, b 1769, m —— Osborn, went to Black River, N. Y.; 46 *Prudence*, b 1772, removed to Camden, N. Y.; 47 *David*, b 1774; 48 *Irena*, b 1775, m twice, and lived in Pennsylvania; 49 *Ard*, b 1777; 50 *Hannah*, b 1780, m Anson, son of Ozias Warner; 51 *Asahel*, b 1782; 52 *Chauncey*, b 1785, removed to Fulton, Ohio; 53 *Susan*, b 1789, m Levi, son of Ozias Warner.

32 JAMES.

JAMES WARNER, son of John and Esther (Scott) Warner, married Eunice, daughter of David Dutton, Jan. 1, 1761, and died May 27, 1819. His wife died May 7, 1815.

Children: 54 *Sarah*, b Oct. 2, 1761; 53 *Noah*, b Aug., 1763, d Sept. 18, 1820; 56 *Lucinda*, b Sept. 20, 1765, m Elijah Hotchkiss; 57 *Eunice*, b April 3, 1769, d Aug. 20, 1769; 58 *James*, b Jan. 25, 1771, d Jan. 15, 1773; 59 *Eunice*, b May 31, 1773, m Eli Terry; 60 *James*, b Nov. 1, 1775.

34 ELIJAH.

ELIJAH WARNER, son of John and Esther (Scott) Warner, married Esther, daughter of Thomas Fenn, Nov. 19, 1767, and lived in Plymouth.

Children: 61 *Lyman*, b May 22, 1768; 62 *Chauncey*, b June 11, 1770, m A. Talmadge; 63 *Rosetta*, b Feb. 25, 1773; 64 *Elijah*; 65 *Apollos*, m Chloe Wilcox of Simsbury.

64 ELIJAH, JR.

ELIJAH WARNER, son of Elijah and Esther (Fenn) Warner, married Clarissa Guernsey, who is now (1874) in her ninety-third year, residing in Plymouth.

Children: 66 *Emeline*, m, 1st, Charles Butler, 2d, Newman Atwater, and lives in Plymouth; 67 *Noah G.*, m Eliza Darrow, lives in Plymouth; 68 *Erastus W.*

68 ERASTUS W.

ERASTUS W. WARNER, son of Elijah and Clarissa (Guernsey) Warner, married Eliza J. Whitlock of Plymouth, Jan. 7, 1842. He removed to Wolcott in 1852, where he still resides, engaged in business as a merchant.

Children : 69 *Sarah Jane*, b April 27, 1843, m Theron Minor, Dec. 1, 1861, lives in Waterbury and has a daughter, Myrtie D., b Oct. 6, 1862; 70 *Elijah H.*, b Oct. 8, 1864, d March 5, 1867; 71 *Clara E.*, b Dec. 24, 1859.

WELTON.

JOHN WELTON was an early settler of Farmington and was one of the eighty-four proprietors of that town in 1672, and a signer of the articles in 1674, and was probably in Waterbury as early as 1679. He died June 18, 1726, and his wife, Mary, died Oct. 18, 1716.

Children: 1 *Abigail*, m, about 1691, Cornelius Bronson of Woodbury; 2 *Mary*, m John Richards, Aug. 17, 1692; 3 *Elizabeth*, m Thomas Griffin; 4 *John*, m Sarah Buck of Weathersfield, March 13, 1706; 5 *Stephen*, m Mary Gaylord, March 4, 1701 or 2; 6 *Richard*, b March, 1680, reputed the first male child of European parents born in Waterbury; 7 *Hannah*, b April 1, 1683, m Thomas Squire, Jr.; 8 *Thomas*, b Feb. 4, 1684 or 5; 9 *George*, b Feb. 3, 1686 or 7; 10 *Elsie*, b Aug., 1690.

6 RICHARD.

RICHARD WELTON, son of John and Mary Welton, married Mary, daughter of Stephen Upson, and lived a few years in Waterbury, then bought of Joseph Gaylord, Jr., in 1708, a house on Buck's Hill, to which place he removed.

Children: 11 *Richard*, b 1701; 12 *John*, b July 13, 1703; 13 *Stephen*, b March 12, 1706; 14 *Mary*, b June 1, 1708; 15 *Thomas*, b Oct. 25, 1710, d Dec. 1, 1780; 16 *Hezekiah*, b Dec. 1, 1713, m Abraham Warner; 17 *Eliakim*, b Jan. 21, 1715; 18 *Tabitha*, b Feb. 17, 1720, m Edward Neal, lived in Southington, afterwards Wolcott; 19 *Ede*, b April 24, 1726, m —— Lewis, d ae. 21.

13 STEPHEN.

STEPHEN WELTON, son of Richard and Mary (Upson) Welton,

GENEALOGIES. 599

married Deborah, daughter of John Sutliff and died April 30, 1759.

Children : 19 *Martha*, b Nov. 19, 1732, d 1735; 20 *Levi*, b Nov. 10, 1734, d 1736; 21 *Martha*, b March 1, 1736, m J. Grilley; 22 *Dinah*, b May 2, 1738; 23 *Levi*, b March 6, 1741; 24 *Stephen*, b Jan. 7, 1744; 25 *Thomas*, b Dec. 22, 1749, d 1751; 26 *Thomas*, b Nov. 22, 1751.

17 ELIAKIM.

ELIAKIM WELTON, son of Richard and Mary (Upson) Welton, married Eunice, daughter of Moses Bronson and settled on Spindle Hill, a little north of John Alcox's place. He died Nov. 20, 1794, aged 79.

Children: 27 *Eliakim*, b Sept. 22, 1736; 28 *Eunice*, b Oct. 19, 1738, m David Roberts; 29 *Avis*, b Aug. 13, 1740, m Thaddeus Barnes; 30 *Richard*, b Oct. 10, 1743, d Feb. 26, 1822; 31 *Eli*, b Oct. 10, 1746; 32 *Moses*, b June 25, 1749; 33 *Aaron*, b Feb. 19, 1752; 34 *Benoni* and 35 *Benjamin*, twins, b Feb. 18, 1756.

26 THOMAS.

THOMAS WELTON, son of Stephen and Deborah (Sutliff) Welton, married, 1st, Abigail, daughter of Lieut. Wm. Hickox, June 22, 1772, who died Jan. 13, 1791, 2d, Ruth Thomas, 3d, Hannah Hill. He settled on the north end of Chestnut Hill, a little south of the Streat Richard's place.

Children: 36 *Seymour*, b July 2, 1772; 37 *Sarah*, b Dec. 18, 1773, d 1774; 38 *Jared*, b July 15, 1774; 39 *Elias*, b July 18, 1776, m Rhoda Prindle of Watertown; 40 *Sarah*, b Dec. 12, 1778, m Levi Hall of Wolcott ; 41 *Chloe*, b Nov. 2, 1789, m John Barnes ; 42 *Lydia*, b July 21, 1783; 43 *Fanny*, b April 1, 1785; 44 *Laura*, b Feb., 1787; 45 *Ransom*, b July 18, 1789, went to Canada ; 46 *Thomas H.* and 47 *Ruth N.*, twins, Ruth married Streat Todd ; 48 *Herschel*, b 1797, d 1842.

27 ELIAKIM, 2D.

ELIAKIM WELTON, son of Eliakim and Eunice (Bronson) Welton, married Amy, daughter of Ebenezer Baldwin, who died Jan. 3, 1829, aged 87. He died June 8, 1821, aged 85. He was an active man in the Episcopal Society, and is still kindly remembered as " Uncle Kim."

Children : 49 *Eben*, b June 24, 1764 ; 50 *Eliakim*, b Dec. 13, 1766 ; 51 *Amy*, b Sept. 25, 1770, d 1770 ; 52 *Joseph*, b Sept. 6, 1771, d 1774; 53 *Mark*, b April 27, 1773 ; 54 *Amy*, b April 4, 1776 ; 55 *Avice*, b March 12, 1779, d 1779 ; 56 *Joseph*, b March 29, 1780 ; 57 *Moses*, b March 16, 1783, d Sept. 14, 1829 ; 58 *Micock*, b March 9, 1787, d 1788.

30 RICHARD.

RICHARD WELTON, son of Eliakim and Eunice (Bronson) Welton, married Margaret, daughter of Ebenezer Warner, April 27, 1766. She died Oct. 19, 1768, and he married, 2d, Hannah Davis, Aug. 7, 1770, who died Dec. 11, 1839.

Children: 59 *Noah*, b Feb. 15, 1767, d Jan. 26, 1847, ae. 80 ; 60 *Richard Warner*, b Oct. 10, 1768, d Dec., 1768 ; 61 *Richard*, b May 10, 1770, d Sept. 26, 1807 ; 62 *Margaret*, b July 2, 1772, m Daniel Steel; 63 *Thomas*, b Dec. 8, 1774, d April 18, 1856, ae. 82 ; 64 *Lydia*, b April 1, 1777, m David Roberts of Burlington; 65 *Hannah*, b Oct. 10, 1779, m David Warner, went to Geneseo, N. Y.; 66 *Joseph Davis*, b April 15, 1783 ; 67 *Bela*, b Sept. 9, 1787, d Oct. 16, 1822.

31 ELI.

ELI WELTON, son of Eliakim and Eunice (Bronson) Welton, married Anna Baldwin July 1, 1771.

Children : 68 *Eli*, b Aug. 10, 1772 ; 69 *Asa*, b Nov. 24, 1773 ; 70 *Phebe*, b Sept. 29, 1775, d 1777 ; 71 *Eunice*, b Aug. 12, 1777 ; 72 *Benoni*, b April 19, 1780; 73 *Anna ;* 74 *Printha*.

32 MOSES.

MOSES WELTON, son of Eliakim and Eunice (Bronson) Welton, married Betta Woster.

Children: 75 *Andrew ;* 76 *Elizur*.

33 AARON.

AARON WELTON, son of Eliakim and Eunice (Bronson) Welton married Zera Bronson, Jan. 13, 1777.

GENEALOGIES. 601

Children: 77 *Tamas*, b Feb. 28, 1778; 78 *Junia*, b Dec., 1779; 79 *Harvey*, b Oct. 28, 1780, d 1782; 80 *Harvey*, b Nov. 2, 1782.

36 SEYMOUR.

SEYMOUR WELTON, son of Thomas and Abigail (Hickox) Welton, married Olive Harrison.

Children: 81 *Harrison*; 82 *Sophronia*; 83 *John P.*

38 JARED.

JARED WELTON, son of Thomas and Abigail (Hickox) Welton, married Philomela Norton.

Children: 84 *Abbe*; 85 *Ziba*; 86 *Emily*; 87 *Orestes*; 88 *Leonard*; 89 *Fanny*; 90 *Delia A.*, m Daniel Clark; 91 *Almira*; 92 *Maryett*.

46 THOMAS H.

THOMAS H. WELTON, son of Thomas and Abigail (Hickox) Welton, married and lived half a mile north of Woodtick.

Child: 93 ——.

48 HERSCHEL.

HERSCHEL WELTON, son of Thomas and Abigail (Hickox) Welton, married Eunice, daughter of David Prindle of Watertown.

Children: 94 *David T.*; 95 *Chauncey P.*, m Jenette Cleaveland and had children, Dwight, Caroline, and Ella; 96 *Sherman E.*; 97 *Hannah A.*; 98 *Ranslin N.*; 99 *Hector E.*; 100 *Herschel O.*

49 EBEN.

EBEN WELTON, son of Eliakim and Amy (Baldwin) Welton, married Sarah, daughter of Titus Barnes and removed to Ohio.

Children: 101 *Avice*; 102 *Sarah*; 103 *Selden*; 104 *Jacob*; 105 *Elisha*; 106 *Caroline*; 107 *Eben*; 108 *Polly*.

50 ELIAKIM, 3D.

ELIAKIM WELTON, son of Eliakim and Amy (Baldwin) Welton, married Loly, daughter of Titus Barnes, Jan. 3, 1788, and removed to Ohio.

Children: 109 *Orasena*, b March 10, 1790, m Thomas Warden; 110 *Micha B.*, b Aug. 13, 1792, m Wealthy Upson; 111 *Sherman P.*, b Oct. 24, 1796, d Oct. 1797; 112 *Sherman P.*, b

Oct. 8, 1798, m Ruth Upson; 113 *Sally M.*, b July 7, 1801, m in Ohio.

53 MARK.

MARK WELTON, son of Eliakim and Amy (Baldwin) Welton, married Sally Davis and removed to the State of New York.

Children: 114 *Samuel;* 115 *Truman;* 116 *Amy;* 117 *Hiram;* 118 *Harriet;* 119 *Almira;* 120 *Dorcas.*

56 JOSEPH.

JOSEPH WELTON, son of Eliakim and Amy (Baldwin) Welton, married Ellen, daughter of John Warner of Plymouth, and removed to the State of New York.

Children: 121 *Norman;* 122 *Charlotte;* 123 *Warner;* 124 *Emeline;* 125 *Eliakim.*

57 MOSES.

MOSES WELTON, son of Eliakim and Amy (Baldwin) Welton, married Huldah, daughter of Titus Hotchkiss, Aug. 20, 1810.

Children: 126 *Milo*, b 1811, d young; 127 *Julia*, b Nov. 22, 1813, m Andrew Hough; 128 *Sarah*, b Feb. 20, 1820, m Franklin Hall; 129 *Huldah*, b Sept. 12, 1823, m Edward Pratt; 130 *Hester*, b April 6, 1825, m Hiram Curtis; 131 *Mary*, b April 25, 1827, m Joel Hungerford.

59 NOAH.

NOAH WELTON, son of Richard and Margaret (Warner) Welton, married, 1st, Nabby Chidsey of East Haven, in 1791, 2d, Ellen Cowles, Dec., 1804, who died Nov. 26, 1848. He lived in Harwinton.

Children: 132 *Miles*, b June 15, 1793; 133 *Margaret A.*, b March 28, 1800, d 1803; 134 *Adaline*, b June 15, 1803, m Willard Hitchcock of Burlington, April 3, 1822, and removed to Vermont; 135 *Nabby*, b Nov. 17, 1805, m Charles Judson, May, 1826; 136 *Margaret A.*, b Jan. 2, 1808, m Enoch Marks, May, 1826; 137 *Noah E.*, b Aug. 12, 1811, d Oct., 1848; 138 *John J.*, b Feb. 2, 1814; 139 *Leicester C.*, b April 20, 1817; 140 *Elvira*, b April 25, 1821, m Rev. Collis Potter of Plymouth, in 1851; 141 *Bela A.*, b Dec. 25, 1823; 142 *Jane*, b July 12, 1829, m Jared Smith of Harwinton in 1854.

GENEALOGIES.

61 RICHARD.

RICHARD WELTON, son of Richard and Margaret (Warner) Welton, married Sarah, daughter of Nathaniel Gunn, March, 1797.

Children: 143 *Artemesia*, b April 15, 1798, m Laurin Frisbie, Nov. 28, 1821; 144 *Edward*, b. Jan. 19, 1800; 145 *Merritt*, b April 5, 1802; 146 *Amy*, b April 18, 1804, m Mortimer Jordan of Alabama; 147 *Hannah M.*, b July 10, 1807, m Nathaniel Hawkins of Alabama.

63 THOMAS.

THOMAS WELTON, son of Richard and Margaret (Warner) Welton, married Sybil Cook of Wallingford, Jan. 3, 1797. She was born Oct. 10, 1778.

Children: 148 *Lyman*, b June 15, 1798; 149 *Evelina*, b Jan. 23, 1800, m Anson Downs, Oct. 26, 1823; 150 *Minerva*, b March 19, 1802, m Burton Payne, Feb. 3, 1828; 151 *Sally D.*, b Sept. 5, 1807, d 1808; 152 *Sally D.*, b June 14, 1810, m Henry Bronson, Oct. 4, 1832; 153 *Nancy*, b April 12, 1812, m Frederic A. Bradley, May 22, 1836.

66 JOSEPH DAVIS.

Rev. JOSEPH D. WELTON, son of Richard and Margaret (Warner) Welton, married Eunice, daughter of Victory Tomlinson. She died Feb. 29, 1832. He died Jan. 16, 1825.

Children: 154 *Julia M.*, b July, 1809, m George Warner; 155 *Hobart V.*, b Oct. 28, 1811; 156 *Joseph*, b May 15, 1814.

67 BELA.

BELA WELTON, son of Richard and Margaret (Warner) Welton, married, April 16, 1817, Polly, daughter of Benjamin Morehouse of Washington, Conn. She was born Nov. 27, 1792.

Children: 157 *Richard*, b Jan. 7, 1820; 158 *Hawley Seymour*, b Oct. 13, 1821.

68 ELI.

ELI WELTON, son of Eli and Anna (Baldwin) Welton, had Children: 159 *Joel*; 160 *Bennet*; 161 *Eli*; 162 *Asa*.

69 ASA.

ASA WELTON, son of Eli and Anna (Baldwin) Welton, married —— Fenn

Children: 163 *Selden;* 164 *Hiram,* m Harriet, daughter of Timothy Ball; 165 *Lyman;* 166 *Emily,* m Simeon Phillips; 167 *Heman.*

94 DAVID T.

DAVID T. WELTON, son of Herschel and Eunice (Prindle) Welton, married, 1st, Polly Nichols, 2d, Caroline Turner.
Children: 168 *Everett;* 169 ———.

95 CHAUNCEY P.

CHAUNCEY P. WELTON, son of Herschel and Eunice (Prindle) Welton, married Jenette Cleaveland.
Children: 170 *Dwight;* 171 *Caroline;* 172 *Ella.*

96 SHERMAN E.

SHERMAN E. WELTON, son of Herschel and Eunice (Prindle) Welton, married Caroline Cleaveland, who died June 15, 1856.
Child: 173 *Hattie.*

98 RANSLIN N.

RANSLIN N. WELTON, son of Herschel and Eunice (Prindle) Welton, married Mary, daughter of Edward Scott.
Children: 174 *Mary;* 175 ———.

132 MILES.

MILES WELTON, son of Noah and Nabby (Chidsey) Welton, married, Jan., 1815, Nancy, daughter of Stephen Graves of East Plymouth.
Children: 175 *Streat C.,* b Sept. 8, 1816; 176 *Ximnus,* b Dec. 16, 1817, d Aug. 9, 1822; 177 *Albert,* b May 7, 1820; 178 *Carlos,* b April 3, 1822; 179 *X. Alanson,* b March 17, 1824; 180 *Ruth Adaline,* b July 14, 1826, m Eben Coll of Plymouth, April, 1845; 181 *Nancy Ann,* b Jan. 25, 1830, m Ralph Humphrey of Ansonia, Nov., 1853; 182 *Major G.,* and 183 *Marvin B.,* twins, b June 21, 1832; 184 *Emily W.,* b April 17, 1836.

137 NOAH E.

NOAH E. WELTON, son of Noah and Ellen (Cowles) Welton, married, 1st, Mehitable Bulkley in 1832, 2d, Lydia J. Chidsey in 1836.

GENEALOGIES.   605

Children : 185 *Charlotte A.;* 186 *Noah J.;* 187 *Ellen J.;* 188 *Seymour H.*

138 JOHN J.

JOHN J. WELTON, son of Noah and Ellen (Cowles) Welton, married Maria Wilcox, April, 1840, who died Sept., 1847.
Children : 189 *Charles*, b 1841 ; 190 *Ellen M.*, b 1846.

139 LEICESTER C.

LEICESTER C. WELTON, son of Noah and Ellen (Cowles) Welton, married Cora Matthews of Bristol, Sept., 1845, lived in Illinois.
Children : 191 *James M.;* 192 *Ellen A.;* 193 *Merritt Hobart.*

144 EDWARD.

EDWARD WELTON, son of Richard and Sarah (Gunn) Welton, married Laura Brown.
Children ; 194 *Richard ;* 195 *Noah A. ;* 196 *Caroline A.;* 197 *Martha A.*

145 MERRITT.

MERRITT WELTON, son of Richard and Sarah (Gunn) Welton, married, removed South, then to California.
Children : 198 *Lamson ;* 199 *Amy ;* 200 *Lydia E.*

148 LYMAN.

LYMAN WELTON, son of Thomas and Sybil (Cook) Welton, married Minerva, daughter of Benjamin Judd, Dec. 24, 1822.
Children : 201 *Henry A.*, b Dec. 2, 1823 ; 202 *Franklin L.*, b Dec. 11, 1827 ; 203 *Nelson J.*, Feb. 15, 1829.

155 HOBART V.

HOBART V. WELTON, son of Joseph D. and Eunice (Tomlinson) Welton, married Adaline, daughter of Luther Richards of Vermont, and lives a little east of Waterbury City.
Children : 204 *Edwin D.*, b 1836 ; 205 *Sarah C.*, b 1839 ; 206 *Harriet A.*, b 1850.

156 JOSEPH.

JOSEPH WELTON, son of Joseph D. and Eunice (Tomlinson) Welton, married Mary, daughter of Seabury Pierpont.

Children: 207 *Heber H.*, b 1837 ; 208 *Eunice C.*, b 1839 ; 209 *Lucy A.*, b 1841.

157 RICHARD.

RICHARD WELTON, son of Bela and Polly (Morehouse) Welton, married Abby Mitchel, May 10, 1853.
Children : 210 *Nellie M. ;* 211 *Richard.*

158 HAWLEY SEYMOUR.

HAWLEY S. WELTON, son of Bela and Polly (Morehouse) Welton, married Eliza Merriam, Dec. 19, 1844.
Children : 212 *Bela*; 213 *Richard.*

167 HEMAN.

HEMAN WELTON, son of Asa and —— (Fenn) Welton, married, 1st, Adaline Blakeslee, 2d, A. Carter.
Children : 214 *Oliver Blakeslee ;* 215 *son.*

175 STREAT C.

STREAT C. WELTON, son of Miles and Nancy (Graves) Welton, married Adaline Smith of Orange, N. J., Sept., 1841.
Children : 216 *John S.* ; 217 *Alanson.*

177 ALBERT.

ALBERT WELTON, son of Miles and Nancy (Graves) Welton, married Susan A. Bidwell of Northfield, Jan., 1842.
Children ; 218 *Francis G.* ; 219 *Mary E.* ; 220 *George W.*

178 CARLOS.

CARLOS WELTON, son of Miles and Nancy (Graves) Welton, married Maria E. Peck of Farmington, Nov., 1846.
Child : 220 *Henry A.*

179 X. ALANSON.

Rev. X. ALANSON WELTON, son of Miles and Nancy (Graves) Welton, an Episcopal clergyman some years in Illinois, married Harriet F. Root of Guilford, Vt., Sept. 4, 1853.
Child : 221 *Ellen E.*

WIARD.

WIARE, WIRD.

SOLOMON WIARD was born in Wolcott in 1780. He married, Dec. 7, 1808, Olive Comes, who was born in Danbury, Jan. 10, 1790. He died July 11, 1829, aged 49. She died Oct. 8, 1869, ae. 78.

Children: 1 *Delila*, b Oct. 9, 1809, m William B. Bailey, May 22, 1827; 2 *Seth*, b April 4, 1811; 3 *Cyrus*, b Jan. 3, 1812; 4 *Edward*, b March 11, 1814, m widow M. H. Smith, in San Francisco, Cal., Dec. 28, 1860; 5 *George*, b Feb. 9, 1816, d Sept. 24, 1821; 6 *Marion*, b Nov. 15, 1817, m Gad Norton, Oct. 23, 1839; 7 *Emma J.*, b May 6, 1820, m William B. Cargill, May 9, 1840; 8 *William*, b Nov. 10, 1821; 9 *George Solomon*, b Sept. 16, 1825; 10 *Infant*, b Nov. 28, 1826; 11 *Harriet;* 12 *Eveline*, b July 3, 1827; 13 *Angeline T.*, b Nov. 14, 1828.

2 SETH.

SETH WIARD, son of Solomon and Olive (Comes) Wiard, married in New York, April 25, 1853, Janette ———.

3 CYRUS.

CYRUS WIARD, son of Solomon and Olive (Comes) Wiard, married in New Fairfield, Aug. 18, 1853, Lucy Chase. He died, April 24, 1873, in Patterson, N. J.

8 WILLIAM.

WILLIAM WIARD, son of Solomon and Olive (Comes) Wiard, married Janette Thomas, Oct. 24, 1837.

Children: 14 *John Edward*, b April 16, 1840, d Feb. 14, 1865; 15 *William F.*, b Jan. 22, 1843; 16 *Francis E.*, b Aug. 18, 1850, d March 1, 1851; 17 *Gerrick Thomas*, b Feb. 16, 1852; 18 *Henry De Forest*, b June 16, 1858.

9 GEORGE SOLOMON.

GEORGE S. WIARD, son of Solomon and Olive (Comes) Wiard, married, Dec. 15, 1844, Nancy M. Sherwood of Naugatuck, and resides in the northeastern part of Wolcott. His wife, Nancy M., died June 19, 1847, ae. 31. He married, 2d, Amanda M. Peck of Wolcott, Jan. 9, 1849.

Children: 19 *Georgianna M.*, b May 10, 1847, d June 17, 1862, ae. 15; 20 *Angeline T.*, b Dec. 14, 1854, m Edward A. Judd, Nov. 28, 1872, and has daughter Grace Judd, b June 6, 1873; 21 *Charles Edward*, b May 21, 1858; 22 *Dora Etta*, b Dec. 24, 1867.

www.ingramcontent.com/pod-product-compliance
Lightning Source LLC
Chambersburg PA
CBHW052128010526
44113CB00034B/941